Rough Consensus and Running Code

Private law has long been the focus of efforts to explain wider developments of law in an era of globalisation. As consumer transactions and corporate activities continue to develop with scant regard to legal and national boundaries, private law theorists have begun to sketch and conceptualise the possible architecture of a transnational legal theory. Drawing a detailed map of the mixed regulatory landscape of 'hard' and 'soft' laws, official, unofficial, direct and indirect modes of regulation, rules, recommendations and principles as well as exploring the concept of governance through disclosure and transparency, this book develops a theoretical framework of transnational legal regulation.

Rough Consensus and Running Code describes and analyses different law-making regimes currently observable in the transnational arena. Its core aim is to reassess the transnational regulation of consumer contracts and corporate governance in light of a dramatic proliferation of rule-creators and compliance mechanisms that can no longer be clearly associated with either the 'state' or the 'market'. The chosen examples from two of the most dynamic legal fields in the transnational arena today serve as backdrops for a comprehensive legal theoretical inquiry into the changing institutional and normative landscape of legal norm-creation.

Hart Monographs in Transnational and International Law: Volume 5

Hart Monographs in Transnational and International Law

Series Editor: Craig Scott, Professor of Law, Osgoode Hall Law School of York University, Toronto.

The objective of this series is to publish high-quality scholarship in public international law and private international law, as well as work that adopts 'transnational law' as its thematic, theoretical or doctrinal focus. The series strives to be a leading forum for work of the following sort:

- critical reappraisals of foundational concepts and core doctrinal principles of both public and private international law, and their operation in practice, including insights drawn from general legal theory;
- analysis and development of conceptions of 'transnational law', including in relation to the role of unofficial law and informal processes in transnational regulation and in relation to theories and studies of 'governance' in transnational spheres; and
- empirical studies of the emergence, evolution and transformation of international and/or transnational legal orders, including accounts and explanations of how law is constructed within different communities of interpretation and practice.

The series will also be home to monographs that explore the interactions between the ever-integrating fields of public and private international law. Of special interest are explorations of the extent to which these interactions are structured by higher-order principles and policies, on the one hand, and by politics and the exercise of various forms of power, on the other.

The series is open to work not only by law scholars but also by scholars from cognate disciplines.

Titles in this series

Volume 1: Terrorism and the State: Rethinking the Rules of State Responsibility
Tal Becker

Volume 2: Transnational Law and Local Struggles: Mining, Communities and the World Bank
David Szablowski

Volume 3: The Institutional Veil in Public and International Law: International Organisations and the Law of Treaties
Catherine Brölmann

Volume 4: Between Governing and Governance: On the Emergence, Function and Form of Europe's Post-National Constellation
Poul Kjaer

Volume 5: Rough Consensus and Running Code: A Theory of Transnational Private Law
Gralf-Peter Calliess and Peer Zumbansen

Rough Consensus and Running Code

A Theory of Transnational Private Law

Gralf-Peter Calliess
and
Peer Zumbansen

•HART•
PUBLISHING
OXFORD AND PORTLAND, OREGON
2010

Published in the United Kingdom by Hart Publishing Ltd
16C Worcester Place, Oxford, OX1 2JW
Telephone: +44 (0)1865 517530
Fax: +44 (0)1865 510710
E-mail: mail@hartpub.co.uk
Website: http://www.hartpub.co.uk

Published in North America (US and Canada) by
Hart Publishing
c/o International Specialized Book Services
920 NE 58th Avenue, Suite 300
Portland, OR 97213-3786
USA
Tel: +1 503 287 3093 or toll-free: (1) 800 944 6190
Fax: +1 503 280 8832
E-mail: orders@isbs.com
Website: http://www.isbs.com

British Library Cataloguing in Publication Data
Data Available

ISBN: 978-1-84113-974-6

Typeset by Compuscript Ltd, Shannon
Printed and bound in Great Britain by
TJ International Ltd, Padstow, Cornwall

Sovereignty is fiction. State legislators have to navigate an ever rising tide of rules, acts of authority, norms and exercises of power beyond their control. Formal law has ceased to be the primary, or the privileged tool for governing society. Under the label of 'transnational law', the authors resurrect the law as a social practice, and they herald in a more timely mission for the law as an academic discipline.

Christoph Engel, Director, Max Planck Institute for Research on Collective Goods, Bonn

World society has long served as a hothouse for the frenzied and disorderly production of widely diverse and disparate legal and social norms. Against the background of current scholarly attempts to understand this process, *Rough Consensus and Running Code* brings us to a new level of awerness. Taking an original approach based on a holistic view of the making, application and enforcement of law, it provides not only a comprehensive overview of the current state of global law, but also a refreshingly efficient framework for the analysis of ongoing transnational legal processes. A milestone in modern legal scholarship.

Marc Amstutz, Professor of Commercial Law, Legal Theory and Sociology of Law at the University of Freiburg

Foreword

Rough Consensus & Running Code is a provocative and important book. Thinking about law often is based on the assumption of a national state that provides legitimacy through political institutional authority, democratic accountability and established enforcement procedures. The authors look at transnational transactions where national states operate through "soft law" or where national states are missing almost entirely or play a very reduced role.

Rough consensus and running code (RCRC) is a concept drawn from the process by which technical standards were developed for the Internet. A nongovernmental organization put forth proposals and asked for comment. The chair announced that a rough consensus had been reached when there was a more or less common core of agreement. The standards were modified as experience suggested future improvements. The process involved "the gradual codification and implementation of law dependent on the consent of the addresses of the norms."

The authors offer several case studies where they see something similar to RCRC operating. They look at the establishment of large-scale "word of mouth" networks on the Internet where potential buyers have access to formalized systems for reporting sellers' reputations. They look at transnational corporate governance, and particularly European approaches, where there is "the unavoidable collision of public, private and hybrid, ceaselessly evolving norm making processes that arise between regulatory arenas populated by actors inside and outside of the nation state."

The authors insist that "law" can be but need not be state-originated, and it can be but need not be privately created or result from a complex interaction between official and unofficial norm-creation. Legitimacy is a major problem. Transnational legal principles are "legitimated not by the authority under which they have been issued but rather from their inherent rational content." The authors insist that they are talking about norms, practices and institutions that are properly called "law." Even if others want to limit the term "law" to normative arrangements, practices and institutions that are part of state action, any theory about law that claims connection to the world must deal with these new regulatory frameworks that exist both inside and outside the regulatory state.

Many of us have called for a new legal realism where we focus seriously on the law in action. *Rough Consensus & Running Code: A Theory of Transnational Private Law* is an important and major step in this direction.

Stewart Macaulay
Professor Emeritus
University of Wisconsin Law School

Preface

This book explores questions of legal theory, philosophy of law as well as legal sociology in the context of a fast evolving transnational regulatory landscape. Aiming to contribute to the theoretical debate on the theme of 'global governance', our project draws on research in transnational law, legal pluralism, new institutional economics, economics of governance, social norms theory and new economic sociology. Starting from the premise that a legal theory of global governance must inevitably grow out of an interdisciplinary inquiry into the relationship between legal and non-legal market regulation, one of the central aims of the book is to make more transparent the methodological challenges facing contemporary legal theory in addressing transnational regulatory phenomena. It will thus begin with a reconstruction of the emergence of the concept of transnational law, as introduced by Phillip Jessup in the 1950s and subsequently follow its development in the context of a fast-evolving and extremely rich set of theoretical approaches to the study of transnational regulation. Against this background, we will discuss both the aspirations and shortcomings of existing approaches to the study of transnational regulatory phenomena, including *lex mercatoria*, transnational commercial law and global governance before suggesting a particular methodological approach, entitled 'Rough Consensus and Running Code' (RCRC). After offsetting this approach from its first use in the context of Internet governance, we apply RCRC to two important areas of transnational commercial activity, consumer contracts on the one hand and corporate governance on the other. While we suggest an interdisciplinary approach as both a necessary and inevitable precondition for the development of transnational legal theory, we argue against a fusing of different disciplinary approaches into a purportedly superior meta-theory. Instead, the hope is, by carefully assessing the theoretical proposals brought forward in the contemporary debate, to provide for a better understanding of the nature and role of legal regulation in the context of emerging regulatory models from a transnational perspective. As a result, the book does not sit exclusively within a particular doctrinal framework nor does it decidedly side with one or other of the theoretical proposals that have been developed in response to the challenges to law arising from global governance. Rather, as a contribution to the study of law in the 'post-national constellation' (Habermas), the book will likely upset a number of traditionally held views about the nature and scope of law, about its relation to the state and about the prospects—may they be dire or utopian— for legal regulation. While we do not purport to develop a coherent, unified theory of 'law beyond the state' we ultimately hope to contribute a number of distinct elements towards ongoing projects that are concerned with the study not only of transnational law as concerned with border crossing regulation, but of the nature of legal regulation in a highly differentiated world society. We understand transnational law primarily as a *methodological* perspective rather than as a demarcated substantive field of law. While we think that every field of law is in fact at the core an expression of a specific methodological programme by which we arbitrarily/decidedly distinguish between, say, contract and property, labour and corporate, or 'public' and 'private' law, transnational law offers, in fact, a particularly rich set of opportunities to explore the methodological architecture that leads to the constitution of legal fields. With transnational law continuing to occupy a space which, from a doctrinal view, is neither captured by private international law ('conflict of laws') nor by public international law ('international law'), this situation presents a welcome opportunity to engage in a series of investigations into evolving regulatory frameworks ('transnational law regimes'), which serve as exemplary case studies in the illustration of the ambivalent form of law today. The study of concrete rules and instruments in the areas of contract law and corporate governance highlighted here should allow the reader to better grasp the connection between the way in which a particular legal framework is evolving and the larger transformation of regulatory entities and processes in both spatial and temporal dimensions.

The starting observation is that today law has become distinctly and irreversibly transnational. It is no longer a choice for the study of law to so 'localise' a rule or instrument as to effectively isolate it from its embeddedness in a hybrid, simultaneously domestic and 'trans'-national regulatory landscape. As such, *transnational law as methodology* formulates a much richer and more ambitious claim than most comparative lawyers, after decades of frustration with the field's struggles for recognition in the academy, would venture to imagine. Transnational law's claim is to understand law as part of a radically opened up regulatory and normative space. This space, constituted by fields of legal, economic, political, cultural consciousness and practice, cannot adequately be depicted by a legal methodology that compares law in, say, jurisdictions A and B—even when the comparatist recognises the intricate dynamics of mutual influences between both jurisdictions, through the identification of 'transplants' or 'migrations' of legal principles. Transnational law—as methodology—picks up on past and present contestations of the relationship between law and society and unfolds these anew in the context of an interdisciplinary assessment of governance models in a global world. Whether law, in a dramatically disembedded global institutional environment, can provide reliable yardsticks for different forms of conflict resolution and power struggles, remains a pressing issue. Learning from early attacks on law's formality by legal sociologists as well as from lasting contestations of law's autonomy by Legal Realists, cultural theorists and Law and Society scholars on both ideological sides (*legal pluralism*, but also *law and economics*), we suggest transnational law as a perspective from which to study law as a particular and yet immensely layered and complex series of arguments about normative arrangements. In a highly differentiated world, however, such normative arguments can no longer simply be put forward from 'universal' or 'objective' vantage points: instead, law appears increasingly functional. From such a perspective, legal arguments constitute a particular social communication, which is occurring in a myriad of highly specialized contexts. On this basis, transnational law provides for a lens through which to study legal structures and their relation to alternative forms of normativity. Transnational law provides a space to inquire into the dynamics of neutralization and re-politicisation of regulatory governance through a critical scrutiny of law's self-proclaimed legitimacy. Such inquiry takes place in light of sobering accounts of law's exhaustion and ineffectiveness—in the face of de-territorialised, 'global' regulatory challenges. Fields such as transitional justice, environmental law or 'global administrative law' and concepts such as 'regulatory capitalism' or 'global legal pluralism' have in recent years become powerful illustrations of the need to study law in a transnational context and for a recognition of law and regulation as being part of an irreversibly trans-jurisdictional search for adequate means to address common and border-crossing concerns. As the economic crisis of 2007–2009 and its embeddedness in a tragically mis-regulated financial system makes abundantly clear, the need to develop adequate transnational legal models will only become more urgent in times to come. It is against this background that we engage in a reflection on the transnational challenge to law regarding two highly prolific and pertinent regulatory areas in the hope of being able to carve out some distinct elements that a transnational legal theory would have to consider.

Such an undertaking is itself embedded in a variety of spaces and times. In the attempt to duly recognise the tremendous inspiration and support we received when working on this study, we would like foremost to acknowledge the ideal settings found at the Collaborative Research Centre (CRC) 597 'Transformations of the State' at the University of Bremen, where the major part of the book was written over the course of three summers (2006–2008). The CRC is itself a telling illustration of the inevitably interdisciplinary context in which such a study must take place and from which its authors have continuously drawn and received inspiration, orientation and critical feedback. The generosity of the CRC's Director/Speaker, Professor Stephan Leibfried, in inviting both co-authors to spend their first of three summers at the Centre for a period of concentrated research and writing, is significantly matched by his sensitivity to fruitful collaborations, intellectual networks and forward-looking and courageous mapping and exploration of themes. We would like to express our appreciation and gratitude to Professor Leibfried and to the German Research Council (*Deutsche*

Forschungsgemeinschaft) for generously facilitating a fruitful environment for the authors in Bremen and to the Social Sciences and Humanities Research Council of Canada (Research Grants # 410-2005-2421, and # 410-2007-0265), the *Hanse Wissenschaftskolleg* in Delmenhorst, Germany, and to University College Dublin School of Law, Ireland, for providing an inspiring and welcoming environment for Peer Zumbansen during the finishing stretch of the manuscript from July to October 2009. In addition, we would like to express our special gratitude to a number of wonderful colleagues in Bremen and beyond for allowing us to work on a book that we think very distinctly expresses the central concern of the 'Transformations of the State' project. As an admittedly ambitious study of regulatory models in transnational spaces, it must pay adequately address the dramatic changes that law's twentieth-century principal orientation points ('government', 'state') and binaries ('public versus private') have been undergoing. As such, these 'Transformations' are—like the transnational law methodology proposed in this book—a lens through which to study the intricate cross-relations between different social science disciplines in their assessment and creation of a complex global world.

In our work for this book we have, in particular, benefited from very helpful comments by Marc Amstutz, Simon Archer, Harry Arthurs, Phillip Bevans, Simon Deakin, Roy Kreitner, Andreas Maurer, Maria Panezi, Oren Perez, Moritz Renner, Colin Scott, Craig Scott, Fenner Stewart, Cynthia Williams, Gunther Teubner, Robert Wai, Rudolf Wiethölter and Mauro Zamboni. For excellent assistance in the finishing stages of the book, we are grateful to Monika Sniegs, Petra Schreiber, Insa Buchmann, Lisa Rieder, Cathérine Jansen and Nadja Alpers in Bremen and Berlin and to Meghan Macdonald and Charles Sherman in Toronto.

Gralf-Peter Calliess & Peer Zumbansen
Bremen, Toronto/Dublin, April 2010

Contents

'Laws and Government are to the Political Bodies of Civil Societies, what the Vital Spirits and Life itself are to the Natural Bodies of Animated Creatures; and as those that study the Anatomy of Dead Carcasses may see, that the chief Organs and nicest Springs more immediately required to continue the Motion of our Machine, are not hard Bones, strong Muscles and Nerves, nor the smooth white Skin that so beautifully covers them, but small trifling Films and little Pipes that are either overlook'd, or else seem inconsiderable to Vulgar Eyes; so they that examine into the Nature of Man, abstract from Art and Education, may observe, that what renders him a Sociable Animal, consists not in his desire of Company, good Nature, Pity, Affability, and other Graces of a fair Outside; but that his vilest and most hateful Qualities are the most necessary Accomplishments to fit him for the largest, and according to the World, the happiest and most flourishing Societies'.

Mandeville, *The Fable of the Bees*, Preface.

'We know very little, in fact, about the structure of global society. How is public power exercised, where are the levers, who are the authorities, and how do they relate to one another? Everywhere we can see the impact of things global, foreign, faraway. How does it all work? How do all the pieces fit together? Are the worlds of politics, markets, and cultural influence held together in a tight structure or is it all more loose and haphazard? Is there more than one global order—how much, in the end, is simply chaos, and how much the work of an invisible hand?'

David Kennedy, *The Mystery of Global Governance* (2009), 38.

Introduction

Private law has long become a case in point for investigations into the nature of legal regulation in the global arena. With consumer transactions and corporate activities continuing to unfold with little regard to jurisdictional or geographical boundaries, private law theorists have to turn their attention to the growing need to critically and constructively explore the relationship between 'hard' and 'soft' laws, official/unofficial, and direct/indirect regulation. This book attempts to develop a framework for a private law regulatory methodology that takes its cues from century-old inquiries in the philosophy of law, legal theory and sociology of law into state-society and public-private relations on the one hand and into fast-evolving transnational normative and institutional 'fields' (Bourdieu) and 'spaces' (Sassen) of new actors and norms on the other.

The risk facing a project that focuses selectively on transnational *private* law may result from its unspecified relation to other complementing, current investigations into the nature and role and even the very possibility of law in the emerging architecture of 'global governance'. Especially today—where scholars, policy-makers and the general public express a deep-seated concern with the lack of coherence, effectiveness and discernable compliance in the context of the 'post-instrumentalist' regulatory paradigm that has come to be associated with the post-welfare state's turn to privatisation, public-private partnerships and delegated norm-creating authority to private actors—a project more or less associated with accompanying theories of 'reflexive', 'responsive', 'learning' and 'adaptive' law might be seen as ill-timed at best?.[1]

Conscious of this pressure and such 'demands' of our time, we attempt to show that a legal theoretical project predominantly grounded in private law and illustrated through a number of private law case studies, indeed offers tremendous potential to illustrate, in particular, the methodological foundations and implications of evolving transnational legal orders. In that spirit, 'Rough Consensus and Running Code' (RCRC) is offered as both an explanatory and a constructive tool to describe, assess and further develop the different law-making regimes, which can be observed in the

[1] William E Scheuerman, 2000; William E Scheuerman, 2004; Michael Blecher, 2009; John Paterson, 2009.

transnational arena. As is true for the changing nature of the institutional framework of actors involved in the transnational production of regulatory norms, the norms themselves seem to fluctuate between so-called official, 'hard' law and unofficial, 'soft law', ranging from standards, recommendations, business practices, best practice guidelines, to codes of conduct and transparency rules. A major challenge, which has been addressed by scholars of public and private international law alike, is how to adequately incorporate this new host of norms into the existing bodies of law. Law and economics scholars such as Robert E Scott and Paul B Stephan have recently raised a number of very important observations with regard to the area of public international law about the need to adopt a new, more differentiated approach to the issue of enforcement in order to adequately account for the 'softer, non-state-based mechanisms of enforcement in the international arena.[2] Such an approach is remarkable at a time when critics of international law have either gathered to carry the discipline off to the grave for its allegedly flagrant lack of effectiveness or to scrutinise it for its purported infringement on states' sovereignty claims.[3] Yet, we contend that even such ambitious theories, which aim at integrating domestic contract law theory and international law theory and international relations, such as the approach taken by Scott and Stephan, would still have to take a wider view on the wealth of emerging normative structures outside of the nation-state. The well-argued connection between contract doctrine and state-to-state relations put forward by Scott and Stephan does allow for a much needed appreciation of the hybrid and mixed regulatory regimes that have been an integral part of the transnational arena; this *terra incognita et obscura* from the point of view of traditional, state-based international law. However, we feel there is 'something rotten' in this state of depiction of *traditional* and *contractual* international law, which Scott and Stephan so eloquently lay out. While their approach manages to integrate a considerable wealth of previously disregarded or dismissed, existing and continuously emerging private, 'informal' and hybrid enforcement regimes, such as arbitration and other examples of private enforcement of international rules, into the framework of 'hard' international law, their general architecture is informed by an understanding of contract law that has its most important roots in a specifically functionalist form of liberalism. With that, while the theory is sensitive to the pressures arising before any judge to adequately assess the competing claims between contested, ill- or non-defined contract terms and the 'social norms' that inform and shape the conflict at hand, this discovery of social norms occurs in an affirmative manner insofar as it

[2] Robert E Scott and Paul B Stephan, 2006.
[3] Jack Goldsmith and Eric Posner, 2005.

continues to treat all stakeholders of a conflict situation as rational choice contracting parties.

As such, the staged meeting of contract law and international law powerfully mirrors the deconstruction that has long been occurring in both fields—contract law and international law. Where in contract law, scholars have in recent times again invested much energy in a persistent attack on judicial activism and general judicial incompetence when it comes to interpreting vague contractual elements in highly complex commercial transactions,[4] a similar exercise in disillusionment has occurred in international law surrounding the problematic role played/not played by the UN and international law in the context of the second Iraq War (2003).[5] In contract law, the pitting of social norms against judicial law-making in contractual arrangements has lead to an intricate collapse of formalism and functionalism in a particular socio-economic and political climate in which—at least until the autumn of 2007, when the first major banks succumbed to the consequences of exuberant investments—private agency in economic affairs was given primacy over concerns of redistribution and 'state interventionism'.[6] The strange, a-historic turn to purportedly simple rules in contract law, then, has been powerfully repeated in international law, where scholars have been applying game theory models to historically evolved, layered and interwoven constellations of international relations.[7]

We share these scholars' interest in international law as probably one of the most intriguing intellectual fields to be studied at this time (next to contract and corporate law, of course!). But, we would like to enrich the current investigations into the legal nature of the emerging global order by further radicalising the correlation between domestic and international legal developments. Pushing the investigative agenda in social norms and rational choice theories of contract and international law, in that sense, further than the current state of scholarship, we argue for a distinct methodological position that we hope will allow us to unfold the rightly felt *inquietude* with regard to the tensions between law and non-law in domestic and international relations much more radically. If prompted to contrast our methodological argument with that brought forward by social norms theorists today, the answer would have to be this: we argue for an understanding of law in the legal pluralist and reflexive law tradition, but in a distinctly post-national, globalised, transnational context.[8]

[4] Eric A Posner, 2000; Robert E Scott, 2004; Robert E Scott, 2000.

[5] Andreas L Paulus, 2004; Nico Krisch, 2005.

[6] For a critical assessment of these developments in contract law, see eg Daniela Caruso, 2006; Ugo Mattei and Fernanda Nicola, 2006, and the contributions to the Symposium '*Governing Contracts: Public and Private Dimensions*' (2007) 14 *Indiana Journal of Global Legal Studies* 181–481, P Zumbansen (ed).

[7] Erin A O'Hara and Larry E Ribstein, 2009; Anne van Aaken, 2009b.

[8] Gunther Teubner, 1997c.

The combination of legal pluralism and reflexive law is important, as it helps us bridge the important differences between the respective origins of both theoretical frameworks with regard to law/non-law as they unfolded on both sides of the Atlantic. But, because legal pluralism was informed largely by a distinct normative (progressive) agenda, and reflexive law occurred in a particular constellation of institutional and socio-economic change often associated with the exhaustion of the welfare state and the rise of neo-liberalism, neither theory is as such the ideal candidate for the development of an innovative and appropriate methodological advance at this time. For that, we wish to upgrade and enrich both approaches in several respects: the legal pluralist agenda must clearly be reformulated in order to combine investigations into 'indigenous' law[9] and into the complex relations between legal and non-legal constitutions of social fields,[10] with the particular challenge arising from an overlapping and interpenetration of human activities, normative standards and conflicts over rights and values. It is here where the legal pluralist agenda unfolds on the transnational level[11] and legal pluralism encounters concerns with global justice.[12] At the same time, reflexive law is and has, indeed, always been bound to shed its domestic skin to address the particular nature of law's embeddedness in a society that we might call—with Luhmann and others—'world society'.[13] Society understood as world society raises a host of extraordinary questions about the possible anchoring points for continuing claims for, contestations of and reconstructions of rights. To the degree that most of Western law has long been understood in its close relationship with and origin in the state,[14] the world society challenge to law, a society without peak or centre,[15] without a distinct institutional framework, an ethical meta-theory or a reliable stratification of social relations, such a theory must have radical consequences for law. Where law, then, is depicted as one among other social rationalities that can be observed in providing more or less coherent explanations of 'society', its relativity in comparison to other social systems becomes frighteningly evident. Where law comes to be understood as one, but not as the *exclusive*, contender for the ordering of social behaviour, for the provision of a normative framework for society, we recognise the pervasiveness of functionalist theories of law already alluded to. The rise of social

[9] Marc Galanter, 1981.

[10] Sally Falk Moore, 1973; John Griffiths, 1986.

[11] Sally Engle Merry, 2006.

[12] Nancy Fraser, 2009; Regina Kreide, 2008.

[13] Niklas Luhmann, 1970; Niklas Luhmann, 1982; Mathias Albert, 2002; Rudolf Stichweh, 2000; see also the comprehensive discussion and treatment of world society by John W Meyer, John Boli, George M Thomas and Francisco O Ramirez, 1997, 145: 'The statelessness of world society also explains, in good measure, the lack of attention of the social sciences to the coherence and impact of world society's cultural and associational properties'.

[14] For an intriguing critique, see Stephan Meder, 2008.

[15] Niklas Luhmann, 1981, 22.

norms and increasingly sophisticated depictions of the correlations between hard and soft laws and between official and unofficial, direct and indirect regulatory instruments, can be seen as a late triumph of reflexive law and at the same time as its magnificent defeat and ironic turn.[16] Adopting the methodology of reflexive law, social norms theory for the most part turns reflexive law's sensitivity to context and its recognition of the inevitable shortcomings of instrumental legal regulation to work for its own ideological programme. The state, which for reflexive law had ceased to live up to the expectations of a social-democratic, social-reformative agenda,[17] eventually became superseded by claims to self-regulation, private ordering and market mechanisms. It is today, amidst a dramatically unfolding financial and economic crisis that the boundaries between the 'state' and the 'market' are allegedly to be redrawn.

We are not convinced by this (non-)use of history. Drawing on evolutionary economic theory and, in particular, on the idea of path dependency, we argue for a more differentiated chronology of 'state' and 'market failures'.[18] While we find that the contours of the very concept of 'institutions' as laid out in work in new institutional economics and evolutionary theory remains wanting,[19] we nevertheless acknowledge the tremendous importance of a continued investigation into the institutional structures of market activities for any project of regulatory governance.[20] At the same time, we admit the certainly evident limitations and omissions of our project, which at its core pursues a *legal* theoretical inquiry, at the price of foregoing a more serious and fruitful engagement with an immensely rich global governance discussion in both institutionalist[21] and philosophical[22] discourses. What emerges from these parallel and overlapping endeavours is the insight that the inquiry into the conditions of global, or transnational governance cannot be separated from an ongoing study of the transformation of states[23] and from a genuinely interdisciplinary assessment of the *meaning* of governance,[24]

[16] Kerry Rittich, 2005; Peer Zumbansen, 2008a.

[17] Gunther Teubner, 1984.

[18] For an intriguing depiction, see Paul A David, 2007.

[19] See, eg: Richard Nelson, 2006, 8: 'a variety of non-market institutions'.

[20] Douglass C North, 1991; Oliver E Williamson, 1996; Avner Greif, 2006.

[21] For excellent explorations of the terrain, see Rodney Bruce Hall and Thomas J Biersteker, 2002 and the contributions to Joseph S Nye and John D Donahue, 2000. See, more recently, Marie-Laure Djelic and Kerstin Sahlin-Andersson, 2006b, as well as, in particular, the following contributions to that volume: Gili S Drori and John W Meyer, 2006, and Göran Ahrne and Nils Brunsson, 2006, and the excellent synthesis and further elaboration by Marie-Laure Djelic and Kerstin Sahlin-Andersson, 2006a, especially 382–83 for the identification of five central 'institutional forces', namely 'scientization', 'marketization', 'organizing', 'moral rationalization', and 'deliberative democracy'.

[22] See, below, ch 2 of this book, for a discussion of the concept of 'cosmopolitan democracy'.

[23] Bengt Jacobson, 2006; Stephan Leibfried and Michael Zürn, 2005.

[24] Marie-Laure Djelic and Kerstin Sahlin-Andersson, 2006a, 382.

a reconceptualisation that began to leave its marks also on the renewed attempts to better link research and teaching.[25]

Our attempt, then, to build on earlier work on reflexive law, integrates these advances in both evolutionary theory and new institutional economics, and unfolds in two steps. First, we think it necessary to further explore the methodological defencelessness of reflexive law against crude assertions of market supremacy and anti-regulatory polemics. In this light, it is important to take another close look at reflexive law's ironic turn in order to contribute to a hopefully richer analysis of the embeddedness of reflexive law in a complex political economy that can only adequately be understood in comparative, historical and spatial terms. This means that a theory of law that wishes to draw inspiration from reflexive law today must learn to incorporate an interdisciplinary host of insights including economics, sociology, regulatory theory, political science and history. Secondly, we think that reflexive law must address head on the challenge to law in the 'post-national constellation'. It is here where we posit that a theory of transnational law can build on the insights from reflexive law and its evolution over the past 30 to 40 years to unfold a rich legal theoretical analysis of the challenges arising around the constitution and regulation of global governance institutions. Contributing to and hopefully enriching current scholarship on (global) legal pluralism,[26] 'global administrative law',[27] our own previous work on transnational law in general,[28] and on transnational private law in particular, applies a reflexive law framework, founded on Luhmannian systems theory, to the study of regulatory regimes outside and beyond the nation state. Yet, because we understand transnational law above all to demarcate a methodological position rather than to identify a perfectly map-able doctrinal field, it is important to recognise that transnational law is better understood as a continuation, as a further elaboration and innovation of reflexive law than as a distinct legal field like, for example, public international law or conflict of laws. Transnational law, in our view, is a further engagement with reflexive law and with the concept of proceduralisation in the sense that it encompasses the particular insights of reflexive law and seeks to render them fruitful in a context of complex, intertwining legal and non-legal regulatory regimes.[29]

[25] See, for example, the representation of 'faculty teaching interests' at Osgoode Hall Law School in Toronto in a small number of integrated 'Knowledge Areas', available at: www.osgoode.yorku.ca/research/knowledge/index.html; see also the proposal for curriculum reform at German law schools by Stephan Leibfried, Christoph Möllers, Christoph Schmid and Peer Zumbansen, 2006.

[26] Paul Schiff Berman, 2007; Ralf Michaels, 2009b; Roger Cotterrell, 2009.

[27] Nico Krisch, Benedict Kingsbury and Richard B Stewart, 2005; Nico Krisch, 2009; for a critical discussion, see BS Chimni, 2005, and Carol Harlow, 2006.

[28] Gralf-Peter Calliess, 2002; Gralf-Peter Calliess, 2007; Gralf-Peter Calliess and Moritz Renner, 2009; Peer Zumbansen, 2006d; Peer Zumbansen, 2006b; Peer Zumbansen, 2008b.

[29] Rudolf Wiethölter, 1985; Rudolf Wiethölter, 1986a; Rudolf Wiethölter, 2006.

Beneath this, certainly, lies a long-standing contestation of the place and the role of law between the competing claims to domination by both economic and political sovereignty.[30] Law's sovereignty and its prerogative over the explosion of markets,[31] we came to learn, would only be ascertainable in negotiating between markets as de-centralised networks of bilateral exchange relations, on the one hand, and corporate actors such as organisations and associations, understood as centrally coordinated networks of corporatist membership relations,[32] on the other. In light of social theory's long-standing preoccupation with reconciling an increasingly sophisticated economic rationality with the overwhelming challenges of political representation,[33] law is irreversibly caught up in the paradoxical dilemma of 'making' or 'finding' rules, of 'direct' or 'indirect' regulation, etc.[34] This dilemma precedes, shapes and informs the present iterations of 'global governance' regimes in their search for law: the demarcation of hard versus soft law[35] or the de- and re-construction of the public/private distinction in international legal theory[36] give ample evidence of the lingering legacies of law's contested sovereignty.

The transnational challenge to legal theory presents itself to the fields and distinct doctrinal frameworks in both public and private international law at a time when both disciplines are already under extreme pressure to adapt their toolkits and even their conceptual frameworks in responding to the challenges arising from increasingly de-centralised and relativised law-making forums. While some scholars of public international law, at present, engage in a critique of law's political and violent nature, others reassert a Realist

[30] See, above all, Bernard Mandeville, 1970; Adam Ferguson, 1995; Adam Smith, 2006; Adam Smith, 1991; contrasting 'rational', 'conscious' governance with the idea of an 'unconscious', 'organic' evolution of order, see Friedrich A von Hayek, 1994, 34–35, distinguishing between a created (made) order and a spontaneous, polycentric order; Friedrich A Hayek, 2006, 193: 'The classical argument for freedom in economic affairs rests on the tacit postulate that the rule of law should govern policy in this as in all other spheres. We cannot understand the nature of the opposition of men like Adam Smith or John Stuart Mill to government "intervention" unless we see it against this background'. See also Friedrich A Hayek, 1973, 35 ('made' and 'grown' orders); see Franz Böhm, 1937; Franz Böhm, 1966, and Ernst-Joachim Mestmäcker, 1995, 117: 'Central to the concept of the economic constitution is the attempt to translate the economic philosophy of the classical national economic theory from the language of national economic theory into the language of law in order to depict free market economy as the legal constitution of economic life' [PZ trans] '*Im Mittelpunkt der Lehre von der Wirtschaftsverfassung steht der Versuch, die Wirtschaftsphilosophie der klassischen Nationalökonomie aus der Sprache der Nationalökonomie in die Sprache des Rechts zu übersetzen, um so die freie Verkehrswirtschaft als die Rechtsverfassung des Wirtschaftslebens nachzuweisen*'; Rudolf Wiethölter, 1965; Rudolf Wiethölter, 2006.

[31] Karl Polanyi, 1944.

[32] Viktor Vanberg, 1982, 76; see also Oliver E Williamson, 1975.

[33] See eg, Crawford Brough Macpherson, 1965, ch VI; Albert O Hirschman, 1970; Albert O Hirschman, 1977.

[34] Vanberg, above; Friedrich A Hayek, 1973, ch 4 'The changing concept of Law'.

[35] See, below, ch 5 of this book.

[36] See eg, A Claire Cutler, 1997; Christine Chinkin, 1999.

perspective on international law, based on rational choice considerations of economic efficiency and individual autonomy.[37] Meanwhile, scholars of private international law see their field challenged through the growing number of cases and instances that defy any continued or renewed attempt at re-domesticating a legal conflict in order to tie it back to a particular jurisdiction.[38] One of the consequences for private international law from the growing number of human rights litigation and internationally launched class action suits to address human rights violations, has been to question central doctrines such as 'forum non conveniens' and state immunity.[39] Other pressures for the field of private international law have emerged from decade-long advances in legal pluralism, law & society and critical legal scholarship with regard to the field's orientation around a state-made legal order. To the degree that private international law experts have been starting to consider the arguments made by these scholars, the field has increasingly been transformed into an important forum for the collision and appreciation of legal and social norms.[40]

Why then, one might ask, would there be a need or even room for an alternative approach to theorising law and global governance, if what we can witness occurring in international law and conflict of laws research is immensely rich and fast evolving? Our proposal of a distinct methodological concept of transnational law grows out of the recognition of the only growing complexity of what Robert Wai has recently referred to as the 'interlegality of transnational private law', which he sees as a promising lens through which to study the normative critical of private law and private international law.[41] The need for this focus results, in turn, from the analytical vacuum that is left between the traditional orientation of both international law and conflict of laws:

> Not only is transnational private law one important normative regime of international business, but it is also identified as providing a good analytical model for understanding the interrelationship among plural norms … An appreciation of private law as concerned with the relationship among plural and transnational normative orders is obscured because subjects of private law and private international law are typically considered separately. When viewed together, a sense

[37] Andrew T Guzman, 2008; Andrew T Guzman and Timothy L Meyer, 2008; for an intriguing discussion of how states compete for stakes in a global jurisdiction game, see Erin A O'Hara and Larry E Ribstein, 2009; see also Joel P Trachtman, 2008, 53: 'In the present context, we may look at an absence of interstate laws regarding prescriptive jurisdiction as the "market": a place where states make ad hoc, individual transactions in jurisdiction'.

[38] Paul Schiff Berman, 2002; Ralf Michaels, 2004; Hannah L Buxbaum, 2009; Craig M Scott, 2001b; Beth Stephens, 2002b.

[39] Excellent: Christopher A Whytock, 2009; see already Craig M Scott, 2001b.

[40] Andreas Fischer-Lescano and Gunther Teubner, 2004; Ralf Michaels, 2005; Paul Schiff Berman, 2005b; Paul Schiff Berman, 2007.

[41] Robert Wai, 2008; see already Robert Wai, 2005; for an elaboration as 'inter-legality' in the context of global sectoral regime collisions, see Fischer-Lescano and Teubner, 2004.

> of the long established task for private law of relating normative orders that challenge state boundaries becomes clearer.[42]

Significant in Wai's observation is the perceived linkage between 'private law, global legal pluralism and transnational governance of business relations', as it takes seriously the need to theorise the place/non-place of law in the continuously evolving framework of mixed, domestic-international, private-public, hard-soft regulation. A similar, equally promising position is taken by Marc Amstutz, who has been arguing for the need to develop a theoretical framework that is sensible to the sociologically constituted nature of legal orders: with regard to the much discussed challenges of harmonising legal fields in the EU, Amstutz emphasises the importance of a harmonisation building on and integrating distinct national legal cultures instead of attempting to level or abolish them. By underscoring the importance of difference, the harmonisation project becomes compatible with a recognition and productive exploitation of different legal cultures. But, even more importantly, harmonisation can then be reconstructed as a sophisticated legal pluralist project, aptly recognising the essential role played by the different legal cultures that are now understood as layered and as constituted in both official and inofficial ways.[43] 'In this specific sense, a constitution is to be understood as a *tool of integration of legal norms into real life processes*'.[44]

Inspired by such advances, we think that one can in fact productively complement and to a degree challenge theoretical approaches in international law that continue to place an exclusive emphasis on 'what people want'. While interventions such as those by Scott and Stephan and, more recently, by Trachtman[45] and O'Hara and Ribstein add an important set of perspectives on the competitive development of norms among states and between private parties and states, through their emphasis on the citizen as a *consumer* of legal norms on a 'law market', we think that another layer of—legal sociological—analysis is crucial. Clearly, as law & economics and, more recently, behavioural economics,[46] have been pointing to the relevance of motivational framework in contractual design and contractual governance, the current state of international law seemed to perfectly lend itself to an application of economic thinking to an area that continues to

42 Robert Wai, 2008, 108.

43 Marc Amstutz and Vaios Karavas, 2009.

44 Marc Amstutz, 2005, 767; but see Christoph Engel, 2004, 198: 'Social scientists often show contempt for a discipline that seems too close to reality to meet hard methodological standards, and too much concerned by pathologies that are beyond the reach of their methodological tools'.

45 Trachtman, 2008; O'Hara and Ribstein, 2009.

46 See, eg the contributions to Cass Sunstein, 2000; now: Richard Thaler and Cass Sunstein, 2008.

appear tragically caught up 'between apology and utopia'.[47] We would argue, however, that a particular layer of this constituted legal 'space' or, to use Saskia Sassen's pervasive term, 'assemblage',[48] cannot fully be captured by such approaches. It is here where we want to argue in favour of a decidedly methodological concept of transnational law that brings together legal pluralism, systems theory and a combination of political theory and political economy.

The concept of 'Rough Consensus and Running Code' (RCRC) proposed here responds to the structural elements of the contemporary regulatory landscape by offering a mixed, public-private, dynamic norm-creation process. RCRC overcomes the described obstacles to effective norm-creation for transnational relations by presenting a form of lawmaking, which does not replace but complements existing modes of norm-creation, either on the nation-state or international level. We understand RCRC to emerge as a particular form of societal self-governance at a time, where domestic and transnational, public and private lawmakers compete over regulatory competency and authority, much in the way this 'competition for jurisdiction' has been described by Scott and Stephan. In our following study we exemplify the conceptual and practical merits of RCRC through two case studies that illustrate the fast evolving developments of transnational norms in the area of consumer contracts and of corporate governance respectively. These case studies are illustrative of the importance of combining a legal pluralist perspective with both a political economy analysis and an understanding of the fundamentally transnational nature of normative evolution today.

[47] Martti Koskenniemi, 2005a; see the Symposium in celebration of the re-issue of this treatise, published in (December 2006) 7(12) *German Law Journal*, available at: www.germanlawjournal.com.

[48] Saskia Sassen, 2006.

1

Law's Elusive Boundaries

I. BORDER CROSSINGS

EVER SINCE PHILIP Jessup delivered the Storrs Lectures on 'Transnational Law' (TL) at Yale Law School in 1956,[1] the concept has occupied an ambivalent place in the theoretical landscapes maintained by scholars of public international law, private international law ('conflict of laws'), human rights law, and legal theory. Aiming to address the empty space left by the existing doctrinal perspectives, TL has always played a more complementing, challenging role than that of consolidating a new, neatly confined field of law.[2] What continues to make Jessup's contribution to our understanding of this particular body of law relevant is the consciousness with which he prepared the ground for a timely and forward-looking depiction of the need to think beyond the clearly demarcated fields of public and private international law. Even if we will argue in this book for a distinct expansion of Jessup's original focus on TL as a field—towards understanding transnational law *as a methodological position*—it is important once more[3] to closely examine Jessup's foray into transnational law's particular character and nature. In contrast to public international law, transnational law, for Jessup, was not confined to relationships among sovereign states. In contrast to the analytical lens applied by conflict of laws scholars, transnational lawyers did not seek to reattach the norms governing a particular situation to the laws of any given nation-state. Instead, TL, as he saw it, consisted of the norms that govern border-crossing transactions of both public—that is governmental—and private, that is individual, collective, commercial or other—actors.[4] To underscore the features of TL, Jessup resorted to

[1] Philip C Jessup, 1956.

[2] See Harold Hongju Koh, 2006, T Alexander Aleinikoff, 2008, and Roger Cotterrell, 2009, 482: 'Legal transnationalism haunts sociology of law or socio-legal studies ... in a somewhat spectral way. It is something seen but not seen; real but not fully real as a presence; mysterious, hard to pin down, and certainly to view clearly and as a whole'.

[3] See, eg Wolfgang Friedmann, Louis Henkin and Oliver Lissitzyn, 1972; Clive M Schmitthoff, 1982; Klaus Peter Berger, 2001a; Emmanuel Gaillard, 2001; Oren Perez, 2003; Christian Tietje and Karsten Nowrot, 2006; Peer Zumbansen, 2006d.

[4] Jessup, 1956, 2–3.

a short set of theatrical scenes, which in themselves constitute a brilliant example of transposing a scholarly argument into a dramatic framework of analogies to illustrate the concept's imaginative potential. In these scenes, Jessup conceptualised TL as providing a framework to analyse the parallel occurrences of regulatory challenges *within and beyond* the state's boundaries. Issues of representation and accountability which could be observed in the domestic arena with increased urgency in an era of government expenditure and bourgeoning government regulation[5] on the one hand and an expanding realm of corporate organisation on the other,[6] found their mirror images in the increasingly powerful, but at the same time, overly opaque and bureaucratic large, international organisations. Jessup's concept of TL, then, not only began to challenge the state-centredness of both public and private international law, it also began to outline the contours of a new perspective from which to study the legal norms that were emerging in the context of new regulatory frameworks inside and outside of the nation-state. Pointing to their non-state nature, Jessup was able to illuminate the intricacies of the fast-emerging normative body, created and consolidated in the context of border-crossing commercial, political and cultural activity.

The consequences of Jessup's concept of TL are both rich and incoherent. Its legacy is that it—perhaps—has none, if we were to measure its success by its ability to enter doctrinal, black-letter legal terminology. Instead, the concept has been spurring legal imagination, spanning from commercial arbitration experts[7] to human rights lawyers,[8] from intellectual property lawyers to legal anthropologists,[9] from contract[10] to tort,[11] property[12] to corporate lawyers.[13] In recent years again, such fields as administrative law and constitutional law, conceived as deeply embedded in a particular nation's political and economic history and as thus understood primarily as *domestic* legal fields, have been discovered as fruitful frameworks by which to more effectively address the regulatory challenges inherent to international organisations.[14]

[5] On this theme, see Charles Reich's seminal article, published just a few years after Jessup's 'Transnational Law': Charles A Reich, 1964; for a later assessment: Charles A Reich, 1990.

[6] A masterful depiction and seminal in its own right: Adolf A Berle, 1954.

[7] Yves Dezalay and Bryant Garth, 1996.

[8] Robert Wai, 2003.

[9] Rosemary J Coombe, 1995.

[10] Gunther Teubner, 1997b; Gralf-Peter Calliess, 2007; Ralf Michaels, 2007a.

[11] Craig M Scott, 2001b.

[12] Daniela Caruso, 2004.

[13] Peer Zumbansen, 2008b.

[14] For constitutional law, see eg Sujit Choudhry, 1999; Mark Tushnet, 2003; Alexandra Kemmerer, 2003; Günter Frankenberg, 2006; for administrative law, see eg Nico Krisch, Benedict Kingsbury and Richard B Stewart, 2005; Andreas Fischer-Lescano, 2008; Anne van Aaken, 2009a; certainly, this transnational dimension of administrative law was already

Meanwhile, as lawyers continue to plough the fields of doctrine and principles of this still young and promising 'field' of law, members of other disciplines have long become equally curious in the normative and regulatory nature of rapidly globalising forms of political and commercial interaction. Economists were among the first scholars to highlight and theorise the historically evolved transnational dimensions of trade and culture in a world economy.[15] This economical work, importantly, built on and complemented research by political scientists who had already been extrapolating the transformations of national and regional political economies under the influence of a globalising economy.[16] From this research emerged the observation that in order to adequately capture the evolutionary dynamics of regulatory models it would be necessary to address and capture—from within established disciplinary methodologies and frameworks—the 'space' between the 'international' and the 'national'. It soon became apparent that the nature of this transnational space had in fact to be understood as itself constructed, instead of being 'found' or 'given'. A crucial instantiation of this recognition was the emergence and subsequent fate of attempts to capture the space between the 'national' and the 'international' through concepts drawn from sociology in the tradition of Max Weber[17] and from political economy in the traditions of Karl Marx,[18] Henry Sumner Maine,[19] Emile Durkheim[20] and Karl Polanyi.[21] As economists and social scientists continued to build on Durkheim's problematisation of the 'non-contractual conditions of contract', one of the most promising advances was clearly the notion of 'embeddedness', mostly associated with Polanyi.[22] Starting with the powerful critique and re-invigoration of the concept and its use in social theory by Granovetter in the 1980s[23], scholars have recently been returning to an assessment of the concept's relevance.[24] Its importance can be seen in the analytical productivity that the concept potentially unfolds in a climate where relations between state and market have—once again—become fundamentally problematic. Informing an increasingly engaged dialogue between

emphasised by a number of conflict of laws scholars: see Christian Joerges, 1972a; Christian Joerges, 1972b; Rudolf Wiethölter, 1977.

15 Karl Marx and Friedrich Engels, 1848; Werner Sombart, 1906; Avner Greif, 2006.

16 See, eg, the important work by Andrew Shonfield, 1965, see also Jonah D Levy, 2006. See also the early analysis by Samuel P Huntington, 1973.

17 Max Weber, 1967.

18 Karl Marx, 1988.

19 Henry Sumner Maine, 1861.

20 Emile Durkheim, 1984.

21 Karl Polanyi, 1944.

22 Importantly, though, Polanyi, in 'The Great Transformation', does not explicitly use the term.

23 Mark Granovetter, 1985; see also Mark Granovetter, 2005.

24 Jens Beckert, 2007; Jens Beckert and Wolfgang Streeck, 2008; Jens Beckert, 2009; Peer Zumbansen, 2009b.

economists, sociologists and lawyers, the idea of embeddedness captures the particular challenges that are facing these disciplines with regard to adequately depicting the tension between different forms of social ordering. Granovetter's intervention in 1985 occurred at a time where law's boundaries were perceived to have become particularly elusive. Writing against the background of an intensifying critique of legal interventionism and juridification—'too much law'[25]—that eventually prepared the ground both for the rise of responsive/reflexive law critiques of 'legal instrumentalism'[26] and for the continuously influential theoretisation of 'law and economics',[27] Granovetter's contribution was crucial in the way that it addressed and emphasised both the promises and challenges of the contemporary fusing of social theory, law and economics.

The ensuing phases of theoretical work done on legal and non-legal social ordering have seen an unfaltering competition between two larger camps of social theory: whereas the juridification critique in the 1980s joined into an already proliferating host of post-legal realism, critical legal studies-informed 'law and society' developments,[28] the conservative attack on the welfare state informed a broad theoretical—and polemical—agenda, that today has given rise to some of the most challenging and powerful explorations of what Johannes Chan—albeit in the context of judicial review of administrative action—recently termed the 'illusory boundary between law and policy'.[29] Central in this boundary-drawing has been the concept of 'institution', most remarkably developed in economic theory, notably in New Institutional Economics (NIE).[30] Today, as NIE has become one of the most influential theoretical influences on social theory and law, Granovetter's approach allows us to both build on and further enrich the institutional analysis put forward by economists, by paying even more attention to the nature and qualities of different institutions that shape economic behaviour. While we are guided by Granovetter's warning against a totalising and eventually insufficiently contoured concept of embeddedness, we think that insights, in particular from legal anthropology, legal pluralism and regulatory theory, are of central importance to better accentuating the nature of institutions, the increasingly sophisticated treatment of which has largely contributed to making NIE such a strong contender for the

[25] Marc Galanter, 2006, 5, 12.

[26] Philippe Nonet and Philip Selznick, 1978; Gunther Teubner, 1983; Gunther Teubner, 1986a.

[27] Richard A Posner, 1973; Oliver E Williamson, 1975; Oliver Williamson, 1985; see the assessment by Richard Swedberg, 2003.

[28] See, eg Lawrence Friedman, 1985; a concise depiction is given by Duncan Kennedy, 2002, and Orly Lobel, 2007.

[29] Johannes Chan, 2008, at 143.

[30] Eg Paul A David, 1994; Paul A David, 2000; Joel Mokyr, 2005.

construction of regulatory theories of global governance.[31] As NIE scholars have been contributing to an extremely rich and lively debate—thereby pushing on the one hand, for a more succinct definition and conceptualisation of the notion of *institution*[32] itself, while on the other, arguing for a new institutional economist theory of (public) international law[33]—NIE has in fact been able to address and further enhance our understanding of emerging governance structures. These advances—themselves building on earlier ground-breaking work in political science[34]—attest to the pertinence of views shared by economists and political scientists that the constantly evolving shape of global markets is informed by a complex and multi-polar combination of public, regulatory action, both inside and outside of the nation-state, together with an increasingly hard-to-discern web of norms, generated by private and semi-public actors.[35] Employing overlapping and mutually complementing notions of 'institutions' or 'regimes', scholars in economics, social sciences and law are bound to continue to engage in further refining a promising inter-disciplinary research agenda.[36]

In recognising as the central challenge for a theoretisation of law and global governance the continued engagement with and contestation of the boundary between legal and non-legal forms of social ordering ('Law vs non-law'), there is much to gain for legal theory from economics and associated theories such as 'social norms' theory and 'new institutional economics', in particular with regard to a much needed further definition of *institutions*.

In Professor Douglass North's words, '[i]nstitutions are the humanly devised constraints that structure political, economic and social interaction. They consist of both informal constraints (sanctions, taboos, customs, traditions, and codes of conduct), and formal rules (laws, property rights)'.[37] In his important study of 1990, he observed: '[a]s defined here, they [institutions] therefore are the framework within which human interaction takes place'.[38] It is against this relatively flexible definition that North has been arguing for the central role of institutions for long-term economic performance. North's contribution to an increasingly interdisciplinary dialogue concerning market regulation in historical perspective can hardly be overestimated.

[31] For a more detailed presentation of this argument, see Peer Zumbansen and Gralf-Peter Calliess, 2010.

[32] For an introduction to these debates, see the introduction and overview by Stefan Voigt, 2002; see also the contributions to Daniele Archibugi and Jonathan Michie, 1997.

[33] Anne van Aaken, 2009b; Joel P Trachtman, 2008.

[34] Kenneth W Abbott, 1989; Anne-Marie Slaughter-Burley, 1993; see the contributions in Stephen D Krasner, 2001.

[35] See, eg Joost Pauwelyn, 2006, 203–205.

[36] Avner Greif and David Laitin, 2004; Avner Greif, 2006; see already Paul R Milgrom, Douglass C North and Barry W Weingast, 1990.

[37] Douglass C North, 1991, 97.

[38] Douglass C North, 1990, 4.

As academic interest in the nature, culture and trajectory of the market[39] among legal scholars, economists, economic historians, geographers and political economists again soared in recent years,[40] Douglass North's insistence on an interdisciplinary, historically grounded analysis of the different institutions that structure market behaviour proved to be a crucial contribution to a more engaged and more challenging exchange between scholars in different disciplines. Building on and eventually substantively expanding his earlier interest in 'institutions' per se, North in his more recent work has adopted a decidedly social-theory perspective, from which he places a central emphasis on the nature and volatility of societal change and on the resulting uncertainty that characterises long-term oriented theorising. Central to this reorientation is the role of intentionality with regard to institutional change.[41] With this, North connects his important institutionalist framework to the increasingly influential[42] work in behavioural finance[43] and behavioural law & economics,[44] and makes thus a powerful argument for the need to take the complexity of market structures and behaviour seriously—a lesson which will continue to inspire future interdisciplinary research not only in corporate finance and corporate governance,[45] but also in economic sociology, geography and regulatory theory.[46] Along with economic geography gaining new attraction for economists and globally oriented policy-makers with regard to regional differences in economic growth and development,[47] and regulatory theory, which over the past 15 years has

[39] See of course already Harrison C White, 1981.

[40] See, eg John Lie, 1997; Ekkehard F Rosenbaum, 2000; Neil Fligstein, 2001; see also the contributions to Victor Nee and Richard Swedberg, 2005b, and Victor Nee and Richard Swedberg, 2005a. Besides the recent renaissance in economic sociology, the contributions by scholars interested in the 'Varieties of Capitalism' are of particular interest in this regard: see eg the landmark volume by Peter A Hall and David Soskice, 2001b, and the preceding work by David Soskice, 1999, and J Rogers Hollingsworth, 1997, as well as Wolfgang Streeck, 2001.

[41] Douglass C North, 2005.

[42] See the hesitant treatment, at the time, by one of the most astute scholars of the ECMH himself: Eugene Fama, 1998, 284: 'anomalies'.

[43] See the foundational work on the Efficient Capital Market Hypothesis (ECMH) by Eugene Fama, 1970; Michael C Jensen, 1970; Ronald J Gilson and Reinier Kraakman, 1984—see also Ronald J Gilson and Reinier Kraakman, 2003, and Lynn Stout, 2003.

[44] See the contributions to Cass Sunstein, 2000; for a very informative discussion and overview, see Lars Klöhn, 2006, 80–153.

[45] See the brilliant example: Ruth Aguilera, Deborah Rupp, Cynthia A Williams and Jyoti Ganapathi, 2004.

[46] As a representative example of work grown out of long-term analysis of the shortcomings of the Efficient (Capital) Market Hypothesis (suggesting that financial markets are informationally efficient), see the scholarship by Richard Thaler: Richard Thaler, 1987; Richard Thaler, 1999; see now Richard Thaler and Cass Sunstein, 2008.

[47] See, eg, the World Bank's 2009 World Development Report '*Reshaping Economic Geography*'; see the contributions to Gordon L Clark, Maryann P Feldman and Meric S Gertler, 2003; see also the famous launch by Paul Krugman in 1992 of 'new economic geography', Paul Krugman, 1992, and Paul Krugman, 1998; see further the relatively recent creation of a new academic journal in this area: *Journal of Economic Geography* (OUP, since 2001),

become something of an umbrella concept for interdisciplinary governance studies,[48] economic sociology has been making important strides, with regard to its engagement both with institutional economics and with law.[49] It is from here that important impulses for a more serious, interdisciplinary study of 'law in context', 'law & society' and 'social norms' in their relation to traditional jurisprudence are likely going to be received still,[50] and it is against this background that this book aims at contributing to an inter-disciplinary research agenda for the study of transnational norms.

II. TOWARDS A LEGAL CRITIQUE OF TRANSNATIONAL GOVERNANCE INSTITUTIONS

In light of the inherent limitations of an effective extension of legal regulatory rules beyond a nation-state's borders, the role and place of law today appear particularly precarious. Law's traditional association with the state's authority to make and to enforce valid law[51] has always sat squarely with what Max Weber called 'extra-state law'—the norms made, for example, by corporatist, ecclesiastical and other entities.[52] Furthermore, given the coercive power to enact norms as law in the first place,[53] the association of law with the state has long been questioned in radical forms.[54] This critique of state-made law—which we will discuss in greater detail in the next chapter—by legal pluralists, together with the varied history of weak or strong, laissez-faire or interventionist governments in Western states' history, has induced a particularly differentiated view with regard to homogeneous

complementing among others the long-standing Economic Geography (Clark University, since 1925).

48 See, eg, the overview by Scott Burris, Michael Kempa and Clifford Shearing, 2008; see also the meanwhile seminal article in legal scholarship by Orly Lobel, 2004; for a refreshing perspective with regard to the EU, see Christoph Möllers, 2006; with regard to global financial regulation, see the important contribution by Julia Black and David Rouch, 2008.

49 See only Victor Nee and Richard Swedberg, 2005a, 795: 'Slowly ... it has been realized by economic sociologists that *law* constitutes a central part of the modern economy'. See, in this context, Richard Swedberg, 2003.

50 See, eg, the definition of 'institution' provided by Nee and Swedberg, *ibid*, 797–8: 'An institution may be conceptualized as a dominant system of interrelated informal and formal elements—customs, shared beliefs, norms, and rules—which actors orient their actions to when they pursue their interests. In this view, institutions are dominant social structures which provide a conduit for social and collective action by facilitating and structuring the interests of actors and enforcing principal agent relationships. It follows from this interest-related definition that institutional change involves not simply remaking the formal rules, but requires the realignment of interests, norms, and power'.

51 The classical statements are Hans Kelsen, 1961; Hans Kelsen, 1941, 50–52; Max Weber, 1967, 11–20.

52 Max Weber, 1967, 19.

53 Robert M Cover, 1986.

54 Robert M Cover, 1983, and Sally Engle Merry, 1988.

or unifying concepts of a legal order.[55] As a growing appreciation of the fast-expanding areas of 'privatisation of law-making'[56] might sometimes be driven by exaggerated beliefs in a 'traditionally' tight correlation between law and the state,[57] the present challenge is indeed one of keeping an eye on the historical facticity of 'private' ordering, on the one hand, and on the evolution of political assessments of 'state responsibilities' and 'societal self-regulation', on the other. Today, there appears to be a consensus among lawyers and sociologists that any legal order is, in reality, always constituted of an amalgamation of official and less official norms, altogether producing and resulting in a dynamic, changing and developing normative order.[58] The different histories[59] of legal reform, protest movements, retrenchment, government expansion, waxings, wanings or retreats of the state, rights movements and the still ongoing evolution of law after the interventionist and welfare states provide telling testimonies of the co-evolution of direct and indirect, official and unofficial forms of legal regulation.[60]

The transnationalisation of this layered, polycentric normative order adds further to the already precarious status of law as 'law'. To be sure, the overwhelmingly economic nature of globalisation[61] has been answered by a number of high-yielding attempts, for example, among public international lawyers to constitutionalise international affairs,[62] or to pursue institutionalist models through a deepened dialogue between public international law and international relations theory.[63] In response, a number of scholars of international law have forcefully challenged law's authority in global governance[64] and thereby provoked a number of hearty responses in defence.[65] This debate provides a number of insights which are relevant to our current investigation. The proliferation of norm-creation activities outside the nation-state points to two developments: on the one hand, it suggests the

[55] See, eg Karl-Heinz Ladeur, 1983; Niklas Luhmann, 1990; Karl-Heinz Ladeur, 1997b, 44.

[56] Johannes Köndgen, 2006.

[57] For an excellent analysis, see Stephan Meder, 2008.

[58] See Sally Falk Moore, 1973; Sally Engle Merry, 1992; Harry W Arthurs, 1988.

[59] See, for the American case, Morton J Horwitz, 1992 (in particular the final chapter); Duncan Kennedy, 2006; Orly Lobel, 2007.

[60] Scholarship in administrative law is particularly telling in that respect: Mark Bevir and RAW Rhodes, 2003; Richard J Stillman II, 2003; Werner Jann, 2003; Robert Elgie, 2003; Alfred C Aman Jr, 1997; for a critical assessment in the context of law & development efforts, see only David Trubek and Marc Galanter, 1974.

[61] Jürgen Osterhammel and Niels P Petersson, 2004.

[62] See, for concise accounts of the pressing challenges, Bardo Fassbender, 1998; Neil Walker, 2003a; Joseph HH Weiler, 2004.

[63] See Andrew Moravcsik, 1997; Oona A Hathaway and Ariel N Lavinbuk, 2006; Kenneth W Abbott, 2006.

[64] Jack Goldsmith and Eric Posner, 2005.

[65] See, eg Detlev F Vagts, 2004; Oona A Hathaway and Ariel N Lavinbuk, 2006; Paul Schiff Berman, 2006.

emergence of an autonomous[66] or, at least, semi-autonomous legal order,[67] which results from societal processes of will-formation and decision-making. The development of such an autonomous legal order would matter methodologically in the sense that it would confirm the legal pluralist contention of a plurality of normative universes and competing official and unofficial normative orders.[68] On the other hand, from the point of view of a *political* legal theory in the tradition of Legal Realism,[69] the proliferation of norm creation outside of the nation-state has inevitably been raising questions about the role of the state in the creation and regulation of societal activities. From the point of view of a public lawyer, the proliferation of private norm creation, then, would foremost be a problem of 'might is right', and what has otherwise been favourably explored as the emergence of a transnational normative order, primarily perceived as the 'dark side of private ordering'.[70] In this highly-charged discourse about law and the state in an era of globalised norm-making, it is necessary to take a much closer look at the conceptual and functional place of 'social norms' and their relation to the 'official' legal order, from which they are allegedly distinct.

III. LAW'S ELUSIVE EMPIRE?

Already at first glance it becomes clear that many examples of a 'global law without a state'[71] do not in fact contain a flat-out rejection of state-based, official law. Rather, examples such as corporate codes of conduct or privately enacted rules in transnational commercial arbitration can be seen as underscoring the increasing complexity of a legal order the building blocks of which originate in regulatory processes that are no longer confined to government actors nor to nation-states alone. This is an important interim observation as it helps to bring some sobriety into otherwise too quickly exhausted discussions of (state-made) law's losing grip on societal affairs.[72] Thus, one of the central challenges of formulating a legal theory of transnational law-making lies in adequately assessing the degree to which the proliferation of norm-creation actors indeed mirrors the history of legal evolution within the nation-state. The methodological concept of TL—and, in particular, of *transnational legal pluralism*, on which our present project

66 For an early, eloquent exposition of this thesis, see Gunther Teubner, 1997c.
67 In close, albeit unmined proximity to SF Moore, see Erich Schanze, 2007.
68 For an excellent overview, see Ralf Michaels, 2009b.
69 For an excellent collection of American and German scholarship see: Christian Joerges and David Trubek, 1985.
70 Curtis J Milhaupt and Mark D West, 2000b.
71 Gunther Teubner, 1997e.
72 In a similar vein: Roger Cotterrell, 2009, 485.

builds[73] and which informs and complements the concurrent project on 'legal certainty on global markets'[74] at the Collaborative Research Centre in Bremen—seeks to draw out the manifold connections between the regulatory experiences, semantic and doctrinal frameworks that evolved within the nation-state and our ongoing attempts to imagine a 'global' or 'post-national' legal order today. From that perspective we can begin to discern the parallels between current troubles of an emerging post-national institutional and legal framework, on the one hand, and preceding institutional transformations that have been marking the nation-state all along, on the other. Our project would be unimaginable without the powerful provocations from within systems theory and legal pluralism in defence of the argument of an emerging, markedly different, 'autonomous'[75] legal order. Yet, we wish to complement this perspective with a particular conceptual, theoretical and historical account of the regulatory transformations of the nation-state,[76] as we believe that these continue to cast an enormous shadow on the way in which we even begin to speak about the challenges for the establishment of a political, legal, normative order on the global level.[77] Our inquiry, thus, necessitates a closer scrutiny of lawyers', economists', sociologists' and other social scientists' assertions of normative frameworks outside—and within—the nation-state.

At the beginning to lay out the building blocks of a theory of transnational private law, there needs to be an engagement with some of the main challenges to conceptualising a new legal field or, as we would like to argue, a new methodological framework for speaking about law. From a methodological perspective, the concept of transnational law challenges some of law's dearly held contentions. Among those, law's origin in a state legal order[78] is surely the most prominent and, as such, at the top of the list of beliefs challenged by the concept of transnational law. However, already a caveat is in order. Whether transnational law and its many progeny, such as *lex mercatoria* (law merchant)[79] or transnational human rights law, should be regarded as 'law' in the traditional sense can remain outside of the present analysis in light of the particular approach to this issue taken here. Confident that decades of exploring the relationship between 'law and society' have produced an impressive set of arguments in support of the *legal nature* of transnational norms, our aim is, on the one hand, to scrutinise

[73] Peer Zumbansen, 2006d; Peer Zumbansen, 2008b; Peer Zumbansen, 2009a.

[74] Gralf-Peter Calliess, 2006; Gralf-Peter Calliess, Thomas Dietz, Wioletta Konradi, Holger Nieswandt and Fabian Sosa, 2007; Gralf-Peter Calliess and Moritz Renner, 2009.

[75] See for this claim, Gunther Teubner, 2004b.

[76] We hereby build on earlier work: see Gralf-Peter Calliess, 1999, and Peer Zumbansen, 2000b.

[77] Peer Zumbansen, 2001b; Gralf-Peter Calliess, 2001.

[78] For an insightful discussion and critique, see Florian F Hoffmann, 2008.

[79] See, eg Clive M Schmitthoff, 1961; Berthold Goldman, 1964; Bruce Benson, 2010.

the particular features of the emergence and unfolding of transnational law, which approximates the current project to parallel efforts in economic sociology, NIE and legal pluralism. On the other hand, this book seeks to offer a critical reading of existing conceptualisations aimed at the *normativity* of the emerging transnational legal order. It is here where it will, for example, become necessary to revisit concepts of 'embeddedness' as developed by Granovetter and ensuing work in economic sociology in order to further scrutinise the tension between 'formal' and 'informal' institutions as well as the particular dynamics of institutional change. Likewise, the concept of 'economic governance', in the form developed by the Nobel Laureate Oliver Williamson, will be further elaborated in order to offer a better grasp of how to distinguish between market and political institutions and, on that basis, to gain a deeper understanding of the normative stakes of combining 'public' and 'private' institutions in the design of governance regimes. Building on some of our and others' previous work regarding the content and nature of transnational law on the one hand[80] and the particular methodological aspects of the concept of transnational law on the other,[81] this book as much focuses on the ways by which norms of transnational law *come into being* as it hopes to further accentuate the challenges that arise from the question 'But, is it law?'. In other words, we remain sceptical towards a distinction between 'form' and 'substance' of transnational law. Central to this project is the contention that the study of transnational processes and institutions through which norms are produced that are subsequently assessed as being either legal or non-legal in nature, is inseparable from the critique of the distinction between law/non-law in the first place.

By studying the emergence of norms that govern transnational processes, we intend to contribute to a better understanding of the different forms of transnational regulation. In that, we are confident that we can enrich the methodological architecture developed by NIE scholars, who have become particularly interested in the interaction of formal and informal norms in governing economic behaviour.[82] With these scholars, we share the belief that social norms do operate within a framework of formal rules, often maintained and reinforced by an institutionalised system of rule enforcement.[83]

At the same time, our aim is to go beyond this observation and to take, as it were, the law more seriously in this context. When studying the wealth

[80] See Sally Engle Merry, 1988; Gunther Teubner, 1997c; Gunther Teubner, 1997b; Peer Zumbansen, 2002a; Gralf-Peter Calliess, 2002; Gralf-Peter Calliess and Moritz Renner, 2009; for an excellent analysis of the similar debate around *lex mercatoria*, see Benson, 2010, and Ursula Stein, 1995.

[81] Peer Zumbansen, 2004c; Peer Zumbansen, 2006d.

[82] See, eg Avner Greif, 2006; Bruce Benson, 1989.

[83] Douglass C North, 2005, 14–15.

of social norms and practices that feed into the creation of binding norms in areas such as those we take up in the case studies in this book—transnational consumer law and transnational corporate governance—we take the view that, despite the manifold forms of informal, 'social' norms operating in this context, a specific emphasis on *law* in this regard is likely to provide us with a better understanding of the nature of the relevant existing regulatory institutions. One of the reasons for being so interested in the role of the law played in the context of regulating consumer contracts (chapter three) or corporate governance (chapter four) is that we contend that law encompasses both informal and formal norms that govern a particular transaction. However, differentiating between social norms on the one hand and 'official', formal norms on the other, in the way that institutional economists tend to do,[84] in our view not only obscures the way in which formal norms are constantly being created, refined and reshaped, but more dramatically, it tends to obscure the fact that the law is constantly called upon to reflect on the way in which it confronts, addresses and eventually incorporates and translates its 'other'. In other, perhaps less intimidating words, this would concern the way in which the legal order is able to translate, to transpose and to integrate informal norms into its 'official body'.[85] This process of translation, transposition and integration is central to an understanding of the law, but is certainly not confined to this internal perspective.

To understand how law constitutes an always necessarily *violent* process of usurpation of social reality, fragility and possibility into a confined and limited space of interpretative hegemony[86] through 'making it law', means to understand not only that a process of transformation of a social norm into an official, 'legal' norm has taken place. Instead, it means to recognise the violence and power that are inherent in this transformation from the informal to the formal. Both violence and power always overshadow private bargaining[87] and thus inform and shape the relationship between public regulation and private ordering, certainly long before the process of transformation is set in motion. This tension between formal and informal law is thus only insufficiently represented in occasional laments on formal law's perceived inadequacy to effectively regulate private parties' behaviour.[88] While such contentions suggest that there is a quasi-natural superiority in private bargaining in comparison to publicly administered, adjudicated conflict resolution, their main thrust is to separate the former from the realm of the latter. Private bargaining, thus portrayed, is presented

[84] Douglass C North, 1991; for an excellent discussion, see Victor Nee and Richard Swedberg, 2005a.

[85] See, eg Gunther Teubner, 1989; Peer Zumbansen, 2007b.

[86] Robert M Cover, 1986; Robert M Cover, 1983.

[87] Robert H Mnookin and Lewis Kornhauser, 1979.

[88] See, eg Eric A Posner, 2000; Robert E Scott, 2000.

as unfolding in a more or less free, uninhibited environment, with the state and its enforcement machinery in place in the background as a pre-emptive or overhanging threat, but ultimately with no further specified bearings on the varied processes of societal bargaining.

By contrast, such representations of private ordering only inadequately capture the role of law in shaping processes of 'private' interaction. These must be understood as always unfolding 'before the law', as so powerfully depicted by Kafka.[89] Building on the contentions by scholars such as Robert Hale[90] and Morris Cohen,[91] we understand processes of private bargaining as constituted by the law. The way in which this constitution takes place is never necessarily a straight-forward one, and certainly no longer so in an age of multiplied sources and sites of law-making.[92] In this regard, the Realists'[93] confidence in re-politicising processes of private, contractual ordering[94] is likely to be unmerited in our days of multi-layered, de-nationalised norm creations.[95] And yet, their insight into the political nature and embeddedness of legal rules in a more complex socio-economic regulatory environment of rights and entitlements, is helpful to address the current depictions of social norms, purportedly unfolding in a realm dominated solely by the will of the parties.

This book, thus, seeks to illuminate the processes by which regulatory structures in areas like consumer law and corporate governance are emerging; how they are conceptualised from a political science, a legal and an economical perspective; and how they might be seen as examples of a new form of global governance regimes. Its project shares certain parallel interests *with* but eventually differs *from* current scholarly endeavours such as Erin O'Hara and Larry Ribstein's 'Law Market',[96] Jens Dammann and Henry Hansmann's proposal of a 'global market for judicial services in contract litigation'[97] and Emanuela Carbonara and Francesco Parisi's 'Market for Legal Rules'.[98] While these scholars lay out a series of intriguing and well-presented arguments concerning federal and global state competition

[89] Franz Kafka, *Before the Law* (1915), available at: www.herzogbr.net/kafka/beforethelaw.htm.

[90] Robert L Hale, 1923.

[91] Morris R Cohen, 1927.

[92] See, eg Julia Black and David Rouch, 2008, 218: 'Political and legal fragmentation is one of the main motivations for formulating market-based, private law solutions and for using regulatory principles which help to create a space within which the markets can make rules.'

[93] *Ibid.*

[94] See the discussion in Peer Zumbansen, 2007b.

[95] Saskia Sassen, 2003.

[96] Erin A O'Hara and Larry E Ribstein, 2009; see already Erin A O'Hara and Larry E Ribstein, 2008.

[97] Jens Dammann and Henry Hansmann, 2008.

[98] Emanuela Carbonara and Francesco Parisi, 2007.

around legal services, the present[99] project aims at a different aspect of such competition. Inspired by foundational work in both regulatory competition[100] and decentralisation[101] the book focuses primarily on the *nature* of competing norms. Building on previous work,[102] the present project seeks to develop a more comprehensive depiction of the *object* of harmonisation or competition; in other words, not of the pursued goals and outcomes but, rather, of what it is that is in fact exposed to pressures of harmonisation or competition. In light of the far-reaching regulatory transformation of states as the principal actors in the harmonisation vs regulatory competition scenario, it seems promising to pierce the traditional conceptual boundaries of the state and to reach within its institutional architecture; only from this perspective will it be possible to glimpse the highly diversified and fragmented landscape of regulatory norms, instruments and institutions that today constitute a state's *legal* structure. We contend that such a norm-oriented perspective is crucial to any promising engagement with harmonisation and regulatory competition. As such, rather than assessing the competition of confined, established legal orders of different national origins, the approach suggested here focuses on the interaction and interpenetration of evolving legal cultures, comprising hard and soft law, official and unofficial norms, promulgated by public, private and hybrid norm-producing entities. Neither explicitly public nor private in nature, pertaining to and originating neither in the nation-state nor exclusively from within international organisations, the evolving normative regimes are bound to fundamentally challenge traditional ways of understanding and speaking of 'law-making'.

Building on a concept of norm creation that was first developed in the context of Internet standards, we suggest that a dynamic process of consensus building and code evolution ('Rough Consensus, Running Code') can adequately capture the interdisciplinary, intricate nature of contemporary, transnational law-making. When unfolding this concept with regard to our fields of interest, it will soon become clear that conceptual challenges arise both from within and from outside our own discipline. From constitutional lawyers, the central challenge to the present concept is probably that it fails satisfactorily to answer the question of legitimacy. From the point of view of economists, the likely weakest element in this concept is the continued emphasis on the *role of law* for an understanding of the tension between formal and informal norms. For the reasons alluded to above with regard to

[99] See in this regard already Gralf-Peter Calliess and Hermann B Hoffmann, 2009b, and Gralf-Peter Calliess and Hermann B Hoffmann, 2009a.

[100] See Henry Manne, 1965.

[101] Charles M Tiebout, 1956; Susan Rose-Ackerman, 1980; Albert Breton, 2000; Brian Galle and Joseph Leahy, 2009.

[102] Gralf-Peter Calliess, 2004; Peer Zumbansen, 2004a; Peer Zumbansen, 2006c; Peer Zumbansen, 2008b.

the problematic distinction between form and substance, we think we can well address these concerns and we will do so later in chapter five.

As regards the concerns raised by constitutional lawyers, we are equally hopeful to be able to show that they rely on an understanding of legitimacy which is not adequate to contemporary forms of norm creation. The constitutionalists' hope for legitimacy continues to be based on a particular, nation-state oriented model of political representation and formal rule-making, whereas our concept, which underlies the idea of global governance regimes, takes a different starting point. Given the different layers and sites of norm creation on the one hand and the mixed, public, private and hybrid nature of norm-makers ('norm entrepreneurs') on the other, a traditional model of political legitimacy might in the end be ill-suited to capture the dynamic and open nature of these regimes' constituencies.

The remainder of this book is structured as follows. The next chapter provides a reconstruction of the theoretical and conceptual context in which the proposal of Rough Consensus and Running Code (RCRC) becomes possible. Much of that chapter addresses the fundamental changes in regulatory frameworks that can be observed within and outside of the nation-state. For that purpose, we review the different approaches of theorising governance structures beyond the nation-state, as put forward by lawyers, economists, political scientists and sociologists. The discussion illustrates the tension between a traditional mode of legal regulation, drawing on norms developed and enforced by state authorities on the one hand, and the vast emergence of private ordering and self-regulatory mechanisms, developed and enforced by private and hybrid, public-private actors on the other. Following Saskia Sassen in her claim that in order to gain an adequate understanding of transnational regulatory regimes, it is essential to acknowledge their *mixed* constitution, consisting of physical as much as of intellectual components, we attempt to work out a *legal theoretical* understanding of these particular regulatory spaces. The emerging transnational 'spaces' or 'global assemblages' are as much a construction as they are a reality.[103] In these spaces, there arises a renewed need to carve out orientations for political action. And, yet, the orientation points are no longer discernable by reliance on traditional binary distinctions such as the public-private divide, an important insight recently promoted by Nancy Fraser.[104] Consequently, one of the tasks confronting us in our work is to engage with and to reach beyond the public-private distinction when developing the conceptual and methodological elements of a theory of transnational law. It is against this background that the concept of 'Rough Consensus and Running Code' is outlined.

[103] Saskia Sassen, 2006.
[104] Nancy Fraser, 2009.

Chapters three and four form the test cases of the conceptual framework laid out here. The concept of RCRC is applied to two distinct regulatory areas, consumer contracts (chapter three) and corporate governance (chapter four), respectively. Both regulatory regimes differ in that they involve specific instruments and relate to particular, different constituent interests. Yet, they resemble each other to a significant degree in that in both areas norm creation has increasingly been transformed through the development of a highly dynamic, and institutionally mixed, complex rule-making process. The rules pertaining to sales contracts can be studied particularly well in the example of consumer protection norms, since these, as experienced in the respective domestic legacies of consumer protection adjudication and legislation,[105] give powerful illustrations of the contested nature of any regulatory strategy in this area. Likewise, the currently, fast-evolving law of corporate governance, which itself has long ceased to be merely of domestic interest, offers important lessons in contemporary law-making studies. Corporate governance norms express a highly complex mix of official, unofficial, hard, soft, domestic and international norms. The resulting transnational law of corporate governance thus serves as a fitting example of RCRC norm creation.

The final chapter five picks up a thread treated lightly in the introductory chapter above, in order to illuminate more clearly the normative and regulatory context in which the current debates over transnational norm creation are taking place. For this purpose follows a discussion of the presently much debated relationship between 'law and *social norms*'. The chapter places this debate in the context of an assessment of *soft law* concepts, on the one hand, and present contestations of *customary international law*, on the other. Stressing the importance of seeing such contestations in 'public' (*international law*) and 'private' (contract, social norms) in connection to current discussions of laws for a global market or a widely proclaimed convergence of corporate governance norms, we conclude by indicating the contours of a legal pluralist theory of transnational law.

[105] Andreas Maurer, 2007; see also Geraint Howells and Thomas Wilhelmsson, 2003.

2

Towards a Theory of Transnational Private Law

I. SEEING THE (GLOBAL) WORLD THROUGH A PRIVATE LAWYER'S EYES

THIS CHAPTER SEEKS to situate our own theoretical premises in the context of contemporary projects of law and globalisation. With such an orientation, the net is—admittedly—cast widely. As will become evident on the pages that follow, a proposal such as that put forward in this book—namely to explore the foundations and prospects of a methodological framework for transnational (private) law—is unavoidably situated in a host of parallel, complementing and challenging theoretical projects concerned with the fate of law outside, and *after* the nation-state. With this perspective in mind, our own proposal grows out of and complements a number of currently discussed concepts of 'global law', but cannot attempt to conclusively assess and evaluate all of them. Instead, we aim at developing a theoretical concept of transnational private law, which we illustrate with case studies from two important fields of transnational norm-creation. As we situate our concept in dialogue with theoretical approaches regarding 'transnational law',[1] 'transnational commercial law',[2] 'global law',[3] 'law *and* globalisation',[4] 'transnational spaces'[5] and 'communities',[6] 'global legal pluralism',[7] 'hard versus soft law',[8] 'law and social norms'[9]

[1] Philip C Jessup, 1956; Craig M Scott, 2009.
[2] Roy Goode, 1997; Ross Cranston, 2007.
[3] Gunther Teubner, 1997e.
[4] Paul Schiff Berman, 2005a; Mathias Reimann, 2004; Peer Zumbansen, 2004b; Craig Scott, 2005.
[5] Richard Ford, 1999; Saskia Sassen, 2006; Saskia Sassen, 2007; Shaunnagh Dorsett and Shaun McVeigh, 2007; T Alexander Aleinikoff, 2008.
[6] Roger Cotterrell, 1997; Roger Cotterrell, 2008.
[7] Paul Schiff Berman, 2007; Ralf Michaels, 2009b.
[8] Kenneth W Abbott and Duncan Snidal, 2000; Christine Chinkin, 1989; see further the contributions to John J. Kirton and Michael J. Trebilcock, 2004; see also the excellent discussion in Larry Catá Backer, 2009, and Gregory Shaffer and Mark A Pollack, 2009.
[9] See Kaushik Basu, 1998; Richard McAdams, 1997; Eric A Posner, 2000; John N Drobak, 2006; for a critical perspective see the author of 'Order without Law', Robert C Ellickson,

or 'law as product',[10] the conceptual boundaries of our own approach are constantly relativised and challenged by these parallel endeavours.

A. Crucial Intersections: *Lex Mercatoria* and Legal Pluralism

Building on the foundations laid in chapter one, we now will offer a more detailed presentation of a concept of Transnational Law, which we develop from a distinctly *private* law perspective. This we believe is justified in several ways: for one, in this present work we continue[11] to build on an extensive scholarship in a 'field' of law that has, despite its continuously being contested with regard to its historical and doctrinal dimensions,[12] contributed immensely to our understanding of privately generated norm regimes: arguably, *lex mercatoria*, or the law merchant, remains one of the most important conceptual laboratories to reflect on the elements of a legal order emerging at a critical distance from the state. As such, *lex mercatoria* has long held a crucial place as much in reflections on the transformation of state regulatory functions[13] as in assessments of the legal nature of post-national or transnational regulatory regimes.[14] From this perspective, the engagement with *lex mercatoria*, in particular commercial arbitration and the privately enacted rules of cross border trade, that reaches back at least more than a century[15] provides ample evidence of a longstanding, critical reflection on the part of private lawyers with regard to the nature of the norms governing transnational commercial transactions. With a close view to the practice of commercial trade, the most influential authors in arguing for the existence and relevance of a 'new law merchant', Clive Schmitthoff and Berthold Goldman, understood *lex mercatoria* to be growing out of

1998; see also the magnificent analysis of the inherent depoliticizing effects of the anti-regulatory efficiency claim advanced by norm proponents, by David Charny, 1996, one of the many outstanding papers in the excellent Symposium Issue on 'Law, Economics, and Norms', published in (1996) 144 *University of Pennsylvania Law Review* 1643–2339; with regard to the 'norms vs regulation' conflict for example in the current debate over a Common Frame of Reference for European Private Law, see, on the one hand: Jan Smits, 2006, and, on the other: Martijn W Hesselink, 2008.

[10] Roberta Romano, 1985; Erin A O'Hara and Larry E Ribstein, 2009; Gralf-Peter Calliess and Hermann B Hoffmann, 2009b; Gralf-Peter Calliess and Hermann B Hoffmann, 2009a; Horst Eidenmüller, 2009.

[11] Gralf-Peter Calliess, 2001; Peer Zumbansen, 2002a; Peer Zumbansen, 2003a.

[12] See, on the one hand: Gunther Teubner, 1997b, and on the other: Albrecht Cordes, 2003.

[13] William E Scheuerman, 2002.

[14] Filip De Ly, 2001; Manfred E Streit and Antje Mangels, 1996; Clive M Schmitthoff, 1964a.

[15] Ernst Zitelmann, 1888; Francis M Burdick, 1902; Wyndam Anstis Beawes, 1923; for a recent discussion of the 'romanticism' of the law merchant story, see Benson, 2010.

an interaction of state and non-state norm-creation[16] and to be evolving towards an 'autonomous law of international trade'.[17] While believing in the universalising and bridging quality of commercial law, cutting across boundaries of legal culture as well as ideology,[18] they underlined the continuously evolving and necessarily 'incomplete' status of this transnational commercial law.[19] As they understood *lex mercatoria* to be embedded within a larger comparative law project pertaining to the universalistic expansion of legal values and the harmonisation and unification of laws,[20] Schmitthoff and Goldman conceptualised *lex mercatoria* and its constitutive elements (custom,[21] institutionalisation) as providing for an important illustration of global markets in search of their law.[22] From this perspective, then, the continuing debate about the legal nature as well as the scope of *lex mercatoria*, including its historical facticity, can be seen in a different light: the seemingly untiring attempts to further add to this longstanding dispute[23] have to be appreciated at a moment in time, where the idea of 'progress' that inspired the beginnings of comparative law has been challenged and comparative law has become something of an umbrella for a vast variety of interdisciplinary critiques of theories of 'sameness' and 'difference'.[24]

[16] Clive M Schmitthoff, 1968; Clive M Schmitthoff, 1961.

[17] Clive M Schmitthoff, 1964c, 5 ('would be one of the most important developments of legal science in our time').

[18] In particular, Schmitthoff emphasised how commercial law rules converged across the boundaries between Capitalist and Socialist countries as well as between common law and civil law legal cultures: Clive M Schmitthoff, 1964c, 3, 4.

[19] Berthold Goldman, 1983, 22.

[20] Konrad Zweigert and Hein Kötz, 1996, 1–2; Rudolf Schlesinger, 1995, 479; Rodolfo Sacco, 2001, 1161: 'comparative legal science triumphs because we are indebted (that is to say, mankind is indebted) to its masterpieces: harmonization, uniformity, and unification of the law'; see also David Kennedy, 1997, 605–6: 'Common to all these comparativisms, of both expertise and erudition, is a stance which we might term "cosmopolitanism," always complexly distanced from what it pictures as governance. Governance is the domain of ideology and political choice, the work of national elites jockeying for position, all dirty stuff for a cosmopolitan. Those who govern are ambitious men, subjective in their political commitments, seeking illegitimate rents and dominion in an unseemly struggle to distribute yesterday's pie rather than working together to bake a larger pie tomorrow. For the cosmopolitan, values are universal and humanist, projects rational and pragmatic, knowledge—of the self as of the other—good for its own sake. The cosmopolitan knows he lives in a world which others rule, but has carved out a niche and made it virtuous'.

[21] Charles Kerr, 1929, 354: 'The Law Merchant, more than any branch of the law, is the direct outgrowth of custom'.

[22] Samuel P Huntington, 1973, 363, highlighting the development and rise to power of the multinational corporation as a direct threat to national regulatory authority.

[23] See, eg, the recent contributions by Nikitas E Hatzimihail, 2008 (providing a reading of Schmitthoff's and Goldman's historical narratives of the development of LM, a reading, however, that in the end is strangely open-ended and inconclusive), and Thomas Schultz, 2008 (an eloquent, sometimes polemic discussion of *lex mercatoria*).

[24] See the excellent work by Pierre Legrand, 2009, 366: 'The lifeworld of the law demands not the abolition of difference, but the deft management of cultural heteronomies, the assumption of pluralism, the acceptance of a coexistence of non-harmonised rationalities, and the steady practice of a politics of inclusion to enlarge the possibility of intelligible

As comparative law continues to evolve into a multi-tiered methodological framework for the study of law and laws,[25] and is thus always in danger of opening up into a battle over primacy of one discipline over another,[26] *lex mercatoria*, too, is of greatest interest for it provides us with a lens through which to study the emergence of private norms, their relation to themselves evolving formalised legal institutions and their further consolidation as fully-fledged regulatory frameworks. As such, our interest in *lex mercatoria* is neither exclusively historical nor doctrinal, but critical. An answer to the question 'Why bother?' seems to us to be more important than to further examine whether *lex mercatoria* 'existed' in this or that form during this or that moment in time, because this line of questioning might hopefully illuminate the place—and, meaning—of speaking about it as *law*.[27]

What the 'historical' accounts of *lex mercatoria*—as opposed to primarily conceptual/theoretical inquiries—tend to ignore is that *lex mercatoria* as concept and idea has attained considerable significance in light of the larger question of how to distinguish between law and non-law. The continuing attempts to grasp its scope and nature speak loudly to the ultimate *undefinedness* of *lex mercatoria*—which as such suggests that a search for historical facts is likely to miss the other existences of *lex mercatoria*. It is from this perspective that we have just approached the debate over *lex mercatoria* as an 'autonomous legal order',[28] something which we found of interest particularly in that this line of questioning allowed us to situate this very effort in a larger context of analysis of changing regulatory landscapes, where the demarcations between public and private, official and unofficial spheres of law-making are being critically examined.[29]

discourse between laws. In short, difference must be understood and the temptation to efface it resisted'.

[25] Annelise Riles, 2006; Peer Zumbansen, 2005b; also Roger Cotterrell, 2009, 492.

[26] Gillian K Hadfield, 2009, 223: 'Most people traveling the interdisciplinary path in law these days are learning that the relationship between the various disciplines on which law can fruitfully call is not, and should not be allowed to devolve into, a battle for dominance between economics, sociology, politics, philosophy, cultural studies and the like. And indeed, the efforts at interdisciplinary thought within legal scholarship and law schools are, in my experience, often farther along than in universities more generally. In my view that is because as legal scholars what holds us together, or at least what can hold us together, is common purpose. One cannot be a legal scholar without sharing the goal of understanding the law'.

[27] See in this respect: Stewart Macaulay, 1986, 449: 'We could plausibly analogise many of these private legal systems to public government if it proved useful to do so. However, we are concerned with studies of the place of law in society, not in writing a dictionary'.

[28] See, eg Berthold Goldman, 1964, 180: 'et à considerer le phénomène sans idée préconçue, on constate que les contrats qui s'y referent ne sont régis ni par la loi d'un État, ni par une loi uniforme adoptée par une Convention entre États, mais bien par les contrats-types euxmêmes'.

[29] Colin Scott, 2008b, 254: 'The development and application of binding rules have never been the sole preserve of governments'. See also Christiana Ochoa, 2008, 13 'any dichotomy which sets state-made law and democracy on one side and private law formation and democratic deficits on the other is going to be overly simple'.

Our interest in *lex mercatoria* is thus, above all, driven by our understanding of this field, concept or 'romantic' idea[30] as a case in point of a larger critical and legal-sociological inquiry into the possibilities and forms, as well as the scope of legal regulation.

Lex mercatoria is an area that is marked in particular by private actors that are creating the 'rules of the game' as well as—in the form of arbitration tribunals—by the institutional framework for the administration of these rules.[31] As already noted, this has prompted endless scholarly debates as to the status of *lex mercatoria* both as historical *fact* and as to its nature as an allegedly *autonomous* legal order.[32] Seemingly, such disputes have remained irresolvable, as many of the contestants' arguments concerning questions of fact ('are there enforceable rules of *lex mercatoria*?'[33]), degree ('did commercial actors rely exclusively on private arbitration or did the enforceability through state courts matter?'[34]), and methodology ('does *lex mercatoria* matter beyond historical—contested[35]—evidence, and does the concept illustrate the functional differentiation and "issue-driven nature" of the legal system?'[36]) often amounted to no more than ships passing in the night. Instead of attempting a final resolution of this discussion, we find its most promising elements to be those concerned with *lex mercatoria* as a *methodological* problem.[37] From that perspective, which is distinct from the understanding of *lex mercatoria* as a method of decision making,[38] the *lex mercatoria* debate ought to be perceived as a continued reflection on the nature and possibility of transnational law,[39] a debate that more *exposes* than resolves the tensions between established nationally-confined, historically-grown legal orders and those regulatory norms that develop outside of these orders—both inside and outside of the nation-state. As such, the challenge of *lex mercatoria* is the challenge of law by its other, by that which is (perhaps) not yet law, which results from private norm-creation and administration

[30] Charles Kerr, 1929, 350: 'The Law Merchant furnishes the legal science its most romantic branch'.

[31] Robert D Cooter, 1996, 1647: 'The new law merchant arises outside the state's apparatus for making law. However, lawmakers are pulled into the affairs of business communities by insiders who look to the state to resolve their disputes and make their laws, and lawmakers are pushed into the affairs of business communities by outsiders who seek to regulate private wealth and power'.

[32] Gunther Teubner, 1997c; see also Felix Dasser, 2001.

[33] See the account by Klaus Peter Berger, 2001a, and in Ursula Stein, 1995.

[34] Erich Schanze, 1986; Albrecht Cordes, 2003.

[35] See, on the one hand, Bruce Benson, 1989, 645, and on the other, Avner Greif, 2006, 314.

[36] Gunther Teubner, 1992b; Gunther Teubner, 1992a; Gunther Teubner, 1997a.

[37] Gralf-Peter Calliess, 2001; Peer Zumbansen, 2002a; Gunther Teubner, 1997d.

[38] See Emmanuel Gaillard, 2001; Thomas E. Carbonneau, 2004; for a discussion and critique see Thomas Schultz, 2008, 671–78.

[39] Peer Zumbansen, 2006d; Ralf Michaels, 2007a.

and which the legal order observes as an exception or a threat.[40] This line of argumentation grows out of a legal pluralist assessment of *lex mercatoria*[41] but, again, goes beyond it: we believe *lex mercatoria* neither to be a 'method of decision making'[42] nor to be constituting an autonomous legal order as such[43]—at least to the degree that such an assertion be made without an ironical stance as to the critical dimension inherent to any definition of law as such.[44] Rather, and this brings us much closer to the interdisciplinary assessments of comparative law and legal pluralism,[45] *lex mercatoria* should foremost be understood as a *methodological* challenge asking us to reflect on the possibility—but also the politics—of 'law', which *can* be but *need not* be state-originating, which *can* be but *need not* be privately created or resulting from a complex interaction between official and un-official norm-creation. It is here, where the real challenge of *lex mercatoria* as a frequently used example for the evolution of an autonomous transnational legal regime becomes most obvious. Precisely because of its multi-layered and, with a view to the interaction of public and private norm-creation and norm-enforcement entities, its *hybrid* nature, the lessons and insights to be gained from *lex mercatoria* for our study of transnational law are important, yet particular. As aptly testified by the exploration of its historical development, *lex mercatoria*'s productive relationship with national contract laws was marked by a continuous evolution of contract legislation and adjudication on the one hand and by the powerful establishment of a transnational commercial community on the other. In Harold Berman's words, the 'universality of international commercial law' was not due only to 'common problems' but also

> due to the fact that such persons—merchants, ship owners, insurance underwriters, bankers and others—whether they act as individuals, corporate entities or as state agencies, form a transnational community which has had a more or less continuous history, despite countless vicissitudes, for some nine centuries.[46]

Once we place *lex mercatoria* in the larger context of an ambitious, ideological comparative law agenda,[47] we are able to recognise the political dimensions of the ubiquitous interest in *lex mercatoria as law*: we noted earlier that we think the question of 'why bother' to be the more promising, the more important question than the final resolution of historical fact or

[40] For a powerful illustration of the two sides of such threats, see only JM Coetzee, *Waiting for the Barbarians* (1982).

[41] Thomas Schultz, 2008, 670: 'The *lex mercatoria* is the flagship of legal pluralism'.

[42] Emmanuel Gaillard, 2001.

[43] Gunther Teubner, 1997b; Gunther Teubner, 2004a.

[44] Kerry Rittich, 2005, 868.

[45] Annelise Riles, 2006.

[46] Harold J Berman, 1987, 236 ('governed by similar legal rules in virtually all countries': *ibid*, 235).

[47] See Jonathan Hill, 1989.

doctrinal systematisation. It seems to us that *lex mercatoria* as an example of a transnational (private) law laboratory prompts, above all, an engagement with the legal theoretical and legal sociological, as well as the political perspectives on the making of law and the evolution of a legal order. It is from such a perspective that we can discern connections between the different contestations regarding *lex mercatoria* on the one hand and a more general critique of global regulatory regimes and transnational law on the other. Seen from a critical distance, *lex mercatoria* becomes less interesting as a contained field (or concept), but more as a starting point to reflect on the evolving forms and phenomena of a post-national 'law without the state'.[48] The institutional formation of such transnational legal regimes raises a particular set of issues relating to the impact of such institutions on the parallel evolving national regulatory, political and socio-economic systems.[49]

Meanwhile, the development of transnational regulatory regimes—such as *lex mercatoria* as part of 'international' or global economic law—presents us with another complex set of questions, primarily related to the 'politics of private law-making' and the constitutional dimensions of private ordering, pertaining to accountability, legitimacy and democratic control, perspectives that have been central to the development of 'new governance' scholarship.[50] Interestingly, these latter aspects seem to find considerably more resonance in the current academic debate: scholars here seem predominantly concerned with ('nagging theoretical'[51]) issues of accountability and legitimacy.[52] As Julia Black and David Rouch recently observed: 'The usual panoply of constitutional mechanisms of accountability and legitimacy which characterises liberal democratic constitutional systems is not necessarily available'.[53] What makes these accountability and legitimacy issues,

[48] Gunther Teubner, 1997e.

[49] See, eg Samuel P Huntington, 1973 (providing for an astute analysis of the complementing and overlapping 'national', 'international', and 'transnational' dimensions of public-private organisations in the global arena and their impact on national systems).

[50] For an insightful discussion, see Kenneth W Abbott and Duncan Snidal, 2009, and Colin Scott, 2008a; for an excellent mapping and scrutiny of the intersecting developments under the umbrella of 'New Legal Realism', see Victoria Nourse and Gregory Shaffer, 2009, in particular part II ('Building From the Old Legal Realism'). See also Amiram Gill, 2008, 471–75, 471: 'Corporate self-regulation and meta-regulation, read against the New Governance literature, capture a central element in the complexity of business law. That is, these regulatory patterns accompany socio-legal changes in market economies, highlighted by the fall of state authority and the rise of private ordering'.

[51] Christopher M Bruner, 2008 (discussing credit rating agencies and the Internet Corporation for Domain Names and Numbers—ICANN—as examples of 'public-private gatekeepers' and their government-like exercise of regulatory authority—*ibid*, at 129, 165).

[52] Bruner, above; Dieter Kerwer, 2005a (assessing credit rating agencies as poignant examples of today's governments' attempts to balance effectiveness with democratic control—by relying on NMRs, *nonmajoritarian regulators*).

[53] Julia Black and David Rouch, 2008 (depicting the system of international financial governance to be distinct from nation-state based understandings of governance), 224.

which have in part been driving the important work in 'global administrative law',[54] particularly intriguing is that they underscore the degree to which the evolving transnational regulatory regimes do not merely raise questions of procedure. Instead, 'private' regulatory regimes such as Credit Rating Agencies or ICANN[55]—like *lex mercatoria*—can be read as outstanding illustrations of the *constitutionalisation* challenges facing the global legal order today. As increasingly specialised, functionally differentiated problem areas and spheres of human and institutional conduct evolve in response to a combination of external impulses and their own particular logic, the law governing these constellations becomes deeply entwined in these complex, layered constitutions. With regard to the emergence of global law, Gunther Teubner and Peter Korth have noted that a

> unitary global law reproduces itself through legal acts which are guided by different programs but are in the end oriented towards the binary code legal/illegal. The unity of global law is just not, as in the nation state, based on the consistency of legal norms structurally secured by the hierarchy of the courts: rather, it is process-based, deriving simply from the modes of connection between legal operations, which transfer binding legality between even highly heterogeneous legal orders.[56]

In perhaps using an exaggerated image, we must imagine law not to be extending its regulatory arm downward from the tip of a hierarchical pyramid, but rather to be embracing constantly evolving institutional permutations.[57] Like a veil, a blanket or a foil, law lays itself onto the surfaces of the emerging institutional body, and through law's transparent, highly lacerable texture it sensitivises and visibilises the anatomy of the evolving torso, its muscles, bones and joints, its strains, injuries and lesions.[58] And yet the faith, which the experience with national constitutional orders has—despite all shortcomings and frustrations—likely nurtured in the West over the course of the twentieth century, carries the substantial risk of being overly and perhaps arrogantly confident as to its 'constitutionalising' powers in an unruly—and unknown—world. What becomes evident through a short-circuiting between the pressing constitutional challenges of global governance and the still painful shortfalls

[54] Benedict Kingsbury, Nico Krisch, Richard B Stewart and Jarrod Wiener, 2005; Kalypso Nicolaidis and Gregory Shaffer, 2005; for critical-sympathetic comments on this project, see Carol Harlow, 2006, BS Chimni, 2005, and Susan Marks, 2006.

[55] See Bruner and Kerwer, above; see also Jochen von Bernstorff, 2004; Viktor Mayer-Schönberger and Malte Ziewitz, 2007.

[56] Gunther Teubner and Peter Korth, 2009, ms at 5, available at: papers.ssrn.com/sol3/papers.cfm?abstract_id=1416041.

[57] See, in this regard, Robert D Cooter, 1994, 216: 'as economies become more complex, efficiency demands more decentralized lawmaking, not less'.

[58] See also Reza Banakar, 2009, for an excellent discussion of the challenges for law to capture social reality.

and exclusionary dynamics of democratic constitutional orders,[59] is that the deeper challenges of our engagement with constitutionalisation lies in facing these deficits.

> 'As we open spaces for conflict and struggle [...] we ought to take a break from the search for a universal ethics. Constitutionalism offers an improved institutional platform from which global ethicists can speak for the universal against those who must be cast out from the community of the universal—just when we need conversation, heterogeneity, interaction, ethical pluralism.'[60]

B. Communities of Interest and Private Governance Regimes: The Conundrum of Transnational Commercial Law

This avenue of inquiry has long been prepared and paved by scholars, practitioners and judges in transnational commercial law. Recognising the role of idealisation, romanticism and 'emotions' in the desire to return to a 'perceived golden age' of commercial law's relative universality,[61] scholars have again and again engaged in laying bare the treacherous and unknown ground on which theories related to the emergence of universal custom, usage and principle emerge. In the face of the concept of transnational commercial law unavoidably raising 'fundamental questions' such as 'What is law?' and 'What are the sources of law?',[62] the further elaboration of a clearly practice-driven inquiry into the fact and scope of this field can only unfold in a rich, interdisciplinary dialogue.[63] While scholars overwhelmingly insist on the importance of empirical evidence to adequately assess the building blocks and 'elements'[64] of transnational commercial law,[65] a claim that is simultaneously raised in the domestic context,[66] there is a similarly recognised urgency as regards the further understanding of the field's theoretical and, importantly, normative underpinnings.[67] Torn between an embracing and a hesitating recognition of the

[59] Catherine Dauvergne, 2008.
[60] David Kennedy, 2009, 67.
[61] Roy Goode, 1997, 5, 35.
[62] Goode, 1997, 4; Alex Stone Sweet, 2006, 637: 'The rise of the new Lex Mercatoria raises deep questions about the nature of law, and about the relationship of law to state power'.
[63] See Lawrence M Friedman, 1996, 69.
[64] Goode, 1997, 4.
[65] Roger Cotterrell, 1998, 185–86; Gregory Shaffer, 2009, ms 7–8.
[66] Marc Galanter, 2006, 12–13.
[67] Harold J Berman, 1995, 1621: 'That humankind, in the aftermath of two world wars, has reached a turning point in its history, that the world has entered a new era of global interdependence, that all inhabitants of Planet Earth share a common destiny, is a historical fact, a political fact, an economic fact, a sociological fact, that has finally penetrated the consciousness of most of earth's inhabitants'. See also Ross Cranston, 2007, 616–17: 'Whether so benign a view of the new transnational commercial law can be taken in general ... depends in every case on the circumstances. Each measure must be tested not only in terms of its contribution

existence of the new law merchant,[68] the current debate reflects a distinct taste for *methodology* in the further elaboration of transnational commercial law and how such a methodological inquiry might shed more light on the emerging contours of an emerging transnational legal order[69] or 'world law'.[70] Couched in a multifaceted array of scholarly inquiries into the origins and trajectories of non-state norms in the transnational arena, such elaboration inevitably finds itself struggling with the contentious field's own history reflecting back on its ambiguous legacy on the one hand,[71] and with parallel jurisprudential introspections and demarcations in legal sub-disciplines, on the other.[72] At the same time, this interest in genealogy and doctrine is complemented and to a significant degree challenged by a set of questions originating in legal theory and legal sociology: where the former primarily focuses on the *nature* of the transnational legal order, the latter raises questions regarding the *nature* and *impact* of transnational norms, apparently only in order to emphasise the more pressing question, namely 'What might the ambiguity of transnational norms tell us about the underlying *distinction* between these norms and law itself?' What makes this inter- and transdisciplinary endeavour so challenging is the tension between the overwhelming evidence with regard to the *facticity* of an emerging transnational legal order and the seemingly irresolvable question regarding its *normative* quality.

Roger Cotterrell remarked in this context, that the difficulty of answering these questions has to be seen against the background of a blurring of boundaries between 'law' and 'society'.[73] 'Law', he writes,

> constitutes society in so far as it is, itself, an aspect of society, a framework and an expression of understandings that enable society to exist. A sociological perspective on legal ideas is necessary to recognise and analyse the intellectual and moral power of law in this respect.[74]

to economic development, but also to social justice'. But see Goode, 1997, 36: 'it is not the function of arbitral awards to develop international jurisprudence. All that matters at the end of the day is that the arbitral tribunal reaches a results that commends itself to the reasonable man as just *in the particular case*'.

[68] See Clive M Schmitthoff, 1961; Lord Justice Mustill, 1987; Cranston, 2007, 597; JH Dalhuisen, 2006, 129; Alex Stone Sweet, 2006, 633.

[69] See only Craig M Scott, 2009.

[70] Harold J Berman, 1995; Rüdiger Voigt, 2008.

[71] See, eg Clive M Schmitthoff, 1961, 131–44; Berhold Goldman, 1979; Lord Justice Mustill, 1987; Klaus Peter Berger, 2001a; Alex Stone Sweet, 2006, 629–37; Ralf Michaels, 2007a, 447–52.

[72] Harold J Berman, 1995, 1617 (suggesting an embracing of international law and transnational law); Friedrich K Juenger, 1995; Friedrich K Juenger, 2000, for a scathing critique of traditional conflicts of law scholarship for its state-centred notion of sovereignty.

[73] Roger Cotterrell, 1998, 176.

[74] Cotterrell, 1998, 182.

Understanding law, then, as a 'social phenomenon',[75] the distinction between law and society does indeed blur: the internal/external distinction is

> replaced by a conception of partial, relatively narrow or specialised participant perspectives on (and in) law, confronting and being confronted by, penetrating, illuminating, and being penetrated and illuminated by, broader, more inclusive perspectives on (and in) law as a social phenomenon.[76]

Such a perspective on law must be understood as an attempt to respond to law's own alleged lack of methodology:[77] a sociological reflection on legal ideas would be to reflect 'methodologically law's own fragmentary varied methodological characteristics'.[78]

In Cotterrell's reading, the blurring between law and society raises significant questions for the demarcation between legal theory and legal sociology, a demarcation that is important for our present inquiry into the nature of the emerging transnational legal order. For Cotterrell, legal theory, in light of a proliferation of non-statist norms and private ordering mechanisms, is in need of 'a genuinely pluralistic approach'.[79] But because we tend to rely on a *juristic* legal theory, our concept of law is still inseparably tied to the notion of the state as the origin of binding, commanding legal norms. Cotterrell is of course right to point out that the pluralism of competing normative orders is by far not limited to the transnational arena, but has always been a constitutive part of the nation-state's legal order,[80] an observation, certainly made by legal pluralist scholars all along. As legal sociology has long been generating crucial insights into the manifold appearances of normativity in society, the question arises how a state-law-based legal theory can be brought together with a legal sociological account of plurality and diversity. Within the transnational realm, a pluralistically designed legal theory, for Cotterrell, would have to accept the impossibility of examining all of the newly-forming contexts, 'communities', and interest

[75] Cotterrell, 1998, 187: '*Sociological* interpretation of legal ideas is not a particular, specialized way of approaching law, merely co-existing with other kinds of understanding. Sociology of law in this particular context is a transdisciplinary enterprise and aspiration to broaden understanding of law as a social phenomenon'.

[76] Cotterrell, 1998, 188.

[77] Cotterrell, 1998, 178: 'Law does not have a "methodology of its own" and borrows methodologies from any discipline that can supply them' (with reference to Jack M Balkin, 1996).

[78] Cotterrell, 1998, 189.

[79] Roger Cotterrell, 2008, 10.

[80] Cotterrell, 2008, 5, 11, invoking the consequences of a 'jurisprudence of difference' with regard to the pressures on law from particular interests and newly formulated 'rights'. See, in this regard, also Lawrence M Friedman, 1996, 79: 'There has been a kind of rights explosion; Jefferson, even Lincoln, would hardly recognize the current system. And the biggest growth areas have had little or nothing to do with classic human rights such as freedom of political speech, the right to vote, and the right to property. Instead, the rights of criminal defendants have gotten a lot of court attention. And there is also a riotous, lush growth of what we might call lifestyle rights—for example, the freedom to talk about sex, and the freedom to have it—on a scale the nineteenth century would have found both shocking and incomprehensible'.

groups that mark the pluralisation of society. While recognising that 'it cannot become sociology', it 'can explore general regulatory problems raised by *basic types* of community and their interaction'.[81]

While this might appear, at first sight and in light of the significant challenges raised by transnational norms with regard to legal certainty, systematisation and structure, a convincing account of how law, methodologically, must be adapted to these new circumstances, this view—upon closer examination—suggests a problematic overburdening of the concept of law. By putting forward a concept of 'pluralistic law',[82] Cotterrell addresses the shift from an understanding of law as functioning in a relatively coherent community, that is guaranteed and stabilised by a centralised political framework, towards a vision of law under 'post-modern' conditions, under which law's aspired unity is as fragmented as that of society.[83] The concept of 'community', for Cotterrell, is the central anchoring point for an ambitious theoretical and sociological framework of the contemporary legal order: in abbreviation, communities are objectively characterised by stable and sustained interaction while they are subjectively marked by a sense of attachment or belonging.[84] Communities are the building blocks of the 'nation', which is itself an 'imagined community' (*Benedict Anderson*)[85] constituted through different types of collective involvement.[86]

> Consequently, state law as expressing the regulatory needs of the nation reflects the regulatory needs and forms of all the fundamental types of collective involvement. Yet, precisely because of the ambiguity of the idea of nation as a community in itself, state law's reflection of these regulatory needs and forms is ambiguous and indirect.[87]

The intriguing and extremely enriching scope of Cotterrell's focus on 'communities' arises from his clear understanding that under pluralistic conditions there can only be highly varied appearances, structures and dynamics of such communities. Although he places the notion of 'trust' at the centre of the subjective dimension of the community,[88] he emphasises that

> the conditions of its creation or maintenance may be different as may the kinds of regulation necessary for its expression and support ... A legal concept of

[81] Cotterrell, 2008, 13.

[82] Roger Cotterrell, 1997, 76; Roger Cotterrell, 2008, 7.

[83] Roger Cotterrell, 1997, 77.

[84] Cotterrell, 1997, 82.

[85] Cotterrell, 1997, 89.

[86] *Ibid*: 'For some purposes it is a traditional community essentially united by the accidents of geography or language, for others a focus on convergent interests of citizens, for yet others a symbol of shared beliefs or a repository of shared values, or an object of veneration and patriotic affection'.

[87] *Ibid.*

[88] Cotterrell, 1997, 86: 'Trust ... is the underpinning of all the many experiences of community—strong and weak, organized or diffuse—that occur in social life'.

community sets an agenda for law; it presents legal analysis with the task of adapting regulation sensitively to current social and cultural diversity.[89]

The emergence of transnational communities further accentuates the aforementioned characteristics and pressures on a law designed to regulate them: Cotterrell remarks that under these conditions

> legal theory's task is not just to analyse, from its traditional standpoints, a range of new transnational legal phenomena. The task is rather to rethink legal theory in a situation in which it is slowly losing its basic modern reference points, the firmly defined jurisdiction of the nation state and the politically organised national society as the terrain from which all legal phenomena can be observed and evaluated.[90]

In recognition of the diversification and pluralisation of communities within the nation-state, it would be a futile attempt to conceptualise a homogeneous global society. Instead, law's task will have to be to adapt to the existence of the fact of 'transnational communities of many kinds'.[91]

The mobilisation of *community* as a key concept to explore the interpenetration of legal theoretical and legal sociological lines of inquiry is, on the basis of extensive studies of the changing nature and appearance of law in social life, indeed promising. It helps to bridge the gap between the already mentioned theoretical-practical elaborations by scholars and practitioners who tend to develop a concept of transnational commercial law through the lens of many specialised, interest-driven communities[92] and a wide array of studies on transnational governance, both with regard to the emerging 'architecture'[93] of disaggregated sovereignties, transgovernmental and transregulatory networks[94] and to the related, pressing issues of accountability, transparency and legitimacy.[95] Seen in this light, the notion of

[89] *Ibid.*

[90] Roger Cotterrell, 2008, 4–5.

[91] Cotterrell, 2008, 5.

[92] Berthold Goldman, 1964, 179: '*Ils emanent d'associations professionelles, ou de groupements d'entreprises plus étroitement intégrées, voire d'entreprises isolées, mais puissantes*'; Clive M Schmitthoff, 1963, 259; Klaus Peter Berger, 2001a: 'This process is detached from domestic legal systems and escapes the realm of domestic lawmakers which is limited to the territory of the respective jurisdiction. Instead, the law is created within the community of merchants doing cross-border trade and commerce, the *societas mercatorum*' (with reference to Berhold Goldman, 1979, 499); JH Dalhuisen, 2006, 158–60; Ross Cranston, 2007, 597, 598; David J Bederman, 2007, 179: 'Transnational corporations, with their newfound power and influence, are certainly starting to weave distinctive threads into the fabric of international law'.

[93] Kal Raustiala, 2002.

[94] Anne-Marie Slaughter, 2004a; Anne-Marie Slaughter, 2004b; see Wolfgang Friedman, 1972, 117.

[95] Kenneth W Abbott and Duncan Snidal, 2000; Raustiala, 2002; Pierre-Hugues Verdier, 2009; Christiana Ochoa, 2008; Jan Aart Scholte, 2008, 323: 'Democracy would therefore need to be reconstructed not only in relation to a reconfigured geography and a restructured regulatory apparatus, but also in relation to concurrent changes in patterns of collective identity'.

community bears considerable potential in an ongoing and further sophisticating study of complex transnational relations, a point we will further explore in the context of contrasting our own conceptual approach with that of cosmopolitan democracy.[96] At this point, it is important to highlight the high degree of overlap and reciprocal enrichment in the presently pursued research agendas in commercial and contract law, international law, regulatory theory and political philosophy. Seen from the concrete applicatory context of transnational commercial activity,[97] many of the already touched upon contestations of *lex mercatoria*'s existence, origin or scope not only play a mere secondary or tertiary role in an understanding of the unfolding and applied legal order,[98] they are furthermore for the most part on a different analytical-critical level from the type of inquiry that leads experts in transnational commercial law to start asking different types of questions. Central here is certainly the idea of 'autonomy', which has again and again instigated heated disputes between different contenders within commercial law as well as between legal historians and legal theoreticians.[99] Berthold Goldman offered an outspoken version of the idea of autonomy, when he asked:

> Ces 'directives de conduite' sont-elles des règles de droit et les comportements qu'elles les déterminent sont-ils juridiques? La question vaut la peine d'être posée, non seulement en raison de l'ampleur et de l'importance des activités qu'elle concerne, mais aussi parce qu'elle fait clairement apparaître certaines des difficultés spécifiques de la separation entre le domaine du droit, et de ce qui lui est étranger.[100]

Taking up Goldman's cue, we can speak of at least a *relative* autonomy of legal rules governing commercial activities.[101] For some participants in

[96] See ch 2 IIC of this book, below.

[97] Berthold Goldman, 1983, 5: 'Whether *lex mercatoria* has the status of law does, however, remain a matter of controversy, at least among scholars'.

[98] Lord Justice Mustill, 1987, 153: 'the *lex mercatoria* simply exists. It springs up spontaneously, in the soil of international trade. It is a growth, not a creation'.

[99] See, eg Gunther Teubner, 1992b; Gunther Teubner, 1997b, on the one hand, and Albrecht Cordes, 2003, on the other.

[100] Berthold Goldman, 1964, 177–78.

[101] Clive M Schmitthoff, 1961, 144: 'The New Law Merchant is in the nature of an "autonomous" law and, as such, it attempts to provide its own legal regulation without reference to, and independent of, any municipal system of law'. Robert D Cooter, 1996, 1647: 'The new law merchant arises outside of the state's apparatus for making law. Lawmakers, however, are pulled into the affairs of business communities by insiders who look to the state to resolve their disputes. Lawmakers are also pushed into the affairs of business communities by outside critics of private wealth and power'. JH Dalhuisen, 2006, 134: 'a new autonomous and independent legal order'; Christopher A Whytock, 2008, 470: 'transnational arbitration is partially, but not completely, autonomous from transnational judicial governance ... transnational litigation to an important extent still relies on domestic courts for enforcement'. See also Lawrence M Friedman, 1996, 72: 'It is a basic postulate of the sociology of law that legal systems are never totally autonomous'.

this debate the questions do not exhaust themselves in an assessment of the legal quality of *lex mercatoria*, but are understood to arise from this concrete field only in relation to an example of transnational legal governance. In other words, the inquiry into the relative or absolute autonomy of *lex mercatoria* from domestic or international, at any rate, state-based legal or judicial intervention, is commonly understood to be but a stand-in for an even more ambitious line of questioning. If a specialised field of social (here, commercial) practice could be seen to give rise to binding and legitimate norms (here, *lex mercatoria*), then we are faced with a set of promising opportunities to ask similar questions as regards the *authors* and *subjects* of these norms, or the *development* or *evolution* of the legal order. These connections are in fact frequently made by weathered experts in transnational commercial law, who—while drawing on a wide range of doctrinal and theoretical, empirical and sociological evidence—never seem to lose sight of why questions relating to the birth and functioning of a legal system were asked in the first place. Beneath the act of making a connection between the 'interests' in a given commercial dispute and the question as to which rules govern the situation, lies unavoidably the question of measure,[102] that is the question regarding the existence and applicability of a meta-code, of a hierarchically higher norm or a set of identifiable values against which the resorted-to custom, usage or general principle should be assessed. Largely, in the area here under review, scholars find it relatively easy to avoid such questions by pointing to the concrete case at hand[103] and, more importantly for our purposes, to the considerably specified and well-identifiable 'interests' among the members of the relevant group. This association of the relevance and meaning of a concrete case with the identifiable interests at hand, however, can easily result in a typifying and objectifying isolation and immunisation of the case from the 'interests', the entirety of which might never have been given effective representation. From the point of view of a substantive theory of law or of Goode's idea of an 'external standard' against which to measure both the quality as well as the alleged universality of interests heard in the case, without such a standard the eventually recognised interest simply becomes an anchoring point on which an outside perception of how *best* to govern the entire situation is fixed. While it may look as if the emphasis was on the subjective dimension of the case (the parties' interests), the failure to problematise the challenges of properly identifying the interests of all affected by a particular agreement, bargaining or contractual regime eventually totalises a small range of interests to represent every conceivable interest. This applies particularly to highly specialised contexts of professional interaction, where the 'rules of the game' tend to

[102] Roy Goode, 1997, 33–34.
[103] Goode, 1997, 36.

win the upper hand over alternative claims or expressions of contestation that are more difficult to verbalise. As Robert Cooter has underlined with regard to judges' task in dealing with custom, their three-fold challenge consists in having, first, to identify 'actual norms that have arisen in specialised business communities', secondly, to 'identify the incentive structure that produced these norms' and, finally, to evaluate 'the efficiency of the incentive structure ... using analytical tools from economics'.[104] It is here, where commercial lawyers' contentions of an emerging transnational commercial law critically overlap with two strands of conceptualising transnational law. One overlapping occurs at the just identified border between a 'law & economics' depiction of *efficient* self-regulation, on the one hand, and a both practice-informed and yet implicitly universalist theorising of transnational commercial law (as a nodal point of 'world law' or a transnational legal order)—as evidenced, for example, in the writings of Harold Berman or Ross Cranston—on the other. To be sure, the short-circuiting of the alleged interests in and around a given case with its efficient resolution can firmly ground itself in long-standing assertions of the need of transnational merchants for adequate, reliable and, thus, efficient, norms. Especially in light of the oft-lamented uncertainty governing transnational commercial activity,[105] it can be argued that the eradication of such uncertainty has to be at the forefront of any attempt to design a set of governing norms. Transnational commercial lawyers have, however, been able to show that there is, in fact, considerably more at stake than 'meets the eye'. Insisting, on the one hand, on the mutually irreducible relevance of private decisions by non-state actors and, on the other, on a system of private law that 'depends on indirectly influencing private ordering and claims through its structure of incentives, and thus must ensure that its content and procedures accord with the expectations and other priorities of private actors',[106] transnational commercial lawyers have long made another short-circuiting, namely between the evolutionary adjustment process of public and private power within the nation-state and the need for a private law theory in the transnational arena, which would allow for an unfolding of a meaningful perspective on questions of bargaining asymmetry, third-party interests or redistribution, even, and especially, *because* of the absence of conventional public/private distinctions and a corresponding institutional framework.[107] Private law theory, rather than becoming a label for a theory of functionally

[104] Robert D Cooter, 1996, 1656.

[105] JH Dalhuisen, 2006, 132: 'international business must inescapably live with a fractured system of laws and with the resulting uncertainty and inequality as well as the inefficiencies this necessarily presents'.

[106] Robert Wai, 2008, 127; see also Rudolf Wiethölter, 1988, 27–28.

[107] Peer Zumbansen, 2007b; Gralf-Peter Calliess and Moritz Renner, 2009; see also Victoria Nourse and Gregory Shaffer, 2009, 93: 'The one (public law) cannot be understood without the other (private ordering)'.

conceived market freedoms,[108] would have to work out ways to identify and problematise the gap between the (legal) norm and the market reality. Such concerns are clearly within the central ambit of encompassing theoretisations of transnational commercial law, which is amply evidenced by the burdensome engagement with parallel developments in international aid, law and development and by the continuing invocation of the importance of the rule of law for transnational commercial regimes.[109] The latter, then, builds important bridges to the longstanding soul-searching into the nature and scope of international law, where we can discern a similar 'turning over' of conventional perceptions and a far-reaching interdisciplinary transformation of circumscribed fields,[110] that echoes Jessup's project of transnational law.[111]

The other overlap that has become visible through law & economics's short-circuiting of the 'interests' in a highly specialised market arena with the facilitation of this very market's functionality, occurs between transnational commercial law's emphasis on the interest-driven, 'self-propelling' evolution of law[112] in highly specialised areas (such as border-crossing commercial activity) and another form of *functional* evolution. As already noted, the emergence of a set of norms, guidelines and codes of conduct governing a circumscribed sphere of social (here, commercial) practice has been taken by many observers to illustrate the coming-into-being of transnational normativity. Some scholars have further scrutinised the scope of the emerging legal order by likening it, for example, either to domestic

[108] For a critique, see Ugo Mattei and Fernanda Nicola, 2006, Daniela Caruso, 2006, and Fernanda Nicola, 2008.

[109] Ross Cranston, 2007, 616: 'If these concerns are addressed, however, it can be strongly argued that important aspects of the new transnational commercial law are as important for the poor as for others'. See also JH Dalhuisen, 2006, 170–71. 'The relevant objective criteria may here foremost emerge from a rule of law test. It is possible to refer in this connection to the rule of law both in an institutional ("law of rules") and substantive ("set of values") sense ... In doing so, the rule of law may not only protect the weak, but it may also promote the successful settlement of disputes, facilitate economic transactions, create a framework for enterprise nationally and internationally, and support an outward-looking perspective'.

[110] Manfred Lachs, 1972, 109, 112; Wolfgang Friedman, 1972, 117; Kal Raustiala, 2006, 423: 'Old orthodoxies are facing challenges and new subfields are growing. Theories from political science, economics, sociology, and other disciplines are increasingly deployed to explain international law'.

[111] Philip C Jessup, 1956; but see Philip C Jessup, 1940, 245: 'The layman and the common lawyer who find it difficult to fit international law into their concept of "law"—a concept which is generally of the Austinian type—usually are alike in asserting that there isn't any international law. They forget that law has many meanings'.

[112] JH Dalhuisen, 2006, 147–48: '[A]ny law must have a self-propelling force to maintain itself, evolve further, and retain its meaning. It is in this connection only too obvious that states, in their intervention in the law through statute or otherwise, often get it wrong or produce for political reasons something that is innately unworkable, obscure, ad hoc, unstable, or perceived as fundamentally unfair (and therefore subject to strong erosive pressures), so that the law with the help of practices and the adjudicatory process must continuously correct and purify itself if only to retain its credibility and move forward'.

private law or to the concept of the Rule of Law, in order to highlight the *constitutional* challenges facing non-state governance regimes. Others chose to concentrate on the related notion of *autonomy* of the emerging normative order. Their approach unfolds in a radicalisation of the functional orientation that transnational commercial lawyers apply to the emergence of specialised governance regimes.[113] This radicalisation occurs with regard to the *function of law* in the construction of the governance regime. From this perspective, law's function is understood as providing for a reconstruction of a social conflict (of any kind, economic, political, moral, religious) as a *legal* one. This does not occur from a hierarchically elevated position, through the application of 'external standards' or on the basis of a presumed *Grundnorm*, but through law's reflexivity. Only through a distinct act of alienating the original conflict from its context, does the conflict become a legal problem.[114] Crucial to this understanding of law and its role 'in society' is the structure of the legal system. Within the framework of autopoietic systems theory, the legal system is at the same time operationally closed and cognitively open.[115] This architectural design allows for a radical positioning of law *in* society. Surpassing the conventional juxtaposition of 'law & society' as two separable spheres or entities, which lay at the heart of legal sociology and conventional socio-legal studies, the concept of autopoietic law reduces law to a communication, marked by the usage of a specific—legal—code. This code alone is what makes a legal communication legal. Because the legal system is both 'closed' and 'open', its code is constantly engaged in a reconstruction of environmental pressure (eg social conflicts) in its own terminology. This outrageously *formalist* side of the law is complemented and constantly challenged by law's reflexivity, through which law is subjected to never-ending evolution, adaptation and transformation.[116] The original legal sociological scrutiny of the nature and the impact of the emerging transnational legal order[117] is now fusing with the legal theoretical depiction of the functioning of the legal system. The legal system that generates legal 'responses' is not by itself in a position to assess their 'success', which can alone be measured by the social system into which the law has 'intervened'.[118] In turn, however, law's 'intervening' function is in fact one of facilitation, irritation, or empowerment, as the case

[113] See, eg JH Dalhuisen, 2006, 134: '[I]t is accepted that law is not created at random and needs some social and economic framework in which it can be articulated and operate, but this framework need not be a state. This approach suggests at the same time a shift away from a territorial approach to law in favor of a more functional one'.

[114] Gunther Teubner and Peer Zumbansen, 2000; Marc Amstutz, 2009, 310.

[115] Niklas Luhmann, 1992a; Gunther Teubner, 1987a, 2.

[116] Gunther Teubner, 1989; Gunther Teubner, 1983; Gunther Teubner, 1984.

[117] Roger Cotterrell, 2008; Gralf-Peter Calliess and Moritz Renner, 2009.

[118] Marc Amstutz, 2009, 311, 312.

may be.[119] Being tied to the state only as a matter of historical contingency, with distinctive evolutionary variances,[120] systems theorists have ventured whether law does/can in fact (continue to) apply the distinction of legal/illegal without its embeddedness in the conventional institutional framework of the nation-state.[121] In this context, the answer could be law's *losing* itself in society, its creeping into the most distant and hidden corners of societal activity in order to perform the above-mentioned functions of facilitation and stabilisation. Marc Amstutz has referred to this process of law's excursions into society as law's 'voyages into society's "*mondes intérieurs*"'.[122] The law, through learning 'to see itself as part of its environment', is now 'forced' by the environment to reflect, that is 'to develop the conceptions of its environment that enable and support its task'.[123] Carrying out this task, the law would visibilise the 'blind spot'[124] in the social system into which it 'intervenes' by, significantly, widening the options, by relativising absolute positions and by opening up a forum for the reflection and proceduralisation of the tension between form and substance, hard and soft, official and unofficial.

This perception of law's function provides for a different understanding of *lex mercatoria*'s 'autonomy'. The resulting notion of autonomy does not so much *blur* the demarcation between law and society, as suggested in the legal sociological reading offered by Roger Cotterrell, but rather problematises the boundary in a reflexive mode. It posits to uphold the boundary in order to emphasise the irreducibility of one sphere onto the other, yet, at the same time no sphere occupies a privileged place. Law, from this perspective, is but a single societal rationality in an inchoate and violent cacophony of competing communications. The differences between the two approaches can, however, be overstated quite easily. Taking a step back from a perhaps too hopeful or optimistic notion of community, which is shaped by the underlying assumption of trust relationships among the community's members and a complementing, stabilising environment, the two approaches have more in common than would have appeared at first. The incessant concern with a threatening or promising congruency between law and society, as reflected in the difficulties of identifying the function of a sociologically informed legal

[119] From the perspective of administrative governance, see in this respect Claudio Franzius, 2006, 234: '*Bereitstellung von Entscheidungshilfen*'.

[120] Ralf Michaels and Nils Jansen, 2007; see also Friedrich K Juenger, 1995, 490: 'The assumption that rules and institutions cannot be called "law" unless they emanate from a sovereign is, of course, thoroughly ahistoric'.

[121] Niklas Luhmann, 2004, 490: 'Therefore it may well be that the current prominence of the legal system and the dependence of society itself and of most of its functional systems on a functioning legal code are nothing but a European anomaly, which might well level off with the evolution of global society'.

[122] Amstutz, 2009, 312.

[123] *Ibid.*

[124] Gunther Teubner, 2007; Amstutz, 2009, 312.

theory and law 'as such',[125] has much in common with the here-described function of law to facilitate and stabilise and to identify a social system's blind spots, dead ends and discursive road blocks. Where both approaches differ, however, is with respect to the understanding of law's embeddedness, context, and *environment*. Adherers to the idea of 'community' in transnational governance inevitably risk being torn between either having to operate with a functionally conceived efficiency regime that protects a narrow, yet identifiable set of interests of the 'transnational business and finance community', or with a (to a certain degree) *substantivised* and as such overburdened concept of community that in Utopian fashion aspires to satisfy objective *and* subjective demands. By contrast, a legal theory steeped in the concept of the functional differentiation of society has considerable difficulties (or, perhaps, even a lack of interest) in such depictions of community. Fearful of 'overburdening' the law with an all-encompassing 'societal' agenda (of economics, politics, culture, religion, morality: in other words, law *as* social theory), systems theorists suggest the use of 'regimes' to depict temporary or, in some cases, lasting clusters or networks of functionally specialised communication. Complementing a strong interest among international relations and public policy scholars in the emergence of 'regimes',[126] systems theorists develop a legal theory of regimes that is based on the recognition of the non-statist, incoherent and hybrid contours of transnational governance.[127] This theory confronts the fragmentation of global law[128] head-on. Recognising the need to adapt to *issues* without the ability to develop responses within a known and stable institutional framework as the central challenge for law in the global arena, the development of legal regime theory seeks to capture an 'issue-driven' evolution of legal governance structures. This concept breaks with conventional territory-based notions of jurisdiction as a further application of the idea of law's differentiation that echoes the differentiation of society into a plural, disharmonious universe of competing rationalities. '[A] wholly new form of conflicts law will emerge; an "inter-systemic conflicts law", derived not from collisions between the distinct nations of private international law, but from collisions between distinct global social sectors'.[129] This conflict is significantly disharmonious, a fact that informs any concept of (global) legal pluralism:[130]

> Global legal pluralism, however, is not simply a result of political pluralism, but is instead the expression of deep contradictions between colliding sectors of a global

[125] See Roger Cotterrell, 1998.
[126] Stephen D Krasner, 2001; Sue Bowden, 2000.
[127] Andreas Fischer-Lescano and Gunther Teubner, 2004; Gunther Teubner, 2004a.
[128] See only Martti Koskenniemi and Paivi Leino, 2002.
[129] Andreas Fischer-Lescano and Gunther Teubner, 2004, 1000, with reference to Gunther Teubner, 1993, 100–101.
[130] Paul Schiff Berman, 2007; Ralf Michaels, 2009b.

> society. At core, the fragmentation of global law is not simply about legal norm collisions or policy-conflicts, but rather has its origin in contradictions between society-wide institutionalised rationalities, which law cannot solve, but which demand a new legal approach to colliding norms.[131]

Rather than assuming a role for law in the resolution of problems of 'injustice' in a pluralist universe of different values, this conception operates with a more radicalised understanding of pluralism: the different rationalities are in constant unavoidable collision because the driving force for societal evolution is the never-ending functional differentiation of various societal rationalities in a 'polycentric' society.[132] In this society the polycentrity of which implies a plurality of self-descriptions of society, each difference becomes the centre of the world, resulting in the emergence of reciprocally conflictual partial rationalities without there being an instance of last resort, a meta-difference that could trump all others.[133] It is important to note that the here used concept of society is one that sees no distinction between a society as drawn up in the confines of the nation-state as compared to one of post-national character.[134] Instead, *world society* comprises 'both' dimensions of society, characterised by simultaneous processes of constitutionalisation and fragmentation in the political and legal system.[135] It is against this background that legal scholars, political scientists and philosophers have been scrutinising the emerging contours of 'world statism' (*Weltstaatlichkeit*)[136] and the possibility of global or, world constitutionalism.[137]

But, how different is systems theory's account of global regime conflicts from legal sociological or critical-political accounts of transnational

[131] Andreas Fischer-Lescano and Gunther Teubner, 2004, 1004.

[132] Fischer-Lescano and Teubner, 2004, 1005: 'The primary motor for this development is an accelerated differentiation of society into autonomous social systems, each of which springs territorial confines and constitutes itself globally. This process is not confined to markets alone but also encompasses science, culture, technology, health, the military, transport, tourism and sport, as well as, albeit in a clearly somewhat retarded form, politics, law and welfare; each of whose current developmental logic has today carved out an autonomous global system'. See also Marcelo Neves, 2009, 78: 'Es geht nicht nur um eine Entwirrung von Gesetz, Macht und Wissen und nicht nur um eine religiöse oder ökonomische Befreiung der Person, sondern es geht um einen umfassenden Vorgang der systemfunktionalen Differenzierung. Dadurch wird die Gesellschaft multizentrisch bzw. polykontextural'.

[133] Neves, 2009, 78; see Marcelo Neves, 2001 for an account of how law's operationability critically depends on structural conditions that cannot be guaranteed in developing countries of 'peripheral modernity'.

[134] Jürgen Habermas, 2001.

[135] Mathias Albert and Rainer Schmalz-Bruns, 2009, 57.

[136] *Ibid*, 67, 69 (arguing that limits to 'de-statisation' (*Entstaatlichung*) are 'compensated through the rudimentary emergence of forms of world statism in the political system of world society'); Andreas Fischer-Lescano and Gunther Teubner, 2007 (highlighting the inadequacies of hierarchising approaches to resolve conflicts between different rationalities and interests); see also Regina Kreide, 2009.

[137] Günter Frankenberg, 2006; Marcelo Neves, 2009; Alec Stone Sweet, 2009; Anne Peters, 2009; Neil Walker, 2009; David Kennedy, 2009.

governance regimes? The first challenge of clarification regarding the parallels between this idea of colliding global sectors and concepts of 'interest-driven', transnational communities arises with regard to the underlying concept of 'law & society'. Concepts of community as used, for example, by Roger Cotterrell,[138] Lawrence Friedman,[139] Jan Aart Scholte[140] or Paul Berman[141] are generally developed against the background of a highly pluralised—domestic or transnational—society. These scholars are all equally aware of the naivity of pictures of homely, harmonious and autonomous '*Gemeinschaften*'. As Richard Ford highlighted in a famous critique of the governmental character of jurisdiction, '[a]ctivity as a member of an enduring political community or group and even long-term alliances are fractured by arbitrary borders that may be periodically redrawn. No affiliation is so important that it cannot be destroyed in the next reapportionment'.[142] Radicalising the notion of a pluralised society as an expression of deeply conflictual social dynamics, Ford scrutinised the political neutralisation inherent to the identification of communities:

> [T]he synthetic jurisdiction constructs a particular type of political subjectivity: a subject whose primary affiliations are either much smaller or much larger than the local community. It encourages privatism—the inward-looking orientation toward self, home and immediate family—and nationalism—the broader-looking affiliation with the nation. The nation, then, is the political entity that the synthetic mode insists is of primary importance. In short, the synthetic mode discourages affiliations that intermediate between the individual (or family) and the state.[143]

As a consequence, the community, which we might at first have desired to celebrate in its autonomy and distinct value, is paradoxically disempowered by deconstructing it as a single-minded unit in relation to centralised political power:

> Territorial jurisdiction is a foundational technology of political liberalism. It defines one of two essential units or 'selves' of liberalism. The liberal concept of

[138] Roger Cotterrell, 1997; Roger Cotterrell, 2008.
[139] Lawrence M Friedman, 1996.
[140] Jan Aart Scholte, 2008, 323–24.
[141] Paul Schiff Berman, 2002, 320–21: 'How are communities appropriately defined in today's world? In what ways might we say that the nation-state is an imagined community, and what other imaginings are possible? How do people actually experience the idea of membership in multiple, overlapping communities? Should citizenship be theorized as one of the many subject positions occupied by people as members of diverse, sometimes non-territorial, collectivities? In what ways is our sense of place and community membership constructed through social forces? And if ideas such as "place," "community," "member," "nation," "citizen," "boundary," and "stranger" are not natural and inevitable, but are instead constructed, imagined, and (sometimes) imposed, what does that say about the presumed 'naturalness' of our geographically based jurisdiction and choice-of-law rules?' [footnotes omitted].
[142] Richard Ford, 1999, 893.
[143] *Ibid*, 893.

> 'self-government' collapses the formal power of a group (perhaps a 'community') to control government with the marginal power of an individual to influence government: the two sovereign selves are the atomistic self of the individual and the communal self of civil society.[144]

These observations illustrate that the critical demarcation of boundaries, which lies at the centre of jurisdiction, has always been a crucial building block in the political structure of society, the allocation of competences and the containment of authority and power. Its correlation with the fading influence of substantivist legal theories of social engineering in a radically differentiated society[145] is reflected in the erosion of distinctions between 'public' or 'private' spheres, actors or norms. Seen in this light, 'jurisdiction' need not only be an instrument of coercion and redistribution but equally one of empowerment, facilitation and authorisation. It is here where theories of jurisdiction with regard to critical legal theory, cosmopolitanism[146] or transnational regulation[147] have their origin.

If there is, however, a distinctive trait by which systems theoretical accounts of regimes and the just-mentioned theories of community differ, it would be what we might call either systems theory's *invisibilisation* of 'justice', or morality concerns, or perhaps the eternal *struggle* with this challenge.[148] To be sure, this does not occur in ignorance of the dramatic consequences of a functionally differentiated world society for claims of representation, equity and redistribution and the resistance against the 'expansionist fervor',[149] especially in the 'Southern hemisphere'. Fischer-Lescano and Teubner admit that

> [s]uch problems are caused by the fragmented and operationally closed functional systems of a global society, which, in their expansionist fervor, create the real problems of the global society, and who, at the same time, make use of global law in order normatively to secure their own highly refined sphere logics.

Drawing on Paul Berman's cosmopolitan theory that aims at developing 'jurisdictional assertions that bind sub-, supra-, or transnational communities' and would include 'a wide range of entities, from official transnational and international regulatory and adjudicative bodies, to non-governmental quasi-legal tribunals, to private standard-setting or regulatory organisations',[150] Fischer-Lescano and Teubner show how the emergence of such highly diversified, particular institutional/normative regimes results in law's task no longer being one of 'resolving' or 'engineering' a specific

144 *Ibid*, 897.
145 Gunther Teubner, 1984.
146 Berman, 2002; Paul Schiff Berman, 2005b.
147 Hannah L Buxbaum, 2006; Hannah L Buxbaum, 2009.
148 See now Gunther Teubner, 2009; see Niklas Luhmann, 2004, 211.
149 Fischer-Lescano and Teubner, 2004, 1008.
150 Berman, 2002, 325.

case with recourse to a centralised or hierarchically elevated authority or a meta-principle.[151]

> Instead, such autonomous societal fragments satisfy their own demands through a direct recourse to law. Increasingly, global private regimes are creating their own substantive law. They have recourse to their own sources of law, which lie outside spheres of national law-making and international treaties.[152]

This process of law's purported *introvertedness* is directly correlated to the system's capacity to address questions of 'justice'. The decisive reformulation of 'justice' concerns in law unfolds through a particular reflexive constitutionalisation process: private governance regimes create 'law' at the outer boundaries of law administered by courts, legislatures and bureaucratic agencies. 'Outside' of this periphery the emerging private governance regimes are closely coupled 'with their own specialised regimes in the legal periphery that they necessarily contribute to a global legal fragmentation'.[153] Law's polycontextualisation thus 'exposes' law to numerous social spheres, which themselves evolve around highly varied 'paradigms of social ordering'.[154] In this light, an appeal to a 'constitutional' or 'political' resolution of a conflict must necessarily be re-directed to an analysis of the polycontextual structure of law itself. Rudolf Wiethölter has repeatedly insisted on the paradox construction of law's legitimacy,[155] and this paradoxical perspective proves particularly helpful to illuminate the evolution of the legal system in the transnational arena. Here,

> [w]e face a paradoxical situation, whereby the legal instance within each regime, which is also a party to the legal collision, must create substantive norms which claim validity for both regimes involved. Transnational substantive norms are created, within a form of mixed law approach, with an eye both to one's own and to the other legal regime, but also with an eye to third party legal orders.[156]

Law's fundamental paradox to produce legitimacy *out of itself* reproduces itself in the collision of different private governance regimes, with regard to law's regulation of specialised social spheres. Law's ultimate 'test' will

[151] See Claudio Franzius, 2009, 37: 'Soweit dieser Rechtsstatus nicht mehr normativ auf eine zentrale Instanz bezogen werden kann, sondern in eine komplementär „zusammengesetzte“ Ordnung des Politischen gestellt ist, *muss* die Sehnsucht nach einer Ursprungs- und Projektionsinstanz, in der einst der Glaube monopolisiert war, später die Souveränität aufgehoben wurde und heute das Wissen gebündelt werden könnte, unerfüllt bleiben'.

[152] Fischer-Lescano and Teubner, 2004, 1010.

[153] Fischer-Lescano and Teubner, 2004, 1014.

[154] Fischer-Lescano and Teubner, 2004, 1015, with reference to Karl-Heinz Ladeur, 1992, 159–67.

[155] Rudolf Wiethölter, 1985, 502: 'The paradox of law in our time in a nutshell is this: for the substantive demands on law (ie for "positive conflict norms"!), which both are indispensable and need to be limited, we have neither criteria nor venues nor procedures'; Rudolf Wiethölter, 1986a; Rudolf Wiethölter, 2006. See also Gunther Teubner, 2006.

[156] Fischer-Lescano and Teubner, 2004, 1022.

be whether and to what degree it is able to 'address' the particular conflicts arising around it. Again, law does not have a direct grasp on a conflict, but needs to alienate it from its social context in order to then reconstruct it through its own distinction between legal and illegal. The legal system's answer to the quest for 'justice' unfolds in its success or failure to 'have an impact', to facilitate the identification of system-internal blind spots and dead-ends. By recognising the legal norm conflicts between different global legal regimes as an 'expression of the fundamental conflicts between organisational principles of social systems',[157] law admits to the inevitability of its exposure to the throes and woes of colliding different social systems and their particular rationalities. In the absence of an elevated and all-encompassing value system, as concentrated, for example, in the sovereign will of a world government or in the towering principles of global constitutionalism,[158] private governance regimes are thrown back onto themselves in the sense that they not only need to constantly fear the inadequacy of their norms ('low-impact', 'irrelevance'[159]) but also the never-ending conflict with other private governance regimes. In this god-less world, and

> in spite of their autonomy, regimes can build on the assumption of common reference points, which is of course nothing but an operative fiction. Building on this fiction, each of them can subordinate themselves to a, necessarily abstract, seemingly common philosophical horizon, to which they orient their own rule-making.[160]

Rather than continuing to dream of a universalistic global value system, private governance regimes and, with them, the theory of transnational governance, must learn to internalise the lessons of human rights critique[161] and assume an ironical attitude towards the attainment of justice. In the process, each regime will likely work out its own particular grammar of a '*common ius non dispositivum*'.[162] Law's transience and frailty and its singing-to-every-tune, then, will turn into its ability to 'deliver justice' the more it succeeds in its facilitating function by its 'openness' to its 'human and natural environment'.[163] It is this receptivity of the legal system to a regime's internal shortcomings and failures that the above-mentioned scholars of transnational commercial law invoke with reference to the need to apply the Rule of Law of otherwise 'autonomous', specialised community

[157] Andreas Fischer-Lescano and Gunther Teubner, 2004, 1024.
[158] See Christian Walter, 2001, and Thomas Cottier, 2009.
[159] Manfred Lachs, 1972, 104.
[160] Fischer-Lescano and Teubner, 2004, 1033.
[161] Makau Mutua, 2002; David Kennedy, 2002; Upendra Baxi, 2005a; Peter Fitzpatrick, 2004; Costas Douzinas, 2007.
[162] Fischer-Lescano and Teubner, 2004, 1034.
[163] Fischer-Lescano and Teubner, 2004, 1037; Georg Nolte, 2008, 32–33; Gregory Shaffer, 2009, 3, 8. See also Claudio Franzius, 2006, 235, who speaks of a 'building of bridges' (*Brückenbau*) through the integration of legislative science into administrative science.

regimes. To be sure, the initial caution that we ought to point to the limits of law rather than exaggerating its hopes and promises, still stands.[164]

The account just rendered has provided us with but a sobering insight into the potential of legal regulation in a heterogenous, disembedded society, which powerfully echoes the transformation of 'law after the welfare state' on the national level over the last 30–40 years. With his usual accuracy, Marc Galanter recently captured this constellation as illustrating the function of 'law and social science' scholarship: '[i]t seeks explanation rather than justification'.[165] The disenchantment with the social engineering potential of law was a result of the structural and normative exhaustion of the ambitious welfarist programmes in the 1960s that entered into unholy communities with a particular quest for emancipation and individualisation. The concurring erosion of collectivism and solidarity eventually provided the fertile ground for social politics that embraced the value of the individual and his/her responsibility in shaping destiny, without the increasingly discredited state considered to be legitimately playing a continued part in this process. This leaves the 'other-directed' individual[166] on her own, with the world around her having become risky and the future uncertain: in the meantime, we strive, shop and hope for the best.

The erosion of a relatively solid institutional framework of justice administration in the context of a pluralising and globalising society driven by technological advance, social emancipation and the dramatic usurpation of the industrial economy by the insatiable golem of borderless finance thus constitutes the unlikely background for the present search for a legal theory. Because such a theory must but can no longer confidently be a social theory of justice, the distinction between law and social scientific projects becomes increasingly fuzzy. Among the most crucial determinants of a legal theoretical inquiry into law making and law enforcement continues to be the understanding of the relation between law and society. But the growing tension between a radically differentiating society and the legal system[167] is now being reassessed in the context of a relativisation of the nation-state as the legal system's definitive reference point in the twentieth century. As such, the context for the analysis of legal regulation such as is pursued in this book is in many ways a still unchartered one.[168] It encompasses the

[164] Fischer-Lescano and Teubner, 2004, 1045: 'In the place of an illusory integration of a differentiated global society, law can only, at the very best, offer a kind of damage limitation'.

[165] Marc Galanter, 2006, 1. See also Gregory Shaffer, 2009, 13: 'While "social science" is never entirely "correct", it is the best way for us to proceed toward a better understanding of the world in which law operates'. See also Gunther Teubner, 1989, and Peer Zumbansen, 2009a.

[166] David Riesman, 1950.

[167] Niklas Luhmann, 1985.

[168] David Kennedy, 2009, 38: 'We know very little, in fact, about the structure of global society. How is public power exercised, where are the levers, who are the authorities, and how do they relate to one another? Everywhere we can see the impact of things global, foreign,

treacherous ground of identifying adequate concepts for the law 'after' the nineteenth-century Rule of Law and the twentieth-century Welfare State. The search for an adequate formula able to depict the current nature of the state becomes intertwined with competing theories assessing the nature of contemporary society, both in the national and a global context. The observations of the relations between law and society from a national and a global perspective must inevitably overlap and it is on this basis that we develop our analysis of private governance regimes from a 'post-national' perspective. The complementary step must be to search out the parallels with 'national' legal theory. As Karl-Heinz Ladeur has repeatedly argued, the recurring attempts to modify the contours of a state-based administrative regulatory science falls short of capturing the particular dynamics of a radically transformed society, which he, in tune with other social scientists,[169] refers to as the 'network society'.[170] These dynamics reflect the emergence of a new cognitive infrastructure of post-modern societies which gives rise to an experimental rationality'.[171] In response to untiring attempts to rescue, resuscitate or vindicate the state by modifying its functionalist labels (eg *risk*, *moderator*, *supervision*, or *guarantor* state[172]), Ladeur traces the radical transformation of an institutionally and normatively embedded liberal society of organisations into a highly fragmented, polycontextual society of networks,[173] the gist of which has tremendous consequences for law and administration both in- and outside of the nation-state.[174] We recognise a radical challenge for a legal theory which has learned to identify the state as the primary law-making and -enforcing authority enthroned 'at the top' of a society that, in turn, is believed to act through collective deliberation to generate consensus: it consists not only in

faraway. How does it all work? How do all the pieces fit together? Are the worlds of politics, markets, and cultural influence held together in a tight structure or is it all more loose and haphazard? Is there more than one global order—how much, in the end, is simply chaos, and how much the work of an invisible hand?'

[169] Jan van Dijk, 1999; Manuel Castells, 1996.

[170] Karl-Heinz Ladeur, 1997b; Karl-Heinz Ladeur, 2000a; Karl-Heinz Ladeur, 2001a; Karl-Heinz Ladeur, 2007; Karl-Heinz Ladeur, 2009. See now the excellent account by Ino Augsberg, Tobias Gostomzyk and Lars Viellechner, 2009, and the other contributions to the Symposium Issue in Honour of Karl-Heinz Ladeur, '*The Law of the Network Society*' in (2009) 10 *German Law Journal* 305–536.

[171] Karl-Heinz Ladeur, 2007, 336–37: 'Each paradigm of decision making in history demands a cognitive infrastructure that is closely linked to the ways that knowledge is generated and stabilized within society as a whole. Decision making in the liberal society is thus not only characterized by its reference to cases, but also its generation and processing of experience, conventions, and patterns that stabilize trust in the reliability of social observations of reality'.

[172] See, eg Gunnar Folke Schuppert, 1999.

[173] Karl-Heinz Ladeur, 2009, 165.

[174] Karl-Heinz Ladeur, 2004a; Lars Viellechner, Ino Augsberg and Peer Zumbansen, 2009; Lars Viellechner, 2009, 525.

turning this image on its head but in substituting the implied—institutional and normative—hierarchy/verticality with the heterarchy and horizontality of networks and their interactions.[175] On this basis, many of the currently discussed processes of the *contracting* state[176] begin to appear in a different light. Despite being characterised through their unfolding against the background of a juxtaposition of 'state' and 'market', neither of these terms can adequately depict the rationality of a specific contractual arrangement. Echoing the long-standing insights of contract lawyers that the denomination of a contract as 'private' says little about its 'public' function,[177] Ladeur underlines the correlation between a contractual arrangement and the context in which it operates and from which it receives valuable impulses. This correlation cannot, however, be captured by what Ladeur refers to a liberal social epistemology, based on which it was possible to demarcate the public and private dimensions of responsibility. In a radically heterogeneous environment the state's lack of adequate knowledge of societal, differentiated contexts only further increases and accentuates the pressure on the constructivist imagination of law.[178] This has significant consequences for our understanding of public, administrative action and, in turn, for our conceptualisation of *private* governance regimes. With regard to the former, Ladeur remarks that

> [t]he administrative act is always limited by the effect of the framing of the observations and information created by the continuity of social expectations, patterns of attributing responsibility, presuppositions of probability, codified relations of cause and effect, normative conventions, and other rules that make up the social epistemology and the cognitive infrastructure of society, which are applied and not reflected in administrative processes.[179]

The 'public contract', a crucial interface between public and private governance, 'is no longer embedded in a "social epistemology" that frames the cognitive environment of individual expectations, but is regarded as being autological without any presupposition'. In this light, all attempts to re-embed administrative action (and, as a mirror image, 'private' ordering) in a comprehensive theory of liberal society must come to this dramatic impasse. The realisation and recognition of the unavailability of an encompassing cognitive (and normative) framework against which 'public' or 'private' action could be designed is crucial for an understanding of the consequences of a fragmented society for liberal social theories

[175] Karl-Heinz Ladeur, 2004b.

[176] For insightful discussions, see Ian Harden, 1992; Jody Freeman, 2000a; Peter Vincent-Jones, 2006; Peter Vincent-Jones, 2007.

[177] See, eg Morris R Cohen, 1932; Friedrich Kessler, 1973; Marc Amstutz, Andreas Abegg and Vagias Karavas, 2007.

[178] Gunther Teubner, 1989.

[179] Karl-Heinz Ladeur, 2007, 337.

that have regularly placed the individual at the centre of their conceptual framework.[180] The fragmentation of society and the ubiquitous emergence of governance processes occur in troubling isolation from a continued emphasis on the individual and its potential, capacity and responsibilities. The failure to make the connection between society's fragmentation and the fundamental erosion of the institutional frameworks of embeddedness of the liberal conception of the individual (family, state school,[181] parliamentary democracy, bowling alleys[182]), however, results in generating a society of 'responsibilisation',[183] characterized by a widening gap between the actual lives of citizens and the spheres of community action alluded to in official discourse. In this context of an ongoing privatisation of public spaces, the oft-praised notion of 'communities'—local, regional, interest-driven or otherwise—turns into a farce. In consequence, a *legal* theory of networks must seek to reinvigorate the concept of civil, constitutional rights by adapting and translating the conventional liberal idea of negative and positive rights into more sophisticated vehicles that are able to facilitate the generation and accessibility of knowledge, which is the key to the ever-fleeting reconstruction of collective identities, a sense of belonging and the meaning of participation.[184] 'The self-organisation of rules, patterns of expectations and behaviour, forms of coordination, knowledge systems etc becomes the core performance of law'.[185]

Before concluding this section, it is important to note that the same reasoning applies to the development of organisations, corporations and regimes—domestic or transnational,[186] a development that is of great

[180] See Christoph Engel, 2004, for an intriguing discussion and analysis of the challenges of hybrid governance for a legal theory that continues to trust to attribute regulatory activity either to the state or to aprivate actor.

[181] Karl-Heinz Ladeur, 2009, 168.

[182] Robert D Putnam, 2000.

[183] See, eg Ronen Shamir, 2008, Garry Gray, 2009, and Carol Harlow, 2009, 91.

[184] Karl-Heinz Ladeur, 2008, 114: '*Gerade weil es in der kontingenten Welt keine „Verständigung" über eine gemeinsame Realitätsbeschreibung oder gemeinsame „Bedürfnisse" (und darüber, wie sie zu befriedigen wären) geben kann, ist die fragmentierte Ordnungsbildung durch ausdifferenzierte Kommunikationssysteme erforderlich*'.

[185] Ladeur, 2008, 114: '*Die Selbstorganisation von Regeln, Erwartungs- und Verhaltensmustern, Koordinationsformen, Wissenssystemen etc wird damit zur eigentlichen Leistung des Rechts*'. [PZ trans]

[186] See, in this regard, Boaventura de Sousa Santos, 2008, 250: 'The social struggles that find expression in the WSF [World Social Forum] do not adequately fit either form of social change sanctioned by western modernity—reform or revolution. Aside from the consensus on non-violence, its modes of struggle are extremely diverse and appear spread out on a continuum between the poles of institution building and insurgency'. See also Ruth Buchanan, 2008, 14: 'Allowing ourselves to re-imagine transnational legal institutions and the politics surrounding them with the metaphor of legal plurality, I argue, might allow us to perceive emerging forms of "global" law, perhaps from unexpected places. The authors of these new forms of global law could well be those "critical beings", those who, like refugees or illegal migrants, find themselves occupying the most inhospitable and interstitial spaces of the transnational order, and who are denied the protection of a settled or determinate law'.

importance in the ongoing discussion of post-national constitutionalism and cosmopolitanism.[187] Because the identification of public or private competence and authority ultimately depended either on the violent usurpation of power or on an encompassing theory of liberal freedoms, the analysis of the rise of the 'network society' can no longer easily resort to the liberal structuring architecture. If the emphasis on the individual and on the promise of private self-organisation is not to result in the invisibilisation of asymmetries and exclusions,[188] it is crucial to apply the network logic also to the institutions that increasingly move into the places formerly held by 'political' or 'private' institutions. The crucial move here consists in the relativisation of the *inside* and *outside* of the organisation. Examples of this shift in perspective exist in great abundance. The currently much discussed 'regulated self-regulation' in highly specialised, 'hybrid' areas of administrative governance illustrates the degree to which it is no longer possible to clearly distinguish between *regulation* and *management*.[189] Similarly, the contestation of the alleged difference between 'contract' and 'organisation'[190] and the deconstruction of the business enterprise as a 'quasi-political' actor[191] are mere forerunners of contemporary, elaborate critiques of contractual and corporate governance.

The preceding illustration of the systems theoretical account of the network logic of global private regimes provides the background against which we can now briefly address the second significant difference to other depictions of the '*interest-driven*' emergence of specialised legal frameworks as offered with regard to examples of transnational business or finance. Whereas these accounts assume, at their basis, the operability of these normative/institutional frameworks not only to *address*, but also to *satisfy* the interests at stake, the legal regime theory described here, as we saw, radically questions this possibility. Irrespective of whether the emergence of an interest-driven, specialised transnational regulatory regime is seen as an illustration of a developing global legal order that encompasses questions of equity and social justice[192] or as a successful regulation of a concrete case in the eyes of the involved parties,[193] in both cases the underlying assumption is one of a *functioning* legal system. The points of contestation arise here with regard to the degree of 'autonomy' from domestic law (courts, administrative regulation) or international law (treaties) and with regard to the scope of the body of norms (universalism v functionalism). Neither

[187] See, eg, David Held, 2000; Daniele Archibugi, 2004; Robyn Eckersly, 2007; Gavin Anderson, 2005.
[188] See Rudolf Stichweh, 2005a, and Antonis Chanos, 2008.
[189] Martin Eifert, 2001; Karl-Heinz Ladeur, 2009, 189.
[190] Terence Daintith and Gunther Teubner, 1986; Rudolf Wiethölter, 1986b.
[191] Adolf A Berle, 1954.
[192] Ross Cranston, 2007; Harold J Berman, 1995.
[193] Roy Goode, 1997, 36.

approach, however, shares the same level of anxiety that informs the systems theoretical account of governance regimes. For this latter account, the anxiety stems from the already mentioned sociological insight into the radical and irreversible functional differentiation of society. Because society is depicted as functionally differentiated, the law can only be understood in relation to this differentiation. It is in this light that the structure of law as 'operationally closed' and 'cognitively open' appears in its most dramatic form. Law's function now appears in a particularly dim light. In light of the dramatic exclusionary dynamics that characterise global functional differentiation in a way that seems to undermine social justice, class- or hierarchy-based social theories,[194] law as just described seems to be complicit in the further differentiation of social systems. Law's seeming complicity in the facilitation of self-propelling governance regimes that adhere to principles of efficiency and cost-reduction[195] provokes a decidedly political critique of the way in which law drives de-formalisation, self-regulation and forms of private ordering that are determined solely with reference to the concrete functional, allegedly 'neutral' quality of a given context.[196] David Levi-Faur's account is worthy to be quoted here at some length:

> The new order of regulatory capitalism, which has been in the making since the 1980s, differs qualitatively from older forms of capitalist governance in its reliance on rules and rule enforcement. It is characterised by (1) a new division of labor between state and society (for example, privatisation), (2) an increase in delegation (remaking the boundaries between the experts and the politicians), (3) proliferation of new technologies of regulation, (4) formalisation of interinstitutional and intrainstitutional relations and the proliferation of mechanisms of self-regulation in the shadow of the state, and (5) the growth in the influence of experts in general and of international networks of experts in particular. It is suggested that this notion of a new order of regulatory capitalism goes beyond privatisation and includes an increase in delegation to autonomous agencies, formalisation of relationships, proliferation of new technologies of regulation in

[194] Marcelo Neves, 2007; Rudolf Stichweh, 2005b, 48: '*Die Frage ist genau die, ob nicht vielfach kompakte Sachverhalte des Ausschlusses aus der Gesellschaft beobachtbar sind, die nicht mehr als soziale Ungleichheit und Schichtung—im Sinne eines Mehr oder Weniger an Teilhabe an sozialen Gütern—beschrieben werden können, die vielmehr eine innergesellschaftliche Trennlinie schaffen, die ein „innen"und ein „außen" deutlich voneinander unterscheidet*'.

[195] Robert D Cooter, 1996; JH Dalhuisen, 2006, 148, 156.

[196] William E Scheuerman, 1999, 3: 'Economic globalization relies overwhelmingly on ad hoc, discretionary, closed, and non-transparent legal forms fundamentally inconsistent with a minimally defensible conception of the rule of law'. See also Daniela Caruso, 2006, 69: 'rhetoric of neutrality'; and David Levi-Faur, 2005, 14: 'The new regulatory order is social, political, and economic. State, markets, and society are not distinct entities. Indeed, regulatory capitalism rests on an understanding of the relations between state and market along a condominium ... The state is embedded in the economic and social order; any change in the state is expected to be reflected in the economy and the society, and vice versa' (footnote omitted).

> both public and private spheres, and the creation of new layers of both national and international regulation.[197]

Against this background, the out-dated, pre-modern depictions of private law as synonymous with self-regulation and the rejection of state-'intervention'[198] that often complements accounts of emerging interest-driven regimes and their aspiration for autonomy are worthy to be read with considerable scepticism.

> Outside the nation state, private law is moving along the same stages of development that it has experienced within state borders for over two centuries—codification into orderly systems, contribution to state-making projects, and eventual enmeshment with policy and ideology.[199]

The crucial constructive element, in this reading, is their 'autonomisation' from the continuing fundamental inquiry into the difference between law and non-law.

Seen from this perspective, systems theory's account of law's *losing itself* in society now appears in a strikingly different light: the notion of 'interest-driven' regimes that follow their own functional logic now appears dangerously close to depictions of global market regimes that are largely sustained by private ordering and are not only not in need of regulatory intervention but are indeed portrayed as being threatened by it. This critique raises the question as to whether, and if so how, a systems theoretical account of a functionally differentiated 'world society' can reckon with the hegemonic and imperialist dynamics of economic rationality in the global collision of societal rationalities.[200] The systems theoretical understanding of governance regimes is informed by the fundamental insight into the non-hierarchical nature of competing interests and societal rationalities. Law's function is no longer understood as unfolding in the direct counter-acting of injustice or the achievement of social justice through 'social engineering'. Based on the insight that there is neither an Archimedean point nor an 'external standard' against which to identify and to measure the necessary steps towards such a goal, law is seen as being *immersed in* and *exposed to* a never-ending 'collision' of competing rationalities. These replace the institutional embeddedness of law in the twentieth-century interventionist and welfare state.[201] From this perspective, it would be important to address the dubious prominence of transnational governance regimes in contemporary assessments of global governance with a considerable dose of hesitation and scepticism.

[197] David Levi-Faur, 2005, 27.
[198] For a critique see only Robert L Hale, 1923.
[199] Daniela Caruso, 2006, 71.
[200] For a still valid analysis, see Karl Marx and Friedrich Engels, 1848; see also Karl Polanyi, 1944.
[201] For an overview, see Jason M Solomon, 2008.

A more outright appreciation of the law's distinct quality—and its limitations—might be necessary to protect the law from either being overburdened with a comprehensive moral agenda in the light of highly diversified societal rationalities or from being neutralised in the face of objectifying concepts of allegedly value-neutral, 'natural' functionalities. Much suggests that it is only on this basis of a fundamental recognition of the correlation between law's evolution and a functionally differentiated society that we can hope for conceptualisations of legal governance in world society to have any currency.

C. Markets as Regulators: It's the Economy, Stupid—Or, is It?

Adopting an understanding of law itself being functionally differentiated, law as an institutionalised system loses its alleged prerogative over the economy, or over society as such. On that basis, then, this emerging understanding of law, derived from a reflection on *lex mercatoria* in recent debates, bears many resemblances with New Institutional Economics (NIE), as we, too, must recognise the particular importance of a more complex definition of institutions, a concept central to NIE and exerting increasing fascination for law.[202] To stay with the example of *lex mercatoria*, the institutions involved in its creation encompass arrangements among contracting parties with regard to choice of law, the constitution of the arbitration panel, and the place of the tribunal. But, they also include norms and principles promulgated—in often contested manner[203]—by institutions such as UNIDROIT, on the one hand,[204] and by awards handed down by arbitration tribunals as well as decisions by domestic courts enforcing arbitral awards, on the other.[205] In that regard, *lex mercatoria* reasserts above all its promise as an important laboratory for the study of the interaction of public and private, state and non-state norms with a view to an erosion of the categorical boundaries used to make these distinctions. The relevance of a particularly rich economic theoretisation of these institutional arrangements in the past is particularly obvious, as the legal imagination regarding the scope and nature of *lex mercatoria* has altogether not only revealed a distinct straining of established legal doctrine and semantics, but has also made it clear that law is not defined in the abstract. As an evolving system of norms clearly associated with neither the 'state' nor the 'market', *lex mercatoria*

[202] See above, ch 1 of this book.

[203] Nicholas Kasirer, 1999, 661 (discussing the choice of translations of key concepts to be at times, 'a neologism at best and, at worst, something of a barbarism').

[204] Michael Joachim Bonell, 1992; Herbert Kronke, 2003.

[205] Christopher A Whytock, 2009, Ms at 21 (describing how domestic courts perform 'jurisdictional global governance' with regard to 'adjudicative authority, prescriptive authority, and enforcement authority').

provides for a powerful illustration of the increased inseparability of questions of form and substance and thus of a complex constellation which will only reveal its nature, promises and perils to an ambitious, interdisciplinary agenda:[206] as the dispute continues over its formal, procedural constitution and its substantive matter in terms of accountability, transparency and legitimacy, it becomes evident how *lex mercatoria* exemplifies an increasing erosion of established categorical boundaries rather than the birth of yet a new field of law. The erosion of these boundaries, however, is not just an event, which would be of interest from the viewpoint of the sociology of law or of legal theory. We can depict a hard political core in this debate and, in particular, in the omnipresent fascination with *lex mercatoria* as an idea. An idea of what? we might ask.

To us, this fascination is inseparable from and tightly interwoven with assertions of 'markets as regulators', which are usually put forward in response to a seemingly irreversible and, at any rate, hopeless loss of sovereignty on the part of the state. As markets are believed to pick up where (exhausted) national governments have left off, they form an integral part of a narrative of natural evolution. In this narrative, conflicts over goals of regulation and principles of political market governance are transposed into strategic options put forward by states engaged in global regulatory competition, or into preferences and choices by market participants as (global) consumers.[207] In these accounts, markets are promoted to assume the role of regulators, however, without any regard to their constituted, legal nature, an insight gained so long ago,[208] that the general amnesia that seems to have taken hold of the market fundamentalists[209] could almost be forgiven. Forgiven, perhaps, if not so much were at stake, then and now: as evidenced by the above-noted examples of transnational governance, there is hardly anything uncontested or straightforward about their institutional or normative constitution. It is thus even more surprising how such narratives are being promulgated in a seemingly undeterred manner, even despite the overwhelmingly obvious need to critically engage with the

[206] With regard to the study of conflict of laws, see only Karen Knop, Ralf Michaels and Annelise Riles, 2008, 3–4, assessing the influence of non-legal research (economics, political science, anthropology) on the study of private international law.

[207] David Kennedy, 1997, 607–608: 'Indeed, international economic law often presses against political or economic differences which can be reinterpreted as protectionist policies, reducing cultural differences to matters of consumer taste ... But the international economic law system also can seem a quite decentralized thing, a politically disengaged process of ongoing interstate bargaining in a marketplace of national regulations. In this mode, international economic law is able to reinterpret and embrace a broad range of cultural and political differences as matters of divergent strategic advantage and to present itself as providing a channel through which a variety of actors, both public and private, can engage in an open-ended process of bargaining in the spirit of free trade and open markets'.

[208] Robert L Hale, 1923; Morris R Cohen, 1927.

[209] Upendra Baxi, 2005b.

meaning of responsibilities ascribed to either 'state' or 'market' today. The 'romance', which as we have seen was so often associated with *lex mercatoria*, appears to inform much of the 'market as regulator' ideas that are promoted in response to alleged regulatory failure.[210] This romantic lens provides a rose-coloured view on the actions of private actors that have over time been entrusted with, or have independently assumed, far-reaching regulatory capacities. As has been observed with regard to the evolution of credit rating agencies[211] or the *Internet Corporation for the Assignment of Names and Numbers* (ICANN),[212] these entities were not emerging through natural evolution, nor were they ever simply filling a regulatory vacuum left by a supposedly exhausted state. Rather, their particular emergence and their role in both the US and the global economy have been assessed to be striking illustrations of a particular form of transnationalism—one referred to by Samuel Huntington to be the 'American mode of expansion'.[213] Huntington, in an early, yet prophetic assessment of the importance of transnational organisations, made the important connection between a particular political claim to national and global sovereignty, on the one hand, and technological development, on the other. In the case of the United States, whose 'penetration of other societies was generally not justified by doctrines of colonialism comparable to those popular in other countries' and 'rarely based on a claim of political or racial superiority' but 'rather on a claim to technological or economic superiority',[214] Huntington noted that the 'pre-eminence of one nation-state in large portions of the world favours the emergence of transnational organisations under the sponsorship and control of that nation-state'.[215] In a similar vein, Christopher Bruner has recently re-emphasised Saskia Sassen's important observation that states have themselves been playing a crucial part in processes of globalisation[216] to make the argument that these particular 'private' regulatory entities represent deeply troubling examples of the state's maintenance of sovereign power—indeed within and beyond its political borders—despite the fact of having delegated far-reaching regulatory power to such entities:

> Although private-sector entities, they nevertheless enjoy the imprimatur of the State; although arising out of de-centralised and informal modes of decision-making in the marketplace, they nevertheless have come to represent a form of decentralised power over their respective domains; although claiming reputational

210 For the field of Public International Law, see Anne van Aaken, 2009b, and the comment by Peer Zumbansen, 2009c.

211 Christopher M Bruner, 2008; Dieter Kerwer, 2005a.

212 Bruner, 2008; Jochen von Bernstorff, 2004; see also Gillian K Hadfield, 2002.

213 Samuel P Huntington, 1973, 344.

214 *Ibid*, 345–46.

215 *Ibid*, 361.

216 Christopher M Bruner, 2008, 130, with reference to Saskia Sassen, 2000, 100–103; see also Saskia Sassen, 2003, and Alfred C Aman Jr, 2004.

> legitimacy rooted in expert knowledge, their power today ultimately derives more substantially from state endorsement of their decisions; and although their authority is rooted in U.S. laws and regulations, their power is projected abroad, and felt acutely by other sovereigns.[217]

The relevance of these observations for the contested relationship between *lex mercatoria* and the state legal order, which we alluded to above, becomes more obvious the more we recognise that the definitional and conceptual challenges to giving a meaningful account of this relation appear to escape the grasp of our legal vocabulary:

> Our unease in describing these entities often expresses itself in the use of imprecise relational terms, such as when we describe them as 'merging into' public authority, or 'hybridising' public and private authority, or 'supplementing' them, or even when ... we describe them as 'gatekeepers' to a market place.[218]

This political assessment of the above examples of private ordering adds a crucial dimension to our present project of developing a theory of transnational private law. The emphasis on the complex relation between state and market that emerges from the preceding observations confirms much of the orientation in the legal and interdisciplinary scholarship which we have found most promising in recent years. In particular, because law continues to be so powerfully—and perhaps, overwhelmingly—challenged by non-legal accounts of social order, to be clear, above all, from economics, any present attempt to outline the basis and contours of a legal theory must engage with that challenge.[219] This challenge, we think, is particularly akin to private law, which, from the perspective of the continental lawyer at least,[220] is a set of norms growing out of society, in a fruitful yet constantly conflictuous exchange with public law, a constellation which is instructive for the answer to the question whether we can speak here of customary law. For Savigny, who juxtaposed the interaction of peoples' law ('*Volksgeist*')

[217] Christopher M Bruner, 2008, 131, 132: 'Ultimately, I argue that this uneasy conflation of public and private characteristics in each case reflects an attempt by the U.S. government to maintain centralized power over a core regulatory function of the given marketplace—an active posture rooted in the Westphalian conception of sovereignty—while cultivating the perception of market-based private ordering—a more hands-off posture reflecting the shift away from autonomous action by States in the face of economic globalization'.

[218] Bruner, above, 167.

[219] Victoria Nourse and Gregory Shaffer, 2009, 64: 'If there is to be a new move in legal theory, we believe that it will neither be simply law "and" some other discipline nor a revival of the New Deal administrative state.'

[220] Franz Wieacker, 1953; Franz Wieacker, 1967, § 27 I.1. '*Die Fortentwicklung des deutschen bürgerlichen Rechts*': '*Mit dem vorsichtigen Zögern, das Pflicht des Richters ist, aber doch mit größerer Beweglichkeit als der romanische oder gar angelsächsische Jurist fand sie [die Rechtsprechung] in neuen Lagen auch neue Entscheidungen; so sehr, daß das wirklich „geltende" Privatrecht, besonders die allgemeinen Lehren und das Schuldrecht, bereits vor 1933 nicht mehr aus dem Gesetzestext hätte abgelesen werden können*'; Karl Renner, 1949; see also the account by John Henry Merryman, 1969.

with lawyers' law ('*Juristenrecht*') in the creation of customary law, all law was created first from custom and peoples' beliefs, later through lawyers and legal science, and thus everywhere through silently working forces, not through the arbitrary acts of a legislature.[221] As often noted by Legal Pluralism scholars, this distinction between the *creation* of law by those with the vested authority and the *emergence* of legal rules out of the life of society is certainly at the heart of any legal theory, be it with regard to the domestic or the international arena. In order to make sense of the norms produced by transnational private governance regimes, this distinction can only be a starting point. As pointed out by Gunther Teubner, ever greater caution is necessary when resorting to ideas of customary law in this context: according to Teubner, the current processes of the making of transnational law are not at all comparable to the slow, unintended evolution of custom as conceived in the domestic context; in contrast, the evolution of transnational law occurs in an extremely fast-moving, multipolar and issue-driven manner, something which leads him to qualify transnational law as *neo-spontaneous law*.[222]

This discussion provides an important backdrop for our current project, which is inevitably struggling between an adequate assessment of highly specialised and issue-driven transnational regulatory fields, on the one hand, and the attempt to work out a more comprehensive methodological concept of transnational law, on the other. While we understand *lex mercatoria* to be deeply embedded in a long-standing intellectual tradition in commercial law,[223] conflict of laws[224] and, arguably, legal pluralism, we think it important to emphasise the particular private law perspective on the regulatory challenges with which *lex mercatoria* is concerned. Purporting to address conflicts among parties engaging in transnational activities for which a fully institutionalised regulatory framework, administered by either domestic courts or global institutions, is not available, *lex mercatoria* captures a particular private law regulatory problem. This is not to say that *lex mercatoria* and other 'private' regulatory regimes dealt with in this regard are defunct of public interest: quite the contrary! We believe the private law perspective to be illustrative of how an issue- and actor-driven approach to law-making cannot as such—and should not—be taken to

[221] Friedrich Karl von Savigny, 1840, 14: '*daß alles Recht … erst durch Sitte und Volksglaube … dann durch Jurisprudenz … erzeugt wird, überall also durch innere stillwirkende Kräfte, nicht durch die Willkühr eines Gesetzgebers*'. ['...that it is first developed by custom and popular faith, next by jurisprudence,—everywhere, therefore, by internal silently-operating powers, not by the arbitrary will of a law-giver.'—Frederick Charles von Savigny (1986) *The Vocation of Our Age for Legislation and Jurisprudence* (Abraham Hayward, transl. 1831) (London, Littlewood & Co), 30.]

[222] Gunther Teubner, 2004a.

[223] Justus Wilhelm Hedemann, 1959; Uwe Blaurock, 1998; Herbert Kronke, 2000.

[224] Christian Joerges, 1972b; Paul Schiff Berman, 2005b; Robert Wai, 2008.

re-establish categorical boundaries between a self-interest-oriented private law here and a common-good-committed public law there. Rather, we find overwhelming evidence from both historical and contemporary private law scholarship and case law with regard to the public interest in private law,[225] something that continues to inform studies of *lex mercatoria* as an example of transnational governance.[226] Drawing in part on an impressive body of regulatory law in the field of environmental risk regulation,[227] we have engaged with this private law perspective already in earlier work, where we have respectively tried to outline conceptual approaches towards changes in administrative governance, in particular the interpenetration of public and private forms of regulation, and the role of private law in these processes.[228] We thus embrace a private law perspective, which is distinctly not based on a clear demarcation from public law as a differently minded regulatory framework, an approach we see as clearly resonating with numerous current treatments of private law regulation.[229] Thus, we are interested in private law as a rich and resourceful repository of legal experimentation in dramatically changing social contexts, something that was long, amply testified to, for example, by Renner,[230] Wieacker[231] and Wiethölter[232] in Germany, by Pound,[233] Llewellyn,[234] Dawson[235] and Macneil[236] in the United States or by Atiyah,[237] Brownsword[238] and Collins[239] in the UK.

D. Law and the Transformation of State Regulatory Functions

Against this background, a further consideration behind our focus on a private law oriented theory of transnational law, and one that had an

[225] Karl Renner, 1949; Franz Wieacker, 1967; Rudolf Wiethölter, 1972b; Rudolf Wiethölter, 1974; for an excellent, recent assessment of this dimension in private law, see Robert Wai, 2008.

[226] See, eg, Alex Stone Sweet, 2006, 632, 641.

[227] Wolfgang Köck, 1995; Wolfgang Köck, 1999; Karl-Heinz Ladeur, 1995; in particular the contributions to Gunther Teubner, Lindsay Farmer and Declan Murphy, 1994.

[228] Gralf-Peter Calliess, 1999; Gralf-Peter Calliess, 2002; Peer Zumbansen, 2000b; Peer Zumbansen, 2003c; Peer Zumbansen, 2003d.

[229] For the field of tort law, see only Peter H Schuck, 1991, and Gert Brüggemeier, 1999; for corporate law, see Kellye Y Testy, 2002, Aaron Dhir, 2006, and PM Vasudev, 2009; see also the wonderful essay by Hugh Collins, 1997.

[230] Karl Renner, 1949.

[231] Franz Wieacker, 1953; Franz Wieacker, 1967.

[232] Rudolf Wiethölter, 1965; Rudolf Wiethölter, 1971; Rudolf Wiethölter, 1972a; Rudolf Wiethölter, 1974.

[233] Roscoe Pound, 1939; see Roscoe Pound, 1932.

[234] Karl Llewellyn, 1930.

[235] John P Dawson, 1947.

[236] Ian R Macneil, 1980; Ian R Macneil, 1985.

[237] Patrick Atiyah, 1979.

[238] Roger Brownsword, 1997.

[239] Hugh Collins, 1999.

important impact on the choice of our case studies, follows from the particular perspective from which private law scholars have been assessing, studying and conceptualising the transformation of state regulatory functions over time—within the nation-state and at some distance from the globalisation of human affairs in the sense of border-crossing commercial and other activities.[240] Long known to comparative law experts working in contract, property or tort law, private law offered in itself manifold illustrations of fast changing domestic regulatory environments, thus providing a basis for observation and analysis of emerging forms of self-regulation and market ordering. What initially drove much comparative private law work was the idea of convergence of regulatory concepts and even universal progress,[241] on the one hand, and a decidedly critical stance regarding the role of law in the rise of capitalism, on the other.[242] Macaulay, re-reading Weber, wrote in 1986:

> Internally, law was rationalised by rule-oriented reasoning, which was manipulated by professionals who shared a legal culture. The justification for this style rested on its contributions to individualism and autonomy from government control. Externally this style of law facilitated private ordering by guaranteeing a framework within which substantive judgments could be made by individuals.[243]

The contribution of comparative law scholarship, which was from its beginning marked by a high degree of methodological introspection,[244] to the emergence of elements of a transnational legal theory can hardly be overestimated, as it laid the groundwork for contemporary critical engagements with regulatory regimes, private ordering and soft law outside of the nation-state.[245] Today, among the numerous examples of transnational regulatory regimes, each prompting extensive and highly specialised scholarship,[246] the EU—as a regulatory space marked by the intersection and overlapping of distinct national cultures, public and private law and direct

[240] Victoria Nourse and Gregory Shaffer, 2009, 110: 'In a world of globalization, the state is constantly reshaped by its need to respond to global market processes and new publicly and privately made transnational legal orders'.

[241] See only Konrad Zweigert and Hein Kötz, 1996, ch 1.

[242] See, eg Vivian Grosswald Curran, 2001; Rodolfo Sacco, 2002; for a powerful assessments of comparative law in the current context of globalization and dramatic technological progress, see Annelise Riles, 1999, 225: 'the perception that law is increasingly transnational, sparked by the expansion of private contractual law and of bodies of transnational law such as European Community Law, for example, as well as by the explosion of opportunities for American law professors to serve as consultants to emerging governments on the writing of laws and constitutions, has rendered the distance between legal systems less pronounced in the consciousness of most lawyers and legal academics.'

[243] Stewart Macaulay, 1986, 493; see also David Trubek, 1972a, and Morton J Horwitz, 1975.

[244] Mathias Reimann, 2002; Ralf Michaels, 2006; see also the critique of Kötz & Zweigert by Jonathan Hill, 1989.

[245] One of the best contributions to this debate: Daniela Caruso, 2006.

[246] See the brillant study by Harm Schepel, 2004.

and indirect regulation in the form of official and unofficial laws, codes of conducts, hard and soft laws, regulations and recommendations—has long been treated with particular zeal by comparative lawyers and regulatory theorists. As Hugh Collins put it: 'Legal discourses of national private law systems have become more complex, with invocations of a broader range of principles than hitherto, including public law and human rights dimensions, and a range of supranational legal orders'.[247] As testified by great scholars of European integration and the Europeanisation of law, the space between Alicante and Helsinki, Galway and Athens has long been recognised as one of the world's most challenging examples of transnational legal evolution.[248]

> Difference and sameness, the core issues of comparative law, have been the European Union's twin challenges from the beginning. The originally neat categories of the unifiable economic, versus the distinctively cultural, have long since become mottled, intertwining and frayed threads, and even the challenge of assessing competing values has become chaotic inasmuch as relevant contexts can be difficult to identify.[249]

In this context, (European) private law, which we will address in more detail later in this chapter as well as in chapter three, continues to offer particularly intriguing lessons about the adaptation and evolution of legal orders in a greater polity, evolving through integration and conflict, competition and harmonisation, globalisation and regionalisation.[250] It is this overwhelming prominence of private law and private law theory in the greater legal imagination of Europe,[251] which provides for an important set of perspectives on the theoretical framework of transnational law, in particular because the European example is illustrative of the far-reaching and complex connections between existing and evolving, 'embedded' legal orders on the one hand and emerging, experimental forms of norm-creation, enforcement and compliance monitoring on the other.[252] The attention paid to the example of Europe in our general framework and our case studies is, however, as promising as it is perilous. The promise of a continued engagement with developments of European law lies, above all, in the seemingly endlessly minable depths of the multilayered and

[247] Hugh Collins, 2008, 270.

[248] See Eric Stein, 1981.

[249] Vivian Grosswald Curran, 2003, 80.

[250] Marc Amstutz, 2005; Marc Amstutz and Vaios Karavas, 2009.

[251] Richard Buxbaum and Klaus J Hopt, 1988; Christian Joerges, 1991; Christian Joerges, 2000; Ernst-Joachim Mestmäcker, 2000; Stefan Grundmann, 2000; Fabrizio Cafaggi and Horatia Muir-Watt, 2008b; Gralf-Peter Calliess and Jens Mertens, 2009.

[252] Fabrizio Cafaggi and Horatia Muir-Watt, 2008a, 2–3: 'By regulatory functions of private law we mean the ability of private law instruments, in particular contract, torts and property to address market failures. This is the result of the decline of the regulatory state and the emergence of new regulatory modes'.

functionally differentiated nature of Europe's legal evolution. In Fabrizio Cafaggi's and Horatia Muir-Watt's succinct formulation: '[t]he intellectual diagram of a hierarchy of norms has turned out to be blatantly inadequate to reflect this complexity'.[253] Yet, its relative dangers, if that term is at all adequate in this context, must be seen in a possible preoccupation with seemingly inexhaustible sets of Europe-related regulatory analysis, concerning fields that must be understood to reflect a specific set of dynamisms, which stem from processes that in fact reach beyond the EU and combine intricate evolutions of europeanisation, globalisation and—certainly—privatisation.[254] In that regard, while we gratefully draw numerous lessons from the well-researched regulatory 'transformation of Europe',[255] we understand our current project to be necessarily—if ambitiously—focused on the role that private law and private law theory can play in the conceptualisation of regulatory regimes in a globalised world.

Against this background, our proposal embraces a distinctly private law orientation which we aim to lay out with a view to the particular role played by private law in the development of transnational regulatory regimes. The concrete examples described in chapters three and four, pertaining to consumer contract law on the one hand and corporate governance regulation on the other, are meant to illustrate the theoretical concept of transnational private law, which we develop in the remainder of this chapter.

II. UBIQUITOUS LAW

A. Normativity versus Realism: Law versus Power

Wherever we find society, we will find law. This Roman maxim, often ascribed to the Dutch jurist and founder of public international law Hugo Grotius,[256] might have inspired modern sociology of law as a metaphor for the assumption, that the globalisation of markets and other social spheres is necessarily accompanied by the emergence of a transnational legal order, despite the absence of a world state as regulator.[257] In recurring debates between Public International Lawyers and International Relations

253 *Ibid*, 7.

254 For an overview, see Ralf Michaels and Nils Jansen, 2007.

255 In reverence to the seminal article by Joseph HH Weiler, 1991.

256 Rodolfo Sacco, 1995, at 456; Philip C Jessup, 1940, 246: 'Perhaps a subconscious human urge, a variety of wishful thinking, seeks to give reality to the ancient maxim: *ubi societas, ibi ius*'.

257 Gunther Teubner, 1997c.

Theorists,[258] the answer to the question of whether law can survive globalisation has generally been tied to the question of the survival of the state. Such debates took many different turns, often oscillating between assessments of the degree of 'legalisation' of existing and emerging global institutions on the one hand[259] and the claim of an emerging global law on the other.[260] Such disputes were informed, certainly, by longstanding concerns with the issue whether we had any right, indeed, to speak of law at all, on the global level.[261] Only gradually did fresh thinking succeed in breaking the deadlock between power and law in order to suggest a more differentiated view on power and authority in response to the 'bare knuckled realism'[262] that had marked the view on International Law during much of the first half of the twentieth century: the work by Harold Lasswell and Myres McDougal was crucial in that regard,[263] and deliberations over the scope and promises of their legacy occupy a central place in present-day discussions on law and politics in a post-Communist-Bloc and post-9/11 world.[264] One of the striking and promising developments unfolding in the allegedly post-ideological aftermath that followed the 'end of history' was a strong interest in interdisciplinary and empirically grounded research, widely shared by different fields and schools of thought. Central here are studies that had for some time already begun to very productively draw on work in cultural studies and anthropology, geography and sociology. Inspired by pioneering post-colonial scholarship from scholars such as Frantz Fanon, Edward Said, Dipesh Chakrabarty or Uday Singh Mehta, scholars in law and anthropology have been rolling out carefully conceptualised research programmes that resulted in significant studies on the emergence, dissemination and practice of rights,[265] transnational law[266] and transitional justice.[267] Parallel to this there has been developing an immensely rich body of theoretical and conceptual work concerned with the much debated and contested nature of transnational and global

[258] Anne-Marie Slaughter-Burley, 1993; Anne-Marie Slaughter, Andrew S Tulumello and Stepan Wood, 1998.

[259] Kenneth W Abbott, Robert O Keohane, Andrew Moravcsik, Anne-Marie Slaughter and Duncan Snidal, 2000.

[260] Gunther Teubner, 1997c; Andreas Fischer-Lescano, 2003; Andreas Fischer-Lescano and Gunther Teubner, 2004.

[261] Steven R Ratner, 1998; Kenneth W Abbott, 1999.

[262] Oona A Hathaway, 2007, 567 with reference to the work by Hans J Morgenthau, 1940, and Edward Hallett Carr, 2001.

[263] Myres McDougal and Harold D Lasswell, 1959; Myres McDougal, 1960; Harold D Lasswell and Myres McDougal, 1992.

[264] See, eg, Richard A Falk, 1995, and Oona A Hathaway, 2007, and the contributions to the same Symposium by Levit, Osofsky, Goodman & Jinks, Berman, Waters and Bratspies.

[265] See eg, Sally Engle Merry, 1992; Annelise Riles, 2005, 2006, and the volume edited by Mark Goodale & Sally Engle Merry, 2007.

[266] Sally Engle Merry, 2006.

[267] Ruti Teitel, 2000; Rosemary Nagy, 2010.

norms.[268] It is in this context that regulatory theory unfolds in close proximity to and through increased dialogue with different developments within Public International Law, including the vivid and mutually enriching dialogue between PIL and International Relations theory[269] or the impressive international legal theory scholarship under the umbrella of 'Third World Approaches to International Law' (TWAIL).[270]

Despite the fact that the relevance of an interdisciplinary dialogue between international law and international relations today appears undisputed, the deliberations concerning the challenges that arise around global governance themselves remain highly charged. Still, much suggests that the impressively interdisciplinary orientation of international legal theory provides a hard ground on which to develop and nurture 'law-oriented approach[es] ... increasingly committed to cosmopolitan values and procedures and to an ethos of global democracy' as drivers of 'international law and the future'.[271] Economists, by contrast, seem to have far fewer solicitudes when it comes to making sense of the emerging normative order of the world: from the viewpoint of New Institutional Economics, global economic governance is likely to mirror if not exacerbate the challenges of sound market regulation that has been marking the past development in OECD (Organisation for Economic Co-operation and Development) countries.[272] For lawyers and economists, then, there appears to be a shared concern with the role and type of regulation likely to govern the irreversibly post-national landscape. It is here that an intriguing debate develops between law(yers) and economics (scholars) about the nature of regulatory institutions and norms outside of the nation state. As we will inquire further below (Chapter 5), one of the foremost arenas of this interdisciplinary exchange occurs in the field of 'social norms'. A brief discussion of this theme is merited at this stage, as it allows us to identify a number of elements that inform the methodological approach taken here with regard to the development of a theory of transnational private law. In discussions in recent years, social norms have regularly been invoked to identify *alternatives* to legal ordering that become necessary in cases of regulatory failure. Social norms theorists have thus been arguing that a recurrence of social norms is warranted where it becomes necessary to 'opt out' of

[268] See, eg, Gregory Shaffer, 2000, 2009; Shaffer & Victoria Nourse, 2009; Schneiderman, 2006.

[269] See Hathaway, 2005; Berman, 2006.

[270] See, eg, M Sornarajah (1997, 2006), Makau Mutua, 1995, Bhupinder S Chimni, 2004, Antony Anghie, 2005, and the contributions to Richard Falk, Balakrishnan Rajagopal and Jacqueline Stevens, 2008.

[271] Richard A Falk, 2008, 24.

[272] Oliver E Williamson, 2005.

inefficient legal systems that have been provided for and administered by the 'state'.[273]

Already, it becomes evident how the mobilisation of social norms touches at the very heart of a legal order, understood as an authoritative and effective system of rule creation and rule enforcement, backed by legitimacy. The here-cited possibility of resorting to social norms by way of a 'back-up' option in cases of regulatory failure raises a number of important and troubling questions as to the deeper relationship or, distinction between the legal system and the allegedly 'alternative' world of social norms. Despite their suggested allusion to scientific factual quality, references to 'failure' or 'inefficiency' belong in the world of normative judgement. That already invites the question whether the invocation of social norms is perhaps a mere misnomer, when what we are really concerned with is a critique—probably from different normative, ideological, political vantage points—of the existing legal (political, economic—regulatory) system as such. Still, there are several considerations that support the importance and even urgency of an engagement with 'social norms'. Foremost, such engagement is likely to prove helpful in allowing lawyers to take a step back from a narrow association of law with the state and to imagine competing concepts of law. In fact, the invitation to rethink the state/law nexus should not meet with too much resistance but instead seems considerably pertinent in a context of globalisation and the absence of world 'government'. The intriguing nature of the social norms challenge to the state/law nexus, however, lies in its arising *before* globalisation, if we may resort to this chronologising illustration for a moment. The social norms critique of legal regulation arises at a time and in a context of existing, historically grown and institutionally differentiated legal systems. It speaks, in other words, to a situation that already existed within the nation state, the very entity and framework that is now being widely—even if mostly unjustifiedly—associated with problems of regulatory capacity and related erosions of sovereignty. Whilst in this book we are concerned with the nature of legal regulation from a *transnational* perspective, the nation-state context of the social norms critique is, as we will argue in more detail throughout this book, of greatest importance for the development of such a transnational legal theory. Leaving aside for a moment the ideological and political motivations of particular invocations of social norms alluded to above, the social norms argument as such proves a very apt and pervasive entry into a larger reflection on the relationship between law and its environment. Social norms raise deeply troubling questions as to their temporal and normative relationship to 'law': do social norms—at some point—become law? Do they constitute, in other words, the 'not yet' of law? Or, are social norms the resistance *against* law, do

[273] Lisa Bernstein, 1992; Eric A Posner, 2000.

they perhaps represent the suppressed and silenced (legal) order? Are social norms, in other words, the possible legitimacy foundation for a constantly evolving legal system?

Given the apparent impossibility of providing clear answers to these questions, the invocation of social norms allows lawyers to gain a more comprehensive understanding of the *evolutionary* nature of the legal and social order. The economist Kaushik Basu's observation made some time ago remains particularly intriguing in this regard:

> There is no reason why we must think of the state as a force opposing private efforts. After all the state itself emerged gradually, from the atomistic actions of individuals. So in some ways the state is itself like a norm. Hence, the state may be viewed as one of the many different instruments through which individuals create order among themselves. Instead of thinking of the law and social norms as alternative systems, or worse, as adversaries, it is possible to treat the legal system as part of the general theory of norms.[274]

This observation powerfully highlights the relevance of a yet incomplete project of a 'general theory'. While the elaboration of such a framework could be an expression of either prophecy or aspiration, Kasu's re-evaluation of the relation between law (the 'state') and social norms empathises that there is something at stake when positioning the two either as separate (or, adversary) or as complementary. It is from this perspective that much of the current critique of adjudication by social norms theorists appears inadequate to address the intricate relation between law and norms as emanations of an evolving system of social order. Instead, the attack on adjudication and the surgical separation of private ordering from political intervention risk missing the deeper conceptual challenge arising from the evolutionary nature of social systems. Motivated more by ideological standpoints ('less state, more freedom') than by insight into the need for an adequately sophisticated theory of social order, the insistence on party 'autonomy' and expertise, for example in the critique brought against private law adjudication in cases of technically sophisticated contractual arrangements, turns a blind eye on the co-evolution of 'formal' and 'informal' systems of ordering.[275] As such, social norms theory runs the danger of aborting the inquiry into the foundations and building blocks of a 'general' theory that would be needed to make sense of the co-existence of formal and informal institutions without forcing them into an allegedly scientific or, neutral relation of hierarchy and superiority *qua* 'efficiency'. Whether 'private' ordering is superior to or more efficient than 'public' ordering depends on the normative standpoint taken with regard to the expected, desired outcome. To contrast 'social norms' with 'law' on the basis that social norms will trump law where the

274 Kaushik Basu, 1998, Ms. 12–13.
275 Moore, 1973.

latter is less efficient, is not a substitute for the answer to the question of what was meant by an 'efficient' system of social order in the first place.

Clearly, the difficulties involved in speaking about social norms and their relation to law illustrates the challenges that any sociological study of formal/informal, public/private, state/market regulation inevitably will have to face. It further illustrates the intriguing parallel renaissance of a law and society perspective on adjudication and 'legal centralism' from both a conservative and a progressive vantage point.[276] It is the shared anxiety between 'Law and Economics' and 'Law and Society' of having to grapple with the task of approaching a complex structured system of formal/informal etc from the viewpoint of a—missing—'general theory', that might explain the intriguing political rebirths that the progressively-minded theories experience, now and again.[277] This shared anxiety, then, also explains the charged nature of any interaction between 'law and economics' scholars and those in the 'law and society' camp. Each side, by admonishing the other's hidden political agenda, risks falling short indeed of actually engaging with the conceptual challenges that confront both—conservative and progressive—projects. The very fact of a widely overlapping methodological apparatus designed to develop a more 'responsive', 'adaptable' and 'learning' law between progressive and conservative legal theories should redirect our attention to the still unanswered questions regarding the distinction between law and social norms.

Needless to say, these anxieties are only going to be exacerbated at the moment where the architects of social order leave the metaphorical four walls of the nation-state. The progressive critique of the alleged 'lawlessness' and a-political, or even de-politicising agenda supposedly pursued by the social norms theorists becomes untameable once it turns its attention to the dire state of 'unholy trinities'[278] and the sobering democracy deficit in global governance.[279] The suspicion regarding the de-politicising agenda of social norms theory gains sharper contours in the context of the absence of a—politically institutionalised and established—effective legal system as represented by the nation-state. The 'global' now must appear as the inevitable abyss of 'lawlessness'. This drawing of connections between the continuing fervent critique of 'interventionist' ordering within the nation-state and the impressive applicability of social norms theory to the global

[276] See, on the one hand, eg, Richard A Posner, 1973; see on the other, eg, David M Trubek, 1972.

[277] With regard to Roscoe Pound's turn against an empiricist foundation for the Realist attack on Legal Formalism, see Horwitz, 1992, 218–20; for a depiction of a politically conservative return to functionalism over the last twenty years, see Kerry Rittich, 2005 and Peer Zumbansen, 2008a.

[278] Richard Peet, 2009.

[279] Von Bogdandy, 2006, 238.

space of commercial interaction is likely to put fear into the heart of those in the law and society and legal pluralism camp, where the pursuit of more 'responsive' or 'authentic' norms was (and remains) motivated by a concern with exclusion and silencing. Again, the apparently solid ground beneath the respective observers prevents an engagement in productive self-irony. What for some constitutes the loss of legal unity, certainty and political-democratic control, is for others merely another instantiation of societal self-regulation, freed from 'paternalistic' judicial intervention, a theme that has long informed claims of a global convergence of legal orders, be it around best principles[280] or economic efficiency[281]—allusions that continue to meet with considerable scepticism.[282]

At this point a note on the development of argument seems in order. The present project proposes an engagement with the law/social norms distinction in order to identify and conceive of building blocks for an analysis of global governance from the viewpoint of legal theory. Meanwhile, the project is conceived from a particular part of law and legal theory that we think to be a particularly well-suited point of departure on a series of inquiries into the legal theoretical challenges of global governance. Conscious of the longstanding attacks launched against any theoretical and, significantly, *doctrinal* edifice that is built on the distinction between public and private law, our concentration on *private* law can only be justified from a reflexive and ironical perspective. By that we mean to engage with the representations of private law as particular and inevitably idiosyncratic ways of describing and constructing social order. As such, we assume that there *is* such a thing as 'private' law. Just as there eventually *was* a field such as labour law, environmental law, and, more recently, say, cyberspace law or the law of transitional justice. Despite the obvious problems associated with the reliance on such impossible distinctions, we contend that to theorise legal ordering from the perspective of such an artificially constructed framework has the advantage of forcing us not only to reflect on the relation between the existing legal theoretical and doctrinal approaches to a legal order of the social and alternative representations of social ordering, but also to remain mindful of the intricate parallels between, on the one hand, the demarcations between law and 'the other' (social norms, legal pluralism, law and society) and, on the other, on the demarcations *within* law itself ('public' law, 'private law', 'corporate law', 'labour' law...). In addition, to do so

[280] Henry Hansmann and Reinier Kraakman, 2001.

[281] Ralf Michaels, 2007b, 1004: 'Law and economics scholars ... argue that the requirements of globalization will pressure legal orders to converge on the level of economic efficiency, because regulatory competition between legal competition makes it impossible for individual legal systems to maintain suboptimal solutions'.

[282] Robert Wai, 2005; Ugo Mattei and Fernanda Nicola, 2006; Horatia Muir-Watt, 2006, 109, discussing the idea of an 'economic due process'.

by sustaining the (impossible-possible) distinction between public and private law[283] is likely to further illustrate the various blind-spots in ongoing depictions of the 'nature' of private law as opposed to that of the state, or the alleged differences between the functions performed by private law, on the one hand, and by public law on the other. There is, indeed, a long line that runs from Felix Cohen's or John Willis's interest in a *functionalist* reconstruction of legal ordering[284] to current assessments of the allegedly limited scope of government in comparison to the self-regulatory capacities of the market that characterized the 'new right' revolution of the early 1980s ushering in the end of Keynesian economics and the neo-liberal turn to 'the three Es of efficiency, economy, and effectiveness'.[285] But then and now, the real question is a normative one, namely what was and is being meant by the function of the state or the market? The distinction itself suggests that both exist in isolation of each other, which leads to the expected consequence that an experience of market failure after a period of 'deregulation' is met by a response of 'more' state. The positing of 'more' or 'less' state of market does not even come close to unpacking the implied understandings of state or market associated with such quantitative haggling. By contrast, the social norms critique of 'too much state', 'too much intervention', and 'too much adjudication' provides a promising opportunity to turn the quantitative perspective into a qualitative one. Which set of goals, what kinds of social utopia are being pursued by social norms? In contrast thereto, what drives 'intervention' at one time, 'deregulation' at another? By placing these questions side by side, it becomes obvious that the references to either 'state' or 'market' refer to different modes of regulation, not that the invocation of market equals the absence of regulation. It follows from this observation that a quantitative representation between 'more' or 'less' market is bound to overlook the still unanswered question as to the goal of the intended regulation—and its normative assessment. The same reasoning applies to the distinction made between law and its other, or 'non-law' as well as to that between different 'fields' within law. Categorisations of this kind belie their own artificial character. This certainly does not mean that they are either irrelevant or nonexistent. They are very real in the way that they represent grown and routinised patterns of order and also because they are constantly being reaffirmed—until that is no longer the case. The historical and cultural relativity of, say, the Continental European distinction between public and private law, is both real and absolute nonsense, if it is meant to explain that public law *is* in fact something else than private law. Of relevance, then, is to realize that the distinction, while having been for some time operational, is anything but

283 Carol Harlow, 1980; A Claire Cutler, 1997; Peer Zumbansen, 2004c.
284 Felix Cohen, 1935; John Willis, 1935.
285 Carol Harlow, 2009, 76.

reliable. As distinctions, those between, say, public and private, corporate and labour law as well as those between law and 'alternative' modes of order, they altogether rest on convention, experience, and coincidence. They exist in relation to what they are meant and taken to represent.

The aim of this book is to contribute to a theory of transnational *private* law. In prioritising and apparently favouring the private law side of the public law/private law divide in this project, we intend to scrutinise anew[286] the arguments put forward in defence of the distinction in the first place. The importance of such an approach is, in our view, underlined for example by the heated debate over the desirably limited role of state action —a debate that has, at the time of writing, however begun to change significantly.[287] Until relatively recently, for most of the 1980s and throughout the 1990s the role of both the state and the law were overwhelmingly depicted as ideally enabling, facilitating, or moderating. The state was depicted as a moderator and monitor of private interests that were themselves allegedly left to self-organisation, unleashing dizzying possibilities of innovation, growth and self-management. The state, when placed in relation to a global society consisting of investors and entrepreneurs, became depicted as having become an institution of last resort. Heavy-handed public regulation was depicted as an untimely, unnecessary concept. The context in which such assertions became popularised was one of exorbitant financial mobility and an overwhelming growth of the financial economy. Meanwhile, taking both a longer and closer look at the development of the regulatory apparatus that accompanied the 'Roaring Nineties' (Stiglitz), scholars have painted very sobering pictures of the state's continued involvement, orchestration and detailed regulation of myriad aspects of the allegedly free-to-self-regulate market.[288] This constellation provides an important backdrop for our decision to focus on the private law dimension of transnational governance. As demonstrated further in this chapter and in our case studies, private law has been an extremely versatile arena for experimentation with different forms of self-regulation, indirect regulation and the introduction of soft-law. Although we draw repeatedly on findings by public law scholars, primarily administrative and environmental law scholars, our main examples are taken from private law, which we understand to provide the regulatory platform for the development of a vast body of transnational market regulation. Our approach to 'private' law in the remainder of the book is mindful of the above made references to the artificial and conventional dimension of distinguishing between public and private law.

[286] For concurring efforts see, eg, the contributions to Jeff Alan Weintraub and Krishan Kumar, 1997, and Mark Freedland and Jean-Bernard Auby, 2006.

[287] See, eg, Paul Krugman, 2008; Robert Skidelsky, 2009.

[288] Carol Harlow, 2009; Stephen Bell and Andrew Hindmoor, 2009.

As such, we do in no way purport to defend either field as self-explanatory or, even less, as objectively given. Meanwhile, our interest in private law is further nurtured by the extremely rich body of work on the regulatory character of private law that well precedes the famous *publicisation* of private law throughout the rise and consolidation of the Western welfare state.[289] Precisely with regard to the highly ambivalent and crucial role played by contract and property in the evolution of legal thought,[290] we find here a sheer inexhaustible—and as regards our project surely inexhausted—reservoir of inquiries and explorations into the regulatory character of private law instruments. Given the high degree of adaptability of private law regulation to changing circumstances in long- and short-term perspective,[291] it has been a highly demanded framework in the continued search for adequately complex law. Lastly, to return here again to the remarks made above with regard to social norms, contract law is doubtless the most vividly discussed field of regulatory law that is competing and in tension with alternative approaches to social ordering. It is with these considerations in mind, that we have chosen to concentrate on private law examples in our attempt to identify constitutive elements of a theory of transnational law.

B. The Transnational: A Realm of Borderless Self-Regulation?

The choice of a private law perspective in the context of analysing evolving forms of transnational norm creation receives further support in light of the high degree of hybrid regulation that marks the transnational space. The apparent legal vacuum on the global level which some see as decline of sovereignty, others as opportunity and still others as the core of a legal pluralist perspective on society,[292] is fast filled by various processes of self-regulation and 'private ordering'.[293] Yet, the move from an embedded, institutionalised and historically evolved national political framework into the great unknown of the global arena continues to be accompanied by fierce

[289] Franz Wieacker, 1967; John N Adams and Roger Brownsword, 1987; Esser, 1996.

[290] Morris R Cohen, 1927; C B Macpherson, 1967.

[291] See Macaulay, 1963; Macneil, 1985; Kreitner, 2005.

[292] Till Müller, 2008, 34–35; Claudio Franzius, 2009, 37: '*Mit dem Souveränitätsbegriff lässt sich der Regulierungsverbund nicht erfassen. Governance, rechtswissenschaftlich reformuliert, unterläuft Begriffe, die für den Staat entwickelt worden sind*'. See also Louis Henkin, 1999, 13: 'What shall we do about the "S word?" I have tipped my hand. We need to address what has happened to traditional notions of sovereignty as a result of forces we have identified, and others, globalization, the market, and cyberspace'. See, in this regard, also Richard Ford, 1999, and Hannah L Buxbaum, 2009.

[293] Marc Galanter, 1981; Oliver Williamson, 2002; Avinash K Dixit, 2004; Robert D Cooter, 1994, 215: 'Rather than proceeding from top to bottom, lawmaking can proceed from bottom to top'.

disputes over categories and distinctions.[294] Depending on one's viewpoint, processes of self-regulation can be categorised as *private* regimes, combining social norms, alternative dispute resolution, and non-legal sanctions, which can then be understood as natural expressions of the market's self-regulatory capabilities.[295] From another perspective, however, they may very well constitute an infringement on the state's regulatory prerogative.[296] While the former can point to the well established, 'spontaneous evolution'[297] of the already alluded to law merchant, or *lex mercatoria*, or to the triumphant story of 'enabling (corporate) law',[298] the continental public lawyer is likely to remain sceptical with regard to the ubiquitous, aspirations of sovereignty displayed by private norm entrepreneurs.[299] Radicalising Weber's rationalisation and disenchantment concept,[300] 'Systems Theory of Law'[301] develops a theory of functional differentiation, which responds to globalisation by ascribing evolutionary priority to 'issue-specific' and 'self-contained non-state legal regimes', which evolve around functionally differentiated spheres of transnational communication and transaction.[302] Doing away with national borders and eventually shuddering at the prospect of law—as such—having been perhaps but a 'European anomaly',[303] this approach has no trust in an exclusive law generating authority ascribed by many to the state, but is left to apply the legal code far into the last corners of societal organisation.

These deconstructions of law's hierarchy, unity and embeddedness raise the question whether and from which standpoint 'private' regimes can and should be understood as law. Under the influence of legal positivism, whereby law was understood as the command of a sovereign backed by force[304] and whereby a close connection, if not an identity between the state and the law, was assumed,[305] much of Western jurisprudence anchored law exclusively in the nation-state.[306] This association of the legal regime with the nation-state facilitated the domestication of political power under the rule of law. The price for the *internal* formalisation and modernisation of private law produced by the nineteenth-century constitutional state

[294] A Claire Cutler, 1997; Christine Chinkin, 1999; Peer Zumbansen, 2004c; Ralf Michaels, 2009b.
[295] Lisa Bernstein, 1992; Lisa Bernstein, 2001; Gillian K Hadfield, 2001.
[296] Paul Kirchhof, 2001; Martin Wolf, 2002.
[297] Friedrich A Hayek, 2002.
[298] For an assessment, see Melvin Eisenberg, 2005.
[299] Felix Hanschmann, 2009.
[300] Max Weber, 1946.
[301] See Niklas Luhmann, 1992a; Niklas Luhmann, 2004; Peer Zumbansen, 2006a.
[302] Andreas Fischer-Lescano and Gunther Teubner, 2004.
[303] Niklas Luhmann, 2004.
[304] John L Austin, 2002.
[305] Hans Kelsen, 1961.
[306] Simon Roberts, 2005; but see Colin Scott, 2008b.

was, however, the nationalisation of the once common European law, the so-called Roman *ius commune*,[307] as well as the decline of the medieval Law Merchant, or *lex mercatoria*.[308]

In order to prevent cross-border trade from suffering from the resulting *external* territorial fragmentation of law, eventually the idea emerged of creating a 'world private law' by means of international treaty harmonisation.[309] This endeavour, however, turned out to be more difficult than expected. More than one hundred years of work within different organisations like the Hague Conference on Private International Law (1893), Unidroit (1926) and UNCITRAL (1966)[310] have resulted in little but fragments, including the 1980–UN Convention on the International Sale of Goods (CISG).[311] The post World War II ideological division into the West, the East, and the South was certainly adding further obstacles, but even after the fall of the Iron Curtain matters did not improve. The negotiations on a Global Judgments Convention, first initiated in the early 1990s in The Hague,[312] quite recently failed for reasons of a purported transatlantic *Justizkonflikt* (Jurisdictional Conflict), which suggests that even the member states to the OECD are unable and/or unwilling to come together to create a common constitution of world trade.[313] At this point, it appears as if hopes for a world private law based on multilateral treaties are in vain.[314]

Certainly, there has been a vivid search for both models of global harmonisation as well as for alternative conceptualisations of law-making: international law scholars, not only those with expertise in international economic or commercial law,[315] have long been seeking alternative paths to achieve legal certainty on a global level. As alluded to above, Philip Jessup's functional concept of transnational law continues to occupy an important place in this effort. Transnational law, for Jessup, was 'all law which regulates actions or events that transcend national frontiers', a definition he put forward with the aim of founding a branch of jurisprudence not only distinct from but also more comprehensive than the state-centred law of nations. Jessup's transnational law comprised national and international as well as public and private law.[316] In a parallel attempt to theorise law on a global level, authors such as Berthold Goldman and

[307] Reinhard Zimmermann, 2001.
[308] Uwe Blaurock, 1998; A Claire Cutler, 2003, 144.
[309] Ernst Zitelmann, 1888; see Klaus Peter Berger, 2001a.
[310] Peer Zumbansen and Maria Panezi, 2008.
[311] See Franco Ferrari, 2005.
[312] Joachim Zekoll, 1998; Vaughan Black, 2000; Michael Traynor, 2000.
[313] Samuel P Baumgartner, 2003; Gralf-Peter Calliess, 2004.
[314] Herbert Kronke, 2003; Herbert Kronke, 2005; Ulrich Drobnig, 2001.
[315] See, eg, Paul B Stephan, 1999, and Joel Trachtman, 2000.
[316] Philip C Jessup, 1956; Peer Zumbansen, 2006d; Christian Tietje and Karsten Nowrot, 2006.

Clive Schmitthoff began, albeit with certain distinctions,[317] to promote a specifically *a*-national understanding of the term transnational law. It was, as we saw, in this context that these authors suggested reviving the medieval Law Merchant in the context of modern international commercial arbitration.[318]

Today the literature on transnational law and the New Law Merchant has become both abundant and extremely diverse, following the logic of world society's functional differentiation. Unsurprisingly, no theoretical consensus on the concept of transnational law seems to be in sight. While these divergences continue to encompass disagreements in substance as well as in method,[319] the evidence from legal practice appears to suggest a certain relaxation of the tenuous opposition between defenders and opponents of a transnational law merchant: looking at this constellation, a number of scholars have been pointing to a distinct '*practice* of transnational law', in light of which the field is held to be too important for it to be buried under inadequately narrow doctrinal and conceptual constructions. Certainly, where the self-proclaimed transnationalist takes comfort in the no doubt lively practice of border-crossing commercial agreements, the indirect dismissal of the question 'But, is it law?' meets with distinct criticism.[320] The undisputed evidence of the existence of rules of *lex mercatoria*[321] does not suffice to make the ghosts disappear that have been haunting us in relation to the nature and relevance of such rules, in particular for our general understanding of law—inside and outside of the nation-state.

Inherent to this continuing brawl are questions of legitimacy. Such questions have always been raised in the context of private law-making[322] and they return in somewhat accentuated fashion in the transnational arena. The absence of a firmly demarcated institutional structure amplifies the already pressing, historical concerns over the role of the state vis-à-vis the market. As such, these concerns have been receiving a great deal of attention: understanding the emergence of 'private authority' in the international arena as a distinctive mark of global governance, we are intrigued by observations by political scientists who question the viability of clean-cut

[317] See above, Chapter 2, A.

[318] Berthold Goldman, 1956; Clive M Schmitthoff, 1964b; Klaus Peter Berger, 2001a.

[319] For a concise discussion, using the example of *lex mercatoria*: Karsten Schmidt, 2007.

[320] See the introduction to and contributions in: Klaus Peter Berger, 2001b; in contrast, see the scathing critique by Thomas Schultz, 2008, 709: 'And so we come to the end of these different lines of argument that all led us to conclude that the *lex mercatoria* is not law, because it is not a legal system, because it cannot be a set of *legal* rules without deriving its non-State juridicity from its belonging to a non-State legal system, and because being a method of rule-selection necessarily relies on the assumption that the *lex mercatoria* is a legal system'.

[321] Karsten Schmidt, 2007, 160: '*Nichtjuristen werden staunen, wie denn über Regeln gestritten wird, deren Existenz doch offenbar festgestellt werden kann*'.

[322] Louis Jaffe, 1937; Robert W Gordon, 1985; Colin Scott, 2008b.

public-private distinctions to delineate spheres of human activity.[323] Of great interest here is the political scientist's treatment of codes of conduct, best practice guidelines and, particularly, standards: studying such forms of private norm-creation through the lens of analogies between national and global regulation, a differentiated picture begins to emerge. Rather than evidencing a blanket loss of state sovereignty, scholars such as Peter Drahos and John Braithwaite have been insisting on a multifunctional assessment of in fact several globalisations. To these globalisations, then, of firms, markets and regulation, Drahos and Braithwaite attribute different forms and processes of a transformation of sovereignty and contend that '[t]here is no reason to think that globalisation strips states of their sovereignty in equal measure'.[324] This re-orientation of focus to the nation-state and its sub-entities[325] as the places 'where the work of globalisation gets done' (S Sassen) has proven crucial for on-the-ground studies of state transformation in a great variety of functional areas.[326] Such studies of the changing landscape of—unequally empowered—*actors* on the one hand[327] and of norms on the other[328] provides important insights into the shifting boundaries between state and non-state, national and global institutions, as well as into the deep transformation of the regulatory apparatus. These echo and parallel a long-standing critique among lawyers with regard to the analytical quality of the public-private distinction in distinguishing areas of law on the one hand and in attributing a particular normative orientation to a legal instrument on the other.[329]

C. Private Ordering and Public Authority: Scrutinising Democratic versus Economic Functions of Law

Given the existence of non-state normative orders in the transnational sphere,[330] the decisive question—for lawyers—seems to be how to reconstruct this social reality from the point of view of 'law'.[331] In an important

[323] Rodney Bruce Hall and Thomas J Biersteker, 2002, 4; A Claire Cutler, 2003.

[324] Peter Drahos and John Braithwaite, 2001, 106, 107.

[325] Saskia Sassen, 1998, 161, 164: 'Major cities in the highly developed world are the terrain where a multiplicity of globalization processes assume concrete, localized forms'.

[326] See, eg, the telling illustrations in Stephan Leibfried and Michael Zürn, 2005, and the study by Jochen Zimmermann, Jörg R Werner and Philipp B Volmer, 2008.

[327] Drahos and Braithwaite, 2001, 124: 'The contest amongst actors is an unequal one'.

[328] Nils Brunsson and Bengt Jacobsson, 2000; Dieter Kerwer, 2005b, 620–28, drawing on a comparative study of soft law approaches for an outline of how the regulatory potential of standards can be assessed from a legitimacy and accountability perspective.

[329] Roscoe Pound, 1939; Martin Bullinger, 1968; Carol Harlow, 1980.

[330] A Claire Cutler, 2003.

[331] Ralf Michaels, 2005; for a more recent presentation of this idea, see Ralf Michaels, 2007a.

chapter, a part of which he first presented in 1980 at Osgoode Hall Law School in Toronto, Stewart Macaulay began with the following observation:

> Much of what we call governing is done by groups that are not part of the institutions established by federal and state constitutions. If governing involves making rules, interpreting them, applying them to specific cases, and sanctioning violations, some or all of this is done by such different clusters of people such as the Mafia, the National Collegiate Association, the American Arbitration Association, those who run large shopping centers, neighborhood associations, and even the regulars at Smokey's tavern. It may be necessary to draw a sharp line between public and private governments such as these in order to think about law, but in reality there is no such division. To the contrary, one finds instead interpenetration, overlapping jurisdictions, and opportunities for both harmony and conflict among public and private governments.[332]

Macaulay's suggestion at the time was to fundamentally upset the state-originates-in-the-state thesis that continued to hold prominence even among those scholars who purported to assume a decidedly sceptical attitude towards law. He proposed, therefore, a distinct 'private government perspective' that would both recognise the effect that private associations had on government and treat dearly held distinctions between public and private spheres as doubtful rather than given.[333] Against the background of an extremely rich, empirically evidenced picture of the manifold overlappings of public and private forms of conflict resolution and norm-creation, Macaulay cautioned against the option of capturing this varied landscape by a mere 'expansion' of the concept of the 'legal system': 'such a move glosses over whether it makes a difference if a particular function is performed publicly or privately'.[334] With reference to Niklas Luhmann's idea of a 'thematisation threshold' (determining the moment of transitioning a 'social' problem into a 'legal' question with largely unpredictable consequences), Macaulay emphasised the importance of studying the place of law in the particular context of different social groups and settings rather than assuming that the role of law in society be determinable in a general fashion.[335] From such an inside perspective, the role of law, in principle regarded as playing a considerable role in establishing legitimacy or providing for symbolic satisfactions, would come to be seen instead as mediated, filtered or distorted by the different layers and overlappings that characterise what Sally Falk Moore famously identified as 'semi-autonomous

[332] Stewart Macaulay, 1986, 445–46.

[333] *Ibid*, 445.

[334] *Ibid*, 471: 'Turning to law usually means withdrawing from the relationship in question, and often one needs support to replace the benefits of the situation rejected. A legal discussion may initiate a chain of events with an unpredictable outcome, and the more uncertain the future, the more support is needed'.

[335] *Ibid*, 472.

fields'.[336] One of the insights gained here was certainly a renewed confirmation of what anti-Formalists had stressed already long before, namely that the transposition of a *social conflict* into a *legal case* was likely to narrow the analytical and potentially emancipatory or empowering range of addressing the 'real' issues at stake, such as economic inequalities, access to justice, education etc by reformulating the conflict with reference to existing concepts of property, freedom and so on.[337] After a review of a great number of theoretical assessments of the transformation of the regulatory landscape during and after welfare state legal-instrumentalism, Macaulay remained fundamentally sceptical with regard to what he found to be 'curiously apolitical' depictions of legal change.[338] With regard to Karl Klare's analysis of the evolution of workers' rights under twentieth-century American trade unionism,[339] Macaulay criticised Klare's overconfidence in these groups' ability 'to write any program they pleased'; assessing Teubner's evolutionary account of law's development from formal, through substantive, to reflexive rationality, Macaulay accused Teubner of omitting from his account 'those who attempt to plan changes or individuals and groups struggling for advantage and power'.[340] In unirritable clairvoyance, Macaulay, roughly 25 years ago predicted: '[r]eflexive rationality would seem only to postpone the day of reckoning for a distinction that Kennedy (1982) tells us is hard to take seriously'.[341] This assessment is, sadly, echoed in present depictions of a dramatic lack of irony in neo-liberal celebrations of societal self-regulation and freedom of contract—without much regard to the always inherently contested and constituted nature of private ordering.[342] In his forward-looking contribution, Macaulay not only provided for an extremely rich portrait of private, and indeed 'mixed', government in the United States, but also put his finger on the open wound of the unresolved questions whether, on the one hand, we should indeed have any reason to trust in the democratic potential of private ordering or whether, on the other, law and its internal logic would be able to unfold its regulatory potential: 'the benefits of a division of labor do not establish that present chains of command are natural or inevitable'.[343]

[336] Sally Falk Moore, 1973.

[337] Macaulay, 1986, 482; see Robert L Hale, 1923, and Morris R Cohen, 1927; see also Gunther Teubner, 1983, 249: 'Legal structures so conceived reinterpret themselves, but in the light of external needs and demands. This means that external changes are neither ignored nor directly reflected according to a "stimulus-response scheme". Rather, they are selectively filtered into legal structures and adapted in accordance with a logic of normative development'.

[338] Macaulay, 1986, 500.

[339] Karl E Klare, 1978.

[340] Macaulay, 1986, 500.

[341] *Ibid*, with reference to Duncan Kennedy, 1982b.

[342] Kerry Rittich, 2005; see also Peer Zumbansen, 2008a.

[343] Macaulay, 1986, 504.

The importance of such critical depictions of private ordering lies in their reminding us of the stickiness of evolutionary change of law and society. Just like through the functionalist lens we are likely to see, in sobering clarity, the increasingly disintegrated and fragmented nature of highly specialised functional spheres,[344] the critical reading of modern society will insist on the relevance of 'purposive' or 'responsive' law,[345] of an untiring contestation of the tension between formal and social equalities, and of the gap between the 'is' and the 'ought to be'.[346] In a benevolently critical discussion of Lisa Bernstein's work on trade usages and private arbitration in the diamond and cotton industries, Macaulay found Bernstein's work to illustrate a

> movement away from what Max Weber called 'substantive rationality', toward his 'formal rationality'. To the extent we ignore custom and courses of dealing and performance, we reinforce the role of the written contract. This, in turn, reinforces the power of those who draft these documents, usually the lawyers who represent those with superior bargaining power.[347]

These two ways of thinking about the role of law in society—one mired in a functionalist depiction of societal subsystems, each evolving according to its own logic, with the law being no exception,[348] and the other one embracing an encompassing theory of society as driven by critique, contestation and an untiring struggle with competing values[349]—seem, to us, to be complementary, not exclusionary. To be sure, such a position inevitably meets with concerns regarding conceptual coherence.[350] We contend, however, that incoherence is unavoidable, given the particularly elusive nature of law as an aspirational concept on the one hand,[351] and law's extremely differentiated forms of appearance on the other.[352] Writing *after* the Legal Realist and Critical Legal Studies' attack on legal formalism and 'classical legal thought',[353] after 'positivism' and 'natural rights' theory, after 'responsive' and 'reflexive law', we are left to operate in yet another highly contested

[344] Gunther Teubner, 1983.

[345] Philippe Nonet and Philip Selznick, 1978.

[346] Erhard Blankenburg, 1984; David Trubek, 1972b; Philip Selznick, 1969.

[347] Stewart Macaulay, 2000, 800.

[348] Niklas Luhmann, 1989a.

[349] Philippe Nonet and Philip Selznick, 1978; Ian R Macneil, 1980; Hugh Collins, 1997; Thomas Wilhelmsson, 2004.

[350] Niklas Luhmann, 1992b.

[351] David M Trubek, 1986, 590–91: 'Weber spoke of rationalization as a "fate", by which he meant an unavoidable development. But this is a tragic fate, for in the end of the process of legal rationalization leads to the denial, not the realization, of the ideals of Western law ... The result, Weber suggested, is that instead of being the shield of liberty, legal rationalization is part of the general process of societal change in which Western society has created rigid structures that enslave us as they seem to promise liberation'.

[352] Rudolf Wiethölter, 1989, 797; Rudolf Wiethölter, 2006.

[353] Duncan Kennedy, 2001a; Duncan Kennedy, 1975.

terrain, which is, as we noted before, characterised by an intricate correlation of overlapping and interpenetrating processes. Much suggests that the present engagement with the role of the state and the nature of legal regulation can only be a highly charged and risky enterprise. In light of the dramatic falsification of assumptions about the respective capacities and roles of state and market that reigned supremely over the closing decades of the twentieth- and well into the first of the twenty-first century,[354] there is little room for complacency. 'All that is solid...'. Our present interest in the idea of private government is thus an admittedly ambitious attempt to identify a timely response to challenges identified as 'Globalisation', 'Europeanisation' and 'Privatisation', because it must at the same time address the long-standing contestations of law and legal regulation.[355] In the present context of a heated debate over the formal and substantive qualities of the rule of law,[356] on the one hand, and over law's contested relevance in what some see as a borderless and pluralist world and others as one dominated by powerful interests,[357] on the other, advances in legal doctrine are inseparable from developments in legal theory, as well as the sociology and philosophy of law. Understanding current inquiries into the nature and role of law in a globalised world as being *political* asks us, above all, to acknowledge the persistence of questions of power, of exclusion and silencing that must be central to a legal theory project of transnational law, but not to attempt to simply equate the present contexts of changed norms and actors with those of *yesterday*.[358] As recently expressed by Regina Kreide, the parallel processes of socialisation (growing importance of non-state actors in the formulation and creation of international rules) and juridification (formalisation ['legalisation'] and 'proceduralisation of infrastructure according to international law')[359] amount to a pressing challenge of legal and democratic theory, in particular with regard to the 'dysfunctionalities' of these parallel developments, of which Kreide observes that

> [t]hey range from the generation of hegemonic, democratically deficient legislation, to its deformalisation and a lack of separation of powers in a multi-leveled system, to the disempowerment of politics and the exclusion of a great part of the global population from access to money, knowledge, power, and judicial outlets for grievances.[360]

[354] Paul Krugman, 2008; Robert Skidelsky, 2009; Christian Marazzi, 2009.
[355] For a promising approach in this vein, see Victoria Nourse and Gregory Shaffer, 2009.
[356] On the one hand: Richard A Posner, 1998a, on the other: Kerry Rittich, 2004; Alvaro Santos, 2006.
[357] Jack Goldsmith and Eric Posner, 2005.
[358] Boaventura de Sousa Santos, 1987.
[359] Regina Kreide, 2009, 18–19.
[360] *Ibid*, 19.

Echoing the far-reaching deformalisation and functionalisation trends we can witness in many areas of domestic law,[361] Kreide observes: '[p]olitical power and the market enter into an alliance that, without being based on a *legal* acquisition of power, cuts across the functional differentiation between right and wrong, government and opposition, haves and have-nots'.[362] Similarly, Nancy Fraser has recently pointed to the particular challenges of transposing the embedded forms of political struggle over redistribution, recognition and representation into a world, in which particularly the last dimension had arguably become very questionable, given the absence of established structures securing, belonging to and participation in the formation of political will.[363] While this view tends to overlook the exclusionary basis on which the contained inclusion structures were inherently based and shielded from the outside,[364] it goes some way in illustrating the tension between something we could refer to as *embeddedness politics* and the emerging politics of transnational governance.

The paradoxical foundation of a contemporary *political* theory of law[365] that is caught between the struggle with past experiences and semantics on the one hand and risk, uncertainty and experimental vocabulary on the other, becomes apparent in the continuing disputes between those that either want to distinguish or to analogise state and non-state forms of rule-making. Echoing the arguments raised in the discussion over *lex mercatoria* as law, some scholars suggest that to underestimate the functional equivalence of private ordering regimes to state-made law (accomplished through the bundling of different mechanisms of private governance into an effective 'private legal system'[366] that would consequently encompass legislation, adjudication and enforcement of norms) would reflect an insufficient understanding of the 'aggregate efficiency of the [private ordering] system',[367] while at the same time furthering the gap between this efficient system and the law, surviving only as an unrealised ideal of a unified effective normative order. To overstate the—existing[368]—constraints of secrecy as one of several indicators of a perceived lack of legitimacy of the private legal system in comparison with state-made law, would occur, however, at the price of ignoring the extremely complex and often intransparent

361 Daniela Caruso, 2006, 69–71; for international law: Manfred Lachs, 1972.
362 *Ibid*, 22, with reference to Hauke Brunkhorst, 2005, 166.
363 Nancy Fraser, 2009.
364 See, eg Antony Anghie, 2006, and Will Kymlicka, 2007. Very instructive is the debate between Seyla Benhabib and her critics in Seyla Benhabib, 2006.
365 See also Victoria Nourse and Gregory Shaffer, 2009, 121, 131, speaking of 'emergent analytics, which is the idea that any dynamic realism takes its concepts from the world and not from disembodied theory.'
366 Lisa Bernstein, 2001, 1726.
367 Lisa Bernstein, 1992, 151.
368 *Ibid*.

relations between state and private actors in contemporary governance.[369] Further, to lament the allegedly *deficient* quality of privately made norms, would equate to a failure to recognise the parallels between presently emerging non-state normative orders and their relationship to the state, on the one hand, and previous assertions and contestations of such developments, on the other.[370] Long before mainstream public law, in particular administrative law, had become productively interested in the (public) governance function of private law arrangements,[371] private lawyers had begun to grapple with ways to adapt their legal categories, concepts and instruments to rapid social changes.[372] The long-standing private law debates centering on the 'constitutionalisation' of the legal order must be seen as a direct outflow of earlier assessments of the public force of private law.[373] They provide a tremendously rich reservoir for current conceptualisation projects of public-private regulatory regimes.

In over-emphasising those aspects of private law that help to enable cross-border exchange through the provision of legal certainty, however, the transnationalists put their trust in a functionalist approach, which risks neglecting the cultural and political dimensions of law. As a result, they almost deliberately produce a variety of standard objections regarding the necessary limits to private autonomy with respect to commutative justice (eg the protection of weaker parties in contract law) as well as public policy (eg the protection of fundamental common values like competition or human rights) and, thus, the legitimacy of privately created transnational law.[374]

As a reaction to such critique, some scholars propose to limit the extent of the private production of law to issue areas in which the state is disinterested because no public policy is involved. Commercial law, where merchants presumably meet on an equal footing, is often offered as example. That this case deserves particular attention was recognised already during our discussion of *lex mercatoria*. The heated nature of this debate can only be explained in so far as *lex mercatoria*, or law merchant illustrates the multifaceted nature of forms of private ordering. From the perspective then of scholars interested in social norms theory,[375] *lex mercatoria* can be seen

[369] See only Carol Harlow, 2009.

[370] Louis Jaffe, 1937; Hans Großmann-Doerth, 1929; Hans Großmann-Doerth, 2005; Franz Böhm, 1960.

[371] From the German discussion, See, eg Wolfgang Hoffmann-Riem, 1997; Martin Bullinger, 1996; Hans-Heinrich Trute, 1996; from the UK debate (with comparative assessments), see Tony Prosser, 1995, and RAW Rhodes, 1994; from the US debate see, eg, the outstanding work by Jody Freeman, 2000b; Jody Freeman, 2000a, and the contributions to Jody Freeman and Martha Minow, 2009.

[372] See, eg, Anton Menger, 1968; Otto Kahn-Freund, 1966, and Franz Wieacker, 1953.

[373] See only Rudolf Wiethölter, 1974.

[374] A Claire Cutler, 2003, 241; see Klaus Peter Berger, 1999, 64, 75.

[375] See the collection in John N Drobak, 2006.

as a powerful illustration of the proliferation of normative regimes without law,[376] while others continue to scrutinise the distinctly 'public' dimensions of such non-state-based forms of transnational regulation.[377] Moving from transnational commercial law back to (domestic) commercial law, there is of course a rich tradition of scrutinising the public-private distinction and the respective rule-making competences of public and private actors in the context of defining the scope of commercial activity and its regulation. One of the sets of questions having arisen in this context is, of course, the long-standing discussion over the importance of trade usages, custom and business practices as relevant sources of party obligations in commercial litigation.[378] Lately, Gillian Hadfield has made a number of important contributions to this debate in a series of papers on commercial law, corporate law and regulatory theory. In her 2001 article on 'Privatising Commercial Law' Hadfield begins with a straight-forward critique of the unjustified costs associated with the state's monopoly over the creation, administration and enforcement of law:

> The state's monopoly over legitimate coercive power is not, in itself, problematic; this monopoly is definitional of the state. The problem lies in the state's monopoly over the rules and procedures governing the application of coercion. Not only does the state enforce a contract, it designs and administers contract law and procedure. And it does so with all the drawbacks of an insulated service provider: unresponsive to costs, reluctant to innovate, bureaucratic in its methods of collecting and processing information, shut off from entrepreneurial creativity and effort. These drawbacks contribute to the high cost of law.[379]

Central to her project is, as a first step, the differentiation of specific functions carried out by a legal system and, as a second, the allocation of these functions to different actors. The fundamental distinction that Hadfield recognises in a legal system is that between the *economic* and the *justice*, or *democratic* functions.[380] In an eclectic yet suggestive list pertaining to the latter function, we find the tasks to 'oversee the institutions of democratic governance, administer the modern welfare state, protect individual rights, ensure social order, and provide a means of non-violent dispute resolution among citizens'.[381] The economic function of the legal system includes, essentially, the provision of the 'structure and the regulation necessary for the operation of efficient markets'.[382] Hadfield suggests that the economic function of the legal system can just as well be assumed by what she calls

376 Peter H Huang and Ho-Mou Wu, 1994; Robert D Cooter, 1994.
377 See Moritz Renner, 2009, and Moritz Renner, 2010.
378 See Lisa Bernstein, 1996, Lisa Bernstein, 1999, and Stewart Macaulay, 2000.
379 Gillian K Hadfield, 2001, 40.
380 See Gillian K Hadfield, 2001, and Gillian K Hadfield, 2000.
381 Hadfield, 2001, 40.
382 *Ibid.*

'private legal regimes'. Assuming that we would here be concerned solely with the relations among corporations, little regard would have to be paid to questions of equity or fairness. Worried that the only pressure on the judicial system that at this time administers, through corporate and contract law, the behaviour of corporations, would be a competitive 'law market'[383]—that is, forum shopping for the 'best' law available—Hadfield refers to the charter competition usually associated with the US state of Delaware[384] and envisages

> a world of truly competitive privatised corporate contract law, [in which] contracting parties would face a marketplace of alternative regimes. Private firms would design packages of substantive and procedural law that would govern the interpretation and enforcement of corporate contracts.[385]

Just as we were beginning to suspect certain analogies between this depiction of commercial law and the 'romance' and symbolic power of the law merchant discussed earlier, Hadfield evokes the 'purely private origins of medieval commercial law'.[386] She makes the point that central to the medieval legal regime is—and, to be sure, much of the current interest in old merchant law likely has to do with—the fact that 'the power to coerce compliance with a legal regime can be decoupled from the function of designing and administering the system according to which that power will be exercised'.[387] Among the decisive characteristics that mark this commercial law is the fact that 'unlike the state law of contract' these 'systems often adopt simple rules and strict rules of interpretation',[388] something that strongly echoes other contemporary assessments of the shortcomings of contract adjudication as contrasted with private parties' bargains.[389] Summarily referring to 'medieval merchants, trade associations, and securities exchanges', Hadfield posits that these private regimes can perfectly well create norms, which can nevertheless come under the scrutiny of adjudicators and policy-makers. In response to eventual concerns regarding the narrowly constructed functional orientation of these private legal systems, she highlights reputation, information technology, organisation and private competition' as the core elements of these systems' basis of legitimacy.[390]

Hadfield's original distinction between the legal system's democratic, or justice function and its economic function was based on the premise that 'privatisation is justifiable only for those areas of law in which efficiency is

[383] For this term, see now Erin A O'Hara and Larry E Ribstein, 2009.
[384] William L Cary, 1974; Ralph K Winter, 1977; Lucian Ayre Bebchuk, 1992; Roberta Romano, 1993.
[385] Hadfield, 2001, 41.
[386] *Ibid.*
[387] *Ibid*, 42.
[388] *Ibid*, 43.
[389] Robert E Scott and George G Triantis, 2006; Robert E Scott, 2007.
[390] Hadfield, 2001, 44–45.

the only value at stake'.[391] Hence, in situations where market efficiency is the sole issue at stake, the competition of different private legal regimes will lead to first-best solutions. Hadfield underlines, however, that such a model is developed for a competition among corporations. In the case of individual citizens, the picture could look somewhat similar or, in fact, very, very different: 'when non-economic values such as justice and due process are at stake, the effort to increase efficiency has to take place within the context of the public regime for reasons of democratic legitimacy'.[392] Historically, Hadfield posits, private legal regimes have only flourished where there was a certain absence of a public law regime. And as a matter of systematic orientation, she holds that public law, instead of disappearing completely,

> will remain crucial where the situation calls for the (public law) system to 'lend' its coercive power to the enforcement of private rules ... The essential task for public law is to identify the points at which public legal structure is needed to facilitate the emergence and maintenance of efficient competition among private legal providers.[393]

With an eye to the overall goal of reducing the 'costs of law in the public sphere',[394] Hadfield concludes that large parts of commercial and corporate law should indeed be privatized,[395] while other areas—such as those covered by the justice function—must not.[396] At the outset of her distinction, which she reiterated in a recent response to work by one of the authors of the present volume,[397] is as we saw the association of 'efficiency' goals with the economic function of a legal system on the one hand and the 'non-efficiency' goals with the justice or, democratic function on the other.[398] Hadfield stresses that efficiency ought not to be understood as a 'scientific or apolitical standard', but as a 'normative, value-laden criterion by which we can evaluate relationships and outcomes in a society'.[399] On this basis, Hadfield acknowledges the impossibility of a neat separation of efficiency from other normative concerns, but resists the idea that this would clearly imply the impossibility of working with a distinction between public and private. Using the example of a contract dispute between different corporate entities, she argues that these disputes (say, over the creation and interpretation of contractual obligations or performance) are exclusively raising issues of efficiency. Because, she says, 'corporate entities are not

391 *Ibid*, 44.
392 *Ibid*, 45.
393 *Ibid*, 45.
394 *Ibid*.
395 See also Gillian K Hadfield and Eric Talley, 2006.
396 Gillian K Hadfield, 2001, 44–45; Gillian K Hadfield, 2002, 263; Gillian K Hadfield and Eric Talley, 2006.
397 Gillian K Hadfield, 2009a.
398 *Ibid*, 241.
399 *Ibid*.

political citizens and do not have moral claims to fair treatment or just distribution'[400]—a distinction she also applies to intellectual property rights held by corporations, not by individuals—she holds on to her contention presented in 2001 that '[a]ny moral or political concerns that are rooted in how the state recognises or rewards individual citizens who produce new works and ideas are a separate matter'.[401] Referring to case studies conducted on European firms purchasing software products and licences in India as one of several instances of intercorporate relations, Hadfield concludes that just as the participating actors design the content of the traded products, they are similarly suited to design 'the optimal legal rules governing the interpretation and implementation of those provisions'.[402] This 'privatisation' however, is importantly qualified: the applicable rules (standards, and norms), despite their private production, can still be regulated by public bodies such as courts, administrators and such.[403] Defending herself against the claim (made by Calliess[404]) that such norm privatisation implies the absence of public law and administration through public actors, she insists on a set of possible combinations of public and private providers of legal services.[405] Explaining this 'embeddedness' of a private norm regime in a set of established institutions and enforcement practices, for example in the field of a contract,[406] Hadfield underlines the continued relevance of what she calls the 'background legal environment'. This nod towards a Hayekian conceptualisation of the facilitative relationship between law (politics, the state) and society (freedom, contracts, individuals)[407] is an important element in Hadfield's project, because it is telling of her awareness of the muddy terrain on which multiple spheres of public and private overlap—not only in the transnational arena[408]—even if she acknowledges that '[t]he pervasive role of publicly provided law in structuring even ostensibly extra-legal enforcement mechanisms takes on a particular salience in the global context'.[409] Since even cross-border transactions, as regards their arbitration (or litigation) and enforcement, cannot avoid a particular juridical touch-down in a particular state,[410] Hadfield

400 *Ibid*, 243
401 *Ibid*, 243.
402 *Ibid*, 245.
403 *Ibid.*
404 Gralf-Peter Calliess, 2009.
405 Gillian K Hadfield, 2009a, 245.
406 *Ibid*, 246.
407 Friedrich A Hayek, 2006, 130, 193–204, 194: 'True, there are good reasons why all government concern with economic matters is suspect'. Friedrich A Hayek, 1973, 113. 'In the ordinary sense of purpose law is therefore not a means to any purpose, but merely a condition for the successful pursuit of most purposes'.
408 Gillian K Hadfield, 2009a, 241.
409 *Ibid*, 248.
410 Robert Wai, 2002.

understands the 'background legal regime' of a given country as 'shaping the legal status of these actions',[411] and it is on this basis that she posits that the distinction between the democratic and economic functions of a legal system ought to be used as an organising principle to differentiate 'between *legal rules or mechanisms* that are measured exclusively in efficiency terms and those that are not'.[412] Because from this perspective, according to Hadfield, some, if not many, transactions or relationships may well raise issues of both efficiency and non-efficiency (democracy, justice), the central application of the distinction lies in the identification of the functions of the legal regimes governing certain transactions or relationships.[413] Using the example of a rule that would permit 'smaller' or 'less sophisticated' firms to rescind a contract within three days without penalty, Hadfield defines such an instance as an expression of fairness, which is external to the values of the parties. In applying such a rule, it would be evaluated in policy terms as regards its success in achieving fairness goals, but there would be no reason to expect that private legal systems on their own would create such a rule. From the standpoint of the private actors that engage in rule creation in this context, fairness is external.[414]

In the article Professor Hadfield responds to, Calliess—as we do in this book—distinguished between a *co-ordinative* and a *regulatory* function of law,[415] a distinction, which we would eventually parallel with the distinction between an economic and a democratic/justice function of the legal system.[416] Hadfield resists that parallel, partially with respect to her concept of the 'background legal system', which for her appears to illustrate that there is no private legal system ever working in a complete normative vacuum. In addition, she lays out four public/private distinctions that in her view must not be conflated into the economic/justice distinction. These four distinctions relate to: (1) the nature of the *relationship* governed (individual-individual vs individual-state); (2) the status of the *provider* of legal services (private vs state entities); (3) the source of the content of legal obligations (parties themselves or the state); and (4) the source of legitimacy (consent or democratic institutions/procedures).

Hadfield suggests that the distinction between economic and justice functions of a legal system, which is not to be lined up with the distinctions between private and public in the above listed four dimensions,[417]

[411] Gillian K Hadfield, 2009a, 248.
[412] *Ibid*, 250.
[413] *Ibid*.
[414] *Ibid*, 251.
[415] Gralf-Peter Calliess, 2009.
[416] See below.
[417] Gillian K Hadfield, 2009a, 243: 'distinguishing the economic and democratic functions of law does not imply that all other public/private dimensions must fall out the same way. Identifying the function of a legal rule as "efficiency" does not tell us whether the rule

is relevant only with regard to the critical public/private dimension of legitimacy.[418] Her claim is that private provision of law, precisely for democratic legitimacy reasons, is only an option for rules solely concerned with efficiency. Her definition of efficiency is crucial in that regard, as it reveals, upon closer inspection, that it is indeed premised on a number of additional, speculative assumptions:

> Legal rules serve exclusively efficiency goals when they can be evaluated in policy terms entirely on the basis of the extent to which they promote the allocation of resources to their highest-valued uses and the production of goods and services with minimal expenditure of resources.[419]

Her assertion that private actors can provide for better rules where only efficiency issues are concerned[420] rests on the assumption of a perfectly competitive market, populated by contracting parties aware of all externalities and 'judges of their own welfare'. This constellation, which Hayek would likely have considered overwhelming, if not unrealistic,[421] makes Hadfield's model considerably vulnerable: even if it were true that all members of a constituent assembly, engaged in devising rules applicable to their dealings, were aware of externalities and competent to assess the future rules' impact on their welfare, this would still not solve the problem of unequal starting points or asymmetric bargaining power relations. Hadfield's assumption of a competitive market appears to ignore long-standing insights into the constituted nature of markets[422] and the impossibility of assigning functional concepts such as 'property' or 'sovereignty' neatly only to one sphere.[423] The Achilles' heal of Hadfield's contention that the 'legitimacy of a private legal regime, with law produced by private entities, rests in the consent of the parties who choose to subject themselves to the regime'[424] consists in us having to assume a free choice on the part of the participating parties. Hadfield's explanation that this constellation would at any rate be an adequate depiction only for inter-corporate relations falls flat if the decisive criterion remains that 'the only public value at stake is the efficiency of

governing private relationships must be supplied by private actors and enforced through private litigation, or find its legitimacy only in the consent of private parties'.

418 *Ibid*, 252.

419 *Ibid.*

420 For an application of this idea in the field of corporate law (private rule making being described as superior to regulatory competition among incorporation states), see Gillian K Hadfield and Eric Talley, 2006.

421 Friedrich Hayek, 1945, reprinted in Friedrich Hayek, 1945, 77: 'the knowledge of the circumstances of which we must make use never exists in concentrated or integrated form but solely as the dispersed its of incomplete and frequently contradictory knowledge which all the separate individuals possess'. 78: 'it is a problem of the utilization of knowledge which is not given to anyone in its totality'.

422 Robert L Hale, 1923.

423 Morris R Cohen, 1927.

424 Gillian K Hadfield, 2009a, 252.

private relations'.[425] The fact alone that corporations interact with each other and that they draw up rules governing 'these' relations does not make these relations 'private'. It is here where Hadfield's earlier contention that her distinction applies not to the content of the rules, but to the rules themselves cannot convince.[426] By having to assume an unrealistic situation of freedom of choice, perfect information (externalities, welfare) as the hallmarks of a private legal system's legitimacy, Hadfield overburdens the members of the system with precisely these utopian conditions that have long been identified with the 'underlying values of public law'.[427] In maintaining the distinction between economic and democratic justice where private legal regimes produce rules based on consent—contrasted with the external imposition of, say, environmental or social standards onto privately enacted corporate governance regimes against the consent of their designers—Hadfield in fact renders the economic function of the private legal system compatible with, or at least not in contrast to, the democratic function.

We thus remain sceptical as to whether this approach can fully illuminate the interplay between and the nature of 'public' and 'private' regulatory regimes, be that in the context of domestic rule-making arrangements or in view of an emerging transnational legal order. As a matter of conceptual coherence, Hadfield's own assertion of the inseparability of efficiency and (other) normative concerns in our view contradicts her claim that we can nevertheless hold on to a distinction between public and private. Although she rightly, in our mind, acknowledges the historical contingency and contextual dependence of such distinctions, something she regards as informing the long-standing misunderstandings between civil and common lawyers,[428] she nonetheless pairs her non-historical, non-contextual assessment of 'corporate disputes' with distinctions between corporations (as legal fictions) and shareholders (as citizens with moral claims). Whether some among them are to be considered 'public' or 'private', however, seems to depend on the *purity* of the relations between them. If they are solely engaging in market operations, they would be from that perspective, eligible members of a *legitimate* private legal system. If they engaged in market operations and related rule-making while even incorporating 'public value' concerns (environment, employees, sustainability), these corporations would also befit a legitimate private legal system. Such rules, she admits, might not 'necessarily satisfy Aristotelian standards of either corrective or distributive justice;

425 *Ibid*.

426 *Ibid*, 244. 'When I speak of the privatisation of commercial contract law, however, I am referring not to the content of the legal obligations per se, but rather to the rules of the regime governing how these obligations will be interpreted and enforced'.

427 See Dawn Oliver, 1997; for a recent application in the area of global organizations, see Armin Bogdandy, Philipp Dann and Matthias Goldmann, 2008.

428 Gillian K Hadfield, 2009a, 239–40.

they will just be the rules that satisfy the demand of these corporations for a mechanism that overcomes the obstacles to moving ahead with the deal'.[429] Where, however, corporations would not consent to the rules promoted by some among them or ordained by an external regulator, this private legal system, due to the absence of consent, would cease to have legitimacy. As noted above, the tight combination of conditions (corporations dealing with corporations, perfect information, consent) weakens rather than strengthens her initial intuition that it might be useful to explore the legitimacy potentials of private governance regimes. But, by persistently applying the economic/justice distinction to constellations that raise both institutional and normative complexities of public and private, she seems to fall short of the promises and potentials of her own project.

As contested by Professor Hadfield, we had previously read her distinction between economic and democratic function of a legal system to be congruent with our own distinction between the *co-ordinative* (or facilitative or enabling) and the *regulatory* dimensions of law.[430] The shared challenge between Professor Hadfield's and our own project remains, that transnational governance regimes can be observed which actually do perform co-ordinative as well as regulatory functions without being compatible with conventional notions of democratic legitimacy. In that context, we are facing the challenge of how to make sense of the public/private conundra in transnational governance regimes in light of the critical discussions around (domestic) commercial law and business customs that occupied us before. As we have said, our central concern with Professor Hadfield's approach arises from her suggestion to juxtapose an efficiency-oriented realm that could be governed by private legal systems, on the one hand, with an allegedly politically laden, 'interventionist' political-legal sphere on the other. We noted that such assertions have long been meeting with substantive, and in our view convincing, contestation[431] and continue to do so.[432] There is no reason to assume that the market is the product of a natural evolution, a sphere which the law in pursuing public interests enters into as an outside, distortive force. To the degree that lawyers speak about the 'market' and to the degree that there is a deliberation about what the market is supposed to do 'on its own' or where it respectively 'fails' or 'succeeds', the market is in itself a legal construct. As a consequence, then, private law theory that is informed by a justice vs efficiency distinction has a hard time explaining the historical facticity of a more-than-a-century-long 'publicisation' or 'materialisation' of private law in response to the changing structures

[429] *Ibid*, 245.

[430] Gralf-Peter Calliess, 2009.

[431] Robert L Hale, 1923; Morris R Cohen, 1927; Rudolf Wiethölter, 1972b; Rudolf Wiethölter, 1986a.

[432] Duncan Kennedy, 2001b; David Campbell, 2007.

of society.[433] Seen through the lens of the public/private distinction, this process continues to prompt heated debates concerning the adequacy of public law 'interventions' into private law[434] or the capacity of private law instruments to pursue public interests.[435] From the viewpoint of our present endeavour to develop a theory of transnational private law, however, its impact is an even further one: the attribution of socio(-legal) conflicts to either 'justice' or 'efficiency', developed against the background of, for example, a highly adjudicated contract, property and corporate law culture, is bound to play a decisive role once it is applied outside of the nation-state. Here lies the real gist of the conflict between the 'traditionalists' and the 'transnationalists'.[436] Too much, indeed, suggests here that we are meant to believe in a renewed 'quérelle des anciens et des modernes', resulting this time in the latter dismissing the former as inadequate and useless in the face of the needs of a global marketplace.[437] Not only does the implied opposition between converging, value-free transnational spaces and stubbornly diverging, politically charged local areas strike us as 'unrealistic',[438] its greater problem is indeed the further implied assumption that global markets are as such distinct from domestic ones. The long quest in legal theory to formulate a legal response to globalising markets and human activity has provided evidence supporting the conclusion that—independently of whether we approach the conundrum of the 'transnational' from within the conceptual edifices of, say, Public International Law, Conflict of Laws, or European Law[439]—the difficulties for a doctrinal lawyer of categorically separating the domestic from the transnational apparently outweigh the justifications offered in defence of an autonomous, self-standing and distinct transnational legal order.[440] From the viewpoint, then, of legal

433 See, eg Franz Wieacker, 1967, David Trubek, 1972a, or Patrick Atiyah, 1979.

434 Uwe Diederichsen, 1997; Duncan Kennedy, 1982a; Peer Zumbansen, 2003b.

435 Gunther Teubner, 1999a; Thomas Wilhelmsson, 2004.

436 Klaus Peter Berger, 1999.

437 See, eg, Michael Joachim Bonell, 2001b; for a critique, see Peer Zumbansen, 2002a; Martin J Doris, 2006, 398.

438 Ralf Michaels, 2007b, 1005: 'This distinction between value-free transnational areas of law that converge, and value-laden local areas of law that do not, is not in accordance with reality'.

439 Luis de Lima Pinheiro, 2001; see also the contributions to Martin Schulte and Rudolf Stichweh, 2008.

440 See, eg, the observations by Karsten Schmidt, 2007, 171: '*Die bestehenden rechtskulturellen Gegensätze sprechen auch unter dem Eindruck der Globalisierung immer noch gegen die Annahme, dass bald ein umfassendes Welt-Gewohnheitsrecht vorhanden sein wird*'. See also David Kennedy, 2009, 58: '[…] I worry that our efforts to comprehend global governance have focused far too much on the authority of agents we see to act within structures we understand. We have paid too little attention to the myriad ways power flows through flows of finances, resources, of affiliation and disaffiliation, the social movements of wills to power, the desire to submit, the experience of triumph and victimization, pride and shame. All these things move like a virus or a fad, but our epidemiology is weak, and our sociology of status convention and emulation at the global level is rudimentary.'

sociology, the picture changes yet again: understanding society as 'world society', the distinctions between the domestic and the transnational appear as a side product and contingent fact from within functional discourses that reconstruct historical developments according to their particular functional code.[441] While the sociological account, which posits society as constituted by functionally differentiated communications—one of which is the legal system,[442] obviously seems to present considerable challenges for a theory of law based on the central role of the state, there appears to be much less anxiety from the viewpoint of economics with regard to this account. This is, at least, the impression we gain from the rather jaunty assertions of a borderless world of commercial transactions.

III. A THEORY OF TRANSNATIONAL PRIVATE LAW

In the remainder of this chapter we set out the basic elements of a theory of transnational private law, which will serve as the conceptual framework for the two examples we explore in the following chapters. In the first part of this section we argue that both the content (substantive dimension) and the authors (procedural dimension) of transnational private law must be categorised as *hybrid* with regard to a traditional distinction between public and private law spheres (Section IIIA). Drawing in particular on New Institutional Economics theories of private ordering and economic governance (IIIB) we then define our concept of *transnational law regimes*, which we develop on the basis of a fundamentally hybrid character of transnational private law (Section IIIC). On that basis, we address the contested issues concerning both the legal status and the legitimacy of such *transnational law regimes*. Building on a conceptual proposal first advanced in the area of Internet standards,[443] we discuss a comprehensive substantive/procedural concept, 'Rough Consensus and Running Code' (RCRC), which we use to conceptualise elements of transnational private law as a way of thinking about a modern theory of customary law (Section IIID).

A. Co-ordination versus Regulation: Revisiting the Public-Private Divide

> 'People do not see law as salient to their lives; at best, it is a background factor with limited impact'.[444]

[441] Niklas Luhmann, 1970.
[442] Niklas Luhmann, 1985; Niklas Luhmann, 1989a; Niklas Luhmann, 2004.
[443] David D Clark, 1992; Andrew L Russell, 2006.
[444] Stewart Macaulay, 1986, 469.

In the era of the Western sovereign nation-state, legal theory for the longest time remained concerned with a distinction between public and private spheres of society on the one hand[445] and competing, non-hierarchical claims of legal pluralism on the other.[446] On the basis of a neat distinction between the public and the private, the state is—assuming a *substantive* role—burdened with the task of minding the public good and looking out for the pursuit of common welfare in a society composed of self-interested individuals.[447] *Procedurally* the state is constructed as a distinct actor, conceived as being in a unique position to institutionally enable the representation of the whole towards the rest of society. A variety of qualifications apply to both dimensions.

On the *substantive* plane, state law is divided into private law and public law. The former is held to be concerned with the relations between individuals; through the guarantee of property rights and the enforcement of contractual agreements, the state facilitates the co-operation of economic actors in markets, among others; this can be called the *co-ordinative function* of law. In contrast, public law would be seen as regulating the activities of the state in relation to the individual; the ambit of thus conceived public law as regulatory law would encompass constitutional law, criminal law, tax law and other branches of administrative law, by which the state directly regulates societal relations with respect to public values, eg free competition, distributive justice, or the protection of the environment; this would be referred to as the *regulatory function* of law.[448] To be sure, both (co-ordinative) private and (regulatory) public law are intrinsically linked to an underlying idea of *justice*: this makes the distinction between co-ordinative and regulatory law blurry and less productive than the proponents, say, of a Private Law Society, would have it. According to these theorists working in the tradition of Friedrich Hayek and the ordo-liberal School of Thought, the distinction between a co-ordinative and a regulatory function of law, respectively associated with private and public law, was crucial for the preservation of a sphere of allegedly uninhibited freedom—represented

[445] See only Max Rheinstein, 1967; Duncan Kennedy, 1982b.

[446] Harry W Arthurs, 1988.

[447] Jacques Chevallier, 2004, 12: '*L'État s'inscrit pleinement dans cette logique de la modernité, caracterisée par l'empire de la Raison et dominée par la figure de l'Individu: element de rationalisation de l'organisation politique, il permet de réaliser un compromis subtil entre le primat accordé à l'individu et la nécessité de creation d'un ordre collectif*'.

[448] For the distinction between *co-ordinative* and *regulatory* standards see Lawrence Lessig, 1999b: 'A coordinating standard is a rule that facilitates an activity that otherwise would not exist. A regulating standard restricts behavior within that activity, according to a policy set by the regulators. A coordinating standard can be imposed from the top down, or emerge from the bottom up; a regulating standard is ordinarily imposed only from the top down. Driving on the right side of the road is a coordinating standard. A speed limit is a regulating standard'. See also Raymund Werle and Eric J Iversen, 2006, 22; Harm Schepel, 2005, 2–6.

by the private law domain.[449] Already here, however, the idea of private law referred to an extremely loaded and enriched understanding of a legal field, which would prove resilient to such clear-cut demarcations. As becomes particularly clear from the relation between private (contract) law and competition law, the ordo-liberal understanding of private law encompassed, on the one hand in a co-ordinative way, rules governing market participants' relations, and on the other, in a regulatory manner, rules to correct market failures.[450] The hybrid nature of private law becomes apparent in the concept of 'economic law', a term that cuts across the public/private divide by capturing the paradoxical impossibility/necessity of the term. The ordo-liberal understanding of private law was enriched with a post-enlightenment understanding of the market participants as political citizens,[451] which made the rules of private law at the same time co-ordinative *and* regulatory. This indirectly relativised the original distinction between the public and the private spheres and, as a consequence, even a critical translation of *economic law* would be difficult. The use of the term by German private law scholars as a particular device to denounce the anti-regulatory impetus harboured by defenders as the hallmark of an uninhibited private sphere that is to be kept free from regulatory 'intervention', must be seen as deeply embedded in a legal culture that has traditionally been working with a distinct—substantive and procedural—separation of public and private law.[452] Yet, the allusion to economic rationality in a large part of, say, contract law thinking with regard to transnational relations seeks to disembed contract law as 'economic law' from this political economy context. By restating contractual governance as 'social norms', the imperialist hegemony of economic rationality in legal thinking[453] assumes the quality of a natural evolution. This, in turn, invites a sustained, critical engagement with its foundations.[454] The large-scale contractualisation in public service delivery[455] in past decades has rightly prompted a host of scholarly, critical analysis,[456] and one of the striking results of this research

[449] Franz Böhm, 1937; Franz Böhm, 1966; Franz Böhm, Wilhelm Eucken and Hans Großmann-Doerth, 1989; for a recent discussion, see Fernanda Nicola, 2008, 144–45.

[450] See David J Gerber, 1998.

[451] Rudolf Wiethölter, 1972b.

[452] For an excellent discussion, see Wiethölter, 1972b, the volume by Heinz-Dieter Assmann, Gert Brüggemeier, Dieter Hart and Christian Joerges, 1980, and Christian Joerges, 1994, 30–32 as well as Christian Joerges, 2004.

[453] See Gunther Teubner, 2007.

[454] This idea is more fully developed in Peer Zumbansen, 2007a.

[455] Peter Vincent-Jones, 2006; see also Ian Harden, 1992 and Jody Freeman, 2000a.

[456] A very fine, differentiated analysis is provided, eg, for the US by Alfred C Aman Jr, 2006, and by Jody Freeman, 2000a, for the UK by Colin Scott, 2004, and Carol Harlow, 2009, and for Germany by Heiko Faber, 1989, Thomas Vesting, 1997, Eberhard Schmidt-Aßmann, 1994, and Wolfgang Hoffmann-Riem, 1997. A true mine is the newly edited Handbook of Administrative Sciences (*Handbuch der Verwaltungsrechtswissenschaft*), W Hoffmann-Riem, E Schmidt-Aßmann and Andreas Voßkuhle (eds), 2006.

is the remaining scepticism with regard to the practical and normative value of the concept of 'efficiency'.[457] While it is true that in many areas of regulation the proof of success is improved economic performance, not only are the ways of bringing that result about much less easily identified, but also the notion of economic performance itself is in no way self-explanatory or value-neutral. In the search of 'better regulation' in a wide range of policy areas, allusions to efficiency abound, often, however, without a convincing commitment to appreciate the regulatory regime in a larger and politically constantly shifting context.[458]

Because transnational law can only be studied as a methodological challenge to reassess the meaning of private and public law dimensions in border-crossing institutional and normative networks,[459] the implied understandings of *economic law* and its relation to *economic governance* deserve particular attention in the realm of border-transcending economic relations.[460] On the *substantive plain*, transnational private, commercial, or business law cannot be purely co-ordinative in nature. Instead it has to deal with both the co-ordinative and regulatory aspects of global economic exchange, since—again in the absence of a world state—there is no distinct sphere of public economic law available. As a result, transnational law regimes in praxis involve and combine both aspects. The already discussed example of *lex mercatoria* is a telling illustration of this intermingling of co-ordinative and regulative aspects in transnational law, as is illustrated by the application of anti-trust provisions by private judges in international commercial arbitration.[461] Similar insights can be won from our two extensive case studies below, dealing with consumer contracts and corporate governance respectively.

It follows from the parallel assessment of private law-making in and outside of the nation-state, that there is and never has been such thing as 'pure' economic law, which would be concerned with efficiency only,[462] unless we expanded the idea of efficiency to cover a very comprehensive set of even conflicting values. Where, however, efficiency is defined in economic terms alone, efficiency would refer to a world of perfect and complete market conditions, something we have questioned already above in the context of our discussion of Hadfield. Whether such an assumption would make sense

[457] See, eg, the observations offered by David Campbell, 2007.

[458] For a critique, see, eg Kerry Rittich, 2005, and Stephen Weatherill, 2007, 4–6.

[459] Karl-Heinz Ladeur, 1997b, 43: 'Theoretical conceptualization must pay due regard to the new phenomenon of overlap amongst the various national, supranational and transnational components of the systems of law, politics and economics, seen as non-personal communication networks'.

[460] Christian Tietje and Karsten Nowrot, 2006, 19–20.

[461] Robert B von Mehren, 2003.

[462] But see Gillian K Hadfield, 2001, 45.

from an economist's perspective[463] is a different matter than how such an assumption unfolds within legal thinking.

Thus, rather than assuming a world in which we would actually be able to draw a neatly cut distinction between a public and a private sphere of norm-making, we suggest pushing the qualifications of *co-ordinative* and *regulatory* that have been associated, respectively, with private and public law, further towards a critical study of how the changing ideas of coordination and regulation influence our understanding of public and private with regard to emerging actors and forms of legal norm-creation. For this effort, we have to reassert some long-standing conceptualisations of the co-ordinative and regulatory functions of law, going back before the ordo-liberal understanding of private law just alluded to. For example, in Aristotle, we find a distinction between commutative and distributive justice,[464] a theory later revisited by Thomas[465] and, with considerable scepticism, by Hobbes.[466] In Hobbes's critique of Aristotle's idea of commutative justice as being not sufficiently interested in the predisposition and choice of the parties themselves, we find a strong expression of an approach to the (private) law governing such societal exchanges the concern of which would be above all the facilitation and co-ordination of these exchanges to proceed in an unfettered, uninhibited manner. From this perspective, private law would be essentially apolitical in content or, in contrast to public law, not inherently interested in the public good. In an excellent essay on the origin and fate of the idea of 'economic justice', CB Macpherson observed that the rise of such an idea was closely tied to the marketisation of societal affairs, as already contemplated by Aristotle and accepted as irreversible by the time of Hobbes's writing.[467] Certainly, and this has correctly been re-emphasised by Professor Hadfield, it would be a misrepresentation to consider the role of common law judges in the creation of private law rules as apolitical.[468] Substantively, the principles governing private law, however, were long depicted as naturalistic, almost technical, neutral—a tradition that continues to persuasively flex its muscles in

[463] For a much more differentiated perspective than some law & economic reception of economic thinking would (like to) have it, see only Douglass C North, 1990, and Douglass C North, 2005.

[464] Aristotle, Nicomachean Ethics, Book V. Another translation for *commutative* justice is *corrective* justice. For an application to Aristotelian Ethics to contract law, see only James Gordley, 1991.

[465] For an excellent discussion, see Crawford Brough Macpherson, 1987.

[466] See, eg DD Raphael, 2001, 74–79.

[467] Crawford Brough Macpherson, 1987, 9: 'Although he was no friend of the rising mercantile order, he saw that it had come to stay'.

[468] Gillian Hadfield, 2009, 241.

contemporary contract law,[469] areas of European private law,[470] and in what has become known as 'social norms theory';[471] all this despite a strong and long-standing critique, powerfully put forward by legal realism at the turn of the century.[472] Considered as exclusively contributing to the functioning of the market, private law thus understood came to be seen as an expression of human freedom with the consequence that private autonomy and private property became functionable as value-neutral concepts.[473] As such, private law rules did not *prima facie* raise issues of legitimacy or accountability. In contrast, public law, associated with a host of regulatory functions and the power to shape societal relations, would generally be subject to standards of legitimacy. From this side of the divide, the allegedly distinct qualities of public and private law were further accentuated by attributing political struggle and democratic consensus to the former and efficiency and value-neutrality to the latter. This depiction of the different qualities of public and private law lies at the heart of much of contemporary thinking in market creation in the law and development context.[474]

Mirroring this *substantive* distinction between public law and private law, we find a particular conceptualisation of the *procedural* characteristics of both fields: on the *procedural plane*, the state is equipped with a monopoly in legitimate law-making, adjudication, and law enforcement.[475] In most cases, *social norms* or *standards* that grow out of societal self-regulation or private ordering are denied the status of law, despite their immense regulatory impact.[476] They may become relevant in the state legal system only indirectly, ie after certain *mechanisms of degradation* are applied: While trade usages and the like are turned into facts through judicial 'deference', other forms of societal self-regulation are domesticated—through both 'incorporation' or 'delegation' as a category with subordinate status when measured on the pre-supposed hierarchy of norms, altogether resulting in a confirmation of the state law supremacy.[477] However, in fields such as arbitration the state leaves some space for private judges to issue arbitral awards, which state courts, in turn, are in a position to recognise and to

469 Among the representative works in this area are Robert E Scott, 2000, and Robert E Scott and George G Triantis, 2006.

470 See the excellent discussion in Fernanda Nicola, 2008, 148–61.

471 Besides the landmark study by Eric A Posner, 2000, see importantly the SSRN Series 'Law, Norms and Informal Order', available at: www.ssrn.com/link/law-norms-informal-order.html, edited by Richard McAdams.

472 For a helpful, monographic review of the Realist scholarship, in particular the importance of Hale, see Barbara H Fried, 1998; see also Joseph W Singer, 1988.

473 For a critique, see, eg Robert L Hale, 1923; John P Dawson, 1947.

474 See, on the one hand, Richard A Posner, 1998a, and on the other, Kerry Rittich, 2002.

475 The term legal centralism is used by Oliver E Williamson, 1983, 520; see also Robert C Ellickson, 1991, 138; Avinash K Dixit, 2004, 2.

476 See, again, Stewart Macaulay, 1986.

477 Ralf Michaels, 2005, at 1209; Ralf Michaels, 2007a.

enforce.[478] As a result, while the private threat and execution of sanctions is strictly limited by public law as the domain of the state, the means of violence and coercion in the private sphere are assigned to fields such as criminal or tort law. Coercion within private law (contract, property, corporate etc) is only indirectly acknowledged as 'economic power' in the form of strike, boycott, discrimination, and other forms of social exclusion, but subjected to strict qualifications regarding their legality. That such a list is anything but complete is, of course, old news.[479]

In Table 1 below, we try to capture this intricate combination of characteristics of public and private law, admittedly by somewhat ironically maintaining the coordinative/regulatory distinction and applying it to public and private law. With that irony in mind, we observe that regulatory issues have traditionally been associated with the state, whereas co-ordinative issues have been associated with private ordering. While state private law is thus seen as limited to the provision of a 'public framework for private ordering', public law is understood as the constitutive legal order, consistent of individual and institutional guarantees. The table thus depicts how a traditional distinction of public and private law contrasts with the overlapping and mutually interpenetrating spheres of public-private interaction, which are marked by a combination of both co-ordinative and regulatory functions.

To be sure, the challenge in a table such as the one provided here consists inadequately if at all depicting the degree to which the purported public/private divide has in fact always been contested and blurred in manifold ways, already under the paradigm of the sovereign nation-state. In alluding to spheres of societal activity the separation between which could be captured by horizontally and vertically dividing lines, the table betrays the complex reality of society. As discussed above, the categorical distinctions between the different boxes both verbalise *and* silence the different legacies of the

Table 1: The Nation-State and the Public/Private Divide

(Issue Area) Substantive / Procedural (Regulator)	Public: Regulation	Private: Coordination
Public: State	Public Law	Private Law
Private: Society	Self-Regulation	Private Ordering

[478] For an introduction, see Alan Redfern and Martin Hunter, 2004; see also Emmanuel Gaillard and John Savage, 1999, paras 1601–607.

[479] OW Holmes J, dissenting in *Vegelahn v Gunter*, 167 Mass 92, 104 (1896).

interests and institutions that have over time been associated with state and society, public and private.

We use this table to capture the different orientations associated with public and private law in the nation-state legal order paradigm. Against this—admittedly, exaggerated—depiction, we hope to adequately address the challenge in understanding the nature of law-making in the transnational realm. As noted already in the introductory chapter and as we will develop in much more detail below, our fundamental premise in conceptualising transnational legal theory is an understanding of 'transnational' as a distinctly methodological orientation. Instead of trying to define the transnational arena as a sphere, territorially different from that of the nation-state, implying issues of jurisdiction, conflict of laws and 'extensions' of domestic law into the non-domestic arena, transnational law is for us, above all, a methodological challenge to rethink the hitherto made experiences with law, legal theory, legal sociology and legal doctrine with regard to relations and human activities that surpass the historically grown and institutionally evolved embeddedness of nation-states. Although we are inescapably bound to recognise and approach questions of legitimacy and redistribution in an 'era of globalisation' based on our experience with the state,[480] the transnational structure of the emerging regulatory order demands a distinct, methodologically critical approach. Such an approach is characterised by a conscious revisiting of known concepts and instruments with regard to their adequacy in the transnational realm. Such a mode of inquiry entails a careful drawing on, and a combining of, concepts and instruments, without simply assuming that their practical utility alone could offer a meaningful assessment of their adequacy.

As had become clear from the early legal sociologist work and, later, from legal pluralism and 'law & society' scholarship, the association of law with the state had at best been a historical contingency, not a definite condition. Central to those endeavours, and to ours, is an analytical-critical orientation that forces us to keep this contingency in mind while pushing us not to forego the learned lessons from the experiences made over time. The challenging combination then of an approach towards the study of law's evolution and embeddedness through a sociological lens on the one hand and the idea that law is merely an argumentative pattern, operating through a central distinction (legal/illegal), on the other, seems to us to make for a most promising starting point from which to begin thinking about a transnational legal theory. As we pass through a sociologically informed reading of the 'transformation' of (domestic) law (as we

[480] Ralf Michaels and Nils Jansen, 2007, 888; Peer Zumbansen, 2000b [Regulatory Patterns of the Modern Welfare State. Learning Experiences between State, Society and Contract]; Peer Zumbansen, 2003c; Peer Zumbansen, 2007c.

knew it) towards the battle over the prospects of law in the 'post-national constellation' (Habermas), we are bound to revisit and relive the long-winding and inseparably intertwined affirmations and contestations of law's formal and functional characteristics. Because *the transnational* is as much a semantic artifice as was previously the *market* or the *state*, when assessing their nature on a legal-sociological basis, we are bound to rediscover similarly unwinding ideological battles over territory and normative stakes when assessing instances of institutional and normative spatialisation.[481] This ties questions—such as whether the transnational marks the liberation of private ordering from welfarist intervention or whether it merely provides for a most sobering perspective on the brutal dynamics of inclusion and exclusion among global human society[482] and the need to critically revisit state-oriented classifications of origins and reasons of migration[483]—back to long-standing assertions of market democracy and 'economic justice',[484] the welfare state[485] and citizenship.[486] Certainly, the attributes of co-ordinative or regulatory orientations of law can only provide for limited guidance back to these contestations.

As already noted with regard to 'economic law', scholars have long been underlining the intertwined and inseparable nature of both co-ordinative and regulatory functions of law:[487] though norms themselves may be enforced through private litigation, their substantive orientation encompasses 'public' values such as free competition, commutative justice or consumer protection, expressed for example in punitive damages awards or in class action suits.[488] Similarly, the procedural dimension of the state, understood to be towering over an otherwise unruly society consisting of self-oriented individuals, has seen an important qualification in the concept of the 'cooperative state'.[489] This and similar depictions testify to a growing

[481] Saskia Sassen, 2006, 1, speaking of an 'epochal transformation'. See also the succinct depiction by Neil Walker, 2010: 'State law, including the frame of state constitutional law, is increasingly rivalled by law otherwise spatially extended, including sub-state law, regional supranational law, transnational domain-specific private ordering, hybrid public-private ordering and, increasingly, new forms of global legal regimes that neither claim universality nor obviously emanate from nor respect the aggregate sovereign will.' (Ms., 33–34)

[482] Marcelo Neves, 2007; Hauke Brunkhorst, 2003, 113, 123: 'The exclusion of a large part of the global population from access to money, knowledge, power, opportunities for legal redress, and so forth is far more dramatic than Marx's impressive analysis of the existence within civil society of a class of excluded persons; this class was at least still included'.

[483] See Seyla Benhabib, 2004, 71–128.

[484] Above all: Crawford Brough Macpherson, 1987.

[485] Gosta Esping-Anderson, 1990; Paul Pierson, 2001.

[486] Mike Wilkinson, 2002; Catherine Dauvergne, 2008.

[487] For the German term '*Wirtschaftsrecht*' see Rudolf Wiethölter, 1972b, and Rudolf Wiethölter, 1986b; see also Dan Wielsch, 2001; Marc Amstutz, 2002.

[488] See Paul D Carrington, 2004, who observes that 'the distinction between public and private law is in America seldom noticed', at 1413, 1416. For comparable developments in German and European private law, see Gerhart Wagner, 2006, 352.

[489] Stephan Hobe, 1998.

recognition that the modern state is not unilaterally intervening in societal affairs from an elevated position, but must instead be conceived as just one player among others. The state as 'moderator', conceived in contrast to the 'interventionist' and regulatory state of the early twentieth century,[490] has in the last decades come to capture the ways in which the state oversees, indirectly steers and catalyses the relevant forces of societal self-regulation by post-interventionist or, 'post-instrumental' means.[491] This depiction, that suggested a notion, frequently commented upon and critiqued, of 'retreat' of the state and a weakening of its regulatory hand,[492] found an early, critical,[493] expression in the concept of 'reflexive law'.[494] Parallel to these advances in legal theory, administrative law scholarship was actively engaged in the development of concepts such as 'new public management' and 'new governance',[495] which made a fast career in capturing the important rise of public-private-partnerships, 'regulated self-regulation',[496] and 'co-regulation' between state, industry, and civil society, mirroring the changing approaches to understanding the relation between state and society.[497] Among the many examples in the area of health care contractualisation and urban infrastructure privatisation such as waste disposal and facilities, one of the most prominent instances of the transformation of public services delivery has been the liberalisation of telecommunications and postal services, that emerged as an impressive example of privatisation and aggressive globalisation from the 1980s onwards.[498]

The level of contestation accompanying such large-scale transformations of formerly nationally embedded infrastructure services testifies to the vivacity of the concerns triggered by these developments. With a global market for the acquisition and privatisation of large-scale infrastructures long in the making,[499] assessments are equally of domestic, comparative and transnational origin.[500] Their multifaceted nature results from the particular constellation in which such developments are perceived.

490 Michael Stolleis, 1989; Orly Lobel, 2004.

491 Gunther Teubner, 1986a; for an early critique, see Peter Nahamowitz, 1985, and Erhard Blankenburg, 1984.

492 For an excellent discussion, see Carol Harlow, 2009.

493 For an assessment of the development of reflexive law, see Peer Zumbansen, 2008a, and Peer Zumbansen, 2009a.

494 Gunther Teubner, 1983; Gunther Teubner, 1993, 64–99; Gralf-Peter Calliess, 1999; Gralf-Peter Calliess, 2002; Peer Zumbansen, 2000b.

495 Lester M Salamon, 2001.

496 See Martin Eifert, 2001, and Martin Eifert, 2006.

497 Wolfgang Schulz and Thorsten Held, 2001; Philippe Moreau Defarges, 2008.

498 Schulz and Held, 2001, 101; Martin Eifert, 1998; an excellent comparative perspective is provided by Viktor Mayer-Schönberger, 2002.

499 See, eg Graeme Guthrie, 2006; Antonio Estache, 2004; see also the overview available at: rru.worldbank.org/Privatization/ (visited 5 October 2009).

500 Harvey Feigenbaum, Jeffrey Henig and Chris Hamnett, 1999; Gregor Richter, 2002.

Understood, by some, as 'consequences of globalisation'[501] that victimise sovereign nation-states, while others understand globalisation as processes that are ultimately driven by domestic policy choices,[502] the fundamental architectonic changes in the national infrastructures in both developed and developing countries have been prompting a long and heated debate over the role and relevance of the state. These changes of domestic political economies are complemented by an almost overwhelming emergence and rapid transformation of governance structures on the transnational level. In the absence of a hierarchically ordered, embedded system of world government that would in any way resemble the political institutional architecture of the nation-state, the 'new world order' (Slaughter) is a beast of a very special political nature[503] and continues to raise yet-to-be-answered questions regarding legitimacy, accountability and participation, something that has been placed at the centre of the fast-growing 'global administrative law' scholarship in recent years. What still remains painfully at the top of the already ambitious research agenda in this area is the question of how to bring insights from national regulatory systems together with the administrative governance conundra on the transnational level. Can privatisation experiences in nation-states with a rich constitutional and administrative history be adequately exploited in order to understand the challenges arising from the interaction among different non-governmental organisations, private standardisation bodies and supra-national political bodies? What lessons can be learned from contestations of the public/private divide in national societies with highly developed civil societal contestation cultures for a much-needed understanding of the plight of the 'losers of globalisation'?

The non-availability of new, unused, fresh concepts to describe the emerging global world in order to better understand it lies at the basis of why our analytical toolkit is disturbingly both inadequate and unavoidable. This situation has been much depicted with regard to the ambiguous nature of a *global public sphere*[504]—representable as a world consumer society or a border-crossing political grass-roots movement. Political philosophers like Regina Kreide observe the following: 'The long-neglected and extremely controversial question regarding the legitimacy of transnational governing institutions emerges more pressing than ever. What normative demands must transnational governance comply with? And when is transnational governance legitimate?'[505] This line of questioning goes to the heart of the contemporary globalisation-governance-legitimacy nexus, as it underlines

[501] Martin Wolf, 2004; Jagdish Bhagwati, 2004.
[502] Saskia Sassen, 2000; Saskia Sassen, 2003; Alfred C Aman Jr, 2004.
[503] See Samuel P Huntington, 1973.
[504] See, eg Mary Kaldor, 2003.
[505] Regina Kreide, 2009, 19.

the urgency of addressing the political challenge raised by the mutually complementing processes of breath-taking institutional growth of both highly formalised and loosely-structured organisations and movements, on the one hand, and the multipolar attempts of 'juridification', on the other. The much noted, yet cautiously assessed absence of world government,[506] has been at the centre of an extremely vivid discussion between political scientists, philosophers, legal scholars and sociologists for many years now: what makes these deliberations so poignant for a legal inquiry such as ours is the wealth of both critical and constructive engagements with the emerging institutional and normative structures on the global level. What current work on global governance contributes to a legal theoretical project on transnational legal theory is to provide for manifold bridges between the philosophical, sociological and ethical debates that have been surrounding transformations of political structures in the nation-state and those we are in the process of observing and assessing today.[507] Central here is the recognition that the problem of the public/private divide returns in the general context of international and transnational law and 'global governance' and that it must be assessed, on the one hand, using the interdisciplinary toolkit that scholars have been assembling over many years of assessing the transformation of the nation-state, but—on the other—by complementing these tools with the emerging insights from both doctrinal and methodological work on the emerging global governance structures. It is against this background that the use of the term 'governance' to depict and identify the different nature of political structures on the global level can only be understood as a starting point, not as a conclusive result.[508]

While the preceding observations can be read to imply a certain impossibility of upholding the distinction between the *substantive* and *procedural* dimensions of law, its continued application is warranted, if only for the reason that it helps us to order the available contributions to the ongoing analysis of the transformation of political institutions and of law on the global level. Complementing, thus, the *substantive* line of inquiry into the nature and orientation of the norms governing transnational activities, on the *procedural* side we are concerned with the institutional dimension of the emerging forms of law-making. Centrally, we find a continuing and, by any measure, dramatic proliferation of norm-entrepreneurs, in other words of producers of guiding rules and in many cases binding norms. The importance of this development not only lies in the overlapping of

[506] Andrew Hurrell, 2007; see Andrew Moravcsik, 2004; Allen Buchanan and Robert O Keohane, 2006.

[507] See, eg the contributions to Benjamin Herborth and Peter Niesen, 2007.

[508] See the contributions to Ernst-Otto Czempiel and James N Rosenau, 1992, and to Meghnad Desai and Paul Redfern, 1995; very instructive: Alfred C Aman Jr, 2001, and Martin Shapiro, 2000; a relatively recent survey of the literature is provided by Renate Mayntz, 2006.

continued pressure exercised by non-state actors to participate in and to influence existing law-making processes institutionalised under Public International Law,[509] but also in the growing relevance of non-state actors as autonomous authors of globally binding rules.[510] As often noted, each single one of these developments constitutes formidable challenges to the state orientation prevalent in Public *Internation*al Law and the legal centralist's conception of the state as a monopolist in the provision of law.[511] The vivid discussions in Public International Law, be it with regard to the field's driving methodologies,[512] achievements[513] or to International Law's connections and overlappings with other fields such as International Relations,[514] Economics,[515] or Ethics[516] testify to a lively engagement with contemporary governance challenges right across the whole discipline.[517] Mirroring the soberingly persuasive contention of the 'transnational as market', scholars interested in an economistic reading of International Law seem to have little trepidation in applying economic order models to map the future landscape of a globalised world: as we have alluded to before, the idea of 'regulatory competition' has thus considerably less difficulty in addressing the multiplication of norm producers as they are perceived to be engaging in an eventually extremely beneficial struggle over the best rules.[518]

What characterises these current inquiries into the prospects of a global legal order is, at best, a genuine multidisciplinary attempt at dissecting the different conceptual elements that have traditionally been understood to amount to a coherent whole.[519] Yet, the crucial difference between the political economy/legal theory debates that accompanied the 'coming of the post-industrial society' (Bell) or of the contestation of the welfare state[520] and those concerned with 'global governance' is the unanswered, often

[509] See, eg Stephan Hobe, 2002, and Karsten Nowrot, 1999.

[510] Nils Brunsson and Bengt Jacobsson, 2000; Oren Perez, 2003.

[511] See, eg the contributions to Neil Walker, 2003b.

[512] See the intriguing comment by Martti Koskenniemi, 1999.

[513] See, eg the essays to the 100th volume of the *American Journal of International Law*, as well as the Special Issues celebrating the 20th Anniversary of the *European Journal of International Law*.

[514] See the excellent depiction by Oona A Hathaway and Ariel N Lavinbuk, 2006.

[515] Jack Goldsmith and Eric Posner, 2005; Andrew T Guzman, 2008.

[516] See, eg Thomas Pogge, 2008.

[517] See in this respect the important work around the notion of the 'disaggregated state' by Anne-Marie Slaughter, who has been exploring the way that private economic and civil society actors have entered the international law arena and started to actively engage in the production of norms and their implementation by alternative modes of governance: Anne-Marie Slaughter, 2002; Anne-Marie Slaughter, 2004a, Anne-Marie Slaughter, 2004b, 12–13.

[518] See, eg Charles M Tiebout, 1956, Konstantine G Gatsios and Peter H Holmes, 1998, and Wolfgang Kerber, 2005.

[519] See the excellent account by Martti Koskenniemi, 2002a, and the recent assessment in Martti Koskenniemi, 2007.

[520] Peer Zumbansen, 2008a, with references.

avoided question of whether law has any role whatsoever to play in the post-national constellation.

B. The Hybrid Character of Transnational Law Regimes

Looking through a transnational lens allows, even forces, us to struggle with the conceptual and semantic artefacts developed in the context of the 'transformation of the nation-state' amidst our attempts to make sense of new actors and new norms on the transnational level.[521] On that basis, the transformation of the state and the challenge of government through numerous assertions of governance, 'new governance' and legal pluralism have important consequences for the understanding of the norms that we see being created from within this emerging global sphere of norm-entrepreneurs. Unsurprisingly, the literature addressing the nature of norms created by sub-state actors and private parties continues to proliferate and has in recent years been differentiating across various increasingly specialised fields. This development that prompts the question as to whether we have even begun to think about a comprehensive theory that would aim to bring together a study of the general direction of an emerging global order with an assessment of the mushrooming highly specialised, functional areas and processes of regulation.[522]

Legal science has its troubles in dealing with the multipolar sources of norms in the domestic arena and these are only exacerbated in the transnational arena. Underscoring their ambiguous status in terms of traditional public international law, which holds the state to be the relevant creator of binding norms, non-state norms are often uncomfortably depicted or dismissed as 'soft law', as mere guidelines or recommendations.[523] The inseparable connection between the substantive and procedural dimensions of (International) law is powerfully underscored in the way that assessments of the legal status and competence of new global actors as 'private law makers'[524] are tightly interwoven with a critique of the quality of the

[521] Peer Zumbansen, 2001a; Joseph HH Weiler, 2004.

[522] For intriguing studies of the EU in this regard, see the contributions to Bruno De Witte, Dominik Hanf and Ellen Vos, 2001.

[523] Jose E Alvarez, 2006, 328–29: 'irrespective of their formally nonbinding status on non-parties, these manifestations of soft law cannot be ignored by international lawyers and, at the very least, form a subsidiary source of international obligation as much as any "judicial opinion" identified in Article 38 of the ICJ's Statute.' See also Christine Chinkin, 1989, and the contributions to John J Kirton and Michael J Trebilcock, 2004.

[524] See, for labour law, Roger Blanpain and Michele Colucci, 2004; Adelle Blackett, 2004; for corporate law: Douglas M Branson, 2000; Peer Zumbansen, 2002b; for commercial arbitration: Filip De Ly, 2001; for contract law: Lisa Bernstein, 1992; for product safety law: Harm Schepel, 2005; for environmental law: Erroll Meidinger, 2006.

norms they produce,[525] the currently reviving debate over customary law offering a troubling illustration of how much still is contested here.[526]

It is against this background of a changing regulatory landscape both at the international and at the domestic level that we must reconceive the scope and nature of norms that govern transnational societal activity. Our examples of consumer contracts and corporate governance codes show a complex interplay between official and unofficial norm-making processes. As far as we wish to refute the contention that only the state can be understood as the author of law, we ascertain the distinctly regulatory quality of norms produced by a growing number of private norm-entrepreneurs such as standardisation bodies, associations and corporations. At the same time, we are not interested in pursuing the concept of such normative orders as 'autonomous', as this has been suggested, for example, in the field of commercial arbitration and the law merchant.[527] As noted during our discussion of *lex mercatoria* above, such an approach would cut off significant learning opportunities regarding the connection between the emergence of non-state law-makers and the increasingly differentiated recognition by mainstream law of such sources of binding norms.[528] A careful study of these connections opens important perspectives on the interplay between different sources of norm-creation, including a better understanding of how the emergence of 'privately made law' can be both a precursor to official law-making and a constituted and delegated process. Both phenomena must be subjected to a comprehensive assessment, including a political critique.[529] As a consequence, while the legal nature of these norms continues to be questioned,[530] the irrepressibly[531] ubiquitous existence of 'official' and 'unofficial', 'hard' and 'soft' norms in domestic and transnational relations speaks to the need of adopting a sociologically and theoretically informed perspective rather than dismissing such developments as contrary to the perception of the state as exclusive author of law. Whereas such dismissals frequently result from an unjustified overstatement of the allegedly autonomous nature of such norms, prompting in return a defence that

[525] Christine Chinkin, 1989 speaks of a 'misleading simplification', 850.

[526] Jack Goldsmith and Eric Posner, 1999; Jack Goldsmith and Eric Posner, 2001; Jack Goldsmith and Eric Posner, 2005; in contrast: Anne van Aaken, 2006; Detlev F Vagts, 2004; Paul Schiff Berman, 2006; see below, ch 5 III of this book, for a discussion of this literature.

[527] See, eg Gunther Teubner, 1997b; Gunther Teubner, 1997c; see also the discussion of *lex mercatoria*, above, ch 2 I of this book.

[528] See the excellent discussion in Johannes Köndgen, 2006.

[529] For an excellent political science critique of the different levels of corporate law making in the United States and in Germany, see the work by John Cioffi: John W Cioffi, 2000b; John W Cioffi, 2006, and his monograph: John W Cioffi, 2010 (ms on file with authors).

[530] See the intriguing, recent observations by Ralf Michaels and Nils Jansen, 2007, who provide a valuable overview of the different positions in the 'is it law?' debate and suggest that the greatest problems in this area are of semantic nature.

[531] Janet Koven Levit, 2008, 57.

reasserts the relevance of the state to legitimise or to delegitimise any form of law-making, the more promising approach to the study of this phase of legal pluralism is, in our view, to take the unresolved role of the state in the production of these norms as a starting point, not as a given. On that basis, then, it is possible to critically engage with the déja vu of seeing concerns regarding distributional consequences,[532] political participation[533] and enforcement[534] to be at the centre of the contested transnational order.

Building on our discussion of both coordinative/regulatory and substantive/procedural orientations of law, we now want to capture the resulting, hybrid nature of norm-creation—in the transnational arena—in the concept of *transnational law regimes* (Table 2, below). These are characterised by a combination and, in fact, inseparability of co-ordinative ('private') and regulatory ('public') dimensions in the *substantive* dimension of law. In the *procedural* dimension of law, in turn, we observe a combination (inseparability) of 'private' (industry) and 'public' (states) as well as civil society actors involved in regulatory efforts of making and implementing what we call *transnational private law*. The hybrid nature of the regime that is captured on the substantive plane by the concept of *economic law* is assumed

Table 2: Transnational Law Regimes

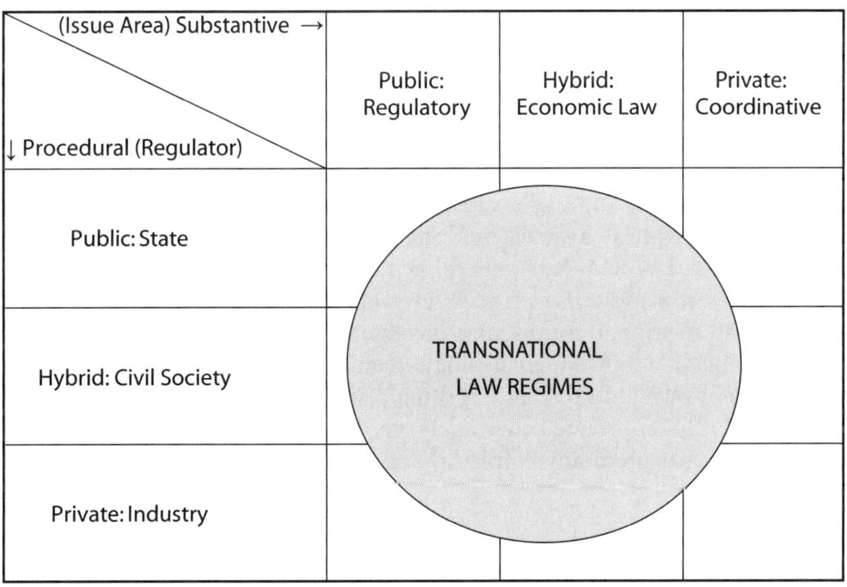

532 Daniela Caruso, 2006.

533 Alfred C Aman Jr, 2001; BS Chimni, 2005.

534 See, eg Samuel P Baumgartner, 2003; in the area of corporate law: Eddy Wymeersch, 2005.

by *civil society* on the procedural plane. Likely to prompt resistance and critique, we nevertheless want to suggest using the term 'transnational *law* regimes' in an attempt to point to their hybrid character, substantively and procedurally, between or beyond the public/private divide, and fundamentally based on a methodological concept of transnational law.

C. The Governance Mode of Transnational Law Regimes

But how exactly are we to understand the existence and operation of transnational law regimes? In the literature on 'law and globalisation' as well as 'law and social norms' we often find the use of the term 'private regime',[535] or even 'private legal system'.[536] The assumption here is that to the degree that the public legal system of a nation-state can be characterised by the three powers of *legislating, adjudicating, and enforcing norms* in a territorially limited jurisdiction, a transnational law regime should equally be able to integrate private governance mechanisms, which perform these three functions, into one effective regime. It is precisely this contention of the purely private nature of such regimes, however, which in our opinion hinders progress in the debate over transnational law. The purported autonomous character of the New Law Merchant, for instance, is often denied by critics of this concept on the basis that the state is lending its power to enforce to arbitral awards under the 1958 New York Convention on the Recognition and Enforcement of Foreign Arbitral Awards. Thus, arbitration for many is merely an example of the traditional technique of delegation of state power to private entities, while others contend that state enforcement is not crucial to the efficacy of arbitration, since it relies predominantly on social sanctions such as reputation and exclusion.[537] Equally it is often contended that international arbitral awards predominantly do apply domestic contract law as opposed to non-state general principles of law.[538] Moreover, where parties to international contracts rely on mechanisms of private ordering such as relational contracting or reputation instead of State contract enforcement to stabilise their business relationship,[539] the proposition that this implies a retreat of the State is often dismissed, because contract parties always did rely on private ordering as well in domestic trade.[540] As a result it seems that despite many empirical surveys on contractual governance in

[535] Gillian K Hadfield, 2001, speaks of 'private legal regimes'; Gunther Teubner, 2004b, speaks of 'private governance regimes'.
[536] Lisa Bernstein, 2001, 1725.
[537] For an empirical evaluation see William Lazonick, 2007, 61 with references to both positions.
[538] For an empirical survey see Fabian Sosa, 2009, 107.
[539] For an empirical survey see Thomas Dietz and Holger Nieswandt, 2009, 87.
[540] See Volkmar Gessner, 2009.

international commerce the question of the existence of a transnational law is simply a question of belief rather than proof: some scholars *want* to see self-regulation and privatisation everywhere, while others simply *want* to see the State still being in control, and both are somehow right.

So how could we advance the discussion? Taking transnational commercial law as an example, we propose—as indicated above—that the problem lies in the inappropriateness of sticking to traditional nineteenth-century concepts like the public/private-divide when analysing the institutional foundations of an emerging sphere of transnational governance. In the following we suggest to overcome the 'black or white'-style of argumentation by *decomposing* the two traditional *modes* of governing business relations, ie public governance through state private law vs. private ordering through self-help or industry self-regulation, into their components. While there are a variety of valuable suggestions to map the governance of business relations, we find the analysis and terminology of Oliver Williamson's 'economics of governance' to be particularly helpful as a starting point, and shall discuss New Institutional Economics' approaches in order to develop a map of governance of cross-border economic exchange which we—drawing on many findings of other authors as well—find to consist of a total of 12 *generic governance mechanisms* (below (i)). In a second step we propose that this map of governance mechanisms is used as a toolbox from which tailor-made solutions for the governance of cross-border commerce are formed, which by virtue of the pragmatism with which public and private elements are *recombined* often are innovative. In an evolutionary process of trial and error those solutions which turn out to be workable are selected and stabilised over time, a process that leads to the emergence of functionally specialised transnational law regimes. Where public or private elements long established within the domestic realm are employed by such transnational law regimes, we argue, they are *disembedded* from their national origin and by their transplantation into the transnational context as well as their recombination with other governance mechanisms receive the status of a *legal mutation*. It is precisely this distinct quality of transnational governance that from a methodological point of view justifies the use of the term transnational private law (below (ii)).

(i) Mapping Economic Governance

The building blocks of transnational law regimes can only be conceived from an interdisciplinary perspective: drawing on the insights gained in our previous discussion of legal pluralism, we will now focus on the 'economics of governance'[541] as part of New Institutional Economics.

[541] This is the case of Williamson's 'transaction cost economics': see Oliver Williamson, 1985, 15.

> The economics of governance is an effort to implement the 'study of good order and workable arrangements', where good order includes both spontaneous order in the market ... and intentional order ... The object is to work out the efficiency logic for managing transactions by alternative modes of governance—principally spot markets, various long term contracts (hybrids), and hierarchies.[542]

Williamson starts his analysis with the classical distinction between markets and hierarchies (firms).[543] An economic actor in need of a product (goods or services) faces the alternatives of 'to make or buy'.[544] Economic actors employ governance mechanisms in order to cope with the intrinsic *uncertainty* involved in co-operation, which is founded in *ex ante* bounded rationality, ie contracting parties' inability to draft 'complete contracts', as well as *ex post* opportunism, ie contracting parties' ability to annihilate part of the mutual gain from co-operation in order to increase their individual share in it.[545] The relevant criteria for choosing a governance mode for a specific transaction under conditions of such uncertainty are *frequency* (occasional/recurrent) from the point of view of the buyer and *asset specificity* with regard to necessary investments made by suppliers (non-specific/mixed/idiosyncratic).[546] Given that the state has the monopoly to define property rights and to enforce contracts (lawfulness),[547] *market governance* is the main governance structure for non-specific transactions, eg the purchase of standard equipment or material. Here, actors mainly rely on market alternatives (prospective exit) and legal rules and litigation (retrospective voice) to protect against opportunism, since the transaction costs of employing additional private governance mechanisms do not pay off. *Unified governance* by means of vertical integration is the most favourable governance mechanism for recurrent transactions with idiosyncratic investment characteristics, eg the site-specific transfer of an intermediate product across successive stages. If in intra-firm trade a problem arises, access to courts is denied (forbearance) and parties—which in this case are not legally distinct persons, but business units of the firm—must resolve their disputes internally by means of hierarchy. The firm, thus, becomes its own court of ultimate appeal.[548]

Private governance comes into focus for transactions with mixed investment characteristics, eg the purchase of customised equipment or

[542] Oliver E Williamson, 2005.

[543] Ronald Coase, 1937; Oliver E Williamson, 1981, 1539.

[544] For the following see Oliver Williamson, 1985, 68; Oliver E Williamson, 1996, 66; Oliver E Williamson, 2005, 3, 11.

[545] Oliver E Williamson, 1996, 9; for a critical stance regarding the distinction between complete and incomplete contracts, see Anna Grandori, 2007, and William W Bratton and Joseph A McCahery, 2001.

[546] Oliver Williamson, 1985, 72–79.

[547] Oliver E Williamson, 2005.

[548] Williamson, 2005, 9–10.

material, as well as for occasional transactions with idiosyncratic investment characteristics, as in the case of the construction of a plant. Here, specialised investments are exposed by the supplier, a fact which poses additional contractual hazards such as premature contract cancellation. The implied risks will either be priced out by the supplier, or the buyer has to offer credible commitments as a relief. Such credible commitments are characteristic for the *hybrid governance*, which best fits long-term relational contracts. Since switching costs rise due to relation-specific investments, the exit option which is characteristic for market governance is of little value. In addition to reliance on the state legal system, contract parties therefore employ mechanisms of private ordering to support the exchange. These may be either bilateral or trilateral. In case of *bilateral governance mechanisms* the immediate parties to an exchange are actively involved in the provision of order, eg by posting hostages (such as entry fees or a deposit), engaging in reciprocal trade, or otherwise embedding the transaction into a self-enforcing arrangement, where the potential benefits of opportunism with regard to a single transaction have to be set off against the disadvantages of a disruption of the long-term business relationship (exit). In the case of *trilateral governance mechanisms* trusted third parties are involved in the provision of private order, eg an escrow agent, a bank issuing a letter of credit, or arbitration institutions offering alternative dispute resolution services.[549]

Because added bureaucratic costs and lower incentive intensity accrue upon taking a transaction out of the market, Williamson concludes that vertical integration is usefully thought of as the governance mode of last resort: 'try markets, try hybrids, and have recourse to the firm only when all else fails'.[550] However, Williamson holds that while the

> main contractual action ... takes places between the parties in the context of private ordering, and court ordering appears late, if at all ... each generic mode of governance (market, hybrid, hierarchy) is supported by and in significant ways is defined by a distinctive form of contract law.[551]

This is obvious for market governance, which relies on state contract law and contract enforcement, and for hierarchy, which relies on state corporate law and property rights enforcement. It is less obvious for hybrids, which, as in the case of long-term contracts, rely on state contract law, but at the same time additional private governance is crucial. Thus, the economics of

549 For the distinction of bilateral and trilateral governance see Oliver Williamson, 1985, 72–77. With special attention to bilateral governance mechanisms see Oliver E Williamson, 1983.

550 Oliver E Williamson, 2005, 12.

551 Oliver Williamson, 1985, 10.

governance is a theory of *private ordering in the shadow of law*, assuming that the state has created and enforces efficacious rules of law.[552]

Insisting on his premise that even in well-developed countries the state's efforts to protect property rights and to enforce contracts are inherently limited, a fact inviting the use of private ordering to infuse order, Williamson acknowledges that circumstances where the state law is 'very costly, slow, unreliable, corrupt, weak, or simply absent'[553] pose *additional* private ordering challenges.[554] Drawing on a vast array of empirical studies, Avinash Dixit recently contributed comprehensive game theoretical analysis to such challenges.[555] Williamson in fact suggests that with regard to his simple scheme of contractual governance choice (*'try markets, try hybrids, and have recourse to the firm only when all else fails'*), in an institutional environment where the government is unable or unwilling to provide adequate protection of property rights and enforcement of contracts, one could substitute the main explaining variable of asset specificity (ie exposure of specialised supplier investments) with property rights (and one should add contract enforcement) hazards with equivalent results.[556]

Thus, under conditions of increasing property rights and contract enforcement hazards (lawlessness) there are three options for the organisation of a non-specific transaction (purchase of standard equipment or material), which in an OECD-country (lawfulness) would be conducted on the unassisted market: (1) the hazards remain unrelieved and the implied risks will be priced out; (2) private governance mechanisms are employed in order to add institutional support through credible commitments (hybrids); and (3) hierarchy is induced by the creation of uniform ownership or other kinds of equity relations (corporate groups, joint ventures, strategic partnerships, etc).[557]

A situation of *lawlessness* is not only pervasive in developing countries and transition economies, but also, for reasons of a lack of state co-operation through multilateral treaties, in *global cross-border trade*. Here, we are confronted with a situation where even parties situated in OECD-countries with an internally well-functioning legal system face added institutional uncertainties resulting from a number of questions: (a) which court will decide (jurisdiction to adjudicate)? (b) which law applies (jurisdiction to

552 See the notion of 'lawfulness' in Oliver E Williamson, 2005, 1–2; see also Avinash K Dixit, 2004, 25.

553 Avinash K Dixit, 2004, 3.

554 Oliver E Williamson, 2005, 14.

555 Avinash K Dixit, 2004.

556 Oliver E Williamson, 2005, 15, fn 24.

557 Barak D Richman, 2004, 2349, rightly observes that it is 'one of the most glaring problems of the legal-centric private ordering literature' to focus on the alternative of public versus private ordering (p 2338) only, while the alternative of firm versus market (p 2348) should be included in the analysis in order to get the full picture. See Gralf-Peter Calliess and Jens Mertens, 2009.

prescribe)? and (c) will a judgment of a court situated in country *A* be recognised and enforced in country *B* (mutual recognition)[558]—the transaction cost economics' scheme introduced above, may provide a good explanation for a governance structure of global markets described as follows:

> Recent estimates suggest that there are about 65,000 TNCs (Transnational Corporations) today, with about 850,000 foreign affiliates across the globe ... (which) account for ... one-third of world exports. Finally, if we take into account the value of TNCs' non-equity relationships (eg international subcontracting, licensing, and contract manufacturers) they would account for even larger shares in the global aggregates mentioned above.[559]

The increasing importance of intra-firm trade within transnational corporate groups (*unified governance*) and of transnational business networks (*bilateral governance*) is one important institutional facet of economic globalisation.[560] However, these modes of transnational contractual governance work in the spirit of 'think global, act local' in that the employed mechanisms of private ordering are functional only in the shadow of national law. By this we mean that TNCs work on the assumption of efficacious state enforcement of the underlying equity and non-equity relationships, based on local contract and corporate laws enforced by local courts.[561]

The same holds true for many *trilateral governance* mechanisms employed by international commerce. One example is international commercial arbitration, the functionality of which depends on the local recognition and enforcement of arbitral awards under the 1958 New York Convention. Other examples of the involvement of trusted third parties in international commercial transactions are letters of credit, escrow services, and indirect import and export.[562] Each of these mechanisms works on the basis of nationalising (part of) the contractual relation for the immediate parties to a cross-border transaction by means of involving banks or merchants as intermediaries, which have specialised in international commerce, often on the basis of relational contracting (bilateral governance) with their foreign counterparts.[563] Thus, instead of supplier *S* contracting directly with buyer

[558] See Dieter Schmidtchen and Hans-Jürgen Schmidt-Trenz, 1990a; Manfred E Streit and Antje Mangels, 1996; see also Gralf-Peter Calliess, 2007; Giesela Rühl, 2008.

[559] UNCTAD, *World Investment Report 2002*, Overview, at 1, available at: www.unctad.org/en/docs/wir2002overview_en.pdf.

[560] See Dieter Schmidtchen and Hans-Jürgen Schmidt-Trenz, 1990b; John H Dunning and Sarianna M Lundan, 2008.

[561] See Gralf-Peter Calliess and Jens Mertens, 2009; in more detail Peter Muchlinski, 2007.

[562] See Dieter Schmidtchen and Hans-Jörg Schmidt-Trenz, 1991; for a more detailed presentation, see Hans-Jürgen Schmidt-Trenz, 1990.

[563] A very good account of the functioning of letters of credit work is provided by Janet Koven Levit, 2007b.

B across jurisdictional borders, in indirect export *S* sells domestically to exporter *E*, who has a self-enforcing long-term relationship with importer *I*, who in turn sells domestically to *B*. But note that the intended transfer of the institutional uncertainties implied in cross-border commerce to specialised third parties works on the assumption that the relations *S* to *E* and *I* to *B* take place under circumstances of lawfulness, ie state enforcement of sales contracts, letters of credit, and the like.[564]

In sum, the *additional* private ordering challenges resulting from the relative lawlessness implied in international commerce when compared to domestic transactions are tackled by employing bilateral as well as trilateral governance mechanisms to infuse order (hybrid governance) or by taking such transactions out of the market (unified governance), where all of these mechanisms in one way or the other take place in the shadow of state law.[565] A central result of our survey of the mechanisms of economic governance is that the embeddedness of transnational economic governance in domestic institutions of state contract enforcement and property rights protection is, generally speaking, undervalued.[566] However, as the intent of this section was to overcome the 'black or white' style of argumentation of the role of public and private institutions in the governance of cross-border commerce by decomposing these institutions into their components, we can—drawing on Williamson's terminology—identify 12 generic governance mechanisms employed by international commerce, an overview of which is given in Table 3 below.

In order to explain this table we should confess that although we draw on the terminology used by Williamson, the categorisation is inspired by a similar table presented by Ellickson, who in presenting his 'theory of norms'

Table 3: Public and Private Governance Mechanisms in International Commerce

Dimension / Regulator	Legislation	Adjudication	Enforcement
Public Trilateral	Parliamentary Act	Courts	Legal Sanctions
Private Trilateral	Social Norms	Arbitration	Social Sanctions
Private Bilateral	Relational Norms	Negotiation	Exit/Hostages
Private Unified	Corporate Norms	Board Decision	Hierarchy

[564] A fact that seems to be undervalued by Hans-Jürgen Schmidt-Trenz, 1990.

[565] Gillian Hadfield, 2009.

[566] Or more precisely, as Avinash K Dixit, 2004, 3, states: 'Thus conventional economic theory does not underestimate the importance of law; rather, the problem is that it takes the existence of a well-functioning institution of state law for granted'. This applies similarly for the legal debate.

develops a 'system of social control' which differentiates between five types of controllers that make rules and administer sanctions: first, second, and third party control, where the latter is split in the three subcategories of informal (reputation-based sanctions), organisational (exclusion), and governmental (legal system) third-party control.[567] However, where Ellickson is not specifically interested in economic governance, but more generally in order without law, we substituted his category of first-party control—meaning the self-control of an actor by personal ethics in relation to another actor—for the economically more relevant internal control of transactions within the hierarchy of the firm (unified governance). This category may be used as well to reflect the issues of corporate governance and corporate social responsibility, where a firm binds itself by means of a code of conduct in relation to actors outside the firm such as potential investors, consumers, or the general public.[568]

With reference to the third column of the table (enforcement mechanisms), the importance lies in the following: rather than drawing a simple line between public (legal) sanctions and private (non-legal) sanctions,[569] we suggest making a further distinction between internal sanctions administered within the hierarchy of a firm, second-party sanctions of one party of a business relation towards the other (which basically entails the termination of a (long-term) business relationship (exit), and—if hostages were provided—the commercial realisation of such securities): Finally, we distinguish social sanctions passed upon the norm offender by third parties, where such social sanction admittedly may be administered informally (reputation) or formally by an organisation such as a trade club or an exchange (exclusion).[570]

(ii) The Recombinant Governance Mode of Transnational Commercial Law

Having mapped the mechanisms employed in the governance of economic transactions, in a second step we intend to evaluate how these mechanisms are used in the practice of cross-border commerce in order to receive a better account of the role of public and private elements in transnational private law. As indicated above, we shall use the New Law Merchant as an example of *transnational market governance*, since it at least with regard to the dimensions of legislation (UNIDROIT Principles, and the like) and adjudication (ICC Court of Arbitration, and the like)

[567] See Robert C Ellickson, 1991, 123, with a table at 131.

[568] See ch 3 of this book for code of conduct based trustmarks in business-to-consumer relations, and ch 4 for corporate governance codes in firm-investor relations.

[569] As proposed, eg by Stephan Panther, 2000.

[570] See Ellickson, 1991, 131; in more detail David Charny, 1990.

falls into the category of private trilateral governance and, like the public contract law enforcement mechanisms, is intended to facilitate arms'-length transactions between legally independent actors as opposed to intra-firm trade.

As noted above, a private legal system which is able to assume the functions of a public legal system in enabling market governance, should bundle private governance mechanisms, which fulfill legislative, adjudicative, and enforcement functions into an effective and operational regime. Among these three functions, the enforcement mechanism is crucial for the contention that a private legal system operates autonomously from state law. Basically, there are three kinds of examples of non-state enforcement mechanisms which operate on the level of private trilateral governance as social sanctions. First, the *reputation mechanism*, which works best in close-knit groups and represents a key case of so-called informal social control. Secondly, the *exclusion mechanism*, which works best in organisations and constitutes formalised social control. Finally, there is the case of *private force*, or *coercion*, which works best in groupings such as the Mafia and is identified under the label of illegal social control.[571] The already mentioned empirical evidence regarding the ancient law merchant as well as from examples studied by Lisa Bernstein of modern trade clubs (eg, in the cotton industry) and specialised exchanges (eg, in the case of diamond traders) testifies to the degree that these groups have been successfully implementing effective and operational private legal systems.[572]

In the context of the institutional organisation of modern cross-border commerce, however, purely private legal systems in praxis are rare. Empirical studies, conducted in the field of global commerce, have revealed that outside business relations in traditional branches with centuries-old local or ethnic ties, there is no evidence of private legal systems. By contrast, in global commerce we can observe *tailor-made governance-cocktails*, which emerge from both a *pragmatic* combination and *innovative* recombination of the 12 governance mechanisms described above. It has been studied in this context, that international law firms play an important role in the strategic choice of different private and public mechanisms. Domestic or international commercial law no longer is perceived as a conclusive

[571] See the overview at Stephan Panther, 2000; the literature on social control is abundant: see David Charny, 1990; John McMillan and Christopher Woodruff, 2000; Curtis J Milhaupt and Mark D West, 2000a; Barak D Richman, 2004; Amitai Aviram, 2004; Neil Cunningham, 2008; a slightly different view is taken by Avinash K Dixit, 2004, 59 (focusing on informal, relation-based enforcement), and 107 (profit-motivated enforcement intermediaries).

[572] For medieval merchants see the important work by Avner Greif, 2006, bringing together more than a decade of research in this area; for contemporary examples see Lisa Bernstein, 1992, 115; Lisa Bernstein, 2001, 1724.

normative framework, but is selectively used as part of the tool-box from which workable solutions are created.[573]

In part, the absence of private legal systems in international commerce may be explained by the fact that state law still is effective, although not necessary in the field of contract law, but rather in the realm of criminal law, tort law, or antitrust laws, under which any operation of social control remains delicate, particularly where its administrators strive for true autonomy from the state. This is obvious for the category of illegal social control conducted by the Mafia,[574] which continues to be qualified and effectively de-legitimised as 'organised crime' and is observed as operational mainly under conditions where the state is very weak or even absent.[575] But it is true as well for forms of social control which are in principle legal, since the state heavily regulates non-legal sanctions and, hence, in effect often suppresses any potential competition to its traditional claim to be the supreme ruler of society: the operation of the reputation mechanisms, for instance, might be jeopardised by the fear of claims for damages or even prosecution for libel and slander under domestic defamation laws.[576] Moreover, the reputation mechanism is tantamount to a group boycott, which as a concerted refusal to deal may constitute an antitrust violation as well as the exclusion of a merchant from a trade club or exchange may constitute an illegal refusal to deal under the essential facilities doctrine.[577] Otherwise individual refusal to deal might be illegal under anti-discrimination laws or simply constitute a breach according to general contract law that provides for damages in case of unjustified cancellation of long-term contracts including memberships.[578]

Where non-legal sanctions such as the reputation and exclusion mechanisms are not suppressed by the threat of illegality under state law, however, it often remains unclear whether or not a legal regime, driven predominantly by private governance mechanisms, operates autonomously from

[573] See Gralf-Peter Calliess, Thomas Dietz, Wioletta Konradi, Holger Nieswandt and Fabian Sosa, 2007.

[574] Diego Gambetta, 1993.

[575] For an excellent discussion, see Curtis J Milhaupt and Mark D West, 2000a, 50: 'private and segmented enforcement of property rights can lead to the entrenchment of small-scale inefficient monopolies, high transaction costs, and a "tragedy of coercion" in which savings from the provision of collective services are dissipated in contests both among firms and between firms and the state'.

[576] Many branch organisations are reluctant to pertain so-called 'black lists' of opportunistic members, because they fear being hauled into court for defamation: see for the example of the software branch Thomas Dietz and Holger Nieswandt, 2009, 87, 94. The reason for this fear is that domestic tort law such as § 824 of the German BGB provides that the person who pertains a black list will bear the burden of proof for the truth of the circulated information on past performance or opportunistic behaviour of a merchant.

[577] Barak D Richman, 2009, 325, 340.

[578] See only Hartmut Oetker, 1994.

the state. This ambiguity relates to the fact that legal and non-legal norms and sanctions in these cases do not work in different directions, but often overlap and eventually support each other in bringing about order.[579] A good example is the New Law Merchant that with regard to the dimension of enforcement simultaneously operates on the basis of social and legal sanctions. This combination effectively contributes to the attractiveness of arbitration for international commerce in light of the absence of an equivalent instrument for international litigation, even if about 99 per cent of arbitral awards continue to be honoured without reliance on state enforcement, arguably for reputation reasons. In fact the 1958 New York Convention appears to have but little positive impact on international trade between member states.[580]

With regard to the dimension of *legislation*, reference is often made to the fact that the New Law Merchant is predominantly based on trade usages which are increasingly codified by private 'norm entrepreneurs' such as the International Chamber of Commerce, for example, by means of model contracts.[581] But reference to trade usages and model contract forms is foreseen as well in national commercial laws administered by state courts.[582] In addition, general principles of contract law are often referenced by arbitral tribunals, collected and formalised in the form of 'private codifications' such as the UNIDROIT Principles of International Commercial Contracts.[583] The latter, however, are explicitly intended to complement the 1980 UN Convention on the Sale of International Goods (CSIG) as a public international law instrument.[584] Thus, in practice we find a *mixture* of publicly and privately made norms for international commerce.[585]

To conclude our evaluation of the New Law Merchant as an example of a transnational law regime, what we find in the institutional organisation of modern cross border commerce is a regime that is characterised by an *institutional mix of public and private governance mechanisms*. Together, they contribute to the implementation of an effective order, which we try to depict in Table 4 below. The relative importance of the different governance mechanisms for the efficacy of that regime is indicated by white (low), light grey (middle), and dark grey (high). However, the individual

[579] See Stephan Panther, 2000.
[580] See Peter T Leeson, 2008.
[581] Peer Zumbansen and Maria Panezi, 2008, no 15.
[582] For a critical discussion, see Lisa Bernstein, 1996, on the one hand, and Stewart Macaulay, 2000, on the other.
[583] Michael Joachim Bonell, 1992; Michael Joachim Bonell, 2007.
[584] www.uncitral.org/uncitral/en/uncitral_texts/sale_goods/1980CISG.html (last visited 16 September 2009).
[585] Empirical evidence on the use of state and non-state legal norms in international commercial arbitration is given by Fabian Sosa, 2009; see also the data provided in Stefan Voigt, 2005.

Table 4: New Law Merchant: Recombinant Governance in a Transnational Law Regime

Dimension / Regulator	Legislation	Adjudication	Enforcement
Public	Parliamentary Act	Courts	Legal Sanctions
Private	Social Norms	Arbitration	Social Sanctions

elements employed by this regime, be they of domestic or international, public or private origin, in the process of their innovative recombination into a denationalised context are disembedded and, thus, fundamentally transformed, and it is exactly this transformation of the elements rather then their public or private origin that legitimates the use of the concept of transnational law regimes.

These findings make us cautious with regard to contentions of an alleged 'privatisation of commercial law', based on the fact that private judges administer private norms. Not only does the continued presence of the state in lending its monopoly on the legitimate use of force to such regimes[586] suggest a more differentiated view, but also the fact that the embeddedness of private ordering in a historically grown and continuously evolving regulatory landscape of co-ordinative/regulatory and substantive/procedural norm creators necessitates a less 'black or white' assessment. The institutional mix of public and private governance mechanisms in transnational law regimes is not adequately captured by an either-or model of private legislation/adjudication on the one hand and public enforcement on the other. Instead, in each of the three dimensions of legislating, adjudicating, and enforcement we can observe the recombination of public and private elements in innovative ways. The possible implications of the thus described *recombinant governance mode of transnational law regimes* cannot appropriately be described by conventional models of the interrelation of public law and private ordering in the nation-state, ie the concepts of incorporation, deference, or delegation.[587] This shall be developed further in the next section.

D. Soft Law, Hard Law, and Legitimacy

The preceding sections have provided a first glance into the extremely complex structure of norm-creation in the transnational arena, with

[586] Gillian K Hadfield, 2001, with many examples.
[587] Ralf Michaels, 2005, 1228–35.

important connections to the transformation of the regulatory landscape of the nation-state. At the same time, our inquiry up to this point has been repeatedly returning to the distinctly methodological challenge in dealing with the proliferation of actors and norms. Beyond a sociological discovery and categorisation of this development, the challenge is methodological as the nature and function of these actors and the norms they produce or are subjected to (continue to) radically question many of the guiding distinctions central to legal thought. We have spent considerable time discussing the fate of the public/private distinction in the transnational arena through an analysis of the co-ordinative/regulatory, as well as the substantive/procedural, dimensions of law in order to shed more light on the interpenetration and overlapping of these dimensions in transnational governance. As we have seen, this challenge to conventional legal thought is not without precursors. Rather, work by political scientists, legal sociologists and legal pluralists have long questioned the clear-cut divide between allegedly separate spheres of norm-creation.[588]

One of the most radical challenges to the long-standing preoccupation among legal scholars to 'resolve' the problem of the public/private distinction was presented by the German sociologist and legal scholar, Niklas Luhmann (1927–98): from the perspective of Luhmann's systems theory, society is a self-reproducing process founded on constant flows of communication, with different communications following specifically coded, 'autopoietic' discourses.[589] According to Luhmann, the generation of norms is subject to the *logic of remembering and forgetting*, ie the selectivity of the communication process, by which some communicative offers for connection are accepted through reference by subsequent communications and others simply fall into oblivion. 'Structures are only real when they are used for linking communicative events; norms, only when they are quoted explicitly or implicitly'.[590] It follows that general principles of law and norms of 'soft law' have their life breathed into them in the very moment of their being referenced in legal discourse, for example in real-life contracting or dispute resolution, which ultimately renders them into 'hard code'. The legal process so understood is characterised by a collapsing of the otherwise distinct notions of creation (legislation) and recognition (adjudication): norms are *condensed and confirmed* in the enduring process of legal discourse.[591] For example, some judgments may attain the status of

[588] Kenneth W Abbott and Duncan Snidal, 2000; Richard Ford, 1999; Gunther Teubner, 1997d.

[589] Niklas Luhmann, 1997, 13; Niklas Luhmann, 2004, 233: 'society communicates and in so doing delineates itself from an external environment. The legal system also communicates and in so doing executes the autopoiesis of society. Society uses language. The legal system also uses language, with only minor variations of the conditions for understanding'.

[590] Niklas Luhmann, 2004, 82.

[591] Niklas Luhmann, 2004, 144: 'logic of condensation and confirmation'.

'leading cases', are included in successive textbook editions and are regularly quoted, while there are statutory provisions that lead a very quiet shelf life with no apparent impact on the 'real world'.

Many areas of transnational governance are marked by numerous non-state norms: model contracts, recommended best practices, codes of conduct, rules and guidelines, general principles, and model laws, among others. For conventional legal theory this abundance of normativity is not necessarily a problem, as the law has developed particular domestication practices through which social norms will become operational within the legal order only after the mentioned methods of degradation (deference, incorporation & delegation) have been applied.[592] As a result, social norms either remain irrelevant for the law, a fact somewhat ambiguously circumscribed as 'soft law', or it is transformed into 'hard code' by an official act of recognition, which *simultaneously* lends legitimacy to the operation of the formerly 'unofficial' norm in the 'official' legal system, a process which has accurately been labelled 'bottom-up transnational law-making'.[593] 'Private law-making', however, becomes a problem where authoritative acts of recognition are largely absent, as is the case in the realm of transnational law regimes. It follows, that legal theory either ignores the social reality of effectively governing transnational law regimes—which is to say: 'it is not law, hence there is no need for legitimacy'—or, the law is in need of an alternative theory allowing to make a distinction between law and non-law and *at the same time* to discriminate between legitimate and illegitimate forms of private law-making—that is to say: 'it is law, hence there is a need—and implied assumption—of legitimacy'.

With regard to the UNIDROIT Principles already mentioned, for example, it is suggested that their legitimacy follows not from *ratione imperii*, but *imperio rationis*:[594] in other words, their governing validity is not derived from the authority by which they have been issued, but rather from their inherent, rational content. Certainly, this prospect seems problematic from the perspective of those in fear of 'government by experts'[595] because it would dramatically seem to dismantle the connection between the authority to make law and the question of who is subject to law. While this fragile nexus lay at the heart of the contestation that shaped nationally embedded legal systems, it certainly does not vanish in the context of transnational governance regimes. Writing in the mid-1950s, Philip Jessup expressed his concerns with a conception that would derive the validity of norms from

592 Ralf Michaels, 2005; Ralf Michaels, 2007b.

593 Janet Koven Levit, 2007a, Janet Koven Levit, 2008; see also David Levi-Faur, 2005, 25.

594 Ulrich Drobnig, 1990, 1151.

595 See the general critique to the 'common core approach' at Ralf Michaels, 2006; for a critique of the European contract law project with regard to its democratic legitimacy, see Gert Brüggemeier et al, 2004, Daniela Caruso, 2004, and Ugo Mattei and Fernanda Nicola, 2006.

an innate or even higher-order rationality.[596] As one way to scrutinise this particular form of inherent validity—perhaps not much unlike Fuller's 'inner morality' of law, which was based on a complex procedural-normative understanding of law won through a long-standing experience in and appreciation of commercial arbitration and the law merchant[597]—Jessup pointed to the relevance of the context in which actors contributed to the creation of norms. Rather than appealing to an inner rationality of such norms, their validity—in very practical terms as regards recognition, compliance and enforcement—was understood to follow from their emergence from within a *transnational situation of human interaction*.

On that basis, to focus solely on the content of the norms in question would provide little guidance for an understanding of their status or, arguably, their validity in a particular, again, institutional *and* normative context, about which we still know too little.[598] What would be of eminent importance for an adequate appreciation of these norms would be this context, which had to be seen as characterised not only by a specific institutional set-up of agents either assuming norm-creation power 'on their own' or upon delegation, but rather by a combination of such shifting constellations, on the one hand, with a possibly very rich or, merely 'functional' and modest, yet altogether *normative* assessment of the binding quality of these norms, on the other. It is this intricate combination of institutional and normative dimensions, which already marked the discussion around *lex mercatoria*.[599]

The tension between privately made norms and state law becomes even more evident once we draw a parallel between this situation in the domestic arena and the heated debate over the status and qualification of customary law in Public International Law.[600] While we will engage with this debate in more detail later in the book (chapter five), this parallel is important to note at this time, as it underscores the recurrence of this very same tension between 'soft' and 'hard', 'unofficial' and 'official', between *law* and *non-law* across the whole range of legal subfields. Similarly to this debate over the sources and genesis of customary international law, there has been a long-standing discussion around 'general principles of law' in Private International Law (PIL). The ongoing dispute around a 'common core', 'uniformity' or 'harmony' of different national private law regimes can be

596 Philip C Jessup, 1956.

597 Lon Fuller, 1964, 41, 43; see also the interpretation by Barry Macload-Cullinane, 1995, 2.

598 David Vogel, 2008, 275.

599 It comes as little surprise, then, that scholars such as Bruce Benson have very productively drawn on Fuller's work in that respect: Bruce Benson, 1989; Macload-Cullinane, 1995, 1, 5–7.

600 See, on the one hand, Jack Goldsmith and Eric Posner, 1999; Jack Goldsmith and Eric Posner, 2005, and Oona A Hathaway and Ariel N Lavinbuk, 2006, and Paul Schiff Berman, 2006, on the other.

taken as an illustration of one of the most fundamentally contested issues in this field. PIL and comparative law scholars have long been engaged in heated debates around the foundations and the politics[601] of the quest for shared values and general principles.[602] One of the outcomes of such efforts has been the initiation of internationally staffed drafting committees to identify, collect and synergise existing rules in specific issue areas. Consequently, PIL and comparative law scholars have been choosing a somewhat practical approach with regard to the lingering ambiguity around the issue of general principles of law. Adopting a functional approach to comparing legal instruments, rules and principles across, for example, different private law systems, a number of international expert committees have been drafting codifications that contain principles aspiring to universal validity and as such capturing what might amount to a 'common core' of national private laws.[603] Sufficiently protected from the otherwise dazzling de- and re-constructions in comparative law methodology,[604] a great number of private law experts have been engaged in years of drafting legal frameworks such as the UNIDROIT *Principles of International Commercial Contracts* and the Lando Commission's *Principles of European Contract Law*.[605] While the former were received very favourably in practice,[606] the latter eventually fused into the more recent elaboration of a *Common Frame of Reference for European Private Law*, the first draft of which was released in 2008[607] and began to prompt an extremely vivid discussion ever since the idea surfaced.[608]

These projects provide for a formidable illustration of the recurrence of the substance/procedure paradox in transnational law-making described above: looking at them from the *substantive* side, the further sophistication and maturing of the Principles (or of the Common Frame of Reference

[601] See only David F Cavers, 1933.

[602] See Otto Kahn-Freund, 1974a, 155: 'What law furnishes the rules of private international law? Obviously this is a fundamental problem of our discipline'. And, *ibid*, at 169: 'Comparative law is the mother of private inter inational law. For centuries the comparative method has been an accepted tool not only of jurists but also of practitioners in this field, a tendency ... re-informced by the general acceptance of the national character of private international law since the end of the 19th century which was accompanied by a shift of emphasis from the solution of particular problems to an exploration of the principles underlying the solutions'. See also Friedrich K Juenger, 1993, 145, 191.

[603] See, eg Mauro Bussani and Ugo Mattei, 1997. See also Ralf Michaels, 2006, 346: 'Comparatists viewed the solutions in different legal systems as responses to common problems, contingent in their form but none the less required by the nature of the problem'.

[604] See the wonderful depiction by Vivian Grosswald Curran, 2003, 72.

[605] Michael Joachim Bonell, 2007; Ole Lando, 2001, 340–42.

[606] Bonell, 2007, 2.

[607] European Research Group on Existing EC Private Law (Acquis Group), available at: www.acquis-group.org/.

[608] See, eg Ole Lando, 1998; Nicholas Kasirer, 2002; Grosswald Curran, 2003 (above), 78: 'The focus on distinctiveness and culture as primordial to understanding law, both one's own and the law of the "other", need not imply a rejection of European legal convergence'.

(CFR), to which we will briefly return below) will in neither case ever be an end-point and still less a resolution of the underlying contestation of the projects' implicit quests for uniformity. Instead, both are examples of the transnational evolution of law, which is marked by the overlapping and mutual interpenetration of substantive and procedural dimensions. The legitimacy concerns that are inherent to the quality and scope of the principles are inseparably tied into the process of their generation and can as such never satisfyingly be put to rest. In other words, without dismissing the long-standing discussion and contestation of 'general principles' as a lost and eventually useless endeavour, its relevance lies in underlining the degree to which the ongoing contestation can only enrich the awareness of the underlying problems of wanting to develop a unified or harmonised legal order.

On the *procedural* side, the UNIDROIT Principles and the CFR illustrate the way in which the constitution of expert committees and the status of the norms resulting from these groups' work remains embedded in two major frameworks, one of which we need to consider as institutional and architectonic, the other one as normative. Regarding the first, the initiation and convening of transnationally staffed and minded expert committees, as in the cases of UNIDROIT and Lando, speaks powerfully to a continuing transformation of both domestic and international law-making. Domestically, there is rich comparative evidence regarding the reliance by state legislatures and courts on private expert committees to prepare and propose later legislative instruments or to draft guidelines and recommendations that, either on their own or through transformation into hard law, attain recognised, legally binding power.[609] Transnationally, the emergence of comitology in the EU law-making process certainly marks one of the most prominent examples of expert law-making.[610] Other examples include the already mentioned case of ICANN,[611] which we will come back to below, or the *Codex Alimentarius*.[612] Furthermore, still on the architectonic side, the Principles, the CFR, ICANN and the *Codex* are of interest not only in terms of the constitution of the committees, but also certainly as regards the *transposition* of the generated norms, rules or standards.[613] As pointed out before in relation to the legal centralist contention that dismisses

[609] Jody Freeman, 1997; Peer Zumbansen, 2002b; Johannes Köndgen, 2006; critically: Martin Wolf, 2002, and Paul Kirchhof, 2001.

[610] One of the best available analyses remains Christian Joerges and Jürgen Neyer, 1997.

[611] See above, ch 1 of this book; Jochen von Bernstorff, 2004.

[612] www.codexalimentarius.net; Alexia Herwig, 2004; for reflections on the eventual emergence of global examples of 'administration without the state', See, eg Eberhard Schmidt-Assmann, 2008, 2067.

[613] Ulrich Drobnig, 1998; see the discussion in Michael Joachim Bonell, 2007; see also the database of arbitral awards and court rulings citing to the UNIDROIT Principles, available at www.unilex.info.

non-state norms as 'non-law', the central question here remains the *status* of the privately generated norms. To the degree that we combine an economic governance with a legal pluralist perspective, the issue of transposition can only be reformulated as one of recognition. The transposition from (allegedly) non-law to law does not occur within the framework of incorporation, deference, or delegation, but through recognition of the legal quality of the privately generated norm. It is important to underline, however, that this recognition always occurs against the background of a comprehensive methodological and critical acknowledgment of the context in which the private generation of (legal) norms occurs. This is crucial, as it serves to further scrutinise the tension that exists between the situation in which the status of these norms *as law* is attained at the moment an official *authority* recognises these norms as law, on the one hand, and that of the relevant *community* recognising the norms as law, on the other. To be sure, if we were to take this distinction at face value, this would amount to a recreation of an inadequate *disentanglement* of the concern with who has an 'official' authority to recognise norms as law and the question of who is affected by and subjected to the binding character of the norms. Our approach, however, attempts to *combine* these two dimensions by applying the same paradoxical perspective to this aspect that we have used to work with the public/private, regulatory/co-ordinative and substantive/procedural dimensions. On that basis, then, we have to assume the implausibility of separating the sphere where official authorities decide over law or non-law from the societal sphere in which the relevant actors recognise legal norms, by the authority these norms exercise over their lives or actions.[614]

It is this distinction between a conventional concept of *transposition of non-law into law* and the paradoxical concept of recognition proposed here, that informs the dispute over the status, for example, of business customs and other norms of merchant law and their 'recognition' by courts.[615] The more obvious, political critique of this situation was, above all, the concern regarding the methodology to explain the mode of incorporation of each kind of social norm into the official legal edifice. Such a critique, however, unfolding now on the *normative* side, must always somehow presuppose a certain model of a legal realist/legal pluralist paradise, characterised by the ability to combine legal plurality with democratic (political) accountability. We contend that to achieve such a state, it has first to be let go. In other words, the legal realist/legal pluralist deconstruction should not be derailed by the incorporation of a hidden normative agenda into what was at the outset and should remain a critical exercise. Our proposal then, in this

[614] On this collapsing of the inside and outside boundaries of organisations, see Karl-Heinz Ladeur, 2009, 189.

[615] Lisa Bernstein, 1996.

context,[616] is to pursue the critical realist/pluralist project without harbouring visions of reconstructing a political system that necessarily or exclusively follows the conventional structures of nation-state politics at the same time. On the one hand, the politics of the emerging forms of norm production between state and market can only follow the comprehensive embeddedness analysis we have suggested here and which must include a recognition of the challenges arising from the parallels between *socialisation* and *juridification* already mentioned. Particularly, the extreme fragmentation of legal processes and normative frameworks, as well as the de-politisation of issue areas through their radical functionalist reinterpretation as technical or efficiency-concerned matters,[617] call for a renewed engagement with the politics of transnational law.

On the other hand, however, we need to further clarify the sphere in which the recognition of norms as law occurs. For this inquiry we can fruitfully draw on a rich discussion concerning the degree of 'affectedness' by norms as put forward by David Held as a central element of his concept of 'cosmopolitan democracy'.[618] Held envisions cosmopolitan democracy as an adequate form of constituting a democratically governed world order outside of the nation-state, an endeavour that has been attracting both enthusiasm as well as scepticism.[619] In light of the vivid contestations surrounding the alleged end of the nation-state and of previously embedded civic identities, political will formation and representation, a project of cosmopolitan democracy needs to develop a framework that effectively addresses the eroding political structures of the globalised nation-state. This is of particular importance in connection with the above-described processes of de-formalisation and de-politisation that have been unfolding in the shadow of a 'neoliberal dystopia of hyper-globalisation',[620] which posit an enormous challenge of any reconstructive politics project. One of the most important features of Held's project is the idea of tying any assessment of democracy to the quality of affectedness by decisions. In a fragmented, post-national world, this is in itself an ambitious criterion as it needs to be established across a whole set of different contexts, identities and associations.[621] 'A citizen's concern is no longer so much "what has my state done

[616] For an application in contract and corporate law, see Peer Zumbansen, 2007b, and Peer Zumbansen, 2008b.

[617] Kerry Rittich, 2002; Regina Kreide, 2009, 20.

[618] See, eg David Held, 1995, Daniele Archibugi and David Held, 1995, and David Held, 2004.

[619] For a proposal to recognise the overly ambitious and ill-founded foundations for a morally conceived concept of post-national cosmopolitan democracy and hence not to give up on the nation-state, see Robyn Eckersley, 2007.

[620] Eckersley, 2007, 679.

[621] Held, 2004; see also David Held, 2006; but see also Roger Cotterrell, 2008, and Jan Aart Scholte, 2008, 311, 323.

about this problem?" as it is "how has the relevant polycentric governance network affected me and my community?" '[622]

As Daniele Archibugi noted in the context of the continuing dispute over the scope and prospects of cosmopolitan democracy,

> [g]lobal democracy is not just the achievement of democracy within each state. Globalisation erodes states' political autonomy and thereby curtails the efficacy of state-based democracy. The stakeholders' communities in a relevant and growing number of specific issues do not necessarily coincide with states' territorial borders. Globalisation engenders new social movements engaged with issues that affect other individuals and communities, even when these are geographically and culturally very distant from their own political community.[623]

Illustrating the challenge of private government regimes described in this book and which needs to be understood as operating in an environment of different fragmented constituencies, audiences, third parties and discourses, Held's notion of 'overlapping communities of fate'[624] describes groups and their members lacking the ability to rely on a democratic process within the political community of one particular state.[625] The concept of such 'communities' is crucial, for example, in the case of religious or other faith-based communities scattered around the world or in that of globally dispersed employees of one multinational firm.[626]

The cosmopolitan democracy answer to such constellations begins with a critique of the inadequate representation of the affected stakeholders through conventional, political institutions. Central here is the contention that democratic theory needs to respond to the growing number of cases in which there is a dramatic divergence between 'a state's political community and those whose interests are most affected'.[627] A key example in this context is certainly that of labour rights, the strengthening of which in the light of an increasingly disembedded sphere of generating, implementing and enforcing such rights has progressed through their (contested) recognition as human rights,[628] their equally problematic protection through codes of conduct[629] or the more recent, ambitiously sophisticated idea of a 'transnational labour citizenship'.[630] Echoing the options, described above, of

[622] Scholte, 2008, 323.
[623] Daniele Archibugi, 2004, 439.
[624] David Held, 1995, 136.
[625] Archibugi, 2004, 443.
[626] *Ibid*.
[627] *Ibid*, 444.
[628] Philip Alston, 2005b.
[629] Harry W Arthurs, 1996; Harry W Arthurs, 2002; Lance Compa and Tashia Hinchliffe-Darricarrère, 1995; Adelle Blackett, 2001; Peer Zumbansen, 2006b.
[630] Jennifer Gordon, 2007; for an earlier elaboration and critique of existing and emerging regulatory enterprises of 'transnational labour regulation' with a specific focus on the need to create protective legal frameworks for citizens in a global economy, see Katherine van Wezel Stone, 1996, and Harry W. Arthurs, 2001.

conceiving of the transnational governance sphere either—from a Systems Theory perspective—as functionally highly differentiated and ultimately 'issue-driven'—or—from a more generally sociological or political theory stand—as 'pluralistic' or 'fragmented', David Held's proposal to use a differentiated concept of affectedness can be seen as approximating both perspectives.

And precisely because the concept has to carry so much—in our reading, institutional and normative—weight, it comes as no surprise that Held's suggestion to focus on decisions' effects on vital interests and human needs is taken by his sympathetic commentators as an invitation for further specification. But regardless of whether one operates with a distinction between 'fundamental, expanded and marginal interests'[631] or different levels of 'strong, moderate and weak interests',[632] neither succeeds in putting the underlying issue at rest, but rather highlights how much is in fact at stake. Thomas Pogge and Regina Kreide emphasise the way *affectedness* needs to be specified by focusing on how institutions—broadly understood to encompass 'norms, regulations, rights and conventions'—determine the prevention or facilitation of access to 'essential resources'.[633] From this perspective, the proposed differentiation between 'fundamental, expanded and marginal interests' becomes more accentuated: arguing that fundamental (subsistence, health, education) and expanded (equal access to participation in public, economic and private life) interests are crucial to identify the effective participation in the law-making processes, this approach puts forward a considerably ambitious and 'inclusive' set of conditions necessary to explain the nexus between legitimacy and affectedness,[634] something that becomes more obvious the more it is tied to institutional reform proposals, for example dealing with the promotion of deliberative practices in the UN General Assembly or the further strengthening of constitutionalisation processes within the EU and international organisations such as the World Trade Organization (WTO), the World Bank or the International Monetary Fund (IMF).[635]

The unceasing interest in private governance regimes on the transnational level, despite pressing and ubiquitously noted legitimacy problems, suggests not only that the dialogue between lawyers and regulatory theorists, sociologists and philosophers has a long way to go but also that it will likely form an important counter-weight to the already important and not always reciprocal influence of economic thinking on legal governance discourses. At this point what emerges from current studies on global governance, socialisation

[631] Kreide, 2009, 28.
[632] David Held, 2004, 373.
[633] Kreide, 2009, 28, with reference to Thomas Pogge, 2008.
[634] Kreide, 2009, 28–29.
[635] *Ibid*, 29.

and juridification is the need for future research to pay particular attention to translation exercises between different disciplines' approaches to the framing of issues around transparency, accountability and legitimacy. Moreover, such a translation effort can only be one, if important, element of a comprehensive engagement with the respectively gained insights into the challenges of identifying structures and contexts of marginalisation and silencing, of empowerment and participation.[636]

With this in mind, the proposal, currently discussed among political philosophers, to combine elements of democratic theory with an ambitious and sophisticated programme of deliberation is a promising advance and one that is of relevance to the parallel searches among legal sociologists and lawyers working on a methodological framework of transnational law. The need, but also the opportunity, to draw out the shared perceptions between legal-doctrinal struggles to make sense of the institutional/normative paradoxes described above and the philosophical investigations into a theory of global/transnational democratic governance are just too obvious. On both sides, the insight into the impressive facticity and vitality of fast proliferating non-traditional forms of representation and norm-creation[637] is frequently contrasted with considerable scepticism towards the ability of new forms of, say, civil society participatory governance at IMF, WTO or ILO (International Labour Organization) level or norm-creation by private governance regimes to meet standards of accountability:

> A democratic transnational government binds deliberation and democratic elements together: without democratic elements it amounts to the exclusion of marginalised minorities, whose position is perpetuated by informal mechanisms through which majority power is exercised. Without deliberation, however, the practice becomes trivial; it does not do justice to the complexity of the problems to be solved, and it becomes less important for those involved, for whom the results are merely decreed.[638]

To be sure, the current debate around 'transnational democratic governance' and, more specifically, around cosmopolitan democracy's notion of *affectedness* and its appropriateness to capture the challenges to post-national democratic ideals certainly had important precursors in discussions around membership and political participation.[639] In other words,

[636] See also Cotterrell who writes: 'People may want not only technically useful law but law that they can see as "truly theirs": law expressing what they see as the distinctive character of their nation or community—even if this is felt rather than understood, and cannot be equated with specific traditions, collective goals, beliefs or values' (Roger Cotterrell, 2009, 497).

[637] Janet Koven Levit, 2008, 62–63.

[638] Kreide, 2009, 33.

[639] See, eg the cautious position taken by Michael Walzer, 1981. See also Joel Rogers and Wolfgang Streeck, 1996, and the highly intriguing work on 'deliberative polyarchy' by Jean Cohen and Charles F Sabel, 1997, which found a later elaboration and further development in Charles F Sabel and Jonathan Zeitlin, 2008.

the critical inquiry into the conditions for congruence between the *authors* of norms and those *subjected* to their rule can be considered to be at the heart of democratic theory. In light of the still unresolved issue even *within* the nation-state, this calls for even more caution when we speak about the conditions for a cosmopolitan *global* order. In the context of our present project, the debate around *affectedness* does not resolve the paradox, identified above, of an inseparable yet tension-laden combination of substance and form, something which we referred to as exemplary of the here conceived *embeddedness politics of transnational governance*. Rather, what is important to note is that the contestation of cosmopolitanism underscores the need to further inquire into the different foundations of transnational governance. Similar to our contention that the need to recognise the mutual interpenetration of the institutional and normative dimensions of private norm-creation is unavoidable in a highly fragmented, functionalised and issue-driven environment that is marked by the absence of a coherently operating institutional structure of politics, we must continue to read the current debate over affectedness as a crucial component of our own discussion of *when* and *how* norms are recognised as law.[640]

E. Rough Consensus and Running Code

The foregoing considerations are crucial for any concept of transnational law in that the recognition of its paradoxical foundations delineate our methodological endeavour from other legal theory projects with regard to Public International Law, Customary Law or Transnational Law in a conventional way. The inseparability of the co-ordinative/regulatory functions of transnational law, together with the paradox of authority and affectedness described above, are missed in theories interested in the identification of 'general principles' or in treatments of customary law as emerging from social or state practice on the international plane. Neither approach can satisfyingly address the tension between legality and legitimacy that is inherent to the authority/affectedness paradox. In light of this situation, we put forward the concept of *Rough Consensus and Running Code* (RCRC) as a methodological approach to productively unfold the dramatic paradox which haunts all transnational law. RCRC allows us to revisit the question 'Is it Law?' by binding the underlying *substantive* concern back into the *procedural* framework specific to transnational (private) law regimes. Accordingly, in the following we will briefly revisit two transnational governance projects—Internet Governance and Private Law Harmonisation—

[640] See only Thomas Pogge, 1992; Daniele Archibugi, 2004; Regina Kreide, 2009; Robyn Eckersley, 2007.

that provided important inspirations for our own project, in order to show how an inquiry into the procedural framework for transnational private law creation is inseparably tied into a larger legitimacy debate.

(i) Internet Governance: Legitimising Open Technical Standards

'We reject kings, presidents and voting. We believe in rough consensus and running code'.[641] In this section we try to unfold the radical proposal that lies beneath this bold exclamation made a few years ago at a time when questions about standardisation and rule-making in the Internet became central after the Internet had become recognised as one of the most challenging contemporary governance *spaces*.[642] In order to safeguard its interoperability as a 'network of networks',[643] the Internet requires global technical standards. The so-called *Request for Comments* procedure (RFC) was developed in order to maintain the quality of standards and to increase the motivation of globally dispersed webmasters for compliance.[644] For the solution of a particular problem a working group chair is appointed, who posts an informal Internet-Draft to facilitate an open mailing list discussion among all interested parties and experts. One of the procedure's striking characteristics is that there is no formal majority voting on standards; instead, consensus is seen to arise out of a deliberative process. Yet, in order to keep the debate from self-destruction through endless loopings of contradicting alternatives or constant 'rebootings', the chair can pronounce a *rough consensus* concerning intermediary or final results. This rough consensus has three implications: In the *social dimension* it captures a near unanimity among the participants (ie, a fairly prevailing opinion), in the *substantial dimension* it points to the existence of a common denominator (ie, a common core), and in the *temporal dimension* it suggests an interim character with regard to potential future improvements (ie, learning aptitude notwithstanding). Where a working group has reached consensus on a new standard, the RFC has to pass a threefold implementation process: at first, the RFC is published as a 'proposed standard' for a period of at least six months, referred to as the *pilot* phase. If the utility of the standard is successfully proven in at least two independent instances, the RFC becomes a 'draft standard', which is recommended for global implementation. It is at this point that the process, which at first was powerfully influenced by the working group and its chair, is subject to a reversal of principal and agent. For it is now up to the Internet community to accept or reject the standard by adopting it in practice: this occurs during the so-called

641 David D Clark, 1992, see also Andrew L Russell, 2006.

642 See, eg Saskia Sassen, 2006, Chapter 7.

643 Lawrence Lessig, 2005, 55.

644 For the following see comprehensively Joseph Reagle, 1990; Andrew L Russell, 2006.

recognition phase. Only if the standard has achieved broad acceptance so that non-compliance with it would jeopardise the interoperability of the Internet, will a network administrator be effectively bound to continue using this exact standard. The RFC thus is turned into a 'full standard' in the *binding* phase. In analogy to IT language, the relevant standard then resembles a *Running Code*, ie a program that functions in practice and is widespread in terms of the installed basis. The binding force of Running Code resembles a 'lock-in', which resembles a 'network effect' in economics parlance.[645] In light of the experimental beginnings of the RFC process, its eventual adoption and elaboration by the Internet Engineering Task Force (IETF) and the World Wide Web Consortium (W3C) are especially noteworthy.[646]

While the parallels between this formulation of Rough Consensus and Running Code and our pursued project of transnational law regimes are evident, some marked differences remain. For one, the role of the 'chair' will probably not be directly translatable into the different regulatory regimes we are concerned with for a more encompassing methodological concept of transnational private law. In light of the described variations among different regimes of transnational law-making, the role of the 'chair' is likely going to be assumed by a wide range of actors. Importantly, however, its designation cannot follow simple rules of, say, hierarchical authority. Instead, given the centrality of the function carried out by the 'chair', its designation must follow the paradoxical nature of the authority/affectedness tension described above. In other words, the role of the chair is never a 'given', but must regularly be scrutinised in light of the specific context, its actors, constituencies and audiences.

Another difference between Internet standards and norms created through transnational law regimes relates to the scope of co-ordination and regulation inherent to these norms. Here, however, what would seem obvious—namely a fairly clear-cut distinction between allegedly 'technical' Internet standards and politically charged transnational governance norms turns out to be extremely treacherous. Not only has it been firmly established that to dismiss Internet rules as merely technical standards would dramatically miss the political and constitutional dimensions of the Internet.[647] At the same time, the technical/political distinction between the Internet and other spheres of norm-creation innocently downplays the challenges of scrutinising the formalising/functionalising dynamics at

[645] Network effects are ascribed to network goods, where the benefit for existing users of a product increases with each additional user, a classical example being a telephone network: see Amitai Aviram, 2003.

[646] See, eg Paul Hoffmann, 2009; L Jean Camp and Charles Vincent, 2004.

[647] Lawrence Lessig, 1999b-a; see also the contributions to Alan B Albarran and David H Goff, 2000.

play in many regulatory areas of the 'off-line' world, which are marked by dramatic de-politicisation developments. Hence, what is of eminent importance in engaging in a translation effort between the innovations in Internet governance theory and transnational law regimes is to make such translations not a one-way effort. Finally, as concerns the specific dynamics of 'spontaneous formation' in the context of Internet rules as in other areas of private governance, evolutionary economists and social norm theorists have much to contribute to the further development of reciprocal learning in this context.[648]

The promises and pitfalls just mentioned of any attempt to draw lessons from the fast-evolving realm of Internet governance for other transnational governance regimes are further accentuated in the case of the Internet Corporation for Assigned Names and Numbers (ICANN). ICANN is a private not-for-profit organisation, responsible, among other things, for the management of the domain name system, ie the global addressing system of the Internet. Domain names could be considered the human-friendly form of otherwise numeric Internet Protocol (IP) addresses. With the commercialisation of the Internet, domain names acquired significance as business identifiers and, as such, their frequent conflicts with intellectual property rights have given rise to a thriving, highly specialised litigation industry. Domain name disputes arise largely from the practice of so-called 'cybersquatting', a pre-emptive registration of trademarks by third parties as domain names. Cybersquatters exploit the first-come, first-served nature of the domain name registration process in order to put the domains on auction or to offer them directly for sale to the company involved at prices far beyond the cost of registration.

In 1998, following a proposal by the US Government,[649] the World Intellectual Property Organisation (WIPO) initiated an extensive international consultations process with regard to the interference of the domain name system with trademarks, especially with a view to establishing a quick, efficient, and cost-effective online dispute resolution procedure for domain name disputes.[650] While an interim report considered arbitration in respect of any intellectual property dispute arising out of a domain name registration, the final report recommended a mandatory administrative procedure. Such a procedure would remain limited to cybersquatting, which was held to be an undoubted infringement of general principles of

[648] For a discussion of the economic model of competition for social lawmaking, see Amitai Aviram, 2004; Andreas Engert, 2006.

[649] See the US Department of Commerce 'White Paper' of 5 June 1998, available at: www.icann.org/general/white-paper-05jun98.htm.

[650] Seventeen consultation meetings were held in 15 different cities throughout the world, and written submissions were received from 334 governments, intergovernmental organizations, professional associations, corporation and individuals. See the Report on the First WIPO Internet Domain Name Process, available at: wipo2.wipo.int/process1/report/index.html.

trademark law as expressed both in international treaties and national case law, and in fact universally condemned throughout the consultation process.[651] Issues not related to trademarks were postponed to be considered in a second consultation process, since the law with respect to trade names, geographical indications and personality rights is less evenly harmonised throughout the world.[652]

As a result, in 1999 ICANN adopted its Uniform Dispute Resolution Policy (UDRP),[653] which all registration service providers, accredited by ICANN as registrars for the generic Top-Level-Domains '.com', '.org', and '.net', incorporated by reference in the registration agreements with their customers, ie the domain name holders.[654] According to the UDRP the registrar will cancel or transfer a registered domain name to a third party (the 'complainant') if it receives an order from an administrative panel of an ICANN-approved dispute resolution service provider to do so, and the registered holder (the 'respondent') has not commenced a lawsuit against the complainant challenging the panel decision within 10 business days after its reception by the registrar. The panel shall issue an order of transfer if the complainant has proved each of the following three elements: (i) the contested domain name is identical or confusingly similar to a trademark or service mark in which the complainant has rights; (ii) the respondent has no rights or legitimate interests in respect of the domain name; and (iii) the domain name has been registered and is being used in bad faith.[655] The UDRP in practice was a resounding success. After 10 years of operation, the number of cases administered by the WIPO Arbitration and Mediation Center, the leading dispute resolution provider under the UDRP, exceeds 16,000.[656] All panel decisions are published on the Internet. Some of them have become leading cases, quoted over and over by other panels and, thus, contributing to an explication and gradual extension of the concept of cybersquatting as contained in the UDRP.[657]

While the WIPO consultation process—which lead to the adoption of the UDRP by ICANN—resembles many elements of Rough Consensus, the UDRP was pushed to become a Running Code by the fact that ICANN, due to its monopoly power, unilaterally imposed the UDRP on domain name holders. Thus, the UDRP was dependent on the consensus of trademark

[651] See First WIPO Report No 174.

[652] The Report on the Second WIPO Domain Name Process is essentially calling for a decision of the international community on a harmonisation of the respective laws as a prerequisite for a uniform dispute resolution policy. The Report is available at: wipo2.wipo.int/process2/report/.

[653] Available at: www.icann.org/dndr/udrp/policy.htm.

[654] For the implementation process see, www.icann.org/udrp/udrp-schedule.htm.

[655] See para 4 a) of the UDRP, while circumstances giving evidence of (ii) and (iii) are outlined in paras 4 b) and c).

[656] See the statistics, available at: www.wipo.int/amc/en/domains/statistics/cases.jsp.

[657] Jay P Kesan and Andres A Gallo, 2005.

holders only who made frequent use of the procedure. Domain name holders (including cybersquatters) in turn can express their discontent with the procedure by contesting panel decisions in state courts, an option which, however, was used rarely. Further qualifying the private governance dimension that characterised the idea of an RFC described above, the example of ICANN's UDRP provides a powerful illustration of the dynamics of public and private interaction that in fact marks a lot of the transnational law regimes we are here interested in. From a methodological perspective, clear-cut demarcations of autonomous law-making areas as they are sometimes put forward in discussions of *lex mercatoria* have relatively little to contribute to a better understanding of the often intertwined processes of regulatory innovation that can be observed.

(ii) Private Law Harmonisation

As we have seen above, the current perspectives on private law unification, or harmonisation by means of multilateral treaty harmonisation under international law are somewhat disillusioning, both from the point of view of norm consumers operating on the European market[658] as well as from those who recognise a troubling orientation of private law harmonisation around principles of efficiency and market functionality.[659] In comparison, the United States' Uniform Commercial Code (UCC) is held to be a particularly significant precedent for the creation of a sufficiently flexible set of guidelines in view of market participants' demands.[660] Paradoxically, the UCC's success is not owed to it being either a 'code' in the traditional continental sense, or even strictly speaking 'uniform' throughout the United States. Rather, the American Law Institute and the National Conference of Commissioners on Uniform State Laws drafted the UCC in the form of a model law, from which follows that the individual States are free to adopt the model law as stated or with modifications. In fact, many States have adopted variations of the model law, but most of the variations are of little or no significance.[661] Such unification of private law through soft law, which in the case of the UCC still has scholars divided over how strong the Code's empirical base really was,[662] can provide a promising concept in transnational governance as well, since the non-binding character of a model law eases the reaching of a consensus, which is central to the concept we lay out below (Section IIIH).[663]

658 Gralf-Peter Calliess, 2007, 474.
659 Ugo Mattei and Fernanda Nicola, 2006; Fernanda Nicola, 2008, see discussion above.
660 In that regard, see Michael Joachim Bonell, 2001a.
661 Michael Joachim Bonell, 2001a, 93.
662 See Saule Omarova, 2009, 914, fn 123: 'early model of the kind of empirically based, collaborative lawmaking endeavor'; but see the critique by Lisa Bernstein, 1999.
663 See Ulrich Drobnig, 2001.

Similarly, the 1985 UNCITRAL Model Law on International Commercial Arbitration discussed before is regarded as a particularly successful example in that regard, having been implemented by 36 States and was used by numerous countries as the standard for the reform of their national arbitration laws.[664]

The model law approach productively dissolves the distinction between law-making and law application: the making of soft law on the level of the norm entrepreneur is decoupled from possibly inadequate attempts to re-attach the law-making authority to an institutional framework similar to that on the nation-state level that is as such not available transnationally. Furthermore, the application of the norms occurs in a crystallisation and compliance process on the level of norm consumers who either reject or embrace the norms. Certainly, the above-mentioned legality (authority) and legitimacy (affectedness) problems can resurface here in a violent manner. In contrast to an openly structured and inclusive law-making procedure that our model envisions, many soft law creations occur without there being a satisfying level of public participation or discourse. As the example of UNCITRAL illustrates, the drafting itself occurs at considerable distance from those eventually 'affected' and, to add to this insulation, given that the drafting of a model law is regularly extremely time and resource consuming, opportunities for reform and adaptation will present themselves only slowly. Finally, model laws are addressed to political legislatures and not to individual law consumers, which adds to a distinct construction of a model law's constituency.

By contrast, private codifications are usually open to revision, adaptation and extension on an ongoing basis.[665] Even more so, the CENTRAL Transnational Law Digest & Bibliography is based on the idea of a 'creeping codification' of transnational law, ie an open list of principles and rules of the *lex mercatoria* that is constantly updated in the light of international arbitral awards, domestic statutes, international conventions, standard contract forms, trade practices and usages, and academic sources, but never completed.[666] Unlike model laws, private codifications are addressed not only to states, but claim to be directly applicable by virtue of private contract parties' choice of law, or indirectly, by state courts and arbitral tribunals in interpreting and supplementing international and domestic law.[667] Indeed, testifying to the relative practical success of the UNIDROIT

[664] Pieter Sanders, 2005.

[665] See, eg the publication of the 2nd edition of the Unidroit Principles in 2004; Michael Joachim Bonell, 2004.

[666] See Klaus Peter Berger, 1999; the TLDB is available online at: www.tldb.net.

[667] The preamble to the Unidroit Principles reads: 'These Principles set forth general rules for international commercial contracts. They shall be applied when the parties have agreed that their contract be governed by them. They may be applied when the parties have agreed that their contract be governed by general principles of law, the lex mercatoria or the like.

Principles, the Internet database Unilex[668] lists a total of 160 court rulings and arbitral awards that, in one way or another, make reference to the Principles.[669] Certainly, the concern regarding a 'government by experts' already mentioned is prevalent in this case as well: private codifications are often drafted by a closed circle of comparative law and other issue-specific experts rather than in a transparent process open to participation by interested parties.

To return once more to the European contract law project: with the European Commission's Communication in 2001, the Action Plan in 2003 and the Communication in October 2004,[670] the Commission had set in motion an open and transparent process of discussion and deliberation, open to interested parties to be joined by written statement and the course and intermediary results of which are accessible through the publication of all related documents on the Internet.[671] The consolidation of fundamental rules of contract law in a non-binding Common Frame of Reference (CFR) was envisioned as a first step. As noted, a first draft CFR was published by the Joint Network on European Private Law at the end of 2008[672] and, again, the CFR drafting process provides, despite the continuing debate over its merits and shortcomings, a powerful illustration of a continuing search not only for more inclusive and responsive norm-creation procedures but also for a legal methodology adequate to the emerging complex legal culture of transnational spaces such as the EU.[673]

They may be applied when the parties have not chosen any law to govern their contract. They may be used to interpret or supplement international uniform law instruments. They may be used to interpret or supplement domestic law. They may serve as a model for national and international legislators'.

[668] See www.unilex.info.

[669] Michael Joachim Bonell, 2007.

[670] Commission of The European Communities, Communication from the Commission to the Council and the European Parliament on European Contract Law, Brussels, 11 July 2001, COM(2001) 398 final; *ibid*, Communication from the Commission to the European Parliament and the Council. 'A More Coherent European Contract Law. An Action Plan', Brussels, 12 February 2003, COM(2003) 68 final; *ibid*, Communication from the Commission to the European Parliament and the Council, 'European Contract Law and the revision of the acquis: the way forward', Brussels, 11 October 2004, COM(2004) 651 final.

[671] For a compilation of the documents concerning the contract law project, see the Homepage of the European Commission, DG Sanco, Safeguarding Consumers' Interests, Ensuring Safe Shopping, European Contract Law, available at: ec.europa.eu/consumers/cons_int/safe_shop/fair_bus_pract/cont_law/index_en.htm.

[672] The coordinator of the network, which encompasses different research groups, is Hans Schulte-Nölke, Professor at the University of Bielefeld. For details, see Joint Network on European Private Law homepage, available at: www.copecl.org/.

[673] In this regard, see Reinhard Zimmermann, 2009, 512: 'All of them require genuinely European, as opposed to national, legal scholarship, based on historical and comparative study ... But none of them is ready to be cast into an official European legal instrument, whatever its name may be'.

To be sure, the important debate over the foundations and aspirations of a 'Common Core' or a Common Frame of Reference for European private law, that reaches beyond the closely involved network of scholars from across Europe, is a key forum for the continued assessment and scrutiny of transnational law-making. To the degree that the heated contestation of premises, starting point and aspirations illustrates the reality of the above outlined politics of transnational embeddedness, it will be a very important contestation site to pay attention to in years to come.[674] As noted before with regard to the fundamentally political dimension of private law in a multilevel and polycentric process of Europeanisation, Globalisation and Privatisation, the CFR debate provides an excellent insight into the struggle over how adequately, on the one hand, to address the still emerging nature of the EU as *polity*, rather than as 'state' or 'market',[675] while—on the other—to experiment with ways to work through the different legacies and legal mindsets of nationally evolved legal cultures.[676]

The European Commission, through the sequenced drafting and publications of focused Communications, the 'Action Plan' and through the establishment of a network of practitioners ('CFR-net'), has provided some corner-stones of a still evolving institutional infrastructure that provides a forum for thought exchange, agenda-setting and norm-drafting. Overall, the CFR is developed with the aim of achieving a broad consensus on the basis of a wide participation of governments, industry, and civil society; at the same time, the involvement of practitioners will lead to an early recognition of implementation issues ('practicability test').[677] Once a 'rough consensus' about the Common Frame of Reference was achieved in the sense outlined above with regard to RCRC, it could, as a first step, be published as a (non-binding) recommendation within the Official Journal of the European Union. Within the realm of commercial activity, these rules could, for example, be applied as chosen law by parties in arbitration proceedings according to the model of the UNIDROIT Principles. In the context of the reform of the 1980 Rome Convention on the Law Applicable to Contractual Obligations the European Commission suggested that contract parties should be allowed to choose particular private codifications

[674] Christian von Bar, 2008; Horst Eidenmüller, Florian Faust, Hans Christoph Grigoleit, Nils Jansen, Gerhard Wagner and Reinhard Zimmermann, 2008.

[675] Christian Joerges, 2004; Christian Joerges, Bo Strath and Peter Wagner, 2005.

[676] Stefan Grundmann, 2008; Ruth Sefton-Green, 2008; for an analysis of 'informational interdependence' of different national governments engaging in policy innovation, see the excellent paper by David Lazer, 2005.

[677] Compare the considerations about a previous 'practicability test' for the CFR, in: COM(2004) 651 final, above n 645, at 3.2.2.

by means of choice of law—having in mind the UNIDROIT principles and the CFR.[678]

In that respect, the CFR could potentially be developed into a so-called 'optional instrument', available by choice of law so that state courts would apply the CFR as law (*recommendation* phase). Only in the case that sufficient practical experience with this instrument could be gained—which would in turn mainly depend on the acceptance of the CFR by contract parties expressed by their choice of law—could it even be imaginable that the degree of obligation associated with the respective CFR rules be raised through a status change from opt-in to opt-out. The rules would then become applicable like state law even in the *absence* of a differing choice of law, as is the case with the CISG.[679] The triggered increase of available interpretations of the CFR as 'precedent' for state courts could result in a decrease in 'opt-outs' by contract parties. Eventually, following this projection, the CFR could transform into a generally accepted practice by contract parties and their counsel (*binding* phase).

From this perspective, the CFR could be seen as an example resembling both the 'rough consensus' and 'running code' dimensions of our model, ie the gradual codification and implementation of law dependent on the consent of the addressees of norms. Yet, in our view, the CFR's merit, at this point in time, can be seen less in providing for an encompassing and effective model of law-making that would satisfy our high standards of authority/affectedness and more as a worthwhile case to explore and pursue further. Where the CFR is still to be enriched and further developed to encompass more private law fields,[680] we contend that there is still more room to further scrutinise its place in a fast-evolving EU regulatory space.

(iii) Modern Customary Law

According to the conceptual framework of RCRC developed here, legal principles collected in private codifications, recommendations, and codes of conduct must build on *rough consensus* if they are to become a *running code* which is to prevail not only in practice but also meet the requirements

[678] This is explained in the commentary to Art 3. *Commission Proposal for a Regulation of the European Parliament and the Council on the Law Applicable to Contractual Obligations (Rome I)*, at 5, COM(2005) 650 final (15 December 2005). For a critique of the choice of non-state law, see Peter Mankowski, 2004.

[679] For the definitions of 'opt-in' and 'opt-out' instruments and an explanation of their relation to choice of law, see COM(2004) 651 final, above n 645, 17; The Convention on the International Sale of Goods (CISG) under this definition is an 'opt-out'-instrument, since Art 6 of the CISG reads: 'The parties may exclude the application of this Convention'.

[680] See Reinhard Zimmermann, 2009.

of legitimacy described above. As emerges from the examples provided here, Internet Governance and CFR, there is both a *focused* and at the same time extremely *open-ended* and boundary-less notion of constituency that is relevant to an elaboration of RCRC in each of these examples. While the design of Internet standards targets Internet users, it is evident that the circle of those 'affected' eventually by such norms is much bigger. The same applies to the realm of private law harmonisation as exemplified by reference to the Common Frame of Reference.

While the target group is constituted, primarily, by 'contracting parties', this specialisation in itself does not capture the reality of the constituency ultimately subjected to the norms. The 'alienating'[681] or 'masquerading' effect of legal formulas, the undoing of which was so central to the Legal Realist enterprise,[682] hides behind assertions of market citizenship, private autonomy and consumers on a 'law market',[683] without much respect paid to the ideological nature of these claims. In that respect, we remain cautious as to the lessons to be learned from both the primary example of RCRC—Internet Governance—as well as from another, prima facie promising case of (European) Private Law Harmonisation. Our interest remains in the further testing of bold claims of cosmopolitan or market citizenship, private autonomy and consumer choice.

In this light, we suggest that RCRC has a lot in common with the—similarly contested—status and validity of customary law, a discussion we will turn to in more detail in the last chapter. Where lawyers may, admittedly cheekily, claim that even customary law has to begin 'somewhere', rough consensus and running code could be understood as a contemporary interpretation of the emergence of customary law norms. In the context of transnational law regimes, RCRC could form an important pillar of a developing concept

Table 5: Rough Consensus & Running Code

RFC Procedure ↓	Rough Consensus	
	Social Dimension	Fairly Prevailing Opinion
	Substantive Dimension	Common Core
	Temporal Dimension	Learning Aptitude
	Running Code	
	Pilot Phase	Proposed Standard
	Recognition Phase	Recommended Standard
	Binding Phase	Full Standard

681 Gunther Teubner and Peer Zumbansen, 2000; Marc Amstutz, 2009, 310–12.
682 Duncan Kennedy, 1973; Joseph W Singer, 1988.
683 Erin A O'Hara and Larry E Ribstein, 2009.

of a global civil society. RCRC could effectively replace the 'silently working forces' so dear to Savigny's depiction of nineteenth-century legal consciousness.[684] The concept of a transnational law regime described here may well provide an adequate substitute for the defining elements of traditional customary law, *consuetudo* (practice and use) and *opinio necessitatis* (recognition of the norm's binding character).

As already powerfully reflected in the parallels between domestic and transnational struggles over legitimate forms of governance,[685] we must no longer confine our search for adequate governance instruments for an effective self-regulation of society[686] to traditional reasoning, or as expressed in models of parliamentary, majoritarian democracies, or formal law-making instruments commonly associated with the Rule of Law. Instead, RCRC may allow us to constructively question the practical and normative relevance of traditional law-making processes, which for too long have been isolated from societal forms of self-regulation.

(iv) The Making of Transnational Private Law

> 'Although not all law is privately made, and most privately made law depends ultimately on the power of the state—power the state lends, dependably and in generous measure—enough law is privately made that we should care'.[687]

Chapters three and four of the book are devoted to exploring the tension between social and legal norms in two fields, which we consider to be telling illustrations of the challenges and promising prospects connected to the here-proposed concept of RCRC. It is here where we can see fierce battles being waged between masked dictators and bold businessmen, where we would hope instead to recognise multifarious societal communications among and between spheres of societal norm production. In this respect, we will have to be aware of the complex concepts of *governance by law* as opposed to *societal governance* under the paradigms of a nineteenth-century society of individuals, a twentieth-century society of groups and organisations and a twenty-first century of networks.[688] It will be against this reconstructive background that we shall illustrate the promising potential of RCRC as an adequate legal governance concept, both for increasingly complex, de-centred domestic regulatory situations[689] and for supra- and transnational spheres of human interaction, where actors are in need of adequately timely and responsive, adaptable forms of legitimate law

684 For an elaboration, see Gralf-Peter Calliess, 2006, ch 5.
685 Colin Scott, 2000; Peer Zumbansen, 2002a; Peer Zumbansen, 2006b.
686 See the brilliant study by Karl-Heinz Ladeur, 2006.
687 David V Snyder, 2003, 373; David V Snyder, 2007.
688 Ladeur, 2006, 5–6; see also Manuel Castells, 1996.
689 Julia Black, 2001.

production.[690] On that basis, the following case studies focus on two areas of private law-making that reflect the larger trends of mixed, public-private and multilevel norm-creation that we have identified as central features of an emerging body of transnational private law. We are focusing on consumer protection regimes on the one hand and on corporate governance codes as regulatory instruments on the other. These areas reveal the complex intersection of privately created norms, codes of conduct, principles and ethics standards with norms generated through statutory law reform on the domestic level and through legislative initiatives by international organisations (as, for example, the European Union or the Organisation for Economic Co-operation and Development (OECD). In studying the hybrid nature of the evolving regulatory regimes that ensue from this complex institutional framework, our traditional core understandings of a centralised or, at least formalised legal norm-making authority[691] are challenged on two levels. The proliferation of norm authors dramatically questions the exclusive claim to legislative authority which is regularly associated with nation-states.[692] This is seen as particularly troubling from the perspective of a state-oriented legal order, because many of the newly emerging entities purporting to generate norms that demand compliance fail to fit classical categories of either public or private entities.[693] Examples of such entities, that must be seen as both public and private in nature, while often made up of private actors who are, however exercising public, norm-generating or administering authority include standard-setting bodies,[694] international organisations,[695] arbitration tribunals,[696] credit rating agencies[697] or, for example, the Forest Stewardship Council.[698]

The proliferation of norm *authors* outside the traditional public-private divide[699] has a dramatic effect on our understanding of the nature of these norms and, with that, of the authority to make binding norms. Where a direct link between an institution with the (constitutional, or) political authority to make laws, on the one hand, and a norm which enjoys wide-spread societal acceptance, while it was not created by any such

[690] See also Gralf-Peter Calliess, 2002.

[691] See only Charles M Tiebout, 1956.

[692] Philip Alston, 2005c.

[693] *Ibid*; for a brilliant historical analysis of the public-private challenge in Public International Law, see Christine Chinkin, 1999; see also with regard to the 19th century legal theory, see Morton J Horwitz, 1992.

[694] A prime example is the International Accounting Standards Board (IASB); see Caroline Bradley, 2005, 177; Robert P Delonis, 2004, 592: 'wholly private organization'.

[695] For example, the Organisation for Economic Development and Co-operation (OECD); see Caroline Bradley, 2005, 139.

[696] Amr Shalakany, 2001; Peer Zumbansen, 2002a.

[697] Timothy J Sinclair, 1994.

[698] See Benedict Kingsbury, Nico Krisch, Richard B. Stewart and Jarrod Wiener, 2005, 2; see further Erroll Meidinger, 2006.

[699] For an illuminating analysis, see A Claire Cutler, 1997.

recognised body, on the other, is broken, the connection between the state and the official legal order is challenged from both sides.[700] As we saw, this erosion of both the institutional and normative elements of the legal order has caught the attention of political scientists and sociologists who have become increasingly interested in private ordering as well as in the recent debate among public international lawyers about the possibility of imagining a constitution as independent from the state.[701] The red thread running through contemporary explorations of governance and law beyond the state remains the question whether and how such new regimes can safeguard equal or functionally equivalent degrees of legitimacy.[702] While traditional public law scholarship has remained sceptical towards acknowledging non-state actors' capacity to satisfy rule-of-law standards in this regard, recent work has rightly been pointing to the need to move beyond either-or approaches to public-private governance institutions and instruments.[703]

At the same time, the resurgence of *lex mercatoria* in the contemporary legal imagination has notably brought a host of further associations with it, in particular those tying it back to its medieval origins.[704] However, where analogies are readily drawn between the stateless, medieval political order of the eleventh century and today's 'Global Bukowina',[705] there seems to be a misconception about the absence/presence and role of the state in both descriptions.[706] The often wholehearted embrace of the allegedly state-less global marketplace where today's merchants, purportedly like their medieval ancestors, enter and engage in border-crossing, de-territorialised trade, custom and arrangements,[707] comes at a high political price. Taking market participants' abilities, competences and freedoms to make rational choices

[700] See, Harold Hongju Koh, 1996; Oren Perez, 2003.

[701] Christian Walter, 2001; for preparatory work, see Gunther Teubner, 1997c; Peer Zumbansen, 2001a. See the important contributions by Andreas Fischer-Lescano, 2002, and Andreas Fischer-Lescano, 2003.

[702] See only Walter Mattli and Tim Büthe, 2005, 227: 'Accountability has therefore been rightly noted as "the most difficult issue" when governance is provided by private actors'; see also Benedict Kingsbury, Nico Krisch, Richard B Stewart and Jarrod Wiener, 2005, 2: 'These evolving regulatory structures are each confronted with demands for transparency, consultation, participation, reasoned decisions, and review mechanisms to promote accountability. These demands, and responses to them, are increasingly framed in terms that have an administrative law character. The growing commonality of these administrative law-type principles and practices is building a unity between otherwise disparate areas of governance'.

[703] David V Snyder, 2003.

[704] Clive M. Schmitthoff, 1982; Albrecht Cordes, 2003.

[705] Gunther Teubner, 1997c.

[706] Anna di Robilant, 2006, 523: 'The two legal experiences, the medieval and the global, although prima facie similar, should be kept distinct. While the defining features of the medieval legal order are the absence of a powerful state in the modern sense and the incompleteness of political control, the global legal order features the re-location of the state rather than its disappearance'.

[707] See, eg Klaus Peter Berger, 2001a.

to buy, to sell and to move about swiftly in 'disembedded markets'[708] for granted, without duly acknowledging the role played by the existing regulatory framework, local socio-economic, cultural and legal conditions, runs the risk of projecting a brave new world into what in fact remains a contested realm of differences and choices.[709] As Anna di Robilant notes,

> [t]he central political forms of capitalism, the nation-state, and the interstate system are now competing for terrain. However, far from receding, the state is re-located, remaining a crucial space in the global landscape, a space in which non-state, local and global actors interact and multiple alliances are formed. Therefore, the neo-medievalist lens proves anachronistic, failing to capture the intricacies of the global horizontal legal order in which the state, though re-located, is still central, being the site of both oppressive power relations as well as unexpected possibilities of emancipation.[710]

While already much earlier work by legal sociologists had explored legal norms that were created by non-state actors,[711] the de-coupling of a constitutional regime (be it a text or an understood framework as in the case of the English constitution) from the nation-state[712] constitutes a new level of radicalising the contention that there can indeed be 'law without the state'.[713] It comes as no surprise then, that the mere suggestion of a constitutional order that would exist in isolation from a state's legal order from which it had been created and received its legitimacy will regularly be met with strong scepticism. At the same time, it does seem obvious that the perceived challenges to a traditional, state-oriented understanding of the legal order are not likely to be put aside that easily. As noted before, the present discussion about public versus private ordering, official versus unofficial law, soft law versus hard law, unfolds in the context of dramatic *transformation* processes of contemporary post-industrial and post-welfare states.[714]

In light of this transformation, we still think that we cannot rightfully claim to be coming to new social and regulatory phenomena empty-handed,

[708] See on this notion first developed by Karl Polanyi, 1944; Kathryn Ibata-Arens, Julian Dierkes and Dirk Zorn, 2006, 2.

[709] William E Scheuerman, 2001; Peer Zumbansen, 2002a.

[710] Anna di Robilant, 2006, 524.

[711] Eugen Ehrlich, 1962; Sally Falk Moore, 1973.

[712] See, eg the contributions by Weiler and Walker in Joseph HH Weiler and Marlene Wind, 2003.

[713] Gunther Teubner, 1997e; Gunther Teubner, 1997d, 768 (highlighting how the 19th-century German legal theorist, Savigny, emphasised how the hierarchical understanding of the nation-state's constitutional order resulted in the dismissal of private rules and arrangements as non-legal); see also David V Snyder, 2003; with considerable scepticism, however, Simon Roberts, 2005.

[714] See only Fritz W Scharpf, 2000 (highlighting the pressure by globalisation politics on domestic welfare regimes and bargaining stability); Matthew Diller, 2000 (for a discussion and analysis of new regulatory instruments in public administration).

ie with a blank conceptual slate. There is a particular burden carried over from the past,[715] and as lawyers, we carry a particularly heavy load in terms of associating law with—or, rather of being unable to *dis*associate law from—a particular understanding of sovereignty.[716] This sovereignty connotation that seems to be inherent to our every mention of law permeates our legal concepts, and this makes it a particularly significant challenge even to begin thinking about privately made law to have any legally recognisable authority.[717]

It has already become clear that these challenges to law arise in different regulatory contexts. It is for this reason that our study of transnational private law cannot be constrained to studying regulatory contexts only outside of the nation-state. In order to begin understanding the scope and content of a transnational private law, it was thus necessary to revisit the ways in which we have been learning to think about the law, to trace, assess and constantly challenge these ways. As mentioned, the current transformation of public and private governance offers important insights for our struggle over effective and legitimate forms of regulation.[718] As we have posited so far, any study of transnational private law-making must take into account the dramatically changed regulatory landscape on the domestic level. It is only against the background of an irreversible transformation of public ordering to entertain, monitor, facilitate or simply acknowledge alternative forms of norm-creation and administration—be that through delegated powers, public-private contracting or authorised or legitimate forms of private ordering—that we can further scrutinise the potential merits of a concept such as RCRC. As we intend to show through our following two case studies, the norms that are created in the areas of consumer contracts and of corporate governance, in specific circumstances amount to law, on equal footing with norms originating from conventionally recognised 'authorities'.[719]

The first case study is concerned with consumer contract law. As has been pointed out, in the modern welfare state private law fulfills both *co-ordinative* and *regulatory functions*, the latter in establishing certain constraints to party autonomy with respect to commutative justice and public policy. The

[715] Reinhart Koselleck, 1979; Reinhart Koselleck, 1981.

[716] David V Snyder, 2003, 413.

[717] David V Snyder, 2003, 419; A Claire Cutler, 2003, 241: 'Processes of juridification, pluralization, and privatization are transforming structures of authority, which implicitly challenges the old Westphalian assumption that a state is a state is a state'.

[718] Paul R Verkuil, 2008, 1–2 (highlighting the constraints of public regulators facing the choice between 'make or buy', following from a non-delegable duty to govern).

[719] See also David V Snyder, 2003, 404: 'The artifacts of private lawmaking are not the result of bargaining over contract terms, nor do they derive from members of a body that is simply deciding how to govern itself, nor are they best described as norms. In the paradigm put forward here, particular groups succeed in governing much wider groups, as shown above, and lawmaking is a better descriptor'.

legislation on the *protection of the consumer*, as the weaker party in business transactions, figures as a prominent example.[720] While consumer protection within domestic markets is a well-established concept, the same does not hold for the international realm, where the enforcement of national protection regimes is hampered by a lack of international co-operation. Until recently this has not posed much of a problem, since consumers rarely engaged in international commerce directly. With the advent of the Internet, however, matters have changed dramatically. In the networked economy, consumers increasingly shop online often without noticing that they get involved in cross-border situations, in which businesses are able to contract around national consumer rights by means of forum shopping and choice of law.[721]

It has been in this context that the issue of *consumer confidence* in business-to-consumer electronic commerce ('B2C e-commerce') entered the global agenda.[722] While states remained reluctant to regulate cross-border consumer contracts by means of multilateral treaties, international organisations called for *co-regulatory* efforts in addressing the issue. Hence, the 1999 OECD Guidelines for Consumer Protection in the Context of Electronic Commerce (the 'OECD Guidelines') read:

> Part II, VIB: Businesses, consumer representatives and governments should work together to continue to use and develop fair, effective and transparent self-regulatory and other policies and procedures, including alternative dispute resolution mechanisms, to address consumer complaints and to resolve consumer disputes arising from business-to-consumer electronic commerce, with special attention to cross-border transactions ... Part III: To achieve the purpose of this Recommendation, Member countries should ... encourage continued private sector leadership that includes the participation of consumer representatives in the development of effective self-regulatory mechanisms that contain specific, substantive rules for dispute resolution and compliance mechanisms.[723]

It is widely accepted that international merchants are able to solve their co-ordination problems by means of private ordering and, therefore, that they should be allowed to opt out of the state's legal system in handing over disputes

[720] See, eg Stefan Grundmann, Wolfgang Kerber and Stephen Weatherill, 2001.

[721] John Rothchild, 1999; Gralf-Peter Calliess, 2006, Chapters 2 and 3.

[722] European Commission, European Initiative for Electronic Commerce, COM(1997) 157 final (all COM-documents cited in this text can be obtained through Eurlex, available at: europa.eu.int/eur-lex/lex/RECH_naturel.do); Federal Trade Commission, Bureau of Consumer Protection, Consumer Protection in the Global Electronic Marketplace, Looking Ahead, September 2000, available at: www.ftc.gov/bcp/icpw/lookingahead/electronicmkpl.pdf; OECD, Consumer Dispute Resolution and Redress in the Global Marketplace, Report of the Committee on Consumer Policy, April 2006, available at: www.oecd.org/dataoecd/26/61/36456184.pdf.

[723] The Guidelines are available at: www.oecd.org/dataoecd/18/13/34023235.pdf; see also OECD, 'Consumers in the Online Market Place. The OECD Guidelines Three Years Later', DSTI/CP (2002)4/Final, available at: www.olis.oecd.org/olis/2002doc.nsf/43bb6130e5e86e5fc12569fa005d004c/af6ec39d8631ca3ac1256cc2005c0edf/$FILE/JT00138646.PDF.

to arbitration under the law merchant.[724] This assumption's underlying rationale is that there is an absence of public interest in international commerce as merchants presumably meet on an equal footing. Regarding consumer contracts, in turn, private ordering is generally not thought to be an effective and legitimate means for achieving the regulatory functions of private law.[725] Thus, the interesting question arises, what the concept of co-regulation promoted by the OECD exactly entails, and whether it could at all work in the context of B2C e-commerce. In our study of transnational consumer contract law we aim at finding an answer.

The second case study, which will explore the nature of law-making that can be observed in these contexts, is taken from the burgeoning field of corporate governance regulation. This area of law illustrates both the challenge and promise held by contemporary law making initiatives as the reform discussion in the field of corporate law is characterised by a vivid public-private interaction in the preparation and drafting of legal texts, an immense proliferation of privately enacted, self-regulatory rules and a constant interchange of law and policy proposals between the national, European and International levels and between government officials, academics and experts. The search for 'good' corporate governance, regularly defined as the backbone of fair competition and overall social and economic welfare, is, simultaneously, taking place in the context of far-reaching concerns regarding national economies' competitiveness and adaptability to the volatile demands of global capital. Prominent voices within the company law scene have been proclaiming the 'end of history of corporate law',[726] aptly pointing to undeniable pressures of international convergence towards a more capital market (law) oriented approach to corporate governance.[727] Some of the highflying observations regarding the universal triumph of shareholder value-oriented corporate governance regimes seem to have been made with too little regard for historical developments, but also for contemporary, highly hybrid reform trends.[728] The latter qualification must also be seen as a comment or complementing thesis to the 'Varieties of Capitalism' scholarship which, certainly ignored by mainstream corporate law scholars, has for a long time now been arguing for distinct historical

[724] Klaus Peter Berger, 1999; Peer Zumbansen, 2002a, 400; see also the critique by A Claire Cutler, 1997.

[725] Gillian K Hadfield, 2001, 40, 45; European Consumer Law Group, Soft Law and the Consumer Interest, ECLG/071/2001–March 2001, available at: europa.eu.int/comm/consumers/policy/eclg/rep03_en.pdf.

[726] See, Henry Hansmann and Reinier Kraakman, 2001; critically: Douglas M Branson, 2001.

[727] Christian Kirchner, 2003.

[728] John W Cioffi, 2006 (highlighting as paradoxical the two features of recent corporate law reform that, first, the expansion of pro-shareholder politics did in fact lead to more regulation and, thus, to more state presence, and that, second, the call for reform was made and pursued by traditional centre-left parties).

starting points of contemporary corporate and finance capitalism.[729] In the following, the stakes of the contemporary debate over corporate governance are to be evaluated close-up, while particular emphasis will be laid on the institutional and procedural embeddedness characterising much of the on-going legal activity in this field. For this purpose, the section will begin with an attempt to define corporate governance before sketching the major poles of the contemporary, often quite polemical dispute over the 'best' model. Following, is a discussion of corporate governance codes as privately enacted rules of conduct, which raise quite a number of constitutional issues related to competences of law-making, binding force etc. As this form of expert norm-setting is a defining feature of law-making procedures in the EU, as for example in the context of the much discussed comitology,[730] the next part of the paper sketches recent developments in European company law making, a field traditionally recently still described as stagnant and arrested.[731] On the European level, the level of normative change in this respect is surely breathtaking. Current developments reach from bold statements made in Luxembourg by the European Court of Justice through legislative initiatives coming from the Commission and the Council to a host of expert recommendations and other private actor initiatives for law reform.[732] Shifting back from the supranational EU law-making level to the national level, the section will focus closer on recent corporate governance developments in Germany. International observers have closely scrutinised developments in this area in Germany, not least because they speak to the intricate domestic politics of law reform in an internationally highly contested area.[733]

[729] See David Soskice, 1999; Peter A Hall and David Soskice, 2001a, esp 4, 14*f*; 24*ff*; Sigurt Vitols, 2001, 338, passim; Gregory Jackson, 2001, 166–70, underlines the weight exercised by transforming international capital markets on historically grown systems of institutional linkages between corporate organization, labour markets and political intervention.

[730] See, eg Ellen Vos, 2000; Christian Joerges and Jürgen Neyer, 1997.

[731] Jan Wouters, 2000.

[732] A glimpse of this development can be had at the European Commission website, available at: ec.europa.eu/internal_market/company/index_en.htm.

[733] See, Cioffi, 2006, above; J Nicholas Ziegler, 2001; Mary O'Sullivan, 2003 (offering a close account and analysis of the German and French states of corporate governance).

3

Transnational Consumer Contracts

'Private lawmaking has not replaced public lawmaking, even in the commercial world, but it is a robust component of commercial and consumer life.'[1]

IN THE FOLLOWING, we intend to examine the potential role of private ordering and co-regulation in the area of cross-border consumer contracts. We start with a survey of the different mechanisms of private ordering, which have developed in e-commerce (Section I). This illustrates that electronic marketplaces fulfill an essential role in bundling different means of private ordering into what we call *transnational law regimes* for consumer protection (Section II). Finally, we aim at demonstrating how states, industry and civil society actors can jointly contribute to the establishment of a *transnational constitution* for such regimes with respect to the regulatory functions of private law (Section III).

I. PRIVATE ORDERING IN B2C E-COMMERCE

There is a plethora of literature on private ordering in commercial relations, describing various governance mechanisms that merchants employ in order to reduce the likelihood of opportunistic behaviour among contractual parties.[2] These mechanisms are generally applied 'in the shadow of law', but their use is rendered essential in a situation of 'lawlessness', eg, in developing countries with inefficient legal systems.[3] The latter situation resembles the one in cross-border commerce in which businesses are confronted with constitutional uncertainties resulting from multi-jurisdictional litigation.[4] We have treated these issues in much more detail above in chapter two. In this part of the book we intend to demonstrate how the governance mechanisms employed by international merchants are increasingly adapted to business and to consumer electronic commerce transactions as well.

[1] David V Snyder, 2003, 374.

[2] Lisa Bernstein, 1992; Bruce L Benson, 1999; Amitai Aviram, 2004; Oliver E Williamson, 2005; Avner Greif, 2006. See as well above in ch 2.

[3] Avinash K Dixit, 2004.

[4] Dieter Schmidtchen and Hans-Jörg Schmidt-Trenz, 1990a; Manfred E Streit and Antje Mangels, 1996.

A. Online Reputation

One important mechanism of contractual governance is reputation: people do not engage in opportunistic behaviour in a certain transaction because they fear that other parties might refrain from entering into future transactions with partners which on the relevant market have a reputation as bad co-operators.[5] But the collection and processing of information on the past performance of potential contract partners is costly, since it usually is not spread in an organised manner but rather spontaneously. For this reason the reputation mechanism is categorised as 'informal third-party control'.[6] It follows that the reputation mechanism works most effectively for high-volume transactions which legitimise the involved information costs, as well as on markets with a limited number of players which interact frequently and thus have a high probability of meeting repeatedly, ie in close-knit homogeneous communities.[7] The interactive communication capabilities of the Internet, however, have enabled the establishment of large-scale, 'word-of-mouth' networks at low cost. Online feedback mechanisms introduced by electronic marketplaces have led to an increasing formalisation of the reputation mechanism.[8] In the following, we shall discuss the 'eBay'-feedback system as an example of the adaptation of the reputation mechanism to the needs of large-scale and small-volume consumer markets with a low probability of repeated transactions.[9]

In order to enter eBay's electronic marketplace, seller and buyer first have to become registered members. eBay offers different procedures for identity check, where the appliance of the most rigorous check is indicated by a symbol attached to the member's name. In the aftermath of every transaction, buyer and seller can mutually assess each other—positively, neutral or negatively—and can briefly justify their decision. Negative assessments can be commented on by the assessed and are allowed to be taken back by mutual agreement. In this way, multiple assessments constitute a rating profile of every member, the quality of which is indicated after the member's name by stars and shooting stars in different colourings. This allows potential transaction partners to get information about each other before completion of a contract.[10] Furthermore, those vendors who on average

[5] Eric A Posner, 2000.

[6] Stephan Panther, 2000.

[7] Peter T Leeson, 2006, at 892, who argues, however, that self-enforcing arrangements work as well in heterogeneous groups.

[8] Chrysanthos Dellarocas, 2003.

[9] David P Baron, 2002; Paul Resnick, Richard Zeckhauser, John Swanson and Kate Lockwood, 2006.

[10] In principle, this only applies to the buyer, as the vendor cannot know the winner of an auction in advance. However, eBay provides sellers with the options of either limiting their offer to buyers from a particular region or with a particular minimum rating profile (buyer requirements) or to block individual buyers on the basis of past experience.

have sold more than 300 items within the last three months or who have generated a turnover of 3,000 Euro and whose ratings are positive to more than 98 per cent receive the status of a 'PowerSeller'. Again, this is indicated by a particular symbol after the member's name. New members and those members who have changed their member name are also indicated by particular symbols. In sum, eBay provides a highly formalised reputation system, which offers its members a high degree of transparency through information about the trustworthiness of potential contractual partners. Shopping with a commercial PowerSeller can be considered as safe as shopping with a traditional high street brand like Marks and Spencer for example. Yet, occasional private sellers can also obtain an impeccable reputation over a longer period of time. In contrast, it is more risky to complete a contract with a new vendor lacking a distinct member profile. In such a case, every member has to consider whether she wants to take such a risk; exceptionally, if higher sums of money are involved, additional precautionary measures are available such as an escrow service, which is further detailed below.

B. Trustmarks and Codes of Conduct

Following the principle 'caveat emptor', trustmarks offer a functional equivalent to trademarks in that both bundle information on a supplier in an easily accessible form and, thus, replace individual investigations into its reputation. Trustmarks are of special importance to Small and Medium-Sized Enterprises (SMEs), which are unable to build up their own trademark on the global electronic marketplace. They are awarded to vendors by a neutral third party, once specific criteria prescribed in a code of conduct have been met.[11] Originally, trustmarks were awarded to products with regard to their technical standard. In principle, trustmarks can also be used to establish socio-ethical standards or to secure compliance with legal norms. Private, state and hybrid institutions can play a crucial part in their award and monitoring. Businesses voluntarily submit themselves to such standards and monitoring, as they hope to gain competitive advantages through the trustmark. The German 'blue angel' and the European 'eco-label' applied such a conception to environmental standards.[12] In the

[11] For the distinction of 'trust' in a vendor and 'reliance' on an independent third party, see Rufus Pichler, 2000.

[12] See Gunther Teubner, Lindsay Farmer and Declan Murphy, 1994; Alexander Pfaff and Chris William Sanchirico, 2000, 189; see also: blauer-engel.de and www.eco-label.com/default.htm; for a survey of environmental trustmarks see: www.label-online.de.

debate over Internet governance, such trustmarks are discussed as a means for the protection of privacy, consumers and children.[13]

Following the Internet euphoria of the late nineties, in B2C e-commerce numerous trustmark schemes have been established, but only a few of those have achieved some significance in the marketplace.[14] Particularly successful has been the 'BBBOnLine Reliability Seal', which, following an initiative by the Canadian and US Chambers of Commerce, is used by more than 55,000 web pages.[15] In order to obtain the seal, an Internet vendor has among other things to become a member of the Better Business Bureau (BBB) located at the headquarters of her business, she has to follow the 'BBB Code of Business Practices', under which she has to subject herself to an alternative dispute resolution procedure that is recommended by BBB.[16]

With more than 5000 certified traders, the private company 'Trusted Shops' is the leading trustmark provider in Europe.[17] Participating traders have to meet certification criteria, which follow current European legal regulations in the field of distance selling and electronic commerce.[18] Furthermore, Trusted Shops assessment encompasses credit ratings, safety technology, price transparency, customer services and privacy issues. In collaboration with credit insurers, Trusted Shops additionally offers a money-back guarantee covering failed delivery, failure to refund after return, and credit card fraud, which is free of cost to buyers. Moreover, Trusted Shops provides a central customer service and dispute resolution procedure. Customers can contact a multi-lingual service centre with any arising issue via phone, email or Internet. According to Trusted Shops, thus far there has been not a single court case filed between a customer and an online shop because of the mediation procedures in place. Certification criteria are continuously revised in collaboration with an advisory board encompassing, among others, members of consumer protection agencies and academics. Participating vendors are informed about new developments in law. All online shops can be accessed via a central portal, which consumers can use to search for particular goods. For all mentioned services vendors pay graded fees according to their turnover. Additionally, for their online shops and advertising campaigns vendors are offered pre-certified web hosting and software solutions. Although big brands have also joined, Trusted Shops remains committed to be a platform that especially allows SMEs to access e-commerce.

13 Ton Wagemans, 2003; Christian Spletter, 2003.

14 See GBDe (Global Business Dialogue on electronic commerce), 2000; see also Fredrik Nordquist, Fredrik Andersson and Eva N Dzepina, 2002.

15 See www.bbb.org/online/consumer/default.aspx.

16 Available at: www.bbb.org/us/bbb-accreditation-standards/.

17 For the following see: www.trustedshops.com/en/trustedshops/index.html.

18 www.trustedshops.com/en/shops/obligations_en.html.

This example highlights that trustmark providers can generate a realm of private order, which rests not only on norms as part of codes of conduct but also on a combination of an insurance for filed payment and alternative dispute resolution procedures. Such an arrangement increases the security level to such an extent that e-shopping is rendered more reliable than traditional bricks-and-mortar business dealings, in which customers have to assert their legal rights in court and in which they carry the risk of the customer's insolvency. The withdrawal of the trustmark itself works as a powerful sanction mechanism. The severity of such a sanction as well as the credibility of its threat, however, depends on the success of the trustmark provider: only if the trustmark has gained some weight within the marketplace can its withdrawal pose a serious competitive disadvantage to vendors. At the same time, only an economically successful trustmark provider can afford to lose vendors as clients. The success of trustmarks depends on three decisive factors usually termed as 'critical mass, financial sustainability, and branding'.[19] As mechanisms of private ordering, trustmarks are network goods by nature.[20] This is the reason why international co-operation between trustmark schemes and both the interlinking with other mechanisms of private ordering (eg, marketplaces, ADR) and the embedding in already existing mechanisms of self-regulation (eg, Chamber of Commerce) seems particularly apposite.

C. Online Dispute Resolution

The notion that the Internet's communicative potential can be used to establish alternative forms of dispute resolution procedures dates back to the mid-1990s.[21] The term 'online dispute resolution' (ODR) covers on the one hand conflicts arising from the use of the Internet itself, such as disputes over domain names or e-commerce transactions, and on the other hand services of alternative dispute resolution provided via the Internet (eADR).[22] The latter includes the whole range of traditional ADR procedures—informal assisted negotiation, mediation and formal arbitration—in so far as the involved parties and a neutral third party communicate via email or via password-protected web pages, electronically exchange documents and

[19] Ton Wagemans, 2003, 14; Julia Hörnle, 2009, 226; A critical stance towards the importance of the trustmark schemes is taken by Jonathan Hill, 2008, 290–302.

[20] Amitai Aviram, 2003.

[21] David G Post, 1995; Martin C Karamon, 1996; Frank A Cona, 1997; Joel B Eisen, 1998; Alejandro E Almaguer and Roland W Baggott, 1998; Robert C Bordone, 1998; Henry H Perritt Jr, 2000a.

[22] Julia Hörnle, 2001; Lousie Ellen Teitz, 2001, at 990; Thomas Schultz, 2004; Lucile M Ponte and Thomas D Cavenagh, 2004; for a comprehensive outline of technologies used in ODR see Julia Hörnle, 2009, 78–86.

photographs ('written proceedings'), and even negotiate simultaneously in chat-rooms, via phone or in videoconferences ('quasi hearings').[23] The type and extent of the use of information and communication technology not only depends on its spread among potential users but also on the aim and type of dispute resolution procedure. When, for example, in international commercial arbitration the formal requirements of the 1958 New York Convention are of concern, high technical standards are necessary, whilst in more informal dispute resolution procedures easily accessible, timely and inexpensive solutions are required.[24]

Moreover, software-supported negotiation systems allow parties to settle disputes without involvement of a neutral third party.[25] Thus, based on game theoretical premises, automatic negotiation systems are offered for those conflicts in which solely the amount of a sum is disputed, such as in insurance cases. Within a 'blind bidding' procedure, the parties submit their offer for a settlement within a number of rounds, yet their offer remains unknown to the opposite party. Then, computer software fixes a binding sum for the settlement based on the arithmetic mean of all offers and given that the final sum remains within a certain range, eg, a difference of 30 per cent.[26] Besides, systems exist that provide parties with a password-protected space for negotiation. Via menu-driven input masks, they allow parties to more closely define the object of dispute, to fix their aims, to deduce their willingness to compromise and to reach voluntary settlement by standardised information about possible ways to resolution.[27] Hence, ODR can be distinguished from more traditional procedures of ADR in that technology takes part as a 'fourth party'.[28]

A study by the Australian Ministry of Justice dating back to 2003 examined 76 ODR web pages worldwide, 42 of which were established in the years 1999–2000 and 19 of which had already ceased to provide their services.[29] Only 24 providers submitted information concerning the number of cases dealt with, and only eight web pages contained statistical information about achieved results.[30] One can assume that those providers that did not present any information were not particularly successful.[31] Among the more successful providers are especially those ODR pages which are linked to a marketplace for e-commerce or which

[23] William Krause, 2001, 460.

[24] Julia Hörnle, 2003.

[25] Arno Lodder and Ernest Thiessen, 2003.

[26] See the survey of providers in Melissa Conley Tyler and Di Bretherton, 2003; Julia Hörnle, 2009, 81–82.

[27] For www.smartsettle.com's offer see Arno Lodder and Ernest Thiessen, 2003, 5.

[28] Ethan Katsh and Janet Rifkin, 2001, 93; Lodder and Thiessen, 2003.

[29] Melissa Conley Tyler and Di Bretherton, 2003, 5; Melissa Conley Tyler, 2004.

[30] Melissa Conley Tyler and Di Bretherton, 2003, 9.

[31] Thomas Schultz, Gabrielle Kaufmann-Kohler and Dirk Bonnet Langer, Vincent, 2001, 67; Gabrielle Kaufmann-Kohler and Thomas Schultz, 2004.

are run by a Chamber of Commerce or an industry association. The reasons for such success may lie in the facts that those pages are easily accessible via the marketplace or the vendor's web page, that they are partly advertised by a trustmark and that they can be used for free or for a minimal charge due to subsidies by the operators of marketplaces and by subscription.[32]

In the following, we introduce the most successful ODR model in the area of B2C e-commerce.[33] 'SquareTrade' is a private company with its headquarters in San Francisco. From 2000 until 2008, when SquareTrade ceased to offer ODR services, it dealt with over one million conflicts linked to 120 countries in five languages. This rendered SquareTrade the market leader for those ODR services dealing with transactions in electronic marketplaces.[34] The dispute resolution procedure was arranged in two phases. At the first level, direct negotiations between the involved parties took place via a secure web page. Communication was organised via interactive input masks, which were constantly revised and improved in the face of new experiences (*software facilitated direct negotiations*). In a majority of cases, the involved parties came to a settlement themselves. If this could not be achieved, each party could call in a mediator at the second level of the procedure. Based on electronic documentation, the mediator was able to quickly gain an overview of the conflict and to support the parties in their quest for a settlement. Following the parties' request, the mediator could even make a non-binding suggestion for a settlement (*online mediation*). Overall, 80 per cent of cases could be resolved by a conjoined settlement, which was obeyed in 98 per cent of cases. The average duration of a procedure was two weeks.

The success of SquareTrade was based on a co-operation agreement with eBay, under which eBay members enjoyed direct negotiations at SquareTrade free of charge and the involvement of a mediator was only US$15. In addition, the SquareTrade mediation process was backed by reputation, since non co-operative behaviour could be sanctioned with negative feedback on eBay. In 2008, however, SquareTrade stopped providing ODR services because eBay changed its feedback policy so that feedback was no longer mutual. Sellers couldn't leave feedback for buyers, so there was no mutuality—hence, nothing to mediate. Meanwhile eBay has built up its own dispute resolution centre, which assists buyers and sellers in solving their problems online.[35]

The example of SquareTrade has proven that cost-effective ODR procedures—even covering cross-border transactions—can be organised

[32] Melissa Conley Tyler and Di Bretherton, 2003, 11.
[33] See Julia Hörnle, 2002; Jonathan Hill, 2008, 284–85.
[34] See the presentation of the Squaretrade President and CEO: Steve Abernethy, 2003.
[35] See resolutioncenter.ebay.com/.

and are affordable for low-volume mass-market transactions. One can record, however, that the success of ODR procedures depends not only on the provision of easily accessible, quick, effective and low-cost dispute resolution, but also on *linkages* with heavily used marketplaces, where online disputes evolve, and on creating *socio-legal bonds* whereby potential dispute parties commit to the process.[36]

D. Method of Payment and Credit Security

In the context of private ordering in e-commerce, the role of payment service providers as *trusted third parties* is of interest. From international commerce it is known that mechanisms such as letters of credit, factoring, forfeiting and credit insurance play a major role in the cushioning of those risks arising out of the consecutive exchange of goods and services.[37] In B2C e-commerce a number of models have been developed which facilitate consumers to carry the burden of the usually required advance payments. These are introduced in the following. More advanced 'real time e-payment' technologies aiming at the simultaneous exchange of services and payments in direct e-commerce with digitised goods remain very much in the future.[38]

In B2C e-commerce payment by credit card is most common.[39] Against widespread fear concerning credit card fraud on the Internet, for consumers this method of payment is the most secure, as payment in e-commerce requires credit card number and period of validity but no signature of the credit card holder. Hence, consumers can take up objections to transactions with the bank issuing their credit card within six weeks after receipt of the credit card statement. According to the so-called 'credit card chargeback' procedure, the vendor has to prove that the payment has taken place with the consent of the credit card holder. Due to the lack of the consumer's signature, this can only be successful if the vendor can prove that he has delivered goods to the consumer and that the consumer has indeed ordered these goods. Failing such proof, eg because the consumer claims not to have made the order, the paid purchase price is refunded and the vendor is subject to a hefty charge. In this way, banks have completely passed on the risks of online fraud to online vendors. Yet, due to possible

[36] The term 'legal bond' being used in a very broad sense, including not only contractual design but also all kinds of 'private ordering' (JP Mifsud Bonnici and CNJ de Vey Mestdagh, 2005).

[37] Siegfried Georg Häberle, 2002.

[38] For the transfer of a 'delivery vs payment' system, well-known from stock market clearings, to B2C e-commerce see European Central Bank, 2004.

[39] Visa is used more often than any other card regarding online shopping, see: www.visaeurope.com/personal/onlineshopping/main.jsp.

abuse through unjustified complaints, in the meantime online vendors have been offered rating systems for credit card customers in order to identify in advance those consumers marked by numerous charge-backs. Somewhat misleadingly termed as consumer protection, yet probably more used to protect vendors, Visa now offers 'Verified by Visa', a system that provides registered customers with an additional password and which allows identification of the customer via a secure 'Visa'-server. Hence, customers cannot claim anymore that they have not ordered particular goods or services.[40]

In the debate on self-regulation in B2C e-commerce, credit card issuers have earlier been discussed as playing an important role in providing effective redress to consumers, since via the 'charge-back' procedure they could enforce decisions issued by ODR service providers.[41] Yet, this would mean that credit card suppliers either provide fair ODR procedures themselves or co-operate with an established ODR provider in this respect, neither of which is the case. In fact, current 'charge-back' procedures are relatively unfair, since vendors are unlikely to succeed in a complaints procedure given the form of evidence necessary, plus they have to carry high costs. Moreover, a fair 'charge-back' procedure should not only cover the absence of card holder authorisation ('I did not do it') but also include other frequently raised complaints, such as 'I did not receive it', 'item not as described', 'item defective', as well as the refund of the purchase price in case of withdrawal and return. In this regard, however, the legal situation differs from country to country: whereas such complaints are ruled out in France, consumers in the US enjoy such rights under the Fair Credit Billing Act. In other countries, the right to complain is stipulated by credit card agreements with the issuing bank. Hence, it remains at the bank's discretion whether it further pursues complaints, which are foreseen in the international 'charge-back' rules of credit card issuers.[42] Finally, the credit card system is unsuitable for small-value transactions due to its tariff scale.

'E-payment' service providers like 'PayPal' take advantage of this gap.[43] PayPal offers to its 56 million users a system of payment that allows the transfer of money to people in 45 countries provided they have an email address. The system requires opening a password-protected PayPal account, to which money can be transferred or for which a direct debit agreement can be authorised. In a protected procedure money can then be transferred via email. The transferred amount is credited to the recipient's

[40] www.visaeurope.com/merchant/handlingvisapayments/cardnotpresent/verifiedbyvisa.jsp.

[41] Henry H Perritt Jr, 2000b; Michael Kumpfmüller, 2008.

[42] OECD, Online Payment Systems for E-Commerce, DSTI/ICCP/IE(2004)18/FINAL, dated 18 April 2006, available at: www.oecd.org/dataoecd/37/19/36736056.pdf, 19.

[43] www.paypal.com; Jonathan Hill, 2008, 290.

PayPal account, which can be opened free of charge even after receipt of the email transfer. Credit can be transferred to a bank account at any time/on each occasion. This standard service is for both parties free of charge, yet there is no payment of interest on credit. PayPal offers special accounts for companies that allow acceptance of credit card payments via PayPal, even if the vendor does not participate in the credit card system. Since PayPal was acquired by eBay in 2002, PayPal offers a special service for eBay auctions. For eBay buyers, who pay via PayPal, a money-back guarantee takes effect in cases where goods are 'not received or significantly not as described' up to a value of US$1,000; for transactions not covered, PayPal provides a 'Buyer Complaint Process' in order to solve complaints. Additionally, PayPal offers support for companies both in averting 'credit card charge backs' and by providing a 'seller protection policy', which covers losses up to US$5,000 provided that the vendor carefully follows particular standards. In the context of settling disputed transactions, PayPal follows a rigid policy of freezing affected credit. Together with PayPal's partly limited attainability, this has led to criticism from companies and customers alike.[44]

Finally, comparable to a letter of credit, 'Escrow.com' offers an online escrow service, the use of which is recommended to customers by eBay for transactions involving higher sums and unknown contractual partners.[45] At first, buyer and seller register via Escrow.com's protected web page and then have to specify their terms of trade: among them a detailed description of the merchandise, its price, the method and insurance of delivery, the way to carry costs and the period in which the buyer has the right to return the goods. Then the buyer deposits the purchase price in an escrow account, Escrow.com informs the vendor about payment receipt, which causes the vendor to dispatch the ordered goods in a way that allows proof of delivery (eg, by United Parcel Services). If the time allowed for returning the goods passes without the buyer's complaint, the purchase price is paid out to the vendor. In case the buyer does not want to keep the goods, she can return them and get back the purchase price (less 0.85 percent as escrow charge) and dispatch costs according to previous agreement, provided that within a specified period the vendor has not objected to the return of the goods. In the latter case, the purchase price remains with Escrow.com without interest payment until buyer and seller have come to a mutual agreement. According to Escrow.com's terms of trade, after 60 days the matter is passed on to the American Arbitration Association (AAA) in order to come to a binding

[44] See the critical web pages www.paypalsucks.com and www.paypalwarning.com where vendors complain that 'PayPal' would deliberately delay complaints for months in order to benefit from the interest for blocked credits. Whereas consumers claim that PayPal would like to withdraw their right to the 'credit card charge back'-procedure.

[45] www.escrow.com; see also the 'Safe Trade program' by www.iloxx.de.

decision. In the meantime, the involved parties are free to turn, for instance, to SquareTrade in order to find an amicable solution, though 'Escrow.com' does not provide any binding rules concerning this procedure.

II. TRANSNATIONAL LAW REGIMES: THE ROLE OF VIRTUAL MARKETPLACES

The above survey of self-regulation in the global electronic marketplace has demonstrated that mechanisms of contractual governance, ranging from reputation and the involvement of trustworthy third parties as intermediaries to alternative dispute resolution—all of which were discussed above in chapter two II, where we introduced the concept of transnational law regimes—have been refined and adapted in order to be used in the field of B2C e-commerce as well. Yet, each of the introduced services alone leaves a number of problems unaddressed. If problems arise after a transaction has been entered into, it is hardly of use that the contractual partner has carefully been chosen on the basis of their reputation according to an individual ratings system or participation in a trustmark scheme. The handling of payments by an escrow service leads to no solution where a dispute has arisen and the parties involved are unable to agree on a particular dispute resolution procedure. Similarly, an ODR procedure is of no use if the resulting settlement is not implemented by the parties involved.[46]

Opportunistic behaviour can occur not only in the parties' direct contractual relationship, but also in the context of private ordering services offered by third parties. For example, a vendor might not only fail to perform as contractually promised, but might in addition fail to respond to a claim brought in an ODR procedure, or might fail to abide by a mutual agreement found in such ODR procedure. However, the efficacy of private ordering can be enhanced by combining different governance mechanisms, especially if it is agreed upon in advance which authority to turn to in case of a dispute, and if the parties' use of ODR procedures can be linked back to online reputation systems on the primary markets. Negative ratings are then given not only to sellers who deliver low-quality goods or to buyers who fail to pay, but also to those who behave unco-operatively in mediation, who do not follow settlements agreed on, or who evade an ongoing ODR procedure of an 'e-payment' provider via a parallel credit card charge-back, and so on.

In international commerce, the necessary *interlinkage* of different private ordering services regularly occurs in relation to an individual transaction. Of course one can find standardised contract clauses such as the 'Incoterms'

[46] Jonathan Hill, 2008, 300–301.

of the International Chamber of Commerce, standard forms for different arrangements concerning letters of credit, and model arbitration clauses referencing the rules of certain arbitration institutions. Yet these are individually tailored by international law firms into a contractual regime as complete as possible.[47] In consumer markets, in turn, there is a higher need for standardisation, which is usually satisfied by companies' general business terms. Due to their unilateral imposition on customers, however, such terms and conditions are hardly suitable to achieve a satisfactory level of consumer protection. In the domestic context, this is the rationale of state intervention through coercive consumer protection laws and judicial review. Similarly, in global B2C e-commerce there exists a demand for a neutral third party that could standardise private ordering services and tie them into effective transnational law regimes.

In this context, operators of virtual marketplaces perform an important function. For, even more than medieval harbours, fairs and marketplaces,[48] operators of electronic marketplaces stand in international competition for suppliers and consumers. In order to attract turnover, it is not only necessary to provide an efficient technical infrastructure, but also to establish a 'safe harbour' policy, which strengthens the trust of potential customers in the fairness of transactions handled in the marketplace. As international stock markets offer additional services for the handling of transactions (clearing) and try to establish standards of transparency and investor protection transcending legal minimum requirements,[49] operators of virtual marketplaces make an effort to establish a market order that both fosters consumer trust and satisfies the needs of small and medium-sized enterprises.

Founded 1995 in California, 'eBay' has developed from an electronic advertisement section, via a platform for online auctions, into the currently most popular site for Internet business between consumers and, especially, small businesses. It encompasses almost 150 million registered users throughout the world and 30 localised web pages ('the world's online marketplace').[50] In order to increase the attractiveness of the marketplace, eBay fosters the public spirit among its users, which leads to the emergence of a private market order.[51] As a virtual marketplace is a network commodity, the benefit of which increases with the number of participants,

[47] Gralf-Peter Calliess and Moritz Renner, 2009.

[48] Avner Greif, 2006.

[49] Johannes Adolff, 2003; Jan Damrau, 2003.

[50] pages.ebay.com/aboutebay/thecompany/companyoverview.html: Currently, 'with millions of buyers and sellers worldwide, eBay offers localized sites in the following markets': Australia, Austria, Belgium, Canada, China, France, Germany, Hong Kong, India, Ireland, Italy, Malaysia, the Netherlands, New Zealand, the Philippines, Poland, Singapore, South Korea, Spain, Sweden, Switzerland, Taiwan, the United Kingdom, and the United States. 'In addition, eBay has a presence in Latin America through its investment MercadoLibre.com'.

[51] pages.ebay.com/aboutebay/community.html.

the level of regulation has only slowly been increased reflecting customers' needs and numbers.[52] As already presented, the core of this market order is a rating system, which has been developed further by the introduction of star ratings and trust symbols. Through co-operation with other providers[53] as well as the buying up of the payment service provider 'PayPal', it has been embedded in a *network* of private ordering services.[54] In addition, eBay offers security tips to buyers and sellers with special attention given to international transactions.[55]

eBay's market order is based on the 'user agreement' and a number of additional 'policies', which regulate the behaviour of members in the marketplace and their relationship with eBay itself.[56] These detailed rules are centrally laid down by eBay, yet they are rooted in closely observed customer habits in the marketplace. They are constantly revised both in exchange with members of eBay fora and in reaction to arising issues becoming evident through the offered protection programmes for buyers and sellers. After termination of the co-operation agreement with SquareTrade, eBay built up its own dispute resolution centre, a fact indicating that ODR services are necessary to stabilise the market order. As a sanction for norm violations, the online reputation mechanism is available (*informal third-party-control*). This mechanism is fostered by eBay via the introduction of a new option for sellers: 'buyer-requirements'. Accordingly, buyers can be excluded who have a negative assessment, frequent 'item not paid' warnings[57] or no PayPal account.[58] On the other hand, eBay itself has the possibility of punishing violations of the market order by imposing sanctions: from warnings, to the temporary freezing of an account, to the exclusion of an involved member (*formal third-party-control*).[59]

Against this backdrop, it is hardly surprising that the literature refers to the regime established by eBay as an autonomous legal order.[60] Although the marketplace is not located outside the state's legal order—especially in Germany numerous judgments concerning eBay transactions have been passed[61]—courts can only partially and indirectly impact on eBay's market

[52] David P Baron, 2002.

[53] Eg eBay Germany co-operates with the escrow service 'iloxx Safetrade', available at: www.iloxx.de.

[54] pages.ebay.com/securitycenter/.

[55] offer.ebay.com/ws/eBayISAPI.dll?GlobalTradeHub&hubType=0.

[56] pages.ebay.com/help/policies: 1. Rules for Buyers, 2. Rules for Sellers, 3. Rules for Everyone, 4. Prohibited and Restricted Items, 5. Rules about Intellectual Property, 6. Feedback, 7. Privacy, 8. Identity.

[57] pages.ebay.de/help/tp/unpaid-item-process.html.

[58] pages.ebay.com/help/sell/buyer-requirements.html.

[59] See § 4 of the user agreement of eBay Germany, available at: pages.ebay.de/help/policies/user-agreement.html?ssPageName=f:f:DE.

[60] Ethan Katsh, Janet Rifkin and Alan Gaitenby, 2000, 705; David P Baron, 2002; Thomas Schultz, 2005.

[61] An up to date collection of verdicts, including many full texts, can be found under: www.internetrecht-rostock.de/ebay-und-internetauktionen.htm.

order. Recently, the German Federal Court (*Bundesgerichtshof*) decided that in the context of eBay auctions consumers have a right to cancel such transactions under the German distance selling provisions within a cooling-off period of two weeks.[62] The exercise of such right, however, contradicts the eBay principle for auctions that purchased goods have to be paid for and that an unpaid for item leads to a warning to the buyer due to his lack of reliability—all this independently of a right to return goods after receipt and inspection by the buyer.[63] Admittedly, eBay does not caution buyers for exercising their statutory right to cancel; yet, the immanent possibility of misuse of the right by its frequent and arbitrary exercise—producing high costs for vendors and eBay due to the necessary refund of commission-fees for auctions—can be tamed via negative feedback from the eBay community. Moreover, the effect of the judgment remains limited to those cases in which German law is applicable. Concerning cross-border transactions, German consumers can refer to the BGH, but they might find little understanding from the international eBay community for behaviour that jeopardises the economic rationale and attraction of online auctions and which consequently questions the market order fundamentally. In the case of a cancellation of an auction with a US seller, the eBay 'private legal system' might hardly help a German consumer to get a refund.

III. REFLEXIVE CONSUMER PROTECTION LAW

Transnational law regimes protecting consumers in the field of global e-commerce have become independent from the legal order of states by linking private rule-making (codes of conduct) with online dispute resolution procedures (ODR), mechanisms of socio-economic sanctioning (reputation, loss of trustmark, exclusion), and private enforcement (money-back guarantee, charge-back). Since a complex variety of such regimes has emerged, we can paint the picture of a *competition among transnational law regimes*, in which different providers of private order

[62] *Bundesgerichtshof* (Federal Court of Justice), decision of 3 November 2004 (VIII ZR 375/03), JurPC Web-Dok. 281/2004, available at: www.jurpc.de/rechtspr/20040281.htm; with critical remarks Ruth Janal, Case Note on the decision by the *Bundesgerichtshof* of 3 November 2004—VIII ZR 375/03 (*Widerrufsrecht bei Internet-Auktion*), JurPC Web-Dok. 4/2005, Abs 27 f., available at: www.jurpc.de/aufsatz/20050004.htm; see also the critical casenote by Gerald Spindler, 2005.

[63] § 9 of the terms of trade of eBay.de, available at: pages.ebay.de/help/policies/user-agreement.html?ssPageName=f:f:DE; see also: pages.ebay.de/help/policies/unpaid-item-process.html. Interestingly, the Amtsgericht Bremen, Decision of 20 October 2005 (16 C 168/O5) recently ruled, that a contractual penalty clause applying in case of an unwarranted exercise of a right to rescission (ie item not paid) is not an unfair business term under the European Unfair Contract Terms Directive (93/13/EEC). Thus, a buyer who refused to pay for a car he purchased by an auction on eBay was ordered to pay damages: www.internetrecht-rostock.de/ebayurteil29.htm.

compete for the trust of vendors and consumers alike.[64] With regard to the substantive consumer protection standards applied by such regimes, the Alternative Dispute Resolution Guidelines agreed on by the Global Business Dialogue on Electronic Commerce (GBDe) and Consumers International in November 2003 read:

> Applicable Rules: One of the principal reasons why business, consumers and governments consider the development of ADR systems to be of such strategic importance for the enhancement of consumer trust in electronic commerce is that such systems can settle disputes in an adequate fashion *without* necessarily engaging in cumbersome, costly, and difficult research on the detailed legal rules that would have to be applied in an official court procedure ... ADR dispute resolution officers *may decide in equity and/or on the basis of codes of conduct.* This flexibility as regards the grounds for ADR decisions provides an opportunity for the development of high standards of consumer protection worldwide (emphasis added).[65]

If ADR providers do not solve conflicts on the basis of state 'legal rules' but on the basis of 'codes of conduct', then substantive consumer contract law is privatised. This privatisation is triggered by a need for simple rules for international consumer contracts, where the application of state law including conflict of laws is 'cumbersome, costly, and difficult'. The thus described combined internationalisation and privatisation leads to what we call 'transnational consumer contract law'.

As mentioned above, private law-making is subject to judicial control for fairness, eg if a business imposes its terms and conditions unilaterally on the consumer in a contract of adhesion. In cases of codes of conduct which are produced and applied by a consumer-protecting transnational law regime, however, things are different. The bilateral contractual relationship between the business and the consumer is *triangularised*, since the transnational law regime comes in as a neutral third party. Here, the consumer is not only a recipient of goods but also a consumer of *private ordering services* supplied by an electronic marketplace like eBay or an ODR provider like SquareTrade, so that a trinity of contractual relationships arises.[66] On the level of the relationship between the immediate parties to a contract (seller and buyer) on the one hand and the provider of private ordering services (eBay) on the other hand, we deal with *reflexive consumer contract law* insofar as the procedural conditions are concerned which render the private generation of substantive consumer contract law rules fair.

[64] As shown below, this competition between transnational law regimes is substantially different, however, from the competition of different state consumer protection regimes as described in Obiora Okafor, 2007, ch 7.

[65] GBDe (Global Business Dialogue on electronic commerce), 2003, 59.

[66] For the arising trinity of potential contractual relationships, see Andreas Hacke, 2001, 31.

The thesis put forward here is that the establishment of effective consumer-protecting transnational law regimes will factually displace state consumer contract law in particular areas of e-commerce, especially in the realm of formally organised virtual marketplaces. This is why the emerging transnational consumer contract law requires an embedding in a procedural constitution of freedom, which at the same time enables the *privatisation of civil law* and adds the necessary *civilisation to private law*. This is to say that state-backed regulation disappears on the substantive level of the primary contract law rules, but should reappear on the meta-level of the secondary rules which ensure that the competition of consumer-protecting transnational law regimes will not lead to a so-called 'race to the bottom' in terms of substantive consumer rights.

In this respect, the necessary constitutionalisation of consumer-protecting transnational law regimes has to distinguish between an interior and an exterior constitution: the emergence of transnational consumer contract law as a legal *system* is, on the one hand, characterised by *reflexivity*, ie the application of a process to itself (eg, making norms on the making of norms, arbitrating over arbitration, self-regulation of self-regulation, etc); hence, societal self-organisation constitutes an interior *spontaneous constitution* of private regimes quasi by itself.[67] On the other hand, private regimes require embedding in a *public framework* that facilitates societal self-organisation as an exercise of party autonomy and at the same time limits it with respect to fairness, third-party interests, and public policy. Here the phenomena of normative reflexivity entrenched in private regimes, as well as their public framework, work as mutually compensatory constitutional orders. In the context of global governance, this renders their boundaries fuzzy. Encompassing the collaboration of state, industry, and civil society actors, they appear as a *hybrid* order,[68] which shall be termed *transnational constitution.*

The establishment of a transnational constitution for cross-border consumer contract law—that is, the making of transnational law (see above chapter two III)—mainly concerns the justification of reflexive institutions which organise the described phenomena of self-regulation and private ordering in a way that, on the one hand, fosters effective redress through alternative mechanisms of consumer protection and, on the other hand, guarantees the fairness and justice of such procedures towards consumers and businesses. In the following, different approaches for the constitutionalisation of consumer-protecting transnational law regimes are introduced. Although both aspects cannot be sharply distinguished, the focus is on the substantial contract law (*rights*) (A) and on the procedural aspects of consumer law (*remedies*) (B).

[67] See Gunther Teubner, 2003.
[68] Christoph Engel, 2001.

A. Reflexive Trustmarks: Contractual Standards of Hybrid Organisations

Trustmarks are awarded on the basis of a catalogue of criteria regularly consolidated in a code of conduct. For the Internet and e-commerce, a plethora of trustmarks is available which on the basis of different criteria aim at enhancing the protection of consumers, children and privacy or any combination of these. While, on the one hand, it is claimed that the best trustmarks prevail due to the invisible hand of competition, it is, on the other hand, feared that due to the wide variety of offers consumers could lose overview and, hence, that the general trust in the industry could vanish.[69] Certainly, a sound regulatory competition between different trustmark schemes only works where consumers are not misled by trustmark providers who apply inferior standards without sufficient monitoring.

In order to increase the transparency in the field of trustmarks, the notion has emerged that quality requirements should be developed in collaboration with states, industry, and consumer associations.[70] In so far as the compliance with minimum requirements established by co-regulation is here rewarded with the award of a secondary trustmark (*trustmark of trustmarks*), we deal with a reflexive form of self-regulation, which even regulates the conditions for its own possibility via self-regulation. Initial approaches to such constitutionalisation have first been developed at the national level (i). From here they can be linked to supranational (ii) and global constitutionalisation (iii) via co-operation.

(i) Secondary Trustmarks at the National Level

On the suggestion of the British government, the Alliance for Electronic Business in collaboration with the Consumers' Association founded a consumer protection initiative in the field of self-regulation in e-commerce in 1999. Its aim was to fix minimum standards in the face of the proliferation of trustmark programmes.[71] For it, the non-profit organisation 'TrustUK' was set up, the board of which consists of representatives of the Chambers of Commerce and of consumer associations. TrustUK established its own trustmark, which is, however, not directly awarded to vendors. As most companies are members of a Chamber of Commerce or of an association that binds its members to a code of practice, these 'code owners' are

[69] For this and the following cf the report of the Irish EU-Presidency presented at the European Consumer Day 2004 Conference 'Building Consumer Confidence in the European Online Marketplace, Dublin Castle, 15 March 2004', p 8, available at: register.consilium.eu.int/pdf/en/04/st09/st09466.en04.pdf.

[70] Fredrik Nordquist, Fredrik Andersson and Eva N Dzepina, 2002.

[71] www.trustuk.org.uk; Jonathan Hill, 2008, 296–98.

granted the licence for the distribution of the trustmark provided that their members' codes are in accordance with TrustUK's minimum requirements. Participating vendors bear either the TrustUK label alone or together with the trustmark of the 'code owner'; if issues arise consumers have to contact the 'owner' directly. Only if the consumer claims that the latter has not settled a dispute in accordance with TrustUK's guidelines is there the possibility to turn to TrustUK directly. Currently, four 'code owners' are accredited to TrustUK, covering more than 4,000 web traders.

The German initiative 'D21' is a network of political parties, enterprises, associations and other institutions ('public-private partnership'). Its aim is to improve the main conditions for Germany to quickly and successfully transit into the information and knowledge society.[72] In July 2002 members of the initiative agreed on the D21 quality criteria for Internet offers ('*D21-Qualitätskriterien für Internet-Angebote*'), which—as amended in 2005[73]—put the OECD Guidelines on the basis of European and German law in concrete terms. Furthermore, the criteria explain and amend the latter. Currently, the D21 initiative recommends five trustmarks meeting its quality criteria.[74] The monitoring and further development of these criteria have been transferred to a trustmark monitoring board, which apart from representatives of participating companies consists of a representative of each of the ministry of economic affairs, the federal data protection office and a consumer association ('*Verbraucherzentrale Bundesverband eV*').[75] However much such initiatives at the national level enhance the transparency of the trustmark market to a certain extent, nevertheless, due to their gearing to national law, they do not contribute much to solving issues of cross-border consumer contracts.[76]

(ii) Supranational Standardisation via Co-Regulation?

With regard to cross-border situations inside the European internal market, the question of which Member State's consumer protection standards shall apply could, in principle, be answered easily, as the minimum standards of consumer contract law are established in the European *acquis communautaire*, ie a variety of EC Directives. Yet, attempts by the European Commission to unify the contract law of the Member States have failed so far, often due to the resistance of consumer associations and national

[72] www.initiatived21.de.

[73] Updated version: www.internet-guetesiegel.de/docs/D21_Qualitaetskriterien_2005.pdf.

[74] www.internet-guetesiegel.de: Apart from Trusted Shops and among others, Euro-Label Deutschland of the EHI, available at: www.shopinfo.net and S@fer-Shopping, available at: www.safer-shopping.de run by the TÜV Süd are part of this initiative.

[75] Carsten Föhlisch, 2004.

[76] Fredrik Nordquist, Fredrik Andersson and Eva N Dzepina, 2002; Jonathan Hill, 2008, 299–300.

governments, which agreed on a minimum harmonisation of consumer rights, but prevented the necessary combination of such measures with the 'country of origin' principle.[77] Hence, one could ask whether it would not be a viable alternative to state-controlled legal harmonisation to generate substantive 'Principles of European Consumer Contracts' via self-regulation, for instance by developing Europe-wide recommended general contract terms,[78] or relating specifically to B2C e-commerce by elaborating a European code of conduct which could be applied in cross-border ADR procedures as institutionalised in the European Extra-Judicial Network (EEJ-Net).[79]

The European Commission, indeed, aims at such a project in the frame of its 'e-confidence' initiative. In its action plan concerning 'eEurope 2005', the following aims are introduced:

> Trust and confidence. By end 2003, the Commission, together with the private sector, consumer organisations and Member States will examine possibilities of establishing a European-wide online dispute resolution system. To facilitate cross-border electronic transactions for SMEs, the Commission will further support the establishment of online information systems on legal issues. The Commission will work with stakeholders on trustmarks requirements with a view to a recommendation on consumer confidence in electronic commerce.[80]

In order to prepare such a recommendation, the Commission has established an 'e-confidence forum' at the Joint Research Centre in the year 2000. In this context, a 'drafting group' comprising members of industry and consumer associations has drawn up 'principles for e-commerce codes of conduct'.[81] On this basis, the European industrial and consumer associations—Union des industries de la Communauté européenne (UNICE) and Bureau Européen des Unions de Consommateurs (BEUC)—have agreed on 'European trustmark requirements' (ETR). For their implementation, a committee of association members shall be established and an 'e-confidence' web page shall be set up. Providers of trustmarks who want to join this portal have to pass an annual assessment of their compliance with the ETR through an independent third party (eg, auditors).[82] Since the announcement of the programme in October 2001, there

[77] See also Gralf-Peter Calliess, 2003b; Gralf-Peter Calliess, 2003a.

[78] European Commission (2003) A More Coherent European Contract Law. An Action Plan, COM(2003) 68 final, 21, at 4.2.

[79] See: ec.europa.eu/consumers/redress/out_of_court/eej_net/index_en.htm.

[80] European Commission, eEurope 2005: An information society for all, An Action Plan to be presented in view of the Sevilla European Council, 21–22 June 2002, COM(2002) 263 final, 15.

[81] On file with authors.

[82] BEUC (Bureau Européen des Unions de Consommatuers/The European Consumers' Organisation) and UNICE (The Confederation of European Business/BUSINESSEUROPE), 2001.

have, however, been no recognisable steps towards the establishment of the system. In November 2004, the Commission finally accepted the failure of the initiative and blamed the industry for a lack of interest in the implementation of the ETR, especially with regard to the financing.[83] This lack of interest may be rooted in the fact that the ETR were developed by association officials who stand more for a traditional industrial society than a modern information society. In addition, it remains unclear how the ETR could contribute to the problems of cross-border B2C e-commerce. In this respect the ETR approach—praised by the Commission—is aiming for a race to the top: '[t]he ETR offer a basis for good online practice. They do not seek to override or replace any mandatory provisions at European level. They are supplementary to legal obligations and do not affect consumers' statutory rights'.[84] In this respect, the ETR accord with consumerists, who demand that 'soft law' generated in the process of self-legislation should lead only to an increase in the level of protection, and under no circumstances to a softening or evasion of those obligatory consumer protection regulations already in place in a consumer's home country (European Consumer Law Group, 2001). Yet, as the ETR refer to nationally applicable law in almost all important points, they appear strangely anaemic and neither guide SMEs to those regulations they should adopt for Europe-wide sales nor do they work as standard for ADR decisions in consequential conflicts. For the solution to the problem of EU-wide cross-border B2C e-commerce is to have uniform legal standards which provide the necessary certainty, and not just another code like the ETR which merely adds to the existing regulatory chaos. One can suspect that the protagonists involved with the ETR are too close to the European legislative process which prevents the 'e-confidence' initiative from becoming an independent stimulus for the generation of certainty of law and justice in the internal market.

At the European level, the 'Euro-Label' system, however, provides a functioning alternative, which was established due to an initiative of the trade association EuroCommerce in 2002.[85] Euro-Label is a network of national trustmark providers from Austria, Germany, France, Spain, Poland and Italy that awards trustmarks on the basis of a common European code of

[83] See European Commission, Commission Staff Working Document, Consumer Confidence in E-Commerce: lessons learned from the e-confidence initiative, SEC(2004) 1390, available at: ec.europa.eu/consumers/cons_int/e-commerce/e-conf_working_doc.pdf.

[84] Appraisal of the European Commission, 2004: 9: 'The Commission Services are of the view that codes such as the ETR are most useful if they contain provisions that set an even higher standard of consumer protection than the protection offered by legislation'. See also BEUC (Bureau Européen des Unions de Consommatuers/The European Consumers' Organisation) and UNICE (The Confederation of European Business/BUSINESSEUROPE), 2001.

[85] www.euro-label.com.

conduct via co-branding. Euro-Label also handles cross-border complaints against its more than 650 certified shops. If in this way issues cannot be resolved, the consumer is referred to the EEJ-Net. The 'European code of conduct' is relatively detailed; instead of sweeping references to nationally applicable law, it details the concrete rules of the *acquis communautaire*. Concerning withdrawals, for instance, it repeats the EU directive on distance contracts, which states that the withdrawal period has to be at least seven working days, does not commence before prior information and delivery and ceases after three months at the latest. Certification, though, happens by national authorities according to local standards. It cannot be foreseen whether the European Codex will be of crucial importance beyond its function as a minimum standard for participating national trustmark providers, for instance in the arbitration of cross-border disputes.[86] Its wording, however, would render it more apposite than the ETR.

(iii) Global Linkage

Already in 2001, the Global Business Dialogue on e-commerce (GBDe) published recommendations concerning trustmarks, including both guidelines for trustmark providers and minimum standards for the codes of conduct applicable to their online traders.[87] Also in 2001, the European umbrella organisation of the Chambers of Commerce, Eurochambres, the mail order firm FEDMA and the US BBBOnline launched the Global Trustmark Alliance (GTA) as a common initiative in order to further develop and implement global standards. Its aim is to unite national and regional trustmark initiatives on the basis of common minimum standards, under the umbrella of the global GTA trustmark, which is intended to be pursued as a co-branding endeavour.[88] In the meantime, the GTA membership has been expanded, especially by Asian organisations, and on the occasion of the annual meeting of the GBDe in November 2004, an organisational committee was installed and given the task of preparing 'best practices'.[89] Given the global reach of the GTA initiative and based on OECD guidelines and the recommendations of the GBDe, it can be expected that the emerging code of conduct will set relevant standards for a transnational consumer contract law.

The involved organisations also intend to co-operate in the handling of cross-border disputes. A good example is the agreement on mutual co-operation in cross-border e-commerce complaints signed by ECOM ADR, a pilot project commissioned by the Japanese Ministry of Economy, Trade and Industry (METI) and operated by Next Generation Electronic Commerce

86 Jonathan Hill, 2008, 316.
87 GBDe (Global Business Dialogue on electronic commerce).
88 See www.bbbonline.org/about/press/2001/042301.asp.
89 GTA (Global Trustmark Alliance), 2004.

Promotion Council of Japan (ECOM),[90] and the US Better Business Bureau in 2002, where complaints from consumers in one country against an e-trader situated in the other country are exchanged and both organisations work together, if necessary assisting in language problems. As of October 2004, 45 complaints from Japanese consumers against US-based companies were forwarded from ECOM-ADR to BBB-Online, and 22 of these disputes had been settled. 12 disputes came to Japan in turn, out of which only two could be settled, while the other cases involved fraud, where eg businesses turned out not to exist at all in Japan.[91] Although ECOM ADR ceased its operations as of March 2006, the quite impressive resolution rate of BBB-Online may be taken as an outlook on how a seamless ODR network for cross-border B2C e-commerce might work in the future.

B. Law-Consumer Protection: ODR Standards and their Implementation

Set down in Article 6(1) of the European Convention for the Protection of Human Rights and Fundamental Freedoms, the 'right to a fair trial' is the codification of the citizen's claim to jurisdiction directly following from the ban on self-help. The Convention frames this claim within the rule of law:

> In the determination of his civil rights and obligations ... everyone is entitled to a fair and public hearing within a reasonable time by an independent and impartial tribunal established by law. Judgement shall be pronounced publicly.[92]

The inherent procedural guarantees are not only the core and heart of the European civil procedure,[93] they also impact on alternative arbitration procedures provided that those are binding to the parties involved.[94] In this way, the European Court of Human Rights has acknowledged that one can give up one's right to access to court, yet such renunciation—for instance as part of an arbitration clause—is only effective if it is voluntary and explicitly expressed. Furthermore, by the judicial review of private arbitration tribunals, the state remains obliged to guarantee the core of fundamental procedural rights, like the right to be heard, judicial independence and procedural neutrality.[95] From the vantage point of ODR procedures in the field of B2C e-commerce, these principles are not only in force for consumer arbitration in a narrow sense, they can also become relevant on the side of companies as they set obligatory and binding procedures, like those in the

[90] See www.ecom.jp/adr/en/index.html; see as well as the outline in Toshiko Sawada, 2004.
[91] Toshiko Sawada, 2004.
[92] conventions.coe.int/Treaty/en/Treaties/Html/005.htm.
[93] Manfred Wolf, 2000.
[94] Susan Schiavetta, 2004.
[95] For the jurisdiction issues, see *ibid*.

case of 'Online Confidence's arbitration procedure concerning amounts in dispute up to 5,000 Euro.'[96]

Yet, even if the parties' right to access to court is not limited in any way, there is demand for principles concerning the transparency and fairness of ODR procedures. Hence, companies which have contractually committed themselves to participate in an online mediation procedure if required by a customer—like in the trustmark programmes of SquareTrade—have to be informed in advance about procedural conditions. In a similar way, the SquareTrade trustmark can only then enhance consumer trust in e-commerce if the consumer is able to form an impression of the course of the procedure and of whether it appears to be fair and reasonable with respect to the neutrality of mediators, to costs, to the promise for the implementation of negotiation results, etc. On this matter, providers of ODR procedures can be subject to certain pre-contractual obligations to inform customers.[97]

In order to render the market for ODR services more transparent and to establish certain minimum standards of fairness under prescribed circumstances, different ODR service providers have (i) suggested different measures in order to guarantee compliance with these principles (ii).

(i) Guidelines for Providers of ODR Procedures

Initially one has to keep in mind that there exists a number of principles for traditional ADR procedures in consumer affairs that special guidelines for B2C e-commerce can build upon: this includes the 15 principles of the 'Due Process Protocol for Mediation and Arbitration of Consumer Disputes' of 1998. The AAA has made compliance with these standards a precondition for consumer arbitration procedures;[98] similarly, it is a precondition for participation in the EEJ-Net to follow the European Commission's recommendations concerning dispute settlement (98/257/EG) and Mediation (2001/310/EG) in consumer affairs.[99] A preliminary outcome of the consultations on the European Commission's 'Green Paper on Alternative Dispute Settlement in Civil and Commercial Matters'[100] is the 'European Code of Conduct for Mediators',[101] which contains a number of ethical principles and which can be adopted by single mediators or institutional providers of mediation procedures.

Based on extensive consultations, the 'Task Force on Electronic Commerce and Alternative Dispute Resolution' of the American Bar Association (ABA)

[96] *Ibid.*

[97] Lucille M Ponte, 2002b; Jonathan Hill, 2008, 315–16.

[98] For the necessicity to adopt the protocol to the Internet see Lucille M Ponte, 2002a.

[99] See ec.europa.eu/consumers/redress/out_of_court/adr_recommendations_en.htm.

[100] For more information, see ec.europa.eu/civiljustice/adr/adr_ec_en.htm.

[101] www.cto.int/Portals/0/docs/adr/adr_ec_code_conduct_en.pdf.

published 'Recommended Best Practices by Online Dispute Resolution Service Providers' in September 2002. These are meant as a non-binding point of orientation for ODR service providers, consumers and trustmark providers and suggest that an ODR service provider informs its users about all relevant features of a procedure in a transparent way.[102] In November 2003 the 'Task Force on Consumer Policy for e-Business' of the International Chamber of Commerce (ICC) has published 'Best Practices for Online Dispute Resolution (ODR) in B2C and C2C transactions', which contain guidelines both for enterprises handling B2C e-commerce and for ODR service providers.[103] At the same time, the Global Business Dialogue on E-Commerce (GBDe) and Consumers International (CI) have agreed on common 'Alternative Dispute Resolution Guidelines' for B2C e-commerce, which contain recommendations for enterprises, ODR service providers, and governments.[104]

(ii) The Implementation of Global ODR Standards

To implement the discussed standards for ODR service providers, a number of measures have been discussed, ranging from self-regulation to national outline legislation. In this context, the role of the state tends to be more emphasised than is usually the case.[105] With respect to transnational consumer contract law, the suggested ODR standards touch upon the relationship between citizens and the state and, hence, they concern the kernel of constitutional law set down in Article 6(1) of the European Convention for the Protection of Human Rights and Fundamental Freedoms. On the one side, such standards have to be developed and spread by institutions that leave no doubt about their neutrality in the face of conflicting interests and thus enjoy the unreserved trust of all involved.[106] Initiatives for self-regulation, led by industry and commerce such as the GBDe or the ICC, do not meet these criteria on their own.[107] On the other side, ODR standards that have been developed with the support of states are advantageous, as they can work as guidelines for judicial review in particular cases. The terms of trade of ODR service providers as well as terms of trade clauses concerning dispute

[102] Michael Kumpfmüller, 2008.

[103] ICC (International Chamber of Commerce), 2003.

[104] GBDe (Global Business Dialogue on electronic commerce), 2003.

[105] Thomas Schultz, 2003; Julia Hörnle, 2009, 246.

[106] See Michael Kumpfmüller, 2008, 32–33; Benjamin G Davis, 2002b; Julia Hörnle, 2009, 238–44.

[107] For this reason the GBDe developed its ADR Guidelines in cooperation with Consumers International. The Guidelines call for governments to initiate 'government accreditation' and/or 'government-backed assessment rules' together with industry and consumer representatives, and on a global level only.

settlement in consumer contracts cannot easily been declared ineffective if they stand in accordance with globally accepted ODR standards.

With the establishment of the EEJ-Net as well as the above-mentioned EU recommendations, the European Commission in particular has demonstrated what a functioning state organisation at the supranational level could contribute. Following this model, the ABA Task Force has discussed the set up of a 'Global Dispute Clearing House', dealing with issues arising out of cross-border consumer contracts, which consumers could turn to if problems emerge and which would be responsible for transferring conflicts to those ODR procedures accredited on the basis of global ODR standards. Furthermore, it was considered whether to establish an ODR trustmark, which can be awarded to those ODR service providers following ODR standards developed by the 'Global Online Standards Commission'.[108]

Yet, the ABA Task Force concludes that the ODR market is not yet mature enough in order to set up binding standards ('not one-size-fits-all'). Moreover, an agreement about such standards in a 'Global Online Standards Commission' under international law is unlikely, due to the apparent divergences, eg, between the USA and the EU concerning the authorisation of consumer arbitration jurisdiction. Additionally, the accreditation of ODR providers with a global ODR trustmark would require substantial financial and personal resources, which would be desirable, yet which seem unachievable. In the current situation, for companies it is of primary importance to avoid disputes by setting up effective consumer complaint procedures ('customer satisfaction systems'). Furthermore, as a first step it is suggested to establish an '*i-ADR-Center*', which is given the task of consolidating information about available dispute resolution procedures on the web ('low-cost, low-profile'). Without being assessed, an ODR provider can initially commit themselves to ODR standards such as the ABA Best Practices. At first financed by the state, such a centre for information could later function as a basis for the more advanced notion of a 'Dispute Clearinghouse' or 'ODR Trustmark Centres'.[109]

More than two years after the ABA recommendations were published, however, the suggested 'i-ADR-Center' has not been established; presumably no sponsor for the project could be found, despite the pursued approach ('low-cost, low-profile'). Taking the EEJ-Net as a blue-print, the UN would actually be the right point of contact. UNECE has indeed organised conferences concerning ODR in 2002 and 2003 in Geneva; in 2004, the third 'UN-Forum on Online Dispute Resolution' took place at the University of Melbourne in co-operation with UNESCA.[110] Due to its chronic lack of financing and efficacy, the UN is hardly able to contribute more than its

[108] Michael Kumpfmüller, 2008, 27; Benjamin G Davis, 2002a.
[109] Michael Kumpfmüller, 2008, 31.
[110] www.odr.info/unforum2004/.

name to the development of global ODR standards. The organisation of the conferences as well as the publication of the results was taken on by academic institutions. For instance, the 'Center for Information Technology and Dispute Resolution' (CITDR) at the University of Massachusetts provides the website www.odr.info, where not only the presentations of the UN-ODR forum are published,[111] but also broad information is available about ODR providers, ODR standards, literature, etc. This actually meets the described functions of the 'i-ADR-Center' suggested by the ABA Task Force.[112] Similar to the Transnational Law Database CENTRAL concerning the *Lex Mercatoria* at the University of Cologne, in the area of transnational consumer contract law science can play an important part through the systematisation of information.[113]

Finally, we would like to introduce the model of state incentives that combines compliance with certain standards and the granting of legal privileges. Thus, the Act on ADR of North Rhine Westphalia couples the accreditation of a mediation institution with the advantage of executing a settlement comparable to a court ruling, provided the standards of transparency and fairness set forth in the Act are complied with.[114] During the political debate on the so-called Brussels-I Regulation, the responsible committee of the European Parliament suggested that in deviation from Article 17 of the Regulation, enterprises should be allowed to introduce a 'choice of court' clause in consumer contracts if in return they subject themselves to an acknowledged out-of-court dispute settlement body.[115] The notion that the state facilitates ADR upon compliance with certain minimum conditions of due process is well established in international commercial arbitration, where arbitral awards corresponding with the requirements outlined in the 1958 New York Convention and the 1985 UNCITRAL Model Law are recognised and enforced by the state.[116] It seems logical, yet hardly realistic to suggest that taking the juridical review of private arbitral awards as a model, compliance with globally accepted ODR standards could be guaranteed by setting up an international public online court, where appeals against outcomes of ODR procedures could be lodged.[117]

[111] www.odr.info/unece2003/index.htm.

[112] Although the information is not always comprehensive and up to date, since ODR.info relies on voluntary contributions mostly by academics.

[113] See, eg the Transnational Law Database on the New Law Merchant established at the Centre for Transnational Law (Professor Klaus-Peter Berger) of the University of Cologne, available at: www.trans-lex.org.

[114] The 'GüSchlG NRW' is available at: www.streitschlichtung.nrw.de/streit/gesetz.php.

[115] Diana Wallis, 2000.

[116] Alan Redfern and Martin Hunter, 2004.

[117] Thomas Schultz, 2003.

IV. RCRC IN THE MAKING OF TRANSNATIONAL CONSUMER CONTRACT LAW

In this chapter we have shown that the private governance mechanisms which have been developed in international commerce between merchants in order to tackle opportunism in cross-border economic exchanges in a situation of constitutional uncertainty—ie the absence of a world state effectively guaranteeing the protection of property rights and the enforcement of contracts—recently have successfully been adapted to the new phenomenon of cross-border electronic commerce between businesses and consumers. Thus, private ordering has proven to be a valuable alternative to state law not only in the apolitical domain of merchant law, where predominantly co-ordinative problems arise, but might as well contribute to the solution of regulatory problems in the area of consumer law, where the protection of weaker parties is at stake. The fact that entrepreneurship in private ordering services led to an extension of its traditional domain—that is the co-ordination of merchants—towards regulatory issues such as the protection of weaker contract parties was the reason why we decided to call the emerging regimes in this area 'transnational law regimes', indicating their ambiguous status somewhere in between or beyond the traditional public-private divide on the *substantive plane* (above, chapter two).

One reason for this successful extension of private ordering is that the protection of consumers is in the rational self-interest of businesses which intend to engage in cross-border commerce with foreign consumers. In order to convince consumers to enter the borderless global retail-market, businesses have to invest in building consumer confidence in electronic commerce by employing various consumer-protecting governance mechanisms. Another reason is the emergence of businesses which do not engage in the *primary markets* for consumer products and services themselves, but act as market makers between other businesses and consumers, and thus, on a *secondary market* for private legal services. These intermediaries are economically interested in attracting a maximum of sellers as well as buyers to participate in their marketplaces. Therefore, it lies in their rational self-interest to act as a neutral party towards both sides of the market, businesses as well as consumers. Electronic marketplaces are, therefore, in a perfect position to effectively bundle different private governance mechanisms into what we call transnational law regimes.

As has been shown in Section III of this chapter, however, a variety of consumer protection concerns remain to be solved. If consumers in the electronic world marketplace are able to choose between different consumer-protecting transnational law regimes, there is the need for transparency with regard to the offered level of protection as well as the effectiveness and fairness of such regimes. In other words, there is a need for substantive as well as procedural minimum standards regarding the private provision of consumer-protecting services, ie 'law-consumer protection'. As such standards for the borderless character of B2C e-commerce have to have a truly transnational character, they are developed outside the traditional international law sphere on the basis of co-regulatory efforts between states, industry, and civil society actors. There can be observed a variety of efforts to establish such global minimum standards, which contribute to the future establishment of a 'transnational constitution' of cross-border consumer contract law. The thus described diffusion of the status and role of actors engaged in regulation was the reason why we decided to call the emerging regimes in this area 'transnational law regimes' on the *procedural plane* (above, chapter two).

As has been shown above in Section III on reflexive consumer protection law, a wide variety of actors are collaborating in an effort to build up a *Rough Consensus* on substantive as well as procedural global minimum standards for consumer protection in B2C e-commerce. However, the multitude of fora in which such minimum standards are discussed and promoted seems to be a serious problem, which limits the likeliness of their transformation into a *Running Code*. The most visible actors in the area of transnational consumer contract law so far have been the OECD in the international public sphere and the Global Trustmark Alliance (GTA) in the private sphere, which is backed by industry initiatives such as the GBDe as well as civil society actors such as Consumers International. Thus, transnational consumer contract law is still in the making, while the above-discussed global standards are still in the pilot phase or in the early recommendation phase. It remains to be decided if the emerged Rough Consensus on these standards will lead to a Running Code in the future. A joint effort by the OECD and the GTA in this regard might be considerably helpful.

4

Transnational Corporate Governance

I. CORPORATE GOVERNANCE CODES

IN THIS CHAPTER, we shift our attention away from transnational consumer contracts in order to explore one of the most dynamic and at the same time scholarly belaboured fields in law today: transnational corporate governance. The chapter comprises two case studies, the first of which focuses on corporate governance codes and the second on executive compensation, or remuneration. Corporate governance codes are an example of the particular dynamics in the area of corporate law making, an area which displays all of the general trends we have so far identified as characteristic of emerging transnational law regimes. More specifically, as we will see, the development, practice and impact of corporate governance codes can be read as a telling illustration of the RCRC model, which we have developed in chapter two. Corporate governance codes such as those at the centre of the first case study are part of the increasingly dense matrix of *transnational corporate governance*. Their very nature—their ambiguity and their oscillation between 'hard' and 'soft' law, between state intervention and market ordering, between, in fact, law and non-law—has been keeping scholars, policy-makers, activists and stakeholders on their toes for years.

Corporate governance codes are woven into the mystic fabric of transnational law, of global governance, of the privatisation of international economic law, and of the 'transformation of the state' and the larger project of law's introspection. Corporate governance codes raise, par excellence, questions of law's identity, questions regarding its demarcation from non-law, its creation, enforcement and impact. As widespread phenomena of corporate law regulation, they embody the challenges we have addressed above—in chapter two—with regard to the notion of 'community'. Our previous discussion of transnational commercial law suggests that even if we conceived of such codes as examples of business 'self-regulation', the ensuing questions of community, legitimacy and effectiveness would still be critical. Even more poignantly than the previous example, corporate law regulation exacerbates the 'third-party effects' of contractual governance in a striking fashion. The identification of the 'parties' at the respective ends of contractual arrangements within and around the corporation as a legal person is only the beginning of unfolding 'the theory of the business enterprise'.[1] As we lay out a definition of corporate governance below, it will become obvious that any such effort is tied into the underlying concept of the business enterprise and its regulation. Is the corporation—under law?—a contract between shareholders (investors) and managers? Is this contract complemented by or distinct from other contractual relations within the corporation? Which contractual relations define the 'purpose' of the corporation? Corporate governance codes are the ghosts in the machine. This machine is the corporation and at the same time it is the transnational creation, expansion and dissemination of rules governing the corporation. An understanding of these rules demands an understanding of the corporation. Is there a way out of this circularity?

Building on our conceptualisation of RCRC in chapter two, this chapter seeks to unfold the transnational dimension of corporate governance 'from within'. Rather than studying the perhaps 'obvious' examples of transnational corporate governance rules as they are evidenced in the *OECD Principles* and the *OECD Guidelines on Multinational Enterprises*,[2] the *UN Global Compact*[3] or the *UN Draft Norms*,[4] this chapter approaches corporate governance from the perspective of transnational *embeddedness* in order to draw out the complex correlations between different levels and spaces of norm creation that characterise corporate governance today and, in fact, make it one of the most fascinating regulatory laboratories. This approach forces us to leave aside in this inquiry, for example, the pressing questions that arise in the context of the regulation of labour rights in corporate codes of conduct.[5] We will also refrain from trying directly to contribute to the extremely rich debate as regards the correlation between the 'soft law' of guidelines and corporate codes of conduct and corporate social responsibility, a correlation that has long been central to any inquiry into the regulation of international business transactions.[6] Closely

[1] Thorstein Veblen, 1958.

[2] www.oecd.org/dataoecd/56/36/1922428.pdf; Jean du Plessis and Claus Luttermann, 2007; Gefion Schuler, 2008; Larry Catá Backer, 2009.

[3] www.unglobalcompact.org/. See George Kell, 2003; Oliver F Williams, 2004; Lynn Bennie, Patrick Bernhagen and Neil J Mitchell, 2007.

[4] UN Economic and Social Council, Norms on the responsibilities of transnational coporations and other business enterprises with regard to human rights. Published on 26 August 2003, available at: www.unhchr.ch/huridocda/huridoca.nsf/(Symbol)/E.CN.4.Sub.2.2003.12.Rev.2.En; see, eg Carolin F Hillemanns, 2003; Surya Deva, 2004; David Weissbrodt and Muria Kruger, 2003, and David Weissbrodt and Muria Kruger, 2005.

[5] See Lance Compa and Tashia Hinchliffe-Darricarrère, 1995; Adelle Blackett, 2004; Harry W Arthurs, 2002; Peer Zumbansen, 2006b.

[6] See, eg Jill Murray, 1998, Thomas McInerney, 2007, Dirk Matten and Jeremy Moon, 2008, and Larry Catá Backer, 2009.

related hereto are the questions that surround the correlation between international organisations and their production of norms, principles, standards and rules.[7]

Instead, this chapter will explore the role of corporate governance codes in an increasingly mixed and decentralised production of corporate law rules and standards. The proliferation of such codes that we turn to now, as well as the ensuing study of standard-setting with regard to executive compensation, illustrate the degree to which corporate governance has long become a *transnational law regime* as defined in chapter two above.

The development of corporate governance codes (CGCs) reflects intricate, domestic and transnational, multi-level processes of norm generation and norm enforcement. Starting from mere factual evidence, the emergence of corporate governance codes in recent years has begun to fundamentally alter the legal landscape of corporate law.[8] Despite their increasingly widespread recognition as indeed an essential element of corporate law,[9] these codes continue to pose particular challenges to legal theory when compared to other, statutory approaches to law-making, as they regularly are drafted by non-state actors such as non-governmental associations, private industry institutes or corporate actors.[10] In general, corporate governance codes are relatively short collections of legal regulations already in force in a particular jurisdiction, that are accompanied by recommendations and suggestions, directed either to private corporations or, in some cases,[11] the law-maker, concerning a company's organisation, its governance rules or disclosure regime as well as its duties towards stakeholders, employees and the environment.[12] Offering a considerable range of flexibility, corporate

[7] See, eg the debate between Alston and Langille with regard to the role of the International Labour Organization and 'core labour standards', Philip Alston, 2003; Brian A Langille, 2005; Philip Alston, 2005a. For a concise reconstruction of the ILO as an international organisation, see Lawrence R Helfer, 2006.

[8] For an overview of so far existing corporate governance codes in various countries, see www.ecgi.org/codes/all_codes.php. For an interesting analysis of how the adoption of the corporate governance code has legitimated Slovenia to adapt the country's company law to international standards rather than having permitted for 'institutional learning', see Nina Cankar, Simon Deakin and Marko Simoneti, 2008.

[9] See Melvin Eisenberg, 2005, 176, 182.

[10] See, for one of the first examples, the German Corporate Governance Code, the interview with Professor Theodor Baums, who chaired the commission that preceded the commission to draft the first German Corporate Governance Code: Theodor Baums, 2001a. For a study and analysis of the work by the American Law Institute on this field, see, eg the contributions to the *Symposium: The American Law Institute's Corporate Governance Project* (1993) *Business Lawyer* 1267; for a discussion of the development in the UK, see, eg Sue Bowden, 2000, John Armour, Simon Deakin and Suzanne J Konzelmann, 2003, and Paul L Davies, 2003. See, for the case of Slovenia, Nina Cankar, Simon Deakin and Marko Simoneti, 2008.

[11] See Ulrich Noack and Dirk Zetzsche, 2005, 6–7.

[12] Christine Mallin, 2005, 19–40; Jennifer Hill, 2005, 376 (highlighting how CGC have tended to be either a response to the absence of governmental regulation or a justification of such absence); Melvin Eisenberg, 2005, 182: 'bodies of standards, principles, or rules that are

governance codes and corporate codes of conduct have become key regulatory instruments in the 'post-regulatory state'.[13] As such, they are of interest both as representative examples of larger transformative trends in post-interventionist, procedural, indirect regulation and as illustrations of far-reaching reform processes in domestic corporate law systems worldwide.[14] The names of such transformations fluctuate between characterisations as 'market-driven reform' and claims to 'universal convergence' of corporate governance systems towards shareholder value.[15] A far-reaching and yet to be fully unpacked *financialisation* of corporate law through capital market law[16] ties path-dependent trajectories of national political economies into the global evolution of markets.[17] This short-circuiting of 'embedded' trajectories of domestic reform, routine and innovation processes in corporate law and securities regulation with the treacherous disembeddedness of global financial markets constitutes the most pressing challenge to present projects of corporate governance reform.[18] The 'convergence vs divergence' debate in corporate law that spurred an almost overwhelming production of comparative assessments on the origins and prospects of different national corporate law systems has only recently begun to ebb,[19] leaving the contestants somewhat wondering where to direct their creative and sometimes polemical energies. This constellation is in many ways a particularly ambivalent one, as the topic as such no longer seems as clearly defined as it was some years ago. Among the discursive topics that appear to be pursued with increasing rigour is the correlation between corporate law and capital markets law in the face of the global financial and economic crisis[20] that has given preceding assessments of this relation a twist of considerable urgency. Other topics currently attracting

promulgated by private institutions, and that have force of some sort although they are not directly backed by state sanctions'.

[13] Colin Scott, 2004; Colin Scott, 2008a.

[14] With regard to the approach taken in the Cadbury Report, see John C Shaw, 1997; for a comparative view of Germany and the UK, see David Seidl, Paul Sanderson and John Roberts, 2009; with considerable skepticism: Nina Cankar, Simon Deakin and Marko Simoneti, 2008 (focusing on the case of Slovenia).

[15] See, on the one hand, Henry Hansmann and Reinier Kraakman, 2001, and, on the other, Cynthia A Williams, 2002, 711–14; Antoine Rebérioux, 2004, and Ronald Dore, 2008.

[16] Werner F Ebke, 2000; Klaus J Hopt, 2003; Friedrich Kübler, 2003; Luca Enriques and Matteo Gatti, 2007a.

[17] See Saskia Sassen, 2005.

[18] See, hereto, the contributions to Klaus J Hopt and Eddy Wymeersch, 2003, and to Klaus J Hopt, Eddy Wymeersch, Hideki Kanda and Harald Baum, 2005.

[19] For an excellent representation of the debate, see Joseph A McCahery, Piet Moerland, Theo Raaijmakers and Luc Renneborg, 2002, and Jeffrey N Gordon and Mark J Roe, 2004.

[20] See, eg *OECD Observer*, No 273 (June 2009): Corporate governance: Lessons from the Crisis, available at: www.oecdobserver.org/news/fullstory.php/aid/2931/Corporate_governance:_Lessons_from_the_financial_crisis.html. 'If there is one major lesson to draw from the financial crisis, it is that corporate governance matters'.

substantial attention are 'not so new' in the sense that current explorations of corporate social responsibilities and Human Rights obligations of multinational or transnational enterprises/corporations (MNEs/TNCs) hark back to historical contestations of the allegedly private nature of a purely profit-driven business enterprise.[21] The critical examination of the possible 'limits of law' vis-à-vis transnational corporate power[22] has fast extended itself into a complex web of regulatory strategies at the core of which scholars have regularly been shifting between questions of re-domesticating (or, litigating) a global corporate actor[23] and devising a regulatory and, very importantly, 'meta'-regulatory[24] (legal) framework adequate to the transnational reality of TNCs. Pursuits with regard to the latter strategy have a history of their own. Detlef Vagts noted 40 years ago: '[a]s the literature about the MNE grows exponentially, the question arises whether the legal profession should not be developing responses to it. As yet it has not: statutory or case law is virtually nonexistent and the secondary coverage is thin'.[25] Over time, such pursuits have often involved parallel or combined efforts to conceptualise corporate accountability at international law and through indirect regulation in the form of corporate codes of conduct.[26] The variety of such attempts is reflective of the 'problem' to which they seek to respond.[27] This chapter is not another attempt to address the question of regulating the transnational corporation as such. Instead, in trying to gain a better understanding for the transnational evolution of law, this chapter seeks to illuminate the connections between the transformation of corporate governance rules within domestic, embedded corporate governance systems—constituted by a historically evolved interaction and correlation between company law, labour law and capital markets law (as well as insolvency law and industrial relations)—and the evolution of rules *for*, *against* and *by* the corporation outside of the nation-state.[28] The corporation, certainly, presents the formidable case in point for the impossibility, as it were,

[21] See, eg Wolfgang G Friedmann, 1957, 164–65, 170–71; Robert Charles Clark, 1981, 569–71.

[22] Cynthia A Williams, 2002, 724; Jan Eijsbouts, 2005.

[23] Heinrich Kronstein, 1952; Raymond Vernon, 1967.

[24] Christine Parker, 2007; see on this concept already Colin Scott, 2003, and Bronwen Morgan, 2003.

[25] Detlev F Vagts, 1969, 739; see also Heinrich Kronstein, 1952, 984: 'Assuming that it is legal theory which should adjust to economic reality and not the reverse, it follows that any "divergence between corporate theory and the underlying economic facts" should be resolved in favor of the latter. Such a divergence does exist, and, despite it, corporate theory has been slow to change'.

[26] See, eg Jonathan I Charney, 1983; Beth Stephens, 2002a; David Kinley and Junko Tadaki, 2004; Sean D Murphy, 2005; Larry Catá Backer, 2006; Sarah Joseph, 2004, and the contributions to Olivier De Schutter, 2006.

[27] Wolfgang G Friedmann, 1957, 173: 'the extension of private corporate power across the confines of State sovereignty is an older as well as a more intractable problem'.

[28] Peter T Muchlinski, 1997; Jean-Philippe Robé, 1997; Peter Hertner, 1998.

for any thinking at all of an existence *outside* of the state. As a legal person it has no 'reality' outside of the legal system.[29] The unquestionable presence and impact of TNCs on the global scale today, however, echoes and further exacerbates the long-standing assertions of corporate 'power', which have always been an integral part of thinking about the corporation on the domestic level.[30] In the following, we posit that a better understanding of the evolution of transnational corporate governance can be gained from studying the way in which the evolution of domestic corporate law-making, through legislation and jurisprudence, through expert committees and corporate actors, is correlated, paralleled, shaped by and *shaping* the production of corporate law rules outside of the nation-state. As such, the examples that inform the following two case studies have to be to a certain degree detailed, even parochial in their illustration of one concrete domestic context in which the production of transnational corporate governance rules is occurring. The spotlight that is directed in the following at the case of Germany can only be justified with regard to the tremendous regulatory transformation which this country has seen in the area of corporate norm-making in the recent decade, a transformation that would not be imaginable without the evolution of transnational institutional and normative 'spaces' that are both embedded and disembedded. The promise of studying the present transformation of German corporate governance lies less in the comparative aspect of 'Rhenish'[31] or 'co-ordinated' capitalism[32] that has inspired corporate law scholars and comparative political economists for decades to contrast institutional design in countries such as the United States and the United Kingdom, on the one hand, and Germany and Japan, on the other,[33] but rather in a necessarily interdisciplinary inquiry into the evolution of norms *between* the domestic and transnational levels, an orientation we will try to capture through an elaboration of Saskia Sassen's concept of 'assemblages'. The research agenda pursued here aims at cutting through the distinct layers of comparative corporate law, economic governance, institutional analysis and regulatory theory in order to illustrate that none of these explanatory frameworks on its own can render an adequate depiction of the complex and ambivalent way in which corporate law norms continue to evolve. Perhaps this is one of the reasons why the convergence vs divergence debate had no clearly discernable outcome, no neat result, no 'winner' or 'loser'. Even if much suggests that corporate governance

[29] John Dewey, 1926.

[30] Adolf A Berle, 1954; Wolfgang G Friedmann, 1957; David Sciulli, 1999; David Millon, 1990; William T Allen, 1992; Paddy Ireland, 2002; William W Bratton, 2005b.

[31] Michel Albert, 1991.

[32] David Soskice, 1999; Sigurt Vitols, 2001.

[33] Detlev Vagts, 1966; Thomas Raiser, 1988; Mark J Roe, 1993; Klaus J Hopt, Hideki Kanda, Mark J Roe, Eddy Wymeersch and Stefan Prigge, 1998; John W Cioffi, 2000b; Ronald Dore, 1973; Peter A Hall and David Soskice, 2001b; Bob Hancké, 2009.

reform projects around the world in recent years displayed a great prominence of shareholder value orientations, and even if the 'end of history for corporate law'[34] had come, the inherent paradoxes of the corporation[35] would in the end likely trump and undermine any universalising theory. The importance of the convergence vs divergence debate today lies, on the one hand, in having provided comparative company lawyers—leaving the polemics aside—with a goldmine of important data to inform future research,[36] and on the other, in having illustrated how an analysis of formal or functional convergence[37] and legal transplants[38] or irritants[39] cannot be disentangled from a critical analysis of how such migrations of standards correlate with changes in the identity of 'legal actors' and the transformation of governing norms and of the regulatory landscape.[40]

The following section will explore the different dimensions of corporate governance codes by first providing a general introduction to the regulatory issues dealt with under the heading of *corporate governance*, before secondly studying the emergence, legal nature and the enforcement of these codes in greater detail. The latter will be addressed in two parts, one of which addresses codes as *alternative* modes of law-making, while the ensuing sub-section deals with one regulatory area in more detail, the case of executive compensation. Both case studies illustrate how corporate governance amounts to a hybrid legal regime, as identified in our RCRC model.

A. Corporate Governance

The law of corporate governance is one of the fastest developing areas in law-making in recent years, and discussions about 'good corporate governance' have for years now been surpassing the confines of academia, occupying media and public debates: '[g]ood corporate governance is a top priority in business worldwide'.[41] Alongside wide-ranging public protest against managers' self-dealing and excessive pay-packages, institutional investors have for years now been moving into the centre of corporate governance rule-making by developing investor protection standards.[42] Surely since the summer of 2002, when President Bush heralded 'Corporate Responsibility'

[34] Henry Hansmann and Reinier Kraakman, 2001; Henry Hansmann, 2006.

[35] See, eg William W Bratton, 2005b.

[36] See Klaus Jürgen Hopt, 2006; David C Donald, 2008.

[37] Ronald J Gilson, 2001.

[38] Katharina Pistor, 2003.

[39] Gunther Teubner, 2001.

[40] Upendra Baxi, 2005b; Daniela Caruso, 2006; David Schneiderman, 2006; Mauro Zamboni, 2007; David Schneiderman, 2008.

[41] Jean du Plessis and Claus Luttermann, 2007, 215.

[42] John C Coffee Jr, 1992; GP Stapeldon, 2000; Friedrich Kübler, 1994.

in the aftermath of the ENRON debacle,[43] corporate governance regulation has come to rank high on national and transnational policy agendas.[44] With other countries learning about their own skeletons in the closet,[45] the high intensity level of policy proposals, domestic and transnational law-making initiatives has been no less than astounding.[46] The worldwide academic and policy discussion of corporate governance, embedded in numerous debates in- and outside of specially empanelled expert commissions, hearings and documented by government and working group reports, symposia, articles and voluminous books, has accompanied an active production of norms on the national and the international level.[47] Issues of general, even public, concern include managers' alleged free-reined authority to dispose of corporate assets as they see fit, the steep amounts of executive compensation packages[48] and the seemingly untamed and untamable power of corporate actors.[49] These questions touch upon long-standing governance, control, legitimacy and accountability problems surrounding the large business

[43] See the ABA Presidential Task Force on Corporate Responsibility: Final Report of March 31, 2003, available at: www.abanet.org/buslaw/corporateresponsibility/final_report.pdf (visited 29 September 2009). The Task Force had been appointed in 2002; see also the *Corporate Responsibility* (CORE) Coalition, founded by Amnesty International, Christian Aid, Friends of the Earth, New Economics and Traidcraft, more available at: www.corporate-responsibility.org/.

[44] See *The Economist*, 13 July 2002: 'American capitalism takes a beating'; Margaret Blair, 2002, 2–3: 'Now, in the spring of 2002, the helium has come out of the formerly high-flying technology and information infrastructure sectors that were leading U.S. economic expansion in the 1990s, and the Enron fiasco and accounting scandals at numerous other corporations have exposed deep flaws in the system that was held up as the model for all the world to follow'.

[45] Roger Adams, 2004: 'As a result of the recent Parmalat case, European attitudes to Enron-like incidents have turned a full 180 degrees from "It can't happen here" to "It has happened—what do we do about it?"'

[46] See, for example, the speech given by SEC Commissioner (as he then was), Paul S Atkins, on 5 February 2003, on '*The Sarbanes Oxley Act: Goals, Content, and Status of Implementation*', available at: www.sec.gov/news/speech/spch020503psa.htm (visited 25 September 2009).

[47] For a selection of fruitful introductions to the over many years burgeoning corporate governance debate, see Klaus J Hopt, Hideki Kanda, Mark J Roe, Eddy Wymeersch and Stefan Prigge, 1998; Joseph A McCahery, Piet Moerland, Theo Raaijmakers and Luc Renneborg, 2002, and Klaus J Hopt, Eddy Wymeersch, Hideki Kanda and Harald Baum, 2005; see the concise overviews of the contemporary regulatory challenges within the EU by Eddy Wymeersch, 2002, and Luca Enriques and Paolo Volpin, 2007.

[48] See the scathing critique by Lucian Ayre Bebchuk and Jesse Fried, 2004; see William W Bratton, 2005a; the scope of executive compensation, its components, allocation and disclosure continues to range high on the political agenda: see, for example, *Frankfurter Allgemeine Zeitung*, 30 June 2008, noting a 20% general increase in CEO pay of German companies listed on the DAX index. On 5 August 2009, the new Law on the Adequacy of Executive Compensation (*Gesetz zur Angemessenheit der Vorstandsvergütung* [*VorstAG*]) entered into force, the full text is available at: www.bmj.de/files/7db813ef5ce3522d02ef3547a4c2f341/3836/gesetz_vorstandsverguetung_VorstAG.pdf (visited 25 September 2009).

[49] See Louis D Brandeis, 1934; Ralph Nader, Mark Green and Joel Seligman, 1974; Richard J Barnet and Ronald E Muller, 1974; David C Korten, 1995.

corporation.[50] The related literature is legion and continues to grow.[51] For the purpose of this chapter, we shall confine ourselves to highlighting a number of central elements in the heightened debate over corporate governance standards before focusing more closely on the specific transnational dimension of corporate governance norms and law-making.

B. Corporate Governance and Political Economy

Corporate Governance relates to the exercise of powers inside the firm: the analytical focus can, for one, be directed to the relationship between the owner (shareholder, principal) and the management (agent). Or, one may focus on the overall organisational structure of the firm. While this also includes the principal-agent ties, it encompasses the other stakeholders in the firm, including employees and creditors. The first, control-oriented approach centres on shareholders as being the prime residual claimants of the firm: therefore, the firm's organisation is governed by the overriding principle of maximising 'shareholder value'. The other, 'stakeholder'-oriented, approach considers the actors in and around the firm and its business with regard to their vested interests in the firm. It sees the firm as *embedded* in a specific legal, economic and political culture, in which it occupies a place as a societal actor. In contrast to the shareholder approach, this perspective takes into account the 'public' services rendered by a large firm in view of employment capacities and overall socio-economic spin-off.[52]

The two definitions lay at the base of the convergence vs divergence debate over different patterns of corporate organisation, which had—ironically—begun to take hold of public policy and academic debates precisely in the moment when the corporate governance world had allegedly already moved towards universal values of capitalist wealth maximation,[53] recognised by some as marking no less than the 'end of history in corporate law'.[54] To be sure, this 'end of history' triumphalism was not invented by company lawyers. When former US State Department Advisor, Francis Fukuyama, published his book on *The End of History and the Last Man*, in the aftermath of the erosion of Communist states in the 1990s, he predicted ethnic and nationalist conflicts to be the successors to the up-till-then

[50] See Adolf A Berle and Gardiner C Means, 1932; Wolfgang G Friedmann, 1957; with regard to Germany, see Detlev Vagts, 1966, and Thomas Raiser, 1988, 115, providing a brief historical outline of the regulatory development.

[51] William W Bratton, 2001; Dalia Tsuk, 2005; Dalia Tsuk Mitchell, (forthcoming).

[52] For a discussion, see William T Allen, 1992, and David Millon, 1990.

[53] See the critical assessment by William Lazonick and Mary O'Sullivan, 2002, and Jennifer Hill, 2005; see also Volkmar Gessner, Richard P Appelbaum and William F Felstiner, 2001, 4–5.

[54] Henry Hansmann and Reinier Kraakman, 2001.

Eastern bloc competition.[55] At the same time, in the shadow of the first Iraq War, the French policy-maker and administrator Michel Albert, published his study *Capitalisme contre Capitalisme*, in which he presented an outline of national capitalist organisation focusing primarily on the French and German (Rhenish, or 'Rhenanian') systems of market and state relations.[56] In what would eventually become recognised as one of the key studies on the path-dependency of institutional change and the pressures of regulatory adaptation in an era of globalisation,[57] Albert described the embeddedness of capitalist organisation within particular historically contingent circumstances, structures of government policy, statutory and social norms and institutional frameworks to emphasise the relevance of such structures for a national economy's sustainable growth and the *longevity* of these very structural conditions. He contrasted the image of the Anglo-Saxon model of market organisation, leaving great room for market incentives, self-regulation and decentralised governance, with the 'other' model of capitalism ('*L'autre capitalisme*').[58] The latter is characterised by long-term investments in firms by banks (and other large, non-financial firms[59]) exercising extensive control rights, cross-holdings on a large scale tying in different industries ('Germany Inc')[60] and a—(so far)—strong role of corporatist collective action pertaining to wage bargaining and lobbying. Much has been written about the merits and the likely demise of these clearly distinguished systems.[61] As noted, one of the 'outcomes' of the otherwise ambivalently open-ended debate about the chances of the respective survival of the shareholder- and stakeholder-oriented models of corporate governance[62] is that the study of corporate governance models against the background of

[55] Francis Fukuyama, 1992; *ibid*, *Trust. The Social Virtues and the Creation of Prosperity* (1995) ch 1.

[56] Michel Albert, 1991, English trans: Capitalism Against Capitalism (1993; Paul Haviland trans).

[57] See, eg, Peter A Hall and David Soskice, 2001a, 4 fn 4 'one of the pioneering works'; Jürgen Hoffmann, 2004; Andreas Busch, 2005, 131; Alain Touraine, 2007, 19–20.

[58] Michel Albert, 1991, 117, 119.

[59] See Jeremy Edwards and Marcus Nibler, 2000, arguing that, in contrast to common opinion, the role of banks as 'insider' controllers of German firms is exaggerated and fails to recognize the strong role played by other large firms in the control of the firm. The authors argue that ownership is more important than the traditionally held assumption that banks play the most important role in German corporate governance.

[60] 'Germany Inc' is the often-used short formula for the densely structured financial and administrative network between German business enterprises and banks, see, for example, Cover Story: 'The Bell Tolls for Germany Inc.: Cosy relations between business, banks and labor are unravelling', Business Week, 15 August 2005, available at: www.businessweek.com/magazine/content/05_33/b3947011_mz001.htm; Peer Zumbansen, 2002; John W Cioffi, 2002.

[61] See, eg Gregory Jackson, 2000; Gregory Jackson, 2001; Ronald Dore, 2000; John W Cioffi, 2000b.

[62] See the excellent paper by Klaus J Hopt, 2002; further on this debate, see the contributions to Jeffrey N Gordon and Mark J Roe, 2004, and to Joseph A McCahery, Piet Moerland, Theo Raaijmakers and Luc Renneborg, 2002; Peer Zumbansen, 2004a.

history and political economy has contributed tremendously to a deeper understanding of the forces that have been shaping this area of law in recent years.[63] From this perspective, the following definition provided by John Cioffi, a legal scholar and political scientist, whose work on comparative corporate governance, the United States and Germany over recent years has significantly contributed to our understanding of the particular dynamics of institutional change of embedded capitalist systems, might best capture the forces at work within the law of corporate governance:

> Corporate governance regimes structure the allocation of power among managers, shareholders, and employees—the principal groups involved in corporate affairs. A tripartite legal structure of company (or corporate) law, securities regulation and labor relations law defines the juridical relationships among these groups and is a central feature of national political economies.[64]

In his book 'Public Law & Private Power', Cioffi uses the term 'juridical nexus' (of securities, company, and labour relations) to capture the 'regulatory framework that structurally allocates power among managers, shareholders, and employees within the corporation'.[65] This definition goes a long way in highlighting the connections between corporate governance norms and the regulatory structures in which they are embedded. By including both securities regulation and labour relations in a thus enlarged concept of corporate governance, it suggests a bridging of the gap that has long come into being between corporate law creation and adjudication but also scholarship and teaching in those fields that have regularly been living separate, 'parallel' lives. Cioffi's definition was not unknown to corporate lawyers. One of its most intimate experts, Melvin Eisenberg, offered a brilliantly concise statement of American corporate law, when he observed '[a]ny body of rules that directly or indirectly addresses the facilitation of corporate transactions or conduct, or the regulation of traditional or positional conflicts of interest, is a part of corporate law'.[66] Similarly, Robert Clark, alerted students of his landmark casebook on corporate law to make every effort to study labour law in order to have a chance to understand their current field of study.[67]

What these assessments suggest, is the need for a richer and deeper understanding of the historical circumstances, the political dynamics and the

[63] See John W Cioffi, 2000a; Colin Crouch, 2005; Wolfgang Streeck, 1997.

[64] John W Cioffi, 2006, 536.

[65] John W Cioffi, 2010, ch 2, on file with authors. Cf Jean du Plessis and Claus Luttermann, 2007, 223: 'A corporate governance model is typically influenced by several legal arrangements such as company law, securities regulation, accounting and auditing standards, insolvency law, contract law, labour law and tax law', an enumeration, however, that tends to isolate and immunise corporate governance from the specific organisational and power structuring functions that eg labour and securities law share with company law in Cioffi's definition.

[66] Melvin Eisenberg, 2005, 176.

[67] Robert C Clark, 1986, 5.

contemporary forces that shape law reform in this area in contrast to the enthusiasm about shareholder value, stock-price euphoria of recent years. The definition of the juridical nexus of corporate governance can reach beyond the already mentioned convergence-divergence dualism by prompting a more differentiated picture of alleged convergence processes. In order to unpack the notion of 'convergence', it is necessary to take a closer look at which elements of corporate law regulation have actually been undergoing change and in which form did this change occur? The juridical nexus perspective demands a careful look at the role of politics, public and private actors to appreciate the causes and prospects of corporate governance reform. As it stands, the contention regarding an allegedly universal transformation of corporate law towards shareholder value, that until very recently has been ardently voiced[68] falls short of explaining how regulatory structures in mature legal systems are in fact adapting to demands of greater investor protection, lower labour costs and more effective management control.[69] Lurking beneath contentions of universal convergence are far-reaching claims about the *limits* of corporate law with regard to the regulation of corporate organisation.[70] The celebration of universally accepted shareholder value standards over many years turned into a triumph over the state's aspiration to regulate the market.

For the longest time this debate among corporate lawyers unfolded in a parallel universe from long-standing historical and comparative studies of institutional and regulatory change, in which corporate governance was among the most actively studied regulatory fields. The 'Varieties of Capitalism' approach (VoC) focused on the framework conditions and regulatory settings of corporate governance regimes with the inclusion of complementing relational frameworks such as industrial relations, co-determination, and vocational training.[71] Central to this work has been the distinction between 'co-ordinated' and 'liberal market economies'.[72] While the former are characterised by a high level of ownership concentration, an institutionalised role of lending investors (banks) in the corporation's governance structure and the representation and participation of employees in the company's decision-making processes, the latter are characterised by stock market liquidity and the absence of employees or their representatives

[68] See, above, and reprinted as Henry Hansmann and Reinier Kraakman, 2002.

[69] Beth Ahlering and Simon Deakin, 2007.

[70] See, eg, Mark J Roe, 2002, 234: 'Lost in the current academic debate (and perhaps lost to policy makers at some international development agencies) is that corporate law does not even try to directly control the costs of basic mismanagement. Other institutions do. For these other institutions (product market competition, incentive compensation, takeovers, shareholder primacy norms, and so on), corporate law (other than for takeovers, which given the usual large premium just sets an outer limit—more about that below) is usually just a supporting prop, not the central institution'.

[71] See, eg Pepper D Culpepper, 1999.

[72] David Soskice, 1999.

from corporate boards. Recently, VoC scholars have begun to critically revisit the CME/LME distinction and to further illuminate the intricate dynamics of legal reform and institutional change within those systems the capacity of which to change had previously been portrayed with great scepticism, mostly with reference to their long-grown, historical and institutional entrenched status.[73] Greater emphasis is now being placed on the interaction of interest groups and on the struggle over particular issues, which are identified and pursued across traditional political lines, such as right and left, conservative and progressive to counter all too rigid descriptions of path-dependent political camps in the battle over law reform.[74] If nothing else, this does already show to what degree a study of contemporary changes in corporate governance depends on a clear view of the various forces at work in this area. At the same time, this research forms an important basis for our contention of emerging hybrid governance regimes, which are characterised by a particular mixture and interaction of public and private, co-ordinative and regulatory elements. In the context of the RCRC model, the recent attention given by VoC scholars to the increasingly flexible governance mixes in corporate law-making allows for a better understanding of the particular ways in which corporate governance reform has been promoted, sometimes even by otherwise unlikely political groupings,[75] but also of the new forms of intertwining formal and informal processes of law-making, as powerfully exemplified by the politics surrounding the drafting and enforcement of corporate governance codes.[76] This differentiation is especially important in a context, where attempts to 'respond' to the crisis are often synonymous with calls for 'more', 'stronger' or 'tougher' regulation. As John Braithwaite noted in a recent book, '[t]he ritual for blaming someone for failures that are system failures is ritualistic in the sense that it seeks to calm critics by giving them a fall guy to chew on instead of fixing the problem'.[77] The rise of the 'post-regulatory' state and the network society, however, illustrate the futility and inadequacy of quantitative assessments of 'more' or 'less' state (meaning government intervention) that turn out to be extremely imprecise in the face of the complexity of the domestic and transnational regulatory landscape. The recent insights by VoC scholars into the changing political economy of corporate

[73] John W Cioffi, 2006; Peter A Gourevitch, 2003, 1835–36 (highlighting the ways in which it has become necessary to focus on issues and interest group politics that may be pursued with no regard to existing party lines or traditional camp politics). Cioffi, above n 65 (forthcoming), suggests moving beyond the political coalition focus put forward in particular by Peter A Gourevitch and James Shinn, 2005, and laying greater emphasis on the constantly re-forming and re-constituting coalitions that drive reform politics.

[74] Peter A Gourevitch, 2003.

[75] Hereto, John W Cioffi, 2002; John C Coffee Jr, 1999, 667.

[76] Peer Zumbansen, 2002b.

[77] John Braithwaite, 2008, 150.

law-making have furthermore illustrated that both transfigurations and demonisations of the 'state' are unhelpful exaggerations. In addition, from a legal sociology perspective, such depictions of the role of the state are likely to miss the nature of non-hierarchical, networked creation of corporate governance norms.

C. Law-Making in Corporate Governance

The German Corporate Governance Code, on which the following section focuses, illuminates the significant characteristics of law-making processes that have been undergoing dramatic changes with regard to the *actors* involved and the *nature of the norms* generated in these processes. These developments have to be placed into the wider context of both highly pressured law reform and regulatory change. In this respect, *reform* does not only concern company law but, more generally involves national, European and international attempts to improve law-making procedures by allowing for a wider inclusion of private actors in rule-making procedures.[78] What is involved from the point of view of democratic theory, is a tension that has long been growing between a functionally reduced, rubber-stamping parliament on the one hand and a fast moving, hardly controllable administration which is in close contact and interaction with private actors, on the other.[79] At the same time, the currently widespread attempts at improving respective national laws on corporate governance and firm organisation[80] must be seen against the background of the considerable pressure to converge towards shareholder value-oriented corporate governance principles.[81]

[78] For developments on the European level, see, eg Kenneth A Armstrong, 2001, 99–100: 'The normative case for a more autonomised transnational civil society … lies in the inclusion of a new constituency of voices, interests and expertise within élite transnational governance'; Kenneth A Armstrong, 2002, 105, qualifies the reaching out to civil society to be more than just a cure to an unsatisfactory supranational parliamentary system, but as a reflection of the EU's development of 'new forms of governance'; *cf* the other contributions in (2002) 8(1) *European Law Journal* and (2009) 15(2) *European Law Journal* edited by Imelda Maher; with particular emphasis on administrative law, see also Carol Harlow, 1999, placing the analysis of contemporary admin. law against the background of 'a global context' and a definite tilt from the interventionist to the regulatory state. The participation of civil society actors and stakeholders in general is, of course, central to the 'global administrative law' project: see, eg Benedict Kingsbury, Nico Krisch, Richard B Stewart and Jarrod Wiener, 2005; Nico Krisch, 2006.

[79] For a powerful reconstruction of the pertinent role of the administration in designing rules 'close to the ground', see the landmark assessment by James W Landis, 1938.

[80] See, the contributions in Dieter Feddersen, Peter Hommelhoff and Uwe H Schneider, 1996; Klaus J Hopt and Eddy Wymeersch, 1997; Theodor Baums, 2001b, Introduction; see, for a list of future items of work in German corporate governance, see, eg: Marcus Lutter, 2002, 85; Holger Fleischer, 2007; Brigitte Haar, 2008.

[81] See, Henry Hansmann and Reinier Kraakman, 2001; critically Douglas M Branson, 2001; Sanford M Jacoby, 2002; see, for an instructive comparison, Steven N Kaplan, 1997; Sigurt Vitols, 2001.

As already alluded to above, such efforts were for years informed by a sense of urgency with regard to getting stakeholder-oriented, closely knit, bank-financed corporate governance systems ready to 'compete' for globally available investments.[82]

These transformations, however, can no longer solely be studied within contained, embedded systems of national political economies. Instead, there is a growing awareness of the fact that the adaptations of historically evolved governance systems display a particular transnational dimension. In light of the globally intertwined business and interaction among firms created under different legal rules, corporate governance rules (as well as securities regulation) have increasingly become a competitive asset on a global 'law market',[83] a market, however, that is not only constituted by sovereign sellers with vested authority in the creation of binding legal norms, but by an amalgamation of national governments, supranational norm-setting institutions such as the OECD or the UN Global Compact as well as private parties such as multinational corporations and interest group representations. Drawing on the observation by Melvin Eisenberg of the four 'essential modules' of corporate law, which he identifies as state statutory law, state judge-made law, federal law and private ordering through soft law,[84] it becomes clear that we can no longer limit our perspectives to national processes of rule creation. Instead, rules and standards are developed and disseminated by transnational actors such as multinationals, stock exchanges (whose listing rules are of overriding importance for domestic and foreign companies), or International Organisations such as the OECD, that altogether must be seen to contribute to the evolution of the transnational law of corporate governance.[85]

This particularly global regulatory landscape has not failed to capture the imagination of scholars of comparative law,[86] regulatory theory[87] and institutional analysis.[88] So, while the economic and financial crisis that has been unfolding since 2007 has frequently been perceived as a failure of regulation and state action,[89] it can no longer be denied that reactions to the crisis—including perhaps calls for 'tougher regulation', as widely promulgated by political leaders around the world in the face of the crisis—will

82 Theodor Baums, 2003.
83 Erin A O'Hara and Larry E Ribstein, 2009; Erin A O'Hara and Larry E Ribstein, 2008; Jens Dammann and Henry Hansmann, 2008; Onnig H Dombalagian, 2008.
84 Melvin Eisenberg, 2005, 176.
85 See hereto Jennifer Hill, 2008, and Julia Black, 2008.
86 Jennifer Hill, 2008.
87 Julia Black and David Rouch, 2008.
88 See, eg the recent monographical study by Andreas Busch, 2009 with case studies on the US, Germany, the UK and Switzerland.
89 Busch, preceding note; Cioffi, 2009, above.

unfold in a tightly interwoven space of governmental collaboration and interaction[90]—both within and beyond the borders of the nation-state.[91] In the field of corporate governance the landscape is not only populated by national governments eagerly engaged in a headstrong pursuit of regulatory reform; complementing such efforts is a vast proliferation of private and mixed public/private, hybrid processes of rule-making, cutting across jurisdictional boundaries and contributing to an increasingly densely woven net of guidelines, best practices, and standards. As will become apparent from the following, the defining feature of the emerging transnational body of corporate governance norms is the intricate resurfacing of the RCRC paradox we described above, pertaining to the inseparability of substantive/procedural, co-ordinative/regulatory and authority/affectedness aspects. As was the case for our discussion of the preceding example of transnational consumer contracts, our focus in this section will not be confined to the *substantive* law governing specific forms of societal activity, which has long remained the hallmark of comparative work in the law of corporate governance;[92] rather, our attention has to turn as well to the dynamics that are unfolding between different levels and sites of rule-making from a *regulatory* perspective. From this combined perspective, the law of corporate governance becomes a prime example of a *transnational law regime*. The intricate embeddedness of regulatory innovation in locally defined governance structures on the one hand, and their integration in transnationally unfolding rule-making processes is characteristic of the current regulatory landscape in corporate governance, as the following example of the German Corporate Governance Code will illustrate. While the evolution of the Code and the legislation arguably having flown out of the Code provides a case in point of the RFC ('request for comments') procedure within our model of Rough Consensus and Running Code, it is an equally powerful denotation of the way in which private ordering maintains an intricately challenging tension with the institutional frameworks for official law-making.

(i) The German Corporate Governance Code as an Example of RCRC

A little bit of legislative history: On 21 June 2002, the German chamber of federal states (*Länder*), the Bundesrat, approved a Bill which had prior to that passed the national parliament (*Bundestag*), and which introduced a number of substantial changes to the German *Aktiengesetz* (Stock Corporation Act).[93] This particular statute had to a large degree been

[90] Howard Davies and David Green, 2008.

[91] Adrienne Héritier and Dirk Lehmkuhl, 2008; Pierre-Hugues Verdier, 2009.

[92] See the excellent study by Detlev Vagts, 1966.

[93] See the *Gesetz zur weiteren Reform des Aktien- und Bilanzrechts, zu Transparenz und Publizität (Transparenz- und Publizitätsgesetz)* [*TraPuG*] (Transparency and Disclosure Act),

contemplated and prepared under the auspices of two specially formed governmental commissions concerned with a reform of German corporate governance. The second of these commissions, the so-called 'Corporate Governance Code-Commission', had been convened with the mandate of taking up the suggestions of the first commission, central to which was the drafting of a voluntary Code of Corporate Governance Rules. Mr Gerhard Cromme, Spokesperson of the supervisory's board of German steel manufacturer ThyssenKrupp,[94] chaired this second commission and presented its work on 26 February 2002 to the Ministry of Justice.[95] Among the many interesting features of the German Corporate Governance Code, which a renowned German corporate governance scholar coined a 'novum' in the system of German legal sources,[96] is its intricate and still largely unresolved legal nature.[97] In the remainder of this first part of this chapter we will formulate a possible answer to this question in the larger context of corporate governance reform as it has been pursued on the domestic, European and transnational levels. In the second part of the chapter, we will focus on the example of executive compensation from a distinctly legal sociological perspective entitled 'transnational legal pluralism'.[98]

From the time of its publication in 2002, the German Corporate Governance Code prompted a vivid debate about its legal or, perhaps, non-legal nature, with assessments ranging from 'soft law'[99] to 'unconstitutional'.[100] That this debate has still not subsided[101] might be explained in light of the particular novelty that the arrival of the idea of a code constituted in Germany.[102] At the same time, its creation could be seen as having been a part of a worldwide surge to draft and to promulgate corporate governance codes.[103] The Code itself includes those *norms* and

adopted by the German Bundestag on 17 May 2002. See also the documentation in *Neue Zeitschrift für Gesellschaftsrecht* (*NZG*), 2002, 78–81, and the comprehensive presentation of the *TraPuG*'s main elements by Heribert Hirte, 2003.

[94] See the relevant information on the Commission at: www.corporate-governance-code.de/index-e.html.

[95] See press release at: www.corporate-governance-code.de/eng/news/presse-20020226.html.

[96] Peter Ulmer, 2002, 152; Wolfgang Seidel, 2004a, 289.

[97] Eberhard Vetter, 2008, 121: 'still not resolved satisfyingly'.

[98] See already Peer Zumbansen, 2008b, and Peer Zumbansen, 2006c.

[99] Marcus Lutter, 2001, 225; critically, Ulmer, 2002, 161.

[100] Wolfgang Seidel, 2004b.

[101] See, eg Jean du Plessis and Ingo Sanger, 2007, 31: 'serious concerns with regard to the constitutionality of the Code'. But see Jan von Hein, 2008, 424–26, arguing for a constitutional form of 'informal governmental action' (*informelles Regierungshandeln*).

[102] Axel von Werder, 2008, 15, fn 6.

[103] See, eg Axel von Werder, 2008, who situates the creation of the German Code within the larger context of a veritable 'international code movement', *ibid*, at 14. See also the list of corporate governance codes listed on the website of the European Corporate Governance Institute, available at: www.ecgi.org/codes/all_codes.php.

regulations that are mandatory corporate law rules, which are already set out in the German Stock Corporation Law. According to its Drafters, the Code's purpose in reiterating these norms here is to provide foreign investors with a transparent and simple introduction to central rules pertinent to the corporate governance rules existing in Germany.[104] Furthermore, the Code includes *recommendations*, which are expressed by the word '*sollen*' (shall) and the observation of which is to be made transparent in an annual statement made by the firm's management.[105] Lastly, the Code contains *suggestions* as to corporate conduct the observation of which is merely 'suggested' but there is no obligation to disclose whether a company has followed these suggestions.[106] The '*comply or disclose*' principle, which is endorsed in the Code with regard to 'recommendations', has been seen as an indirect enforceability anchor in the Code, whereby it could be seen to lose its genuinely voluntary character.[107] That the Code in fact attains an at least indirect mandatory character, is suggested by the enactment of Section 161 in the German Stock Corporation Act (*AktG*), whereby the legislature actually introduced the disclosure duty into codified law.[108] But, does this suffice to make the Code a piece of enforceable legislation? Others have argued that even if there was a disclosure obligation with regard to the company's compliance with the Code's recommendations, it would be wrong to perceive the Code itself as 'law'. The latter, so it was argued,[109] would only be the case if the recommendations themselves were being made obligatory, which, arguably, they are not.[110] These opposing viewpoints illustrate the underlying central difficulty: it is clear, that the Code's practical relevance is to be seen in its effect on the actual *behaviour* of firms,[111] something which appears to have continuously accrued with each

[104] German Corporate Governance Code, Foreword available at: www.corporate-governance-code.de/eng/kodex/1.html: 'This German Corporate Governance Code (the "Code") presents essential statutory regulations for the management and supervision (governance) of German listed companies and contains internationally and nationally recognized standards for good and responsible governance. The Code aims at making the German Corporate Governance system transparent and understandable. Its purpose is to promote the trust of international and national investors, customers, employees and the general public in the management and supervision of listed German stock corporations'.

[105] See the German Corporate Governance Code, Preface, 2, available at: www.corporate-governance-code.de/index-e.html.

[106] *Ibid.*

[107] Wolfgang Seidel, 2004a; Wolfgang Seidel, 2004b; Markus Heintzen, 2004.

[108] The quality and assessment of this obligatory annual 'explanation' must certainly be disputed. See, eg Martin Peltzer, 2002b, 594; Gerald Spindler, 2008, annotations 12–79, in particular 14–16; Henrik-Michael Ringleb, 2008, annotations 46–65, in particular 47 (no obligation to justify non-compliance of Kodex norms). Ringleb suggests to substitute the often 'confusing' notion of 'comply or explain' by 'comply or disclose'.

[109] Ringleb, 2008, annotations 51–65 ; Axel von Werder, 2002; Christoph H Seibt, 2002.

[110] Marcus Lutter, 2002, 86, with regard to informations and suggestions.

[111] Christoph H Seibt, 2003.

passing year.[112] Whether or not firms do comply with the code's dispositions relating, eg, to transparency and disclosure of executive compensation[113] (a part of the *Kodex* that spurred concrete legislative action leading up to the entering into force of a federal statute on the adequacy of executive compensation in August 2009[114]), the publication of the firm's reports on the Internet,[115] or the facilitating of personal exercise of shareholders' voting rights[116] will, according to the rules established by the Code, remain within the discretion of the company.[117] Again, the Code explicitly foresees that companies do not have to comply with 'recommendations'. And yet they are *obliged*—under Section 161 *AktG*—to issue an annual account of whether or not they did comply.[118] The annual monitoring of the Code's 'acceptance' has revealed consistently growing numbers of German major corporations to be observing the Code.[119]

A systematic interpretation alone of the Code's three-fold structure with *information*, *recommendations* and *suggestions*, which would aim at determining the legal nature of each of the Code's components in concert with the others and, lastly, within the general structure of the Code, does not appear to yield a clear-cut result. While the merely informative sections on the one hand and the suggestions on the other can remain outside the ambit of such a line of inquiry, the Code's recommendations invite further inspection. The mentioned disclosure obligation is in itself intriguing, if not problematic.[120] While identifying criminal sanctions against the disclosing director in the case of an incorrect declaration (Section 400 *AktG*), neither the statute nor the Code suggests how such incorrectness could be ascertained. This can be interpreted as meaning that the legislator did not wish to or did not imagine how to put in place a tight monitoring system that goes beyond the registration of whether the declaration has been made at all, the failure of which is sanctioned in the *Handelsgesetzbuch* [*HGB*] (Commercial Code). What is likely, then, is that the legislator, keeping in line with the regulatory spirit of the Code itself, did in turn aim at

[112] Jürgen van Kann and Mira Eigler, 2007, 1733.

[113] Very critically, Martin Wolf, 2002, 60.

[114] See *Gesetz zur Angemessenheit der Vorstandsvergütung* [*VorstAG*]; full text at: www.bmj.de/files/7db813ef5ce3522d02ef3547a4c2f341/3836/gesetz_vorstandsverguetung_VorstAG.pdf. For an assessment, see eg Klaus-Stefan Hohenstatt, 2009, Björn Gaul and Alexandra Janz, 2009, and, from inside the responsible Ministry, Ulrich Seibert, 2009.

[115] See, eg, Section 2.3.1 of the Cromme commission's German Corporate Governance Code.

[116] German Corporate Governance Code, Section 2.3.3.

[117] German Corporate Governance Code, Section 1: Foreword, differentiating between voluntary recommendations ('shall'), suggestions ('should', 'can'), and legally compelling provisions, according to existing law.

[118] See Section 16 Transparency and Disclosure Act.

[119] Van Kann and Eigler, 2007, 1733.

[120] For a list of the extensive, even monographical literature on this provision, see Gerald Spindler, 2008, before annotation 1.

inducing an *indirect* enforcement mechanism into the law, the functionality of which, however, is unfolding entirely outside of the statutory realm. Where companies fail to correctly disclose their compliance or non-compliance, so it might be argued, the market—that is, the investors—will adequately act on this communication. Surely, such a perspective is not without problems: even if in theory the market were to react to a declaration incorrectly issued or not issued at all by devaluing the company's shares, there would still remain considerable burden of proof challenges to establish liability.[121] Rejecting as well a number of other legal grounds for liability due to the legal—non-binding—nature of the Code,[122] the effect of Section 161 would merely be the initiation of a *shaming* process, playing out on a *market for reputation*, something we have already discussed in the context of chapter three. From this perspective, however, it remains doubtful how the Stock Corporation Act, a statutory public norm, which commands a private actor, here a stock corporation, to disclose annually whether it has complied with a non-binding set of recommendations, can be compatible with an enforcement processs through shaming, which unfolds outside of the state.

But, perhaps, this perspective is inadequate to capture the particular combination of *co-ordinative/regulatory* dimensions reflected in the Code. The preceding discussion suggested that our conceptualisation of the enforcement qualities of the Corporate Governance Code is informed by our understanding of the distinction between a statutory norm of law set by the state, on the one hand, and a non-binding norm of non-law, on the other. The linkage between law and non-law as established by Section 161 leads us to further entrench this unquestioned distinction where, perhaps, we should recognise that it was an inappropriate one to begin with. Whether or not the Code is law might not be answerable with regard to its enforcement mechanism, but perhaps better with a view to its authorship. It is here, where the relevance of the above proposed RCRC model to depict such incremental ways of rule-making becomes central. We will lay this out in detail in the following sub-section.

(ii) Who Makes Company Law?

If the answer to whether or not a norm is to be recognised as law depends on the authoritative process to enact legal norms, then we have to take a closer look at the process through which the Corporate Governance Code was enacted. Under German constitutional law, the right to initiate legislative proposals lies with the government and with the *Bundestag* and the

121 Gerald Spindler, 2008, annotation 63.
122 Spindler, 2008, annotations 63–77.

Bundesrat, the federal parliament and the representation of the Federal states respectively.[123] This in fact is the starting observation of those scholars who are opposed to norm-making by private expert groups. These scholars characterise instances where a government seeks societal approval for envisioned legislative projects from private interest groups, as examples of an on-going and proliferating 'deparlamentarisation'.[124] Their critique is directed, in particular, against the norm-production by societal groups such as expert groups, commissions or associations the work of which is at times based on an ambivalent form of public authorisation.[125]

This scepticism, however, appears overdrawn. First of all, it has long been recognised by adminstrative and constitutional law scholars that the state is highly dependent on the expert input from societal actors in carrying out 'its' legislative and administrative functions.[126] Furthermore, it is clear that with the growing complexity of societal relations and, correspondingly, a growing demand for sophisticated and increasingly responsive governance forms that are sensitive to the networked, non-hierarchical structure of society,[127] any form of norm-production and implementation has become an extremely fragile process of risk-taking and of trial-and-error. In light of the particular governance challenges arising in contemporary, complex societies, an allegedly clear-cut distinction between public and private governance schemes, built on the image of a sovereign, knowledgable state presiding over a fragmented, market-society, fails to grasp the intricate forms of public-private governance mechanisms, of knowledge sharing and experimental politics and regulation that characterise contemporary law-making.[128] In this light, the insistence on the state keeping a safe distance from private knowledge, bears little explanatory value for our understanding of contemporary forms of governance.

The second strand of critique of corporate governance codes and the associated form of private law-making was directed against the real *effect* emanating from such codes and practices. Given the already noted, particular co-ordinative/regulatory nature of the Code, it is not surprising that it has met with criticism regarding its purportedly absent legislative basis.[129] While some scholars expressed their support of this form of installing

[123] See, Art 76 para 2 *Grundgesetz* (German Basic Law).

[124] See, Martin Wolf, 2002; Paul Kirchhof, 2001; Paul Kirchhof, 2000, 690.

[125] Kirchhof, 2001, above, arguing that parliaments, but not such private commissions are mandated to produce legal norms; see also Wolfgang Seidel, 2004b, arguing that the Code remains a public norm, which was drafted without proper law-making authority.

[126] See already Richard B Stewart, 1975; Jody Freeman, 1997.

[127] Gunther Teubner, 1987b; Karl-Heinz Ladeur, 1999; Karl-Heinz Ladeur, 2007; Karl-Heinz Ladeur, 2009.

[128] See, eg Michael Power, 1997; Michael Power, 2005; Ladeur, 2009.

[129] See Wolfgang Seidel, 2004a; Paul Kirchhof, 2004; Ulrich Noack, 2002, 620, calling the Code drafted by the Cromme-Commission, 'a peculiar set of rules' ('*ein Regelwerk von eigenartiger Gestalt*'); Martin Peltzer, 2002b, 593, highlights the fact that the the Code has

a forum in order to solicit dispersed and urgently needed expertise, feeding into concrete law-making proposals for the Federal legislature,[130] others pointed to various drawbacks of this particular form of law-making.[131] One of the main contentions concerns the alleged 'exclusion' of the parliament from the actual process of conceptualising and preparing of the legislative proposal.[132] In this respect, it has been alleged that the solicitation of experts into the open parliamentary arena would make the law's genesis more transparent and, ultimately, render it more legitimate.[133] Another critical issue concerns the fundamental question whether or not a private body of experts is or *should* in fact be entitled and authorised to draw up binding law.[134]

In this concrete case of the German Corporate Governance Code, the mandate to form a commission the task of which would be to draft the first such Corporate Governance Code, came from the Chancellor and the Ministry of Justice. At the time, it was widely debated among German legal scholars whether this would suffice to provide a legitimation for the Commission's work on the one hand, or whether this would amount to rendering both the Commission and the Code public in nature, on the other.[135] The reasons in support of the argument that they are public must seem rather exotic to non-continental readers, especially when scholars defending this view began referring to the German Eagle Seal, which is placed on the cover of the Code.[136] In turn, then, another look at the Code reveals a number of significant elements that can be taken to respond to the mentioned critique. The work of both commissions, that of 2000–01, chaired by Mr Baums, and that of 2001–02, chaired by Mr Cromme, is of interest not only because it outlines significant reform perspectives and proposals leading to concrete legislative proposals. Moreover, the commissions'

been drafted without a legislative authorisation nor democratic legitimisation; see, even more polemically, Paul Kirchhof, 2001.

[130] See, eg Theodor Baums, 2001a.

[131] See, eg Martin Wolf, 2002, 59, 60; in the same vein Paul Kirchhof, 2001, 1332, 1333, critically observing a 'deparlamentarisation' (*Entparlamentisierung*) both with regard to the EU's (ie the Council's) appropriation of law-making sectors formerly reserved by the Member States and the executive's practice on the national level of seeking consensus with market players before pushing this consensus through the parliament; see already *ibid*, ZGR 2000, 609; for a thorough discussion of private law-making, See Ferdinand Kirchhof, 1987; in the US American context, the canonical text is Louis Jaffe, 1937; see also Jody Freeman, 2000a; Jody Freeman, 2000b.

[132] See, Martin Wolf, 2002; Paul Kirchhof, 2001.

[133] *Ibid.*

[134] *Ibid.*

[135] See Seidel, *Der Deutsche Corporate Governance Kodex—eine private oder doch eine staatliche Regelung?*, above, (explicitly adopting the view that both the Commission and the Code are public in nature); likewise Markus Heintzen, 2004.

[136] See www.ixos.com/german-corporate-governance-code-en.pdf; Wolfgang Seidel, 2004a, 287.

activities mark significant examples of integrating scientific expertise into law-making procedures.[137] In fact, in view of the work actually presented by the two commissions—the first presenting its Report and the recommendation to the Ministry to initiate a Code Commission in July of 2001, and the second Commission, which in February 2002 presented the first draft of the Code—it can be well disputed if any binding law had in fact been adopted *by* these Commissions. The proposals of the first Commission were both an encompassing survey of current company law, drawn up against the background of increasing pressure to react to international capital markets' demands, and a presentation of recommended amendments to the existing law, referring to both statutory law changes and to the drafting of a Code.[138] Thus, while sometimes very concrete proposals for changes to be enacted through normal legislative procedures were included in the first Commission's report, the Commission by itself did *not* formulate norms.[139] However thin the line between the Commission's report and what the parliament later adopted in form of the Transparency and Disclosure Act, which amended the Stock Corporation Act, the report itself did not contain binding law.

To be sure, the case is more complicated with regard to the Code, which was drafted by the second Commission upon a recommendation by the preceding Commission.[140] The Code Commission did draw up a corporate governance code, the provisions of which clearly build upon and endorse the Transparency and Disclosure Act and, importantly, the already mentioned comply-or-explain rule in Section 161 of the Stock Corporation Act. It is against this concrete background of the first and second commissions, that we can now return to answer the original question about the Code's legal nature. This procedure is itself reflective of the changing forms of law-making that are characteristic of contemporary law reform processes.

As to the first strand of critique, it can easily be maintained that different forms of soliciting information by experts in order to prepare (legislative) processes of law making are not at all anything new or unheard of.[141] Quite

[137] For a discussion of the procedure and quality of this know-how integration, see Theodor Baums, 2001a.

[138] See Martin Peltzer, 2002b, 593; Ulrich Seibert, 2002, 608.

[139] For Joachim Schulze-Osterloh, 2001, 1436, it goes without saying that these norms are not 'law', which leads him to find the term 'soft law' as used by Marcus Lutter (in ZGR 2001, 225) *misleading*.

[140] This is acknowledged by both the Federal Justice Minister, Mrs Däubler-Gmelin, and the commission's Chairperson, Mr Gerhard Cromme in their statement before the press on the occasion of the the publication of the Commission's report, available at: www.corporate-governance-code.de/eng/news/presse-20020226.html.

[141] See, eg the examples given by Matthias Schmidt-Preuss, 1996, and also the reflections by Udo Di Fabio, 1996; *cf* Karl-Heinz Ladeur, 2001b, 63: '*Der Staatsapparat büßt seine Rolle in der Mediation und Aggregierung des allgemeinen Handlungswissens und eines allgemeinen Regelbestandes ein und wird selbst zum Manager fragmentierter begrenzter Interventionen auf der Grundlage spezialisierten Wissens*'. [The state apparatus relinquishes its role in mediating

to the contrary, the inclusion of private expertise into law making processes is not only common practice but, arguably, unavoidable in view of an ever proliferating and further dispersing body of societal, private knowledge[142] on which the state has always been dependent. This holds true even if this state is no longer neither the nineteenth-century interventionist state reserving the right to govern and shape the market nor the twentieth-century, modern welfare state as broker and mediator of societal conflicts and interests through different patterns of juridification.[143] The post-modern, 'Supervisory' State, as contemporary public governance is sometimes coined in political science or legal scholarship,[144] can fulfill its function only to the degree that both its information-intake procedures and regulatory instruments are suited to a fast evolving, heterarchical societal production of norms and knowledge.[145] The emerging and changing forms of 'informal' and 'procedural' political conflict resolution and public-private governance reshape the face not only of today's nation-states[146] but, clearly, also that of international politics.[147] Yet, the soliciting of expert opinions from a group of experts engaging in serious research and analysis in order to undertake a requested analysis differs

and aggregating general action knowledge to become itself a manager of fragmented, limited interventions on the basis of specialized knowledge. [Trans PZ]

[142] See, again, Karl-Heinz Ladeur, 2000b, esp 13, 19–20; Karl-Heinz Ladeur, 1999, 31–33; Karl-Heinz Ladeur, 2001b, 63, arguing that 'specialized bodies of knowledge' (*spezialisierte Wissensbestände*) can only with great difficulty be traced back to commonly shared expectations and shared knowledge; see, Peter Hommelhoff and Martin Schwab, 2001, 694, suggesting that, for example, in the allegedly fast-evolving field of accounting standards but also in many other areas of corporate or commercial law policy, neither the parliament nor the executive were capable to provide for the necessary expert knowledge, see also, *ibid*, 700; in the same vein, Havermann, 2000, 698, with regard to innovative forms of product design and distribution as well as new financial instruments.

[143] See, Gralf-Peter Calliess, 1999, 55–70, for a discussion of different connotations of contemporary 'statehood' (*Staatlichkeit*); Gunther Teubner, 1987b, 4: 'juridification describes a reality which is not merely a problem of jurists, nor a national phenomenon. *Verrechtlichung* does not only spring from the well-known Teutonic tendency towards over-regulation, so the discussion of the problem is not confined to German jurisprudence. Although national divergences exist ... the phenomenon is universal, and the debate international and interdisciplinary'.

[144] See, eg Helmut Willke, 1997; Armin von Bogdandy, 1995; Peer Zumbansen, 2000b, 43, 286–94.

[145] See, eg Karl-Heinz Ladeur, 2001b; Karl-Heinz Ladeur, 2006; with regard to supranational law making: Joanne Scott and David Trubek, 2002, 3.

[146] See, Peter Hommelhoff and Martin Schwab, 2001, 698: '*Die Einbindung privater Gremien scheint gegenwärtig nicht mehr nur punktuell-vereinzelt, sondern generell zum Mittel moderner Rechtssetzungstechnik heranzuwachsen*'. [The inclusion of private bodies is no longer a punctual-singular occurrence, but has generally grown into an instrument of modern law making. PZ trans].

[147] See, eg Michael Zürn, 2001, 39; Christoph Knill and Dirk Lehmkuhl, 2002, 41. See also the EU Commission's communication of 13 June 2000, regarding standard setting in the field of corporate accounting, where the Commission explicitly plans to nominate 'highly qualified experts' for a comparative review of IAS (international accounting standards) and the EU's own directives on accounting.

fundamentally from what has long since been practised in contemporary parliamentary life: the invitation of experts to parliamentary hearings and interrogations.[148] This does indeed prompt a whole new array of questions pertaining to the issue of introducing expert knowledge into both parliamentary and bureaucratic law and decision-making processes.[149] Yet, in idealising rational debate and open deliberation on the parliamentary floor,[150] one runs the danger of overburdening parliamentary democracy, which has always been characterised by the structured chaos of public debate, the biasedness of prepared and party-line guided speeches as well as by the division between a handful of experts on the one hand and a majority of laymen with regard to specific topics on the other.[151] Only where such exclusive emphasis is laid upon parliament-based forms of law-making, can the fact that government commissions work 'outside' the parliament, paint such a negative image of 'behind closed doors' politics.[152] While this does not have to mean taking up an older Schmittian critique of parliamentary democracy—in which the correct observation pertained to the ineffectiveness of the parliamentary body to engage in productive deliberation, thereby not being able to confront the 'arcane practice of lobbying, haggling and consensus-seeking which took place behind executive doors[153]—the scepticism towards commissions is justified where it points to the parliament's exclusion from its own soliciting and hearing of experts. Indeed, there is a difference between convening a commission of experts and later presenting their findings to the parliamentary assembly and the invitation and open hearing before the congress assembly.[154]

[148] See Paul Kirchhof, 2001, 1332–33, who strongly contrasts expert commissions and pre-legislative bargaining between the government and market players to expert hearings taking place before the parliamentary assembly.

[149] This is certainly not a mere national issue: see, for example, for the case of the EU, Ellen Vos, 2000, 40–41, discussing the participation of 'civil society'; see also Martin Shapiro, 2000, discussing administrative law's contribution to global cooperation and networks, and Kenneth A Armstrong, 2001, with particular reference to the EU's experimentation with 'new forms of governance' in connection with the Commission's 'White Paper on Governance'. Another example is the extremely fruitful series of expert and stakeholder consultations led by the UN Special Representative on Business & Human Rights, Professor John Ruggie, available at: see www.business-humanrights.org/SpecialRepPortal/Home.

[150] Paul Kirchhof, 2000, 681: 'Das parlamentarische Verfahren der öffentlichen Diskussion verbürgt das staatlich erreichbare Maß an Vernünftigkeit und Gemeinwohlverbindlichkeit des Gesetzesinhalts'. [The parliamentary procedure of the public discussion guarantees the degree of rationality and common welfare of the law's content that the state may attain. PZ trans].

[151] See, Martin Peltzer, 2002a, 12–13, for an instructive analogy to the impossibility of rational deliberations within a supervisory board of 20 members, providing the ground for the insertion of new members by other ways of decision making.

[152] See Paul Kirchhof, 2001, 1333, speaking of, secretive governmental conversations' (*verschwiegene Regierungsgespräche*); this notion is picked up by Peter Hommelhoff and Martin Schwab, 2001, 707.

[153] See the *locus classicus*, Carl Schmitt, 1988.

[154] See Paul Kirchhof, 2000, 689: '*Das Parlament ist sachverständig kraft Wahl, spezialisiert sich in den jeweiligen Ausschüssen, bedient sich im übrigen in Anhörungen des in Staat und Gesellschaft verfügbaren Sachverstands … Das Demokratieprinzip baut darauf, dass der*

The task at this point then is to merge the perspectives. The rightist critique of parliamentarism in the name of a virtual, even utopian world of unimpaired and rational parliamentary discussions à la Schmitt,[155] did a lot of damage to the concept of parliamentary rule as such, but also helped to see parliamentary rule in its separation-of-powers context. In particular, this critique and its further elaborations, also from the political left,[156] can productively be taken as an occasion to take a closer look at contemporary administrative law-making processes, where a substantial sharing of law-making power with private actors is—rightly and readily being seen as normal.[157]

The second critique mounted against 'private' law-making bodies such as the two recent government commissions on corporate governance is harder to refute. The core issue appears to be whether or not privately enacted norms may be given binding effect towards third parties to the norm generation. While an intuitive answer would suggest a clear 'no', the matter at stake here does indeed escape such a straight-forward assessment. While it is commonplace in private law that contractual obligations concern foremost and only the contracting parties,[158] we have been witnessing a decisive evolutionary development in the public (constitutional) governance of private contract law to recognise the social role played by private transactions.[159] Indeed, it is not unknown to private law litigation, that contracts between two (or more) parties often unfold effects upon third parties to the contractual

Sachverständige seinen Sachverstand weitergeben kann, das Parlament für sachverständigen Rat zugänglich ist'. [The parliament is knowledgeable by election, specializing itself in its committees and otherwise serves itself the expertise which is available in state and society ... The democratic principle relies on the Expert passing on his expertise and that the parliament is receptive to expert advice. PZ trans].

155 We may also mention one of Carl Schmitt's most influential pupils, Ernst Forsthoff: see Ernst Forsthoff, 1971, and the excellent article by Ilse Staff, 1987. See also Fritz Ossenbühl, 2000, 7–9, with explicit references to Forsthoff's diagnosis of the pressure resulting from technological progress on parliamentary law-making.

156 See Volker Neumann, 1981.

157 Alfred C Aman Jr, 1997, 90; Matthias Schmidt-Preuss, 1996; see also Klaus Günther, 1990; Jody Freeman, 2000b, 592–93; Martin Shapiro, 2000, 369: 'Today, elected and nonelected government officers, nongovernmental organizations, political parties, interest groups, policy entrepreneurs, "epistemic communities", and "networks" are all relevant actors in the decision-making processes that produce government action'.

158 See, eg Hugh Collins, 1999, 23; Michael Bäuerle, 2001, 65, describing the different ordering function of private (contract) law and public (administrative) law; see also Murray Hunt, 1997, 38, recognizing both the need and the emergence of a 'modern conception of constitutionalism', which reaches beyond a strictly parliamentarian vision of law making; see also Martin Peltzer, 2002a, 11.

159 See Murray Hunt, 1997; Hugh Collins, 1999, 46; Michael Bäuerle, 2001, 121, 123; Dieter Hart, 1987; Dieter Hart, 1984; see Hestermeyer, Report on the BGH's Jurisprudence in Private Law, in: *The Annual of German & European Law* (R Miller and P Zumbansen (eds) (Oxford/New York, Berghahn, 2004), Section C II.

agreement.[160] And yet, the here suggested connection between contractual private ordering and the setting of norms by commissions might, however, be misleading. As we have seen, it is not entirely clear, whether or not the commissions are in fact 'private' by nature. This can be doubted at least in those cases where government officials are participating in the commission's work, such as was the case in the first Commission of 2000–01.[161] While the Code Commission[162] was made up only of private actors, ie representatives of large firms or academic institutions, the Commission's personnel might also not entirely provide the answer to the question as to whether any of these commissions is furnished with the proper competence to enact binding law. More importantly, then, is the nature of the Commission's empannelling. Where the Commission is convened upon the initiative and request by the government, there is indeed considerable reason to qualify it to be more 'public' in nature than if it were upon the initiative of a commercial actor, such as a bank or another private interest group.[163]

After the preceding discussion, we are likely to still feel unsatisfied with an ultimately inconclusive attempt at answering the question regarding the Code's legal nature with regard to the constitution of the drafting Commission. The result, however, we suggest, was entirely predictable if not inevitable, given the starting premises. If anything, this discussion has begun to illustrate the inadequacy of the public/private distinction to capture what we have in chapter two referred to as the paradoxical constitution of transnational law making. In the following section, we will further explain the inadequacy of the attempt to explain the legal nature of the Code through a designation of its norms or its authors as either public *or* private.

(iii) Corporate Law-Making Between State and Society

The discussion of the rise of governance in contemporary law making reflects a wide-ranging interest, but also a high level of concern with what

160 See, eg the jurisprudence of the *Bundesgerichtshof* (BGH–Federal Court of Justice) concerning third party effects of expert testimony contracts: BGH, JZ 2000, 725; earlier BGH, in (1979) *Neue Juristische Wochenschrift* 1595; BGH, in (1982) *NJW* 2431, and BGH, in (1984) *NJW* 355; BGHZ 127, 378; BGHZ 138, 157; see also BGHZ 133, 168; for a discussion of this jurisprudence, see Basil Markesinis and Hannes Unberath, 2002, 265–88; Peer Zumbansen, 2000a; see already Friedrich Kessler, 1973 and the contributions to David Campbell, Hugh Collins and John Wightman, 2003.

161 See, again, the Report of the (First) Government Commission Corporate Governance, chaired by Professor Theodor Baums, section B.

162 See Martin Wolf, 2002, note 3; see the list of members of the (Second) Government Commission Corporate Governance, chaired by Dr Gerhard Cromme, available at: www.corporate-governance-code.de/eng/mitglieder/index.html; see the Code at: www.corporate-governance-code.de/eng/download/CorGov_Endfassung_E.pdf.

163 Latter examples include the code commissions for the Deutsche Bank, the 'Berliner Initiativkreis' and the 'Frankfurt Commission', all mentioned in Martin Peltzer, 2002a, 11.

is being perceived as a 'privatisation of law'.[164] As Colin Scott recently noted, 'recognition of private legislation reflects both a desire to better understand the diffuse nature of capacities underpinning regulatory and wider governance practices and a concern respecting the legitimacy of such non-governmental rule making'.[165] This combination of 'desire' and 'concern' originates from a persisting association of law and its creation with the public, state sphere, while informal and private ordering remains relegated to the private, market realm. Throughout our discussion up to this point and in particular in our first case study on consumer protection, we have been arguing against this dualistic distinction, which we hold to be inadequate to grasp the ways in which both hybrid and private forms of norm generation can produce norms with regulatory functions.

(iv) The Reform of German Corporate Governance: The Intricacies of Rough Consensus and Running Code

The example of the German Corporate Governance Code illustrates our model of *Rough Consensus and Running Code* in the following way. The German government, facing immense domestic and international pressure to reform its corporate law regime so as to make German companies more attractive for global investors, was aware of the reform obstacles existing in the contemporary German political economy. At the same time, the government was well aware of the potential of societal ('market') self-regulation, as was declared by the Ministry of Justice on the occasion of being presented with the Commission's Corporate Governance Code in February 2002. Furthermore, the German government was hardly taking a revolutionary step when inviting a Commission to draft this instrument. Even if the legislative project of drafting a national civil code in the latter part of the nineteenth century was of course in many ways different to the drafting of the Corporate Governance Code in 2002, the Schröder government's initiation of the Commission, which was markedly referred to as a 'Government Commission', also bears some important resemblances to its historical forerunner. In both instances, the government drew on private expert knowledge in preparing a comprehensive legislative instrument, the regulatory impact of which was perceived as being so large that its delegation to a commission of experts promised to channel otherwise conflicting and perhaps irresolvable positions through a discursive, outcome-oriented process. Certainly, the government's initiation of this norm-generation process remained ambivalent at best with regard to the legal nature of the Code growing out of the commission's work. The striking characteristic of

[164] See the survey by Johannes Köndgen, 2006.
[165] Colin Scott, 2008b, 254.

both the process of the Code's drafting and of the Code itself remains, it seems, its *hybrid* nature between a non-binding, voluntary, 'private' regulatory instrument, on the one hand, and a document linked to a statutory disclosure obligation by a federal law, on the other. Yet, neither dimension adequately depicts the dynamics that shape the emergence of the idea of a Code, the evolution of its drafting, the intriguingly open-ended nature of the discussion around the legal nature of both the norms of the Code and of the Code itself. Instead, the discussion has made it far too clear that the repeated attempts to solve this mystery—by effectively avoiding the question 'public' or 'private' through designating the Code as *hybrid* and by referring to its norms as 'soft law'—achieve just that, namely to avoid the underlying conundrum of how to integrate such governance processes into a much-needed new legal theoretical methodology and doctrine. To us, the example of the German Corporate Governance Code is intriguing because its coming into being is reflective of its embeddedness both in a complex, historically evolved political economy that was historically sceptical with regard to private law-making and market ordering[166] and in a fast-evolving transnational regulatory landscape in which public and private actors—as 'norm entrepreneurs'—not only compete in striving to make 'better rules' but in a much richer fashion overlap, intertwine, collaborate and antagonise, thereby contributing to a constantly changing space that Saskia Sassen has referred to as both institutional *and* normative. From the perspective of RCRC, the transnational regulatory landscape that *is* corporate governance today, is marked by the unavoidable collision of public, private and hybrid, ceaselessly evolving norm-making processes that arise between regulatory arenas populated by actors inside and outside of the nation-state. These norm-making processes we have identified above as being messy in the sense that the identification of either co-ordinative or regulatory functions can no longer occur on the basis of distinguishing between the public or private nature of the actors involved. Instead, the norm-making processes have to be seen as *law generating* when and where we are willing to recognise the inseparability of the co-ordinative/regulatory dimension from the authority/affectedness dimension of these processes.

Against this background, what can be learned from this example for other contemporary forms of law-making? Recognising a growing interest among legal scholars in the origins and prospects of what is conventionally referred to as a 'privatisation of law',[167] we need to emphasise that the *regulatory* function of the Code does not follow from the state's enactment of a statutory disclosure obligation, as was repeatedly argued by those identifying the Code as a public regulatory instrument. What we have

166 See Hans Großmann-Doerth, 2005; Dieter Hart, 1984.

167 Johannes Köndgen, 2006; Georg Borges, 2003.

above identified as an unsatisfactory answer to the question of whether or not the Code is law, resulted from the recognition that in fact not only the underlying drafting process but also the envisioned enforcement mechanism are intriguingly complex and arguably open-ended for a reason. The government did not make the Code directly or indirectly enforceable, when it enacted the disclosure requirement, as it did not itself enact an ultimately effective sanctioning mechanism for the case of non-disclosure or deficient disclosure. Instead, the government's action in this regard illustrates what we have before identified as the defining features of the RCRC model. The Code can only fulfill its function of influencing corporate behaviour (and, as such, rendering German corporations more competitive) if a sufficient number of market participants endorse the Code's rules to make them matter. In that sense, a rough consensus regarding the Code's normative obligations must exist for it to have any influence on the corporate landscape. This rough consensus need not encompass each and every one of the Code's recommendations or, perhaps even less so, its suggestions. Instead, it suffices that there is among market participants a far-reaching agreement—a rough consensus—as to the binding quality of the Code's content. That this is the case has been verified by a number of empirical studies since its publication.[168] Secondly, the particular quality of the Code's three-pronged regulatory scheme of information (restatements), recommendations and suggestions in connection with the statutory disclosure requirements for recommendations leads to a complex constellation of the Code's regulatory impact. Where a rough consensus is being attained, it might set into motion the generation and crystallisation of a *customary law* of corporate governance norms, namely with the passage of time and an increasing acceptance of the Code among market participants. With the crystallisation of certain corporate governance rules, parts of the law of corporate governance can develop into a regime, which can further develop and solidify in the future. In light of such an incremental growth of norms through piloting (drafting a code), implementing (publishing it) and enforcing them (through a communication obligation set by the state on the one hand, and a market shaming process, on the other), the Code can contribute to the growth of a corporate governance regime, which can become ever more comprehensive, while at the same time being more flexible, open and adaptive to changes than a statutory provision would be. Seen in this light, the Code is illustrative of how recommendations can be made to enter a regulatory realm, which is occupied by both public and private norm-entrepreneurs, including the state that is pursuing corporate law reform, and private actors such as banks, investments funds and expert groups who are calling for

[168] Axel von Werder, Till Talaulicar and Georg L Kolat, 2003; Peter Oser, Christian Orth and Dominic Wader, 2003; Jürgen van Kann and Mira Eigler, 2007.

new rules governing corporate conduct, but also other stakeholders such as unions and business ethics propagators. From this perspective, the Code denotes how recommendations can increasingly be recognised as 'rules to be followed', long before they may grow into widely accepted norms of 'good governance'. That the latter is not oriented towards a reductionist concept of market efficiency is maintained by connecting the co-ordinative/regulatory dimension with that of authority/affectedness. It is against this background, then, that we need to not only return again to the original question of whether the Code is law, but also to dare asking whether we have been asking the right question.

As suggested, the perspective taken vis-à-vis reform issues relating to corporate governance has for the longest time been informed by both a public-private, official-non-official distinction between law and non-law and by a deeply felt scepticism about the chances for the law reform of historically grown, path-dependent norms and institutions, not only in 'Germany Incorporated'.[169] And, indeed, the legacies with which we have been struggling are weighty. In the face of these legacies, we have put forward an approach that seeks to draw out the institutional and methodological dimensions of norm-setting and law-making in the context of increasingly 'privatised' law-making forms. As it stands, law reform continues to be conceptualised largely with regard to a dualistic perception of state regulation and 'intervention', on the one hand, and market order and self-regulation, on the other. Traditionally, the German choice was thus: '[t]o regulate or not to regulate'. And the traditional answer was, indeed, to regulate.[170] The realm of options for the protection of shareholders' interests has thus been perceived to range from coercive, binding law ('vested rights') to an approach of entrusting this protection to the capital market. In the latter extreme, the shareholder's position as that of a rights-holder in a corporation would basically be seen as a tradable asset, the value of which would be determined by the market, not by 'the law'.[171] There is, certainly, much more to be said to this set of alternatives, and the dramatic substitution of post-ENRON corporate governance reform[172] by an overwhelming task to

[169] Peter A Hall and David Soskice, 2001a.

[170] See, hereto the brillant account by Gerald Spindler, 1998, 53, 57, stressing the different approach taken by American corporate law, which—for the most part—was state law and in turn 'enabling' law, giving firms great discretion in designing their governing law. 'Corporate law' as such, then, serves for one as framework providing default rules, while it does, on federal level, contain a considerable number of binding rules pertaining to safeguard investors's interest and the trust in the capital market; Peter Ulmer, 2002, 178–79, contemplating the code's allegedly meager achievements as to further de-regulate corporate law; but see Jeffrey N Gordon, 1999, see also, Werner F Ebke, 1998, 109–12.

[171] Gerald Spindler, 1998, 59.

[172] Interestingly, commentators were quick to point out the futility of premature European trimphancy with regard to the events in corporate America at the time of Enron and WorldCom's collapse: see *The Economist*, 13 July 2002, 54, denouncing any pride in 'Europe's

come to terms with the current financial and economic crisis underscores the dimensions of the task faced.

But it is against this background that—on both sides of the Atlantic—the search for 'good governance' in company law will continue. It will do so by involving the wide range of public, private and hybrid law-making forms which we have increasingly grown accustomed to. For this, valuable lessons can be drawn from earlier examples of self-regulation (eg standard contracts), as well as from other, contemporary developments in other fields (eg transnational commercial law). The rich spectrum of experiences on the national, European and international level is reflective of an on-going search for ways to adequately mobilise societal knowledge while being aware and conscious of divergent national trajectories of socio-legal and economic development. The enactment of the German Corporate Governance Code and the installation and indeed highly effective continuation of a 'standing commission' to review its acceptance and the need for amendments are both illustrations of a change in approach to law reform in a politically highly contested area. At the same time, the development of codes, in Germany as in many other countries around the world, by private and public actors, both domestically and transnationally, gives testimony of an emerging legal regime that can no longer adequately be relegated to either a state or market realm. Instead, the emerging regime of a transnational law of corporate governance is characterised by its 'spatial' character, both with regard to its normative scope and its institutional origin.

II. TRANSNATIONAL CORPORATE GOVERNANCE AND EXECUTIVE COMPENSATION

This section addresses the regulation of executive compensation and in particular the disclosure requirements as developed in the EU in recent years as as another example of a transnational law regime, displaying all of the features of recombinant governance developed in chapter two. In looking at this example through the lens of RCRC, we suggest to study the regulation of executive compensation as part of an emerging *transnational law regime* of corporate governance.[173] The defining feature of this body of law must be seen in the intricate combination of, again, substantive/procedural, co-ordinative/regulatory and authority/affectedness dimensions. After our preceding discussion of the making of norms of transnational private law

gentle form of Capitalism' in light (or shadow, for that matter) of highly disputable governmental interventions at the side of falling corporate giants.

[173] In this regard Klaus-Stefan Hohenstatt, 2009, 1351, highlighting the need to acknowledge levels of executive remuneration in the context of global capital markets and commercial affairs.

has laid out the structure of recombinant governance in the examples of consumer contracts and corporate governance codes, we use our third example to suggest that RCRC has to be seen as an important building block of a distinct methodological approach in legal theory, which shall be referred to as 'transnational legal pluralism'.[174]

A. The Transnational Embeddedness of European Corporate Governance Regulation

The European Commission's corporate governance agenda occupies a unique place within the European imagination. Since the beginning, the 'European company law scene'[175] has occupied regulators and policy-makers inside and outside of Europe, and recent innovations and changes in approaches to regulatory governance have given this area a set of note-worthy turns.[176] The arrival of 'new governance' in the area of European Corporate Governance Regulation (ECGR) brings the already charged interests and dynamics that are at stake in this area into much sharper contours. New Governance (NG) is itself a label for a tremendously challenging and provoking trajectory for the EU's transnational governance. Ever since 'governance' entered the scene through the Commission's '*White Paper on European Governance*' in 2001,[177] the spectre of a fundamental transformation of law-making has been haunting Europe.[178] The Commission's definition of governance as 'a very versatile one ... being used in connection with several contemporary social sciences, especially economics and political science', and as one originating 'from the need of economics (as regards corporate governance) and political science (as regards State governance) for an all-embracing concept capable of conveying diverse meanings not covered by the traditional term "government"'[179] is very open-ended and leaves one wondering whether the definition is meant to conclude or open an inquiry into the changing nature of market regulation.[180]

[174] The following draws in particular on Peer Zumbansen, 2006d, and Peer Zumbansen, 2008b.

[175] Clive M Schmitthoff, 1973.

[176] For excellent accounts, see Richard Buxbaum and Klaus J Hopt, 1988, ch 3, Jan Wouters, 2000, Mathias Habersack, 2003, Stefan Grundmann, 2004, Luca Enriques and Paolo Volpin, 2007.

[177] 'European Governance. A White Paper' COM(2001) 428 final, dated 25 July 2001, available at: aei.pitt.edu/1188/01/european_governance_wp_COM_2001_428.pdf.

[178] See Fritz W Scharpf, 1999, the contributions in Christian Joerges, Yves Mény and Joseph HH Weiler, 2001, and the analysis by David Trubek and Louise G Trubek, 2005.

[179] European Commission: 'GOVERNANCE', available at: ec.europa.eu/governance/index_en.htm.

[180] See Christoph Möllers, 2006 (for a critique of the omnipresent resorting to a still poorly defined and demarcated concept).

Without intending to overly strain the Commission's reference to corporate governance in the cited definition, the following observations will nevertheless point to particular complementarities between the EU's ongoing construction process and the unfolding *European Corporate Governance Matrix*. The varied history of European corporate law regulation is marked by the diversity of interests and concerns invested in this area of regulation.[181] While the legislative record was, until recently, not altogether comprehensive,[182] ECGR has in recent years become one of the most vibrant sectors of norm-creation and regulatory interaction. As such, ECGR has become a regulatory universe of its own, with a large portfolio within the Commission's Internal Market division and a seemingly tireless expert community feeding into the policy- and norm-making process at every turn. With ECGR long having left the confines of the European Court of Justice, the Council and Parliament, it has expanded into an extremely versatile, comparative and transnational legal laboratory. As a result, ECGR constitutes a *semi-autonomous* field, comprising both hard law and social norms, which are in a constant relation of complementarity, fusion and irritation.[183] As such, ECGR presents formidable challenges for legal, economic, sociological or political analysis. From the point of view of legal pluralism, the particularity and intricacy of ECGR lie in its mixed constitution of law and 'social norms'.[184] Seen through the legal pluralist lens, ECGR develops as a co-evolutionary process, where the imposition of law—which encompasses regulations, directives, recommendations and judgments—is both shaping and being shaped by the norms evolving outside of its imposition. Similar to the unpredictability of consequences and effects of rights/principles-transplants,[185] ECGR faces enormous challenges in terms of legal certainty and strategy, given its many sources of potential disturbance, irritation, and complementing points due to its complex regulatory agenda. In view of the challenges facing the EU from its substantive enlargement in 2004, Silvana Sciarra observed:

> As the tradition of comparative legal scholarship in Europe has taught us, the attempt to pursue a 'transplant' of legal institutions uncritically is both a sign of

[181] Richard Buxbaum and Klaus J Hopt, 1988, 193: 'In light of the economic importance and volume of transnational corporate activity on the one hand, and the numerous and sometimes fundamental differences in the various company and particularly capital market laws on the other, the endeavor to bring about European legal harmonization seems bold, if not indeed utopian'.

[182] For an overview of the legislative acts in the area of company law up to 2000, see Jan Wouters, 2000, and Vanessa Edwards, 1999; for a more recent discussion of state and prospects of EC company law making, see Klaus J Hopt, 2005; for a continuously updated listing of directives, regulations and recommendations, see the website of the European Commission at: ec.europa.eu/internal_market/company/index_en.htm.

[183] Sally Falk Moore, 1973; Gunther Teubner, 1999b.

[184] Peer Zumbansen, 2006c; see generally Sally Engle Merry, 1988; Harry Arthurs and Claire Mummé, 2007.

[185] Gunther Teubner, 2001; Katharina Pistor, 2003.

> disregard for traditions different from the one to be transplanted, and, very often, is an inefficient solution.[186]

Adding to the difficulties arising from the multilevel and multi-stakeholder dimension in company law regulation in Europe, ECGR has been amplifying the tensions that underlie the conceptual and architectural distinction between 'company' and 'capital market' law, which are deeply embedded in a country's history of market regulation.[187] Struggling with competing policy goals regarding the enhancement of market freedoms as they relate to capital market rules on the one hand and to corporate governance law on the other, ECGR is driven to actualise 'the best of both worlds'. To the degree that we adopt John Cioffi's definition of corporate governance to encompass the 'judirical nexus' of company law, labour law and securities regulation,[188] the ECJ's 2007 decisions in *Viking* and *Laval* fall squarely within this conflict zone.[189] Yet, while corporate law itself appears to continue to withstand all attempts at de-construction and de-mystification by other conceptual frameworks as to what corporations do,[190] ECGR finds itself deeply involved in and seemingly inseparable from a large, ever-so amorphous market-building project. The 'function' of the firm, as necessarily implicated within ECGR, must now extend far beyond the financial-organisational dimensions that have recently again been depicted as the 'what', 'how' and 'why' of corporate law.[191] Within the European project, in particular after the Lisbon Summit of 2000[192] and its more recent re-invigoration in form of a 'social makeover',[193] corporate law has become a strategic token in a complex multilevel governance game that brings a much wider range of players to the policy-making table than any Single Market regulation unit would reasonably want to assume responsibility for.

[186] Silvana Sciarra, 2004, 155 (with reference to Otto Kahn-Freund, 1974b).

[187] Rudolf Wiethölter, 1961; Richard Buxbaum and Klaus J Hopt, 1988, 193; Friedrich Kübler, 2001; Hanno Merkt, 2003; Horst Eidenmüller, 2007; Niamh Moloney, 2003; José M Garrido García, 2005, 761: 'One of the most debated areas'; for the US, see Roberta Romano, 2005.

[188] John W Cioffi, 2010, ch 2.

[189] See Christian Joerges and Florian Rödl, 2009 and Simon Deakin, 2008; see also the contributions to Rogert Blanpain, 2009.

[190] See Robert C Clark, 1986, 5 (regarding the importance of incorporating labour law into one's study of business corporations).

[191] Reinier Kraakman, Paul L Davies, Henry Hansmann, Gérard Hertig, Klaus J Hopt, Hideki Kanda and Edward B Rock, 2004.

[192] The Lisbon Special European Council (March 2000): Towards a Europe of Innovation and Knowledge, available at: europa.eu/legislation_summaries/education_training_youth/general_framework/c10241_en.htm.

[193] 'Euractiv: Lisbon Agenda gets social makeover' (18 March 2008), reporting on the 13–14 March 2008 Summit's recommendations to move away from its purely 'growth and jobs' focus of the past three years and to put the environment and citizens more 'in the foreground', available at: www.euractiv.com/en/innovation/eu-lisbon-agenda-gets-social-makeover/article-171013.

While the to-do-list for ECGR only seems to keep growing in view of pressing competitive, social, environmental and monitoring demands,[194] it has in fact always been evolving in a particularly accentuated and contested field of contrasting and competing Member State agendas in pursuit of national prosperity, of which corporate and capital market law had always been a central building block.[195] As such, ECGR has never sat comfortably within the wider market integration agenda. The real challenges of company law harmonisation, however, became impressively obvious during the exhausting struggle over the adoption of a regulation concerning the creation of the European Company statute, originally initiated already in the 1970s, and eventually passed after many more compromises, in 2001.[196] Another illustration of how ECGR has been inextricably caught up in the European 'Varieties of Capitalism'[197] was, without doubt, the long contest over a European Takeover Directive,[198] which resulted in 2004 in a Directive full of loopholes and opt-out clauses.[199] A few years later, Eddy Wymeersch called the moment of adopting the Directive a 'provisional semi-final point in a process that has taken more than 17 years, and according to some even more than 30 years on the way to opening up the European markets for corporate control'.[200] At the time, André Nilsen observed that 'the Takeover Directive sees light after a long and acrimonious journey through the institutional labyrinth in Brussels'.[201]

As the regulatory trajectory of ECGR continues to unfold, we must be even more sensitive to the degree to which this enterprise remains deeply embedded in the particular dynamics of multilevel governance of European integration, on the one hand,[202] and the globalisation of markets and

[194] See the Commission's Action Plan of 2003 '*Modernising Company Law and Enhancing Corporate Governance in the European Union—A Plan to Move Forward*' COM(2003) 284 final; see also the Director General's for Internal Market and Services' Summary Report of 2007 on the 'Consultation and Hearing on Future Priorities on the Action Plan'; on the tasks lying ahead, see Klaus J Hopt, 2005 and Luca Enriques and Paolo Volpin, 2007.

[195] John W Cioffi and Stephen S Cohen, 2000; Luca Enriques and Matteo Gatti, 2007b.

[196] Erik Werlauff, 2003; Christoph Teichmann, 2003.

[197] Peter A Hall and David Soskice, 2001b.

[198] See Ronald J Gilson, 1992, and Eddy Wymeersch, 1992.

[199] For the history, see Christian Kirchner and Richard W Painter, 2002; Peer Zumbansen, 2004a; for a recent analysis, see Blanaid Clarke, 'Takeover Regulation: Through the Looking Glass', (2007) CLPE *Comparative Research in Law & Political Economy Research Paper* No 18, available at: www.comparativeresearch.net/papers.jsp, and Ben M Clift, 2009; for a US-UK comparative perspective, see John Armour and David Skeel Jr, 2007.

[200] Eddy Wymeersch, 'The Takeover Bid Directive, Light and Darkness' (January 2008) *Financial Law Institute Working Paper* No 2008-01, available at: ssrn.com/abstract=1086987, at 2.

[201] André Nilsen, 2004, 1.

[202] See Markus Jachtenfuchs, 2001; Ian Bache and Matthew Flinders, 2004; but see Charles F Sabel and Jonathan Zeitlin, 2008.

regulatory processes, on the other.[203] Under such conditions, an assessment of the concrete forms of norm-creation presents great challenges due to ECGR's complex appearances ranging from 'hard' to 'soft' law to norms that are developed, promulgated and disseminated by a panoply of public and private actors.[204] Therefore, instead of trying to free ECGR from its embeddedness in this complex regulatory environment, the emphasis must be on the exact opposite. Precisely by embracing the embeddedness of ECGR as a *transnational law regime* can we begin to better see the concrete as well as the amorphous forms of change. The ECGR's transnational embeddedness is here understood in the following four dimensions:

- ECGR is informed by the policy and legislative dynamics between corporate law and capital-market law (securities regulation) as well as between corporate law and labour law, reflecting categorisations of functionally separable legal areas that can be found in all advanced industrialised societies and that are increasingly challenged through global forces of rule-making;
- ECGR is entangled in the European 'Varieties of Capitalism' with regard to corporate and labour regulation, as evidenced for example in the struggle over the Takeover Directive and the statute of the *Societas Europaea*;
- ECGR as part of the larger project towards the completion of the European internal market,[205] in particular in the post-Lisbon environment of 'knowledge society' politics within the EU;[206]
- ECGR as a *semi-autonomous field* is marked by a vibrant and yet precarious, always threatened balance between official law-making, transnational consultations, expert committee preparatory work, recommendations, communications and standardisation, that we see unfolding on the domestic, EU-supranational and transnational levels.

This complex categorisation of embeddedness prompts further study in order to draw out the correlations between the ECGR and the unfolding

[203] See, eg Dani Rodrik, 2000; David S Law, 'Globalization and the Future of Constitutional Rights', (2008) *Northwestern University Law Review* 1–82, at 31: 'Although globalization appears to have levelled off in the world's wealthiest countries in recent years—and the "social" component, in particular, now lags behind the "economic" and the "political" components—the overall trend across all countries remains one of increasing globalization'.

[204] For a succinct account of this regulatory development, see David Trubek and Louise G Trubek, 2005.

[205] Catherine Barnard and Simon Deakin, 2002.

[206] See the Presidency Conclusions of the Council of the European Union [7652/08], 13–14 March 2008, available at: www.consilium.europa.eu/ueDocs/cms_Data/docs/pressData/en/ec/99410.pdf, 4: 'The implementation of the broad-based innovation strategy is key to realising EU ambitions in the area'. For an intriguing historical background, see Dominique Pestre, 2007, available at: ec.europa.eu/research/science-society/document_library/pdf_06/historical-perspectives_en.pdf.

forms of 'new' and 'experimental' governance in the EU. The next section will work out the connections between the transnational legal pluralism of ECGR and emerging, parallel forms of transnational norm-creation by focusing on the disclosure of executive compensation. The emergence of de-territorialised, hybrid regulatory regimes, consisting of both hard and soft norms governing particular elements of corporate governance accentuates the degree to which ECGR has come under pressure to facilitate quasi-neutral, 'best' practices in 'good corporate governance'. This *normalisation* of corporate governance standards illustrates, in turn, how the transnationalisation of the European Company Law scene is at the same time deeply issue-driven and functionalist in nature. As a result, corporate governance regulation presents formidable challenges with a view to developing adequate enabling rules for corporate actors in highly competitive global markets while not frustrating critics' attempts at preventing the insulation of emerging regulatory processes from normative critique. In 2007, Simon Deakin, one of the most astute observers of European corporate governance, noted[207] how expert groups such as the European Corporate Governance Forum,[208] while importantly building on recent experiences with the Winter I and II groups and their vital contribution to break the deadlock over the Takeover Directive, nevertheless reinforce and further accentuate the drive towards a 'right' standard in corporate governance regulation despite the declarations that many years of debating the convergence and divergence of corporate governance standards[209] should support the view that 'no one size fits all'.[210]

Building on earlier work by Zumbansen and Deakin we will suggest that a combination of *transnational legal pluralism*[211] and *reflexive corporate governance*[212] can best address this challenge. With ECGR constituting an intricate combination of both substantive and procedural aspects, displaying co-evolving and intertwined processes of law vs social norms negotiation, dissemination and alternative 'enforcement' modes, ECGR goes *beyond* and reaches *across* categories through which comparative company

207 Simon Deakin, 2007.

208 See the website at: ec.europa.eu/internal_market/company/ecgforum/index_en.htm.

209 See, eg Jeffrey N Gordon, 1999; Ronald J Gilson, 2001; Eddy Wymeersch, 2002.

210 See Frits Bolkestein, *Corporate Governance in the European Union*, Speech of 18 October 2004 on the occasion of the Inauguration of the ECGF in The Hague, available at: europa.eu/rapid/pressReleasesAction.do?reference=SPEECH/04/460&format=PDF&aged=1&language=EN&guiLanguage=en; see Jaap Winter, 2002a, 9, 72.

211 Peer Zumbansen, 2006d; Peer Zumbansen, 2006c; Peer Zumbansen, 2008c; Peer Zumbansen, 2008b.

212 Simon Deakin, 2001; Simon Deakin, 2003; Simon Deakin, 2007.

law scholars have so far been assessing the function of the corporation[213] and the rules governing its behaviour.[214]

B. 'New' and 'Experimentalist Governance' in European Corporate Law Regulation: RCRC as Transnational Legal Pluralism

Any assessment of emerging forms of corporate governance regulation in Europe has to build on the fast-growing body of scholarship by legal sociology and conflicts of laws scholars,[215] on the one hand, and comparative company law experts, on the other.[216] The present challenge consists in the facilitation of a mutually enriching dialogue and exchange between this scholarship and the ongoing exploration of EU governance, which remains—due to its complexity of levels and contexts of regulation—for the most part a domain almost exclusively belaboured by EU-focused regulatory theorists. One important area of 'overlap' between EU regulatory and Corporate Governance scholarship is marked by the tension between 'harmonisation' and 'regulatory competition'. This perspective has for years been informing a fruitful comparative inquiry into the different conditions in particular between the US federal organisation of corporate law-making (States) and securities regulation (federal).[217] Recent years have seen significant process in reaching beyond the obvious obstacles to comparisons, on the one hand, by focusing more clearly on the evolving flexible and hybrid forms of regulation in Europe[218] and, on the other, by further developing the underlying comparative methodologies.[219] Again, the emphasis on the particular nature of the emerging regulatory spaces—as being both *embedded* in established regulatory practices from within the Member States and *disembedded* in terms of evolving within a dramatically globalising market—points to the difficulties of disentangling any assessment of ECGR

[213] Reinier Kraakman, Paul L Davies, Henry Hansmann, Gérard Hertig, Klaus J Hopt, Hideki Kanda and Edward B Rock, 2004; see Mark J Roe, 1998.

[214] Rafael La Porta, Florencio Lopez-de-Silanes, Andrei Shleifer and Robert W Vishny, 1998; Rafael La Porta, Florencio Lopez-de-Silanes and Andrei Shleifer, 2008; see the critique by Simon Deakin, 'Corporate Governance and Human Development', Tanner Lectures presented at the University of Oxford, February 2008, ms on file with authors; Beth Ahlering and Simon Deakin, 2007; Udo C Braendle, 2006; Mathias M Siems and Simon Deakin, 2009; Mathias M Siems, 2007; John Armour, Simon Deakin, Priya Lele and Mathias M Siems, 2009; Holger Spamann, 2009; Ralf Michaels, 2009a; Mark J Roe, 2006.

[215] Annelise Riles, 2005; Ralf Michaels, 2005; Ralf Michaels, 2007a; Paul Schiff Berman, 2007.

[216] See, eg Klaus J Hopt and Patrick C Leyens, 2004.

[217] See Richard Buxbaum, 1986, and David Charny, 1991; Stefano Lombardo, 2002.

[218] Simon Deakin, 2001; John Armour, 2005; Gérard Hertig and Joseph A McCahery, 2007.

[219] See Klaus-Jürgen Hopt, 2006; David C Donald, 2008; Ralf Michaels, 2009a.

from the larger project of European integration which is itself inescapably and always tied to processes of globalisation of capital, labour, and rights.

It is against this background that we contend that the particular challenges facing ECGR must be studied through the lens of transnational law and, more specifically, through the emerging prism of *transnational legal pluralism* that serves as an illustration of the concept of RCRC which we propose here. The connection of observations of the transformation of public and private international law towards 'transnational law'[220] and the legal-sociological and anthropological work on legal pluralism offers important insights into a better understanding of current trajectories of functionally determined regulatory areas. As noted above, ECGR must be understood as a functional field, determined by its semi-autonomous nature with regard to its tension between law/norms and politics/market. ECGR emerges through the co-evolution of the different functional dynamics, which drive corporate organisation. At the same time, the fast-emerging forms of new corporate organisation such as private equity vehicles and hedge funds seem to defy an organisation-oriented assessment of the firm in favour of a differently positioned analysis of contemporary corporate forms. As scholars re-visit and re-contextualise the 'end-of-history' thesis in comparative corporate governance scholarship and the Berle-Means paradigm of corporate organisation and its related governance issues,[221] the dramatic mortgage-loan meltdown in the spring of 2008 points to the need of a comprehensive reassessment of the corporate governance approach for an understanding of the financial structures of the corporate form and the contested aspiration of financial markets regulation.[222]

(i) The Polarities of EU Governance: Global Competitiveness and Political-Economic Integration

But even before the current financial and ecomomic crisis began to unfold its impact on governments around the world, it was obvious that the study of transnational regulatory spaces such as the ECGR requires a decisive move towards an interdisciplinary research agenda. ECGR has to be seen in the context of a highly diversified series of norm-setting processes resulting in a veritable explosion of corporate governance codes in Europe and elsewhere. With the proliferation of corporate governance codes, influenced and pushed by international and transnational activities of norm-setting,

[220] Philip C Jessup, 1956.

[221] See William W Bratton and Michael L Wachter, 2007; Dalia Tsuk, 2005.

[222] Marcel Kahan/Edward B Rock, 'Hedge Fund Activism in the Enforcement of Bondholder Rights', *NYU Law and Economics Research Paper* No 08-02, available at: ssrn.com/abstract=1093387; see Sanford Jacoby, 2008, 'Finance and Labor: Perspectives on Risk, Inequality, and Democracy', available at: ssrn.com/abstract=1020843.

discussion and thought exchange,[223] it has become increasingly difficult to identify a single institution or author of a set of norms. Instead, much of the production and dissemination of corporate governance rules operates through the migration of standards[224] and a cross-fertilisation of norms. A distinct feature of this de-territorialised production of norms is the radical challenge these processes pose for our understanding of what we call *law proper*. The dissemination of corporate governance codes, disclosure standards and rules, best practices and codes of conduct, affects the entire juridical nexus of corporate governance, as the de-centralisation of norm-producers is repeated, mirrored and reflected in the hybridisation of the norms themselves. It is in this sense, that the study of the proliferation of corporate governance codes and company law production in general and of the rules of remuneration disclosure in particular feeds into the broader research inquiry into the changing face of legal regulation in globally integrated marketplaces, to which our book aims to contribute.

To be sure, a concept such as RCRC, developed to capture the particular regulatory dynamics of emerging norm-creating fields, stands neither autonomously nor uncontestedly within the marketplace of ideas. Conceptual work on new regulatory modes of governance has been occupying scholars of public and private law all throughout the twentieth century, preceded and interspersed by assessments of the anthropological and sociological underpinnings of law throughout.[225] The study of governance in the EU has been a most productive and fruitful field of research, given its manifold instantiations of multilevel and polycontextual norm-creation.[226] As we seek to illustrate, it is important to reassess a concept as ambitious as RCRC against the far-advanced conceptual background of contemporary governance studies, as we can find them in the example of the EU. 'New' or alternative modes of governance have been emerging in response and reaction to the regulatory challenges that inevitably arise from these distinct variances in 'Member States' regulatory design. The most remarkable regulatory innovation in recent years is without doubt the so-called Open Method of Co-ordination (OMC), which, since its emergence during the 1990s in the realm of politically contested national, economic and employment policies, was formally adopted at the 2000 Lisbon Summit. Its defining feature has been the *proceduralisation* of regulatory governance

[223] See, eg ECGI, INSEAD, Euroshareholders.
[224] See for a comparable analysis of migrating human rights standards, Craig Scott and Robert Wai, 2004.
[225] Eugen Ehrlich, 1962; Georges Gurvitch, 1947; Sally Falk Moore, 1973; Sally Engle Merry, 1988; Gunther Teubner, 1983; Peer Zumbansen, 2008a.
[226] See Joseph HH Weiler, 1991; Fritz W Scharpf, 1999; Jean Cohen and Charles F Sabel, 1997; Oliver Gerstenberg, 1997; Charles F Sabel and Jonathan Zeitlin, 2008.

by benchmarking and disseminating non-binding objectives and standards across a growing body of regulatory areas.[227]

> In the years following the Lisbon Summit, the OMC ... appeared to have become the governance instrument of choice for EU policymaking in complex, domestically sensitive areas, where diversity among the Member States precludes harmonisation but inaction is politically unacceptable, and where widespread strategic uncertainty recommends mutual learning at the national as well as the European level.[228]

The departure of the OMC from the more rigid norm-generation and enforcement programme of the 'Community Method' has been both welcomed and criticised.[229] What Francis Snyder identified as 'the challenge of sites' facing the European Constitutionalist project,[230] indeed constitutes the framework for the proliferating norm-generation processes of ECGR. As the example of regulating the disclosure requirements for executive compensation illustrates, ECGR is marked by a deep, underlying tension between increasingly decentralised, indirect regulatory forms on the one hand and vaguely defined and yet broadly conceived policy goals against which the adequacy and the success of lower-level norm-setting processes will be measured, on the other. At the same time, EU internal corporate governance negotiations are increasingly becoming disembedded from the exclusionary European context as they are complemented and shaped by those norms and principles ('best practices' and 'guidelines' that are disseminated on the transnational level, promulgated, for example, by actors such as the OECD).[231] This interrelation between norm-creation spheres such as the EU and the OECD is even more poignant, as the respective proliferation of different regulatory norms, principles, guidelines etc[232] contributes to a constellation that tends to escape a clear-cut conflict of laws agenda. To the degree that national, regional as well as *issue-driven* legal cultures, such as the already mentioned *lex mercatoria* or our present example of corporate governance, are increasingly marked by a complex juxtaposition of hard and soft rules, the dynamics of regulatory interaction previously conceived through the lens of private international law, now prompt a much more sophisticated, inter- or, *trans*disciplinary approach.[233]

[227] Dermot Hodson and Imelda Maher, 2001.
[228] Charles F Sabel and Jonathan Zeitlin, 2008, 292.
[229] See, eg Joanne Scott and David Trubek, 2002.
[230] Francis Snyder, 2004b, 13.
[231] See the OECD Principles of Corporate Governance, revised edn 2004, available at: www.ecgi.org/codes/documents/principles_en_final.pdf.
[232] Jean du Plessis and Claus Luttermann, 2007, 222–23: 'The OECD Principles emphasise the point that a corporate governance framework typically comprises elements of legislation, regulation, self-regulatory arrangements, voluntary commitments and business practices that are the result of a country's specific circumstances, history and tradition'.
[233] In this regard, see the essay by Karen Knop, Ralf Michaels and Annelise Riles, 2008.

Studying ECGR as a particularly open-ended and contestable practice[234] suggests strong corollaries between ECGR and emerging general forms of 'new'[235] or 'experimental' EU governance,[236] on the one hand, and between ECGR and transnational governance forms in corporate and labour law, on the other.[237] On the 'inside' of the European integration process, recent years have seen a tremendous drive towards the creation of ever-more flexible forms of indirect regulation, benchmarking and rule/standards production through expert groups and advisory committees, while on the 'outside' ECGR has long become entangled in global highly charged competition over the most effective corporate governance standards as part of an emerging trasnational private law.[238] We need to pay close attention to the particular dynamics between the regulatory innovation on the 'inside' and the regulatory competition on the 'outside'. Precisely the innovation advances in the evolution of the EU's regulatory architecture, as exemplified in the Open Method of Co-ordination as one of the most contentiously debated developments in recent years, may reveal the pressing dangers of new governance and an embrace of market ordering. Paradoxically, the operational method of the OMC, originally designed to promote greater flexibility and pressure to foster a race to the top in social standards, might turn out to transform itself in the context of the ECGR into an engine towards 'best practice in corporate governance'. The utilitarian, soft-law approach, which increasingly marks ECGR, leads to considerably different results than would have been hoped for in other areas of the OMC. In view of the earlier described tensions between different regulatory trajectories of corporate governance—consisting of an amalgamation of company law, securities regulation, taxation and insolvency law—the pursuit of 'best practices' is threatened to be determined by a considerably narrower scope of functional concerns. By emphasising the need to ensure the economic performance and, connected herewith, the integrity and stability of financial institutions, corporate governance as a regulatory field is gradually being immunised against the more complex regulatory context we have seen unfold over the course of the twentieth century.[239]

(ii) Reflexive Corporate Governance

As the globalisation of corporate activity and finance has over the last 20 years successfully been undermining any attempt at effectively

[234] See Norbert Reich, 2005, 307: 'Governance is concerned with achieving this balance between legitimate and illegitimate uses of autonomy'.
[235] Critically, Scott and Trubek, 2002, above; see also Kenneth A Armstrong, 2002; Christine Parker and John Braithwaite, 2003; Colin Scott, 2007.
[236] Sabel and Zeitlin, 2008, above.
[237] Peer Zumbansen, 2006b.
[238] Daniela Caruso, 2006.
[239] See, eg Adolf A Berle, 1954; Mark J Roe, 1997; Erik Berglöf and Ernst-Ludwig von Thadden, 2000.

re-domesticating corporate governance into the previously contained political economies of nation-states, a more appropriate conceptual approach might be to argue for the need for a transnationalisation of corporate governance regulation. In the case of ECGR this would mean first to recognise the need for a differentiated assessment of different nation-state regulatory experiences and their presently continuing variations and innovations.[240] The next step would then not consist in 'translating' specific regulatory instruments onto the transnational sphere, but, instead, in fostering a radically functionalist understanding of corporate governance. Such an approach would go beyond the now abundant references to 'best practices', which owe their content more to the ideological battles out of which they are emerging than to a truly functionalist governance model. Such a model would have to be developed on the basis of an understanding of the transnationally embedded firm in mind. Building on work on 'reflexive law' in the area of corporate governance and corporate environmental responsibilities,[241] a more adequate governance approach would start with the corporation itself, complementing simultaneously continuing assessments of the organisational functionalities of the corporation.[242] While such a refined functionalist approach to corporate governance is still at the beginning,[243] its promise lies in the pursuit of governance models that are evolving directly out of the practice, management and operation of complex business entities on uncertain markets.

This approach would place a particular emphasis on self-regulation, which would in turn create additional pressure on the regulatory systems with a mandatory-law approach to corporate law,[244] *reflexive corporate governance* would eventually emerge as a more adequate and flexible approach to corporate law regulation while—at the same time—not necessarily being insulated from ongoing assessments of this hybrid regulatory enterprise. Instead of reacting to the long, tiresome and frustrating harmonisation attempts in European company law by turning to expert rule and market governance, reflexive corporate governance allows for a clearer view of how political governance and corporate self-regulation can be mutually reinforcing and optimising through the constant exposure of regulatory choices and practices to scrutiny. The prime advantage of this approach would be that the regulatory challenges facing today's transnational corporations could be assessed in correlation with the ongoing

[240] For the example of Germany, see Ulrich Noack and Dirk A Zetzsche, 2007.
[241] Gunther Teubner, 1988; Eric Orts, 1995; Karl-Heinz Ladeur, 1997a.
[242] Reinier Kraakman, Paul L Davies, Henry Hansmann, Gérard Hertig, Klaus J Hopt, Hideki Kanda and Edward B Rock, 2004.
[243] For the example of a transnational regulatory framework of corporate environmental responsibilities of Multinational Chemical Enterprises, see the excellent study by Martin Herberg, 2007.
[244] See Klaus J Hopt, 2002.

transformation of the political economies in which companies are legally constituted.[245] A reflexive approach to corporate governance is even more pressing as the dramatically unfolding debate over a reassessment of the alleged transition from a 'real economy' to a 'financial economy'[246] suggests that neither a return to embedded capitalism corporate governance regulation nor an undeterred belief in the 'end of history of corporate law'[247] with its dubious promises of triumphant shareholder value maximisation are a viable option. This means that what would previously have been an interest-pluralist assessment of choices in corporate governance regulation, in view of allegedly opposed and eventually irreconcilable stakeholder interests, can now be transposed into a more comprehensive and contextual analysis of the corporation's functions, in particular, of its embeddedness in operational and regulatory practices.

(iii) European Corporate Governance Regulation and RCRC

Against this background, it is important to contextualise ECGR, on the one hand, within the otherwise unfolding dynamics of hybrid governance modes within the EU and, on the other, within the here proposed framework of RCRC. Echoing long-standing legitimacy concerns with regard to the OMC, recent explorations of 'new', 'experimentalist' or 'informal'[248] governance critically address the instrumentalisation of decentralised self-governance in service of a larger 'whole', the problem being that both the accessibility of the implied, overall political goal along with the now available regulatory modes have arguably become even more precarious.[249] As Charles Sabel and Jonathan Zeitlin emphasise, the persistent legitimacy critique vis à vis soft and hybrid governance forms 'crucially overlooks the underlying architecture of public rule making in the EU: the fundamental design for law-making, and the way this design transforms the distinct elements of EU governance by connecting them into a novel whole'.[250] The particular challenge arising from these forms of governance is, however, the growing pressure on actors participating in multi-level norm-creation processes to effectively identify the desired output and the co-ordination elements necessary for its realisation.

[245] For the observation that even the ECJ's decision in *Centros* and others since 1999, which facilitated greater corporate mobility, have neither significantly induced more foreign incorporation nor more regulatory competition, see William W Bratton, Joseph A McCahery and Erik PM Vermeulen, 2008.

[246] Frank Partnoy, 2007.

[247] Henry Hansmann and Reinier Kraakman, 2001; Henry Hansmann, 2006.

[248] Burkhard Eberlein and Edgar Grande, 2005.

[249] Giandomenico Majone, 2005.

[250] Charles F Sabel and Jonathan Zeitlin, 2008, 273.

> The difficulty … and the open secret of administrative law in both the EU and the USA, is that it is very often—regularly?—the case that no actor among those seeking to coordinate their efforts has a precise enough idea of the goal either to give precise instructions to the others or reliably recognise when their actions do or don't serve the specified end.[251]

In defence of what they call 'experimentalist governance', Sabel and Zeitlin extrapolate the legitimacy potentials of the 'recursive redefinition of means and ends' at its heart by pointing out that under conditions of complex regulatory challenges an accountability model designed for a hierarchical principal-agent relation is no longer adequate.[252] Instead of assessing whether the agent did comply with a rule set by the principal, the agent is expected to provide 'a good explanation for choosing, in the light of fresh knowledge, one way of advancing a common, albeit somewhat indeterminate project (as all projects are)'. Correspondingly, '[p]eer review becomes in turn dynamic accountability—accountability that anticipates the transformation of rules in use—and dynamic accountability becomes the key to "anomalous" administrative law'.[253] The authors certainly recognise the limitations of the proposed endorsement of experimental governance, when they address the tension between the described participatory processes and democracy. But, their response is radical: while acknowledging the unavailability of a large-scale democratic justification of the new system of governance, Sabel and Zeitlin emphasise how accountability-through-peer review can help destabilise 'entrenched forms of authority—starting with, but not limited to technical authority'.[254] Importantly, they argue that the

> diffusion of procedural commitments to transparency and participation in EU networked governance has had a democratising destabilisation effect in terms of stimulating demands to widen the circle of actors and alternatives involved in policy making at the national as well as the European level.[255]

What renders this account important for our study of transnational (corporate) governance as an example of RCRC is the intricate public-private mix of regulatory actors, on the one hand, and the correlation of experimentalist governance with the particular integrationist agenda of the EU, on the other. Seen through the lens of Sabel's and Zeitlin's model, ECGR on the one hand radicalises the particular traits of nationally evolved, distinct legal, socio-economic cultures, now reflected in the straining of traditional law-making powers, competences, authorities and modes. On the other hand, ECGR illustrates the emergence of hybrid regulatory regimes across

[251] *Ibid*, 304.
[252] *Ibid.*
[253] *Ibid*, 305.
[254] *Ibid*, 313.
[255] *Ibid*, 315–16.

traditional political and jurisdictional boundaries. Sabel's and Zeitlin's depiction of contemporary EU 'experimentalist' governance modes thus underscores the deeper complexity of tying the assessment of ECGR into the context of *European* governance. As the following case study of regulating executive compensation disclosure will illustrate, the particular challenges in this context inevitably arise from the intersection of national and transnational law-making in an overall already hotly contested regulatory area. There has been and continues to be considerable pressure on European corporations to become more 'attractive' to foreign investors, first, by both changing core corporate governance rules, and secondly, by substantively expanding corporations' disclosure portfolios. The peculiar trajectory of the European attempt at introducing standards regarding the disclosure of executive compensation can be used to highlight the persistent tension between 'old' and 'new' EU governance.

C. The Case of Executive Compensation

At the core of this small case study is the 'law' governing the disclosure of executive compensation in large, publicly traded business corporations. In recent years, there has been much development in this area, mostly initiated by public resistance against high pay packages for corporate leaders all too often now associated with excessive rent-seeking and fraudulent behaviour.[256] Academic work alone on the issue of executive compensation—while having grown with the rise in real-world compensation during the 1990s 'bull market'—has eventually outgrown this development.[257] Even a superficial survey of the media and the scholarly literature suggests that the topic has not ceased to attract immense attention—from the academic and policy advisory circles to the media and the general public. The mood regarding the subject, however, might have—or so we hope—matured over time, not least in light of the troubling revelations of severance and

[256] See eg 'Fat Cats Feeding—Executive Pay', *The Economist*, 11 October 2003, US edn, available at: www.econ.umn.edu/~edgar/Economist.pdf (observing a 60% increase of media mentionings of 'fat cats' between 2002 and 2003, making executive pay corporate governance's greatest worry); 'CEO pay: Fat Cats turn to low fat', *The Economist*, 5 March 2005, print edition, p 14 (warning against a continuation of 'lavish' payments to CEOs—including ousted ones); see also Sandeep Gopalan, 'Say on Pay, and the SEC Disclosure Rules: Expressive Law and CEO Compensation' (2008) *Pepperdine Law Review* (forthcoming), available at: ssrn.com/abstract=1096647, 1: 'Excessive CEO compensation is the *cause celebre* of current corporate law'. Similarly, Richard Smerdon observed that remuneration is perceived by some as 'the only governance issue'. Smerdon, 2004, 115.

[257] See, eg Lucian A Bebchuk, David I Walker and Jesse M Fried, 2002, 753; Lucian Ayre Bebchuk and Jesse Fried, 2004; Marcus Lutter, 2006; Björn Gaul and Alexandra Janz, 2009; Klaus-Stefan Hohenstatt, 2009; for an insider's perspective of the Federal Ministry, see Ulrich Seibert, 2009.

compensation packages for 'bailed-out' banks and companies in the more recent past. With allegedly or potentially everyone driving a BMW in parts of California a few years ago, the perception of success in the market was that it was generally accompanied and documented by steep increases in management pay. With Bernard Ebbers convicted by a jury that remained utterly unimpressed by his pleas of ignorance vis-à-vis the fraudulent events in Enron,[258] today's discussion about executive compensation seems again to be moving in another direction. Generally, the attitudes rank from scepticism to outright hostility with regard to compensation programmes.[259] In the shadow of the dramatic and existential destruction of real capital and life-long earnings with the collapse of the dot.com market in 2002[260] and the irritating distribution of generous pay packages to departing CEOs of companies rescued by tax-payers in 2008–09, it is hardly surprising that management pay has again risen to the fore of public attention.[261] While now is not the time to further pursue the deeper problems that surround executive compensation as a core regulatory field within corporate governance, it suffices to note that the European law-maker was well aware of the close connection between the substantive and procedural regulation of executive compensation and the particular culture of distinct corporate law systems. In fact, what makes the discussion of executive compensation so interesting is that we can recognise a set of much more fundamental questions[262] that underlie the different contentions about competences to determine compensation packages. These questions concern our understanding and concept of the corporation as a regulatory object, subject and space.

While the extreme amounts being distributed to top management surely remain on academics',[263] policy-makers' and the public's mind, the intriguing discussion we are here interested in, addresses this problem from another perspective, a perspective on the regulatory structure of executive

[258] Carrie Johnson, 'Ebbers Gets 25-Year Sentence For Role in WorldCom Fraud', *Washington Post*, 14 July 2005; available at: www.washingtonpost.com/wp-dyn/content/article/2005/07/13/AR2005071300516.html; see also Johnson, 'Enron's Lay Dies Of Heart Attack. Convicted Founder Faced Life in Prison', *Washington Post*, 6 July 2006; available at: www.washingtonpost.com/wp-dyn/content/article/2006/07/05/AR2006070500523.html (reporting on heart attack of convicted former Enron chairman, Kenneth Lay).

[259] See Knowledge @ Wharton: 'SEC's Spotlight on Executive Pay. Will it make a Difference?', 8 February 2006.

[260] For a concise account of Enron's downfall, see William W Bratton, 2002; see also Simon Deakin and Suzanne J Konzelmann, 2004.

[261] Besides numerous instances of post-ENRON press coverage, see from the academic debate Bebchuk et al, 2002; Bebchuk and Fried, 2004; Randall S Thomas, 2004; Franklin G Snyder, 2003; Michael C Jensen, Kevin J Murphy and Eric G Wruck, 2004.

[262] See Paddy Ireland, 2005.

[263] William W Bratton, 2005a, 1561: 'CEO compensation has ballooned (9–10), with total remuneration increasing by more than eleven times in the past thirty years'.

compensation, the related competences[264] and its disclosure.[265] Here, we encounter the important debate about mandatory vs voluntary disclosure, a discussion, which powerfully began to emerge in the context of government regulation following the financial scandals of firms such as ENRON, WorldCom and Tyco, and which reflects long-standing and dramatically urgent deliberations over state vs market-based approaches to corporate governance and securities regulation.[266] Central to this discussion over the merits or drawbacks of voluntary vs mandatory disclosure is their fundamental recognition as regulatory means. As convincingly reiterated by Cynthia Williams, the recognition of disclosure as a regulatory instrument, certainly, goes back a long time, at least to the work done by Brandeis, Berle and Means.[267] The more recent discussion focuses predominantly on the positive effects (or the lack thereof) of the US government's regulatory initiatives after ENRON, most notably the Sarbanes-Oxley Act of 2002,[268] which has meanwhile come under heavy fire.[269] This focus on the disclosure of corporate earnings prompts us to explore the intertwining of substantive standards and formal procedures, as it plays out in this area. Whereas the

[264] See Stephen M Bainbridge, 2005.

[265] Lucian Ayre Bebchuk and Jesse Fried, 2004, 212–13; Stephen M Bainbridge, 2005, 1655 (noting the impediments in particular for small shareholders to make effective use of the wealth of disclosed information, leaving mostly professional, institutional investors to make informed choices on the basis of corporate disclosure); for a comparative overview of developments in Europe, see Luca Enriques and Paolo Volpin, 2007, 132–35.

[266] Roberta Romano, 1998; Roberta Romano, 2002; Steven Choi, 2000; see Robert A Prentice, 2006, 781: 'A company can benefit when it develops a reputation for disclosing accurate information to investors. In theory, then, we should not need an SEC to enforce voluntary, accurate disclosure. Corporate practices of the last decade or so, however, stand in marked contrast to economic theory'. Prentice, therefore, argues against models of voluntary disclosure and even regulatory competition. See, *ibid*, 816: 'In the end, voluntary full disclosure seldom occurs in the real world'.

[267] Cynthia A Williams, 1999, 1211, with references to Louis D Brandeis, 1914, and to Adolf A Berle and Gardiner C Means, 1932. But, see also James W Landis, 1938 (highlighting the necessity of a strong SEC to regulate corporate disclosure practices).

[268] Public Company Accounting Reform and Investor Protection (Sarbanes-Oxley) Act, Pub L No 107–204, 116 Stat 745 (2002) (codified as amended in scattered sections of 15, 18 USC).

[269] Jenny Strasburg, 'Corporate Backlash over Sarbanes-Oxley', *San Francisco Chronicle*, 23 March 2005, available at: www.sfgate.com/cgi-bin/article.cgi?f=/c/a/2005/03/23/BUGVCBR78D43.DTL; Tracey L Coenen, 'Reflections on Sarbanes-Oxley Act of 2002', *Wisconsin Law Journal*, published 13 August 2007, available at: www.sequence-inc.com/index.php?option=com_content&task=view&id=43&Itemid=22; Roberta Romano, 2005 (noting that the Federal Government's legislative initiative leading up to the 2002 Sarbanes-Oxley Act encroached upon the States' competence in corporate law making, calling the Act 'not just a considerable change in law, but also a departure in the mode of regulation. The federal regime had until then consisted primarily of disclosure requirements rather than substantive corporate governance mandates, which were traditionally left to state corporate law'. (*Ibid*, 1523); see also Hudson T Hollister, 2005, 463: 'corporate-governance regulation in the 1930s was a matter of state, not national law, so the SEC's task for both U.S. and foreign corporations was one of requiring financial reports, rather than mandating governance structures'.

substantial issue at hand is primarily the adequacy—meaning the amount—of a compensation scheme, the secondary, procedural issue concerns the question whether investors, directors or managers should be authorised to establish the amount of compensation to be allocated to the company's top management.[270] Connected to this procedural issue is the question how executive compensation is regulated, in other words, whether the regulation of executive compensation should be left in the discretion of the corporate actor or whether it should be designated mandatory, state-made law.

(i) Breaking the Political Deadlock: Governance by Expertise

While it has often been repeated that there is no universally optimal system of corporate governance and that, despite upheld claims of an 'end of history in corporate law', there is much likelihood of continued divergences and persistence of distinct regimes, the case of management compensation powerfully illustrates the particular dynamics within ECGR. As the harmonisation of hard law in the area of company law seems to be out of reach,[271] soft-law harmonisation is offered as a potentially far more efficient approach to regulatory reform. Since company law experts in the 1970s had harboured a strong hope for a flourishing harmonisation programme of company laws in Europe,[272] the ensuing decades must receive a much more reserved assessment. Over time it became apparent that harmonisation could not be achieved in many central areas of company law given the substantial, political, socio-economic and legal differences of company law organisation in the European Member States.[273] Instead, the European Commission as the principle initiator of European-wide company law legislation pursued various projects in the area of capital market and securities law. Recently, much of this well-known status quo has come into greater movement. Among the events and developments that have contributed to a notable increase in legislative activity in this area are the already mentioned *Societas Europaea* and the Takeover Directive, the ECJ's judgment in *Centros* and later decisions in 2002, 2003 and 2004, and a fourth—and in many ways very promising—development, which had been initiated by the Commission amidst of the turmoil surrounding the deliberations around the Takeover Directive. In 2002, the Commission mandated the so-called High-Level Group of Company Law Experts under the chairmanship of Dutch law professor, Jaap Winter, to prepare a comprehensive

[270] In most US corporate law jurisdictions, the directors of a corporation have the competence to determine the amount of compensation for managers.

[271] Jan Wouters, 2000; Simon Deakin, 2001; Peer Zumbansen, 2006c; Luca Enriques and Paolo Volpin, 2007.

[272] See above all Clive M Schmitthoff, 1973.

[273] See Klaus J Hopt, 2002.

report to facilitate the Directive's adoption.[274] Shortly after the Group had submitted its report, the Commission requested another study, the mandate for which eventually constituted the starting point for an entirely new wave of European company law-making. When the Winter-Group submitted its 'Report of the High-Level Group of Company Law Experts on A Modern Regulatory Framework for Company Law in Europe' in November 2002 (the 'Winter II' report), it did no less than present an outline, blueprint and wish-list for future legislative projects for the European company law legislator.[275] Based on the Winter II report, the Commission drafted a concise outline of future legislative projects, the 'Modernising Company Law and Enhancing Corporate Governance in the European Union—A Plan to Move Forward', the so-called 'Action Plan'.[276] Given the wide range of issues addressed in its Action Plan, including, inter alia, corporate governance disclosure, strengthening of shareholder rights, modernising corporate boards and co-ordinating the corporate governance efforts of Member States,[277] the Commission invited public comments designed to assist it in the realisation and implementation of the Action Plan's agenda.[278] When, in November 2003, the Directorate General Internal Market, the Commission's subdivision responsible for company law, issued a synthesis of the responses received on the Action Plan,[279] it highlighted the overwhelming public support for the attempt embodied in the Action Plan to work towards a higher capital market efficiency and enhanced confidence in the market.[280] It further reiterated that many participants in the consultation process had stressed the necessity of a 'fully integrated approach combining self-regulatory market solutions, adequate co-ordination of corporate governance codes and legislation where necessary' while recognising that there cannot be a one-size-fits-all solution[281] for corporate governance in Europe. In light of the continuing differing company law structures in Europe and the differences in the political economies among Member States, it had been the long-standing and uncontested consensus not to pursue a uniform corporate governance model but to enhance better transparency, communication and *learning* across Member State borders.[282]

[274] See the report Jaap Winter, 2002b.
[275] Jaap Winter, 2002a.
[276] Action Plan, COM(2003) 284 final, available at: eur-lex.europa.eu/LexUriServ/site/en/com/2003/com2003_0284en01.pdf.
[277] *Ibid*, 10–17.
[278] *Ibid*, 22.
[279] Synthesis, available at: ec.europa.eu/internal_market/company/docs/modern/governance-consult-responses_en.pdf.
[280] *Ibid*, 5.
[281] *Ibid*, 6.
[282] According to EU Internal Market Commissioner, Charlie McCreevy, in a speech at the Corporate Governance Forum on 20 January 2005, there is neither need nor political will for a European wide corporate governance code: 'We *see* no need for this at present and the adoption

(ii) Executive Compensation: Governance by Transparency

Among the issues more recently pursued by the lawmakers in Brussels, however, was a European-wide regime for executive compensation. Already highlighted in the Winter II report,[283] the Action Plan of May 2003 re-emphasised the need for an initiative in this regard, which would basically be oriented around the central principles of shareholder approval and full, ie individualised, disclosure of the compensation schemes.[284] The Commission acted in this regard by issuing, on 14 December 2004, the Recommendation:[285] '[f]ostering an appropriate regime for the remuneration of directors of listed companies'.[286] Under paragraph (3) of the recitals to the Recommendation, the Commission highlighted the central role of the compensation scheme's disclosure for good corporate governance: '[t]he disclosure of accurate and timely information by the issuers of securities builds sustained investor confidence and constitutes an important tool for promoting sound corporate governance throughout the Community'.[287] One of the remarkable features of this Recommendation was that it addressed questions of disclosure over any substantive issues related to directors' remuneration. While the Recommendation subsequently addressed 'remuneration policy', 'remuneration of individual directors', 'share-based remuneration', and 'information', its central focus was on issues of transparency, disclosure and effective communication of the compensation details to shareholders and investors. The Commission addressed this Recommendation to the Member States[288] and underlined the necessity of Member States taking 'all appropriate measures' to ensure that companies registered in their jurisdictions have regard to this Recommendation.[289] The Recommendation did in very explicit terms highlight the political embeddedness of the remuneration regime within the greater system of corporate governance. Paragraph (2) of the recitals to the Recommendation reads:

> remuneration is one of the key areas where executive directors may have a conflict of interest and where due account should be taken of the interests of shareholders.

of such a code, if it were even possible, would be an inevitable and possibly messy political compromise, which would be unlikely to achieve full information for investors about the key corporate governance rules'. Available at: europa.eu/rapid/pressReleasesAction.do?reference=SPEECH/05/26&format=HTML&aged=1&language=EN&guiLanguage=en; see also Action Plan, above n 276, 11: 'no need for an EU corporate governance code'.

283 Jaap Winter, 2002a, 9, 64–67.

284 Action Plan, above n 276, 16.

285 A recommendation is a non-binding act by the Commission, pursuant to Art 211 EC Treaty second indent, to 'deliver opinions on matters dealt with this in this Treaty, if it expressly provides so or if the Commission considers it necessary'.

286 European Commission, Recommendation 2004/913/EC, of 14 December 2004, OJ L 385/55, available at: eur-lex.europa.eu/LexUriServ/site/en/oj/2004/l_385/l_38520041229en00550059.pdf.

287 *Ibid.*

288 *Ibid*, Section V, Point 8.2.

289 *Ibid*, Section 1, Point 1.1.

> Remuneration systems should therefore be subjected to appropriate governance controls, based on adequate information rights. In this respect, it is important to respect fully the diversity of corporate governance systems within the Community, which reflect different Member States' views about the roles of corporations and of bodies responsible for the determination of policy on the remuneration of directors, and the remuneration of individual directors.[290]

This section expresses—in very simple terms—one of the most compelling features of European company law development, ie the great divergence between different company law traditions and histories.[291] While the history of ECGR has long been marked by this struggle over nationally distinct corporate governance regimes,[292] more recent accounts document the origins, causes and prospects for change.[293] As already alluded to, the regulatory changes taking place in Brussels and in various Member States strongly reflect trends of parallel law-making initiatives that on the one hand involve official norm-setting bodies such as the Commission and the Member States' parliaments, and on the other, non-state actors, expert commissions and private enterprises, complementing or accompanying the official law-making processes through an amalgam of private, informal law-making regimes.[294] The particular challenge lies in the *proliferation of sites, levels and forms of law making*. As we can see from the brief account of the German response to the European Commission Recommendation below, norms are sometimes the result of a highly intricate and unpredictable political process, during which the legislative initiative moves back and forth between domestic and supranational (*Berlin–Brussels*) and between unofficial and official law-makers (*Expert Commission–Federal Legislator*).

The Commission's Recommendation of December 2004 soon began to trigger reactions in Member States, which—according to Point 8.1. of the Recommendation—were 'invited to take the necessary measures to promote the application ... by 30 June 2006'. According to the legally non-binding nature of this regulatory instrument,[295] Member States were then invited 'to notify the Commission of measures taken in accordance with this Recommendation in order to allow the Commission to monitor closely the situation and, on this basis, to assess the need for further measures'. Not only did the Recommendation appear to be just about one of the most

[290] *Ibid*, recital (2).

[291] See, eg the brief accounts in Mark J Roe, 2003; see, from a political economy perspective, Ronald Dore, 2000.

[292] See the classical account by Clive M Schmitthoff, 1973; for a more recent observation and overview, see Klaus J Hopt, 2002.

[293] Gérard Hertig, 2000; Peer Zumbansen, 2004a.

[294] See Theodor Baums, 2001a.

[295] See the decision by the Regional Court (*Landgericht*) Munich of 31 January 2008 [5 HK 15082/07], published in *BetriebsBerater* 2008, 9, with a comment by R Thümmel.

elegant, non-coercive and perhaps most permeating legal instruments in a highly politically contested regulatory environment, but it also might have offered just the right amount of pressure and substance to allow Member States to domestically pursue certain policies that otherwise might have proven too politically sensitive. The following section will trace these developments as they unfolded in Germany.

D. 'Germany Inc' and Executive Compensation

Executive compensation came onto the corporate law reform agenda in two steps. The first one occurred with the introduction of disclosure obligations for German stock corporations,[296] the second, more recent one was concerned with the adequacy of pay packages as such. This legislation is particularly interesting when seen in light of the ongoing corporate governance reforms in Germany on the one hand and the initiatives in this regard from the European Commission. While Germany had for some years been undergoing what is without doubt the most comprehensive overhaul of company and securities law reform in decades,[297] the dynamics of this process can only be adequately assessed in light of the greater discussion surrounding the already noted, alleged need to adapt 'Germany Inc' to a globally integrated market environment where investor confidence is key to gaining access to capital from large institutional investors.[298] It is further necessary to understand the particular quality of contemporary law reform in corporate governance, as we touched on in the first section of this chapter. As we discussed in the context of the emergence of the Corporate Governance Code, this regulatory field is neither purely public nor private in nature. Moreover, the intricate interaction between the government, a semi-public, semi-private expert commission, and industry representatives in a far-reaching public debate over mandatory vs voluntary disclosure of CEO earnings suggests that, rather than resolving the issue *in favour* or

[296] See the *Gesetz über die Offenlegung der Vorstandsvergütungen* [*VorstOG*] (Federal CEO Earnings Disclosure Act) of 3 August 2005, published in *Bundesgesetzblatt* [*BGBl*] (Federal Gazette) 2005 vol I, p 2267, available at: www.bmj.bund.de/files/-/1382/VorstOG.pdf; for the draft and the ensuing discussion, see *Bundesministerium der Justiz* (Federal Ministry of Justice), Press release, 11 March 2005, '*Eckpunkte eines Gesetzentwurfs "Individualisierte Offenlegung der Gehälter von Vorstandsmitgliedern von Aktiengesellschaften" vorgestellt*', available at: www.bmj.de/enid/0,0/Presse/Pressemitteilungen_58.html?druck=1&presseartikel_id=1906; *see* also 'Grüne bemängeln Gesetzentwurf', *Netzeitung*, 11 March 2005 (citing the critique voiced by members of the Green Party (*Die Grünen*) targeting the option for the general shareholder assembly adopting a non-disclosure possibility for management earnings with a ¾ majority).

[297] For overviews, see Ulrich Noack and Dirk Zetzsche, 2005; Patrick C Leyens, 2005; Ulrich Noack and Dirk A Zetzsche, 2007 (highlighting the current dynamism of 'service-oriented law making and innovative reforms').

[298] John W Cioffi, 2006.

against mandatory disclosure, the outcome of the struggle depends in reality on a complex and even unpredictable set of developments that unfold in a volatile and hybrid regulatory environment. This means that even where we can note distinct elements of private, 'market' ordering, we are here dealing with a straight-forward example of a radically de-centralised and de-hierarchised law making enterprise nor with a top-down, government-made legal regime. Instead, similar to the observations made with regard to the emergence of and the role played by the Code, the development of law-making in Germany in this area underscores the particular nature of this regulatory area which brings together all of the elements identified in our RCRC model.

Executive compensation came onto the radar of German corporate law reformers mainly as a result of the pressure of the international discussion over excessive CEO pay packages and management self-dealing, alluded to above, that for many commentators underscored the ultimate powerlessness of investors to effectively constrain fraudulent and otherwise illicit behavior among managers. At a time marked by an enormous growth in share ownership across many states' populations—either through direct acquisition of corporate shares or through indirect participation resulting from the marketisation of employees' pension funds—executive compensation has to be seen as an an *issue* emerging in a particular regulatory, political and cultural context. Once it emerges, however, it quickly attains an almost universal connotation, which in turn disembeds it from often sticky, historical contexts of contestation and ultimately leads to the de-politicisation of the underlying strategic choices.[299] Thus manager pay almost becomes another 'essential' element of corporate law.[300] Once debated within a distinct, historically-evolving political economy, the contested issue moves from its embeddedness in a particular context[301] into a sphere in which it assumes the functional status of a global regulatory challenge.[302] It is this process,

[299] See Robert J Shiller, 2005, Chapter 6 for an intriguing discussion of populist beliefs in the promises of 'new eras'; see also Sassen, 2006, 247, 248: 'The key concern here is the fact that the global financial markets are not only capable of deploying raw power but also have produced a logic that now is seen as setting the criteria for "proper" economic policy'. See also Robert B Reich, 2007, 7: 'As a result, consumers and investors had access to more choices and better deals. But the institutions that had negotiated the spread of wealth and protect what citizens valued in common began to disappear. Giant firms that dominated entire industries, retreated, and labor unions shrank. Regulatory agencies faded. CEOs could no longer be corporate statesmen. And as the intensifying competition among companies spilled over into politics, elected officials became less concerned with attracting money for their campaigns. Lobbyists swarmed over Washington and other capital cities seeking laws and rules that would give them a competitive advantage (or avoid competitive disadvantage) relative to their rivals, wielding greater and greater influence over decision-making. Thus did supercapitalism replace democratic capitalism'.

[300] See John Armour, Henry Hansmann and Reinier Kraakman, 2009.

[301] Ronald J Gilson, 1992; John C Coffee Jr, 1999; David Charny, 1991.

[302] See the critique by Douglas M Branson, 2001.

which prompts our emphasis on the paradoxical combination of substantive and procedural dimensions that lies at the heart of our concept of RCRC. If share ownership was indeed 'universal' in the sense that it was a fundamental expression of fully-fledged, universal shareholder democracy, then the idea of a rough consensus regarding, for example, the essentials of corporate law would relate to mere facticity. Where, however, we are concerned with continuously contested areas of coordination and regulation, the importance lies in the fragile balance between the recognition of rough consensus and the ensuing emergence of running code. This space becomes ever more fragile the less homogeneous the 'affected community' and the more contested the underlying substantive dilemma.

Thus prompted to reach beyond the historical origins of particular institutions, their alleged starting points and ensuing trajectories, lock-ins and aberrations,[303] we must look more closely at the particular dynamics of regulatory change occurring with regard to both the institutional framework and the normative content that can be found in a particular field. The following, concluding account of the regulatory response in Germany to the Commission's advances regarding management pay illustrates the 'stakes' of RCRC.

(i) The Political Economy of Corporate Governance Reform in Germany

(a) Governing 'Germany Inc'

For the longest time, the governing norm for executive compensation in German stock corporations has been section 87(1) *Aktiengesetz* (Stock Corporation Act). It reads:

> In setting up the total earnings for each member of the Management Board (Salary, Profit participation, Compensation, Insurances, Provisions and auxiliary remunerations of any type), the Supervisory Board must ensure that the total earnings remain appropriate in relation to the tasks of the Manager and the state of the company. This correspondingly is true also of retirement pay, payments to heirs and related payments.[304]

The norm's most prominent and governing feature is both its explicitness and implicitness. The law demands that the remuneration of members of a stock corporation's executive, or managing board must be proportionate

303 Mark J Roe, 1996.

304 German original: '*Der Aufsichtsrat hat bei der Festsetzung der Gesamtbezüge des einzelnen Vorstandsmitglieds (Gehalt, Gewinnbeteiligungen, Aufwandsentschädigungen, Versicherungsentgelte, Provisionen und Nebenleistungen jeder Art) dafür zu sorgen, daß die Gesamtbezüge in einem angemessenen Verhältnis zu den Aufgaben des Vorstandsmitglieds und zur Lage der Gesellschaft stehen. Dies gilt sinngemäß für Ruhegehalt, Hinterbliebenenbezüge und Leistungen verwandter Art*'. [trans, PZ]

(*angemessen*) to the tasks of the board member and to the situation of the company (*Lage der Gesellschaft*). That is its explicitness. The implicitness of the norm can be seen in its silence as regards further specification and substantiation of this appropriateness. While there has been *some* discussion in Germany with regard to the level of appropriateness in executive pay, this has been comparatively less than elsewhere. Largely responsible for the relative acquiescence of the wider public in what German managers earn might be a simultaneous awareness that the German *Vorstandssprecher* and *Vorstandsmitglieder* (CEOs and managers) generally earn strikingly less than their peers in New York or Los Angeles.[305]

While in Germany, as in elsewhere, financial scandals in recent years had led to public concern about excessive management pay[306] and the public's irritation with scandalously lavish pay packages for managers of 'failed banks' and other bailed-out companies seems universal today, the related law making activity was at first remarkably limited to questions of procedure, in particular to the rules governing disclosure of management earnings. German stock corporations are obliged under section 285 No 9 *Handelsgesetzbuch* (Commercial Code) to identify in their annual report the collective sum of compensation earned by the collectivity, be it the board of managers or the supervisory council. While this obligation extends to different categories of remuneration—salary, boni and options—it used to stop short of demanding disclosure of individual earnings of board members. In the meantime, following the drafting of the Corporate Governance Code, some initial advance was made towards a commitment of German industry to *disclose* individualised corporate earnings. Intermittently, however, policy-makers, industry leaders and lobbyists disagreed about the need to comply with the Code's recommendations.[307] A legislative proposal introduced by the Ministry of Justice in March 2005 changed this state of

[305] Finfacts Ireland, 30 March 2006: 'Global Executive Pay 2006; Senior executives in the US earn the highest salaries', available at: www.finfacts.com/irelandbusinessnews/publish/article_10005367.shtml; Jay W Lorsch, 'Rising CEO Pay: What Directors Should Do', *Harvard Business School Working Knowledge*, 13 August 2006, available at: hbswk.hbs.edu/item/5490.html: 'Ask any thoughtful corporate board member what they are most concerned about these days, and it is not Sarbanes-Oxley. It is CEO pay'.

[306] Ulrich Papendick, '*Welche Konzernchefs zuviel verdienen*' (Which corporate bosses earn too much, trans PZ), *Manager Magazin*, 23 June 2005, available at: www.manager-magazin.de/unternehmen/vorstandsgehaelter/0,2828,361510,00.html; '*Europa Vergleich: Deutsche Bosse verdienen zu viel*' (European comparison: German bosses earn too much), *Der Spiegel*, 23 June 2006, available at: www.spiegel.de/wirtschaft/0,1518,422959,00.html.

[307] Last amended version (18 June 2009), available at: www.corporate-governance-code.de/ger/download/kodex_2009/D_CorGov_Endfassung_Juni_2009_markiert.pdf; see the Press Release of the Commission of 18 April 2008, stating that level of compliance has been increasingly steadily, available at: www.corporate-governance-code.de/eng/download/080418_Pressemitteilung_2008_en.pdf.

ambivalence.[308] According to the new provisions, which came into force on 1 January 2006, companies are obliged to disclose detailed management earnings.[309] This constituted a dramatic change to the prior regime under section 285 No 9 *Handelsgesetzbuch*. Yet, the real degree to which the new legislation departed from the previous rules can only be discerned when appreciated against the background of the political and regulatory climate that prevailed before and after the introduction of the new law. For this, we must again look to the proliferation of corporate governance codes generally and to the German example as a telling illustration: what became strikingly clear was that the introduction of self-introductory instruments in the area of company law constitutes a challenge to traditional understandings of legislative authority as perceived by German scholars as well as government officials. While there seems to be a wide-ranging consensus on the need to improve investor confidence, at the centre of which we find calls for greater corporate transparency and better accountability, much of which is endorsed in the recommendations and suggestions of the Code, the concerns about its still not fully resolved constitutional status on the one hand and questions of voluntary compliance on the other continue to be problematic. The fate of the Corporate Earnings Disclosure Law of 2005 is a most telling illustration of this ambiguity. In her speech relating to the draft legislation, the Justice Minister noted in November 2004 that '[t]he Principle of societal self-regulation lies at the roots of the success of corporate governance. Rightfully this principle has received international support and many followers'.[310] The Minister went on to highlight the reasons why her government should at this time not pursue the adoption of a public Act but instead expand the support basis for further voluntary compliance with the Code's recommendation to disclose individual earnings. The Minister noted that

> also in this area *norms* included in the Code are better than rigid statutory laws [given that] especially in this sensible field voluntary changes of heart and self-regulation are more advantageous than state coercion. That is why we prefer—against many other voices—the economy's self-regulation through a flexible

[308] Then Federal Minister of Justice, Brigitte Zypries, justified the regulatory advance with the failure of companies to voluntarily disclose their management earnings. See 'Corporate Governance: Zypries fordert gläserne Vorstandsgehälter', *Manager-Magazin* 14 May 2005, available at: www.manager-magazin.de/unternehmen/vorstandsgehaelter/0,2828,299768,00.html.

[309] See *Gesetz über die Offenlegung der Vorstandsvergütungen* (Law Concerning the Disclosure of Management Earnings) of 3 August 2005, published in *Bundesgesetzblatt* (Federal Gazette) 2005, vol I, p 2267, available at: www.publicgovernance.de/pdf/vorstog_aug_05.pdf.

[310] '*Das Prinzip der gesellschaftlichen Selbstregulierung begründet den Erfolg von Corporate Governance. Dieses Prinzip hat zu Recht auch international Anerkennung erhalten und zahlreiche Anhänger gefunden*'. [trans, PZ]

> recommendation of the Code. From our point of view, therefore there is no need to pass a statutory law regulating the disclosure of corporate earnings.[311]

The mood, however, changed within a matter of months. In fact, already in the summer of 2004, the Minister had underscored her commitment to industry self-regulation, emphasising simultaneously, however, that she would pursue a legislative solution by mid-2005, if industry bosses proved resilient towards the Code's recommendations.[312] Much of the drive for this change of mind, however, turned out to come from a direction which only few would have expected. None other than the chairman of the first Corporate Governance Commission of 2001—which had prepared not only the most comprehensive task list for the company law legislator in the post-War era, but also had called in its final report for the installation of a second commission mandated to draft the Corporate Governance Code[313]—Professor Theodor Baums, was yet to become the leading voice for a statutory regulation of corporate earnings disclosure. In many weeks of lobbying in early 2005, Professor Baums castigated German industry leaders for not complying with the recommendations of the Code to disclose their earnings in an individualised form:

> Concerning an obligation to disclose corporate earnings, the Code postulates this already today. Unfortunately, however, there is a consensus among approximately two-thirds of all DAX corporations not to follow these recommendations of the Code. In our view, this constitutes a veritable abuse of that instrument. And it is for this reason that the Federal Justice Minister is rightfully threatening with a statutory obligation. The EU Commission holds a similar view.[314]

[311] See Federal Minister of Justice as she then was, Brigitte Zypries, above: '*Allerdings halte ich auch in diesem Bereich Regelungen im Rahmen des Kodex für besser als rigide gesetzliche Vorschriften. Denn gerade auch auf diesem sensiblen Feld sind freiwilliges Umdenken und Selbstregulierung vorteilhafter als staatlicher Zwang. Daher bevorzuge ich–trotz vieler anderer Stimmen—weiterhin die Selbstregulierung der Wirtschaft über eine flexible Kodexvorgabe. Es besteht deshalb aus meiner Sicht kein Anlass, die Offenlegungspflicht bereits jetzt nach so kurzer Zeit gesetzlich zu normieren*'. [trans, PZ].

[312] '*Politik erhöht Druck auf Unternehmen zur Offenlegung der Manager-Bezüge*', Netzeitung.de, 2 August 2004, available at: www.netzeitung.de/wirtschaft/wirtschaftspolitik/298430.html; see also Wendelin Wiedeking (CEO, Porsche), '*Wie man das Thema auch wendet, es kommt immer Unsinn heraus*'. (Regardless from which perspective you look at the issue, it always turns out to be nonsense, [our translation]) in *Frankfurter Allgemeine Zeitung*, No 64, 17 March 2005.

[313] Theodor Baums, 2001a.

[314] Andreas Nölting, '*Von gierigen Vorständen und albernen Vergleichen*' (Interview with Theodor Baums), *Manager Magazin*, 26 April 2004, available at: www.manager-magazin.de/unternehmen/vorstandsgehaelter/0,2828,305446-3,00.html. See, *ibid*, '*Was die Offenlegungspflicht angeht, so besteht sie nach dem Kodex schon heute. Es gibt aber leider eine Übereinstimmung von etwa zwei Drittel der Dax-Unternehmen darüber, dass man sich an diese Empfehlungen des Corporate-Governance-Kodex nicht hält. Das ist meines Erachtens ein klarer Missbrauch dieses Instruments. Und das bedeutet, dass die Bundesjustizministerin Recht hat mit ihrer Drohung, dass wir eine gesetzliche Vorgabe haben müssen. Die EU-Kommission sieht das ähnlich*'. [trans PZ]

(b) Hybridisation of Law-Making: The Return of the State?

Consider this development, first, in light of the euphoric declarations regarding the value of a newly discovered ability of the German economy to modernise itself through the means of self-regulation. Secondly, try to look at this turn of events in light of the fragility of the embeddedness of corporate and industry self-regulation in the larger regulatory culture. To speak, like Professor Baums did in the cited interview, of an 'abuse' of the Code by companies mutually agreeing not to provide an individualised disclosure of their management compensation schemes, appears to turn the idea of self-regulation on its head. This is even more remarkable as Professor Baums had himself highlighted the innovative and reform potential of self-regulation, which he studied with his commission between 2000 and 2001, before submitting his final report to the German government in July 2001.[315] Likewise, the Justice Minister underlined the success of corporate self-regulation through Corporate Governance Codes, referring specifically to the recently revised Corporate Governance Principles drafted by the OECD.[316]

The regulatory origin and scope of the recent German legislation is of particular interest in that it underlines the above-suggested hybridisation of the norms governing this field. While the Ministry makes it very clear that it deems earnings disclosure of management to be of vital importance for the rebuilding and strengthening of international investor confidence in German firms, the draft foresaw the possibility for the shareholder assembly to vote against disclosure with a ¾ majority.[317] Certainly, this promptly contested option powerfully underscores the political dilemma the legislator was facing in this area. Given the stern and outspoken resistance of influential industry leaders, in the months leading up the draft law, against an obligation to disclose management earnings, the option clause must have appeared a reasonable compromise. But, with regard to the perspective taken here on the changing shape of reforming a fast evolving and highly sensitive area such as company law, the larger questions lie elsewhere. The remuneration dispute is but the tip of the iceberg of the long-standing struggle over adequate ways of valuating the firm and, with it, a richer assessment of what is at stake in the current shareholder value debate. Clearly, Ferrarini, Moloney and Vespro are right in their assertion that '[i]t is easier to find problems than solutions in this field'.[318]

[315] Theodor Baums, 2001a (Interview with Peer Zumbansen).

[316] Federal Minister of Justice, Brigitte Zypries, Speech before the Annual *Handelsblatt* Conference, 18 November 2004.

[317] See *Gesetz über die Offenlegung der Vorstandsvergütungen*, above, Art 1(2), inserting a new para 5 into section 286 *Aktiengesetz* [*AktG*] (Stock Corporation Law).

[318] Guido Ferrarini, Niamh Moloney and Cristina Vespro, 2003, 66.

The developments in the years following the disclosure legislation provide a telling illustration of the continuing interplay between official policy-making and market self-regulation. But, again, the picture is ultimately ambiguous. While we might be inclined to see the recently adopted federal statute on the 'adequacy of management compensation' as a clear sign of the State's firm regulatory hand, at least two complementing developments suggest a more differentiated view. For one, the global financial crisis proved to provide an important stage on which to re-direct the discussion around management pay from disclosure to substance. But, in addition, the law that entered into force in August 2009, refrains from putting forward concrete regulations pertaining to the amount of pay. Instead, the law recognises the relevance played by previously exaggerated compensation incentives that had allegedly driven corporate managers to an exclusive orientation of their resources towards a short-term increase in shareholder value. In response, the Ministry of Justice defends its recent legislation by arguing for the importance to tie compensation expectations to a consideration of longterm development prospects of the firm. In light of the one-sided focus on share value maximisation, the Ministry posits that 'the time has come for politics to readjust the regulatory architecture.'[319] The central feature of the new legislation is the tying of flexible compensation elements to the management's consideration of long-term development prospects. This is a striking example of the above described idea of 'reflexive corporate governance': in recognising the limits in adequately determining the 'right' amount a manager should be paid across a highly diverse group of business corporations, the legislator—undeniably—pursues a distinct political agenda when it draws on a long-standing, critical assessment of the role and place of the business corporation in society, which in Germany has traditionally been placing considerable value on the longterm development prospects of the firm.[320] At the same time, the legislator does not reject but instead acknowledges and embraces past innovations in terms of individually conceptualised compensation mechanisms. This allows the legislator to instrumentalise the existing, diverse array of compensation avenues along the lines of its desired political intervention. Injecting a longterm monitoring process to assess to which degree managers have pursued different goals believed to be in the interest of the corporation, the legislator has taken decisive steps towards a strengthening of the supervisory board in assuming its legally prescribed role in determining 'adequate' compensation. Some of this legislation's features are likely to occupy commentators for some time to come, including the regulator's decision to create a 4-year period before the end of which no option may be exercised by a manager or, the stipulation

[319] Press Release, Federal Ministry of Justice, 18 June 2009: '*Es ist an der Zeit, dass die Politik den Ordnungsrahmen neu justiert*'.

[320] Thomas Raiser, 1988.

that manager pay be determined not by a small executive committee, but by the entire supervisory council, rendering the determination of management pay 'more transparent'.[321] In addition, the increased liability risks for the supervisory board for having distributed 'inadequate' compensation to managers, underscores not only the legislator's commitment to follow through on longstanding attempts towards a strengthening of the supervisory board, but also indicates that the determination of management pay is one of the board's central tasks.[322]

(ii) Transnational Corporate Governance as Spatio-Temporal Assemblage

To be sure, another striking feature of this recent regulatory intervention from Berlin, which will likely continue to deprive commentators of sleep when trying to give more concrete meaning to new terms such as the 'sustainable development of the corporation'[323] or old ones, such as the 'inequity' of a continued maintenance of management pay at the same rate,[324] which the legislator decided to leave in the original section 87 *AktG*, is its correlation with parallel rule making developments and knowledge generation in this field. One instance of an implied reception of the norms included in the Code is the identification of the 'future development prospects of the corporation' in 4.2.2. of the Code as one of the guiding criteria that the supervisory board has to consider when determining the amount of compensation. Such a specification of the management's task and its correlation to the adequacy of remuneration was missing in the previous formulation of the relevant statute in section 87 *AktG*. It is noteworthy, however, that this correlation between the Ministry's policy making and the larger regulatory environment is not regularly mirrored in the federal statute representing a crystallisation or 'hardening' of the soft norms laid down, for example, in a guideline such as the German Corporate Governance Code. Whereas the Code, in 5.3.4., designates that the supervisory board may delegate the determination of management pay to one or more committees, the federal legislator opted for the opposite for the reasons indicated above.

As suggested before, corporate governance needs to be understood as a transnational law regime, which is constituted through a complex interaction and overlapping of public and private rule making processes. The development of a regulatory regime pertaining to executive compensation is a case in point, as we have begun to illustrate with regard to the development within the EU and in the case of Germany's recent legislation. A constitutive element of this

[321] Press release, Federal Ministry of Justice, above n 319.

[322] See, in more detail, www.bmj.de/managergehaelter.

[323] *Gesetz zur Angemessenheit der Vorstandsvergütung* [*VorstAG*], Art 1, 1. a) '*nachhaltige Unternehmensentwicklung*'.

[324] *Ibid*, b.

regime is, thus, on the one hand, its ongoing evolutionary state-of-becoming and, on the other, its experimental and open-ended nature, which is illustrated, for example, by the continuous changes made to the transnational body of norms that regulate management pay. The above-mentioned interpretation challenges with regard to the 'sustainable' clause which was inserted into the list of criteria to be considered when determining the scope of remuneration, appear in a different light, once the frame of reference is widened. The adoption of such an enlarged horizon proved crucial in the work of the German Corporate Governance Commission when drafting its first report 2001, for which it relied on numerous accounts of similar drafting experiences in other countries such as the United Kingdom.[325] The discussion around the obligations under the 'comply or disclose' principle which governs the German Code occurs in constant exchange and dialogue with its British forerunner model,[326] thereby further deepening the ever deepening comparative corporate governance research agendas.[327] Another indication of how the inclusion of the reference to the sustainability prospect of the corporation's development into the German law reflects on a transnational corporate governance debate in a time of dramatic crisis, is US President Obama's unveiling of his administration's 'Plan to Reshape Financial Regulation': laying out the core features of this Plan on 17 June 2009, the President highlighted the emphasis on the creation of 'new standards and guidelines to align executive compensation with long-term shareholder value'.[328] Such developments grow out of and are in constant reciprocal exchange with ongoing scholarly debates of the future prospect of corporate governance, which is *inter alia* marked by a stubborn rejection of value maximisation principles, displaying, instead, a long-standing interest in trust building, relational contracting and sustained commitments.[329]

In conclusion, we want to push the concept of corporate governance as a transnational law regime a little further in order to more adequately capture the intricate intertwining of highly charged political-economy and path dependency dimensions (*co-ordinated market economy vs liberal market economy*; *harmonisation vs regulatory competition*; *convergence vs divergence*) and issue-driven, functionalist as well as organisational dimensions that shape the concrete evolution of the business firm and feed back into the evolving body of rules governing the corporation. As suggested before with regard to the emergence of transnational law regimes, the realm in which these parallel and overlapping developments between public and private rule

[325] Theodor Baums, 2001a.

[326] See, eg Marita Körner, 2004; David Seidl, Paul Sanderson and John Roberts, 2009.

[327] In this respect, see Paul L Davies, 2001, and Paul L Davies, 2003.

[328] See Practising Law Institute: Understanding the Securities Laws 2009, PLI Order No 18186 (September–December), White & Case LLP, Client Alert.

[329] See, eg James A Fanto, 2009, and Robert H Frank, 1996.

making and knowledge creation, dissemination and implementation occur, can best be captured by the notion of 'space' as prominently advanced by Saskia Sassen,[330] who has now further elaborated this notion towards a concept of 'mixed assemblages'. Focusing on 'a new spatio-temporal order', Sassen has been continuing her important work on the relevance of a *spatial* analysis of governance changes and globalisation.[331] Charging the notion of assemblage with an admittedly complex and ambitious combination of spatial and temporal aspects, Sassen pursues her longstanding interest in the ways in which globalisation processes cannot be properly understood without taking into account the local, 'national' conditions and transformations that bring them about. She acknowledges that the analyis of how 'the insertion of this novel spatio-temporal order alters the national' is 'a process in the making'.[332] While one of Sassen's prominent examples is the highly sophisticated space of global finance, in particular the case of derivatives trading markets that she conceives as a space to be constituted through an intricate combination of institutional innovation and knowledge,[333] we want to argue for a similar understanding of transnational corporate governance. As we have tried to show in this chapter, corporate governance is a case in point of a fast-evolving, transnational regulatory laboratory. It displays nothing less than a constant *re-combination* of the paradoxical public/private, co-ordinative/regulatory, substantive/procedural and authority/affectedness dimensions, which we have identified to lie at the heart of contemporary governance regimes. Sassen's still evolving concept of assemblage contributes to our own model of RCRC a further accentuation of the tension between the regime's time and space dimensions. Insofar as RCRC emphasises, on the one hand, the development of a regulatory regime from *pilot* to *recognition* on to *binding* phase,[334] while it seeks to capture the problem of space or *community* through reference to the authority/affectedness paradox, on the other, Sassen's insistence on the spatio-temporal order productively complements this architecture by insisting on the importance of juxtaposing a political economy perspective on the emergence and exercise of power with a keen interest in the emergence of knowledge-driven regulatory realms. The challenge of transnational law regimes, then, studied through the lens of RCRC and Sassen's assemblages, consists in depriving us of conventional tools to designate public or private actors engaging in the production of legal norms. Instead, both theoretical concepts suggest that we must approach fields such as transnational contract law or transnational corporate governance as fundamentally challenging our nation-state based

[330] See recently Saskia Sassen, 2006, Chapter 8.
[331] See Saskia Sassen, 1991; Saskia Sassen, 2003.
[332] Sassen, 2006, 378.
[333] Sassen, 2006, 348–9.
[334] See above, ch 2, III E.(i) of this book.

conceptual framework. To acknowledge that transnational law regimes, as here exemplified with reference to corporate governance, emerge through a complex recombination of institutional and normative elements, can thus only be the first step. Applying the conceptual framework of RCRC and placing the unavoidable recurrence of the just mentioned four paradoxical distinctions at the centre of the ensuing assessment of a regime is the next step. Finally, to expose and to sustain the paradox simultaneity of the national and the global, as suggested by Sassen's notion of spatio-temporal assemblage, is the concluding, crucial step towards an—admittedly highly ambitious—reconceptualisation of transnational legal theory.

As corporate governance scholarship continues to sharpen its lens for deeper structures of formal/informal norm-creation and the particular socio-economic cultures[335] in which different hybrid regulatory approaches emerge, it becomes evident to which degree 'comparative corporate governance'[336] is being transformed into an inter-disciplinary area of regulatory analysis. Our focus on the way in which corporate governance principles are migrating in between different national political economies on the one hand and emerging, constantly reshaping regulatory spaces, for which Marc Amstutz has poignantly used the term of 'interlegality',[337] on the other, informs and accentuates our perceptions not only for the existing *differences* in national corporate laws, but more importantly for the fact that conventionally viewed 'national corporate governance systems' have long become transnationally constituted spaces of institutional and normative interaction and contestation. They are, thus, anything but peaceful, embedded legal orders. Instead, they are marked by a fundamental regulatory transformation in which social norms and 'soft law' become intertwined, changed, adapted and interwoven within a regulatory environment which itself is no longer stable.

Following up on the example of transnational consumer contracts, the case of corporate governance reform, which we studied in this chapter, illustrates the degree to which the contested issues and the successively made proposals that grew out of a far-reaching and open-eyed gathering of information and evidence by national and supra-national policy-makers, expert committees and scholars were of a veritable *transnational* nature, emerging from parallel reform efforts in other countries, among private and non-state actors around the world. In that sense,[338] domestic company law reform must be seen as part of an emerging transnational legal pluralism. Its defining feature is the fundamental contestation of the very distinction that legal pluralism has always struggled with: that between law and non-law.

[335] See Amir N Licht, 2001.

[336] Mark J Roe, 1998.

[337] Marc Amstutz, 2005; see also Marc Amstutz and Vaios Karavas, 2006—engl: Marc Amstutz and Vaios Karavas, 2009.

[338] Robert Wai, 2005, 475–76, refers to examples of transnational human rights litigation.

E. Transnational Corporate Governance Regulation as RCRC

Corporate governance norms provide a telling example of the transformation of traditional state-originating, official norm-setting in favour of increasingly de-centralised, multi-level processes of norm production. At the same time, not only are norms produced on more levels; the nature of these norms themselves has been changing dramatically. What our assessment of the present trajectories of ECGR and the case study of Germany's efforts as regards corporate governance reform illuminated is the particular nature of the regulation of business conduct and corporations in globally interdependent activity spheres (marketisation), fundamentally changing national political economies (privatisation) and a dramatic expansion of issue-driven, functionalist regulatory regimes (scientisation).[339] This constellation, however, suggests nothing less than a fundamental contestation and erosion of boundaries between state and non-state actors, official and unofficial law, public and private ordering.[340] What is important at this point is to repeat the observation made earlier, that the novelty of this blurring of boundaries between traditional norm-creating and -executing spheres appears as a direct result of a specific historical experience of a particular framework of socio-economic, political-legal regulation that characterised the twentieth century rise of the Social and Welfare State.[341] This experience has been aptly identified and premeditated by turn-of-the-century sociologists and lawyers, and powerfully captured by Max Weber's sobering assessment of the disenchantment of modernity.[342] Irredeemably thrown into the iron cage of modern rationalisation,[343] contemporary hopes are pinned—if at all—on a transformative realisation of emerging self-regulatory potentials.[344] It is against this narrative that we have conceptualised our model of RCRC.

Studying European Corporate Governance Regulation as a key case of RCRC has allowed us to better appreciate the complexities that accompany the emergence of such a transnational law regime. This transnational regulatory framework can only be understood against the background and in light of the complex, intertwined nature of corporate governance regulation between national and European competitiveness, European integration dynamics and the increasingly transnational nature of firm's operations and

[339] For an excellent demarcation of these dimensions, see Gili S Drori and John W Meyer, 2006.

[340] See, eg Volkmar Gessner, Richard P Appelbaum and William F Felstiner, 2001; Volkmar Gessner, 2009; Francis Snyder, 2004a; Katharina Pistor, 2003.

[341] Niklas Luhmann, 1990; Michael Stolleis, 1989.

[342] Max Weber, 1930; Max Weber, 1967; David Trubek, 1972a; Rudolf Wiethölter, 1985; Gunther Teubner, 1983; Gralf-Peter Calliess, 1999; Peer Zumbansen, 2000b.

[343] Richard Sennett, 2006.

[344] Jean Cohen and Charles F Sabel, 1997; Oliver Gerstenberg, 1997; critically William E Scheuerman, 2004.

regulations. Our concept of RCRC, which we suggest as an illustration of transnational legal pluralism, ambitiously seeks to acknowledge these learning experiences in order to productively integrate them into an enriched concept of regulatory governance. RCRC, as outlined above, can powerfully capture the particular dynamics of transnational corporate governance regulation through its structuring capacities of distinguishing between the substantive and procedural dimensions of contemporary norm-creation. The particular promise of RCRC here lies in its capacity to draw conceptual lines between the experimentation with norm-creating processes, which are understood as contextualised learning processes ('rough consensus') on the one hand, and the assessment of emerging normative bodies on the other ('running code'). Again, the promise of RCRC lies in its sensitivity with regard to knowledge emanating from concrete regulatory contexts that are recognised as norm proposals. Within the process of disseminating such norm proposals, they are gradually evolving into programs of regulation. Emerging into a still evolving running code, such norm programs remain fully assessable from any factual or normative standpoint, while not sacrificing their ongoing regulatory function. As such, our model strives—not unlike competing governance concepts—for coherence, applicability and, ultimately, legitimacy. It is based on this consideration that we will in the concluding chapter place RCRC in the context of competing and emerging transnational governance concepts.

5

Rough Consensus and Running Code in Context

'A post-industrial society must discover ways to decentralize not only commodity production, but also significant ways of lawmaking.'[1]

IN OUR CONCLUDING chapter, we place the RCRC model in the context of three existing concepts that address the relationship and tension between law and non-law that we have identified as the fundamental challenge facing all concepts of transnational governance. We contend that these approaches—social norms theory, soft law and customary law—are respectively in need of further development to adequately address the complexity of the transnational law regimes that the concept of RCRC aims to capture.

I. LAW AND SOCIAL NORMS

Any treatment of so vast a topic should be prefaced with a caveat. To speak about 'law and social norms' is, of course, to speak about law as such. Sociologists have traditionally been interested by the tension between formalised orders and social norms, which eventually became inseparable from an inquiry into the respective nature of each. In a sense, we are all Weberians, Durkheimians and Ehrlichs now, just as we all eventually became, as legal theorists, regardless of which political colour, 'legal realists',[2] only to turn into 'economists', ie another form of realist, at a later stage. No one can deny, thus, that all along much has been at stake. To negotiate between 'intervention' and 'social order', between 'regulation' and 'co-ordination', has never been *l'art pour l'art*. This is evident with regard to legal sociologists' interest in traditional social structures as much as for their assessment of that tension between intervention and private ordering in politically and economically sensitive fields. The inquiry into law and social norms has, through time, played a more or less significant role in the evolution of legal consciousness, which almost

[1] Robert D Cooter, 1993, 418.
[2] Joseph W Singer, 1988.

suggests that to speak, today, of 'social norms theory' and to do so in the belief of circumscribing a containable and overseeable research agenda, is—well—surprising. What makes the current interest in social norms so intriguing, however, is the wealth of unanswered questions, questions that demand heightened attention and treatment particularly in times of social and regulatory transformation. Similarly to the surge in legal theorists' interest in the co-existence of several legal orders[3] and in the impact of rights and regulation on existing and continuously evolving societal orders,[4] the current interest in the troubling relationship is concerned with the role of law in a highly complex social environment. 'Social norms theory', if in fact there were such a programme, would certainly have to take these past developments into account. Such acknowledgments, however, are inevitably going to unfold either as narratives of defeat or as hailings of triumph. There is simply nothing neutral about this relationship.

While the relationship between 'law and social norms' has thus long been the subject of intense scholarly debate, recent contributions made by law & economics (L&E) scholars have given the discussion a particular twist.[5] In the context of an increasingly complex regulatory environment populated by public and private, domestic and transnational 'norm entrepreneurs',[6] social norms are perceived as efficient rules, developed by 'many specialised business communities' to govern social behaviour.[7] Social norms bear particular importance for L&E scholars in that they are portrayed as providing for an altogether more efficient form of ordering.[8] The attention given to social norms by L&E scholars constitutes a relative novelty and late arrival when compared to the earlier displayed interest in institutions of formal law[9] or adjudication.[10] Robert Ellickson, one of the leading scholars of private ordering,[11] has associated this new interest among L&E scholars in social norms with the fact that 'many disciplines increasingly [are] emphasising the significance of the informal glue that holds a society together'.[12] While sociologists' research on norms had for a long time

[3] Sally Falk Moore, 1973; Marc Galanter, 1981; John Griffiths, 1986; Sally Engle Merry, 1988.

[4] Erhard Blankenburg, Ekkehard Klausa, Hubert Rottleuthner and Ralf Rogowski, 1980; Gunther Teubner, 1986b; Gunther Teubner, 1986a; Orly Lobel, 2007; Peer Zumbansen, 2009a.

[5] See, in particular, Richard H McAdams, 1997, 342: 'But because norms are a relatively new subject for law and economics, there is as yet no consensus about certain basic theoretical propositions, including, most importantly, the meaning of norm'. Eric A Posner, 2000; Richard A Posner, 1998b; see the critique by Robert C Ellickson, 1998.

[6] Cass Sunstein, 1996, 909.

[7] Robert D Cooter and Thomas Ulen, 2004, 439; Lisa Bernstein, 1992.

[8] Cooter and Ulen, 440.

[9] See, eg Ronald Coase, 1960; Robert C Ellickson, 1998, 540.

[10] Paul H Rubin, 1977; George L Priest, 1977.

[11] Robert C Ellickson, 1991.

[12] Robert C Ellickson, 1998, 541.

failed to exert significant influence on other fields, perhaps because of the field's preoccupation with groups as 'operative agents' as compared to L&E scholars' respective focus on 'methodological individualism',[13] obviously much has since come into motion.[14] At the same time, the central question as to the primacy of either law or social norms remains open, even among L&E scholars.[15]

This current soul-searching is important for our present inquiry because it illustrates the contentious relationship between 'official' and 'unofficial law', that we have touched on repeatedly in our study and which reflects on a problem which is central to different, contemporary studies of governance regimes.[16] This problem strikingly re-emphasises the distinction between *co-ordinative* and *regulatory* functions that we have conventionally associated with private and public law, respectively. The model of RCRC proposed here seeks to re-incorporate this viewpoint in the form of an unavoidable paradox rather than as a distinction. As we noted in chapter two in the context of our discussion of the distinction between 'economic' and 'democratic', or 'justice' functions of law,[17] we contend that the attempt to distinguish between these functions and to associate different institutional and normative frameworks with each, fails to acknowledge the paradoxical quality of the original distinction. That this is not merely a fight over words becomes clear, when the emphasis on the value of social norms is coupled with a particularly formal depiction of the 'state', namely a state that is seen to merely embody a framework-providing institution for private ordering, which by contrast exists autonomously from the political realm of the state.[18] By disentangling the two sides from one another, the underlying complexity of the state/market distinction is neutralised.

It is crucial to note, however, that the current interest among legal scholars in social norms goes beyond what could otherwise be seen as expression of a surge in neo-liberal legal theory. The intriguing challenge arising from social norms for legal scholars is its ideological ambiguity: that social norms *precede*, *relate to*, *are in contestation of* and *in constant exchange with* the established, institutionalised and formalised legal order, is the shared

[13] Ellickson, 1998, above, 542; see also Robert D Cooter, 1993, at 426: 'Of course, sociology is not an unqualified improvement over abstract economic theory'.

[14] See the references in Ellickson, 1998, fns 22–24, and *ibid*, 543, noting that towards the mid-1990s, norms had become the 'hottest topic in the legal academy'; see also the Symposium on Law and Norms in Corporate Law, published in the 1996 volume of the *University of Pennsylvania Law Review*; see also the contributions in Richard P Appelbaum, William F Felstiner and Volkmar Gessner, 2001, and in John N Drobak, 2006.

[15] Ellickson, 1998, 551–52.

[16] See, eg David V Snyder, 2003; Simon Deakin, 2002; Gralf-Peter Calliess, 2002; Peer Zumbansen, 2002b; Peer Zumbansen, 2006b.

[17] See Gillian Hadfield, 2009.

[18] For a discussion, see above, ch 2 of this book.

starting point for both law & economics and law & society approaches.[19] Our interest, in turn, begins precisely with this observation: the noted ideological openness of social norms at the outset informs our search for a legal theory of transnational governance regimes and prompts us to dismiss simplifying associations of social norms with either a neo-liberal critique of political 'intervention'[20] or a romanticising embrace of local norms.[21] On that basis and in light of a vivid exploration of social norms in contemporary legal and economic scholarship,[22] we want to merely highlight at this point where we see overlaps and tensions between RCRC and the present surge in 'social norms' theory in legal scholarship.

Eric Posner, in a powerful reformulation of an L&E position on law and social norms, recently underlined how the latter provide an efficient *regulatory* tool, in particular in light of the continuously rising costs of invoking the state legal system.[23] In his book, Posner emphasises that in contract law relationships, parties do not avoid breaching their mutual agreements for fear of the other's invocation of the legal system, but rather, because the parties are worried about the costs arising from a judicial conflict. Contractual parties, in Posner's view, are hesitant to rely on the court to resolve conflicts, as courts are bound to misunderstand the existing practices in contemporary commercial relations. Not only do parties here abstain from (over-) burdening courts, which they anyway hold to be incompetent,[24] but they positively rely on their respective willingness to engage with the other in a way that is efficient for both sides, involving 'reputation, ethnic and family connections and other elements of non-legal regulation'.[25] 'The Chance of winning a contract suit is pretty much random'.[26]

The social norms theorists are right—as many did before them—to draw attention to an eventually deficient knowledge base or lack of expertise on the side of the court to adequately assess all specificities of highly technical contractual arrangements. It is evident that 'matters of law' assume a radical degree of complexity in comparison to the growing sophistication of the arrangements and conflicts that find their way into the courtroom.[27] A similar critique—directed at competence and the risk of increased costs

[19] John N Drobak, 2006, Introduction, 1.

[20] For a powerful refutation, see already Robert L Hale, 1923.

[21] For this point, see only John Griffiths, 1986.

[22] See only the SSRN series 'Law, Norms and Informal Order', edited by Richard McAdams.

[23] Eric A Posner, 2000, 148.

[24] *Ibid*, 152: 'Courts have trouble understanding the simplest of business relationships'.

[25] *Ibid*, 153.

[26] *Ibid*. Meanwhile, the uncertainty regarding the judicial resolution of a case is an inherent element of 'risk' in the legal system and is as such a thorn not only in the side of law & economics.

[27] Gunther Teubner and Peer Zumbansen, 2000.

of adjudication—applies to private courts operating, for example, in the context of commercial dealings in relatively contained communities:

> [T]hese various communities and agencies would have very strong incentives to seek out judges for both inter- and intracommunity dispute resolutions who not only have reputations for impartiality, but for issuing clear, easily interpretable opinions available as a guide in settling future disputes—that is, precedents. Judges who provide such opinions would garner much more business (if not all the business) than judges who issue vague, uninterpretable, or secret opinions. Why? Simply because disputes are costly and always raise the specter of potential violence.[28]

There is another dimension to the critique of courts that is implicated in some of the excitement about 'social norms', which has to do with what this critique leaves unsaid. This perspective on parties' agreements, concluded, administered and often enforced in considerable distance from a court, of course, builds on much older, but also differently situated work on the role of informal agreements in the area of contractual relations, most significantly elaborated by scholars like Stewart Macaulay and Ian Macneil.[29] Their work on relational contracts, intricately situated 'between contract' and 'organisation',[30] and on 'private government',[31] laid the ground for ensuing research into organisational models that go beyond the classical, one-off focus of contractual agreements[32] and eventually provide a framework for adaptive governance and flexible relational design.[33] Common to all such assessments was a continued awareness of the challenge of designating such governance regimes as private or public.[34] Importantly, the interest in relational contracting was arguably not driven by the belief in cosy social relationships in friendly communities[35]—instead, as Michael Power, has recently emphasised, there is nothing merely technocratic or strategic about 'soft' social ordering tools such as 'reputation':

> The category of reputation is not simply or only a 'boundary object' spanning management sub-fields like marketing, accounting, and human resources. Crucially, it has also emerged from the continuing conceptual, legal, and ethical dynamic in which the boundary between organisations, their environments,

[28] Bruce L Benson, 1990, 36.

[29] Stewart Macaulay, 1963; Ian R Macneil, 1985.

[30] See also Terence Daintith and Gunther Teubner, 1986.

[31] Stewart Macaulay, 1986.

[32] John P Esser, 1996; David Campbell, 1997; David Campbell, 2001; Orly Lobel, 2004, 383 (emphasising how the use of relational agreements between bureaucracies and citizens strengthens the interface between both).

[33] See Jody Freeman, 2000a, 171: 'the contract becomes a framework and a set of default rules that will help direct future gap filling'.

[34] Lester M Salamon, 2001; see already Carol Harlow, 1980, 249: 'The intervention of a static "public/private" classification can only hinder this development by blinding us to obvious parallels and encouraging uneven growth'.

[35] On this see Gunther Teubner, 2000, and the response by Ian R Macneil, 2000.

> and society as a whole is negotiated. So, while the notion of 'reputational asset' suggests a logic of instrumentalisation within management practice, in fact this asset derives its value from a complex field of social and economic interdependencies, an institutional field from which organisations derive social legitimacy.[36]

Against the background of these advances in contract[37] but also administrative law,[38] the current research by L&E scholars on the relation of social norms to contractual arrangements does not appear to be motivated by an interest in these preceding and parallel discussions among administrative law scholars and relational contract theorists. While these scholars continue to explore the shifting boundaries between public and private and push our understanding of emerging contractual regimes further,[39] this debate is surprisingly absent in contemporary L&E discussions. Does this suggest that L&E scholars' interest in social norms is primarily driven by a determination to keep contractual governance autonomous and 'free'—of politics? Such an assessment, however, would presuppose that the celebration of private ordering was itself neutral to begin with. Quite the contrary is true. While *economic theory* pervasively inform L&E's pursuit of the relevance and role of social norms in societal—private—ordering,[40] the insulation of this inquiry from earlier *legal sociological* and *legal pluralist theory* in fact weakens the L&E agenda. By disentangling 'social norms theory' from parallel efforts in studying contracts, organisations and networks from a legal sociology perspective,[41] L&E scholars forego highly promising research avenues towards a more adequate understanding of the dynamics between law and norms. As we have tried to show in the context of our presentation of RCRC, even sophisticated theories of economic governance following Williamson or Dixit need to be complemented by a distinctly legal theoretical perspective in order to carve out the specific legitimacy challenges inherent to the studied phenomena of private ordering.

Without a real engagement with the legal and sociological history of contract law, its critique is in danger of falling flat and of turning into ideology. Attacks on judges' alleged *incompetence*[42] or on the inevitably

[36] Michael Power, 2007, 133.

[37] Marc Amstutz, Andreas Abegg and Vaios Karavas, 2007.

[38] Harm Schepel, 2005, 259–84 (discussing developments in US administrative law and the changing features of the non-delegation doctrine); see also Paul R Verkuil, 2008.

[39] Elizabeth Mertz, 2006, 919: 'Unhappily for such dreams of a streamlined world in which courts become largely unnecessary—and, indeed, in which disputes themselves essentially end before they begin—empirical researchers studying language have in recent years only moved further in the direction of demonstrating the integral role of context in anchoring human meaning and communication'. See also Victoria Nourse and Gregory Shaffer, 2009, 108: '[...]new legal realists generally oppose a neo-formalist conception of judging that is blind to real-life behavior and to the institutional implications of judicial decision making'.

[40] See the excellent essay by Richard H McAdams, 1997.

[41] See now the contributions to Marc Amstutz and Gunther Teubner, 2009.

[42] Eric A Posner, 2000, 154.

high costs of adjudication cut off the ties between the present state of contractual governance and its evolution through a complex overlapping of private ordering, legislation and adjudication.[43] As such, the endorsement of social norms by L&E scholars effectively removes contract law from a long-standing development of conflict negotiation, for which *contract law* provides a most powerful framework.[44] As L&E scholars argue in favour of a re-formalisation of contract law in order to *free* it from judicial activism (and, incompetence), the debate turns inevitably political. The implicitly desired return to a formal contract law regime, through a literal interpretation under very restricted circumstances, and accompanied and supplemented by a system of social norms, resounds strangely in light of a history of contract law, which over the course of the twentieth century had increasingly become 'publicised'.[45] Contract law, through the assumption of regulatory and redistributory functions,[46] had been a central pillar of Western states' regulatory framework. As such, a critique of contract law becomes a critique of the welfare state and with that a critique of the role of the state vis-à-vis the economy—a line of reasoning informing an understanding of private law, which the Legal Realists already in the 1920s identified as an inadequate and misleading representation of the law governing contemporary market relations.[47] L&E's recent interest in social norms then appears to be but a new attempt to re-establish a private, purified and neutral system of private law, uninhibited by activist judges, consumer protection lobbyists and concepts of constitutionalised contractual governance.[48]

The tensions between this conceptualisation of the law/social norms distinction and that which informs our model of *Rough Consensus and Running Code* are manifest. While the celebration of private ordering thrives on enthusiasm for social norms, the demarcation of what is law and non-law in RCRC has turned out to be much more problematic. We have tried to take the distinctions that inform the question about law and non-law seriously: whether we are dealing with the public/private, the regulatory/co-ordinative, the substantive/procedural or the authority/affectedness distinction, we ought not to try to overcome any of them.

[43] Hugh Collins, 1999; Dieter Hart, 1987.

[44] For the idea of contract as framework, see Roy Kreitner, 2005, 111: 'The conflicts of interest perspective I have proposed here challenges economic thinking to compare things whose comparison is difficult, with tools that do not promise precision. At the same time, it attempts to expand the set of tools to make such comparisons. The conflicts of interest perspective may run aground trying to account instrumentally for things whose value lies beyond instrumentality, but one may hope that the failure would be enlightening'.

[45] Franz Wieacker, 1967.

[46] See, eg Anthony T Kronman, 1980; Peer Zumbansen, 2000b, Chapter C.

[47] Robert L Hale, 1923; Morris R Cohen, 1927; for a succinct discussion and critique, see also Roy Kreitner, 2007.

[48] Peer Zumbansen, 2003b.

Instead, the task is in sustaining them as constitutive paradoxes of a legal order. The inseparability of the respective sides is the decisive feature which lies at the heart of a legal order. As such, our concept of law is shaped by the constant awareness of its very fragility on the one hand,[49] its violence on the other.[50] At the same time, RCRC had a more modest aim as well. In unfolding its different elements through an interlocking sequence of experimental rule-making (*pilot*, *recognition*, *binding* phases) and assessment (RFC), we have tried to show how RCRC can allow us to better understand even highly specialised, issue-driven rule-making processes in areas. But, acknowledging the ambitious nature of our proposal, we need to emphasise that RCRC is but a model struggling in each of its architectural parts with the underlying tension between law and non-law. In trying to go beyond traditional concepts to explain the gap between 'official' and 'unofficial' law, we have developed RCRC as a model for law-making in contexts that are marked by a dramatic fragmentation of political institutional authority, democratic accountability and established enforcement procedures.[51] Like present projects on social norms, we are interested in the potential of private ordering and are thus equally wary of conventional attempts to domesticate processes of societal orders through inadequate attempts to either 'bring the state back in' or de-legitimise private ordering as such. But unlike social norms theorists, we contend that even a rudimentary concept of transnational law regimes must acknowledge the paradoxical nature of the underlying distinctions. Law in that sense, then, is what we do not yet have.

On this basis, the following discussion of soft law and customary law can be considerably brief. Its relevance for the project pursued here lies primarily in drawing out some of the obvious connections and touching points between these concepts and our model of RCRC. As such, the next section cannot in any way attempt to provide a comprehensive overview of soft law, but will merely draw on a small section of a vast discussion in the hope of highlighting a number of the shared concerns and remaining differences.

II. SOFT LAW

A. Asking the Right Questions?

That there are norms not made by the state, which still exercise coordinative and regulatory functions, has long ceased to be a secret for

[49] Reinhart Koselleck, 2000; Peer Zumbansen, 2007b; Peer Zumbansen, 2008a, 771.
[50] Robert M Cover, 1983; Robert M Cover, 1986; Marc Amstutz and Vaios Karavas, 2009.
[51] For an excellent illustration of this constellation, see Adrienne Héritier and Dirk Lehmkuhl, 2008.

legal sociologists[52] and, within private law, in particular for commercial lawyers.[53] Unsurprisingly, both the theoretical dimensions and the practical implications of 'soft law' have repeatedly been the subject of scholarly scrutiny and analysis.[54] Such scrutiny appears inevitable in light of an understanding of law as an allegedly closed and coherent order, and we discussed *lex mercatoria* as a powerful illustration of soft law for any unified, institutionalised theory of law.[55] On the domestic level, other phenomena that are associated with the concept of 'soft law' include, among others, 'social labeling, voluntary corporate codes of conduct, private accreditation, and certification by nongovernmental actors'.[56] In recent years, much attention has in fact been directed at standard-setting bodies and at the role of privately generated standards in environmental legislation or tort litigation.[57] Such norms have long been considered to be more than merely technical standards.[58] For example, in the area of environmental legislation in general and emissions regulation in particular, the level of 'acceptable' emissions cannot realistically be determined outside of a context of normative assessment of that very acceptability.[59] Another example of privately generated norms on both the domestic and transnational level is provided by accounting rules.[60] In Germany, the generation of accounting rules had for the longest time been a matter of commercial custom, and the Commercial Code had long recognised the existence of such private norms.[61] In comparison with technical standard norms, the political character of accounting rules is even more evident.[62] When drafting these norms, the expert body inevitably faces questions regarding the goals pursued (eg *creditor vs investor protection*) or the standards' compatibility with international norms. This last example may serve as a powerful illustration of the crystallisation process through which non-legal norms such as accounting standards,

[52] Eugen Ehrlich, 1962; Sally Falk Moore, 1973.

[53] Nathan Isaacs, 1917; Paul R Milgrom, Douglass C North and Barry W Weingast, 1990, 20–21 (describing how mercantile courts operated outside of the state's judicial realm).

[54] Anna di Robilant, 2006, 500: 'The notion of soft law reflects two major trends in the globalization of law: the striking multiplication of producers of law and, in turn, of bodies of law and the privatization of legal regimes. A negative concept of soft law usually amounts to a critique of the state-centered vertical and hierarchical law-making model. A positive definition, however, appears more problematic, given the multiplicity and the complexity of soft legal regimes'.

[55] Above, ch 2 I. A of this book.

[56] Orly Lobel, 2004, 389 (footnote omitted).

[57] See the excellent overview in Johannes Köndgen, 2006, 481–86.

[58] For an excellent analysis, see only Harm Schepel, 2005.

[59] Köndgen, 2006, 482.

[60] Jens Wüstemann and Sonja Kierzek, 2007; Sebastian Botzem and Sigrid Quack, 2006; Jochen Zimmermann, Jörg R Werner and Philipp B Volmer, 2008.

[61] Köndgen, 2006, 487.

[62] Walter Mattli, 2003; Walter Mattli and Tim Büthe, 2003; Shyam Sunder, 2005; Yuri Biondi and Tomo Suzuki, 2007.

which arose out of recognised commercial customs, are transposed into a formalised and functioning regulatory framework.[63] The setting in which this process takes place in Germany is characterised by a public law-maker that mandates a private body to generate norms and to advise the government on their further implementation. In a next step, the government publishes these rules in the *Bundesanzeiger* (Federal Bulletin) and thereby renders these norms *quasi-public*.[64] The institutional dimension, however, is crucially complemented by a highly intriguing normative side: as in the example described by Lisa Bernstein, the real issue at stake is the effective design of a process at the end of which stand norms that are accepted by the relevant *community*.[65]

The previous section makes it all too clear that such regulatory regimes unfold in a critical zone of proximity and distance between actors that can no longer satisfyingly be exclusively associated with either the private or public sphere. From our point of view, the exercise of public authority by private parties occurs not on the basis of delegation or deference, but has a paradoxical, simultaneous origin. The fact that private actors exercise public authority, is—from a legal perspective—relatively unproblematic, if not irrelevant. In fact, the problems arise from the perspective of politics, where the institutional designation of 'public' or 'private' actors bears significance for the allocation and exercise of power.[66] While the question whether an actor is public or private is thus interesting to the lawyer to the degree that it might or might not resonate with previous accounts of who was in charge of what and which rights were associated with each constellation, law has otherwise little to say about the changes in the grounds of legitimacy of the transformation of the regulatory architecture. Law is interested in itself, that is, in its proper functioning. Whether the law is able to fulfill the function of addressing conflicts of an economic, political or religious nature and 'translate' them into a legal problem and to solve this problem as it (the legal system) has done all along, does not depend on whether a case comes before a civil or an administrative court. It depends on whether there is a process by which a case gets *resolved*. The designation of private or public authority to draft, enforce and adjudicate legal rules is not a legal problem, the effectiveness of carrying out this function is.

Both the lawyer and the political scientist who studies and scrutinises the change in the institutional architecture for law, power and government (or, governance), can address this institutional transformation within the

[63] Sunder, 2005.

[64] Johannes Köndgen, 2006, 491.

[65] Lisa Bernstein, 1996.

[66] Very instructive in this regard is Colin Scott, 2004, 163–64 with regard to the de-hierarchisation of control instances.

nation-state relatively easily. The lawyer will likely do so through the lens of administrative and constitutional law, the political scientist will resort to an increasingly sophisticated institutional analysis.[67] The problems, however, arise for both where the institutional conditions are not only absent (no 'world government'), but also where the transnational competition and 'interlegality' between 'public' or 'private' actors in the creation and enforcement of rules escape the analytical and doctrinal toolkit of both law and political science. 'Globalisation', then, continues to be a Pandora's box for lawyers[68] as much as for political scientists.[69] And, yet, we are 'borne back ceaselessly' to such inquiries. As Fleur Johns surmised:

> Perhaps legal scholars' persistent preoccupation with law in a changing world manifests an intuitive appreciation of the errant instability of our legal understandings? Perhaps, moreover, this instability extends *beyond* the difficulty of maintaining laws' correlation to something that we call the Real World? ... Each time that we produce law to match the world, we produce world to match the law, and vice versa.[70]

B. Soft Law as Embarrassment

It is against this background that 'soft law' surfaces as a highly charged concept and idea, as a reference to a fundamental embarrassment in the face of a radical transformation of the known regulatory landscape. Christine Chinkin noted years ago that these 'variables [of soft law], coupled with the inherent contradictions in any concept of soft law, highlight the challenges presented to the structure and substance of the traditional international legal order by the increasing use of soft law norms'.[71] Across legal fields, domestic and international, the turn to soft law is ubiquitous, it has become, as Jacob Gersen and Eric Posner note, 'all the rage'.[72] Unsurprisingly, the explanations and interpretations of this development abound. What makes the current inquiry into the meaning, relevance and direction of soft law important for our present discussion, is the increasingly wide-spread recognition that an engagement with 'soft law' touches on a number of fundamental pillars of the legal system, and that makes the endeavour not

[67] See Robert E Goodin, 2003, 366–67, introducing a differentiated accountability regime for the state, market and third sector. See also Colin Scott, 2004, 164.

[68] Paul Schiff Berman, 2005a.

[69] Adrienne Héritier and Dirk Lehmkuhl, 2008.

[70] Fleur Johns, 2004, 475.

[71] Christine Chinkin, 1989, 850; see also Michael Bothe, 1980, unfolding an intriguing dialogue between International Law and IR; from this perspective, see of course Oona Hathaway, 2005.

[72] Jacob E Gersen and Eric A Posner, 2008, 1.

only worthwhile, but also highly challenging.[73] Dinah Shelton, in a recent handbook entry, underlined the fact that

> [in] any community, efforts to resolve social problems do not invariably take the form of law. Societies strive to maintain order, prevent and resolve conflicts, and assure justice in the distribution and use of resources not only through law, but through other means of action.[74]

Echoing the observations by legal sociologists and legal anthropologists in a plethora of studies, these remarks implicitly point to the numerous parallel efforts among lawyers in a host of specialised areas to come to terms with the gap between hard and soft law. In international law, given its particular structure, the interest in soft law often seems motivated by a greater concern for the development of the field as such and its capacity to transform political claims into rights.[75] Where international lawyers consider soft law in many cases to be the precursor and testing ground for ensuing treaty law,[76] the gap between hard and soft law is scrutinised as a zone in which a transposition occurs of something into something else. This opens the perspective for a more targeted assessment of how this transposition actually occurs, and why.

As the 'variables' of soft law continue to proliferate, the anxieties regarding its (legal)[77] nature, its accountability and legitimacy have become legendary.[78] But as the previous observations suggest, much of this unrest is directly tied to the different sites of contestation on which we find references to soft law. Precisely because *soft* law can be seen as a starting point to reflect on the origin of a legal order, the—positive and negative—excitement over the relation between soft and hard law tells us a lot about the contestants' understanding of law to begin with. Unlike legal sociologically oriented international or, for example, constitutional lawyers,[79] positivists will

[73] See already Tadeusz Gruchalla-Wesierski, 1984, 42, emphasising that differences in economic (and other) interests and strategies often prompt international actors to resort to soft law; similarly Robert E Scott and Paul B Stephan, 2006, 110; see also Kal Raustiala, 2005, and Dinah L Shelton, 2008, highlighting a surge in soft law, which allows states discretion in political action rather than to bind themselves in law.

[74] Shelton, 2008, 2.

[75] David Kennedy, 2005.

[76] Shelton, 2008, 7.

[77] Jack Goldsmith and Eric Posner, 2005, 81–82: 'The literature usually labels nonlegal international agreements "soft law". We avoid this label because nonlegal agreements are not binding under international law (or any other law), so it is confusing to call them law, soft or otherwise'. Compare this with Jan Klabbers, 2007, and Jan Klabbers, 1998, 387: 'the simplicity of the law, knowing only categories of legal or illegal, in force or not in force, binding or not binding, makes it possible to survive in this complex world. It is the simplifying rigor of law, the way in which it can translate complexity into something we can handle, which makes law such a useful tool'.

[78] David Trubek and Louise G Trubek, 2005.

[79] See the wonderful essay by Ernest A Young, 2007, 408, 473: 'If you seek the Constitution, look around you. It is much bigger than you think. If we look for it through functional

juxtapose soft law with a specific image of the legal system—at the outside of which they situate soft law—that often amounts to an exaggerated depiction of a highly unified, coherent, formalised and effective and functioning system of order.[80] However, to juxtapose soft law regimes with such a hyperbolically crafted model of the rule-of-law, ultimately seeks to immunise the latter against all methodological contestations that could have their point of departure in the fundamental question underlying soft law—*what* is law?

Legal critique throughout the twentieth century[81] has revealed numerous shortcomings in democratic systems as to their propagated ideals of representability and accountability, something that received renewed attention in the context of a far-reaching debate with regard to the legitimacy of non-governmental organisations.[82] In the attempt to better understand the problem, or *promise* of soft law as provocation, we need to engage to approximate legal theory and doctrine with regulatory analysis of contemporary forms of public and private ordering on the domestic[83] and transnational levels.[84] This would likely open a promising perspective on the way in which the boundaries between 'hard' and 'soft' law have become porous and mirror the constantly shifting weights between state and market institutions in producing and administering rules and norms. Soft law's true embarrassment, however, might still lie elsewhere:[85] perhaps in the fact that our present preoccupations with the absence of world 'government' and with the proliferation of highly varied forms of transnational regulatory governance can at best be seen as transient endeavours in the face of the dramatic challenges that confront a theory of transnational law today, a theory that must reckon with the extremely multifaceted nature of social identities, cultural practices and functional idiosyncrasies of world society.

eyes—that is, if we seek to identify the set of legal norms that actually constitute our public legal order—then the "Constitution" will include not only the canonical document but a host of statutes, regulatory materials, federal common law rules, and established practices. This Article has only scratched the surface of the theoretical, doctrinal, and pedagogical implications of viewing constitutionalism from this perspective. The basic point, however, should be clear: constitutional scholars need to quit drawing rigid lines around the legal materials that interest them—and hence around their scholarly discipline—and engage the constitution outside the Constitution'.

80 For a recent restatement, see Jean D'Aspremont, 2008.

81 See only Carl Schmitt, 1988.

82 Christoph Schreuer, 1993; Karsten Nowrot, 1999.

83 Peer Zumbansen, 2003c; Orly Lobel, 2004.

84 Philip Alston, 2005c; Peter J Spiro, 2002; Eberhard Schmidt-Assmann, 2008.

85 David Kennedy, 2009, 59: 'It is disheartening that while the world fractures so many of our debates about global governance are content merely to embroider the habits of the technical class, decorating their management with intellectual filigree. So much scholarship today is simply a brief for the significance and vitality of a narrow professional culture and sensibility. Its authors struggle for political rapprochement between a center-right attuned to market failures and a center-left that has lost faith in its own nostalgia for what it remembers as the potent regulatory and administrative state of earlier days'.

III. CUSTOMARY INTERNATIONAL LAW (AND ITS LIMITS)

Like 'soft' law, customary law touches on the painful root of law. The search for customary law is likely to expose the foulness, violence or tragedy that might be at the basis of a legal order. Or, perhaps, the aspirations of a timid mind, or a wicked one. Society's silent workings or crude power?

> It is not actually possible to describe what a system of privately produced law and order would be like in modern society because one cannot describe what does not exist, and, more fundamentally, guesses based on historic privatised systems (and there have been many) or current trends in privatisation may miss the mark substantively.[86]

Likewise, scholars have referred to customary international law as 'the most rudimentary of legal obligations',[87] while others, embracing the perspective on power that we think inevitable in any engagement with customary law remarked: '[i]t is constitutional in that it involves the allocation among various institutions ... of legal power, that is, the authority to enact rules and to reach decisions that will be regarded as properly binding those affected by them'.[88] At the heart of customary law, then, is—again—the gap, bridge, transition or abyss—between that which is and that which is not, might be, or ought to be. In other words, the question that returns is the same which has run a red thread through our foregoing discussions of 'norms' as of 'soft law' and which informs the project of this book: '[w]hat is it, above mere behavior, that makes the behavior normative?'[89]

The ubiquitous turn to unofficial norms, indirect regulation and the reliance on soft law, particularly in politically highly contested regulatory areas, which we looked at in the previous section, leads us to take another look at the area of international law, and here particularly at customary international law. The, at present, very heated discussion among public international lawyers over the value and merits or, even the existence of customary law seems to bear some resemblance to our previous observations regarding 'norms' or 'soft law'. But, unlike these two, the discussion around customary law is comparably more violent and agitated. Here, we can hear loud voices defending the nation-state's sovereignty against the onslaught of allegedly amorphous and threatening norms of customary law.

We believe that the current debate among international lawyers and political scientists over scope and content of customary international law (CIL) is of significance for our present attempt to outline both the premises and structure of a transnational private law. This debate was primarily spurred

86 Bruce L Benson, 1990, 25.
87 Andrew T Guzman and Timothy L Meyer, 2008, 197.
88 Lon Fuller, 1964, 128–29.
89 Alan Watson, 1985, 44.

by a series of articles[90] by Jack Goldsmith and Eric Posner and eventually culminated in a book, published in 2005.[91] While this discussion, which meanwhile has been feeding into a wide-reaching exploration of the premises of international law as such,[92] evolved around core issues in the field of public international law, the analysis undertaken of CIL has much to say to our present project. In particular, where Professors Goldsmith and Posner and their interlocutors address the complex nature of CIL, both with regard to an actor-centred institutionalism and a normative focus on rules, the parallel challenges between their public international law inquiry and our transnational law inquiry become apparent.

A. Elements of Customary International Law

The relevance of the customary international law (CIL) discussion for our own exploration of a transnational private law primarily follows from the similarities between the doctrinal and conceptual challenges, which are facing both public international law and an emerging of transnational private law. Among these similarities, the *role of new actors* in the global institutional architecture, on the one hand, and the *changing nature of norms* produced in the respective regimes, on the other, figure most prominently. This may be summarised in the following way. For the discussion of CIL within the framework of public international law, the conventional starting point is the enumeration of sources in Article 38 of the ICJ statute.[93] The famously ambiguous formula of '*international custom, as evidence of a general practice accepted as law*' both represents and endorses an exclusively state-centred understanding of public international law, based on the principle of a consensus-driven commitment to peaceful relationships among

[90] Jack Goldsmith and Eric Posner, 1999; Jack Goldsmith and Eric Posner, 2000; Jack Goldsmith and Eric Posner, 2001.

[91] Jack Goldsmith and Eric Posner, 2005.

[92] See Detlev F Vagts, 2004; Anne van Aaken, 2006; Andrew T Guzman, 2006; Oona A Hathaway and Ariel N Lavinbuk, 2006; Paul Schiff Berman, 2006; Balakrishnan Rajagopal, 2006.

[93] Art 38 of the Statute of the International Court of Justice reads as follows:

1. The Court, whose function is to decide in accordance with international law such disputes as are submitted to it, shall apply:
   a. international conventions, whether general or particular, establishing rules expressly recognized by the contesting states;
   b. international custom, as evidence of a general practice accepted as law;
   c. the general principles of law recognized by civilized nations;
   d. subject to the provisions of Article 59, judicial decisions and the teachings of the most highly qualified publicists of the various nations, as subsidiary means for the determination of rules of law.
2. This provision shall not prejudice the power of the Court to decide a case ex aequo et bono, if the parties agree thereto.

states.[94] The factual and psychological elements, which are contained in the formula, 'general practice' and 'accepted as law',[95] constitute the two defining poles of this legal source. And regardless of how obviously problematic each of these poles is in terms of its clear demarcation, interpretation and application,[96] their centrality in defining customary law as one of the most important sources of public international law is widely acknowledged. CIL, from this perspective, constitutes one fundamental pillar of public international law and is as such understood and interpreted from within international law's conceptual architecture and framework. From this it follows that as CIL is applied as part of the enumerated list of sources of public international law in Article 38, it is not obvious how and, even, *why* CIL should invite a less state-centred interpretation.

And yet, at the same time, the current debate over CIL provides ample evidence to what degree the state-centredness of public international law and with it, of CIL, has been challenged up to this moment in time. These challenges, to no one's surprise, arise from a changing understanding among international legal scholars of both the actors and the norms in public international law. While references to the increasing relevance of non-state, sub-state or non-governmental actors abound,[97] these are accompanied by an increasing awareness that the changing nature of norms, in particular in the field of human rights, has begun to have an impact on the normative landscape within which the definition of CIL has been operational for the longest time.[98] In comparison, the rules and institutions of transnational private law that we have so far looked at, begin to crystallise precisely in those areas where state-centred models of legal order find their limits. The long-perceived arrival of transnational corporate[99] and other private, non-state actors in the areas of commerce,[100] knowledge transfer,[101] human rights advocacy,[102] interest group representation and political lobbying[103] has been documented not only in ever recurring discussions among public international lawyers on whether and how to acknowledge this change in the actor landscape,[104] but has also been highly instrumental in fuelling

[94] Hedley Bull, 1977.

[95] See Art 38(1)b of the ICJ Statute, cited above note 93.

[96] Goldsmith and Posner, 1999 certainly leave no instance out to point to these inherent shortcomings, see 'A Theory of Customary International Law', 1114; Goldsmith and Posner, 2000, 645.

[97] See, eg Rainer Hofmann and Nils Geissler, 1998; R Higgott, G Underhill and A Bieler, 2000; Menno Kamminga, 2005; Philip Alston, 2005c.

[98] Craig M Scott, 2001b; Craig Scott and Robert Wai, 2004; Peer Zumbansen, 2005a.

[99] Peter Cornelius and Bruce Kogut, 2003; Peer Zumbansen, 2006b.

[100] Clive M Schmitthoff, 1982.

[101] Rudolf Stichweh, 1999.

[102] Beth Stephens, 2001.

[103] Nico Krisch, Benedict Kingsbury and Richard B Stewart, 2005.

[104] See only Kindred and others, 2006, *International Law as Chiefly Applied in Canada*, 7th edn; Kamminga, 2005, above.

civil society initiatives worldwide.[105] While this development concerns the 'proliferation of private actors', much commented upon in recent years,[106] from an *institutionalist* perspective, its *normative* aspects concern the changes in the applicability of norms to govern the ensuing new relationships, that don't fit easily into the existing analytical scheme of state-state or private-private relations.[107] Transnational law, in our discussion so far, is on the one hand, characterised by this mixture of public and private regulatory elements. On the other hand, however, we understand transnational law as a distinctly methodological challenge presenting itself in legal theory. It is here where the institutionalist interest diverges from the legal theoretical one, as highlighted in our discussion of soft law in the previous section. The institutionalist reference to public or private actors that are engaged in the production of 'public' or 'private' norms has in itself little meaning for law. The institutional transformation is mirrored in the legal system as a proliferation of specialised legal answers, norms and instruments of regulatory fields, the labels for which eventually find their way into textbooks: transnational human rights litigation,[108] telecommunication law,[109] international environmental law,[110] corporate social responsibility[111] or accounting.[112]

The developments in these areas all reflect an intricate transformation of the defining features of the particular regime, with respect to both actors and norms being produced. The actors in these areas are situated somewhere *between* state and society, and from an institutionalist perspective pose radical questions concerning accountability and legitimacy.[113] In addition, these norms pose *compatibility* problems in relation to existing bodies of state-made law,[114] which we have touched upon at different points in this book. While, from an administrative law perspective, one might be tempted to recognise these developments merely as a form of delegated authority, we have contended that the fact that many of these new norm regimes develop and unfold 'from below', without state initiation—both in the domestic and the transnational arenas—as issue-driven, contextually arising regimes, weakens the reference to conventional administrative law. In the domestic

[105] See, eg the Global Governance and Civil Society Project by Mary Kaldor and Helmut Anheier at the London School of Economics, available at: www.lse.ac.uk/Depts/global/2research.htm.

[106] See only Anne-Marie Slaughter, 2004b; Alston, 2005 *Not-a-cat syndrome.*

[107] A fine illustration of the accompanying proliferation of theoretical discourses is provided by Paul Schiff Berman, 2005a, while Fleur Johns, 2007 engages in an excellent legal realist deconstruction.

[108] Scott, Torture as tort, above; Sarah Joseph, 2004.

[109] Liora Salter, 1999; Viktor Mayer-Schönberger, 2002.

[110] John J Kirton and Michael J Trebilcock, 2004; Jaye Ellis, 2006.

[111] See eg David Weissbrodt and Muria Kruger, 2005.

[112] Bernhard Grossfeld, 2003.

[113] Nico Krisch, 2009.

[114] Ralf Michaels, 2005, 1211.

context, the debate has long remained preoccupied with questions of capture, delegation or privatisation,[115] and the Cinderella of administrative science still lies waiting to be effectively kissed by legal pluralism. On the transnational level, where, too, there is no clear demarcation of 'public' or 'private', analogies between transnational norm-creation and domestic administrative bodies promise little assistance to adequately capture the quality of the newly forming order. In recent years, legal scholarship has begun to put increasing emphasis on exploring this realm of norm production between the nation-state and an emerging global sphere. A striking feature of this work is the discernible renewed interest in taking seriously the connections between legal structures and rights discourses within and beyond the nation-state,[116] connections that necessarily have to draw on previous contestations, for example, of 'formal' law or the unity of the legal order.[117]

B. Ships Passing in the Night?

As the following section will illustrate, too much of the legal discussion around CIL is not a legal discussion, in that it is not interested in the underlying legal theoretical questions that are inseparably connected with customary law. Instead, many contemporary statements with regard to CIL are at best institutionalist in nature and spirit. The current discussion offers a welcome opportunity to reflect on the promises of introducing economic thinking and game theoretic modelling into the interplay of public international law and international relations.[118] However, it falls short of making the connections outlined above between the global governance challenges on the one hand and the way in which legitimacy, accountability and sovereignty debates have within the nation-state—from a critical perspective—always been seen as crucial to any assessment of the legal order, on the other. All scholars—despite deep-running ideological differences—correctly understand the CIL discussion to be part of a larger critique of public international law as a normative order.[119] We aim to complement this discussion by a methodological and critical dimension, which informs our definition of transnational law and as a result shapes our concept of RCRC. From this perspective, we are troubled by what we

[115] Excellent analysis, at different points of the development, by Richard B Stewart, 1975, and Jody Freeman, 1997.

[116] See the path-breaking work by Alfred C Aman Jr, 1997; Alfred C Aman Jr, 2004.

[117] Fleur Johns, 2007.

[118] See, eg Andrew T Guzman, 2008; Andrew T Guzman and Timothy L Meyer, 2008; Anne van Aaken, 2009b.

[119] See, on the one hand, Jack Goldsmith and Eric Posner, 2005; and on the other: Nico Krisch, 2005; Detlev F Vagts, 2004.

identify as the hidden agenda of the current attack on CIL, namely the promotion of a model of legal authority which is based less on the recognition of law's paradoxical origin (law binds those who are governed by it), than on a crude identification of egotistic actors operating on a competitive market for influence and power. The refutation of customary international law as 'inexistent',[120] then, ignores and invisibilises the connections between that which makes customary law a problem and that which defines law itself: the distinction between law and non-law. This distinction matters, to us, not in a positivist sense (can we see law?), but as an expression of a fundamental concern over what we aim to achieve by referring to law in the first place. Law, in our understanding, arises only in the moment it is invoked. The hastened refutation of customary international law as incompatible with an international legal order that should best be described through the lens of rational choice theory, rids us of previous experiences with the creation and destruction of law, with its defeat or triumph[121] and, instead, subsumes law to a contained toolkit for strategic behaviour. From that perspective, there would be no room for a methodologically driven model of transnational private law as we propose here: instead, the emphasis on actors' rational behaviour and a minimalist 'intervention' of public authority other than enforcing the parties' will, reverses and ultimately negates the developments that have marked the evolution of law in the twentieth century, which include a significant expansion of the scope of private law to incorporate elements of public ordering, social welfare and constitutional self-government.[122] The current lament over the purported loss of private autonomy in domestic discourses about private law in general, and contract law in particular,[123] feeds into the rejection of CIL on the international level by fuelling a larger normative attack on an understanding of law, for which legal norms have always been *hybrid* in the sense that they result out of a complex mixture of state-originating norms and societal ordering, violence and coincidence, things said and unsaid.

C. The Attack on Customary International Law

We shall now briefly suggest a number of points that one might consider in reaction to this representation and eventual dismissal of CIL. Our critique hereby follows two strands: one is to highlight what we deem to be internal shortcomings of the conceptual suggestions made, in particular by Professors Goldsmith and Posner in their recent work on CIL. The other

[120] Goldsmith and Posner, 2005, 81–82.
[121] Reinhart Koselleck, 2000.
[122] Peer Zumbansen, 2002a; Duncan Kennedy, 2003; Kerry Rittich, 2004.
[123] See, eg Charles Fried, 1981; Michael J Trebilcock, 1993; Ernest Weinrib, 1995.

strand of our reaction sets out to make a number of suggestions growing out of our observation that the current debate about CIL falls short of fully realising the potential of current developments in transnational law, which could provide a fruitful basis for future development of the field.

The present debate over CIL as it unfolded over the past few years, can at least in part be traced back to three articles and a book, written in 1999, 2001 and 2005, in which Professors Goldsmith and Posner purported to offer a 'theory of customary international law'. While it was based on arguments taken from game theory and rational choice, a closer look suggests that this project is in fact reflective of a deeper scepticism with regard to the normative value of international law as such. To set the stage for the presentation of their theory, they painted a devastatingly bleak portrait of CIL. In their parlance, CIL remains 'a puzzle [lacking] a centralised executive enforcer, and a centralised, authoritative decision maker', while the 'content of CIL seems to track the interests of powerful nations. The origins of CIL rules are not understood'.[124] Furthermore, they highlighted that

> [w]e do not know why nations comply with CIL, or even what it means for a nation to comply with CIL. And we lack an explanation for the many changes in CIL rules over time. CIL's standard definition raises perennial, and unanswered, questions. It is unclear which state acts count as evidence of a custom, or how broad or consistent state practice must be to satisfy the custom requirement. It is also unclear what it means for a nation to follow a custom from a sense of legal obligation, or how one determines whether such an obligation exists.[125]

Given this state of affairs, Professors Goldsmith and Posner suggested an altogether different approach to thinking about CIL. In their reading, which they base on a number of more or less thoroughly historically and systematically selected and explored case studies, states cannot convincingly be thought to act out of a sense of legal obligation. Where others (judges, commentators) have recognised state action as reflective of a will to comply with binding norms,[126] Professors Goldsmith and Posner emphasise that, rather than being an example of legal compliance, the leading American case in Public International Law, *The Paquete Habana* of 1900, concerns a factual situation that was determined purely by self-interested and cost-calculating motives rather than by a commitment to governing norms of international law. In the eyes of Professors Goldsmith and Posner, the case had little to do with the endorsement of a customary norm of international law whereby a combatant state must spare the commercial vessels of the enemy. The fact that such boats were not seized was due merely to what Professors Goldsmith and Posner call a specific combination of several considerations, each of which can stand on its

[124] Jack Goldsmith and Eric Posner, 1999, 1114.
[125] *Ibid.*
[126] See, eg *The Paquete Habana*, 175 US 677 (1900) 700.

own in motivating state behaviour, that is without regard to the recognition of a legal obligation. Instead of reflecting a commitment to a recognised, binding norm of international law, the state's behaviour should rightly be understood solely as an expression of the state's lack of interest—for strategic and financial reasons—to engage the enemy in such confrontation.[127] This interpretation by Professors Goldsmith and Posner is of particular relevance with regard to one of the two defining elements of CIL, the so-called psychological element—*opinio iuris*. This element complements the factual element of CIL, as expressed by state action. In Professors Goldsmith and Posner's reading of CIL, no one has yet offered any solid proof that states have acted or do act out of a sense of being compelled to do so by a certain body of law. In contrast, on their reading, states' behaviour is determined by one or more of the following four elements: *coincidence of interest*, *coercion*, *co-ordination*, *co-operation*. In application of their consequentialist reading of state behaviour, Professors Goldsmith and Posner want to recognise state behaviour—even where oral reference is made to existing norms of international law—merely as a *coincidence* between the state's national self-interest and that laid out in international law, without, however any genuine concern for the commitment of, say, other states to a particular norm. The second of their disputable contentions sees virtually no instance of multilateral concern in one state's action in the international realm: instead, in Professors Goldsmith and Posner's view, all that drives a state's actions with regard to another state, is its belief that by engaging in *co-ordination* with another state, the own state's self-interest can be promoted. This element feeds into a summary rejection of CIL by which Professors Goldsmith and Posner question the supposedly universal scope of CIL. Against this, they observe that 'many apparently cooperative universal behavioral regularities are illusory'. Rather, they argue, most of the instances cited in support of the existence of a universal body of CIL must be read as in fact cases of bilateral behaviour, giving testimony then to a state's strategic exploitation of its bargaining position.[128]

A case in point for such universally existing customary norms must surely be the existence and expansion of human rights norms.[129] The authors indeed do not shy away from citing the case of genocide and the absence of a widespread state practice in engaging in genocide as evidence of their theory. In fact, their observation is so drastic, that it deserves to be quoted here:

> the absence of genocide reflects a coincidence of interest. Both before and after the development of the ostensible international law prohibition in this century, nations rarely committed genocide. Most nations lack any reason to commit

[127] Jack Goldsmith and Eric Posner, 2000, 645: 'simply no interest'.
[128] Jack Goldsmith and Eric Posner, 1999, 1129.
[129] Paul Beaumont, 2002; Carol Harlow, 2002.

genocide, and even nations with a reason to do so find it very costly in military, economic, or moral terms.[130]

The third element of their scathing reading of CIL is *co-operation*. Co-operation requires, at times, a more differentiated choice making on the part of the state, which may find itself in situations where abstention from an otherwise favoured approach is believed to further one's own goals in the long run. Their last element, *coercion*, may express the conceptual return already indicated to a power-relations oriented dismissal of international law in the brightest colours. Coercion, according to Professors Goldsmith and Posner, is exerted where one state is in the position to force another state to abide by the other's force. International law, in that instance, has nothing left on its body, it is left naked for all to see. Or, is it?

As we have seen, Professors Goldsmith and Posner's concept of CIL centrally evolves around the definition of national interest and actors' rational behaviour. More than anything else a state's consideration of the benefits, pay-offs and costs, according to Professors Goldsmith and Posner, drives its behaviour.[131] This leads them to the conclusion that CIL must readily be understood as nothing but a 'label attached to certain behavioral regularities resulting from states pursuing their self-interest'.[132] As a consequence, their attack on the psychological element of CIL is no less than fierce. Professors Goldsmith and Posner read *opinio juris* as a 'conclusion about a practice's status as international law; it does not explain how a widespread and uniform practice becomes law'.[133] This certainly goes very far in dismissing a legal order, which must be, as follows from its recognised sources—Article 38 of the ICJ Statute—understood as a complex and fragile normative and institutional, evolutionary[134] framework. The thrust of this attack primarily comes from its purported normative nihilism, in other words the authors' resistance to engage in a discussion over why we ought to believe in international law in the first place. Some have wondered in this respect, whether such a critique can be presented as a mere technical exercise without taking responsibility for the normative consequences.[135] There has been a long-running thematisation of international law's frailty in relationship to bare-handed

[130] Jack Goldsmith and Eric Posner, 1999, 1173; for a repetition of this, see Jack Goldsmith and Eric Posner, 2000, 668.

[131] Jack Goldsmith and Eric Posner, 1999, 1168; Jack Goldsmith and Eric Posner, 2000, 660.

[132] Jack Goldsmith and Eric Posner, 2000, 662.

[133] Jack Goldsmith and Eric Posner, 1999, 1118.

[134] For the idea of a constitution as an evolutionary achievement, see Niklas Luhmann, 1989b.

[135] See hereto also Detlev F Vagts, 2004; Anne van Aaken, 2006, 289, 307; Oona A Hathaway and Ariel N Lavinbuk, 2006, 1404, 1405: 'What began as the "new American foreign affairs law" and a disdain for the incorporation of customary international law (CIL) by U.S. courts has developed into a revisionism deeply critical of all international law scholarship, with Professors Goldsmith and Posner at the forefront' (footnotes omitted).

struggles over power and international domination[136] in international legal scholarship.[137] The (for many) promising outcome of this closer dialogue between the two disciplines (Private International Law and International Relations) consisted in overcoming much of the long-held reciprocal disdain for the other discipline's central contentions. In fact, after much soul searching, political scientists and international legal scholars did in fact recognise the potential of seeing their field through a two-glassed lens.[138] To no one's surprise, then, must a new attempt at dismissing international law from an allegedly uncompromising rationalist perspective arouse resistance from the camp of enlightened International Law/International Relations scholars. As recently emphasised by Professor Hathaway and Ariel Lavinbuk, Professors Goldsmith and Posner's attack on customary international law does not provide a new critique of the power-discourses underlying international law. Instead, their project places them at a forefront of those promoting a revisionist agenda of international policy that has its origin in a number of sound convictions regarding the federal agenda in US constitutional law and a strong endorsement of international sovereignty within the foreign policy agenda.[139] 'They do not explain, for example, which interests matter, how they are formed, or how we are to discover them. We are left with a theory of state behavior that explains too much and hence too little'.[140] Indeed, by driving again a deep wedge in between the disciplines of international law and international relations, Professors Goldsmith and Posner fail to contribute much insight to a meanwhile very differentiated interdisciplinary discussion, which, in light of the increasing political challenge to international law's normativity,[141] is in the process of incorporating ever more theoretical insights from neighbouring disciplines.[142]

D. Customary International Law in the Making of Global Law

Carrying this analysis further, we shall next focus on Professors Goldsmith and Posner's argument regarding a state's self-interest and the economistic

[136] Nico Krisch, 2005; see also the brilliant analysis by Jürgen Habermas, 2004 (trans Jürgen Habermas, 2006).

[137] Kenneth W Abbott, 1989; Anne Marie Slaughter-Burley, 1993; Peer Zumbansen, 2001a [*The Past Future of International Law*]; Oona Hathaway, 2005, 469, 470–71: 'As long as there was no sovereign power to manage enforcement, critics argued, international law was meaningless. Regarding it as otherwise was not just unrealistic but dangerous' (footnotes omitted); David Kennedy, 2009.

[138] Harold Hongju Koh, 1997.

[139] Oona A Hathaway and Ariel N Lavinbuk, 2006, 1414.

[140] Oona A Hathaway and Ariel N Lavinbuk, 2006, 1406.

[141] See, with regard to the law of occupation, the brilliant analysis of recent developments by Eyal Benvenisti, 2004, Introduction.

[142] Paul Schiff Berman, 2005a.

focus on pay-offs to highlight the specific contentions made by the authors with regard to CIL but also to lay out the connection between their position and one in international law in general. In building further on the analogy between international law and private law developed above, we argue that the deeper trends towards a *deformalisation* of international law, in particular in the aftermath of the Kosovo crisis and with increasing intensity since the (second) Iraq War, must be read as expressions of the serious crisis in which the field finds itself,[143] and that this crisis has deep repercussions for our discussion of denationalised, private law regimes. In both areas we find the same reverence to problematic, ultimately unproductive distinctions. The thrust of the re-introduction just described of 'law and politics' into international law and that of 'law/non-law' in the area of transnational private law is to dis-embed legal norms from the societal debates in which they must have their democratic origin and place them further from the procedural and constitutional framework in which they can be safeguarded. The result of this movement is the de-politicisation of both international law and private law.

Professors Goldsmith and Posner validate a state's action purely on the assumption that it was motivated by a cost-analysis and that the state (or, its leadership) expected a return for its action.[144] This, however, begs several questions at once, and it is not altogether clear what the authors' answer would be. Surely, a given factual situation can always be interpreted in light of a more or less crude assessment of the costs incurred by this or that action. At the same time, it is also clear that the focus on costs can only be a starting point, if we are dealing with such complexly structured actors as states. States, not even taken in a most abstract ideal-type situation, could never adequately be reduced to one-track-mind bearing actors.[145] It is clear that a state's action will always have a panoply of effects as they trickle down and outward into a nation's complex web of institutions, norms and customs. On that basis it is difficult to accept their proposition, that we should dismiss the thought of a state acting out of a legal obligation on the premise that that state acted in fact with a specific pay-off in mind. In fact, it seems unrealistic not to interpret a state's behaviour as set against the background and in the context of a particular, historically-grown socio-economic and normative setting, which in an era of the 'open state'[146] includes the 'international'.

> [A] policymaker's idea of what is in the state's interest is always and necessarily affected by ideas of appropriate action, and these ideas are likely to be shaped—

[143] See, in this respect, the Special Issue on Habermas' Divided West, in (January 2009) 10 *German Law Journal*.
[144] Jack Goldsmith and Eric Posner, 1999, 1132.
[145] Florian F Hoffmann, 2008.
[146] Stephan Hobe, 1998; Udo Di Fabio, 1998; Udo Di Fabio, 2001.

> even if unconsciously—by legal norms, including the norms of international law.[147]

And, as David Kennedy, underlined,

> [w]hen the international/national issue is framed as a question of the relationship between law and politics or law and fact, as a question of the possibility of international law itself, there is some overlap with the traditional problems of jurisprudence—the problem of normativity or adjudication, the translatability of power into right, the legitimacy of political discretion and so forth.[148]

In our view, additional problems arise from Professors Goldsmith and Posner's ultimately too narrow focus on states in understanding the current scope of CIL. In exclusively focusing on states as relevant actors (and as authors of norms), they omit from their view those who try to make themselves heard outside of the state universe, namely groups, peoples, non-state actors, all of which have found their way into the list of 'subjects of international law' in classroom textbooks. Furthermore, this interest in the state alone misses the opportunity to engage with the normative premise of international law as such.[149]

Evidence for the latter is amply provided by the impressive growth in *transnational human rights litigation*.[150] The ever increasing recognition of border-crossing scandalisation of human rights violations[151] that informs and shapes the proliferation of human rights focused special tribunals[152] and the unceasing pressure by human rights litigators upon domestic courts, as well as the mounting pressure upon the international community to acknowledge human rights claims brought by various aboriginal groups and collectivities, give compelling proof of fundamental changes occurring within the normative framework of international law. Crucial for such developments is their non-linearity. The significance of contemporary developments in human rights law must in fact be seen in its manifold and fragmented manifestation, that reflects on the many places and spaces of emerging and nascent human rights regimes rather than on a uniformly proceeding development of a closed body of rules.[153] The latter, to be sure, would also be the least likely scenario given the ever more disputed nature of human rights to begin with.[154] While Professors Goldsmith and Posner do not refute the facticity of these developments, they seem unwilling to

[147] Paul Schiff Berman, 2006, 1265, 1267.

[148] David Kennedy, 1994, 338.

[149] But see Jürgen Habermas, 2006.

[150] Craig M Scott, 2001a; Beth Stephens, 2001.

[151] Andreas Fischer-Lescano, 2003.

[152] Roger P Alford, 2000; Cesare PR Romano, 1999; see already the predictions by Manley O Hudson, 1944.

[153] Martti Koskenniemi, 2005b; Martti Koskenniemi and Paivi Leino, 2002; Andreas Fischer-Lescano, 2002; Sundhya Pahuja, 2008.

[154] For an introduction to this discussion, see Upendra Baxi, 2005a.

acknowledge the deeper normative consequences of the proliferation of human rights. In light of the worldwide advances in the protection of human rights, coupled with an ever more differentiated critique of the underlying, universalist, post-colonial origins of human rights concepts,[155] their contention that human rights developments are owed simply to improvements in information technology and the ensuing cost-reductions for states to monitor human rights out of instrumentalist considerations[156] can only appear startling.

Their narrow treatment of human rights developments echoes what Philip Alston recently observed with regard to the discussion of human rights in connection to the changing landscape of international actors. According to Alston, the current treatment of non-state actors succeeds in de-legitimising all those rights discourses that are not associated with the state. Operating with a negative, exclusionary and labelling definition of non-state actors, the international legal order can feel safe and unchallenged by entities that are denied autonomous voices to define themselves. The 'not-a-cat-syndrome' in international law with regard to non-state actors reduces these to only something that they are not,[157] without allowing for a learning process through which we could begin to discern the particular form of legal norm-creation and political action originating from non-state actors. This has dramatic consequences for the rights bound up in these non-state actors, groups and collectivities. They are negated as official rights from the beginning, as their origin is not—because they are not states—recognised as legitimate. The deconstruction of customary international law, as presented by Professors Goldsmith and Posner, has the potential—intended or not—to silence those that have hitherto been excluded from the international legal order. From within the conceptual framework of public international law, they set out to eradicate those elements that have always been considered a most essential source for the continuing growth of international law. By attacking CIL as being too fragmented, incoherent and 'confusing',[158] Professors Goldsmith and Posner question the normative foundations of the international legal order as such.[159] Instead of embracing the fragmented and dynamic, constantly evolving nature that CIL shares with any evolving legal order struggling with its own institutional and normative legacies,[160] they turn it into the opposite, declaring it a sign of weakness and decay. With customary law constituting the soft source, the soul and beating heart

155 See only Antony Anghie, 2005.

156 Jack Goldsmith and Eric Posner, 2000, 670.

157 Philip Alston, 2005c.

158 Goldsmith and Posner, 2005, 83.

159 See for this assessment, also the brillant analysis by Paul Schiff Berman, 2006, 1265, 1279.

160 Peer Zumbansen, 2001a.

of a constantly disputed and self-critical legal order, its dismissal amounts to a turning away from international law as such.

It is here, finally, that the correlation between this discourse in international law and transnational private law becomes crystal clear. In both areas, the process of de-formalisation leads to an irreversible dismissal of norms—in international law declared as incoherent and non-binding and in private law as non-law—from the realm of sheer force. Whereas politics' function is to reign over the international order, that of social norms, or the market, is to determine the outcome of conflict in the private realm.

IV. TRANSNATIONAL PRIVATE LAW: HARD LAW, SOFT LAW, REFLEXIVE LAW AND THE CONDITIONS FOR PRIVATE LAW-MAKING

From the perspective of legal theory, the transnational production of law unavoidably confronts it with the law/non-law distinction. Several escape routes seem available. While soft law can be used in order to provide for a procedure of constant revision and update, its counterpart, hard law, refers to a set of norms from which the rest is being distinguished but toward which it optimally will lean. The tension between the policy aims pursued by legal intervention and the difficulties arising with their implementation characterises the modern state's learning experiences in steering clear of flooding civil society with regulatory law, while struggling to safeguard a constitutional level of legal and social protection.[161] The emergence of responsive, reflexive and post-instrumental law is an expression of the increasing awareness of the shortcomings of regulatory law as to the concrete circumstances and its addressees at a time where the state has become institutionally and normatively exhausted.[162] To matter, law had to learn to become more sensitive to the intrinsic value of contextually framed societal practices and customs.[163]

In this book we have proposed the concept of 'rough consensus and running code' as a promising new approach to address the challenges arising in contemporary regulatory governance. There were at least two compelling reasons that lead us to reach beyond the so-far available concept of using law as a regulatory instrument for an increasingly transnationalising world of societal interaction. One reason arose from the dramatic expansion of regulatory fields, both territorial and de-territorial in nature. This growth in regulatory fields was, as we saw, complemented by a continuing proliferation of norm-creating actors. While we were able to assert that these 'norm entrepreneurs' were either acting by delegation from government agencies

161 See Gunther Teubner, 1987b, 6–19.
162 Jürgen Habermas, 1989.
163 Hereto, see Gunther Teubner, 1983; Gunther Teubner and Helmut Willke, 1984.

or by self-authorisation, this alone hardly proved helpful in assessing their particular institutional nature. As evidenced through our examples in consumer protection law and in corporate governance regulation, the expert commissions, associations, standardisation organisations, private enterprise and other non-state actors acting in these areas escape a clear-cut divide between public or private actors and thereby challenge traditional regulatory approaches in their roots. These institutions' mixed legal status correlates, as we saw, in dramatic fashion, with a changing type of norms, that these actors generate and disseminate. In this context, it became more than obvious that the mere replacement of a hierarchy of norms, with which we are acquainted in the nation-state, by a heterarchic transnational order alone might suffice to answer questions regarding the sociological dimension of a legal order.[164] Yet, it can hardly satisfy our query into understanding the particular nature of this new legal order in substantive terms.

We thus explored the promise of 'rough consensus and running code' as both a constructive and a methodological model to describe, assess and further develop the different law-making regimes, which can be observed in the transnational arena. As said before, the changed institutional status of the actors involved correlated with the norms themselves ranging from so-called official, 'hard' law to unofficial, 'soft law', in turn including and encompassing standards, recommendations, business practices, best practice guidelines, codes of conduct and transparency rules. While much contemporary scholarship contents itself with offering, to be sure, a desperately needed, sociological and institutionalist analysis of the changes in the regulatory landscape, we saw how this description often is offered to merely disguise much deeper contestations of *legal* regulation in the first place. Drawing together contemporary assessments from contract, corporate, administrative and public international law scholars alike, we observed how much of allegedly factual statements were in truth based on a rejection of a normative mandate for legal regulation as such. Reading current legal scholarship in view of the larger, underlying vision of social order that the authors were pursuing, contributed to a better understanding of the present political economy of legal scholarship. But, apart from the perceived scepticism among some scholars with regard to law's regulatory and normative potential, the problems depicted by scholars of all backgrounds alike, continue to be very real. As such, a major challenge, repeatedly addressed by scholars of public and private international law alike, has been how (if, at all) to adequately incorporate this new host of norms into the existing bodies of law. Even with the best of intentions of the lawyers and policy-makers involved, the described transnational proliferation of societal interaction and norm-creation that has dramatically been de-centring

[164] Hans Kelsen, 1941, 50; Max Weber, 1967, 11.

the site of contestation, protest and legitimation outside of the nation-state, continues to challenge scholars of public and private international law at a crucial time. Both disciplines have, for some time now, been under extreme pressure to adapt their respective concepts and tools in response to developments which increasingly challenge and relativise the state's law-making capacities. A closer look at the way in which, for example, scholars in public international law, are currently choosing to address these challenges, proved to be revealing as much as sobering. At the same time that some scholars of public international law remain committed to a critique of law's and, particularly now, public international law's, deeply political and violent nature,[165] others are offering a whole-hearted reassertion of Realist perspectives on international law, based on rational choice considerations of economic efficiency and individual autonomy, that were, probably for the wrong reasons, long believed to be lost.[166] This current explosive mix of views in public international law is of crucial importance for ongoing assessments of the role of law in contemporary regulatory design, both in research and teaching.[167]

Similar tensions can be perceived in public international law's sister discipline: some scholars of private international law have crucially argued in favour of having their field recognised as being fundamentally challenged through the growing number of cases and instances that defy any attempt at re-domesticating a legal conflict and at tying it back to a particular jurisdiction.[168] One of the consequences for private international law of the growth in human rights litigation and in internationally launched class action suits to address human rights violations, has been to question central doctrines such as 'forum non conveniens' and state immunity. Again this trickles down even to the first year, civil procedure university curriculum.[169] But, how easy is it in fact to determine the direction in which a field, historically grown, is likely to develop in the next few decades, and to what degree can the law school curriculum be opened to such developments? Private international law, like other legal fields, continues to evolve in communication with and contestation from legal pluralism, law and society, and critical legal scholarship, and thus remains a promising, methodologically rich enterprise[170] that needs to find its way into the curriculum not merely as an 'add-on' or, luxury item in one's legal education.[171]

[165] Antony Anghie, 2005; Balakrishnan Rajagopal, 2003; Martti Koskenniemi, 2002b.

[166] Oona A Hathaway and Ariel N Lavinbuk, 2006.

[167] Anita Bernstein, 2007; Harry W Arthurs, 2005; Craig Scott, 2005.

[168] Craig M Scott, 2001b; Ralf Michaels, 2004; Robert Wai, 2005.

[169] Bob Carlson, 2003.

[170] Karen Knop, Ralf Michaels and Annelise Riles, 2008; Robert Wai, 2008; Gunther Teubner, 2004b.

[171] Craig Scott, 2005; Harold Hongju Koh, 2006, 751; Peer Zumbansen, 2006d, 748–50 'transnational legal education'; Elizabeth Mertz, 2007, 512–13; Anita Bernstein, 2007.

Against this background of deep changes in the self-description and outlook of legal fields, the exploration of a concept such as 'rough consensus and running code' proposed a mixed, public-private, dynamic norm-creation process. We proposed RCRC in order to explore venues of overcoming obstacles to effective norm-creation for transnational relations by presenting a form of law-making which does not replace but complements existing modes of norm-creation on different regulatory levels. We have described and asserted RCRC to be emerging as a particular form of societal self-governance at a time where domestic and transnational, public and private law-makers compete over regulatory competency and authority. As such, our argument has been both practical and substantive.

Bibliography

Abbott, Kenneth W (1989) 'Modern International Relations Theory: A Prospectus for International Lawyers' 14 *Yale Journal of International Law* 335.

—— (1999) 'International Relations Theory, International Law and the Regime Governing Atrocities in Internal Conflicts (Symposium on Method in International Law)' 93(2) *American Journal of International Law* 361.

—— (2006) 'Toward a Richer Institutionalism for International Law and Policy' 1 *Journal of International Law & International Relations* 9.

Abbott, Kenneth W and others (2000) 'The Concept of Legalization' 54(3) *International Organization* 1.

Abbott, Kenneth W and Snidal, Duncan (2000) 'Hard and Soft Law in International Governance' 54(3) *International Organization* 421.

—— (2009) 'Strengthening International Regulation Through Transnational New Governance: Overcoming the Orchestration Deficit' 42 *Vanderbilt Journal of Transnational Law* 501.

Abernethy, Steve (2003) 'Building Large-Scale Online Dispute Resolution & Trustmark Systems' in Ethan Katsh and Choi (eds), *Online Dispute Resolution (ODR), Papers and Proceedings of the 2003 United Nations Forum on ODR.*

Adams, John N and Brownsword, Roger (1987) 'The Ideologies of Contract' 7 *Legal Studies* 205.

Adams, Roger, 'Enron to Parmalat: Now Europe needs to declare war on fraud', *International Herald Tribune (web edition)* (14 January 2004) available at: www.iht.com/articles/2004/01/14/edadams_ed3_.php.

Adolff, Johannes (2003) 'Europäisches Gesellschaftsrecht: Vom Wettbewerb der nationalen Rechtsordnungen zum Systemwettbewerb der Börsen?' in Carl-Heinz Witt (ed), *Privatisierung des Privatrechts—rechtliche Gestaltung ohne staatlichen Zwang [Jahrbuch Junger Zivilrechtswissenschaftler 2002]* (Stuttgart ua, Boorberg) 61–92.

Aguilera, Ruth and others (2004) 'Putting the S Back in Corporate Social Responsibility: a Multi-Level Theory of Social Change in Organizations' 32(3) *Academy of Management Review* 836.

Ahlering, Beth and Deakin, Simon (2007) 'Labor Regulation, Corporate Governance, and Legal Origin: A Case of Institutional Complementarity?' 41 *Law & Society Review* 865.

Ahrne, Göran and Brunsson, Nils (2006) 'Organizing the World' in Marie-Laure Djelic and Kerstin Sahlin-Andersson (eds), *Transnational Governance Institutional Dynamics of Regulation* (Cambridge, Cambridge University Press) 74–94.

Albarran, Alan B and Goff, David H (eds) (2000) *Understanding the Web: Social, Political, and Economic Dimensions of the Internet* (Ames IA, Iowa State Press).

Albert, Mathias (2002) *Zur Politik der Weltgesellschaft. Identität und Recht im Kontext internationaler Vergesellschaftung* (Weilerswist, Velbrück Wissenschaft).

Albert, Mathias and Schmalz-Bruns, Rainer (2009) 'Antinomien der Global Governance: Mehr Weltstaatlichkeit, weniger Demokratie?' in Hauke Brunkhorst (ed), *Soziale Welt (Sonderband 18): Demokratie in der Weltgesellschaft* (Baden-Baden, Nomos) 57–74.

Albert, Michel (1991) *Capitalisme contre Capitalisme* (Paris, Editions du Seuil).

Aleinikoff, T Alexander (2008) 'Transnational Spaces: Norms and Legitimacy' 33 *Yale Journal of International Law* 479.

Alford, Roger P (2000) 'The Proliferation of International Courts and Tribunals: International Adjudication in Ascendance' 94 *American Society of International Law Proceedings* 160.

Allen, William T (1992) 'Our Schizophrenic Conception of the Business Corporation' 14 *Cardozo Law Review* 261.

Almaguer, Alejandro E and Baggott, Roland W (1998) 'Shaping New Legal Frontiers: Dispute Resolution for the Internet' 13 *Ohio State Journal on Dispute Resolution* 711.

Alston, Philip (2003) '"Core Labour Standards" and the Transformation of the International Labour Rights Regime' 15(3) *European Journal of International Law* 457.

—— (2005a) 'Facing up to the Complexities of the ILO's Core Labour Standards' 16(3) *European Journal of International Law* 467.

—— (2005b) 'Labour Rights as Human Rights: The Not So Happy State of the Art' in Philip Alston (ed), *Labour Rights as Human Rights* (Oxford/New York, Oxford University Press) 1–24.

—— (2005c) 'The "Not-a-Cat" Syndrome: Can the International Human Rights Regime Accommodate Non-State Actors?' in Philip Alston (ed), *Non-State Actors and Human Rights* (Oxford/New York, Oxford University Press) 3–25.

Alvarez, Jose E (2006) 'International Organizations: Then and Now' 100 *American Journal of International Law* 324.

Aman Jr, Alfred C (1997) 'Administrative Law for a New Century' in Michael Taggart (ed), *The Province of Administrative Law* (Oxford/Portland OR, Hart Publishing) 90–107.

—— (2001) 'The Limits of Globalization and the Future of Administrative Law: From Government to Governance' 8 *Indiana Journal of Global Legal Studies* 379.

—— (2004) *The Democracy Deficit* (New York, New York University Press).

—— (2006) *Administrative Law and Process,* 2nd edn (Newark NJ, Lexis Nexis).

Amstutz, Marc (2002) *Evolutorisches Wirtschaftsrecht* (Baden-Baden, Nomos).

—— (2005) 'In-Between Worlds: Marleasing and the Emergence of Interlegality in Legal Reasoning' 11(6) *European Law Journal* 766.

—— (2009) 'The Constitution of Contractual Networks' in Marc Amstutz and Gunther Teubner (eds), *Networks Legal Issues of Multilateral Co-operation* (Oxford UK/Portland OR, Hart Publishing) 309–46.

Amstutz, Marc, Abegg, Andreas and Karavas, Vaios (2007) 'Civil Society Constitutionalism: The Power of Contract Law' 14(2) *Indiana Journal of Global Legal Studies* 235.

Amstutz, Marc and Karavas, Vaios (2006) 'Rechtsmutation: Zu Genese und Evolution des Rechts im transnationalen Raum' 6 *Rechtsgeschichte* 14.

—— (2010) 'The Mutation of Law: On the Genesis and Evolution of Transnational Law' in Peer Zumbansen and Oren Perez (eds), *Law After Luhmann: Legal Sociology in the World Society* (forthcoming).

Amstutz, Marc and Teubner, Gunther (eds) (2009) *Networks. Legal Issues of Multilateral Co-operation* (Oxford/Portland OR, Hart Publishing).

Anderson, Gavin (2005) *Constitutional Rights After Globalization* (Oxford/ Portland OR, Hart Publishing).

Anghie, Antony (2005) *Imperialism, Sovereignty and the Making of International Law* (Cambridge, Cambridge University Press).

—— (2006) 'The Evolution of International Law: colonial and postcolonial realities' 27(5) *Third World Quarterly* 739.

Appelbaum, Richard P, Felstiner, William F and Gessner, Volkmar (eds) (2001) *Rules and Networks. The Legal Culture of Global Business Transactions* (Oxford/Portland OR, Hart Publishing).

Archibugi, Daniele (2004) 'Cosmopolitan Democracy and Its Critics: A Review' 10(3) *European Journal of International Relations* 437.

Archibugi, Daniele and Held, David (eds) (1995) *Cosmopolitan Democracy: An Agenda for a New World Order* (Cambridge, Polity Press).

Archibugi, Daniele and Michie, Jonathan (eds) (1997) *Technology, Globalisation and Economic Performance* (Cambridge, Cambridge University Press).

Armour, John (2005) 'Who Should Make Corporate Law? EC Legislation versus Regulatory Competition' 55 *Current Legal Problems* 369.

Armour, John, Deakin, Simon and Konzelmann, Suzanne J (2003) 'Shareholder Primacy and the Trajectory of UK Corporate Governance' 41 *British Journal of Industrial Relations* 531.

Armour, John and others (2009) 'How Do Legal Rules Evolve? Evidence from a Cross-Country Comparison of Shareholder, Creditor, and Worker Protection' 57 *American Journal of Comparative Law* 579.

Armour, John, Hansmann, Henry and Kraakman, Reinier (2009) 'The Essential Elements of Corporate Law' in Kraakman, Armour, Hansmann, Davies, Enriques, Hansmann, Hertig, Hopt, Kanda and Rock (eds), *The Anatomy of Corporate Law*, 2nd edn, at: ssrn.com/abstract=1436551.

Armour, John and Skeel Jr, David (2007) 'Who Writes the Rules for Hostile Takeovers, and Why?—The Peculiar Divergence of U.S. and U.K. Takeover Regulation' 95 *Georgetown Law Journal* 1727.

Armstrong, Kenneth A (2001) 'Civil Society and the White Paper—Bridging or Jumping the Gaps?' in Christian Joerges, Yves Meny and Joseph HH Weiler (eds), *Mountain or Molehill? A Critical Appraisal on the Commission White Paper on Governance* (Cambridge MA/London, Harvard Law School Jean Monnet Working Paper No 6/01) 95–102.

—— (2002) 'Rediscovering Civil Society: The European Union and the White Paper on Governance' 8 *European Law Journal* 102.

Arthurs, Harry and Mummé, Claire (2007) 'From Governance to Political Economy: Insights from a Study of Relations between Corporations and Workers' 45(3) *Osgoode Hall Law Journal* 439.

Arthurs, Harry W (1988) *Without the Law: Administrative Justice and Legal Pluralism in Nineteenth Century England* (Toronto, University of Toronto Press).

—— (1996) 'Labor Law Without the State' 46(1) *University of Toronto Law Journal* 1.

—— (2001) 'Reinventing Labor Law for the Global Economy: The Benjamin Aaron Lecture' 22(2) *Berkeley Journal of Employment and Labor Law* 271.

—— (2002) 'Private Ordering and Workers' Rights in the Global Economy: Corporate Codes of Conduct as a Regime of Labour Market Regulation' in Joanne Conaghan, Richard Michael Fischl and Karl Klare (eds), *Labour Law in an Era of Globalization Transformative Practices and Possibilities* (Oxford/New York, Oxford University Press) 471–87.

—— (2005) 'Madly Off In One Direction: McGill's New Integrated, Poly-Jural, Trans-Systemic Law Program' 50(4) *McGill Law Journal* 707.

Assmann, Heinz-Dieter and others (1980) *Wirtschaftsrecht als Kritik des Privatrechts* (Königstein Ts, Athenäum).

Atiyah, Patrick (1979) *The Rise and Fall of Freedom of Contract* (Oxford, Oxford University Press).

Augsberg, Ino, Gostomzyk, Tobias and Viellechner, Lars (2009) *Denken in Netzwerken. Zur Rechts- und Gesellschaftstheorie Karl-Heinz Ladeurs* (Tübingen, Mohr Siebeck).

Austin, John L (2002) *Lectures on Jurisprudence, or The Philosophy of Positive Law (1879)*, 4th edn, R Campbell (ed) (Bristol, Thoemmes Press).

Aviram, Amitai (2003) 'A Network Effects Analysis of Private Ordering' *Berkeley Olin Program in Law & Economics, Working Paper 80*: repositories.cdlib.org/cgi/viewcontent.cgi?article=1079&context=blewp.

—— (2004) 'A Paradox of Spontaneous Formation: The Evolution of Private Legal Systems' 22 *Yale Law & Policy Review* 1.

Bache, Ian and Flinders, Matthew (eds) (2004) *Multi-level Governance* (Oxford/New York, Oxford University Press).

Bainbridge, Stephen M (2005) 'Executive Compensation: Who Decides?' 83 *Texas Law Review* 1615.

Balkin, Jack M (1996) 'Interdisciplinarity as Colonization' 53 *Washington & Lee Law Review* 949.

Banakar, Reza (2009) 'Law Through Sociology's Looking Glass: Conflict and Competition in Sociological Studies of Law' *The ISA Handbook in Contemporary Sociology* 58.

Barnard, Catherine and Deakin, Simon (2002) 'Market Access and Regulatory Competition' in Catherine Barnard and Joanne Scott (eds), *The Law of the Single European Market: Unpacking the Premises* (Oxford/Portland OR, Hart Publishing) 197.

Barnet, Richard J and Muller, Ronald E (1974) *Global Reach: The Power of the Multinational Corporations* (New York City, Simon and Schuster).

Baron, David P (2002) 'Private Ordering on the Internet: The EBay Community of Traders' 4(3) *Business and Politics (Online Version)* Article 1.

Basu, Kaushik (1998) 'Social Norms and the Law', in Peter Newman (ed), *The New Palgrave Dictionary of Economics and the Law* (Basingstoke, Palgrave Macmillan), available at: http://ssrn.com/abstract=42840.

Bäuerle, Michael (2001) *Vertragsfreiheit und Grundgesetz. Normativität und Faktizität individueller Vertragsfreiheit in verfassungsrechtlicher Perspektive* (Baden-Baden, Nomos).

Baumgartner, Samuel P (2003) *The Proposed Hague Convention on Jurisdiction and Foreign Judgements* (Tübingen, Mohr Siebeck).

Baums, Theodor (2001a) 'Interview: Reforming German Corporate Governance: Inside a Law Making Process of a Very New Nature' 2(12) *German Law Journal* at: www.germanlawjournal.com/past_issues.php?id=43.

—— (2003) 'Company Law Reform in Germany' 3 *Journal of Corporate Law Studies* 181.

—— (ed) (2001b) *Bericht der Regierungskommission Corporate Governance. Unternehmensführung, Unternehmenskontrolle, Modernisierung des Aktienrechts* (Cologne, Otto Schmidt).

Baxi, Upendra (2005a) *The Death of Human Rights*, 2nd edn (Oxford/New York, Oxford University Press).

—— (2005b) 'Market Fundamentalisms: Business Ethics at the Altar of Human Rights' 5(1) *Human Rights Law Review* 1.

Beaumont, Paul (2002) 'Human Rights: Some Recent Developments and Their Impact on Convergence and Divergence of Law in Europe' in Paul Beaumont, Carole Lyons and Neil Walker (eds), *Convergence & Divergence in European Public Law* (Oxford/Portland OR, Hart Publishing) 151–75.

Beawes, Wyndam Anstis (1923) *The Romance of the Law Merchant* (London, Sweet & Maxwell).

Bebchuk, Lucian Ayre (1992) 'Federalism and the Corporation: The Desirable Limits on State Competition in Corporate Law' 105 *Harvard Law Review* 1437.

Bebchuk, Lucian A, Walker, David I and Fried, Jesse M (2002) 'Management and Control of the Modern Business Corporation: Executive Compensation and Takeovers' 69 *University of Chicago Law Review* 751.

Bebchuk, Lucian Ayre and Fried, Jesse (2004) *Pay Without Performance. The Unfulfilled Promise of Executive Compensation* (Cambridge MA/London, Harvard University Press).

Beckert, Jens (2007) 'The Great Transformation of Embeddedness. Karl Polanyi and the New Economic Sociology' *Max-Planck-Institut für Gesellschaftsforschung, MPIfG Discussion Paper 07/1*.

—— (2009) 'The social order of markets' 38 *Theory and Society* 245.

Beckert, Jens and Streeck, Wolfgang (2008) 'Economic Sociology and Political Economy. A Programmatic Perspective' *MPIfG Working Paper 08/4*, at: www.mpifg.de/pu/workpap/wp08.

Bederman, David J (2007) 'Diversity and Permeability in Transnational Governance' 57 *Emory Law Journal* 171.

Bell, Stephen and Hindmoor, Andrew (2009) *Rethinking Governance. The Centrality of the State in Modern Society* (Cambridge, Cambridge University Press).

Benhabib, Seyla (2004) *The Rights of Others. Aliens, Residents and Citizens* (Cambridge, Cambridge University Press).

Benhabib, Seyla, Waldron, Jeremy, Honig Bonnie and Kymlicka, Will (2006) *Another Cosmopolitanism* (Oxford/New York, Oxford University Press).

Bennie, Lynn, Bernhagen, Patrick and Mitchell, Neil J (2007) 'The Logic of Transnational Action: The Good Corporation and the Global Compact' 55 *Political Studies* 733.

Benson, Bruce (1989) 'The Spontaneous Evolution of Commercial Law' 55 *Southern Economic Journal* 644.

—— (1990) 'Customary Law with Private Means of Resolving Disputes and Dispensing Justice: A Description of a Modern System of Law and Order without State Coercion' IX(2) *The Journal of Libertarian Studies* 25.

—— (1999) 'To Arbitrate or to Litigate: That is the Question' 8(2) *European Journal of Law & Economics* 91.

—— (2010) 'The Lex Mercatoria Story: How Romantic Is It?' in Peer Zumbansen and Gralf-Peter Calliess (eds), *Law, Economics and Evolutionary Theory* (Cheltenham, Edward Elgar, forthcoming).

Benvenisti, Eyal (2004) *The International Law of Occupation [1993], with a new preface to the paperback edition* (Princeton NJ, Princeton University Press).

Berger, Klaus Peter (1999) *The Creeping Codification of the Lex Mercatoria* (The Hague, Kluwer Law International).

—— (2001a) 'The New Law Merchant and the Global Market Place. A 21st Century View of Transnational Commercial Law' in Klaus Peter Berger (ed), *The Practice of Transnational Law* (The Hague, Kluwer Law International) 1–22.

—— (ed) (2001b) *The Practice of Transnational Law* (The Hague, Kluwer Law International).

Berglöf, Erik and Thadden, Ernst-Ludwig von (2000) 'The changing corporate governance paradigm: implications for developing and transition economies' in Stephen S Cohen and Gavin Boyd (eds), *Corporate Governance and Globalization Long Range Planning Issues* (Cheltenham/Northampton MA, Edward Elgar) 275–306.

Berle, Adolf A (1954) *The 20th Century Capitalist Revolution* (New York, Harcourt, Brace & World).

Berle, Adolf A and Means, Gardiner C (1932) *The Modern Corporation and Private Property* (Brunswick NJ/London, Transaction Publishers).

Berman, Harold J (1987) 'The Law of International Commercial Transactions (*Lex Mercatoria*)' 2 *Emory Journal of International Dispute Resolution* 235.

—— (1995) 'World Law' 18 *Fordham International Law Journal* 1617.

Berman, Paul Schiff (2002) 'The Globalization of Jurisdiction' 151 *University of Pennsylvania Law Review* 311.

—— (2005a) 'From International Law to Law and Globalization' 43 *Columbia Journal of Transnational Law* 485.

—— (2005b) 'Towards A Cosmopolitan Vision Of Conflict Of Laws: Redefining Governmental Interests In A Global Era' 153 *University of Pennsylvania Law Review* 1819.

—— (2006) 'Seeing Beyond the Limits of International Law: Jack L Goldsmith/ Eric A Posner, The Limits of International Law' 84(5) *Texas Law Review* 1265.

—— (2007) 'Global Legal Pluralism' 80(6) *Southern California Law Review* 1155.

Bernstein, Anita (2007) 'On Nourishing the Curriculum with a transnational law lagniappe, New York Law School'. *Public Law and Legal Theory Research Paper Series 06/07*: ssrn.com/abstract=987347.

Bernstein, Lisa (1992) 'Opting out of the Legal System: Extralegal Contractual Relations in the Diamond Industry' 21 *Journal of Legal Studies* 115.

—— (1996) 'Merchant Law in a Merchant Court: Rethinking the Code's Search for Immanent Business Norms' 144 *University of Pennsylvania Law Review* 1765.

—— (1999) 'Formalism in Commercial Law: The Questionable Empirical Basis of Article 2's Incorporation Strategy: A Preliminary Study' 66 *University of Chicago Law Review* 710.

—— (2001) 'Private Commercial Law in the Cotton Industry: Creating Cooperation Through Rules, Norms, and Institutions' 99 *Michigan Law Review* 1724.

Bernstorff, Jochen von (2004) 'The Structural Limitations of Network Governance: ICANN as a Case in Point' in Gunther Teubner, Christian Joerges and Inger-Johanne Sand (eds), *Transnational Governance and Constitutionalism* (Oxford/Portland OR, Hart Publishing) 257–81.

BEUC (Bureau Européen des Unions de Consommatuers/The European Consumers' Organisation) and UNICE (The Confederation of European Business/BUSINESSEUROPE) (2001) e-Confidence project.

Bevir, Mark and Rhodes, RAW (2003) 'Searching for Civil Society: Changing Patterns of Governance in Britain' 81(1) *Public Administration* 41.

Bhagwati, Jagdish (2004) *In Defense of Globalization* (New York, Oxford University Press).

Biondi, Yuri and Suzuki, Tomo (2007) 'Socio-Economic Impacts of International Accounting Standards: An Introduction' 5(4) *Socio-Economic Review* 585.

Black, Julia (2001) 'Decentering Regulation: The Role of Regulation and Self-Regulation in a "Post-Regulatory" World' 54 *Current Legal Problems* 103.

—— (2008) 'Constructing and Contesting Legitimacy and Accountability in Polycentric Regulatory Regimes' *LSE Law, Society and Economy Working Papers 2/2008*: ssrn.com/abstract=1091783.

Black, Julia and Rouch, David (2008) 'The development of global markets as rule-makers: engagement and legitimacy' *Law and Financial Markets Review* 218.

Black, Vaughan (2000) 'Commodifying Justice for Global Free Trade: The Proposed Hague Judgments Convention' 37 *Osgoode Hall Law Journal* 237.

Blackett, Adelle (2001) 'Global Governance, Legal Pluralism and the Decentered State: A Labor Law Critique of Codes of Corporate Conduct' 8 *Indiana Journal of Global Legal Studies* 401.

—— (2004) 'Codes of Corporate Conduct and the Labour Law Regulatory State in Developing Countries' in John J Kirton and Michael J Trebilcock (eds), *Hard Choices, Soft Law Voluntary Standards in Global Trade, Environment and Social Governance* (Aldershot, Ashgate) 121–33.

Blair, Margaret (2002) 'Post-Enron Reflections on Comparative Corporate Governance', *Social Science Research Network*: papers.ssrn.com/paper.taf?abstract_id=316663.

Blankenburg, Erhard (1984) 'The Poverty of Evolutionism: a critique of Teubner's case for "reflexive law"' 18 *Law & Society Review* 273.

Blankenburg, Erhard and others (eds) (1980) *Alternative Rechtsformen und Alternativen zum Recht* (Düsseldorf, Jahrbuch für Rechtssoziologie und Rechtstheorie, Bertelsmann).

Blanpain, Roger and Colucci, Michele (2004) *The Globalization of Labour Standards. The Soft Law Track* (The Hague, Kluwer Law International).

Blanpain, Rogert (ed) (2009) *The Laval and Viking Cases. Freedom of Services and Establishment v. Industrial Conflict in the European Economic Area and Russia* (Alphen van den Rijn, Kluwer Law International).

Blaurock, Uwe (1998) 'The Law of Transnational Commerce' in Franco Ferrari (ed), *The Unification of International Commercial Law* (Baden-Baden, Nomos) 9–25.

Blecher, Michael (2009) 'Reclaiming the Common, or On Beginning and End of the (Legal) System' in Gralf-Peter Calliess, Andreas Fischer-Lescano, Dan Wielsch and Peer Zumbansen (eds), *Soziologische Jurisprudenz Festschrift für Gunther Teubner zum 65 Geburtstag* (Berlin/New York, Walter de Gruyter) 3–18.

Bogdandy, Armin von (2006) 'Constitutionalism in International Law: Comment on a Proposal from Germany' 47 *Harvard International Law Journal* 223.

Bogdandy, Armin von, Dann, Philipp and Goldmann, Matthias (2008) 'Developing the Publicness of Public International Law' 9(11) *German Law Journal* 1375.

Bogdandy, Armin von (1995) 'Sittlicher Interventions—oder vermittelnder Supervisionsstaat?' 81 *Archiv für Rechts- und Sozialphilosophie* 102.

Böhm, Franz (1937) *Die Ordnung der Wirtschaft als geschichtliche Aufgabe und rechtsschöpferische Leistung* (Stuttgart/Berlin, Kohlhammer).

—— (1960) 'Das Problem der privaten Macht' in Franz Böhm (ed), *Reden und Schriften* (Karlsruhe, CF Müller) 25–45.

—— (1966) 'Privatrechtsgesellschaft und Marktwirtschaft' 17 *ORDO* 75.

Böhm, Franz, Eucken, Wilhelm and Großmann-Doerth, Hans (1989) 'The Ordo Manifesto of 1936' in Alan Peacock and Hans Willgerodt (eds), *Germany's Social Market Economy: Origins and Evolution* (London, Palgrave Macmillan).

Bonell, Michael Joachim (1992) 'Unification of Law by Non-Legislative Means: The UNIDROIT Draft Principles of International Commercial Contracts' 40 *American Journal of International Law* 617.

—— (2001a) 'Creating International Legislation for the Twenty-First Century: Do We Need a Global Commercial Code?' 106 *Dickinson Law Review* 87.

—— (2004) 'UNIDROIT Principles 2004—A Further Step Towards a Global Contract Law' *Uniform Commercial Code Law Journal* 49.

—— (2007) 'Towards a Legislative Codification of the UNIDROIT Principles?' *Modern Law for Global Commerce Congress to celebrate the fortieth annual session of UNCITRAL, Vienna 9–12 July 2007*: www.cnudmi.org/pdf/english/congress/Bonell.pdf.

Bonnici, JP Mifsud and de Vey Mestdagh, CNJ (2005) 'Right Vision, Wrong Expectations: The European Union and Self-regulation of Harmful Internet Content' 14(2) *Information & Communications Technology Law* 133.

Bordone, Robert C (1998) 'Electronic Online Dispute Resolution: A Systems Approach—Potential, Problems, and a Proposal' 3 *Harvard Negotiation Law Review* 175.

Borges, Georg (2003) 'Selbstregulierung im Gesellschaftsrecht—zur Bindung an Corporate Governance-Kodices' 32 *Zeitschrift für Unternehmens- und Gesellschaftsrecht* 508.

Bothe, Michael (1980) 'Legal and Non-Legal Norms—A Meaningful Distinction in International Relations?' 11 *Netherlands Yearbook of International Law* 65.

Botzem, Sebastian and Quack, Sigrid (2006) 'Contested rules and shifting boundaries: International standard-setting in accounting' in Marie-Laure Djelic and Kerstin Sahlin-Andersson (eds), *Transnational Governance Institutional Dynamics of Regulation* (Cambridge, Cambridge University Press) 266–86.

Bowden, Sue (2000) 'Corporate Governance in a Political Climate: The Impact of Public Policy Regimes on Corporate Governance in the UK' in John Parkinson, Gavin Kelly and Andrew Gamble (eds), *The Political Economy of the Company* (Oxford/Portland OR, Hart Publishing) 175–94.

Bradley, Caroline (2005) 'Private International Law-Making for the Financial Markets' 29 *Fordham International Law Journal* 127.

Braendle, Udo C (2006) 'Shareholder Protection in the USA and Germany—"Law and Finance" Revisited' 7(3) *German Law Journal* 257.

Braithwaite, John (2008) *Regulatory Capitalism. How it Works, Ideas for Making it Work Better* (Cheltenham, Edward Elgar).

Brandeis, Louis D (1914) *Other People's Money and How the Bankers Use It* (New York, Harper's Torch Books).

—— (1934) *The Curse of Bigness* (New York, Viking).

Branson, Douglas M (2000) 'Teaching Comparative Corporate Governance: The Significance of "Soft Law" and International Institutions' 34 *Georgia Law Review* 669.

—— (2001) 'The Very Uncertain Prospect of "Global" Convergence in Corporate Governance' 34 *Cornell International Law Journal* 321.

Bratton, William W (2001) 'Berle and Means Reconsidered at the Century's Turn' 26 *Journal of Corporate Law* 737.

—— (2002) 'Enron and the Dark Side of Shareholder Value' 76 *Tulane Law Review* 1275.

—— (2005a) 'The Academic Tournament over Executive Compensation' 93 *California Law Review* 1557.

—— (2005b) 'Welfare, Dialectic, and Mediation in Corporate Law' 2 *Berkeley Business Law Journal* 59.

Bratton, William W and McCahery, Joseph A (2001) 'Incomplete Contracts Theories of the Firm and Comparative Corporate Governance' 2(3) *Theoretical Inquiries in Law* Article 7.

Bratton, William W, McCahery, Joseph A and Vermeulen, Erik PM (2008) 'How does Corporate Mobility Affect Lawmaking? A Comparative Analysis', *ECGI Working Paper No 91/2008*: ssrn.com/abstract=1086667.

Bratton, William W and Wachter, Michael L (2007) *Shareholder Primacy's Corporatist Origins: Adolf Berle and The Modern Corporation*, available at: ssrn.com/abstract=1021273.

Breton, Albert (2000) 'Federalism and Decentralization: Ownership Rights and the Superiority of Federalism' 30(2) *Publius: The Journal of Federalism* 1.

Brownsword, Roger (1997) 'Contract Law, Co-operation, and Good Faith: The Movement from Static to Dynamic Market Individualism' in Simon Deakin and Jonathan Michie (eds), *Contracts, Co-operation, and Competition Studies in Economics, Management and Law* (Oxford/New York, Oxford University Press) 255–84.

Brüggemeier, Gert (1999) *Prinzipien des Haftungsrechts* (Nomos, Baden-Baden).

Brüggemeier, Gert, Bussani, M, Collins, H, Colombo Ciacchi, A, Comandé, G, Fabre-Magnan, M, Grundmann, S, Hesselink, M, Joerges, C, Lurger, B, Ugo, M, Meli, M, Rutgers, J, Schmidt, C, Smith, J, Sefton-Green, R, Muir-Watt H and Wilhelmsson T (2004) 'Social Justice in European Contract Law: a Manifesto' 10(6) *European Law Journal* 653.

Bruner, Christopher M (2008) 'States, Markets, and Gatekeepers: Public-Private Regulatory Regimes in an Era of Economic Globalization' 30 *Michigan Journal of International Law* 125.

Brunkhorst, Hauke (2005) *Solidarity. From Civic Friendship to a Global Legal Community*, Jeffrey Flynn (trans) (Cambridge MA, MIT Press).

Brunsson, Nils and Jacobsson, Bengt (2000) *A World of Standards* (Oxford/ New York, Oxford University Press).

Buchanan, Allen and Keohane, Robert O (2006) 'The Legitimacy of Global Governance' 20 *Ethics and International Affairs* 4.

Buchanan, Ruth (2008) 'Reconceptualizing Law and Politics in the Transnational: Constitutional and Legal Approaches', *CLPE Research Paper No 19/2008*: ssrn. com/abstract=1167722.

Bull, Hedley (1977) *The Anarchical Society: A Study of Order in World Politics* (New York, Columbia University Press).

Bullinger, Martin (1968) *Öffentliches Recht und Privatrecht. Studien über Sinn und Funktion einer Unterscheidung* (Stuttgart, Kohlhammer).

—— (1996) 'Die funktionelle Unterscheidung von öffentlichem Recht und Privatrecht als Beitrag zur Beweglichkeit von Verwaltung und Wirtschaft in Europa' in Wolfgang Hoffmann-Riem and Eberhard Schmidt-Assmann (eds), *Öffentliches Recht und Privatrecht als wechselseitige Auffangordnungen* (Baden-Baden, Nomos) 239–60.

Burdick, Francis M (1902) 'What is the Law Merchant?' 2 *Columbia Law Review* 470.

Burris, Scott, Kempa, Michael and Shearing, Clifford (2008) 'Changes in Governance: A Cross-Disciplinary Review of Current Scholarship' 41(1) *Akron Law Review* 1.

Busch, Andreas (2005) 'Globalisation and National Varieties of Capitalism: The Contested Viability of the "German Model"' 14(2) *German Politics* 125.

—— (2009) *Banking Regulation and Globalization* (Oxford, Oxford University Press).

Bussani, Mauro and Mattei, Ugo (1997) 'The Common Core Approach to European Private Law' 3 *Columbia Journal of European Law* 339.

Buxbaum, Hannah L (2006) 'Transnational Regulatory Litigation' 46 *Virginia Journal of International Law* 251.

—— (2009) 'Territory, Territoriality, and the Resolution of Jurisdictional Conflict' 57 *American Journal of Comparative Law* 631.

Buxbaum, Richard (1986) 'Federal Aspects of Corporate Law and Theory' in Terence Daintith and Gunther Teubner (eds), *Contract and Organisation Legal Analysis in the Light of Economic and Social Theory* (Berlin/New York, Walter de Gruyter) 274–92.

Buxbaum, Richard and Hopt, Klaus J (1988) *Legal Harmonization and the Business Enterprise. Corporate and Capital Market Law Harmonization Policy in Europe and the U.S.A.* (Berlin/New York, Integration Through Law, Walter de Gruyter).

Cafaggi, Fabrizio and Muir-Watt, Horatia (2008a) 'Introduction' in Fabrizio Cafaggi and Horatia Muir-Watt (eds), *Making European Law Governance Design* (Cheltenham, Edward Elgar) 1–36.

—— (eds) (2008b) *Making European Law Governance Design* (Cheltenham, Edward Elgar).

Calliess, Gralf-Peter (1999) *Prozedurales Recht* (Baden-Baden, Nomos).

—— (2001) 'Lex Mercatoria: A Reflexive Law Guide To An Autonomous Legal System': www.germanlawjournal.com/article.php?id=109.

—— (2002) 'Reflexive Transnational Law. The Privatisation of Civil Law and the Civilisation of Private Law' 23 *Zeitschrift für Rechtssoziologie* 185.

—— (2003a) 'Coherence and Consistency in European Consumer Contract Law: A Progress Report' 4(4) *German Law Journal No 4*.

—— (2003b) 'Das Zivilrecht der Zivilgesellschaft. Die abendländische Rechtstradition, das internationale Privatrecht und der Verbraucherschutz' in Christian Joerges and Gunther Teubner (eds), *Rechtverfassungsrecht Recht-Fertigung zwischen Privatrecht und Gesellschaftstheorie* (Baden-Baden, Nomos) 239–69.

—— (2004) 'Value-added Norms, Local Litigation and Global Enforcement: why the Brussels-Philosophy failed in The Hague' 5(12) *German Law Journal* 1489.

—— (2006) *Grenzüberschreitende Verbraucherverträge. Rechtssicherheit und Gerechtigkeit auf dem elektronischen Weltmarktplatz* (Tübingen, Jus Privatum, Mohr Siebeck).

—— (2007) 'The Making of Transnational Contract Law' 14(2) *Indiana Journal of Global Legal Studies* 469.

—— (2009) 'Transnational Civil Regimes: Economic Globalization and the Evolution of Commercial Law' in Volkmar Gessner (ed), *Contractual Certainty in International Trade Empirical Studies and Theoretical Debates on Institutional Support for Global Economic Exchanges* (Oxford/Portland OR, Hart Publishing) 215–38.

Calliess, Gralf-Peter and others (2007) 'Transformations of Commercial Law. New Forms of Legal Certainty for Globalised Exchange Processes?' in Achim Hurrelman, Stephan Leibfried, Kerstin Martens and Peter Mayer (eds), *Transforming the Golden Age Nation State* (Basingstoke, Palgrave Macmillan) 83–108.

Calliess, Gralf-Peter and Hoffmann, Hermann B (2009a) 'Effektive Justizdienstleistungen für den globalen Handel' 42(1) *Zeitschrift für Rechtspolitik* 1.

—— (2009b) 'Judicial Services for Global Commerce—Made in Germany?' 10(2) *German Law Journal* 115.

Calliess, Gralf-Peter and Mertens, Jens (2009) 'Private Law and Competition Policy in the Global Economy': ssrncom/abstract=1413257.

Calliess, Gralf-Peter and Renner, Moritz (2009) 'Between Law and Social Norms: The Evolution of Global Governance' 22(2) *Ratio Juris* 260.

Camp, L Jean and Vincent, Charles (2004) 'Setting Standards: Looking to the Internet for Models of Governance', available at: ssrncom/abstract=615201.

Campbell, David (1997) 'The Relational Constitution of Contract and the Limits of "Economics": Kenneth Arrow on the Social Background of Markets' in Simon Deakin and Jonathan Michie (eds), *Contracts, Co-operation, and Competition Studies in Economics, Management and Law* (Oxford/New York, Oxford University Press) 307–36.

—— (2001) 'Ian Macneil and the Relational Theory of Contract' in David Campbell (ed), *The Relational Theory of Contract: Selected Works of Ian Macneil* 3.

—— (2007) 'Relational Contract and the Nature of Private Ordering: A Comment on Vincent-Jones' 14(2) *Indiana Journal of Global Legal Studies* 279.

Campbell, David, Collins, Hugh and Wightman, John (eds) (2003) *Implicit Dimensions of Contract. Discrete, Relational and Network Contracts* (Oxford/Portland, OR, European Private Law Theory, Hart Publishing).

Cankar, Nina, Deakin, Simon and Simoneti, Marko (2008) 'The Reflexive Properties of Corporate Governance Codes: The Reception of the "Comply or Explain" Approach in Slovenia', *Cambridge Centre for Business Research CBR Working Paper 371*: www.cbr.cam.ac.uk/pdf/WP371.pdf.

Carbonara, Emanuela and Parisi, Francesco (2007) 'Choice of Law and Legal Evolution: Rethinking the Market for Legal Rules', *University of Minnesota Legal Studies Research Paper No 07-38*: ssrn.com/abstract=1011376.

Carbonneau, Thomas E (2004) 'Arbitral Law-Making' 25 *Michigan Journal of International Law* 1183.

Carlson, Bob (2003) 'Why Slavery Reparations are Good for Civil Procedure Class' 47 *St Louis University Law Journal* 139.

Carr, Edward Hallett (2001) *The Twenty Years' Crisis, 1919–1939: An Introduction to the Study of International Relations [1939] (with a new introduction by Michael Cox)* (Basingstoke, Palgrave Macmillan).

Carrington, Paul D (2004) 'The American Tradition of Private Law Enforcement' 5(12) *German Law Journal* 1413.

Caruso, Daniela (2004) 'Private Law and Public Stakes in European Integration: the case of Property' 10(6) *European Law Journal* 751.

—— (2006) 'Private Law and State-Making in the Age of Globalization' 39 *New York University Journal of International Law & Politics* 1.

Cary, William L (1974) 'Federalism and Corporate Law: Reflections Upon Delaware' 83 *Yale Law Journal* 663.

Castells, Manuel (1996) *The Rise of the Network Society, The Information Age: Economy, Society and Culture*, vol I [2nd edn, 2000] (Cambridge MA/Oxford, Blackwell).

Catá Backer, Larry (2006) 'Multinational Corporations, Transnational Law: The United Nations' Norms on the Responsibilities of Transnational Corporations as Harbinger of Corporate Social Responsibility in International Law' 37 *Columbia Human Rights Law Review* 287.

—— (2009) 'The OECD Guidelines for Multinational Corporations: Using Soft Law to Operationalize a Transnational System of Corporate Governance' *Law at the End of the Day (Blog)*: lcbackerblog.blogspot.com/2009/03/oecd.

Cavers, David F (1933) 'A Critique of the Choice-of-Law Problem' 47 *Harvard Law Review* 173.

Chan, Johannes (2008) 'Administrative law, politics and governance. The Hong Kong Experience' in Tom Ginsburg and Albert YH Chen (eds), *Administrative Law and Governance in Asia Comparative Perspectives* (London/New York, Routledge) 143–74.

Chanos, Antonis (2008) 'Demokratie in der Weltgesellschaft—Inklusion/Exklusion als neuer Metacode?' 39(2/3) *Rechtstheorie Sonderheft Weltrecht*, Martin Schulte & Rudolf Stichweh (eds) 383.

Charney, Jonathan I (1983) 'Transnational Corporations and Developing Public International Law' *Duke Law Journal* 748.

Charny, David (1990) 'Non-Legal Sanctions in Commercial Relationships' 104 *Harvard Law Review* 375.

—— (1991) 'Competition among Jurisdictions in Formulating Corporate Rules: An American Perspective on the "Race to the Bottom" in the European Communities' 32(2) *Harvard International Law Journal* 423.

—— (1996) 'Illusions of a Spontaneous Order: "Norms" in Contractual Relationships' 144 *University of Pennsylvania Law Review* 1841.

—— (1999) 'The New Formalism in Contract' 66 *University of Chicago Law Review* 842.

Chevallier, Jacques (2004) *L'État post-moderne*, 2ême édn (Paris, LGDJ).

Chimni, Bhupinder S (2004) 'International Institutions Today: An Imperial Global State in the Making' 15 *European Journal of International Law* 1.

—— (2005) 'Cooption and Resistance: Two Faces of Global Administrative Law', *IILJ International Law and Justice Working Papers 2005/16*.

Chinkin, Christine (1989) 'The Challenge of Soft Law: Development and Change in International Law' 38 *International & Comparative Law Quarterly* 850.

—— (1999) 'A Critique of the Public/Private Distinction' 10 *European Journal of International Law* 387.

Choi, Steven (2000) 'Regulating Investors Not Issuers: A Market-Based Proposal' 88 *California Law Review* 279.

Choudhry, Sujit (1999) 'Globalization in Search of Justification: Toward a Theory of Comparative Constitutional Interpretation' *Indiana Law Journal* 819.

Cioffi, John W (2000a) 'Governing Globalization? The State, Law, and Structural Change in Corporate Governance' 27(4) *Journal of Law and Society* 572.

—— (2000b) 'State of the Art: A Review Essay on Comparative Corporate Governance: The State of the Art and Emerging Research' 48 *American Journal of Comparative Law* 501.

—— (2002) 'Restructuring "Germany Inc.": The Politics of Corporate Governance Reform in Germany and the European Union' 24(4) *Law & Policy* 355.

—— (2006) 'Corporate Governance Reform, Regulatory Politics, and the Foundations of Finance Capitalism in the United States and Germany' 7(6) *German Law Journal* 533.

—— (2010) *Public Law and Private Power: Corporate Governance Reform in the United States and Germany in an Age of Finance Capitalism* (forthcoming) (Ithaca NY, Cornell University Press).

Cioffi, John W and Cohen, Stephen S (2000) 'The state, law and corporate governance: the advantage of forwardness' in Stephen S Cohen and Gavin Boyd (eds), *Corporate Governance and Globalization Long Range Planning Issues* (Cheltenham/Northampton MA, Edward Elgar) 307–49.

Clark, David D (1992) 'A Cloudy Crystal Ball: Visions of the Future', *Plenary Presentation at 24th meeting of the Internet Engineering Task Force, Cambridge, Massachusetts, 13–17 July 1992* (ietf20.isoc.org/videos/future_ietf_92.pdf).

Clark, Gordon L, Feldman, Maryann P and Gertler, Meric S (eds) (2003) *Oxford Handbook of Economic Geography* (Oxford, Oxford University Press).

Clark, Robert C (1986) *Corporate Law* (Boston MA, Brown & Little).

Clark, Robert Charles (1981) 'The Four Stages of Capitalism: Reflections on Investment Management Treaties' 94 *Harvard Law Review* 561.

Clift, Ben M (2009) 'The Second Time as Farce? The EU Takeover Directive, the Clash of Capitalisms and the Hamstrung Harmonization of European (and French) Corporate Governance' 47(1) *Journal of Common Market Studies* 55.

Coase, Ronald (1937) 'The Nature of the Firm' 4 *Economica* 386.

—— (1960) 'The Problem of Social Cost' 3 *Journal of Law and Economics* 1.

Coffee Jr, John C (1992) 'Liquidity versus Control: The Institutional Investor as Corporate Monitor' in Klaus J Hopt and Eddy Wymeersch (eds), *European Takeovers Law and Practice* (London et al, Butterworths) 315–48.

—— (1999) 'The Future as History: The Prospects of Global Convergence in Corporate Governance and Its Implications' 93 *Northwestern University Law Review* 641.

Cohen, Jean and Sabel, Charles F (1997) 'Directly-deliberative polyarchy' 3 *European Law Journal* 313.

Cohen, Felix S (1935) 'Transcendental Nonsense and the Functional Approach' 35 *Columbia Law Review* 809.

Cohen, Morris R (1927) 'Property and Sovereignty' 13 *Cornell Law Quarterly* 8.

—— (1932) 'The Basis of Contract' 46(4) *Harvard Law Review* 553.

Collins, Hugh (1997) 'The Voice of the Community in Private Law Discourse' 3(4) *European Law Journal* 407.

—— (1999) *Regulating Contracts* (Oxford/New York, Oxford University Press).

—— (2008) 'Governance implications for the European Union of the changing character of private law' in Fabrizio Cafaggi and Horatia Muir-Watt (eds), *Making European Law Governance Design* (Cheltenham, Edward Elgar) 269–86.

Compa, Lance and Hinchliffe-Darricarrère, Tashia (1995) 'Enforcing International Labor Rights Through Corporate Codes of Conduct' 33 *Columbia Journal of Transnational Law* 663.

Cona, Frank A (1997) 'Application of Online Systems in Alternative Dispute Resolution' 45 *Buffalo Law Review* 975.

Coombe, Rosemary J (1995) 'The Cultural Life of Things: Anthropological Approaches to Law and Society in Conditions of Globalization' 10 *American University Journal of International Law & Policy* 791.

Cooter, Robert D (1993) 'Against Legal Centrism. Review of Robert C. Ellickson, Order Without Law. How Neighbors Settle Disputes' 81 *California Law Review* 417.

—— (1994) 'Structural Adjudication and the New Law Merchant: A Model of Decentralized Law' 14 *International Review of Law and Economics* 215.

—— (1996) 'Decentralized Law for a Complex Economy: The Structural Approach to Adjudicating the New Law Merchant' 144(5) *University of Pennsylvania Law Review* 1643.

Cooter, Robert D and Ulen, Thomas (2004) *Law & Economics*, 4th edn (Boston MA, Pearson).

Cordes, Albrecht (2003) 'The Search for a Medieval Lex Mercatoria' 5 *Oxford University Comparative Law Forum*: ouclf.iuscomp.org/articles/cordes.shtml.

Cornelius, Peter and Kogut, Bruce (2003) 'Creating the Responsible Firm: In Search for a New Corporate Governance Paradigm' 4(1) *German Law Journal* 45.

Cotterrell, Roger (1997) 'A Legal Concept of Community' 12(2) *Canadian Journal of Law & Society* 75.

—— (1998) 'Why Must Legal Ideas Be Interpreted Sociologically?' 25(2) *Canadian Journal of Law and Society* 171.

—— (2008) 'Transnational Communities and the Concept of Law' 21(1) *Ratio Juris* 1.

—— (2009) 'Spectres of Transnationalism: Changing Terrains of Sociology of Law' 36(4) *Canadian Journal of Law and Society* 481.

Cottier, Thomas (2009) 'Multilayered Governance, Pluralism, and Moral Conflict' 16 *Indiana Journal of Global Legal Studies* 647.

Cover, Robert M (1983) 'Nomos and Narrative' 97 *Harvard Law Review* 4.

—— (1986) 'Violence and the Word' 95 *Yale Law Journal* 1601.

Cranston, Ross (2007) 'Theorizing Transnational Commercial Law' 42 *Texas International Law Journal* 597.

Crouch, Colin (2005) 'Models of Capitalism' 10(4) *New Political Economy* 439.

Culpepper, Pepper D (1999) 'The Future of the High-Skill Equlibrium in Germany' 15(1) *Oxford Review of Economic Policy* 43.

Cunningham, Neil (2008) 'Private Ordering, Self-Regulation and Futures Markets: A Comparative Study of Informal Social Control' 13(4) *Law & Policy* 297.

Cutler, A Claire (1997) 'Artifice, Ideology and Paradox: the Public/Private Distinction in International Law' 4(2) *Review of International Political Economy* 261.

—— (2003) *Private Power and Global Authority: Transnational Merchant Law in the Global Economy* (Cambridge, Cambridge University Press).

Czempiel, Ernst-Otto and Rosenau, James N (eds) (1992) *Governance without Government: Order and Change in World Politics* (Cambridge, Cambridge University Press).

D'Aspremont, Jean (2008) 'Softness in International Law: A Self-Serving Quest for New Legal Materials' 19 *European Journal of International Law* 1075.

Daintith, Terence and Teubner, Gunther (eds) (1986) *Contract and Organisation. Legal Analysis in the Light of Economic and Social Theory* (Berlin/New York, Walter de Gruyter).

Dalhuisen, JH (2006) 'Legal Orders and their Manifestation: The Operation of the International Commercial and Financial Legal Order and its Lex Mercatoria' 24 *Berkeley Journal of International Law* 129.

Dammann, Jens and Hansmann, Henry (2008) 'Globalizing Commercial Litigation' 94 *Cornell Law Review* 1.

Damrau, Jan (2003) *Selbstregulierung im Kapitalmarktrecht, Eine rechtsökonomische Analyse der Normsetzung der deutschen Börsen und ihrer Träger* (Berlin, Tenea).

Dasser, Felix (2001) 'Lex Mercatoria—Critical Comments on a Tricky Topic' in Volkmar Gessner, Richard P Appelbaum and William F Felstiner (eds), *Rules and Networks The Legal Culture of Global Business Transactions* (Oxford/Portland OR, Hart Publishing) 189–200.

Dauvergne, Catherine (2008) *Making People Illegal: What Globalization Means for Migration and Law* (Cambridge, Cambridge University Press).

David, Paul A (1994) 'Why Are Institutions the "Carriers of History"?: Path Dependence and the Evolution of Conventions, Organizations and Institutions' 5 *Structural Change and Economic Dynamics* 205.

—— (2000) 'Path dependence, its critics and the quest for "historical economics"' in Pierre Garrouste and Stavros Ioannides (eds), *Evolution and Path Dependence in Economic Ideas: Past and Present* (Cheltenham, Edward Elgar).

—— (2007) 'Path Dependence—A Foundational Concept For Historical Social Science' 1(2) *Cliometrica—The Journal of Historical Economics and Econometric*

History 91 (reprinted in P Zumbansen and G-P Calliess (eds), *Law, Economics and Evolutionary Theory* (Cheltenham, Edward Elgar, 2010)).

Davies, Howard and Green, David (2008) *Global Financial Regulation. The Essential Guide* (Cambridge/Malden MA, Polity Press).

Davies, Paul L (2001) 'Struktur der Unternehmensführung in Großbritannien und in Deutschland: Konvergenz oder fortbestehende Divergenz?' 30 *Zeitschrift für Unternehmens- und Gesellschaftsrecht* 269.

—— (2003) 'Shareholder Value, Company Law, and Securities Markets Law: A British View' in Klaus J Hopt and Eddy Wymeersch (eds), *Capital Markets and Company Law* (Oxford/New York, Oxford University Press) 261–88.

Davis, Benjamin G (2002a) 'Building the Seamless Dispute Resolution Web: A Status Report on The American Bar Association Task Force on E-Commerce and Alternative Dispute Resolution' 8 *Texas Wesleyan Law Review* 529.

Dawson, John P (1947) 'Economic Duress—An Essay in Perspective' 45(3) *Michigan Law Review* 253.

De Schutter, Olivier (ed) (2006) *Transnational Corporations and Human Rights* (Oxford/Portland OR, Hart Publishing).

De Witte, Bruno, Hanf, Dominik and Vos, Ellen (eds) (2001) *The Many Faces of Differentiation in EU Law* (Antwerpen, Oxford & New York, Intersentia).

Deakin, Simon (2001) 'Regulatory Competition versus Reflexive Harmonisation in European Company Law' in Daniel C Esty and Damien Geradin (eds), *Regulatory Competition and Economic Integration Comparative Perspectives* (Oxford/New York, Oxford University Press) 190–217.

—— (2002) 'The Many Futures of the Contract of Employment' in Joanne Conaghan, Richard Michael Fischl and Karl Klare (eds), *Labour Law in an Era of Globalization Transformative Practices & Possibilities* (London/New York, Oxford University Press) 177–96.

—— (2003) 'Reflexive Governance in the Public Interest' *Proposal for a Research Project, 2 September 2003* (unpublished).

—— (2007) 'Reflexive Governance and European Company Law' in *CLPE Research Paper Series 2007*: www.comparativeresearch.net.

—— (2008) 'Regulatory Competition in Europe after Laval', *Cambridge Centre for Business Research CBR Working Paper 364*: www.cbr.cam.ac.uk/pdf/WP364.pdf.

Deakin, Simon and Konzelmann, Suzanne J (2004) 'Learning from Enron' 12(2) *Corporate Governance* 134.

Defarges, Philippe Moreau (2008) *La Gouvernance* (Paris, Que Sais-je? PUF).

Dellarocas, Chrysanthos (2003) 'The Digitization of Word of Mouth: Promise and Challenges of Online Feedback Mechanisms' 49 *Management Science* 1407.

Delonis, Robert P (2004) 'International Financial Standards and Codes: Mandatory Regulation without Representation' 36 *New York University Journal of International Law & Politics* 563.

Desai, Meghnad and Redfern, Paul (eds) (1995) *Global Governance: Ethics and Economics of the World Order* (London, Pinter).

Deva, Surya (2004) 'UN's Human Rights Norms for transnational corporations and other business enterprises: an imperfect step in the right direction?' 10 *ILSA Journal of International and Comparative Law* 493.

Dewey, John (1926) 'The Historic Background of Corporate Legal Personality' 35(6) *Yale Law Journal* 655.

Dezalay, Yves and Garth, Bryant (1996) *Dealing in Virtue: International Commercial Arbitration and the Construction of a Transnational Legal Order* (Chicago IL, Chicago University Press).

Dhir, Aaron (2006) 'Realigning the Corporate Building Blocks: Shareholder Proposals as a Vehicle for Achieving Corporate Social and Human Rights Accountability' 43(2) *American Business Law Journal* 365.

Di Fabio, Udo (1996) 'Verwaltung und Verwaltungsrecht zwischen gesellschaftlicher Selbstregulierung und staatlicher Steuerung' 56 *Veröffentlichungen der Vereinigung der Deutschen Staatsrechtslehrer* 235.

—— (1998) *Das Recht offener Staaten* (Tübingen, Siebeck Mohr).

—— (2001) *Der Verfassungsstaat in der Weltgesellschaft* (Tübingen, Mohr (Siebeck)).

di Robilant, Anna (2006) 'Genealogies of Soft Law' 54 *American Journal of Comparative Law* 499.

Diederichsen, Uwe (1997) 'Die Selbstbehauptung des Privatrechts gegenüber dem Grundgesetz' *Jura* 57.

Dietz, Thomas and Nieswandt, Holger (2009) 'The Emergence of Transnational Cooperation in the Software-Industry' in Volkmar Gessner (ed), *Contractual Certainty in International Trade Empirical Studies and Theoretical Debates on Institutional Support for Global Economic Exchanges* (Oxford/Portland OR, Hart Publishing) 87.

Dijk, Jan van (1999) *The Network Society* (London, Sage).

Diller, Matthew (2000) 'The Revolution in Welfare Administration: Rules, Discretion and Entrepreneurial Government' 75 *New York University Law Review* 1121.

Dixit, Avinash K (2004) *Lawlessness and Economics. Alternative Modes of Governance* (Princeton NJ/Oxford, Princetown University Press).

Djelic, Marie-Laure and Sahlin-Andersson, Kerstin (2006a) 'Institutional dynamics in a re-ordering world' in Marie-Laure Djelic and Kerstin Sahlin-Andersson (eds), *Transnational Governance Institutional Dynamics of Regulation* (Cambridge, Cambridge University Press) 375–97.

—— (2006b) 'Introduction: A world of governance: The rise of transnational regulation' in Marie-Laure Djelic and Kerstin Sahlin-Andersson (eds), *Transnational Governance Institutional Dynamics of Regulation* (Cambridge, Cambridge University Press) 1–28.

Dombalagian, Onnig H (2008) 'Choice of Law and Capital Markets Regulation' 82 *Tulane Law Review* 1903.

Donald, David C (2008) 'Approaching Comparative Company Law' 14 *Fordham Journal of Corporate and Financial Law* 83.

Dore, Ronald (1973) *British Factory—Japanese Factory. The Origins of National Diversity in Industrial Relations* (Berkeley/Los Angeles CA, University of California University Press).

—— (2000) *Stock Market Capitalism: Welfare Capitalism. Japan and Germany versus the Anglo-Saxons* (Oxford/New York, Oxford University Press).

—— (2008) 'Financialization of the Global Economy' 17(6) *Industrial and Corporate Change* 1097.

Doris, Martin J (2006) 'The Continued Resonance and Challenge of the "Ius Commune" in Modern European Contract Law' 34(2) *International Journal of Legal Information* 391.

Dorsett, Shaunnagh and McVeigh, Shaun (2007) 'Questions of jurisdiction' in Shaun McVeigh (ed), *Jurisprudence of Jurisdiction* (Oxford/New York, Routledge-Cavendish) 1–18.

Douzinas, Costas (2007) *Human Rights and Empire: The Political Philosophy of Cosmopolitianism* (Abingdon/New York, Routledge-Cavendish).

Drahos, Peter and Braithwaite, John (2001) 'The Globalisation of Regulation' 9(1) *Journal of Political Philosophy* 103.

Drobak, John N (ed) (2006) *Norms and the Law* (Cambridge, Cambridge University Press).

Drobnig, Ulrich (1990) 'Ein Vertragsrecht für Europa' in Jürgen F Baur, Klaus J Hopt and K Peter Mailänder (eds), *Festschrift für Ernst Steindorff zum 70 Geburtstag am 13 März 1990* (Berlin/New York, Walter de Gruyter) 1141–54.

—— (1998) 'The UNIDROIT Principles in the Conflict of Laws' *Uniform Law Review/Revue de droit uniforme* 385.

—— (2001) 'Vereinheitlichung von Zivilrecht durch soft law: neuere Erfahrungen und Einsichten' in Jürgen Basedow, Ulrich Drobnig, Reinhard Ellger, Klaus J Hopt, Hein Kötz, Rainer Kulms and Ernst-Joachim Mestmäcker (eds), *Aufbruch nach Europa 75 Jahre Max-Planck-Institut für Privatrecht* (Tübingen, Mohr Siebeck) 745–56.

Drori, Gili S and Meyer, John W (2006) 'Scientization: Making a World safe for organizing' in Marie-Laure Djelic and Kerstin Sahlin-Andersson (eds), *Transnational Governance Institutional Dynamics of Regulation* (Cambridge, Cambridge University Press) 31–52.

du Plessis, Jean and Luttermann, Claus (2007) 'Corporate Governance in the EU, the OECD Principles of Corporate Governance and Corporate Governance in Selected Other Jurisdictions' in Jean J du Plessis, Bernhard Großfeld, Claus Luttermann, Ingo Saenger and Otto Sandrock (eds), *German Corporate Governance in International and European Context* (Berlin, Heidelberg & New York, Springer) 215–56.

du Plessis, Jean and Sanger, Ingo (2007) 'An Overview of the Corporate Governance Debate in Germany' in Jean J du Plessis, Bernhard Großfeld, Claus Luttermann, Ingo Saenger and Otto Sandrock (eds), *German Corporate Governance in International and European Context* (Berlin, Heidelberg & New York, Springer) 9–36.

Dunning, John H and Lundan, Sarianna M (2008) *Multinational Enterprises and the Global Economy*, 2nd edn (Cheltenham, Edward Elgar).

Durkheim, Emile (1984) *The Division of Labor in Society [1893]*, WD Halls (trans) (New York, Free Press).

Eberlein, Burkhard and Grande, Edgar (2005) 'Beyond Delegation: Transnational Regulatory Regimes and the EU Regulatory State' 12 *Journal of European Public Policy* 89.

Ebke, Werner F (1998) 'Die Zukunft der Rechtsetzung in multijurisdiktionalen Rechtsordnungen: Wettbewerb der Rechtsordnungen oder zentrale Regelungsvorgabe—am Beispiel des Gesellschafts- und Unternehmensrechts' in Christian J Meier-Schatz (ed), *Die Zukunft des Rechts* (St Gallen, Helbing & Lichtenhahn) 106–27.

—— (2000) 'Accounting, Auditing and Global Capital Markets' in Theodor Baums, Klaus J Hopt and Norbert Horn (eds), *Corporations, Capital Markets and*

Business in the Law Liber Amicorum Richard M Buxbaum (London et al, Kluwer Law International) 113–36.

Eckersley, Robyn (2007) 'From cosmopolitan nationalism to cosmopolitan democracy' 33 *Review of International Studies* 675.

Edwards, Jeremy and Nibler, Marcus (2000) 'Corporate governance in Germany: The role of banks and ownership concentration' 15(31) *Economic Policy* 237.

Edwards, Vanessa (1999) *EC Company Law* (Oxford/New York, Oxford University Press).

Ehrlich, Eugen (1962) *Fundamental Principles of the Sociology of Law* (originally published in German as *Grundlegung der Soziologie des Rechts [1913]*) (New York, Russell & Russell).

Eidenmüller, Horst (2007) 'Forschungsperspektiven im Unternehmensrecht' 62 *Juristenzeitung* 487.

—— (2009) 'Recht als Produkt' 64 *Juristenzeitung* 641.

Eidenmüller, Horst and others (2008) 'The Common Frame of Reference for European Private Law—Policy Choices and Codification Problems' 28(4) *Oxford Journal of Legal Studies* 659.

Eifert, Martin (1998) *Grundversorgung mit Telekommunikationsleistungen im Gewährleistungsstaat* (Baden-Baden, Nomos).

—— (2001) 'Regulierte Selbstregulierung und lernende Verwaltung' *Regulierte Selbstregulierung als Steuerungskonzept des Gewährleistungsstaates (Die Verwaltung, Beiheft 4)* 137.

—— (2006) 'Regulierungsstrategien' in Wolfgang Hoffmann-Riem, Eberhard Schmidt-Assmann and Andreas Voßkuhle (eds), *Grundlagen des Verwaltungsrechts Band I: Methoden Maßstäbe Aufgaben Organisation* (München, CH Beck) 1237–310.

Eijsbouts, Jan (2005) 'Corporate Social Responsibility: A Matter of Principle(s), Law or Both?' in Sven Dumoulin, Theo Raaijmakers and Arie Tervoort (eds), *Tussen Themis en Mercurius, bedijfsjuridische bijdragen aan een Europese beleidsconcurrentie* (The Hague, Kluwer International) 83–96.

Eisen, Joel B (1998) 'Are We Ready for Mediation in Cyberspace?' *Brigham Young University Law Review* 1305.

Eisenberg, Melvin (2005) 'The Architecture of American Corporate Law: Facilitation and Regulation' 2 *Berkeley Business Law Journal* 167.

Elgie, Robert (2003) 'Governance Traditions and Narratives in Public Sector Reform in Contemporary France' 81(1) *Public Administration* 141.

Ellickson, Robert C (1991) *Order without Law: How Neighbors Settle Disputes* (Cambridge MA/London, Harvard University Press).

—— (1998) 'Law and Economics Discovers Social Norms' 27 (June) *Journal of Legal Studies* 537.

Ellis, Jaye (2006) 'Has International Law Outgrown Trail Smelter?' in Russell Miller and Rebecca Bratspies (eds), *Transboundary Harm: Lessons from the Trail Smelter Arbitration* (Cambridge, Cambridge University Press).

Engel, Christoph (2001) 'Hybrid Governance Across National Jurisdictions as a Challenge to Constitutional Law' 2 *European Business Organization Law Review* 569.

—— (2004) 'A Constitutional Framework for Private Governance' 5(3) *German Law Journal* 197.

Engert, Andreas (2006) 'Norms, Rationality, and Communication: A Reputation Theory of Social Norms' 92(2) *Archiv für Rechts- und Sozialphilosophie* 335.

Enriques, Luca and Gatti, Matteo (2007a) 'EC Reforms of Corporate Governance and Capital Markets Law: Do They Tackle Insiders' Opportunism?' 28(1) *Northwestern Journal of International Law and Business* 1.

—— (2007b) 'Is There a Uniform EU Securities Law After the Financial Services Action Plan?', *Proceedings of the 7th Nordic Company Law Conference*: ssrn.com/abstract=982282.

Enriques, Luca and Volpin, Paolo (2007) 'Corporate Governance Reforms in Continental Europe' 21(1) *Journal of Economic Perspectives* 117.

Esping-Anderson, Gosta (1990) *The Three Worlds of Welfare Capitalism* (Princeton NJ, Princeton University Press).

Esser, John P (1996) 'Institutionalizing Industry: The Changing Forms for Contract' *Law and Social Inquiry* 593.

Estache, Antonio (2004) 'Emerging Infrastructure Policy Issues in Developing Countries: A Survey of the Recent Economic Literature' *World Bank Policy Research Working Paper No 3442*: ssrn.com/abstract=625320.

Faber, Heiko (1989) 'Vorüberlegungen zu einer Theorie des Verwaltungsrechts der industriellen Gesellschaft' in Ekkehart Stein and Heiko Faber (eds), *Auf einem dritten Weg Festschrift für Helmut Ridder* (Neuwied, Luchterhand) 293–300.

Falk, Richard A (1995) 'Casting the Spell: The New Haven School of International Law' 104 *Yale Law Journal* 1991.

—— (2008) 'International Law and the Future' in Richard A Falk, Balakrishnan Rajagopal and Jacqueline Stevens (eds), *International Law and the Future* (London/New York, Routledge Cavendish) 23–33.

Falk, Richard A, Rajagopal, Balakrishnan and Stevens, Jacqueline (eds) (2008) *International Law and the Third World* (London/New York, Routledge Cavendish).

Fama, Eugene (1970) 'Efficient Capital Markets: A Review of Theory and Empirical Work' 31(2) *Journal of Finance* 383.

—— (1998) 'Market Efficiency, long-term returns, and behavioral finance' 49(3) *Journal of Financial Economics* 283.

Fanto, James A (2009) 'Recognizing the 'Bad Barrel' in Public Business Firms: Social and Organizational Factors in Misconduct by Senior Decision-Makers' 57 *Buffalo Law Review* 1.

Fassbender, Bardo (1998) 'The United Nations Charter as Constitution of the International Community' 36 *Columbia Journal of Transnational Law* 529.

Feddersen, Dieter, Hommelhoff, Peter and Schneider, Uwe H (eds) (1996) *Corporate Governance. Optimierung der Unternehmensführung und der Unternehmenskontrolle im deutschen und amerikanischen Aktienrecht* (Köln, Otto Schmidt).

Feigenbaum, Harvey, Henig, Jeffrey and Hamnett, Chris (1999) *Shrinking the State: The Political Underpinnings of Privatization* (Cambridge, Cambridge University Press).

Ferguson, Adam (1995) *An Essay on the History of Civil Society [1767]* (Cambridge, Cambridge University Press).

Ferrari, Franco (ed) (2005) *Quo vadis CISG? Celebrating the 25th anniversary of the United Nations Convention on Contracts for the International Sale of Goods* (Munich, Sellier European Law Publishers).

Ferrarini, Guido, Moloney, Niamh and Vespro, Cristina (2003) 'Executive Compensation in the EU: Comparative Law and Practice', *ECGI Working Paper Series in Law, No 09/2003*.

Fischer-Lescano, Andreas (2002) 'Globalverfassung, Verfassung der Weltgesellschaft' 88(3) *Archiv für Rechts- und Sozialphilosophie* 349.

—— (2003) 'Die Emergenz der Globalverfassung' 63 *Zeitschrift für ausländisches öffentliches Recht und Völkerrecht* 717.

—— (2008) 'Transnationales Verwaltungsrecht' 62 *Juristenzeitung* 373.

Fischer-Lescano, Andreas and Teubner, Gunther (2004) 'Regime-Collisions: The Vain Search for Legal Unity in the Fragmentation of Global Law' 25 *Michigan Journal of International Law* 999.

—— (2007) 'Fragmentierung des Weltrechts: Vernetzung globaler Regimes statt etatistischer Rechtseinheit' in Mathias Albert and Rudolf Stichweh (eds), *Weltstaat und Weltstaatlichkeit: Beobachtungen globaler politischer Strukturbildung* (Wiesbaden, Verlag für Sozialwissenschaft) 37–61.

Fitzpatrick, Peter (2004) 'Terminal Legality? Human Rights and Critical Being' in Peter Fitzpatrick and Patricia Tuitt (eds), *Critical Beings Law, Nation and the Global Subject* (Aldershot, Ashgate) 119–36.

Fleischer, Holger (2007) 'Zur Zukunft der gesellschafts- und kapitalmarktrechtlichen Forschung' *Zeitschrift für Unternehmens- und Gesellschaftsrecht* 500.

Fligstein, Neil (2001) *The Architecture of Markets. An Economic Sociology of Twenty-First-Century Capitalist Societies* (Princeton NJ, Princeton University Press).

Föhlisch, Carsten (2004) 'Bedeutung der Gütesiegel im Internet für den Verbraucherschutz und Funktion des D21 Gütesiegel-Boards aus Sicht eines Anbieters' *Presentation at the D21 Gütesiegelkongress on 27 September 2004*: www.foehlisch.de/docs/Foehlisch_D21_Guetesiegel_Kongress_Berlin_2004.pdf.

Ford, Richard (1999) 'Law's Territory (A History of Jurisdiction)' 97 *Michigan Law Review* 843.

Forsthoff, Ernst (1971) *Der Staat der Industriegesellschaft* (Munich, CH Beck).

Frank, Robert H (1996) 'Can Socially Responsible Firms Survive in a Competitive Environment?' in David M Messick and Ann E Tenbrunsel (eds), *Codes of Conduct: Behavioral Research into Business Ethics* (New York, Russell Sage) 86–103.

Frankenberg, Günter (2006) 'Comparing Constitutions: Ideas, Ideals, and Ideology—Toward a Layered Narrative' 4 *International Journal of Constitutional Law* 439.

Franzius, Claudio (2006) 'Modalitäten und Wirkungsformen der Steuerung durch Recht' in Wolfgang Hoffmann-Riem, Eberhard Schmidt-Aßmann and Andreas Voßkuhle (eds), *Grundlagen des Verwaltungsrechts, Band 1: Methoden—Maßstäbe—Aufgaben—Organisation* (Munich, CH Beck) 177–237.

—— (2009) 'Warum Governance?' 42(1) *Kritische Justiz* 25.

Fraser, Nancy (2009) *Scales of Justice. Reimagining Political Space in a Globalizing World* (New York, Columbia University Press).

Freedland, Mark and Auby, Jean-Bernard (eds) (2006) *The Public Law/Private Law Divide (Une Entente Assez Cordiale?)* (Oxford/Portland OR, Hart Publishing).

Freeman, Jody (1997) 'Collaborative Governance in the Administrative State' 45 *University of California at Los Angeles Law Review* 1.

—— (2000a) 'The Contracting State' 28 *Florida State University Law Review* 155.
—— (2000b) 'The Private Role in Public Governance' 75 *New York University Law Review* 543.
Freeman, Jody and Minow, Martha (eds) (2009) *Government by Contract: Outsourcing and American Democracy* (Cambridge MA/London, Harvard University Press).
Fried, Barbara H (1998) *The Progressive Assault in Laissez Faire: Robert Hale and the First Law and Economics Movement* (Cambridge MA, Harvard University Press).
Fried, Charles (1981) *Contract as Promise* (Cambridge MA, Harvard University Press).
Friedman, Lawrence M (1985) 'Legal culture and the welfare state' in Gunther Teubner (ed), *Dilemmas of Law in the Welfare State* (Berlin/New York, Walter de Gruyter) 13–27.
—— (1996) 'Borders: On the Emerging Sociology of Transnational Law' 32 *Stanford Law Review* 65.
Friedmann, Wolfgang G (1957) 'Corporate Power, Government by Private Groups, and the Law' 57(2) *Columbia Law Review* 155.
—— (1972) 'Human Welfare and International Law—A Reordering of Priorities' in Wolfgang Friedmann, Louis Henkin and Oliver Lissitzyn (eds), *Transnational Law in a Changing Society Essays in the Honor of Philip C Jessup* (New York, Columbia University Press) 113–34.
Friedmann, Wolfgang, Henkin, Louis and Lissitzyn, Oliver (eds) (1972) *Transnational Law in a Changing Society. Essays in the Honor of Philip C. Jessup* (New York, Columbia University Press).
Fukuyama, Francis (1992) *The End of History and the Last Man* (New York, Macmillan).
Fuller, Lon (1964) *The Morality of Law* (New Haven CT/London, Yale University Press).
Gaillard, Emmanuel (2001) 'Transnational Law: A Legal System or a Method of Decision Making?' in Klaus Peter Berger (ed), *The Practice of Transnational Law* (The Hague, Kluwer Law International) 53–65.
Gaillard, Emmanuel and Savage, John (eds) (1999) *Fouchard Gaillard Goldman On International Commercial Arbitration* (Kluwer Law International, The Hague, Boston & London).
Galanter, Marc (1981) 'Justice in many rooms: Courts, Private Ordering and Indigenous Law' 19 *Journal of Legal Pluralism* 1.
—— (2006) 'In the Winter of our Discontent: Law, Anti-Law, and Social Science' (2) *Annual Review of Law & Social Sciences* 1.
Galle, Brian and Leahy, Joseph (2009) 'Laboratories of Democracy? Policy Innovation in Decentralized Governments' 58 *Emory Law Journal* 1333.
Gambetta, Diego (1993) *The Sicilian Mafia: The Business of Private Protection* (Cambridge MA, Harvard University Press).
García, José M Garrido (2005) 'Company Law and Capital Markets Law' 69 *Rabels Zeitschrift für Ausländisches und Internationales Privatrecht* 761.
Gatsios, Konstantine G and Holmes, Peter H (1998) 'Regulatory Competition' in Peter Newman (ed), *The New Palgrave Dictionary of Law and Economics*, vol 3 (London, Macmillan) 271–5.

Gaul, Björn and Janz, Alexandra (2009) 'Wahlkampfgetöse im Aktienrecht: Gesetzliche Begrenzung der Vorstandsvergütung und Änderungen der Aufsichtsratstätigkeit' 26(15) *Neue Zeitschrift für Arbeitsrecht* 809.

GBDe (Global Business Dialogue on electronic commerce) 'Trustmarks': www.gbd-e.org/pubs/Tokyo_Recommendations_2001.pdf.

—— (2000) 'Miami Recommendations': www.gbd-e.org/pubs/Miami_Recommendations_2000.pdf.

—— (2003) 'New York Recommendations': www.gbd-e.org/pubs/NYC_Recommendations_2003.pdf.

Gerber, David J (1998) *Law and Competition in Twentieth Century Europe. Protecting Prometheus* (Oxford, Clarendon Press).

Gersen, Jacob E and Posner, Eric A (2008) 'Soft Law' *University of Chicago Public Law and Legal Theory Working Paper No 213*: ssrn.com/abstract=1113537.

Gerstenberg, Oliver (1997) 'Law's Polyarchy: A Comment on Cohen and Sabel' 3 *European Law Journal* 343.

Gessner, Volkmar (2009) 'Theories of Change—The Governance of Business Transactions in Globalising Economies' in Volkmar Gessner (ed), *Contractual Certainty in International Trade Empirical Studies and Theoretical Debates on Institutional Support for Global Economic Exchanges* (Oxford/Portland OR, Hart Publishing).

Gessner, Volkmar, Appelbaum, Richard P and Felstiner, William F (2001) 'Introduction: The Legal Culture of Global Business Transactions' in Volkmar Gessner, Richard P Appelbaum and William F Felstiner (eds), *Rules and Networks: The Legal Culture of Global Business Transactions* (Oxford/Portland OR, Hart Publishing) 1–36.

Gill, Amiram (2008) 'Corporate Governance as Social Responsibility: A Research Agenda' 26 *Berkeley Journal of International Law* 452.

Gilson, Ronald J (1992) 'The Political Ecology of Takeovers: Thoughts on Harmonizing the European Corporate Governance Environment' in Klaus J Hopt and Eddy Wymeersch (eds), *European Takeovers Law and Practice* (London et al, Butterworths) 49–74.

—— (2001) 'Globalizing Corporate Governance: Convergence of Form or Function?' 49 *American Journal of Comparative Law* 329.

Gilson, Ronald J and Kraakman, Reinier (1984) 'The Mechanisms of Market Efficiency' 70 *Virginia Law Review* 549.

—— (2003) 'The Mechanisms of Market Efficiency Twenty Years Later: The Hindsight Bias' 28 *Journal of Corporate Law* 715.

Goldman, Berhold (1979) 'La Lex Mercatoria dans les Contrats et l'Arbitrage International: Réalités et Perspectives' 106 *Clunet* 475.

Goldman, Berthold (1956) 'Arbitrage International et droit commun des nations' *Revue de l'Arbitrage* 115.

—— (1964) 'Frontières du droit et "lex mercatoria"' 13 *Archives de la Philosophie de Droit* 177.

—— (1983) 'Lex Mercatoria' 3 *Forum Internationale* 3.

Goldsmith, Jack and Posner, Eric (1999) 'A Theory of Customary International Law' 66 *University of Chicago Law Review* 1113.

—— (2000) 'Understanding the Resemblance between Modern and Traditional Customary International Law' 40 *Virginia Journal of International Law* 639.

—— (2001) 'Further Thoughts on Customary International Law' 23 *Michigan Journal of International Law* 191.

—— (2005) *The Limits of International Law* (Cambridge MA/London, Harvard University Press).

Goodale, Mark and Merry, Sally Engle (eds) *The Practice of Human Rights. Tracking Law Between the Local and the Global* (Cambridge, UK, Cambridge University Press).

Goode, Roy (1997) 'Usage and Its Reception in Transnational Commercial Law' 46 (1) *International & Comparative Law Quarterly* 1.

Goodin, Robert E (2003) 'Democratic Accountability: the Distinctiveness of the Third Sector' 44 *Archives europées de sociologie* 359.

Gordley, James (1991) *The Philosophical Origins of Modern Contract Doctrine* (Oxford, Oxford University Press).

Gordon, Jeffrey N (1999) 'Pathways to Corporate Governance? Two Steps on the Road to Shareholder Capitalism in Germany' 5 *Columbia Journal of European Law* 219.

Gordon, Jeffrey N and Roe, Mark J (eds) (2004) *Convergence and Persistence in Corporate Governance* (Cambridge, Cambridge University Press).

Gordon, Jennifer (2007) 'Transnational Labor Citizenship' 80 *Southern California Law Review* 503.

Gordon, Robert W (1985) 'Macaulay, Macneil, and the Discovery of Solidarity and Power in Contract Law' *Wisconsin Law Review* 565.

Gourevitch, Peter A (2003) 'The Politics of Corporate Governance Regulation' 112 *Yale Law Journal* 1829.

Gourevitch, Peter A and Shinn, James (2005) *Political Power and Corporate Control. The New Global Politics of Corporate Governance* (Princeton NJ/Oxford, Princeton University Press).

Grandori, Anna (2007) *Associational Contracts and Firm-Like Organization* (ssrn.com/abstract=986286).

Granovetter, Mark (1985) 'Economic Action and Social Structure: The Problem of Embeddedness' 91 *American Journal of Sociology* 481.

—— (2005) 'The Impact of Social Structure on Economic Outcomes' 19(1) *Journal of Economic Perspectives* 33.

Gray, Garry (2009) 'The Responsibilization Strategy of Health and Safety: Neo-Liberalism and the Reconfiguration of Individual Responsibility for Risk' 49(3) *British Journal of Criminology* 326.

Greif, Avner (2006) *Institutions and the Path to the Modern Economy. Lessons from Medieval Trade* (Cambridge, Cambridge University Press).

Greif, Avner and Laitin, David (2004) 'A theory of endogenous institutional change' 98(4) *American Political Science Review* 633.

Griffiths, John (1986) 'What is Legal Pluralism?' 24(1) *Journal of Legal Pluralism and Unofficial Law* 1.

Grossfeld, Bernhard (2003) 'Comparative Corporate Governance: Generally Accepted Accounting Principles v. International Accounting Standards' 28 *North Carolina Journal of International Law & Commercial Regulation* 847.

Großmann-Doerth, Hans (1929) 'Der Jurist und das autonome Recht des Welthandels' 58 *Juristische Wochenschrift* 3447.

—— (2005) 'Selbstgeschaffenes Recht der Wirtschaft und staatliches Recht [1933]' in Uwe Blaurock, Nils Goldschmidt and Alexander Hollerbach (eds), *Das selbstgeschaffene Recht der Wirtschaft Zum Gedenken an Hans Großmann-Doerth (1894–1944)* (Tübingen, Mohr Siebeck) 77–96.

Grosswald Curran, Vivian (2001) 'Rethinking Hermann Kantorowicz: Free law, American legal realism and the legacy of anti-formalism' in Annelise Riles (ed), *Rethinking the Masters of Comparative Law* (Oxford/Portland OR, Hart Publishing) 66–93.

—— (2003) 'On the Shoulders of Schlesinger: The Trento Common Core of European Private Law Project' 1(1) *European Review of Private Law* 66.

Gruchalla-Wesierski, Tadeusz (1984) 'A Framework for Understanding "Soft Law"' 30 *McGill Law Journal* 37.

Grundmann, Stefan (2000) 'General Principles of Private Law and Ius Commune Modernum as Applicable Law?' in Theodor Baums, Klaus J Hopt and Norbert Horn (eds), *Corporations, Capital Markets and Business in the Law Liber Amicorum Richard M Buxbaum* (London et al, Kluwer Law International) 213–34.

—— (2004) *Europäisches Gesellschaftsrecht. Eine systematische Darstellung unter Einbeziehung des Kapitalmarktrechts* (Heidelberg, CF Müller).

—— (2008) 'The Structure of the DCFR—Which Approach for Today's Contract Law?' 4(3) *European Review of Contract Law* 225.

Grundmann, Stefan, Kerber, Wolfgang and Weatherill, Stephen (eds) (2001) *Party Autonomy and the Role of Information in the Internal Market* (Berlin/New York, Walter de Gruyter).

GTA (Global Trustmark Alliance) (2004) 'Plans for global online consumer protection network take shape, Trustmark organizations in Asia, Europe and the Americas join global alliance': www.globaltrustmarkalliance.org/press/113004.asp.

Günther, Klaus (1990) 'Der Wandel der Staatsaufgaben und die Krise des regulativen Rechts' in Dieter Grimm (ed), *Wachsende Staatsaufgaben—sinkende Steuerungsfähigkeit des Rechts* (Baden-Baden, Nomos) 51–68.

Gurvitch, Georges (1947) *Sociology of Law* (originally published in French as *Problèmes de la sociologie du droit*) (London, Routledge and Kegan Paul).

Guthrie, Graeme (2006) 'Regulating Infrastructure: The Impact on Risk and Investment' 44(4) *Journal of Economic Literature* 925.

Guzman, Andrew T (2006) 'Saving Customary International Law' 27 *Michigan Journal of International Law* 115.

—— (2008) *How International Law Works. A Rational Choice Theory* (Oxford, Oxford University Press).

Guzman, Andrew T and Meyer, Timothy L (2008) 'Customary International Law in the 21st Century' in Rebecca Bratspies and Russell Miller (eds), *Progress in International Law* (The Hague, Martin Niejhouf) 197–218.

Haar, Brigitte (2008) 'Law and Finance—Kapitalmarktentwicklung in interdisziplinärer Perspektive' 63 *Juristenzeitung* 964.

Häberle, Siegfried Georg (ed) (2002) *Handbuch für Kaufrecht, Rechtsdurchsetzung und Zahlungssicherung im Außenhandel* (Munich/Vienna, Oldenbourg).

Habermas, Jürgen (1989) 'The New Obscurity: The Crisis of the Welfare State and the Exhaustion of Utopian Energies [1985]' in Jürgen Habermas (ed), *The*

New Conservatism Cultural Criticism and the Historians' Debate, Shierry Weber Nicholsen (ed and trans) (Cambridge MA, MIT Press) 48–70.

—— (2001) *The Postnational Constellation* (Cambridge MA, MIT Press).

—— (2004) 'Hat die Konstitutionalisierung des Völkerrechts noch eine Chance?' in J Habermas, *Der gespaltene Westen* (Frankfurt, Suhrkamp) 113.

—— (2006) *The Divided West* (Cambridge/Malden MA, Polity Press).

Habersack, Mathias (2003) *Europäisches Gesellschaftsrecht*, 2. Aufl (München, CH Beck).

Hacke, Andreas (2001) *Der ADR-Vertrag, Vertragsrecht und vertragliche Gestaltung der Mediation und anderer alternativer Kon-fliktlösungsverfahren* (Heidelberg, Recht und Wirtschaft).

Hadfield, Gillian K (2000) 'The Price of Law: How the Market for Lawyers Distorts the Justice System' 98 *Michigan Law Review* 953.

—— (2001) 'Privatizing Commercial Law' *Regulation* 40.

—— (2002) 'Privatizing Commercial Law: Lessons From Icann' 6 *Journal of Small & Emerging Business Law* 257.

—— (2009a) 'The Public and the Private in the Provision of Law for Global Services' in Volkmar Gessner (ed), *Contractual Certainty in International Trade Empirical Studies and Theoretical Debates on Institutional Support for Global Economic Exchanges* (Oxford/Portland OR, Hart Publishing) 239–56.

—— (2009b) 'The Strategy of Methodology: The Virtues of Being Reductionist for Comparative Law' 59(2) *University of Toronto Law Journal* 223.

Hadfield, Gillian K and Talley, Eric (2006) 'On Public versus Private Provision of Corporate Law' 22 (2) *Journal of Law, Economics & Organization* 414.

Hale, Robert L (1923) 'Coercion and Distribution in a Supposedly Non-Coercive State' 38(3) *Political Science Quarterly* 470.

Hall, Peter A and Soskice, David (2001a) 'An Introduction to Varieties of Capitalism' in Peter A Hall and David Soskice (eds), *Varieties of Capitalism The Institutional Foundations of Comparative Advantage* (Oxford/New York, Oxford University Press) 1–68.

—— (eds) (2001b) *Varieties of Capitalism. The Institutional Foundations of Comparative Advantage* (Oxford/New York, Oxford University Press).

Hall, Rodney Bruce and Biersteker, Thomas J (2002) 'The Emergence of Private Authority in the International System' in Rodney Bruce Hall and Thomas J Biersteker (eds), *The Emergence of Private Authority in Global Governance* (Cambridge, Cambridge University Press) 3–20.

Hancké, Bob (ed) (2009) *Debating Varieties of Capitalism. A Reader* (Oxford, Oxford University Press).

Hanschmann, Felix (2009) 'Theorie transnationaler Rechtsprozesse' in Sonja Buckel, Ralph Christensen and Andreas Fischer-Lescano (eds), *Neue Theorien des Rechts*, 2 Ed (Stuttgart, UTB) 375–99.

Hansmann, Henry (2006) 'How Close is the End of History?' 31 *Journal of Corporate Law* 745.

Hansmann, Henry and Kraakman, Reinier (2001) 'The End of History for Corporate Law' 89 *Georgetown Law Journal* 439.

—— (2002) 'Toward a Single Model of Corporate Law?' in Joseph A McCahery, Piet Moerland, Theo Raaijmakers and Luc Renneborg (eds), *Corporate Governance Regimes Convergence and Diversity* (Oxford/New York, Oxford University Press) 56–82.

Harden, Ian (1992) *The Contracting State* (Buckingham, Open University Press).
Harlow, Carol (1980) '"Public" and 'Private" Law: Definition without Distinction' 43(3) *Modern Law Review* 241.
—— (1999) 'European Administrative Law and the Global Challenge' in Paul Craig and Gráinne de Búrca (eds), *The Evolution of EU Law* (Oxford/New York, Oxford University Press) 261–85.
—— (2002) 'Voices of Difference in a Plural Community' in Paul Beaumont, Carole Lyons and Neil Walker (eds), *Convergence & Divergence in European Public Law* (Oxford/Portland OR, Hart Publishing) 199–24.
—— (2006) 'Global Administrative Law: The Quest for Principles and Values' 17 *European Journal of International Law* 187.
—— (2009) 'The 'Hidden Paw' of the State and the Publicisation of Private Law' in David Dyzenhaus, Murray Hunt and Grant Huscroft (eds), *A Simple Common Lawyer Essays in Honour of Michael Taggart* (Oxford/Portland OR, Hart Publishing) 75–97.
Hart, Dieter (1984) 'Zur konzeptionellen Entwicklung des Vertragsrechts' 29 *Die Aktiengesellschaft* 66.
—— (1987) 'Einleitung vor §§ 116 ff. BGB' in Rudolf Wassermann (ed), *Alternativkommentar BGB,* 1 Band (Neuwied, Luchterhand).
Hathaway, Oona A (2005) 'Between Power and Principle: An Integrated Theory of International Law' 72 *University of Chicago Law Review* 469.
—— (2007) 'The Continuing Influence of the New Haven School' 32 *Yale Journal of International Law* 565.
Hathaway, Oona A and Lavinbuk, Ariel N (2006) 'Rationalism and Revisionism in International Law' 119 *Harvard Law Review* 1404.
Hatzimihail, Nikitas E (2008) 'The Many Lives—and Faces—of *Lex Mercatoria*: History as Genealogy in International Business Law' 71 *Law & Contemporary Problems* 169.
Havermann, Hans (2000) 'Private Regelsetzung aus der Sicht des Handelsbilanzrechts' *Zeitschrift für Unternehmensrecht* 693.
Hayek [von], Friedrich A (1945) 'The Use of Knowledge in Society' 35 *American Economic Review* 519.
—— (1973) *Law, Legislation and Liberty. Vol. 1: Rules and Order* (Chicago IL, University of Chicago Press).
—— (1994) 'Arten der Ordnung' (originally (1963) 14 *ORDO* 1) in Hayek, *Freiburger Studien, Gesammelte Aufsatze*, 2nd edn (Tübingen, Mohr Siebeck) 32, reprint of 1st edn [1969].
—— (2002) 'Competition as a Discovery Procedure' (originally published in German [1968]; Marcellus S Snow (trans)) 5(3) *Quarterly Journal of Austrian Economics* 9.
—— (2006) *The Constitution of Liberty [1960]* (London/New York, Routledge).
Hedemann, Justus Wilhelm (1959) 'Das Wirtschaftsrecht, Rückblick und Abschied' in Rolf Dietz, Hans Carl Nipperdey and Eugen Ulmer (eds), *Beiträge zum Arbeits-, Wirtschafts- und Zivilrecht* (München/Berlin, CH Beck) 377–412.
Hein, Jan von (2008) *Die Rezeption US-amerikanischen Gesellschaftsrechts in Deutschland* (Tübingen, Mohr Siebeck).
Heintzen, Markus (2004) 'Der Deutsche Corporate Governance Kodex aus der Sicht des deutschen Verfassungsrechts' 25(41) *Zeitschrift für Wirtschaftsrecht* 1933.
Held, David (1995) *Democracy and the Global Order* (Cambridge, Polity Press).

—— (2000) 'The changing contours of political community: Rethinking democracy in the context of globalization' in Barry Holden (ed) *Global Democracy. Key Debates* (London, Routledge), 17–31.

—— (2004) 'Democratic Accountability and Political Effectiveness from a Cosmopolitan Perspective' 39(2) *Government and Opposition* 364.

—— (2006) 'Cosmopolitanism' *Stanford Encyclopedia of Philosophy* (28 November 2006): plato.stanford.edu/entries/cosmopolitanism.

Helfer, Lawrence R (2006) 'Understanding Change in International Organizations: Globalization and Innovation in the ILO' 59(3) *Vanderbilt Law Review* 649.

Henkin, Louis (1999) 'That "S" Word: Sovereignty, and Globalization, and Human Rights, et cetera' 68 *Fordham Law Review* 1.

Herberg, Martin (2007) *Globalisierung und private Selbstregulierung: Umweltschutz in multinationalen Unternehmen* (Frankfurt, Campus).

Herborth, Benjamin and Niesen, Peter (eds), (2007) *Anarchie der kommunikativen Freiheit: Jürgen Habermas und die Theorie der internationalen Politik* (Frankfurt, Suhrkamp).

Héritier, Adrienne and Lehmkuhl, Dirk (2008) 'The Shadow of Hierarchy and New Modes of Governance' 28 (1) *Journal of Public Policy* 1.

Hertig, Gérard (2000) 'Western Europe's Corporate Governance Dilemma' in Theodor Baums, Klaus J. Hopt and Norbert Horn (eds), *Corporations, Capital Markets and Business in the Law Liber Amicorum Richard M Buxbaum* (London et al, Kluwer Law International) 265–82.

Hertig, Gérard and McCahery, Joseph A. (2007) 'Optional rather than Mandatory EU Company Law: Framework and Specific Proposals' *European Company and Financial Law Review* 341.

Hertner, Peter (1998) 'Corporate Governance and Multinational Enterprise in Historical Perspective' in Klaus J Hopt, Hideki Kanda, Mark J Roe, Eddy Wymeersch and Stefan Prigge (eds), *Comparative Corporate Governance—The State of the Art and Emerging Research* (Oxford, Clarendon Press) 41–59.

Herwig, Alexia (2004) 'Transnational Governance Regimes for Foods Derived from Bio-Technology and their Legitimacy' in Gunther Teubner, Christian Joerges and Inger-Johanne Sand (eds), *Transnational Governance and Constitutionalism* (Oxford and Portland OR, Hart Publishing) 199–221.

Hesselink, Martijn W (2008) 'A spontaneous order for Europe? Why Hayek's libertarianism is not the right way forward for European private law', *Centre for the Study of European Contract Law, Working Paper Series No 2008/07*: ssrn.com/abstract=1270566.

Higgott, R, Underhill, G and Bieler, A (eds) (2000) *Non-State Actors and Authority in the Global System* (London, Routledge).

Hill, Jennifer (2005) 'Regulatory Responses to Global Corporate Scandals' 23 *Wisconsin International Law Journal* 367.

—— (2008) 'Regulatory Show and Tell: Lessons from International Statutory Regimes' 33 *Delaware Journal of Corporate Law* 819.

Hill, Jonathan (1989) 'Comparative Law, Law Reform and Legal Theory' 9 *Oxford Journal of Legal Studies* 101.

—— (2008) *Cross-Border Consumer Contracts* (Oxford, Oxford University Press).

Hillemanns, Carolin F (2003) 'UN Norms on the Responsibilities of Transnational Corporations and Other Business Enterprises with regard to Human Rights' 4 *German Law Journal* 1065.

Hirschman, Albert O (1970) *Exit, Voice, and Loyalty. Responses to Decline in Firms, Organizations, and States* (Cambridge MA, Harvard University Press).

—— (1977) *The Passions and the Interests. Political Arguments for Capitalism before Its Triumph* (Princeton NJ, Princeton University Press).

Hirte, Heribert (2003) *Das Transparenz- und Publizitätsgesetz* (Munich, Beck).

Hobe, Stephan (1998) *Der offene Verfassungsstaat zwischen Souveränität und Interdependenz. Eine Studie zur Wandlung des deutschen Staatsbegriffs der deutschsprachigen Staatslehre im Kontext internationaler institutionalisierter Kooperation* (Berlin, Duncker & Humblot).

—— (2002) 'The Era of Globalisation as a Challenge to International Law' 40 *Duquesne Law Review* 655.

Hodson, Dermot and Maher, Imelda (2001) 'The Open Method as a New Mode of Governance: The Case of Soft Economic Policy Coordination' 39 *Journal of Common Market Studies* 719.

Hoffmann-Riem, Wolfgang (1997) 'Tendenzen in der Verwaltungsrechtsentwicklung' 50 *Die Öffentliche Vervaltung* 433.

Hoffmann, Florian F (2008) 'In Quite a State: Trials and Tribulations of an Old Concept in New Times' in Russell A Miller and Rebecca Bratspies (eds), *Progress in International Law* (The Hague, Martin Nijhoff) 263–88.

Hoffmann, Jürgen (2004) 'Co-ordinated Continental European Market Economies Under Pressure From Globalisation: Germany's "Rhineland capitalism"' 5(8) *German Law Journal* 985.

Hoffmann, Paul (2009) 'The Tao of IETF: A Novice's Guide to the Internet Engineering Task Force', *IETF Internet Draft 28 June 2009*: www.ietf.org/tao.html.

Hofmann, Rainer and Geissler, Nils (eds) (1998) *Non-State Actors as New Subjects of International Law—From the Traditional State Order Towards the Law of the Global Community. Proceedings of an International Syposium at the Walter Schücking Institute of International Law, Kiel, March 25–28, 1998* (Berlin, Duncker & Humblot).

Hohenstatt, Klaus-Stefan (2009) 'Das Gesetz zur Angemessenheit der Vorstandsvergütung' 30(29) *Zeitschrift für Wirtschaftsrecht* 1349.

Hollingsworth, J Rogers (1997) 'The Institutional Embeddedness of American Capitalism' in Colin Crouch and Wolfgang Streeck (eds), *Political Economy of Modern Capitalism Mapping Convergence and Diversity* (London, Sage) 133–47.

Hollister, Hudson T (2005) '"Shock Therapy" for Aktiengesellschaften: Can the Sarbanes-Oxley Certification Requirements Transform German Corporate Culture, Practice and Prospects?' 25 *Northwestern Journal of International Law & Business* 453.

Hommelhoff, Peter and Schwab, Martin (2001) 'Staats-ersetzende Privatgremien im Unternehmensrecht' in Walter Drenseck and Roman Seer (eds), *Festschrift für Heinrich Wilhelm Kruse zum 70 Geburtstag* (Cologne, Otto Schmidt Verlag) 693–718.

Hopt, Klaus-Jürgen (2006) 'Comparative Company Law' in Mathias Reimann and Reinhard Zimmermann (eds), *Oxford Handbook of Comparative Law* (Oxford/New York, Oxford University Press) 1161–91.

Hopt, Klaus J (2002) 'Common Principles of Corporate Governance in Europe?' in Joseph A McCahery, Piet Moerland, Theo Raaijmakers and Luc Renneborg (eds), *Corporate Governance Regimes Convergence and Diversity* (Oxford/New York, Oxford University Press) 175–204.

—— (2003) 'Corporate Governance in Germany' in Klaus J Hopt and Eddy Wymeersch (eds), *Capital Markets and Company Law* (Oxford/New York, Oxford University Press) 289–326.

—— (2005) 'European Company Law and Corporate Governance: Where does the Action Plan of the European Commission Lead?' in Klaus J Hopt, Eddy Wymeersch, Hideki Kanda and Harald Baum (eds), *Corporate Governance in Context* (Oxford/New York, Oxford University Press), 119–42.

Hopt, Klaus J and others (eds) (1998) *Comparative Corporate Governance. The State of the Art and Emerging Research* (Oxford/New York, Oxford University Press).

—— (2005) *Corporate Governance in Context. Corporations, States and Markets in Europe, Japan and the US* (Oxford/New York, Oxford University Press).

Hopt, Klaus J and Leyens, Patrick C (2004) 'Board Models in Europe. Recent Developments of Internal Corporate Governance Structures in Germany, the United Kingdom, France and Italy'. *ECGI Law Working Paper No 18/2004*: ssrn.com/abstract=487944.

Hopt, Klaus J and Wymeersch, Eddy (1997) *Comparative Corporate Governance—Essays and Materials* (Berlin/New York, Walter de Gruyter).

—— (eds) (2003) *Capital Markets and Company Law* (Oxford/New York, Oxford University Press).

Hopt, Klaus Jürgen (2006) 'Comparative Company Law' in Mathias Reimann and Reinhard Zimmermann (eds), *Oxford Handbook of Comparative Law* (Oxford/New York, Oxford University Press) 1161–91.

Hörnle, Julia (2001) 'Disputes Solved in Cyberspace and the Rule of Law' *Journal of Information, Law and Technology.*

—— (2002) 'Online Dispute Resolution in Business to Consumer E-commerce Transactions' *The Journal of Information, Law and Technology*: www2.warwick.ac.uk/fac/soc/law/elj/jilt/2002_2/hornle/.

—— (2003) 'Online Dispute Resolution: More than the Emperor's New Clothes' in Ethan Katsh and Daewon Choi (eds) *Online Dispute Resolution (ODR), Papers and Proceedings of the 2003 United Nations Forum on ODR* (Geneva, University of Massachusetts Amherst, Center for Information Technology and Dispute Resolution), www.odr.info/unece2003/pdf/Hornle.pdf.

—— (2009) *Cross-border Internet Dispute Resolution* (Cambridge, Cambridge University Press).

Horwitz, Morton J (1975) 'The Rise of Legal Formalism' 19(4) *American Journal of Legal History* 251.

—— (1992) *The Transformation of American Law 1870–1960* (Oxford/New York, Oxford University Press).

Howells, Geraint and Wilhelmsson, Thomas (2003) 'EC Consumer Law: Has it Come of Age?' 28(3) *European Law Review* 370.

Huang, Peter H and Wu, Ho-Mou (1994) 'More Order Without More Law: A Theory of Social Norms and Organizational Cultures' 10(2) *Journal of Law, Economics and Organization* 390.

Hudson, Manley O (1944) *International Tribunals. Past and Future* (Washington, Carnegie Endowment for International Peace and Brookings Institution).

Hunt, Murray (1997) 'Constitutionalism and the Contractualisation of Government in the United Kingdom' in Michael Taggart (ed), *The Province of Administrative Law* (Oxford/Portland OR, Hart Publishing) 21–39.

Huntington, Samuel P (1973) 'Transnational Organizations in World Politics' 25(3) *World Politics* 333.

Hurrell, Andrew (2007) *On Global Order. Power, Values and the Constitution of International Society* (Oxford, Oxford University Press).

Ibata-Arens, Kathryn, Dierkes, Julian and Zorn, Dirk (2006) 'Guest Editors' Introduction: Theoretical Introduction to the Special Issue on the Embedded Enterprise' 7(1) *Enterprise & Society* 1.

ICC (International Chamber of Commerce) (2003) Tools for e-Business, Resolving disputes online—Best practices for Online Dispute Resolution (ODR) in B2C and C2C transactions.

Ireland, Paddy (2002) 'History, Critical Legal Studies and the Mysterious Disappearance of Capitalism' 65(1) *Modern Law Review* 120.

—— (2005) 'Shareholder Primacy and the Distribution of Wealth' 68(1) *Modern Law Review* 49.

Isaacs, Nathan (1917) 'The Standardizing of Contracts' 27 *Yale Law Journal* 34.

Jachtenfuchs, Markus (2001) 'The Governance Approach to European Integration' 39(2) *Journal of Common Market Studies* 245.

Jackson, Gregory (2000) 'Comparative Corporate Governance: Sociological Perspectives' in John Parkinson, Gavin Kelly and Andrew Gamble (eds), *The Political Economy of the Company* (Oxford/Portland OR, Hart Publishing) 265–87.

—— (2001) 'The Origins of Nonliberal Corporate Governance in Germany and Japan' in Wolfgang Streeck and Kozo Yamamura (eds), *The Origins of Nonliberal Capitalism* (Ithaca NY, Cornell University Press) 121–70.

Jacobson, Bengt (2006) 'Regulated regulators: Global trends of state transformation' in Marie-Laure Djelic and Kerstin Sahlin-Andersson (eds), *Transnational Governance Institutional Dynamics of Regulation* (Cambridge, Cambridge University Press) 205–24.

Jacoby, Sanford M (2002) 'Corporate Governance in Comparative Perspective: Prospects for Convergence' 22(5) *Comparative Labor Law & Policy Journal* 5.

Jaffe, Louis (1937) 'Law Making by Private Groups' 51 *Harvard Law Review* 201.

Jann, Werner (2003) 'State, Administration and Governance in Germany: Competing Traditions and Dominant Narratives' 81(1) *Public Administration* 95.

Jensen, Michael C (1970) 'Some anomalous evidence regarding market efficiency' 6(2/3) *Journal of Financial Economics* 95.

Jensen, Michael C, Murphy, Kevin J and Wruck, Eric G (2004) 'Remuneration: Where we've been, how we got here, what are the problems, and how to fix them', *ECGI Working Paper Series in Law, No 44/2004*.

Jessup, Philip C (1940) 'The Reality of International Law' 18(2) *Foreign Affairs* 244.

—— (1956) *Transnational Law* (New Haven CT, Storrs Lectures in Jurisprudence at Yale Law School, Yale University Press).

Joerges, Christian (1972a) 'Die klassische Konzeption des Internationalen Privatrechts und das Recht des unlauteren Wettbewerbs' 36(3) *Rabels Zeitschrift für Ausländisches und Internationales Privatrecht* 421.

—— (1972b) *Zum Funktionswandel des Kollisionsrechts. Die 'Governmental Interest Analysis' und die 'Krise des Internationalen Privatrechts'* (Berlin/Tübingen, Walter de Gruyter/Siebeck Mohr).

—— (1991) 'Markt ohne Staat?—Die Wirtschaftsverfassung der Gemeinschaft und die regulative Politik' in Rudolf Wildenmann (ed), *Staatswerdung Europas? Optionen für eine Europäische Union* (Baden-Baden, Nomos) 225–67.

—— (1994) 'Economic Law, the Nation-State and the Maastricht Treaty' in Renaud Dehousse (ed), *Europe after Maastricht: An Ever Closer Union?* (Munich, Beck) 29–62.

—— (2000) 'The Science of Private Law and the Nation-State' in Francis Snyder (ed), *The Europeanization of Law The Legal Effects of European Integration* (Oxford/Portland OR, Hart Publishing) 47–82.

—— (2004) 'The Challenges of Europeanization in the Realm of Private Law: A Plea for a New Legal Discipline' 14 *Duke Journal of Comparative & International Law* 149.

Joerges, Christian, Mény, Yves and Weiler, Joseph HH (eds) (2001) *Mountain or Molehill? A Critical Appraisal on the Commission White Paper on Governance, Jean Monnet Working Paper No 6/01* (Cambridge MA/London, Harvard Law School).

Joerges, Christian and Neyer, Jürgen (1997) 'From Intergovernmental Bargaining to Deliberative Political Processes: The Constitutionalisation of Comitology' 3(3) *European Law Journal* 273.

Joerges, Christian and Rödl, Florian (2009) 'Informal Politics, Formalised Law and the Social Deficit of European Integration: Reflections after the Judgments of the ECJ in Viking and Laval' 15(1) *European Law Journal* 1.

Joerges, Christian, Strath, Bo and Wagner, Peter (eds) (2005) *The Economy as a Polity. The Political Constitution of Contemporary Capitalism* (London, Cavendish).

Joerges, Christian and Trubek, David (eds) (1985) *Critical Legal Thought: An American-German Debate* (Baden-Baden, Nomos).

Johns, Fleur (2004) 'On Writing Dangerously' 26 *Sydney Law Review* 473.

—— (2007) 'Performing Power: The Deal, Corporate Rule, and the Constitution of Global Legal Order' 34(1) *Journal of Law and Society* 116.

Joseph, Sarah (2004) *Corporations and Transnational Human Rights Litigation* (Portland OR/London, Hart Publishing).

Juenger, Friedrich K (1993) *Choice of Law and Multistate Justice* (Transnational Publishers).

—— (1995) 'American Conflicts Scholarship and the New Law Merchant' 28 *Vanderbilt Journal of Transnational Law* 487.

—— (2000) 'The Lex Mercatoria and Private International Law' 60 *Louisiana Law Review* 1133.

Kahn-Freund, Otto (1966) 'Das soziale Ideal des Reichsarbeitsgerichts (1931)' in Thilo Ramm (ed), *Arbeitsrecht und Politik Quellentexte 1918–1933* (Neuwied, Luchterhand) 149.

—— (1974a) 'General Problems of private international law' (III) *Recueil des Cours* 139.

—— (1974b) 'On Use and Misuse of Comparative Law' 37 *Modern Law Review* 1.

Kaldor, Mary (2003) *Global Civil Society: An Answer to War* (Cambridge, Polity Press).

Kamminga, Menno (2005) 'The Evolving Status of NGOs under International Law: A Threat to the Inter-State System?' in Philip Alston (ed), *Non-state Actors and Human Rights* (Oxford/New York, Oxford University Press) 93–112.

Kaplan, Steven N (1997) 'Corporate Governance and Corporate Performance: A Comparison of Germany, Japan and the U.S.' in Klaus J Hopt and Eddy Wymeersch (eds), *Comparative Corporate Governance Essays and Materials* (Berlin/New York, Walter de Gruyter) 195–210.

Karamon, Martin C (1996) 'ADR on the Internet' 11 *Ohio State Journal on Dispute Resolution* 537.

Kasirer, Nicholas (1999) '*Lex*-icographie mercatoria' 47 *American Journal of Comparative Law* 653.

—— (2002) 'The Common Core of European Private Law in Boxes and Bundles' 10 *European Review of Private Law* 417.

Katsh, Ethan and Rifkin, Janet (2001) *Online Dispute Resolution: Resolving Conflicts in Cyberspace* (San Francisco).

Katsh, Ethan, Rifkin, Janet and Gaitenby, Alan (2000) 'E-Commerce, E-Disputes, and E-Dispute Resolution: In the Shadow of "eBay Law"' 15 *Ohio State Journal on Dispute Resolution* 705.

Kaufmann-Kohler, Gabrielle and Schultz, Thomas (2004) *Online Dispute Resolution: Challenges for Contemporary Justice*.

Kell, George (2003) 'The Global Compact. Origins, Operations, Progress, Challenges' 11 *Journal of Corporate Citizenship* 35.

Kelsen, Hans (1941) 'The Pure Theory of Law and Analytical Jurisprudence' 55 *Harvard Law Review* 44.

—— (1961) *General Theory of Law and State [1945]*, Wedberg (trans) (New York, Russell & Russell).

Kemmerer, Alexandra (2003) 'Constitutional Law as Work of Art—Experts' Eyes: Judges of the World Examine the Constitution of Europe' 4(8) *German Law Journal* 859.

Kennedy, David (1994) 'A New World Order: Yesterday, Today, and Tomorrow' 4 *Transnational Law and Contemporary Problems* 329.

—— (1997) 'New Approaches to Comparative Law: Comparativism and International Governance' *Utah Law Review* 545.

—— (2002) 'The International Human Rights Movement: Part of the Problem?' 15 *Harvard Human Rights Journal* 101.

—— (2005) 'Challenging Expert Rule: The Politics of Global Governance' 27 *Sydney Journal of International Law* 5.

—— (2009) 'The Mystery of Global Governance' in Jeffrey L. Dunoff and Joel P. Trachtman (eds) *Ruling the World? Constitutionalism, international law and global governance* (Cambridge, UK, Cambridge University Press), 37–68.

Kennedy, Duncan (1973) 'Legal Formality' 2 (June) *Journal of Legal Studies* 351.

—— (1975) *The Rise and Fall of Classical Legal Thought* (Washington DC, Beard Books).

—— (1982a) 'Distributive and Paternalist Motives in Contract and Tort Law, with Special Reference to Compulsory Terms and Unequal Bargaining Power' 41 *Maryland Law Review* 563.

—— (1982b) 'The Stages of the Decline of the Public/Private Distinction' 130 *University of Pennsylvania Law Review* 1349.

—— (2001a) 'Afterword: A Semiotics of Critique' 22 (March) *Cardozo Law Review* 1147.

—— (2001b) 'The Political Stakes in 'Merely Technical' Issues in Contract Law' 10 *European Review of Private Law* 7.

—— (2002) 'The Critique of Rights in Critical Legal Studies' in Wendy Brown and Janet Halley (eds), *Left Legalism/Left Critique* (Durham NC, Duke University Press) 178–228.

—— (2003) 'Two Globalizations of Law and Legal Thought: 1850–1968' 36 *Suffolk Law Review* 631.

—— (2006) 'Three Globalizations of Law and Legal Thought: 1850–2000' in David Trubek and Alvaro Santos (eds), *The New Law and Economic Development* (Cambridge, Cambridge University Press) 19–73.

Kerber, Wolfgang (2005) 'Applying Evolutionary Economics to Economic Policy: The Example of Competitive Federalism' in Kurt Dopfer (ed), *Economics, Evolution and the State: The Governance of Complexity* (Cheltenham, Edward Elgar) 296–324.

Kerr, Charles (1929) 'The Origin and Development of the Law Merchant' 15(4) *Virginia Law Review* 350.

Kerwer, Dieter (2005a) 'Holding Global Regulators Accountable: The Case of Credit Rating Agencies' 18(3) *Governance* 453.

—— (2005b) 'Rules that Many Use: Standards and Global Regulation' 18(4) *Governance: An International Journal of Policy, Administration, and Institutions* 611.

Kesan, Jay P and Gallo, Andres A (2005) 'The Market for Private Dispute Resolution Services—An Empirical Re-Assessment of ICANN-UDRP Performance' 11 *Michigan Telecommunications & Technology Law Review* 285.

Kessler, Friedrich (1973) 'Die soziale Funktion des Vertrages zugunsten Dritter' in Klaus Müller and Hermann Soell (eds), *Rechtswissenschaft und Gesetzgebung Festschrift für Eduard Wahl zum siebzigsten Geburtstag* (Heidelberg, Carl Winter Universitätsverlag) 81.

Kingsbury, Benedict and others (2005) 'Global Governance as Administration—National and Transnational Approaches to Global Administrative Law' 68 *Law & Contemporary Problems* 1.

Kinley, David and Tadaki, Junko (2004) 'From Walk to Talk: The Emergence of Human Rights Responsibilities for Corporations at International Law' 44 *Virginia Journal of International Law* 931.

Kirchhof, Ferdinand (1987) *Private Rechtsetzung* (Berlin, Duncker & Humblot).

Kirchhof, Paul (2000) 'Gesetzgebung und private Regelsetzung als Geltungsgrund für Rechnungslegungspflichten?' 29 *Zeitschrift für Unternehmensrecht* 681.

—— (2001) 'Demokratie ohne parlamentarische Gesetzgebung?' 54 *Neue Juristische Wochenschrift* 1332.

—— (2004) 'Das Parlament als Mitte der Demokratie' in Peter M. Huber, Michael Brenner and Markus Möstl (eds), *Der Staat des Grundgesetzes—Kontinuität und Wandel Festschrift für Peter Badura zum 70 Geburtstag* (Tübingen, Mohr Siebeck) 237–62.

Kirchner, Christian (2003) 'Shareholder Value: A New Standard for Company Conduct' in Klaus J Hopt and Eddy Wymeersch (eds), *Capital Markets and Company Law* (Oxford/New York, Oxford University Press) 341–54.

Kirchner, Christian and Painter, Richard W (2002) 'Takeover Defenses under Delaware Law, the Proposed Thirteenth EU Directive and the New German Takeover Law: Comparison and Recommendations for Reform' 50(3) *American Journal of Comparative Law* 451.

Kirton, John J and Trebilcock, Michael J (eds) (2004) *Hard Choices, Soft Law. Voluntary Standards in Global Trade, Environment and Social Governance* (Aldershot, Ashgate).

Klabbers, Jan (1998) 'The Undesirability of Soft Law' 67 *Nordic Journal of International Law* 381.

—— (2007) 'Reflections on Soft International Law in a Privatized World' www.helsinki.fi/eci/Publications/JKSoft_law_and_public.pdf.

—— (2009) 'The Bridge Crack'd: A Critical Look at Interdisciplinary Relations' 23 *International Relations* 119.

Klare, Karl E (1978) 'Judicial Deradicalization of the Wagner Act and the Origins of Modern Legal Consciousness, 1937–1941' 62 *Minnesota Law Review* 265.

Klöhn, Lars (2006) *Kapitalmarkt, Spekulation und Behavioral Finance. Eine interdisziplinäre und vergleichende Analyse zum Fluch und Segen der Spekulation und ihrer Regulierung durch Markt und Recht* (Berlin, Duncker & Humblot).

Knill, Christoph and Lehmkuhl, Dirk (2002) 'Private Actors and the State: Internationalization and Changing Patterns of Governance' 15(1) *Governance: An International Journal of Policy, Administration, and Institutions* 41.

Knop, Karen, Michaels, Ralf and Riles, Annelise (2008) 'Transdisciplinary Conflict of Laws: Introduction' 71 *Law & Contemporary Problems* 1.

Köck, Wolfgang (1995) 'Umweltschutzsichernde Betriebsorganisation als Gegenstand des Umweltrechts: Die EG-"Öko-Audit"-Verordnung' *Juristenzeitung* 643.

—— (1999) 'Grundzüge des Risikomanagements im Umweltrecht' in Alfons Bora (ed) *Rechtliches Risikomanagement Form, Funktion und Leistungsfähigkeit des Rechts in der Risikogesellschaft* (Berlin, Duncker & Humblot) 129.

Koh, Harold Hongju (1996) 'Transnational Legal Process' 75 *Nebraska Law Review* 181.

—— (1997) 'Why Do Nations Obey International Law?' 106 *Yale Law Journal* 2599.

—— (2006) 'Why Transnational Law Matters' 24 *Pennsylvania State International Law Review* 745.

Köndgen, Johannes (2006) 'Privatisierung des Rechts. *Private Governance* zwischen Deregulierung und Rekonstitutionalisierung' 206 *Archiv für die civilistische Praxis* 477.

Körner, Marita (2004) 'Comply or disclose—Erklärung nach § 161 AktG und Außenhaftung des Vorstands' *Neue Zeitschrift für Gesellschaftsrecht* 1148.

Korten, David C (1995) *When Corporations Rule the World* (San Francisco CA, Barrett-Koehler Publishers and Kumerian Press).

Koselleck, Reinhart (1979) '"Erfahrungsraum" und "Erfahrungshorizont"—zwei historische Kategorien (1975)' *R Koselleck, Vergangene Zukunft* (Frankfurt, Suhrkamp) 349.

—— (1981) 'Modernity and the Planes of Historicity' 10 *Economy and Society* 166.

—— (2000) 'Geschichte, Recht und Gerechtigkeit (1986)' *Zeitgeschichten Studien zur Historik* (Frankfurt, Suhrkamp) 336–58.

Koskenniemi, Martti (1999) 'Letter to the Editors of the Symposium' 93(2) *American Journal of International Law* 351.

—— (2002a) *The Gentle Civilizer of Nations: The Rise and Fall of International Law 1870–1960 (Hersch Lauterpacht Memorial Lectures)* (Cambridge, Cambridge University Press).

—— (2002b) '"The Lady Doth Protest Too Much". Kosovo, and the Turn to Ethics in International Law' 65 *Modern Law Review* 159.

—— (2005a) *From Apology to Utopia. The Structure of International Legal Argument (1989)* (Cambridge, Cambridge University Press).

—— (2005b) 'International Law in Europe: Between Tradition and Renewal' 16(1) *European Journal of International Law* 113.

—— (2007) 'The Fate of Public International Law: Between Technique and Politics' 70(1) *Modern Law Review* 1.

Koskenniemi, Martti and Leino, Paivi (2002) 'Fragmentation of International Law? Postmodern Anxieties' 15 *Leiden Journal of International Law* 553.

Kraakman, Reinier and others (2004) *The Anatomy of Corporate Law. A Comparative and Functional Approach* (Oxford/New York, Oxford University Press).

Krasner, Stephen D (ed) (2001) *International Regimes* (Ithaca NY, Cornell University Press).

Krause, William (2001) 'Do You Want to Step Outside? An Overview of Online Alternative Dispute Resolution' 19 *John Marshall Journal of Computer & Information Law* 457.

Kreide, Regina (2008) 'Transnational Governance and Human Rights: The Obligations of Private Actors in the Global Context' in Christian Joerges and Poul F Kjaer (eds), *Transnational Standards of Social Protection Contrasting European and International Governance* (Oslo, ARENA Centre for European Studies) 133–56.

—— (2009) 'The Ambivalence of Juridification. On Legitimate Governance in the International Context' 2 *Global Justice: Theory Practice Rhetoric* 18.

Kreitner, Roy (2005) 'Frameworks of Cooperation: Competing, Conflicting, and Joined Interests in Contract and its Surroundings' 6 *Theoretical Inquiries in Law* 59.

—— (2007) *Calculating Promises. The Emergence of Modern American Contract Doctrine* (Stanford CA, Stanford University Press).

Krisch, Nico (2005) 'International Law in Times of Hegemony: Unequal Power and the Shaping of the International Legal Order' 16(3) *European Journal of International Law* 369.

—— (2006) 'The Pluralism of Global Administrative Law' 17 *European Journal of International Law* 247.

—— (2009) 'Global Administrative Law and the Constitutional Ambition' *LSE Law, Society and Economy Working Papers 10/2009*: ssrn.com/abstract=1344788.

Krisch, Nico, Kingsbury, Benedict and Stewart, Richard B (2005) 'The Emergence of Global Administrative Law' 68 *Law and Contemporary Problems* 15.

Kronke, Herbert (2000) 'International Uniform Commercial Law Conventions: Advantages, Disadvantages, Criteria for Choice' 5 *Uniform Law Review* 13.

—— (2003) 'UNIDROIT 75th Anniversary Congress on Worldwide Harmonisation of Private Law and Regional Economic Integration: Hypotheses, Certainties and Open Questions' 8 *Uniform Law Review* 10.

—— (2005) 'Methodical Freedom and Organizational Constraints in the Development of Transnational Commercial Law' 51 *Loyola Law Review* 287.

Kronman, Anthony T (1980) 'Contract Law and Distributive Justice' 89 *Yale Law Journal* 472.

Kronstein, Heinrich (1952) 'The Nationality of International Enterprises' 52(8) *Columbia Law Review* 983.

Krugman, Paul (1992) *Geography and Trade* (Cambridge MA, MIT Press).

—— (1998) 'What's new about the new economic geography?' 14(2) *Oxford Review of Economics & Politics* 7.

—— (2008) *The Return of Depression Economics and the Crisis of 2008* (New York & London, Norton).

Kübler, Friedrich (1994) 'Institutional Investors and Corporate Governance: A German Perspective' in Theodor Baums, Richard Buxbaum and Klaus J Hopt (eds), *Institutional Investors and Corporate Governance* (Berlin/New York, Walter de Gruyter) 565–79.

—— (2001) 'The Impact of Equity Markets on Business Organization: Some Comparative Observations Regarding Differences in the Evolution of Corporate Structures' 2 *European Business Organization Law Review* 669.

—— (2003) 'The Rules of Capital Under Pressure of the Securities Markets' in Klaus J Hopt and Eddy Wymeersch (eds), *Capital Markets and Company Law* (Oxford/New York, Oxford University Press) 95–114.

Kumpfmüller, Michael (2008) *Nachricht an alle* (Köln, Kiepenheuer & Witsch).

Kymlicka, Will (2007) *Multicultural Odysseys: Navigating the New International Politics of Diversity* (Oxford/New York, Oxford University Press).

La Porta, Rafael, Lopez-de-Silanes, Florencio and Shleifer, Andrei (2008) 'The economic consequences of legal origins' 46(2) *Journal of Economic Literature* 285.

La Porta, Rafael and others (1998) 'Law and finance' 106 *Journal of Political Economy* 1113.

Lachs, Manfred (1972) 'Some Reflections on Substance and Form in International Law' in Wolfgang Friedmann, Louis Henkin and Oliver Lissitzyn (eds), *Transnational Law in a Changing Society* (New York, Columbia University Press) 99–112.

Ladeur, Karl-Heinz (1983) '"Abwägung"—ein neues Rechtsparadigma? Von der Einheit der Rechtsordnung zur Pluralität der Rechtsdiskurse' 69 *Archiv für Rechts- und Sozialphilosophie* 463.

—— (1992) *Postmoderne Rechtstheorie* (Berlin, Duncker & Humblot).

—— (1994) 'Subjektive Rechte und Theorie der Prozeduralisierung: Vom Universalismus des Rechts zur rechtlichen Modellbildung unter Ungewißheitsbedingungen' 40(1) *Kritische Justiz* 42.

—— (1995) *Das Umweltrecht der Wissensgesellschaft* (Berlin, Duncker & Humblot).

—— (1997a) 'Die Prozeduralisierung des Unternehmens' in Dieter Hart (ed), *Privatrecht im "Risikostaat"* (Baden-Baden, Nomos) 137–54.

—— (1997b) 'Towards a Legal Theory of Supranationality—The Viability of the Network Concept' 3(1) *European Law Journal* 33.

—— (1999) 'The Theory of Autopoiesis as an Approach to a Better Understanding of Postmodern Law' *EUI Working Paper Law No 99/3*.

—— (2000a) 'Die rechtswissenschaftliche Methodendiskussion und die Bewältigung des gesellschaftlichen Wandels' 64 *Rabels Zeitschrift für Ausländisches und Internationales Privatrecht* 60.

—— (2000b) *Negative Freiheitsrechte und gesellschaftliche Selbstorganisation* (Tübingen, Mohr Siebeck).

—— (2000c) 'Privatisierung öffentlicher Aufgaben und die Notwendigkeit der Entwicklung eines neuen Informationsverwaltungsrechts' in Wolfgang Hoffmann-Riem and Eberhard Schmidt-Assmann (eds) *Verwaltungsrecht in der Informationsgesellschaft* (Baden-Baden, Schriften zur Reform des Verwaltungsrechts, Nomos) 225–56.

—— (2001a) 'Die Regulierung von Selbstregulierung und die Herausbildung einer "Logik der Netzwerke"' *Regulierte Selbstregulierung als Steuerungskonzept des Gewährleistungsstaates (Die Verwaltung, Beiheft 4)* 59.

—— (2001b) 'Die Regulierung von Selbstregulierung und die Herausbildung einer "Logik der Netzwerke"' *(Die Verwaltung, Beiheft 4)* 59.

—— (2004a) 'Globalization and Public Governance—A Contradiction?' in Karl-Heinz Ladeur (ed), *Public Governance in the Age of Globalization* (Aldershot, Ashgate) 1.

—— (2004b) 'Globalization and the Conversion of Democracy to Polycentric Networks: Can Democracy Survive the End of the Nation-State?' in Karl-Heinz Ladeur (ed), *Public Governance in the Age of Globalization* (Aldershot, Ashgate) 89.

—— (2006) *Der Staat gegen die Gesellschaft* (Tübingen, Mohr Siebeck).

—— (2007) 'The Role of Contracts and Networks in Public Governance: The Importance of the "Social Epistemology" of Decision-Making' 14(2) *Indiana Journal of Global Legal Studies* 329.

—— (2008) 'Das subjektive Recht und der Wunsch nach Gerechtigkeit als sein Parasit' 29(1) *Zeitschrift für Rechtssoziologie* 109.

—— (2009) 'Der Staat der "Gesellschaft der Netzwerke". Zur Notwendigkeit der Fortentwicklung des Paradigmas des "Gewährleistungsstaates"' 48(2) *Der Staat* 163.

Landis, James W (1938) *The Administrative Process* (New Haven CT, Yale University Press).

Lando, Ole (1998) 'The Common Core of European Private Law and the Principles of European Contract Law' 21 *Hastings International and Comparative Law Review* 809.

—— (2001) 'Salient Features of the Principles of European Contract Law: A Comparison with the UCC' 13 *Pace International Law Review* 339.

Langille, Brian A (2005) 'Core Labour Rights—The True Story (Reply to Alston)' 16(3) *European Journal of International Law* 409.

Lasswell, Harold D and McDougal, Myres (1992) Jurisprudence for a Free Society: Studies in Law, Science and Policy (Dordrecht, Martinus Nijhoff).

Lazer, David (2005) 'Regulatory Capitalism as a Networked Order: The International System as an Informational Network' 598 *Annals of the American Academy of Political and Social Science* 52.

Lazonick, William (2007) 'Varieties of Capitalism and Innovative Enterprise' 24 *Comparative Social Research* 21.

Lazonick, William and O'Sullivan, Mary (2002) 'Maximizing Shareholder Value: A New Ideology for Corporate Governance' in William Lazonick and Mary O'Sullivan (eds), *Corporate Governance and Sustainable Prosperity* (London, Palgrave Macmillan) 11–36.

Leeson, Peter T (2006) 'Cooperation and Conflict, Evidence on Self-Enforcing Arrangements and Heterogeneous Groups' 65(4) *American Journal of Economics & Sociology* 891.

—— (2008) 'How Important is State Enforcement For Trade?' 10(1) *American Law and Economics Review* 61.

Legrand, Pierre (2009) 'Comparative Legal Studies and the Matter of Authenticity' 1(2) *Journal of Comparative Law* 365.

Leibfried, Stephan and others (2006) 'Redefining the Traditional Pillars of German Legal Studies and Setting the Stage for Contemporary Interdisciplinary Research' 7(8) *German Law Journal* 661.

Leibfried, Stephan and Zürn, Michael (eds) (2005) *Transformations of the State?* (Cambridge, Cambridge University Press).

Lessig, Lawrence (1998) 'The New Chicago School' 27(2) *Journal of Legal Studies* 661.

—— (1999a) *Code and other Laws of Cyberspace* (New York, Basic Books).

—— (1999b) 'The limits in open code: regulatory standards and the future of the net' 14(2) *Berkeley Technology Law Journal* 759.

—— (2005) 'Commons on the Wires' in John Hartley (ed) *Creative Industries* (Malden MA/Oxford, Blackwell) 55–69.

Levi-Faur, David (2005) 'The Global Diffusion of Regulatory Capitalism' 598 *The Annals of The American Academy of Political and Social Science* 12.

Levit, Janet Koven (2007a) 'Bottom-Up International Lawmaking: Reflections on the New Haven School of International Law' 32 *Yale Journal of International Law* 393.

—— (2007b) 'Bottom-Up Lawmaking through a Pluralist Lens: The ICC Banking Commission and the Transnational Regulation of Letters of Credit' 57 *Emory Law Journal* 1147.

—— (2008) 'Bottom-Up Lawmaking: The Private Origins of Transnational Law' 15(1) *Indiana Journal of Global Legal Studies* 49.

Levy, Jonah D. (2006) 'The State Also Rises: The Roots of Contemporary State Activism' in Jonah D. Levy (ed), *The State after Statism New State Activities in the Age of Liberalization* (Cambridge MA/London, Harvard University Press) 1–28.

Leyens, Patrick C (2005) 'German Company Law: Recent Developments and Future Challenges' 6 *German Law Journal* 1407.

Licht, Amir N (2001) 'The Mother of all Path-Dependencies: Towards a Cross-Cultural Theory of Corporate Governance Systems' 26 *Delaware Journal of Corporate Law* 147.

Lie, John (1997) 'Sociology of markets' 23 *Annual Review of Sociology* 341.

Llewellyn, Karl (1930) 'What Price Contract?—An Essay in Perspective' 40 *Yale Law Journal* 704.

Lobel, Orly (2004) 'The Renew Deal: The Fall of Regulation and the Rise of Governance in Contemporary Legal Thought' 89 *Minnesota Law Review* 342.

—— (2007) 'The Paradox of Extralegal Activism: Critical Legal Consciousness and Transformative Politics' 120 *Harvard Law Review* 937.

Lodder, Arno and Thiessen, Ernest (2003) 'The Role of Artificial Intelligence in Online Dispute Resolution' in Ethan Katsh and Daewon Choi (eds), *Online Dispute Resolution (ODR), Papers and Proceedings of the 2003 United Nations*

Forum on ODR (Geneva, University of Massachusetts Amherst, Center for Information Technology and Dispute Resolution): www.odr.info/unece2003/pdf/lodder_thiessen.pdf.

Lombardo, Stefano (2002) *Regulatory Competition in Company Law in the European Community. Prerequisites and Limits* (Frankfurt et al, Peter Lang).

Luhmann, Niklas (1970) 'Die Weltgesellschaft' 57 *Archiv für Rechts- und Sozialphilosophie* 1.

—— (1981) *Politische Theorie im Wohlfahrtsstaat* (München, Olzog).

—— (1982) 'The World Society as a Social System' 8 *International Journal of General Systems* 131.

—— (1985) *A Sociological Theory of Law* (London, Routledge Kegan & Paul).

—— (1989a) 'Law as a Social System' 83 *Northwestern University Law Review* 136.

—— (1989b) 'Verfassung als evolutionäre Errungenschaft' 9 *Rechtshistorisches Journal* 176.

—— (1990) *Political Theory in the Welfare State* [1981], John Bednarz Jr (trans) (Berlin/New York, Walter de Gruyter).

—— (1992a) 'Operational closure and structural coupling: the differentiation of the legal system' 13 *Cardozo Law Review* 1419.

—— (1992b) 'Some Problems with Reflexive Law' in Gunther Teubner and Alberto Febbrajo (eds), *State, Law and Economy as Autopoietic Systems* (Berlin & New York, Walter de Gruyter) 389–412.

—— (1997) *Die Gesellschaft der Gesellschaft* (Frankfurt, Suhrkamp).

—— (2004) *Law as a Social System*, K Ziegert (trans), F Kastner, D Schiff, R Nobles, R Ziegert (eds) (Oxford/New York, Oxford University Press).

Lutter, Marcus (2001) 'Vergleichende Corporate Governance—Die deutsche Sicht' 30 *European Company Law Review* 224.

—— (2002) 'Die Kontrolle der gesellschaftsrechtlichen Organe: Corporate Governance—ein internationales Thema' 24 *Jura* 83.

—— (2006) 'Aktienrechtliche Aspekte der angemessenen Vorstandsvergütung' 27 *Zeitschrift für Wirtschaftsrecht* 733.

Ly, Filip De (2001) 'Lex Mercatoria (New Law Merchant): Globalisation and International Self-Regulation' in Volkmar Gessner, Richard P Appelbaum and William F Felstiner (eds), *Rules and Networks The Legal Culture of Global Business Transactions* (Oxford/Portland OR, Hart Publishing) 159–88.

Macaulay, Stewart (1963) 'Non-contractual Relations in Business: A Preliminary Study' 28 *American Sociological Review* 55.

—— (1986) 'Private Government' in Leon Lipson and Stanton Wheeler (eds), *Law and the Social Sciences* (Washington DC, Russell Sage) 445–518.

—— (2000) 'Relational Contracts Floating on a Sea of Custom? Thoughts about the Ideas of Ian Macneil and Lisa Bernstein' 94(3) *Northwestern University Law Review* 775.

Macload-Cullinane, Barry (1995) 'Lon L. Fuller and the Enterprise of Law' (22) *Legal Notes*: www.libertarian.co.uk/lapubs/legan/legan022.pdf.

Macneil, Ian R (1980) *The New Social Contract. An Inquiry into Modern Contractual Relations* (New Haven CT/London, Yale University Press).

—— (1985) 'Relational Contract: What we do and what we do not know' *Wisconsin Law Review* 483.

—— (2000) 'Contracting Worlds and Essential Contract Theory' 9(3) *Social & Legal Studies* 431.

Macpherson, Crawford Brough (1965) *The Political Theory of Possessive Individualism. Hobbes to Locke* [1962] (Oxford, Oxford Clarendon Press).

—— (1987) 'The Rise and Fall of Economic Justice' in Macpherson, *The Rise and Fall of Economic Justice, and other Essays. The role of state, class and property in twentieth-century democracy* (Toronto, University of Toronto Press) 1.

Maine, Henry Sumner (1861) *Ancient Law. Its connection with the early history of society, and its relation to modern ideas* (London, John Murray).

Majone, Giandomenico (2005) *Dilemmas of European Integration: The Ambiguities and Pitfalls of Integration by Stealth* (Oxford, Oxford University Press).

Mallin, Christine (2005) *Corporate Governance* (Oxford/New York, Oxford University Press).

Mandeville, Bernard de (1970) *The Fable of the Bees* [1714], edited with an introduction by Philip Barth (London, Penguin).

Mankowski, Peter (2004) 'Stillschweigende Rechtswahl und wählbares Recht' in Stefan Leible (ed), *Das Grünbuch zum Internationalen Vertragsrecht* (München, Sellier) 63.

Manne, Henry (1965) 'Mergers and the Market for Corporate Control' 73 *Journal of Political Economy* 110.

Marazzi, Christian (2009) *The Violence of Financial Capitalism* (Cambridge, MA, Semiotext(e))

Markesinis, Basil and Unberath, Hannes (2002) *The German Law of Torts*, 5th edn (Oxford/Portland OR, Hart Publishing).

Marks, Susan (2006) 'Naming Global Administrative Law' 37 *New York University Journal of International Law and Politics* 995.

Marx, Karl (1988) *The Economic and Philosophic Manuscripts of 1844* (Amherst, NY, Prometheus Books).

Marx, Karl and Engels, Friedrich (1848) *Das kommunistische Manifest* (Berlin, Dietz).

Mattei, Ugo and Nicola, Fernanda (2006) 'A "Social Dimension" in European Private Law? The Call for Setting a Progressive Agenda' 41(1) *New England Law Review* 1.

Matten, Dirk and Moon, Jeremy (2008) '"Implicit" and "Explicit" CSR—A conceptual framework for a comparative understanding of corporate social responsibility' 33(2) *Academy of Management Review* 404.

Mattli, Walter (2003) 'Public and Private Governance in Setting International Accounting Standards' in Miles Kahler and David Lake (eds), *Governance in a Global Economy* (Princeton NJ, Princeton University Press) 199–225.

Mattli, Walter and Büthe, Tim (2003) 'Setting International Standards: Technological Rationality or Primacy of Power?' 56(1) *World Politics* 1.

—— (2005) 'Global Private Governance: Lessons from a National Model of Setting Standards in Accounting' 68 *Law & Contemporary Problems* 225.

Maurer, Andreas (2007) 'Consumer Protection and Social Models of Continental and Anglo-American Contract Law and the Transnational Outlook' 14(2) *Indiana Journal of Global Legal Studies* 353.

Mayer-Schönberger, Viktor (2002) 'Governing Networks: Telecommunication Deregulation in Europe and the United States' 27 *Brooklyn Journal of International Law* 819.

Mayer-Schönberger, Viktor and Ziewitz, Malte (2007) 'Jefferson Rebuffed: The United States and the Future of Internet Governance' 8 *Columbia Science and Technology Law Review* 188.

Mayntz, Renate (2006) 'From government to governance: Political steering in modern societies' in Dirk Scheer and Frieder Rubik (eds), *Governance of Integrated Product Policy* (Aizlewood Mill, Greenleaf Publishing) 18–25.

McAdams, Richard H (1997) 'The Origin, Development, and Regulation of Norms' 96 *Michigan Law Review* 338.

McCahery, Joseph A and others (eds) (2002) *Corporate Governance Regimes. Convergence and Diversity* (Oxford/New York, Oxford University Press).

McDougal, Myres (1960) *Studies in World Public Order.*

McDougal, Myres and Lasswell, Harold D (1959) 'The Identification and Appraisal of Diverse Systems of Public Order' 53 *American Journal of International Law* 1.

McInerney, Thomas (2007) 'Putting Regulation Before Responsibility: Towards Binding Norms of Corporate Social Responsibility' 40 *Cornell International Law Journal* 171.

McMillan, John and Woodruff, Christopher (2000) 'Private Order under Dysfunctional Public Order' 98 *Michigan Law Review* 2421.

Meder, Stephan (2008) *Ius non scriptum—Traditionen privater Rechtssetzung* (Tübingen, Mohr Siebeck).

Meidinger, Erroll (2006) 'The Administrative Law of Global Private-Public Regulation: the Case of Forestry' 17 *European Journal of International Law* 47.

Menger, Anton (1968) *Das Bürgerliche Recht und die besitzlosen Volksklassen (1890)* (Darmstadt, Wissenschaftliche Buchgesellschaft).

Merkt, Hanno (2003) 'Zum Verhältnis von Kapitalmarktrecht und Gesellschaftsrecht in der Diskussion um die Corporate Governance' 48 *Die Aktiengesellchaft* 126.

Merry, Sally Engle (1988) 'Legal Pluralism' 22(5) *Law & Society Review* 869.

—— (1992) 'Anthropology, Law, and Transnational Processes' 21 *Annual Review of Anthropology* 357.

—— (2006) 'New Legal Realism and the Ethnography of Transnational Law' 31(4) *Law & Social Inquiry* 975.

Merryman, John Henry (1969) *The Civil Law Tradition. An Introduction to the Legal Systems of Western Europe and Latin America* (Stanford CA, Stanford University Press).

Mertz, Elizabeth (2006) 'An Afterword: Tapping the Promise of Relational Contract Theory—'Real' Legal Language and a New Legal Realism' 94 *Northwestern University Law Review* 909.

—— (2007) 'Inside the Law School Classroom: Toward a New Legal Realist Pedagogy' 60 *Vanderbilt Law Review* 483.

Mestmäcker, Ernst-Joachim (1995) 'Wirtschaftsordnung und Geschichtsgesetz' in Red. Ludwig-Erhard Stiftung Martin Lambert (ed), *Wirtschaftsordnung als Aufgabe Zum 100 Geburtstag von Franz Böhm* (Krefeld, Sinus-Verlag) 111–36.

—— (2000) 'Marktversagen und Staatsversagen in der Europäischen Union' in Stefan Grundmann (ed), *Systembildung und Systemlücken in Kerngebieten des Europäischen Privatrechts* (Tübingen, Mohr Siebeck) 53–65.

Meyer, John W and others (1997) 'World Society and the Nation-State' 103(1) *American Journal of Sociology* 144.

Michaels, Ralf (2004) 'Territorial Jurisdiction after Territoriality' in Jan Pieter Slot and Mielle Bulterman (eds), *Globalisation and Jurisdiction* (The Hague, Kluwer Law International) 105–30.

—— (2005) 'The Re-State-Ment of Non-State Law: The State, Choice of Law, and the Challenge from Global Legal Pluralism' 51 *Wayne Law Review* 1209.

—— (2006) 'The Functional Method in Comparative Law' in Mathias Reimann and Reinhard Zimmermann (eds), *Oxford Handbook of Comparative Law* (Oxford/ New York, Oxford University Press) 339–82.

—— (2007a) 'The True New Lex Mercatoria: Law Beyond the State' 14 *Indiana Journal of Global Legal Studies* 447.

—— (2007b) 'Two Paradigms of Jurisdiction' 27 *Michigan Journal of International Law* 1003.

—— (2009a) 'Comparative Law by Numbers? Legal Origins Thesis, Doing Business Reports, and the Silence of Traditional Comparative Law' 57 *American Journal of Comparative Law* 765.

—— (2009b) 'Global Legal Pluralism', *Duke Public Law & Legal Theory Research Paper No 259*: papers.ssrn.com/sol3/papers.cfm?abstract_id=1430395.

Michaels, Ralf and Jansen, Nils (2007) 'Private Law Beyond the State? Europeanization, Globalization, Privatization' 55 *American Journal of Comparative Law* 843.

Milgrom, Paul R, North, Douglass C and Weingast, Barry W (1990) 'The Role of Institutions in the Revival of Trade: The Law Merchant, Private Judges and the Champagne Fairs' 2 *Economics & Politics* 1.

Milhaupt, Curtis J and West, Mark D (2000) 'The Dark Side of Private Ordering: An Institutional and Empirical Analysis of Organized Crime' 67 *University of Chicago Law Review* 41.

Millon, David (1990) 'Theories of the Corporation' *Duke Law Journal* 201.

Mnookin, Robert H and Kornhauser, Lewis (1979) 'Bargaining in the Shadow of the Law: The Case of Divorce' 88 *Yale Law Journal* 950.

Mokyr, Joel (2005) 'The Knowledge Society: Theoretical and Historical Underpinnings': facultywcasnorthwesternedu/~jmokyr/UnitednationsPDF.

Möllers, Christoph (2006) 'European Governance: Meaning and Value of a Concept' 43 *Common Market Law Review* 313.

Moloney, Niamh (2003) 'New Frontiers in EC Capital Markets Law: From Market Construction to Market Regulation' 40(4) *Common Market Law Review* 809.

Moore, Sally Falk (1973) 'Law and Social Change: the semi-autonomous field as an appropriate subject of study' 7 *Law & Society Review* 719.

Moravcsik, Andrew (1997) 'Taking Preferences Seriously: A Liberal Theory of International Politics' 51(4) *International Organization* 513.

—— (2004) 'Is there a Democratic Deficit in World Politics?' 39 *Government and Opposition* 336.

Morgan, Bronwen (2003) 'The economization of politics: Meta-regulation as a form of nonjudicial legality' 12(4) *Social & Legal Studies* 489.

Morgenthau, Hans J (1940) 'Positivism, Functionalism, and International Law' 34 *American Journal of International Law* 260.

Muchlinski, Peter (2007) *Multinational Enterprises and the Law*, 2nd edn (Oxford, Oxford University Press).

Muchlinski, Peter T (1997) '"Global Bukowina" Examined: Viewing the Multinational Enterprise as a Transnational Law-making Community' in Gunther Teubner (ed), *Global Law Without A State* (Dartmouth, Aldershot) 79–108.

Muir-Watt, Horatia (2006) 'Integration and Diversity: The Conflict of law as a Regulatory Tool' in Fabrizio Cafaggi (ed), *The Institutional Framework of European Private Law* (Oxford, Oxford University Press) 107–48.

Müller, Till (2008) 'Customary Transnational Law: Attacking the Last Resort of State Sovereignty' 15(1) *Indiana Journal of Global Legal Studies* 19.

Murphy, Sean D (2005) 'Taking Multinational Corporate Codes Of Conduct To The Next Level' 43 *Columbia Journal of Transnational Law* 389.

Murray, Jill (1998) 'Corporate Codes of Conduct and Labour Standards' *ILO Publication* at: www.itcilo.it/english/actrav/telearn/global/ilo/guide/jill.htm.

Mustill, Lord Justice (1987) 'The New *Lex Mercatoria*: The First Twenty-Five Years' in Maarten Bos and Ian Brownlie (eds), *Liber Amicorum for the Rt Hon Lord Wilberforce* (Oxford, Clarendon Press) 149–83.

Mutua, Makau (2002) *Human Rights: A Political and Cultural Critique* (Philadelphia PA, University of Pennsylvania Press).

—— (1995) 'The Ideology of Human Rights' 36 *Virginia Journal of International Law* 589.

Nader, Ralph, Green, Mark and Seligman, Joel (1974) *Corporate Power in America* (New York, Norton).

Nagy, Rosemary (2010) 'Transitional Justice as Global Project: Critical Reflections' in Peer Zumbansen & Ruth Buchanan (eds) *Human Rights, Development and Transitional Justice: A Reader* (Oxford/Portland, OR, Hart Publishing), *forthcoming*.

Nahamowitz, Peter (1985) '"Reflexives Recht": Das unmögliche Ideal eines post-interventionistischen Steuerungskonzepts' 6(1) *Zeitschrift für Rechtssoziologie* 29.

Nee, Victor and Swedberg, Richard (2005a) 'Economic Sociology and New Institutional Economics' in Claude Ménard and Mary M Shirley (eds), *Handbook of New Institutional Economics* (Heidelberg, Springer) 789–818.

—— (eds) (2005b) *The Economic Sociology of Capitalism* (Princeton NJ, Princeton University Press).

Nelson, Richard (2006) 'Economic Development From the Perspective of Evolutionary Economic Theory' *Working Papers in Technology Governance and Economic Dynamics no 2*, available at: hum.ttu.ee/wp/paper2.pdf.

Neumann, Volker (1981) 'Verfassungstheorien politischer Antipoden: Otto Kirchheimer und Carl Schmitt' 14 *Kritische Justiz* 235.

Neves, Marcelo (2001) 'From the Autopoiesis to the Allopoiesis of Law' 28 *Journal of Law and Society* 242.

—— (2007) 'Grenzen der Autonomie des Rechts in einer asymmetrischen Weltgesellschaft: Von Luhmann zu Kelsen' 93 *Archiv für Rechts- und Sozialphilosophie* 363.

—— (2009) 'Transversale Verfassungen? Konstitutionalismus: Vom Staat zur Weltgesellschaft' in Hauke Brunkhorst (ed), *Soziale Welt (Sonderband 18): Demokratie in der Weltgesellschaft* (Baden-Baden, Nomos) 75–97.

Nicola, Fernanda (2008) 'Transatlanticism: Constitutional Asymmetry and Selective Reception of U.S. Law and Economics in the Formation of European Private Law' 16 *Cardozo Journal of International and Comparative Law* 101.

Nicolaidis, Kalypso and Shaffer, Gregory (2005) 'Transnational Mutual Recognition Regimes: Governance without Global Government' 68 *Law & Contemporary Problems* 263.

Nilsen, André (2004) 'The EU Takeover Directive and the Competitiveness of European Industry' *The Oxford Council on Good Governance* www.oxfordgovernance.org/fileadmin/Publications/EY001.pdf.

Noack, Ulrich (2002) 'Neuerungen im Recht der Hauptversammlung durch das Transparenz- und Publizitätsgesetz und den Deutschen Corporate Governance Kodex' 55 *Der Betrieb* 620.

Noack, Ulrich and Zetzsche, Dirk (2005) 'Corporate Governance in Germany: The Second Decade', *Center for Business & Corporate Law (CBC) Research Paper Series WP No 0010* [ssrn.com/abstract=646761].

Noack, Ulrich and Zetzsche, Dirk A (2007) 'Germany's Corporate and Financial Law 2007: (Getting) Ready for Competition' *CBC Research Paper Series WP No 0028* [ssrn.com/abstract=986357].

Nolte, Georg (2008) 'Kulturelle Vielfalt als Herausforderung für das Völkerrecht' in Georg Nolte, Helen Keller, Armin von Bogdandy, Heinz-Peter Mansel, Andrea Büchler and Christian Walter (eds), *Pluralistische Gesellschaften und Internationales Recht* (Heidelberg, CF Müller) 1–37.

Nonet, Philippe and Selznick, Philip (1978) *Law and Society in Transition. Toward Responsive Law* (New York, Octagon Books).

Nordquist, Fredrik, Andersson, Fredrik and Dzepina, Eva N (2002) 'Trusting the Trustmark?, 17th BILETA Annual Conference': www.bileta.ac.uk/Document%20Library/1/Trusting%20the%20Trustmark.pdf.

North, Douglass C (1990) *Institutions, Institutional Change and Economic Performance* (Cambridge, Cambridge University Press).

—— (1991) 'Institutions' 5(1) *Journal of Economic Perspectives* 97.

—— (2005) *Understanding the Process of Economic Change* (Princeton NJ/Oxford, Princeton University Press).

Nowrot, Karsten (1999) 'Legal Consequences of Globalization: The Status of Non-Governmental Organizations under International Law' 6 *Indiana Journal of Global Legal Studies* 579.

Nye, Joseph S and Donahue, John D (eds) (2000) *Governance in a Globalizing World* (Washington DC, Brookings).

O'Hara, Erin A and Ribstein, Larry E (2008) 'Rules and Institutions in Developing a Law Market: Views from the U.S. and Europe' 82 *Tulane Law Review* 2147.

—— (2009) *The Law Market* (Oxford, Oxford University Press).

O'Sullivan, Mary (2003) 'The political economy of comparative corporate governance' 10(1) *Review of International Politics and Economics* 23.

Ochoa, Christiana (2008) 'The Relationship of Participatory Democracy to Participatory Law Formation' 15(1) *Indiana Journal of Global Legal Studies* 5.

Oetker, Hartmut (1994) *Das Dauerschuldverhältnis und seine Beendigung* (Tübingen, Siebeck Mohr).

Okafor, Obiora (2007) *The African Human Rights System, Activist Forces and International Institutions* (Cambridge, Cambridge University Press).

Oliver, Dawn (1997) 'The Underlying Values of Public and Private Law' in Michael Taggart (ed), *The Province of Administrative Law* (Oxford/Portland OR, Hart Publishing) 217–42.

Omarova, Saule (2009) 'Risks, Rules, and Institutions: A Process for Reforming Financial Regulation' 39 *University of Memphis Law Review* 881.

Orts, Eric (1995) 'Reflexive Environmental Law' 89 *Northwestern University Law Review* 1227.

Oser, Peter, Orth, Christian and Wader, Dominic (2003) 'Die Umsetzung des Deutschen Corporate Governance Kodex in der Praxis' 56 *Der Betrieb* 1337.

Ossenbühl, Fritz (2000) *Die Not des Gesetzgebers im naturwissenschaftlich-technischen Zeitalter* (Opladen, Nordrhein-Westfälische Akademie der Wissenschaften, Westdeutscher Verlag).

Osterhammel, Jürgen and Petersson, Niels P (2004) *Globalization: A Short History* (Princeton NJ/Oxford, Princeton University Press).

Pahuja, Sundhya (2008) 'Rights as Regulation: The Integration of Development and Human Rights' in Bronwyn Morgan (ed), *The Intersection of Rights and Regulation* (London, Ashgate) 167–91.

Panther, Stephan (2000) 'Non-Legal Sanctions' in Boudewijn Bouckaert and Gerrit De Geest (eds), *Encyclopedia of Law and Economics Vol I* (Cheltenham, Edward Elgar): encyclo.findlaw.com/0780book.pdf.

Parker, Christine (2007) 'Meta-Regulation: Legal Accountability to Corporate Social Responsibility' in Doreen McBarnet, Aurora Voiculescu and Tom Campbell (eds), *The New Corporate Accountability: Corporate Social Responsibility and the Law* (Cambridge, Cambridge University Press) 207–38.

Parker, Christine and Braithwaite, John (2003) 'Regulation' in Peter Cane and Mark Tushnet (eds), *The Oxford Handbook of Legal Studies* (Oxford/New York, Oxford University Press) 119–45.

Partnoy, Frank (2007) 'Financial Innovation and Corporate Law' *University of San Diego Legal Studies Research Paper No 07-89*: ssrn.com/abstract=976931.

Paterson, John (2009) 'Reflexive Law: challenges and choices' in Gralf-Peter Calliess, Andreas Fischer-Lescano, Dan Wielsch and Peer Zumbansen (eds), *Soziologische Jurisprudenz Festschrift für Gunther Teubner zum 65 Geburtstag* (Berlin & New York, Walter de Gruyter), 503–16.

Paulus, Andreas L (2004) 'The War Against Iraq and the Future of International Law: Hegemony or Pluralism?' 25 *Michigan Journal of International Law* 691.

Pauwelyn, Joost (2006) 'Non-Traditional Patterns of Global Regulation: Is the WTO 'Missing the Boat'?' in Christian Joerges and Ernst-Ulrich Petersmann (eds), *Constitutionalism, Multilevel Trade Governance and Social Regulation* (Oxford/Portland OR, Hart Publishing) 199–227.

Peet, Richard (2009) *Unholy Trinity. The IMF, Worldbank and WTO* 2nd edn (London & New York, Zed Books).

Peltzer, Martin (2002a) 'Corporate Governance Codices als zusätzliche Pflichtenbestimmung für den Aufsichtsrat' 5 *Neue Zeitschrift für Gesellschaftsrecht* 10.

—— (2002b) 'Handlungsbedarf in Sachen Corporate Governance' *Neue Zeitschrift für Gesellschaftsrecht* 593.

Perez, Oren (2003) 'Normative Creativity and Global Legal Pluralism: Reflections on the Democratic Critique of Transnational Law' 10 *Indiana Journal of Global Legal Studies* 25.

Perritt Jr, Henry H (2000a) 'Dispute Resolution in Cyberspace: Demand for New Forms of ADR' 15 *Ohio State Journal on Dispute Resolution* 675.

—— (2000b) 'The Internet is changing the Public International Legal System' 88 *Kentucky Law Review* 885.

Pestre, Dominique (2007) 'Science, Society and Politics. Knowledge Societies from Historical Perspective' *Report to the Science, Economy and Society Directorate at the European Commission*: ec.europa.eu/research/science.

Peters, Anne (2009) 'The Merits of Global Constitutionalism' 16 *Indiana Journal of Global Legal Studies* 397.

Pfaff, Alexander and Sanchirico, Chris William (2000) 'Environmental self-auditing: setting the proper incentives for discovery and correction of environmental harm' 16(1) *Journal of Law, Economics and Organization* 189.

Pichler, Rufus (2000) *Trust and Reliance—Enforcement and Compliance: Enhancing Consumer Confidence in the Electronic Marketplace*, JSM Thesis (Stanford CA, Stanford University).

Pierson, Paul (ed) (2001) *The New Politics of the Welfare State* (Oxford/New York, Oxford University Press).

Pinheiro, Luis de Lima (2001) 'The 'Denationalization' of Transnational Relationships—Regulation of Transnational Relationships by Public International Law, European Community Law and Transnational Law' in Jürgen Basedow, Ulrich Drobnig, Reinhard Ellger, Klaus J Hopt, Hein Kötz, Rainer Kulms and Ernst-Joachim Mestmäcker (eds), *Aufbruch nach Europa 75 Jahre Max-Planck-Institut für Privatrecht* (Tübingen, Mohr Siebeck) 429–46.

Pistor, Katharina (2003) 'Of Legal Transplants, Legal Irritants, and Economic Development' in Peter Cornelius and Bruce Kogut (eds), *Corporate Governance and Capital Flows in a Global Economy* (Oxford/New York, Oxford University Press) 347–66.

Pogge, Thomas (1992) 'Cosmopolitanism and Sovereignty' 103(1) *Ethics* 48.

—— (2008) *World Poverty and Human Rights,* 2nd edn *(1st edn 2002)* (London, Polity Press).

Polanyi, Karl (1944) *The Great Transformation. The Political and Economic Origins of our Time* (Boston MA, Beacon Press).

Ponte, Lucile M. and Cavenagh, Thomas D. (2004) *Cyberjustice: Online Dispute Resolution* (Upper Saddle River NJ, Prentice Hall).

Ponte, Lucille M (2002a) 'Boosting Consumer Confidence in E-Business: Recommendations for Establishing Fair and Effective Dispute Resolution Programs for B2C Online Transactions' 12 *Albany Law Journal of Science and Technology* 441.

—— (2002b) 'Broadening Traditional ADR Notions of Disclosure: Special Considerations for Posting Conflict Resolution Policies and Programs on E-Business Web Sites' 17 *Ohio State Journal on Dispute Resolution* 321.

Posner, Eric A (2000) *Law and Social Norms* (Cambridge MA/London, Harvard University Press).

Posner, Richard A (1973) *Economic Analysis of Law* (Boston MA, Little Brown).

—— (1998a) 'Creating a Legal Framework for Economic Development' 13(1) *The World Bank Research Observer* 1.

—— (1998b) 'Social Norms, Social Meaning, and the Economic Analysis of Law' 27(2) *Journal of Legal Studies* 553.

Post, David G (1995) 'Anarchy, State, and the Internet: An Essay on Law-Making in Cyberspace' www.temple.edu/Lawschool/dpost/Anarchy.html.

Pound, Roscoe (1910) 'Law in Books and Law in Action' 44 *American Law Review* 12.
—— (1932) 'The New Feudalism' 16 *American Bar Association Journal* 553.
—— (1939) 'Public Law and Private Law' 24(4) *Cornell Law Quarterly* 469.
Power, Michael (1997) *The Audit Society: Rituals of Verification* (Oxford/New York, Oxford University Press).
—— (2005) 'Enterprise Risk Management and the Organization of Uncertainty in Financial Institutions' in Karin Knorr Cetina and Alex Preda (eds), *The Sociology of Financial Markets* (Oxford/New York, Oxford University Press) 250–68.
—— (2007) *Organized Uncertainty. Designing a World of Risk Management* (Oxford, Oxford University Press).
Prentice, Robert A (2006) 'The Inevitability of a Strong SEC' 91 *Cornell Law Review* 775.
Priest, George L (1977) 'The Common Law Process and the Selection of Efficient Rules' 6(1) *Journal of Legal Studies* 65.
Prosser, Tony (1995) 'The State, Constitutions and Implementing Economic Policy: Privatization and Regulation in the UK, France and the USA' 4 *Social & Legal Studies* 507.
Putnam, Robert D. (2000) *Bowling Alone. The Collapse and Revival of American Community* (New York, Simon & Schuster).
Raiser, Thomas (1988) 'The Theory of Enterprise Law in the Federal Republic of Germany' 36(1) *American Journal of Comparative Law* 111.
Rajagopal, Balakrishnan (2003) 'International Law and Social Movements: Challenges of Theorizing Resistance' 41 *Columbia Journal of Transnational Law* 397.
—— (2006) 'Martti Koskenniemi's *From Apology to Utopia*: A Reflection' 7 *German Law Journal* 1089.
Raphael, DD (2001) *Concepts of Justice* (Oxford, Oxford University Press).
Ratner, Steven R (1998) 'International Law: The Trials of Global Norms' *Foreign Affairs* 65.
Raustiala, Kal (2002) 'The Architecture of International Cooperation: Transgovernmental Networks and the Future of International Law' 43 *Virginia Journal of International Law* 1.
—— (2005) 'Form and Substance in International Agreements' 50 *Harvard International Law Journal* 231.
—— (2006) 'Refining the Limits of International Law' 34 *Georgia Journal of International and Comparative Law* 423.
Reagle, Joseph (1990) 'Why the Internet is Good. Community Governance That Works' *Berkman Center Working Draft*: cyber.law.harvard.edu/archived_content/people/reagle/regulation.
Rebérioux, Antoine (2004) 'The end of history in corporate governance? A critical appraisal' *Amsterdam Research Centre for Corporate Governance Regulation*, Inaugural Workshop 17–18 December 2004: www.arccgor.nl/uploads/File/Reberioux%20Amsterdam%202.pdf.
Redfern, Alan and Hunter, Martin (2004) *Law and Practice of International Commercial Arbitration*, 4th edn.
Reich, Charles A (1964) 'The New Property' 73 *Yale Law Journal* 733.
—— (1990) 'Beyond The New Property: An Ecological View of Due Process' 56 *Brooklyn Law Review* 731.

Reich, Norbert (2005) *Understanding EU Law. Objectives, Principles and Methods of Community Law*, 2nd edn (Antwerpen/Oxford, Intersentia).

Reich, Robert B (2007) *Supercapitalism. The Transformation of Business, Democracy, and Everyday Life* (New York, Vintage).

Reimann, Mathias (2002) 'The Progress and Failure of Comparative Law in the Second Half of the Twentieth Century' 50 *Am J Comp L* 671.

—— (2004) 'From the Law of Nations to Transnational Law: Why We Need a New Basic Course for the International Curriculum' 22 *Pennsylvania State International Law Review* 397.

Renner, Karl (1949) *The Institutions of Private Law and their social functions* (orig. German 1929) (London, Routledge and Kegan Paul).

Renner, Moritz (2009) 'Towards a Hierarchy of Norms in Transnational Law?' 26(4) *Journal of International Arbitration* 533.

—— (2010) 'The Dialectics of Transnational Economic Constitutionalism' in Christian Joerges and Josef Falke (eds), *The Social Embeddedness of Transnational Markets* (Oxford and Portland OR, Hart Publishing), *forthcoming*.

Resnick, Paul and others (2006) 'The Value of Reputation on eBay: A Controlled Experiment' 9(2) *Experimental Economics* 79.

Rheinstein, Max (1967) 'Introduction' *Max Weber on Law in Economy and Society* xvii.

Rhodes, RAW (1994) 'The Hollowing Out of the State: The Changing Nature of the Public Service in Britain' 65 *Political Quarterly* 137.

Richman, Barak D (2004) 'Firms, Courts, and Reputation Mechanisms: Towards a Positive Theory of Private Ordering' 104 *Columbia Law Review* 2328.

—— (2009) 'The Antitrust of Reputation Mechanisms: Institutional Economics and Concerted Refusals to Deal' 94 *Virginia Law Review* 325.

Richter, Gregor (2002) *Privatisierung und Funktionswandel der freien Wohlfahrtspflege. Strategien in nationalen und europäischen Sozialmärkten* (Baden-Baden, Forschung und Entwicklung in der Sozialwirtschaft, Nomos).

Riesman, David (1950) *The Lonely Crowd. A Study of the Changing American Character* (New Haven, Yale University Press).

Riles, Annelise (1999) 'Wigmore's Treasure Box: Comparative Law in the Era of Information' 40 *Harvard International Law Journal* 221.

—— (2005) 'A New Agenda for the Cultural Study of Law: Taking on the Technicalities' 53 *Buffalo Law Review* 973.

—— (2006) 'Comparative Law and Socio-Legal Studies' in Mathias Reimann and Reinhard Zimmermann (eds), *Oxford Handbook of Comparative Law* (Oxford/New York, Oxford University Press) 775–814.

Ringleb, Henrik-Michael (2008) 'Preamble to German Corporate Governance Commentary' in Henrik-Michael Ringleb, Thomas Kremer, Marcus Lutter and Axel von Werder (eds), *Kommentar zum Deutschen Corporate Governance Kodex [Kodex-Kommentar]* (Munich, CH Beck) 16–35.

Rittich, Kerry (2002) *Recharacterizing Restructuring. Law, Distribution and Gender in Market Reform* (The Hague, The Erik Castrén Institute Monographs on International Law and Human Rights, Kluwer Law International).

—— (2004) 'The Future of Law and Development: Second Generation Reforms and the Incorporation of the Social' 26 *Michigan Journal of International Law* 199.

—— (2005) 'Functionalism and Formalism: Their latest Incarnations in Contemporary Development and Governance Debates' 55 *University of Toronto Law Journal* 853.

Robé, Jean-Philippe (1997) 'Multinational Enterprises: The Constitution of a Pluralistic Legal Order' in Gunther Teubner (ed), *Global Law Without A State* (Dartmouth, Aldershot) 45–77.

Roberts, Simon (2005) 'After Government? On Representing Law Without the State' 68 *Modern Law Review* 1.

Rodrik, Dani (2000) 'Governance of Economic Globalization' in Joseph S. Nye and John D. Donahue (eds), *Governance in a Globalizing World* (Washington DC, Brookings) 347–65.

Roe, Mark J (1993) 'Some Differences in Corporate Structure in Germany, Japan, and the United States' 102 *Yale Law Journal* 1927.

—— (1996) 'Chaos and Evolution in Law and Economics' 109 *Harvard Law Review* 641.

—— (1997) 'Path Dependence, Political Options and Governance Systems' in Klaus J Hopt and Eddy Wymeersch (eds), *Comparative Corporate Governance Essays and Materials* (Berlin/New York, Walter de Gruyter) 165–84.

—— (1998) 'Comparative corporate governance' in Peter Newman (ed), *The New Palgrave Dictionary of Economics and the Law* (New York, Palgrave Macmillan) 339–46.

—— (2002) 'Corporate Law's Limits' 31 *J Legal Studies* 233.

—— (2003) *Political Determinants of Corporate Governance* (Oxford/New York, Oxford University Press).

—— (2006) 'Legal origins, politics and modern stock markets' 120 *Harvard Law Review* 460.

Rogers, Joel and Streeck, Wolfgang (eds) (1996) *Works Councils: Consultation, Representation, and Cooperation in Industrial Relations* (Chicago IL, University of Chicago Press).

Romano, Cesare PR (1999) 'The Proliferation of International Judicial Bodies: The Pieces of the Puzzle' 31 *New York University Journal of International Law and Policy* 709.

Romano, Roberta (1985) 'Law as Product: Some Pieces of the Incorporation Puzzle' 1 *Journal of Law, Economics and Organizations* 225.

—— (1993) *The Genius of American Corporate Law* (The American Enterprise Institute Press).

—— (1998) 'Empowering Investors: A Market Approach to Securities Regulation' 107 *Yale Law Journal* 2359.

—— (2002) 'Less is More: Making Institutional Investor Activism a Valuable Mechanism of Corporate Governance' in Joseph A McCahery, Piet Moerland, Theo Raaijmakers and Luc Renneborg (eds), *Corporate Governance Regimes Convergence and Diversity* (Oxford/New York, Oxford University Press) 507–66.

—— (2005) 'The Sarbanes-Oxley Act and the Making of Quack Corporate Governance' 114 *Yale Law Journal* 1521.

Rose-Ackerman, Susan (1980) 'Risk Taking and Reelection: Does Federalism Promote Innovation?' 9(3) *Journal of Legal Studies* 593.

Rosenbaum, Ekkehard F (2000) 'What is a market? On the methodology of a contested concept' LVIII (4) *Review of Social Economy* 455.

Rothchild, John (1999) 'Protecting the Digital Consumer: The Limits of Cyberspace Utopianism' 74 *Indiana Law Journal* 893.

Rubin, Paul H. (1977) 'Why is the Common Law Efficient?' 6(1) *Journal of Legal Studies* 51.

Rühl, Giesela (2008) 'Effizienzprobleme bei grenzüberschreitenden Rechtsstreitigkeiten' *German Working Papers in Law and Economics No 17* www.bepress.com/cgi/viewcontent.cgi?article=1247&context=gwp.

Russell, Andrew L (2006) "Rough Consensus and Running Code' and the Internet-OSI Standards War' 28(3) *IEEE Annals of the History of Computing* 48.

Sabel, Charles F and Zeitlin, Jonathan (2008) 'Learning from Difference: The New Architecture of Experimentalist Governance in the EU' 14(3) *European Law Journal* 271.

Sacco, Rodolfo (1995) 'Mute Law' 43 *American Journal of Comparative Law* 455.

—— (2001) 'Diversity and Uniformity in the Law' 49 *American Journal of Comparative Law* 171.

—— (2002) 'Souvernirs d'un vieux comparatiste' *ZEuP* 727.

Salamon, Lester M (2001) 'The New Governance and the Tools of Public Action: An Introduction' 28 *Fordham Urban Law Journal* 1611.

Salter, Liora (1999) 'The Standards Regime for Communication and Information Technologies' in A. Claire Cutler, Virginia Haufler and Tony Porter (eds), *Private Authority and International Affairs* (Albany NY, State University of New York Press) 97–127.

Sanders, Pieter (2005) 'UNCITRAL's Model Law on International and Commercial Arbitration: Present Situation and Future' 21 *Arbitration International* 443.

Santos, Alvaro (2006) 'The World Bank's Uses of the 'Rule of Law' Promise in Economic Development' in David Trubek and Alvaro Santos (eds), *The New Law and Economic Development A Critical Appraisal* (Cambridge, Cambridge University Press) 253–300.

Sassen, Saskia (1991) *The Global City* (Princeton NJ, Princeton University Press).

—— (1998) *Globalization and Its Discontents. Essays on the New Mobility of People and Money* (New York, The New Press).

—— (2000) 'The State and Globalization' in Joseph S Nye and John D Donahue (eds), *Governance in a Globalizing World* (Washington DC, Brookings Institution) 91.

—— (2003) 'Globalization or denationalization?' 10(1) *Review of International Political Economy* 1.

—— (2005) 'The Embeddedness of Electronic Markets: The Case of Global Capital Markets' in Karin Knorr Cetina and Alex Preda (eds), *The Sociology of Financial Markets* (Oxford/New York, Oxford University Press) 17–37.

—— (2006) *Territory—Authority—Rights. From Medieval to Global Assemblages* (Princeton NJ/Oxford, Princeton University Press).

—— (2007) 'The Places and Spaces of the Global: An Expanded Analytic Terrain' in David Held and Anthony McGrew (eds), *Globalization Theory Approaches and Controversies* (London, Polity Press) 79–105.

Savigny, Friedrich Carl von (1840) *Vom Beruf unserer Zeit für Gesetzgebung und Rechtswissenschaft* 3rd edn (Heidelberg, Mohr, first published 1814).

Sawada, Toshiko (2004) 'Cross-border Transactions on E-Commerce and the Role of ADR': www.ecom.jp/adr/en/html/Full%20text%20incl.%20reference.pdf.

Schanze, Erich (1986) *Investitionsverträge im internationalen Wirtschaftsrecht* (Frankfurt, Metzner).
—— (2007) 'International Standards. Functions and links to law' in Christian Brütsch and Dirk Lehmkuhl (eds), *Law and Legalization in Transnational Relations* (Abingdon/New York, Routledge) 166–84.
Scharpf, Fritz W (1999) *Governing Europe. Effective and Democratic?* (Oxford/New York, Oxford University Press).
—— (2000) 'The viability of advanced welfare states in the international economy: vulnerabilities and options' 7(2) *Journal of European Public Policy* 190.
Schepel, Harm (2004) 'Constituting Private Governance Regimes: Standards Bodies in American Law' in Christian Joerges, Inger-Johanne Sand and Gunther Teubner (eds), *Transnational Governance and Constitutionalism* (Oxford/Portland OR, Hart Publishing) 161–88.
—— (2005) *The Constitution of Private Governance. Product Standards in the Regulation of Integrating Markets* (Oxford/Portland OR, International Studies in Private Law Theory, Hart Publishing).
Scheuerman, William E (1999) 'Economic Globalization and the Rule of Law' 6(1) *Constellations* 3.
—— (2000) 'Reflexive Law and the Challenges of Globalization' 8(4) *Journal of Political Philosophy* 1.
—— (2001) 'Global Law in our High Speed Economy' in Volkmar Gessner, Richard P Appelbaum and William F Felstiner (eds), *Rules and Networks The Legal Culture of Global Business Transactions* (Oxford/Portland OR, Hart Publishing) 103–21.
—— (2002) 'Franz Neumann—Legal Theorist of Globalization?' 35(1) *Kritische Justiz* 79.
—— (2004) 'Democratic Experimentalism or Capitalist Synchronization? Critical Reflections on Directly-Deliberative Polyarchy' 17(1) *Canadian Journal of Law & Jurisprudence* 101.
Schiavetta, Susan (2004) 'The Relationship Between e-ADR and Article 6 of the European Convention of Human Rights pursuant to the Case Law of the European Court of Human Rights' *Journal of Information, Law and Technology*.
Schlesinger, Rudolf (1995) 'The Past and Future of Comparative Law' 43(3) *American Journal of Comparative Law* 477.
Schmidt-Aßmann, Eberhard (1994) 'Flexibilität und Innovationsoffenheit als Entwicklungsperspektiven des Verwaltungsrechts' in Wolfgang Hoffmann-Riem and Eberhard Schmidt-Aßmann (eds), *Flexibilität und Innovation des Verwaltungshandelns* (Baden-Baden, Nomos) 407–24.
—— (2008) 'The Internationalization of Administrative Relations as a Challenge for Administrative Law Scholarship' 9(11) *German Law Journal* 2061.
Schmidt-Preuss, Matthias (1996) 'Verwaltung und Verwaltungsrecht zwischen gesellschaftlicher Selbstregulierung und staatlicher Steuerung' 56 *Veröffentlichungen der Vereinigung der Deutschen Staatsrechtslehrer* 160.
Schmidt-Trenz, Hans-Jörg (1990) *Außenhandel und Territorialität des Rechts, Grundlegung einer Neuen Institutionenökonomik des Außenhandels* (Baden-Baden, Nomos).
Schmidt, Karsten (2007) 'Lex mercatoria: Allheilmittel? Rätsel? Chimäre?' in Junichi Murakami, Hans-Peter Marutschke and Karl Riesenhuber (eds),

Globalisierung und Recht: Beiträge Japans und Deutschlands zu einer internationalen Rechtsordnung im 21 Jahrhundert (Berlin/New York, Walter de Gruyter) 153–74.

Schmidtchen, Dieter and Schmidt-Trenz, Hans-Jörg (1991) 'Private International Trade in the Shadow of the Territoriality of Law: Why Does It Work?' 58 *Southern Economic Journal* 329.

Schmidtchen, Dieter and Schmidt-Trenz, Hans-Jörg (1990a) 'The Division of Labour is limited by the extent of the Law' 1 *Constitutional Political Economy* 1.

—— (1990b) 'New Institutional Economics of International Transactions. Constitutional Uncertainty and the Creation of Institutions in Foreign Trade as exemplified by the Multinational Firm' 9 *Jahrbuch für Neue Politische Ökonomie* 3.

Schmitt, Carl (1988) *The Crisis of Parliamentary Democracy* [1926], Ellen Kennedy (trans) (Cambridge MA, Studies in Contemporary German Social Thought, MIT Press).

Schmitthoff, Clive M (1961) 'International Business Law: A New Law Merchant' 2 *Current Law and Social Problems* 129.

—— (1963) 'The New Sources of the Law of International Trade' 15 *International Social Science Journal* 259.

—— (1964a) 'Das neue Recht des Welthandels' 28 *Rabels Zeitschrift für Ausländisches und Internationales Privatrecht* 47.

—— (1964b) 'Das neue Recht des Welthandels' 28 *Rabels Zeitschrift für Ausländisches und Internationales Privatrecht* 47.

—— (1964c) 'The Law of International Trade, its Growth, Formulation and Operation' in Clive Schmitthoff (ed), *The Sources of the Law of International Trade* (New York, Praeger) 3–38.

—— (1968) 'The Unification of the Law of International Trade' *Journal of Business Law* 105.

—— (1973) 'The Future of the European Company Law Scene' in Clive Schmitthoff (ed), *The Harmonisation of European Company Law* (London, The UK National Committee of Comparative Law) 3–27.

—— (1982) 'Nature and Evolution of the Transnational Law of Commercial Transactions' in Norbert Horn and Clive Schmitthoff (eds), *The Transnational Law of International Commercial Transactions* (Dordrecht, Deventer) 19–31.

Schneiderman, David (2006) 'Transnational Legality and the Immobilization of Local Agency' 2 *Annual Review of Law and Social Sciences* 387.

—— (2008) 'Realising Rights in an Era of Economic Globalisation: Discourse Theory, Investor Rights, and Broad-Based Black Economic Empowerment' in Wenhua Shan, Penelope Simons and Dalvinder Singh (eds), *Redefining Sovereignty in International Economic Law* (Oxford/Portland OR, Hart Publishing) 429–44.

Scholte, Jan Aart (2008) 'Reconstructing Contemporary Democracy' 15(1) *Indiana Journal of Global Legal Studies* 305.

Schreuer, Christoph (1993) 'The Waning of the Sovereign State: Towards a New Paradigm for International Law?' 4 *European Journal of International Law* 447.

Schuck, Peter H (1991) *Tort Law and the Public Interest: Competition, Innovation, and Consumer Welfare* (New York, WH Norton).

Schuler, Gefion (2008) 'Effective Governance through Decentralized Soft Implementation: The OECD Guidelines for Multinational Enterprises' 9(11) *German Law Journal* 1754.

Schulte, Martin and Stichweh, Rudolf (eds) (2008) *Weltrecht* (Berlin, Duncker & Humblot).

Schultz, Thomas (2003) 'An Essay on the Role of Government for ODR: Theoretical Considerations about the Future of ODR (2004)' in Ethan Katsh and D Choi (eds), *Online Dispute Resolution (ODR), Papers and Proceedings of the 2003 United Nations Forum on ODR*: www.odr.info/unece2003/pdf/Schultz.pdf.

—— (2004) 'Does Online Dispute Resolution Need Governmental Intervention? The Case for Architectures of Control and Trust' 71 *North Carolina Journal of Law & Technology* 71.

—— (2005) 'eBay: un système juridique en formation?' 22 *Revue du Droit des Technologies et de l'Information* 27.

—— (2008) 'Some Critical Comments on the Juridicity of Lex Mercatoria' X *Yearbook of Private International Law* 667.

Schultz, Thomas, Kaufmann-Kohler, Gabrielle, Langer, Dirk and Bonnet, Vincent (2001) *Online Dispute Resolution: The State of the Art and the Issues, E-Com Research Project of the University of Geneva* (Geneva).

Schulz, Wolfgang and Held, Thorsten (2001) 'Regulated Self-Regulation as a Form of Modern Government' Interim Report, October 2001', available at: wwwhans-bredow-institutde/publikationen/apapiere/8selfregpdf.

Schulze-Osterloh, Joachim (2001) 'Das deutsche Gesellschaftsrecht im Banne der Globalisierung' 22 *Zeitschrift für Insolvenzpraxis* 1433.

Schuppert, Gunnar Folke (1999) 'Zur notwendigen Neubestimmung der Staatsaufsicht im verantwortungsteilenden Verwaltungsstaat' in Gunnar Folke Schuppert (ed), *Jenseits von Privatisierung und 'schlankem' Staat* (Baden-Baden, Nomos) 299–329.

Sciarra, Silvana (2004) 'The Convergence of European Labour and Social Rights: Opening to the Open Method of Coordination' in George A Bermann and Katharina Pistor (eds), *Law and Governance in an Enlarged European Union* (Oxford/Portland OR, Hart Publishing) 155–75.

Sciulli, David (1999) *Corporations vs. the Court: Private Power, Public Interests* (Boulder CO, Lynne Rienner Publishers).

Scott, Colin (2000) 'Accountability in the Regulatory State' 27(1) *Journal of Law and Society* 38.

—— (2003) 'Speaking softly without big sticks: Meta-regulation and public sector audit' 25(3) *Law & Policy* 203.

—— (2004) 'Regulation in the Age of Governance: The Rise of the Post Regulatory State' in Jacint Jordana and David Levi-Faur (eds), *The Politics of Regulation: Institutions and Regulatory Reforms for the Age of Governance* (Cheltenham, Edward Elgar) 145–74.

—— (2007) 'New-ish Governance and the Legitimacy of the EU' 3(5) *CLPE Comparative Research in Law & Political Economy Research Paper.*

—— (2008a) 'Reflexive governance, meta-regulation and corporate social responsibility: the "Heineken effect"' in Nina Boeger, Rachel Murray and Charlotte Villiers (eds), *Perspectives on Corporate Social Responsibility* (Cheltenham, Edward Elgar) 170–85.

—— (2008b) 'Regulating private legislation' in Fabrizio Cafaggi and Horatia Muir-Watt (eds), *Making European Law Governance Design* (Cheltenham, Edward Elgar) 254–86.

Scott, Craig (2005) 'A Core Curriculum for the Transnational Legal Education of JD and LLB Students: Surveying the Approach of the International, Comparative and Transnational Law Program at Osgoode Hall Law School' 23 *Penn State International Law Review* 757.

Scott, Craig M (2001a) '*Introduction to* Torture as Tort: *From Sudan to Canada to Somalia*' in Craig M Scott (ed), *Torture as Tort* (Oxford/Portland OR, Hart Publishing) 3–44.

—— (2001b) 'Translating Torture into Transnational Tort: Conceptual Divides in the Debate on Corporate Accountability for Human Rights Harms' in Craig M. Scott (ed), *Torture as Tort* (Oxford/Portland OR, Hart Publishing) 45–63.

—— (2009) '"Transnational Law" as Proto-Concept: Three Conceptions' 10 *German Law Journal* 859.

Scott, Craig and Wai, Robert (2004) 'Transnational Governance of Corporate Conduct through the Migration of Human Rights Norms: The Potential of Transnational "Private" Litigation' in Christian Joerges, Inger-Johanne Sand and Gunther Teubner (eds), *Transnational Governance and Constitutionalism* (Oxford/Portland OR, Hart Publishing) 287–319.

Scott, Joanne and Trubek, David (2002) 'Mind the Gap: Law and New Approaches to Governance in the European Union' 8(1) *European Law Journal* 1.

Scott, Robert E (2000) 'The Case for Formalism in Relational Contract' 94 *Northwestern University Law Review* 847.

—— (2004) 'The Death of Contract Law' 54(4) *University of Toronto Law Journal* 369.

—— (2007) '*Hoffmann v. Red Owl Stores* and the Myth of Precontractual Reliance' 68 *Ohio State Law Journal* 71.

Scott, Robert E and Stephan, Paul B (2006) *The Limits of Leviathan. Contract Theory and the Enforcement of International Law* (Cambridge, Cambridge University Press).

Scott, Robert E and Triantis, George G (2006) 'Anticipating Litigation in Contract Design' 115 *Yale Law Journal* 814.

Sefton-Green, Ruth (2008) 'Sense and Sensibilities: The DCFR and the Preservation of Cultural and Linguistic Plurality' 4(3) *European Review of Contract Law* 281.

Seibert, Ulrich (2002) 'Das "TransPuG"' *Neue Zeitschrift für Gesellschaftsrecht* 608.

—— (2009) 'Das VorstAG—Regelungen zur Angemessenheit der Vorstandsvergütung und zum Aufsichtsrat' 63 *Wertpapiermitteilungen* 1489.

Seibt, Christoph H (2002) 'Deutscher Corporate Governance Kodex und Entsprechenserklärung (§ 161 AktG-E)' 47(5) *Die Aktiengesellschaft* 249.

—— (2003) 'Deutscher Corporate Governance Kodex: Antworten auf Zweifelsfragen der Praxis' 48(9) *Die Aktiengesellschaft* 465.

Seidel, Wolfgang (2004a) 'Der Deutsche Corporate Governance Kodex—eine private oder doch eine staatliche Regelung?' 25(7) *Zeitschrift für Wirtschaftsrecht* 285.

—— (2004b) 'Kodex ohne Rechtsgrundlage' 23 *Neue Zeitschrift für Gesellschaftsrecht* 1095.

Seidl, David, Sanderson, Paul and Roberts, John (2009) 'Applying "Comply-or-Explain": Conformance with Codes of Corporate Governance in the UK and Germany' *Cambridge Centre for Business Research CBR Working Paper 389*: www.cbr.cam.ac.uk/pdf/WP389.pdf.

Selznick, Philip (1969) *Law, society, and industrial justice* (New Haven CT, Yale University Press).
Sennett, Richard (2006) *The Culture of the New Capitalism* (New Haven CT, Yale University Press).
Shaffer, Gregory (2000) 'Globalization and Social Protection: The Impact of EU and International Rules in the Ratcheting Up of U.S. Data Privacy Standards 25 *Yale Journal of International Law* 1.
—— (2009) 'A Call for New Legal Realism in International Law: The Need for Method (Melvin C Steen Inaugural Lecture)' *University of Minnesota Legal Studies Research Paper No 09-02*: ssrn.com/abstract=1323912.
Shaffer, Gregory and Nourse, Victoria (2009) 'Varieties of New Legal Realism: Can a New World Order Prompt a New Legal Theory?' 95 *Cornell Law Review* 61.
Shaffer, Gregory and Pollack, Mark A (2009) 'Hard vs. Soft Law: Alternatives, Complements and Antagonists in International Governance' *University of Minnesota Legal Studies Research Paper No 09-23*: ssrn.com/abstract=1426123.
Shalakany, Amr (2001) 'Arbitration and the Third World: A Plea for Reassessing Bias Under the Spector of Neoliberalism' 41 *Harvard International Law Journal* 419.
Shamir, Ronen (2008) 'The age of responsibilization: on market-embedded morality' 37(1) *Economy and Society* 1.
Shapiro, Martin (2000) 'Administrative Law Unbounded: Reflections on Government and Governance' 8 *Indiana Journal of Global Studies* 369.
Shaw, John C (1997) 'The Cadbury Report, Two Years Later' in Klaus J Hopt and Eddy Wymeersch (eds), *Comparative Corporate Governance Essays and Materials* (Berlin/New York, Walter de Gruyter) 21–45.
Shelton, Dinah L (2008) 'Soft Law' in *Handbook of International Law* (London, Routledge): ssrn.com/abstract=1003387.
Shiller, Robert J (2005) *Irrational Exuberance*, 2nd edn (New York et al, Currency Doubleday).
Shonfield, Andrew (1965) *Modern Capitalism. The Changing Balance of Public and Private Power* (London/New York/Toronto, Oxford University Press).
Siems, Mathias M (2007) 'Legal Origins: Reconciling Law & Finance and Comparative Law' 52 *McGill Law Journal* 55.
Siems, Mathias M and Deakin, Simon (2009) 'Comparative Law and Finance: Past, Present and Future Research' *Journal of Institutional and Theoretical Economics*: ssrn.com/abstract=1428247.
Sinclair, Timothy J (1994) 'Passing Judgment: Credit Rating Processes as Regulatory Mechanisms of Governance in the Emerging World Order' 1 *Review of International Political Economy* 133.
Singer, Joseph W (1988) 'Legal Realism Now' 76 *California Law Review* 465.
Skidelsky, Robert (2009) *Keynes. The Return of the Master* (London, Allen Lane).
Slaughter-Burley, Anne-Marie (1993) 'International Law and International Relations Theory: A Dual Agenda' 87 *American Journal of International Law* 205.
Slaughter, Anne-Marie (2002) 'Breaking Out: The Proliferation of Actors in the International System' in Yves Dezalay and Bryant Garth (eds), *Global Prescriptions, The Production, Exportation, and Importation of a New Legal Orthodoxy* (Ann Arbor MI, University of Michigan Press) 12–36.

—— (2004a) 'Disaggregated Sovereignty: Towards the Public Accountability of Global Government Networks' 39(2) *Government and Opposition* 159.

—— (2004b) *A New World Order* (Princeton NJ, Princeton University Press).

Slaughter, Anne-Marie, Tulumello, Andrew S and Wood, Stepan (1998) 'International Law and International Relations Theory: A New Generation of Interdisciplinary Scholarship' 92 *American Journal of International Law* 367.

Smerdon, Richard (2004) *A Practical Guide to Corporate Governance* (London, Sweet & Maxwell).

Smith, Adam (1991) *Wealth of Nations* [1776] (Amherst NY, Prometheus Books).

—— (2006) *The Theory of Moral Sentiments* [1759], 6th edn [1760] (Mineola NY, Dover Publications).

Smits, Jan (2006) 'European Private Law: a Plea for a Spontaneous Legal Order' in Deidre Curtin, Jan Smits, André Klip and Joseph McCahery (eds), *European Integration and Law* (Antwerp/Oxford, Intersentia) 85.

Snyder, David V (2003) 'Private Lawmaking' 64 *Ohio State Law Journal* 371.

—— (2007) 'Molecular Federalism and the Structures of Private Lawmaking' 14(2) *Indiana Journal of Global Legal Studies* 419.

Snyder, Francis (2004a) 'Economic Globalisation and the Law in the 21st Century' in Austin Sarat (ed), *The Blackwell Companion to Law and Society* (New York/ Oxford, Blackwell) 624–40.

—— (2004b) 'European Constitutionalism in the 21st Century' in Takis Tridimas and Paolisa Nebbia (eds), *European Union Law for the Twenty-First Century*, vol 1 (Oxford/Portland OR, Hart Publishing) 9–16.

Snyder, Franklin G (2003) 'More Pieces of the CEO Compensation Puzzle' 28 *Delaware Journal of Corporate Law* 129.

Solomon, Jason M (2008) 'Law and Governance in the 21st Century Regulatory State' 86(4) *Texas Law Review* 819.

Sombart, Werner (1906) *Der moderne Kapitalismus. Historisch-systematische Darstellung des gesamteuropäischen Wirtschaftslebens von seinen Anfängen bis zur Gegenwart* (Munich, dtv).

Sornarajah, M (1997) 'Power and Justice in International Law' *Singapore Journal of International and Comparative Law* 28.

—— (2006) 'Power and Justice: Third World Resistance in International Law' *Singapore Yearbook of International Law* 19.

Sosa, Fabian (2009) 'Cross-Border Dispute Resolution From the Perspective of Midsized Law Firms: The Example of International Commercial Arbitration' in Volkmar Gessner (ed), *Contractual Certainty in International Trade Empirical Studies and Theoretical Debates on Institutional Support for Global Economic Exchanges* (Oxford/Portland OR, Hart Publishing) 107–56.

Soskice, David (1999) 'Divergent Production Regimes: Coordinated and Uncoordinated Market Economies in the 1980s and 1990s' in Herbert Kitschelt, Peter Lange, Gary Marks and John D Stephens (eds), *Continuity and Change in Contemporary Capitalism* (Cambridge, Cambridge University Press) 101–34.

Sousa Santos, Boaventura de (1987) 'Law: A Map of Misreading. Toward a Postmodern Conception of Law' 14(3) *Journal of Law & Society* 279.

—— (2008) 'The World Social Forum and the Global Left' 36(2) *Politics & Society* 247.

Spamann, Holger (2009) 'Contemporary Legal Transplants—Legal Families and the Diffusion of (Corporate) Law' *Brigham Young University Law Review*: http://ssrn.com/abstract=1411704.

Spindler, Gerald (1998) 'Deregulierung des Aktienrechts?' 43 *Die Aktiengesellschaft* 53.

—— (2005) 'Internet-Auctions versus Consumer Protection: The Case of the Distance Selling Directive' 6(3) *German Law Journal* 725.

—— (2008) 'Commentary to § 161 AktG' in Karsten Schmidt and Marcus Lutter (eds) *Aktiengesetz Kommentar* (Köln, Otto Schmidt) fns 1–79.

Spiro, Peter J (2002) 'Accounting for NGOs' 3 *Chicago Journal of International Law* 161.

Spletter, Christian (2003) *The Significance of Trustmarks in B2C E-Commerce*, LLM Thesis, University of Strathclyde (Strathclyde).

Staff, Ilse (1987) 'Die Wahrung staatlicher Ordnung. Ein Beitrag zum technologischen Staat und seinen rechten Propheten Carl Schmitt und Ernst Forsthoff' *Leviathan* 141.

Stapeldon, GP (2000) 'Institutional Investors: What Are Their Responsibilities as Shareholders?' in John Parkinson, Gavin Kelly and Andrew Gamble (eds), *The Political Economy of the Company* (Oxford/Portland OR, Hart Publishing) 195–231.

Stein, Eric (1981) 'Lawyers, Judges, and the Making of a Transnational Constitution' 75(1) *American Journal of International Law* 1.

Stein, Ursula (1995) *Lex Mercatoria. Realität und Theorie* (Frankfurt, Juristische Abhandlungen, Vittorio Klostermann).

Stephan, Paul B (1999) 'The Futility of Unification and Harmonization in International Economic Law' *Virginia Journal of International Law* 743.

Stephens, Beth (2001) 'Taking Pride in International Human Rights Litigation' 2 *Chicago Journal of International Law* 485.

—— (2002a) 'The Amorality of Profit: Transnational Corporations and Human Rights' 20 *Berkeley Journal of International Law* 45.

—— (2002b) 'Translating Filártiga: A Comparative and International Law Analysis of Domestic Remedies for International Human Rights Violations' 27 *Yale Journal of International Law* 1.

Stewart, Richard B (1975) 'The Reformation of American Administrative Law' 88 *Harvard Law Review* 1669.

Stichweh, Rudolf (1999) 'Globalisierung von Wirtschaft und Wissenschaft: Produktion und Transfer wissenschaftlichen Wissens in zwei Funktionssystemen der modernen Gesellschaft' 5 *Soziale Systeme* 27.

—— (2000) *Die Weltgesellschaft. Soziologische Analysen* (Frankfurt, Suhrkamp).

—— (2005a) *Inklusion und Exklusion. Studien zur Gesellschaftstheorie* (transcript, Bielefeld).

—— (2005b) 'Inklusion/Exklusion, funktionale Differenzierung und die Theorie der Weltgesellschaft' *Stichweh, Inklusion und Exklusion Studien zur Gesellschaftstheorie* (transcript, Bielefeld) 45.

Stillman II, Richard J (2003) 'Twenty-First Century United States Governance: Statecraft and the Peculiar Governing Paradox it Perpetuates' 81(1) *Public Administration* 19.

Stolleis, Michael (1989) 'Die Entstehung des Interventionsstaates und das öffentliche Recht' 11 *Zeitschrift für Neuere Rechtgeschichte* 129.

Stone, Katherine van Wezel (1996) 'Labour in the Global Economy: Four Approaches to Transnational Labour Regulation' in Joseph McCahery, William W Bratton, Sol Picciotto and Colin Scott (eds), *International Regulatory Competition and Coordination Perspectives on Economic Regulation in Europe and the United States* (Oxford, Clarendon Press) 445–77.

Stone Sweet, Alec (2009) 'Constitutionalism, Legal Pluralism, and International Regimes' 16 *Indiana Journal of Global Legal Studies* 621.

Stone Sweet, Alex (2006) 'The new Lex Mercatoria and transnational governance' 13(5) *Journal of European Public Policy* 627.

Stout, Lynn (2003) 'The Mechanisms of Market Inefficiency: An Introduction to the New Finance' 28 *Journal of Corporate Law* 635.

Streeck, Wolfgang (1997) 'German Capitalism: Does it exist? Can it survive?' in Colin Crouch and Wolfgang Streeck (eds), *Political Economy of Modern Capitalism* (London, Sage) 33–54.

—— (2001) 'Introduction: Explorations into the Origins of Nonliberal Capitalism in Germany and Japan' in Wolfgang Streeck and Kozo Yamamura (eds), *The Origins of Nonliberal Capitalism* (Ithaca NY, Cornell University Press) 1–38.

Streit, Manfred E and Mangels, Antje (1996) 'Privatautonomes Recht und grenzüberschreitende Transaktionen' 47 *ORDO* 73.

Sunder, Shyam (2005) 'Minding our manners: Accounting as social norms' 37 *The British Accounting Review* 367.

Sunstein, Cass (1996) 'Social Norms and Social Roles' 96 *Columbia Law Review* 903.

—— (ed) (2000) *Behavioural Law & Economics* (Chicago IL, University of Chicago Press).

Swedberg, Richard (2003) 'The Case for an Economic Sociology of Law' 32 *Theory and Society* 1.

Taggart, Michael (1997) 'The Province of Administrative Law Determined?' in Michael Taggart (ed), *The Province of Administrative Law* (Oxford/Portland OR, Hart Publishing) 1–20.

Teichmann, Christoph (2003) 'The European Company—A Challenge to Academics, Legislatures and Practitioners' 4(4) *German Law Journal* 309.

Teitel, Ruti (2000), *Transitional Justice* (Oxford, Oxford University Press, 2000).

Teitz, Lousie Ellen (2001) 'Providing Legal Services for the Middle Class in Cyberspace: The Promise and Challenge of On-Line Dispute Resolution' 70 *Fordham Law Review* 985.

Testy, Kellye Y (2002) 'Linking Progressive Corporate Law with Progressive Social Movements' 76 *Tulane Law Review* 1227.

Teubner, Gunther (1983) 'Substantive and Reflexive Elements in Modern Law' 17 *Law & Society Review* 239.

—— (1984) 'Autopoiesis in Law and Society: A Rejoinder to Blankenburg' 18(2) *Law & Society Review* 201.

—— (1986a) 'After Legal Instrumentalism? Strategic Models of Post-regulatory Law' in Gunther Teubner (ed), *Dilemmas of Law in the Welfare State* (Berlin/New York, Walter de Gruyter) 299–325.

—— (1987a) 'Introduction to Autopoietic Law' in Gunther Teubner (ed), *Autopoietic Law: A New Approach to Law and Society* (Berlin/New York, Walter de Gruyter) 1–11.

—— (1987b) 'Juridification—Concepts, Aspects, Limits, Solutions' in Gunther Teubner (ed), *Juridification of Social Spheres* (Berlin/New York, Walter de Gruyter) 3–48.

—— (1988) 'Enterprise Corporatism: New Industrial Policy and the "Essence" of the Legal Person' 36(1) *American Journal of Comparative Law* 130.

—— (1989) 'How the Law Thinks: Toward a Constructivist Epistemology of Law' 23(5) *Law & Society Review* 727.

—— (1992a) 'Regulatory Law: Chronicle of a Death Foretold' 1 *Social & Legal Studies* 451.

—— (1992b) 'The Two Faces of Janus: Rethinking Legal Pluralism' 13 *Cardozo Law Review* 1443.

—— (1993) *Law as an Autopoeitic System* (Oxford/Cambridge, Blackwell).

—— (1997a) 'Altera pars audiatur: Law in the Collision of Discourses' in Richard Rawlings (ed), *Law, Society and Economy* (Oxford/New York, Oxford University Press) 149–76.

—— (1997b) 'Breaking Frames: The Global Interplay of Legal and Social Systems' 45 *American Journal of Comparative Law* 145.

—— (1997c) '"Global Bukowina": Legal Pluralism in the World Society' in Gunther Teubner (ed), *Global Law Without A State* (Dartmouth, Aldershot) 3–28.

—— (1997d) 'The King's Many Bodies: The Self-Deconstruction of Law's Hierarchy' 31(4) *Law & Society Review* 763.

—— (1999a) 'After Privatisation? The Many Autonomies of Private Law' in Thomas Wilhelmsson and Samuli Hurri (eds), *From Dissonance to Sense: Welfare State Expectations, Privatisation and Private Law* (Aldershot, Ashgate) 51–82.

—— (1999b) 'Eigensinnige Produktionsregimes: Zur Ko-evolution von Wirtschaft und Recht in den *varieties of capitalism*' 5(1) *Soziale Systeme* 7.

—— (2000) 'Contracting Worlds: The Many Autonomies of Private Law' 9(3) *Social & Legal Studies* 399.

—— (2001) 'Legal Irritants: How Unifying Law Ends Up In New Divergences' in Peter A. Hall and David Soskice (eds), *Varieties of Capitalism The Institutional Foundations of Comparative Advantage* (Oxford/New York, Oxford University Press) 417–41.

—— (2003) *Netzwerk als Vertragsverbund. Virtuelle Unternehmen, Franchising, Just-in-time in sozialwissenschaftlicher und juristischer Sicht* (Baden-Baden, Internationale Studien zur Privatrechtstheorie, Nomos).

—— (2004a) 'Global Private Regimes: Neo-spontaneous law and dual constitution of autonomous sectors in world society?' in Karl-Heinz Ladeur (ed), *Globalization and Public Governance* (Aldershot, Ashgate) 71–87.

—— (2004b) 'Societal Constitutionalism: Alternatives to State-Centred Constitutional Theory?' in Christian Joerges, Inger-Johanne Sand and Gunther Teubner (eds), *Constitutionalism and Transnational Governance* (Oxford/Portland OR, Hart Publishing) 3–28.

—— (2006) 'Dealing With Paradoxes: Luhmann, Wiethölter, Derrida' in Oren Perez and Gunther Teubner (eds), *Paradoxes and Inconsistencies in Law* (Oxford/Portland OR, Hart Publishing) 41–64.

—— (2007) 'In the Blind Spot: The Hybridization of Contracting' 8(1) *Theoretical Inquiries in Law* 51.

—— (2009) 'Self-subversive Justice: Contingency or Transcendency Formula of Law?' 72 *Modern Law Review* 1.

—— (ed) (1986b) *Dilemmas of Law in the Welfare State* (Berlin/New York, Walter de Gruyter).

—— (ed) (1997e) *Global Law Without A State* (Dartmouth, Aldershot).

Teubner, Gunther, Farmer, Lindsay and Murphy, Declan (eds) (1994) *Environmental Law and Ecological Responsibility: The Concept and Practice of Ecological Self-Organization* (London, Wiley).

Teubner, Gunther and Korth, Peter (2009) 'Two Kinds of Legal Pluralism: Collision of Laws in the Double Fragmentation of World Society' in Margaret Young (ed), *Regime Interaction in International Law: Theoretical and Practical Challenges*, forthcoming, available at: papers.ssrn.com/sol3/papers.cfm?abstract_id=1416041.

Teubner, Gunther and Willke, Helmut (1984) 'Kontext und Autonomie: Gesellschaftliche Selbststeuerung durch reflexives Recht' 6(1) *Zeitschrift für Rechtssoziologie* 4.

Teubner, Gunther and Zumbansen, Peer (2000) 'Rechtsverfremdungen: Zum gesellschaftlichen Mehrwert des zwölften Kamels' 21(1) *Zeitschrift für Rechtssoziologie* 189.

Thaler, Richard (1987) 'Anomalies—The January Effect' 1(1) *Journal of Economic Perspectives* 197.

—— (1999) 'The End of Behavioral Finance' 55(6) *Financial Analysts Journal* 12.

Thaler, Richard and Sunstein, Cass (2008) *Nudge. Improving Decisions about Health, Wealth and Happiness* (New Haven CT, Yale University Press).

Thomas, Randall S (2004) 'Explaining the International CEO Pay Gap: Board Capture or Market Driven?' 57 *Vanderbilt Law Review* 1171.

Tiebout, Charles M (1956) 'A Pure Theory of Local Expenditures' 64(5) *Journal of Political Economy* 416.

Tietje, Christian and Nowrot, Karsten (2006) *Laying Conceptual Ghosts of the Past to rest: The Rise of Philip C. Jessup's 'Transnational Law' in the Regulatory Governance of the International Economic System* (Essays in Transnational Law 50/2006) 17–55.

Touraine, Alain (2007) *A New Paradigm for Understanding Today's World* (originally in French [2005] *Un nouveau paradigme pour comprendre le monde d'aujourd'hui*) (Cambridge, Polity Press).

Trachtman, Joel (2000) 'Regulatory Competition and Regulatory Jurisdiction' 3 *Journal of International Economic Law* 331.

Trachtman, Joel P (2008) *The Economic Structure of International Law* (Cambridge MA, Harvard University Press).

Traynor, Michael (2000) 'An Introductory Framework for Analyzing the Proposed Hague Convention on Jurisdiction and Foreign Judgments in Civil and Commercial Matters: U.S. and European Perspectives' 6 *Annual Survey of International & Comparative Law* 1.

Trebilcock, Michael J (1993) *The Limits of Freedom of Contract* (Cambridge MA, Harvard University Press).

Trubek, David M (1972a) 'Max Weber on Law and the Rise of Capitalism' *Wisconsin Law Review* 720.

—— (1972b) 'Toward a Social Theory of Law: An Essay on the Study of Law and Development' 82(1) *Yale Law Journal* 1.

—— (1986) 'Max Weber's Tragic modernism and the study of law in society' 20 *Law & Society Review* 573.

Trubek, David and Galanter, Marc (1974) 'Scholars in Self-Estrangement: Some Reflections on the Crisis in Law and Development Studies in the United States' *Wisconsin Law Review* 1062.

Trubek, David and Trubek, Louise G (2005) 'Hard and Soft Law in the Construction of Social Europe: the Role of the Open Method of Coordination' 11(3) *European Law Journal* 343.

Trute, Hans-Heinrich (1996) 'Wechselseitige Verzahnungen zwischen Privatecht und öffentlichem Recht' in Wolfgang Hoffmann-Riem and Eberhard Schmidt-Assmann (eds), *Öffentliches Recht und Privatrecht als wechselseitige Auffangordnungen* (Baden-Baden, Nomos) 167–223.

Tsuk, Dalia (2005) 'From Pluralism to Individualism: Berle and Means and 20th Century American Legal Thought' 30 *Law & Social Inquiry* 179.

Tsuk Mitchell, Dalia (*forthcoming*) 'Legitimating Power: The Changing Status of the Board of Directors' in Peer Zumbansen and Cynthia Williams (eds), *The Embedded Firm: Labour, Corporate Governance and Finance Capitalism.*

Tushnet, Mark (2003) 'Transnational/Domestic Constitutional Law' 27 *Loyola of Los Angeles Law Review* 239.

Tyler, Melissa Conley (2004) '115 and Counting: The State of ODR 2004' in Melissa Conley Tyler, Ethan Katsh and D Choi (eds), *Proceedings of the Third Annual Forum on Online Dispute Resolution.*

Tyler, Melissa Conley and Bretherton, Di (2003) 'Seventy-six and Counting: An Analysis of ODR Sites. A Report of Research Conducted for the Department of Justice, Victoria, Australia' in Katsh and Choi (eds), *Online Dispute Resolution (ODR), Papers and Proceedings of the 2003 United Nations Forum on ODR.*

Ulmer, Peter (2002) 'Der deutsche Corporate Governance Kodex—ein neues Regulierungsinstrument für börsennotierte Aktiengesellschaften' 166 *Zeitschrift fur das Gesamte Handelsrecht und Wirtschaftsrecht* 150.

Vagts, Detlev F (1966) 'Reforming the 'Modern Corporation': Perspectives from the German' 80 *Harvard Law Review* 23.

—— (1969) 'The Multinational Enterprise: A New Challenge for Transnational Law' 83 *Harvard Law Review* 739.

—— (2004) 'International Relations Looks at Customary International Law: A Traditionalist's Defence' 15 *European Journal of International Law* 1031.

van Aaken, Anne (2006) 'To do away with International Law? Some Limits to the "Limits of International Law"' 17 *European Journal of International Law* 289.

—— (2009a) 'Democracy in Times of Transnational Administrative Law. The Case of Financial Markets' in Hauke Brunkhorst (ed), *Soziale Welt (Sonderband 18): Demokratie in der Weltgesellschaft* (Baden-Baden, Nomos) 195–212.

—— (2009b) 'Effectuating Public International Law Through Market Mechanisms?' 165(1) *Journal of Institutional and Theoretical Economics* 33.

van Kann, Jürgen and Eigler, Mira (2007) 'Aktuelle Neuerungen des Corporate Governance Kodex' 39 *Deutsche Zeitschrift für Steuerrecht* 1730.

Vanberg, Viktor (1982) *Markt und Organisation. Individualistische Sozialtheorie und das Problem korporativen Handelns* (Tübingen, Mohr Siebeck).

Vasudev, PM (2009) 'Credit Derivatives and Risk Management: Corporate Governance in the Sarbanes-Oxley World' (4) *Journal of Business Law* 331.

Veblen, Thorstein (1958) *The Theory of Business Enterprise* [1904] (New York, Mentor Books).

Verdier, Pierre-Hugues (2009) 'Transnational Regulatory Networks and Their Limits' 34 *Yale Journal of International Law* 113.

Verkuil, Paul R (2008) 'Outsourcing and the Duty to Govern' in Jody Freeman and Martha Minow (eds), *Governance by Design* (Cambridge MA/London, Harvard University Press) 310–34.

Vernon, Raymond (1967) 'Multinational Enterprise & National Sovereignty' *Harvard Business Review* 156.

Vesting, Thomas (1997) 'Wiederkehr der bürgerlichen Gesellschaft und ihres Rechts? Zur neueren Diskussion über das Verhältnis von öffentlichem Recht und Privatrecht' in Hans Schlosser (ed), *Bürgerliches Gesetzbuch 1896–1996 Ringvorlesung der Juristischen Fakultät Augsburg* (Heidelberg, CF Müller) 183–202.

Vetter, Eberhard (2008) 'Der Deutsche Corporate Governance Kodex nur ein zahnloser Tiger? Zur Bedeutung von § 161 AktG für Beschlüsse der Hauptversammlung' (4) *Neue Zeitschrift für Gesellschaftsrecht* 121.

Viellechner, Lars (2009) 'The Network of Networks: Karl-Heinz Ladeur's Theory of Law and Globalization' 10(4) *German Law Journal* 515.

Viellechner, Lars, Augsberg, Ino and Zumbansen, Peer (2009) 'Introduction to the Special Issue: The Law of the Network Society' 10(4) *German Law Journal* 305.

Vincent-Jones, Peter (2006) *The New Public Contracting. Regulation, Responsiveness, Relationality* (Oxford/New York, Oxford University Press).

—— (2007) 'The New Public Contracting: Public versus Private Ordering?' 14 (2) *Indiana Journal of Global Legal Studies* 259.

Vitols, Sigurt (2001) 'Varieties of Corporate Governance: Comparing Germany and the UK' in Peter A Hall and David Soskice (eds), *Varieties of Capitalism The Institutional Foundations of Comparative Advantage* (Oxford/New York, Oxford University Press) 337–60.

Vogel, David (2008) 'Private Global Business Regulation' 11 *Annual Review of Political Science* 261.

Voigt, Rüdiger (2008) 'Weltrecht—Entsteht eine "dritte Rechtsordnung"?' 39(2/3) *Rechtstheorie Sonderheft Weltrecht* (Martin Schulte & Rudolf Stichweh (eds)) 357.

Voigt, Stefan (2002) *Neue Institutionenökonomik* (Tübingen, Mohr Siebeck (UTB)).

—— (2005) 'Are International Merchants Stupid?—A Natural Experiment Refutes the Legal Origin Theory' *International Centre for Economic Research Working Paper No 21/2005*: ssrn.com/abstract=813624.

von Bar, Christian (2008) 'A Common Frame of Reference for European Private Law—Academic Efforts and Political Realities' 23 *Tulane European and Civil Law Forum* 37.

von Mehren, Robert B (2003) 'The Eco-Swiss Case and International Arbitration' 19 *Arbitration International* 465.

von Werder, Axel (2008) 'Preamble to the Commentary on the German Corporate Governance Code, 3rd ed.' in Henrik-Michael Ringleb, Thomas Kremer, Marcus

Lutter and Axel von Werder (eds), *Kommentar zum Deutschen Corporate Governance Kodex Kodex-Kommentar*, 3rd edn (München, CH Beck) 13–16.

Vos, Ellen (2000) 'EU Committees: the evolution of Unforeseen Institutional Actors in European Product Regulation' in Christian Joerges and Ellen Vos (eds), *EU Committees: Social Regulation, Law and Politics* (Oxford/Portland OR, Hart Publishing) 19–47.

Wagemans, Ton (2003) *An introduction to the labelling of websites, Presentation at the European Commission DG Information Society conference 'Quality labels for websites—alternative approaches to content rating'*, available at: <http://europa.eu.int/information_society/activities/sip/docs/pdf/reports/qual_lab_bkgd.pdf.

Wagner, Gerhart (2006) 'Prävention und Verhaltenssteuerung durch Privatrecht—Anmaßung oder legitime Aufgabe?' 206 *Archiv für die civilistische Praxis* 352.

Wai, Robert (2002) 'Transnational Liftoff and Juridical Touchdown: The Regulatory Function of Private International Law in an Era of Globalization' 40 *Columbia Journal of Transnational Law* 209.

—— (2003) 'Countering, Branding, Dealing: Using Economic and Social Rights in and around the International Trade Regime' 14(1) *European Journal of International Law* 35.

—— (2005) 'Transnational Private Law and Private Ordering in Contested Global Society' 46 *Harvard International Law Journal* 471.

—— (2008) 'The Interlegality of Transnational Private Law' 71 *Law & Contemporary Problems* 107.

Walker, Neil (2003a) 'Postnational Constitutionalism and the problem of translation' in Joseph HH Weiler and Marlene Wind (eds), *European Constitutionalism Beyond the State* (Cambridge, Cambridge University Press) 27–54.

—— (ed) (2003b) *Sovereignty in Transition* (Oxford/Portland OR, Hart Publishing).

—— (2009) 'Taking Constitutionalism Beyond the State' in Rainer Nickel (ed) Conflict of Laws and Laws of Conflict in Europe and Beyond. Patterns of Supranational and Transnational Juridification (Oslo, Arena), 277–308.

—— (2010), 'Out of Place and Out of Time: Law's Fading Coordinates' 14 *Edinburgh Law Review* 13, available at: http://ssrn.com/abstract=1367591.

Wallis, Diana (2000) *Report on the proposal for a Council regulation on jurisdiction and the recognition and enforcement of judgments in civil and commercial matters—Committee on Legal Affairs and the Internal Market.*

Walter, Christian (2001) 'Constitutionalizing (Inter)national Governance—Possibilities and Limits to the Development of an Inernational Constitutional Law' 44 *German Yearbook of International Law* 170.

Walzer, Michael (1981) 'The Distribution of Membership' in Peter G Brown and Henry Shue (eds), *Boundaries: National Autonomy and Its Limits* (Lanham MD, Rowman & Littlefield), 1.

Watson, Alan (1985) *The Evolution of Law* (Baltimore/London, Johns Hopkins Press).

Weatherill, Stephen (2007) 'The Challenge of Better Regulation' in Stephen Weatherill (ed), *Better Regulation* (Oxford/Portland OR, Hart Publishing) 1–18.

Weber, Max (1930) *The Protestant Ethics and the Spirit of Capitalism* [1904–05], Talcott Parsons (trans) (New York, Charles Scribner's Sons).

—— (1946) 'Science as Vocation (1918)' in HH Gerth and C Wright Mills (eds), *From Max Weber: Essays in Sociology* (New York, Oxford University Press) 129–56.

—— (1967) *On Law in Economy and Society* (originally in German, *Wirtschaft und Gesellschaft*, 2nd edn [1925]), E Shils and M Rheinstein (trans), M Rheinstein (ed) (New York, Simon Schuster).

Weiler, Joseph HH (1991) 'The Transformation of Europe' *Yale Law Journal* 2403.

—— (2004) 'The Geology of International Law—Governance, Democracy and Legitimacy' 64 *Zeitschrift für ausländisches öffentliches Recht und Völkerrecht* 547.

Weiler, Joseph HH and Wind, Marlene (eds) (2003) *European Constitutionalism Beyond the State* (Cambridge, Cambridge University Press).

Weinrib, Ernest (1995) *The Idea of Private Law* (Cambridge MA, Harvard University Press).

Weintraub, Jeff Alan and Kumar, Krishan (eds) (1997) *Public and Private in Thought and Practice: Perspectives on a Grand Dichotomy* (Chicago IL, University of Chicago Press).

Weissbrodt, David and Kruger, Muria (2003) 'Norms on the responsibilities of Transnational Corporations and other Businesses enterprises with Regard to Human Rights' 97(4) *American Journal of Comparative Law* 901.

—— (2005) 'Human Rights Responsibilities of Business as Non-State Actors' in Philip Alston (ed), *Non-state Actors and Human Rights* (Oxford/New York, Oxford University Press) 315–50.

Werder, Axel von (2002) 'Der Deutsche Corporate Governance-Kodex—Grundlagen und Einzelbestimmungen' 55 *Der Betrieb* 801.

Werder, Axel von, Talaulicar, Till and Kolat, Georg L (2003) 'Kodex Report 2003: Die Akzeptanz der Empfehlungen des Deutschen Corporate Governance Kodex' 56 *Der Betrieb* 1857.

Werlauff, Erik (2003) 'The SE Company—A New Common European Company from 8 October 2004' 14(1) *European Business Law Review* 85.

Werle, Raymund and Iversen, Eric J (2006) 'Promoting Legitimacy in Technical Standardization' 2 *Science, Technology & Innovation Studies* 19.

White, Harrison C (1981) 'Where Do Markets Come From?' 87 *American Journal of Sociology* 517.

Whytock, Christopher A (2008) 'Litigation, Arbitration, and the Transnational Shadow of the Law' 18 *Duke Journal of Comparative and International Law* 449.

—— (2009) 'Domestic Courts and Global Governance' 84 *Tulane Law Review forthcoming* (available at: ssrn.com/abstract=923907).

Wieacker, Franz (1953) *Das Sozialmodell der klassischen Privatrechtsgesetzbücher und die Entwicklung der modernen Gesellschaft* (Karlsruhe, CF Müller).

—— (1967) *Privatrechtsgeschichte der Neuzeit unter besonderer Berücksichtigung der deutschen Entwicklung* (Göttingen, Vandenhoeck & Ruprecht).

Wielsch, Dan (2001) *Freiheit und Funktion. Zur Struktur- und Theoriegeschichte des Rechts der Wirtschaftsgesellschaft* (Baden-Baden, Nomos).

Wiethölter, Rudolf (1961) *Interessen und Organisation der Aktiengesellschaft im amerikanischen und deutschen Recht* (Karlsruhe, Berkeley-Kölner Rechtsstudien, CF Müller).

—— (1965) 'Die Position des Wirtschaftsrechts im sozialen Rechtsstaat' in Helmut Coing, Heinrich Kronstein and Ernst-Joachim Mestmäcker (eds), *Wirtschaftsordnung und Rechtsordnung, Festschrift für Franz Böhm zum 70 Geburtstag* (Tübingen, Siebeck Mohr) 41–62.

—— (1971) 'Die Wirtschaftspraxis als Rechtsquelle' in Paul Bockelmann (ed), *Das Rechtswesen—Lenker oder Spiegel der Gesellschaft?* (München, Piper) 165–85.

—— (1972a) 'Artikel Bürgerliches Recht' in Axel Görlitz (ed), *Handlexikon zur Rechtswissenschaft* (Darmstadt, Wissenschaftliche Buchgesellschaft) 47–55.

—— (1972b) 'Artikel Wirtschaftsrecht' in Axel Görlitz (ed), *Handlexikon zur Rechtswissenschaft* (Darmstadt, Wissenschaftliche Buchgesellschaft) 531–9.

—— (1974) 'Privatrecht als Gesellschaftstheorie?' in Fritz Baur, Josef Esser, Friedrich Kübler and Ernst Steindorff (eds), *Funktionswandel der Privatrechtsin stitutionen Festschrift für Ludwig Raiser zum 70 Geburtstag* (Tübingen, Siebeck Mohr) 645–95.

—— (1977) 'Begriffs- oder Interessenjurisprudenz—falsche Fronten im IPR und Wirtschaftsverfassungsrecht' in Alexander Lüderitz and Jochen Schröder (eds), *Internationales Privatrecht und Rechtsvergleichung im Ausgang des 20 Jahrhunderts* (Frankfurt, Alfred Metzner Verlag) 213–63.

—— (1985) 'Proceduralization of the Category of Law' in Christian Joerges and David Trubek (eds), *Critical Legal Thought: An American-German Debate* (Baden-Baden, Nomos) 501–10.

—— (1986a) 'Materialization and Proceduralization in Modern Law' in Gunther Teubner (ed), *Dilemmas of Law in the Welfare State* (Berlin/New York, Walter de Gruyter) 221–49.

—— (1986b) 'Social Science Models in Economic Law' in Terence Daintith and Gunther Teubner (eds), *Contract and Organisation Legal Analysis in the Light of Economic and Social Theory* (Berlin/New York, Walter de Gruyter) 52–67.

—— (1988) 'Zum Fortbildungsrecht der (richterlichen) Rechtsfortbildung' 3 *Kritische Vierteljahresschrift für Gesetzgebung und Rechtswissenschaft* 1.

—— (1989) 'Ist unserem Recht der Prozess zu machen?' in Axel Honneth, Thomas McCarthy, Claus Offe and Albrecht Wellmer (eds), *Zwischenbetrachtungen im Prozess der Aufklärung Jürgen Habermas zum 60 Geburtstag* (Frankfurt, Suhrkamp) 794–812.

—— (2006) 'Just-ifications of a Law of Society' in Oren Perez and Gunther Teubner (eds), *Paradoxes and Inconsistencies in the Law* (Oxford/Portland OR, Hart Publishing) 65–75.

Wilhelmsson, Thomas (2004) 'Varieties of Welfarism in European Contract Law' 10(6) *European Law Journal* 712.

Wilkinson, Mike (2002) 'Postnationalism, (Dis)organised civil society and Democracy in the European Union: Is Constitutionalism Part of the Solution or Part of the Problem?' 9 *German Law Journal*: www.germanlawjournal.com/past_issues.php?id=192.

Williams, Cynthia A (1999) 'The Securities and Exchange Commission and Corporate Social Transparency' 112 *Harvard Law Review* 1197.

—— (2002) 'Corporate Social Responsibility in an Era of Economic Globalization' 35(3) *University of California at Davis Law Review* 705.

Williams, Oliver F (2004) 'The UN Global Compact: The Challenge and the Promise' 14(4) *Business Ethics Quarterly* 755.

Williamson, Oliver (1985) *The Economic Institutions of Capitalism* (New York/London, Free Press/MacMillan).

—— (2002) 'The Lens of Contract: Private Ordering' 92(2) *American Economic Review* 438.

Williamson, Oliver E (1975) *Markets and Hierarchies. Analysis and Antitrust Implications* (New York, Free Press).

—— (1981) 'The Modern Corporation: Origins, Evolution, Attributes' 19(4) *Journal of Economic Literature* 1537.

—— (1983) 'Credible Commitments: Using Hostages to Support Exchange' 73 *American Economic Review* 519.

—— (1996) *The Mechanisms of Governance* (Oxford, Oxford University Press).

—— (2005) 'The Economics of Governance' 95(1) *American Economic Review* 1.

Willis, John (1935) 'Three Approaches to Administrative Law: The Judicial, the Conceptual, and the Functional' 1 *University of Toronto Law Journal* 53.

Willke, Helmut (1997) *Supervision des Staates* (Frankfurt, Suhrkamp).

Winter, Jaap (2002a) 'Report of the High Level Group of Company Law Experts on A Modern Regulatory Framework for Company Law in Europe' at: ec.europa.eu/internal_market/company/docs/modern/report_en.pdf.

—— (2002b) 'Report of the High Level Group of Company Law Experts on Issues related to Takeover Bids' at: europa.eu.int/comm/internal_market/company/docs/takeoverbids/2002.

Winter, Ralph K (1977) 'State Law, Shareholder Protection, and the Theory of the Corporation' 6 *Journal of Legal Studies* 251.

Wolf, Manfred (2000) 'Zivilprozessuale Verfahrensgarantien in Art. 6 I EMRK als Grundlage eines europäischen Zivilprozeßrechts' in Gerhard Köbler, Meinhard Heinze and Wolfgang Hromadka (eds), *Europas universale rechtsordnungspolitische Aufgabe im Recht des dritten Jahrtausends Festschrift Alfred Söllner* (München, CH Beck) 1279–96.

Wolf, Martin (2002) 'Corporate Governance. Der Import angelsächsicher "Self-Regulation" im Widerstreit zum deutschen Parlamentsvorbehalt' 35 *Zeitschrift für Rechtspolitik* 59.

—— (2004) *Why Globalization Works* (New Haven CT, Yale University Press).

Wouters, Jan (2000) 'European Company Law: Quo Vadis?' 37 *Common Market Law Review* 257.

Wüstemann, Jens and Kierzek, Sonja (2007) 'Transnational legalization of accounting: the case of international financial reporting standards' in Christian Brütsch and Dirk Lehmkuhl (eds), *Law and Legalization in Transnational Relations* (Abingdon/New York, Routledge) 33–57.

Wymeersch, Eddy (1992) 'Problems of the Regulation of Takeover Bids in Western Europe: A Comparative Survey' in Klaus J Hopt and Eddy Wymeersch (eds), *European Takeovers Law and Practice* (London et al, Butterworths) 95–131.

—— (2002) 'Convergence or Divergence in Corporate Governance Patterns in Western Europe?' in Joseph A McCahery, Piet Moerland, Theo Raaijmakers and Luc Renneborg (eds), *Corporate Governance Regimes Convergence and Diversity* (Oxford/New York, Oxford University Press) 230–47.

—— (2005) 'Enforcement of Corporate Governance Codes' *ECGI Law Working Paper No 46/2005*.

Young, Ernest A (2007) 'The Constitution outside the Constitution' 117 *Yale Law Journal* 408.

Zamboni, Mauro (2007) 'Globalization and Law-Making: Time to Shift a Legal Theory's Paradigm' 1(1) *Legisprudence* 125.

Zekoll, Joachim (1998) 'Codification in the Twenty-First Century' 31 *University of California at Davis Law Review* 655.
Ziegler, J Nicholas (2001) 'Corporate Governance in Germany: Toward a New Transnational Politics?' in Steven Weber (ed), *Globalization and the European political economy* (New York, Columbia University Press) 197–228.
Zimmermann, Jochen, Werner, Jörg R and Volmer, Philipp B (2008) *Global Governance in Accounting. Rebalancing Public Power and Private Commitment* (Basingstoke, Palgrave Macmillan).
Zimmermann, Reinhard (2001) *Roman Law, Contemporary Law, European Law* (Oxford/New York, Clarendon Law Lectures, Oxford University Press).
—— (2009) 'The Present State of European Private Law' 57 *American Journal of Comparative Law* 479.
Zitelmann, Ernst (1888) 'Die Möglichkeit eines Weltrechts' *Allgemeine Österreichische Gerichts-Zeitung* 193.
Zumbansen, Peer (2000a) 'Drittschützende Wirkung eines Anwaltvertrages und verdeckte Sacheinlage' 55 *Juristenzeitung* 442.
—— (2000b) *Ordnungsmuster im modernen Wohlfahrtsstaat. Lernerfahrungen zwischen Staat, Gesellschaft und Vertrag* (Baden-Baden, Nomos).
—— (2001a) 'Die vergangene Zukunft des Völkerrechts' 34(1) *Kritische Justiz* 46.
—— (2001b) 'Spiegelungen von Staat und Gesellschaft: Governance-Erfahrungen in der Globalisierungsdebatte' *Archiv für Rechts- und Sozialphilosophie (Beiheft 79)* 13.
—— (2002) 'Germany Inc. Eroding?—Board Structure, CEO and Rhenish Capitalism' 3(6) *German Law Journal*: www.germanlawjournal.com/article.php?id=156.
—— (2002a) 'Piercing the Legal Veil: Commercial Arbitration and Transnational Law' 8(3) *European Law Journal* 400.
—— (2002b) 'The Privatization of Corporate Law? Corporate Governance Codes and Commercial Self-Regulation' 3 *Juridikum* 136.
—— (2003a) 'Lex mercatoria: Zum Geltungsanspruch transnationalen Rechts' 67(4) *Rabels Zeitschrift fur Auslandisches und Internationales Privatrecht* 637.
—— (2003b) 'Public Values, Private Contracts and the Colliding Worlds of Family and Market' 11(1) *Feminist Legal Studies* 73.
—— (2003c) 'Quod Omnes Tangit: Globalization, Welfare Regimes and Entitlements' in Eyal Benvenisti and Georg Nolte (eds), *The Welfare State, Globalization, and International Law* (Berlin, Springer) 135–73.
—— (2003d) 'Vertragsregimes im "Dritten Sektor": Zur Verortung des Verwaltungsrechts angesichts des Zusammenwachsens privat- und öffentlich-rechtlicher Handlungsformen' in W Rainer Walz, Karsten Schmidt and Hein Kötz (eds), *Non Profit Law Yearbook* (Köln, Heymanns) 61–85.
—— (2004a) 'European Corporate Law and National Divergences: The Case of Takeover Law' 3(3) *Washington University Global Studies Law Review* 867.
—— (2004b) 'Globalization and the Law: Deciphering the Message of Transnational Human Rights Litigation' 5 *German Law Journal* 1499.
—— (2004c) 'Sustaining Paradox Boundaries: Perspectives on the Internal Affairs in Domestic and International Law' 15(1) *European Journal of International Law* 197.
—— (2005a) 'Beyond Territoriality: The Case of Transnational Human Rights Litigation' (Fall 2005) *ConWEB Paper 4/2005* at: www.qub.ac.uk/schools/

School of Politics International Studies and Philosophy/Research/PaperSeries/ ConWEBPapers/.

—— (2005b) 'Comparative Law's Coming of Age? Twenty Years after "Critical Comparisons"' 6(7) *German Law Journal* 1073.

—— (2006a) 'Book Review: Niklas Luhmann's Law as a Social System (2004)' 15(3) *Social & Legal Studies* 453.

—— (2006b) 'The Parallel Worlds of Corporate Governance and Labor Law' 13 *Indiana Journal of Global Studies* 261.

—— (2006c) 'Spaces and Places: A Systems Theory Approach to Regulatory Competition in European Company Law' 12(4) *European Law Journal* 534.

—— (2006d) 'Transnational Law' in Jan Smits (ed), *Encyclopedia of Comparative Law* (Cheltenham, Edward Elgar) 738–54.

—— (2007a) 'Introduction: Private Ordering in a Globalizing World: Still Searching for the Basis of Contract' 14(2) *Indiana Journal of Global Legal Studies* 181.

—— (2007b) 'The Law of Society: Governance Through Contract' 14(2) *Indiana Journal of Global Legal Studies* 191.

—— (2007c) 'Transnational Law and Societal Memory' in Scott Veitch (ed), *Law and the Politics of Reconciliation* (Aldershot, Ashgate) 129–46.

—— (2008a) 'Law After the Welfare State: Formalism, Functionalism and the Ironic Turn of Reflexive Law' 56 *American Journal of Comparative Law* 769.

—— (2008b) "New Governance' in European Corporate Governance Regulation as Transnational Legal Pluralism' 15(2) *European Law Journal* 246.

—— (2008c) 'Varieties of capitalism and the learning firm: corporate governance and labour in the context of contemporary developments in European and German company law' in Nina Boeger, Rachel Murray and Charlotte Villiers (eds), *Perspectives on Corporate Social Responsibility* (Cheltenham, Edward Elgar) 113–43.

—— (2009a) 'Law's Effectiveness and Law's Knowledge: Reflections from Legal Sociology and Legal Theory' 10(4) *German Law Journal* 417.

—— (2009b) 'The Next 'Great Transformation' of Markets and States in the Transnational Space: Global Assemblages of Corporate Governance & Financial Market Regulation' *CLPE Research Paper 11/2009* available at: ssrn.com/ abstract=1415463.

—— (2009c) 'The State as Black Box and the Market as Regulator' 165(1) *Journal of Institutional and Theoretical Economics* 62.

Zumbansen, Peer and Calliess, Gralf-Peter (2010) 'Law, Economics & Evolutionary Theory: An Introduction' in Peer Zumbansen and Gralf-Peter Calliess (eds), *Law, Economics & Evolutionary Theory* (Cheltenham, Edward Elgar), *forthcoming.*

Zumbansen, Peer and Panezi, Maria (2008) 'UNCITRAL' *Max Planck Encyclopedia of Public International Law*, 2nd edn: www.mpepil.com.

Zürn, Michael (2001) 'Sovereignty and Law in a Denationalised World' in Volkmar Gessner, Richard P Appelbaum and William F Felstiner (eds), *Rules and Networks The Legal Culture of Global Business Transactions* (Oxford/Portland OR, Hart Publishing) 39–71.

Zweigert, Konrad and Kötz, Hein (1996) *An Introduction to Comparative Law*, 3rd edn (Oxford/New York, Oxford University Press).

Index